Why Religion Went Obsolete

Why Religion Went Obsolete

The Demise of Traditional Faith in America

CHRISTIAN SMITH

OXFORD
UNIVERSITY PRESS

Oxford University Press is a department of the University of Oxford.
It furthers the University's objective of excellence in research, scholarship,
and education by publishing worldwide. Oxford is a registered trade mark of
Oxford University Press in the UK and certain other countries.

Published in the United States of America by Oxford University Press
198 Madison Avenue, New York, NY 10016, United States of America.

© Oxford University Press 2025

All rights reserved. No part of this publication may be reproduced, stored in a retrieval system, transmitted, used for text and data mining, or used for training artificial intelligence, in any form or by any means, without the prior permission in writing of Oxford University Press, or as expressly permitted by law, by license or under terms agreed with the appropriate reprographics rights organization. Inquiries concerning reproduction outside the scope of the above should be sent to the Rights Department, Oxford University Press, at the address above.

You must not circulate this work in any other form
and you must impose this same condition on any acquirer

Library of Congress Cataloging-in-Publication Data
Names: Smith, Christian, 1960– author.
Title: Why religion went obsolete : the demise of traditional faith in America / Christian Smith.
Description: New York, NY, United States of America : Oxford University Press, [2025] |
Includes bibliographical references and index.
Identifiers: LCCN 2024038636 (print) | LCCN 2024038637 (ebook) |
ISBN 9780197800737 (hardback) | ISBN 9780197800751 (epub) |
ISBN 9780197800768 | ISBN 9780197800775
Subjects: LCSH: Church attendance—United States. |
Non-church-affiliated people—United States. |
Church membership—United States. | Public worship—United States.
Classification: LCC BV652.5 .S63 2025 (print) | LCC BV652.5 (ebook) |
DDC 254/.5—dc23/eng/20241212
LC record available at https://lccn.loc.gov/2024038636
LC ebook record available at https://lccn.loc.gov/2024038637

DOI: 10.1093/oso/9780197800737.001.0001

Printed by Sheridan Books, Inc., United States of America

The manufacturer's authorised representative in the EU for product safety is Oxford University Press España S.A. of El Parque Empresarial San Fernando de Henares, Avenida de Castilla, 2 – 28830 Madrid (www.oup.es/en or product.safety@oup.com). OUP España S.A. also acts as importer into Spain of products made by the manufacturer.

Contents

Acknowledgments ix
About the Companion Website xi

Introduction 1
   Key Concepts 2
   Two Decades of Converging Perfect Storms 12
   The Empirical Evidence 13
   On Interviews, Culture, and Historical Causes 17
   Last Thoughts 19

I SETTING THE STAGE

1. What Needs Explaining 23
   US Religious Affiliation 23
   US Religious Service Attendance 26
   Average Age of Regular Religious Service Attenders 28
   Knowing God Exists 29
   The Rise of "Not Religious" Americans 30
   Identifying as "Spiritual but Not Religious" 31
   Church Closings 31
   Confidence in Religious Institutions 33
   Ratings of Clergy Honesty and Ethical Standards 35
   Are Survey Measures of Religion Valid Indicators? 36
   Dispatches from the Front by Religion Leaders 37
   Conclusion 41

2. Religion Is Good When... 44
   Conclusion 59

3. Some Complex Ways Culture Changes 60
   Population Ecology Species Decline 60
   Avalanche Science 61
   Cultural Mismatch 62
   Particulate Matter in the Atmosphere 64
   Delayed, Nonlinear Change 65
   Adoption of Innovation 67
   Crowding Out 68
   Professional Control over Expert Knowledge 69
   Conclusion 70

II PERFECT STORMS CONVERGING

4. Long-Term Social Trends — 73
   - Higher Education for the Masses — 73
   - Women Entering the Paid Workforce — 75
   - The Deinstitutionalization of Marriage and Family — 76
   - Declining Participation in Face-to-Face Membership Organizations — 83
   - Triumphant Mass Consumerism — 85
   - Intensifying Expressive Individualism — 89
   - From Materialist to Postmaterialist Culture — 94
   - Rise of Emerging Adulthood — 96
   - Conclusion — 99

5. The Developing Religious Environment — 100
   - Mainline Protestant (Cultural Triumph and) Organizational Decline — 100
   - Catholic Organizational Weakening — 103
   - Moralizing of Religion, Downplaying Transcendence — 107
   - The Rise of Televangelism and the Religious Right — 117
   - The Spread of Eastern Religions and the New Age Movement — 121
   - The Ersatz "Warfare of Science and Religion" Narrative — 122
   - Declining Confidence in Organized Religion — 125
   - Obsolescence Postponed: Institutional Momentum and Diversion in the 1980s — 125
   - Conclusion — 127

6. The 1990s: Beginning of the End — 128
   - End of the Cold War — 128
   - Ascendant Neoliberalism Capitalism — 129
   - The Digital Revolution — 138
   - Pop Postmodernism — 150
   - Multicultural Education — 163
   - Millennial Geographical Mobility to Cities — 165
   - The Rise of Intensive Parenting — 168
   - "Not Religious" as an Acceptable Identity Option — 170
   - Conclusion — 172

7. The 2000s: Obsolescence Assured — 173
   - September 11, 2001 — 173
   - The New Atheism — 178
   - A Third Sexual Revolution — 183
   - LGBTQ+ Mainstreamed — 194
   - Religious Pluralism and National Identity — 200
   - Identity Politics and the Sacralizing of Partisan Politics — 208
   - Crucibles of Despair: The War on Terror, Political Polarization, Global Warming — 208

The Disappearing American Dream	214
Good Without God	218
"Spiritual but Not Religious"	223
The Continued Rise of the Religious "Nones"	226
Conclusion	228

8. Religious Self-Destructions ... 229
   - Religious Scandals ... 229
   - Evangelical Mission Drift ... 248
   - Evangelical Me-and-God Spirituality ... 254
   - Evangelical Biblicist Foundationalist Epistemology ... 258
   - Evangelical Purity Campaigns ... 262
   - Denominational Culture Wars ... 267
   - Religion as a Tool for Social Control ... 271
   - Congregational Stalwart Power-Hoarding Boomers ... 272
   - Conclusion ... 275

III THE AFTERMATH

9. Contours of the Millennial Zeitgeist ... 279
   - The Cultural Tenor of Successive Decades ... 280
   - Thematic Tones of the Age ... 283
   - Toward a Formal Analytics of the Millennial Zeitgeist ... 284
     - Time Duration ... 284
     - Spatial and Social Scope ... 285
     - Narrative Course ... 286
     - Characteristic "Carrying" Groups and Media ... 287
     - Crucial Events ... 287
     - Embodying Public Figures and Celebrities ... 288
     - Symbolic and Artistic Expressions ... 290
     - Styles of Attire and Presentation of Self ... 291
     - Common Slogans ... 293
     - A Caveat ... 294
   - The Defining Grunge Rock (and Mismatched Christian Counterparts) ... 294
   - The Zeitgeist in Expert Advice ... 296
   - An Analytical Model of Zeitgeist Cultural Assumptions ... 297
   - The Reality of Re-Enchantment ... 330
   - Conclusion: Why the Zeitgeist Made Religion Obsolete ... 336

10. Through the Exit Doors ... 339
    - Religious Turn-Offs ... 340
    - Explanations for Leaving Religion ... 345
    - Comparing Other Accounts of Disaffiliation ... 349

Three Important Minority Traditions	352
Jewish Millennials	353
Black Protestant Millennials	356
Mormon Millennials	360
Conclusion	364
Conclusion	**365**
Damned If It Do, Damned If It Don't	367
Not by Secularization Alone	368
And the Future?	369
Appendix: The Changing Social Locations of Religious Nones, 1970s–2010s	375
Notes	385
Index	421

Acknowledgments

This book would not exist without the work of my fantastic "LZ Gang" research team: Claire Cataldo, Matt Coetzee, Ainsley Gibbs, Tricia McCormack, Mary Quirk, Bridget Ritz, Nicole Tonetti, and Mary Grace Walsh. I could not have wished for a more capable and enjoyable group of collaborators with whom to work. Thank you! May we all meet again in Saugatuck someday. Tryce Prince of the University of Illinois Chicago also made key contributions in interview data collection and analyses. David Voas of University College London was exceptionally generous with his time and talents in providing me important data analyses for Chapter 1, for which I am immensely grateful. Eric Morgan of the Notre Dame Hesburgh Library conducted invaluable searches of media corpuses for me. Bruce Barr and Jessica Torres of the University of Chicago's National Opinion Research Center's AmeriSpeak Survey contributed valuable professional services and support, as did Alan Cooperman, Greg Smith, and Michael Rotolo of the Pew Research Center. I owe much gratitude to the good people at the Notre Dame Rome Global Gateway for their hospitality and support during the spring of 2023—thanks to Silvia Dall'Olio, Alice Bartolomei, Antonella Piccinin, Anna Ricigliano, Vitamaria Papa, Costanza Montanari, Jim Schwarten, Danilo Domenici, and Simone De Cristofaris. Thank you, too, to Dean Sarah Mustillo for inviting me to serve as the inaugural Pizzo Family Rome Scholars Program scholar. Thanks to Linda Woodhead of Kings College London for expert consulting about survey questions related to re-enchanted culture and to Bobby Duffy of the same for a helpful conversation about generations. John Evans of the University of California San Diego and Nicolette Manglos-Weber of Boston University read the manuscript in its entirety and provided insightful feedback. I also benefited from comments received from audiences at the Emory University Candler School of Theology Alonzo L. McDonald Family Distinguished Lecture Series and a Wheaton College Billy Graham Center presentation; I especially appreciate the critical comments of Frank Lechner and Ted Smith. Others who variously helped along the way include Galen Watts, Terry McDonnell, Matthew Guest, Yaakov Ariel, Bo McCready, Lenny Delorenzo, Phil Schwadel, Brad

Gregory, Tracy Wickham, Dave Odom, Jim Brockmole, Justin Farrell, Ilana Horwitz, James Hunter, Melissa Wiginton, Tom Tweed, Brett Robinson, Aleze Fulbright, Nadia Beider, Prince Rivers, Keith Anderson, Steve Vaisey, Melinda Denton, Rick Lawrence, Joel Carpenter, Chanon Ross, Mark Chaves, Rob Tonetti, Jim and Kathleen Littleton, Cassandra Sever, Tracy Wickham, and Zachary Smith. My Oxford editor, Theo Calderara, worked hard to make my argument more accessible to general readers; Carlene Bauer also lent her considerable line-editing skills to that end. Finally, research for the book was generously funded by the Lilly Endowment Inc. I greatly appreciate the trust, guidance, and support of Jessicah Duckworth, Chris Coble, and Clay Robbins.

About the Companion Website

https://global.oup.com/us/companion.websites/9780197800737/

Oxford has created a website to accompany *Why Religion Went Obsolete: The Demise of Traditional Faith in America*, in order to provide material that cannot be made available in a book, namely Appendix A: Research Methodology and Appendix B: Additional Interview Quotes. The reader is encouraged to consult this resource in conjunction with the book.

The appendixes available online are indicated in the text with Oxford's symbol ⏵.

Introduction

Americans have lost faith in traditional religion.

Over the past three decades, America's historic religious traditions have suffered major losses. Rates of both belief and belonging are in decline. The number of Americans identifying as "not religious" has increased remarkably. Calling oneself "spiritual but not religious" is now commonplace. While many Baby Boomers have retained their received religious ties, each generation of Americans since has been much less religious than the one that came before. Traditional American religion is caught in a spiral of decline.

And it is not just the numbers. Traditional religion has lost much of its cultural influence. Religious organizations have been reeling from recurrent revelations of sexual and financial scandals and cover-ups. Public trust in "organized religion" has declined significantly. American cultural norms and laws, especially regarding marriage, sexuality, and family, have been rewritten in ways that conflict with many traditional religious teachings. Non-religious and non-Christian Americans have increasingly pushed back on religion's influence on public life and sought greater influence of their own.[1] Many clergy and pastoral workers report that their messages are getting much less traction with people on the ground.

Until the 1990s, traditional American religion appeared in many ways to be alive and well. As recently as the George W. Bush era, the United States was seen as the last bastion of religion in the industrialized world—the exception to the secularization that prevailed in western Europe. No longer. The tide has turned.

Crucially, these religious losses are concentrated among younger generations, which means that—barring unlikely religious revivals among youth—the losses will not just continue but accelerate as less-religious younger Americans replace older more-religious ones and fewer and fewer American children are raised by religious parents.

That much is evident. What is less clear is exactly *why* this is happening. The growing ranks of religiously disaffiliated Americans offer researchers their own accounts. These explanations are helpful but not entirely satisfying, however.[2] Religious leaders, for their part, tend to focus on the inadequacies of their programs and communications and their struggles to retool for greater appeal and relevance.[3] Journalists have, with some success, tried to explain religion's decline.[4] And many scholars have offered thoughtful accounts, mostly correct as far as they go—but also, I think, incomplete.[5] Consequently, we know a lot more about the fact *that* traditional American religion has suffered big losses than we do about *why* this is so.

This book seeks to correct that discrepancy, attempting to explain why Americans have lost faith in traditional religion.

It offers five distinctive contributions. First, it demonstrates the importance of a *wide range* of causal factors often ignored by previous accounts to deepen appreciation for the breadth and complexity of the forces that influence religious outcomes. The story is more complicated than the ones told so far. Second, I introduce in this book the concept of religious *obsolescence* as a distinct way to understand the fate of American religion. Religion has not merely declined; it has become culturally obsolete. Or so I will argue. Third, this book moves beyond statistics and interviews to explore the larger *cultural environment*—the "zeitgeist"—during which American religion declined and that reflected that decline. What was the "spirit of the age" in which American religion became obsolete? Fourth, the analysis here raises the bar on *evidentiary rigor* by introducing quantitative measures of big-picture cultural changes over time, relying, when possible, on empirical indicators of cultural trends. Fifth, this book introduces an *alternative narrative* to the "secularization" thesis, suggesting that something more complicated and interesting has transpired that requires a more creative conceptual description than traditional secularization theory offers. Religious losses do not automatically translate into secular gains—that zero-sum mentality is misleading. There are other possibilities out there, and this book advances new ways of thinking about them.

Key Concepts

Before we get to the heart of the argument, it will be helpful to define some key terms and explain some of this book's key ideas.

Traditional Religion. By this term I mean religious groups that have existed for multiple generations; that have established practices, doctrines, organizational structures, and cultures that are solidified in authoritative texts; and that would not be considered novel, fringe, or "alternative" by the mainstream population. Specifically, I include in this category mainline Protestantism, Roman Catholicism, Black Protestantism, white evangelical Protestantism, most Pentecostal charismatic churches, Eastern Orthodox churches, Judaism, the Church of Jesus Christ of Latter Day Saints (LDS or Mormons), and most religious sects and denominations that have separated from the above traditions and organizations over doctrinal and lifestyle differences as long as they remain subcultural and not countercultural (e.g., Adventists and Holiness churches). Americans often call this collection of groups "organized religion," "established religion," and "institutional religion." I largely avoid those terms, however, since most non-traditional religions are also usually organized, established, and institutionalized to some degree. Being part of traditional religion in the United States normally means a person identifying with one specific tradition and becoming a member of a local congregation in which they participate and invest at least minimally.

What the category "traditional religion" does *not* include are various pagan groups, Wicca, witchcraft, "cults," magic practices, esoteric movements, fortune telling, astrology, paranormal enthusiasms, strongly countercultural sects, popular trends in individualistic spirituality, quasi-religions (such as UFO chasers and ghost hunters), and various other new religious movements.

What about Islamic, Hindu, Buddhist, Sikh, Jain, and other minority religious groups? Should they count as traditional American religions? There is no obvious answer. These clearly are traditional religions sharing many of the defining characteristics named above. Yet they are not traditional in the American context. Most Americans see them as distinct from Catholicism, evangelicalism, Judaism, and so on. To the extent that they self-consciously lay claim and seek to carry forward what they understand to be their authentic, historically inherited religious traditions, I am tempted to include them within the category of traditional American religion. Yet because of their largely "alternative" status in terms of the cultural mainstream, their close connection with recent immigrant ethnic groups, and as sources of syncretistic beliefs of many New Age and other new religious movements in the United States, I will not count them for present purposes as American traditional religions. Furthermore, I do not think the sociological processes examined in this book shaped these religions in the same ways they influenced clearly American traditional religions. In some ways, they belong to the category of traditional religion, but in other ways, in the United States, they—especially Buddhism—represent alternatives. Given this ambivalence, I leave this an open question and defer for insight to further empirical investigations rather than try to decide here on abstract, a priori, theoretical grounds.

Certain of these practices—not just major world religions but paganism, magic, and astrology—descend from traditions that are countless millennia older than some I am counting as "traditional," like Mormonism, which is less than 200 years old. But, in the United States, culturally speaking, I would argue that Mormonism now belongs to traditional religion whereas paganism does not. That paradox illustrates the cultural relativity partly determining such categorizations. Access to mainstream cultural capital is part of what makes a religion "traditional." You might call this a tautology—a "traditional American religion" is a religion that Americans consider traditional—but that is because cultural stature is part of what we are attempting to address, which is critical if we are to understand the seismic shift that has occurred in the past 30 years.

To avoid repetition, I will not often use the full phrase "traditional American religion." When I say simply "religion" or "American religion," I will always mean traditional religion as defined here.

Unplanned Obsolescence. This book argues that traditional American religion has become obsolete among younger generations and, increasingly, older ones. Something becomes obsolete when most people feel it is no longer useful or needed because something else has superseded it in function, efficiency, value, or interest. Obsolete connotes outdated or old-fashioned, in the sense of being "put out of business" or style by some innovation, incompatible larger trend, or perceived change in functional need.[6] The invention of the automobile made the horse and buggy obsolete. Electronic calculators made the slide rule obsolete. Electric typewriters suffered the same fate with the arrival of desktop computers. When something becomes obsolete, however, it is not simply that it is rarely used. There is also a mental shift. Obsolete items are simply less likely to cross anyone's mind. When people can ask Alexa to play any song, they rarely think about vinyl records. And so obsolete items become decreasingly familiar to most people and, in time, associated with bygone eras.

Some clarifications are crucial for what follows. First, obsolete does not mean "useless" or "failed." It just means having been superseded by alternatives that most users deem preferable. Existing electric typewriters can still type letters as well as they ever did. Most people just prefer computers.

Analogously, traditional religion still works well for some Americans. Most people simply prefer alternatives. Second, obsolete does not mean totally abandoned or extinct. Some people still can and do use obsolete items because they are familiar, less expensive, viewed with affection, or as a matter of principle. At this very moment, some people are no doubt happily listening to music on cassette tapes or watching DVDs, just as many Americans are still practicing traditional religion.

Third, most tools, ideas, products, and practices depend on other items and support systems to be useful. A humming electric typewriter is useless if one cannot buy the ink ribbon it requires or find a repair technician when it breaks. The model of a stay-at-home mother with a breadwinning husband doesn't work so well when all the other wives in the neighborhood are away at their paid jobs every workday—it's lonely. Lots of things go together in "packages," so even obsolete items that are still functional become harder to maintain when others have moved on to alternatives. That adds extra "systemic" pressures, making increasingly obsolete things more definitely so. Similarly, some functional items are only useful when many other people are also using or joining them. Think about telegraphs, two-way pagers, community choirs, fax machines, social networks, even email—their usefulness depends on the participation of a critical mass of others. This is called a "network effect." Obsolescence is thus determined partly by what most people prefer, aside from the wishes of any specific user.

Finally, not all obsolescence is about perceived improvements in function. Some items go obsolete simply as a matter of fashion. There are few functional differences among, for example, boot-cut, flare, skinny, or bell-bottom jeans. Yet these have all gone obsolete across the decades, sometimes within single years, when "everyone" knows not be caught dead wearing the wrong style. The reasons behind non-functional fashion obsolescence are various, including industry profit motives and the human desire to belong. Once such shifts start gaining momentum, people notice and can be pulled into such trends—some more consequential than clothing styles, like ones that affect religion.

To capture the "feel" of the kind of obsolescence that I argue has beset American religion, consider changes in the popularity of different genres of films. Specifically, think about Westerns. Over time, different genres increase and decline in popularity and thus production. Some genres enjoy long, steady growth and sometimes spikes of popularity. Others endure long downward trends. Bo McCready, who works for Apple analytics and is a public ambassador for the interactive visual data analytics platform Tableau, used genre tags on IMDB, the Internet Movie Database, to track the number of films of different genres released between 1910 and 2018. Figure I.1 shows the results of his analysis. We see there that some genres—including Action, Crime, and Fantasy—have enjoyed sustained popularity. Others, especially Thriller and Horror, have seen long-term growth. Documentaries have become popular in recent decades. Still others, like War and Musicals, tell their own interesting stories. But the most illustrative for our purposes is the Western. The Western never dominated film production, peaking at just above 10% of all releases around 1950. More noticeable, however, is the Western's drastic decline since then, interrupted only temporarily by a modest revival in the late 1960s and early 1970s. After that, Westerns virtually disappeared.

The fate of Western movies in the late twentieth century can, I think, help us grasp the *subjective feel* of obsolescence as I mean it here. The obsolescence of Westerns cannot be described or explained as merely a decline in

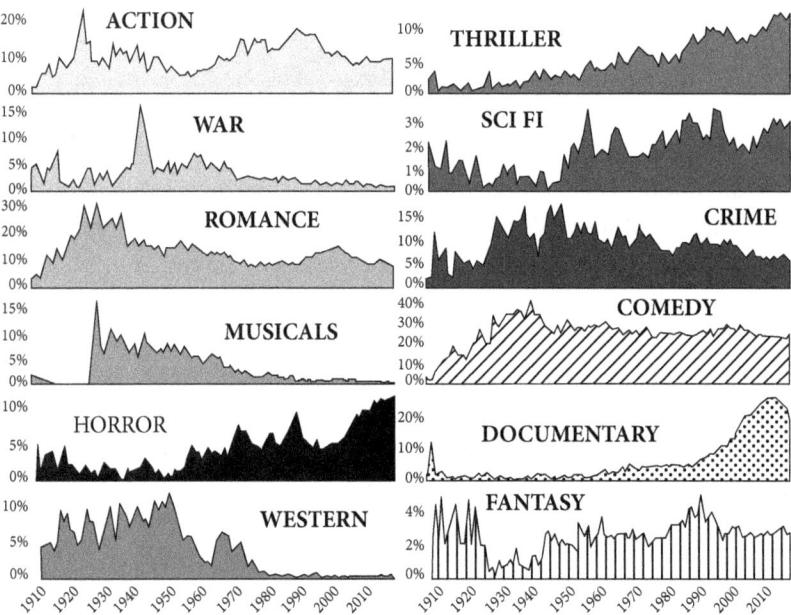

Figure I.1 Film genre popularity, 1910–2018.
Source: Bo McCready, using IMDB genre tags, on Tableau public, used with permission.
Note: vertical axis ranges are unstandardized but can be interactively standardized for comparison on the source website, https://public.tableau.com/app/profile/bo.mccready8742/viz/FilmGenrePopularity-1910-2018/GenreRelativePopularity.

quality that increasingly sophisticated audiences grew tired of. Many tacky Westerns were produced over the decades, but that is true of all film genres. Many outstanding Westerns were also produced. Furthermore, some of the most beloved American entertainers have starred in Westerns, including John Wayne, Gary Cooper, James Stewart, Henry Fonda, Elvis Presley, Paul Newman, and Clint Eastwood. Western roles were not second-class acting jobs. So, aside from the puzzle of exactly why Westerns became obsolete, the question for present purpose remains: What are the *qualities* that *subjectively* strike viewers so they just *feel* or *know* something to be obsolete? What *exactly* about cowboys, Indians, outlaws, sheriffs, and chases on horseback *feels* passé, outmoded, and worn out? Considering such questions helps provide clues about the subjective character of obsolescence. This book attempts to understand and explain how religious obsolescence feels.

Finally, what do I mean by emphasizing *unplanned* obsolescence? A good deal of product obsolescence is intentionally engineered by design. An appliance that could, for a slightly higher cost, be built to last three times longer is purposefully designed to break in, say, four years, forcing the consumer to purchase another. Cell phone software updates are intentionally designed not to work well on "old" models in order to prompt upgrades to new phones. That obsolescence is planned. However, we will see, very few of the causes of religion's obsolescence in recent decades were like that. Nearly all were unplanned.

I have argued elsewhere that in other eras and spheres of American life, religious secularization was the result of purposeful anti-religious activism.[7] It sometimes happens. But not in the present case. Some religious leaders claim that purposefully anti-religious actors ("secular humanists") have intentionally wielded ideologies ("secular humanism," "wokeism") through institutions they control ("The Media," universities) to attack traditional religion and morality. That is not absolutely false, but it grossly exaggerates the power of anti-religious activism. It also ignores the many ways that religion has been the agent of its own demise (more on this later). The bottom line: very little of what caused American religion's obsolescence was planned or intended by anti-religious agents. That is a crucial point.

Culture. This is a book about religion. But more broadly, it is a book about culture. The idea of "culture" is central to my argument and so requires some explanation. My account does not depend on one particular theory of culture nor am I offering any theoretical innovation. Most standard social science definitions will do as long as we maintain some crucial conceptual distinctions.[8] I take a general *cognitive* and *practice* view of culture, conceiving it as a stock of *learned human knowledge*—both knowledge *about* things and knowledge of *how to do things*—acquired through socialization and modified through creative reconfiguration, which people deploy to live functional and meaningful lives. In this view, culture per se consists of the categories, assumptions, beliefs, values, skills, and other practical know-how possessed in minds and bodies.[9] Culture provides descriptive "models *of*" reality and prescriptive "models *for*" living in that reality. Culture's "models of" supply representations of the way things *are*. Culture's "models for" prescribe how one should act within those realities. In short, "culture" is learned knowledge about reality and how to live in it.

Cultural models do not always map well onto the actual realities of life, society, and the world. Cultural models are social constructions largely inherited from the past, which often lag behind lived experience on the ground. Major cultural changes often occur when there are significant *mismatches* between received cultural models and experienced reality. When enough people find their models no longer describe the realities they see or fail to help them navigate those realities, they may question and revise those models. This was one of the major reasons that traditional religion became obsolete. Younger Americans' expectations of religion clashed with their lived experiences in a dramatically changing society. A number of external developments fostered that mismatch, including technological developments, economic transformations, and cultural innovations. The assumption that religion was credible and valuable gave way.

Culture is in many ways self-reinforcing. We humans use culture (the knowledge we have accumulated) to create products or objects— clothing, graffiti, dance performances, recipes, parties, rules of etiquette, myths, computers, you name it—that we collectively call "culture." Culture is thus, in complex ways, subjective and objective, mental and material, internal and external, personal and public. It does not suffice to view culture only as what individuals think and believe or only as some collective property of a group—both are necessary, and observing the mutual causal interactions between them is crucial.[10] Complicating matters, people can also internalize external cultural objects and turn them into personal culture as knowledge. For instance, memorizing your grandmother's handwritten apple pie recipe (a cultural object) turns it into part of one's own internal culture (how-to knowledge).

The entire external social world of cultural objects that people generate, inhabit, and sustain by living constantly "acts back" on them, primarily reinforcing their internal culture as knowledge but also sometimes revising it. The production of cultural objects in the external, physical world imbues that world of products with an apparent "objective facticity." A cultural object no longer seems like a mere creation of human cognition and activity but instead an independently existent fact of reality impinging from the outside. An organization founded by a group of people (a cultural object), for instance, takes on an institutional independence that can then use its bylaws to expel those same founders and alter their beliefs (culture as knowledge) about such organizations. So, while people use culture to produce cultural objects, those same objects in turn produce and influence one's internal notions about culture. The causal effects flow in both directions. This book tells the story of how sociocultural developments over the past 30 years acted on post-Boomer Americans in ways that made most of them believe that traditional religion was not relevant, valuable, or attractive.

People must *share* culture at least somewhat within and across their social groups in order to function. But culture also *varies* between people and groups, especially in large, diverse, pluralistic societies. The traditional idea of culture as systems of ideas commonly embraced by all members of tribes or societies is inaccurate. As much as cultures can seem like orderly systems, they are also often internally disjointed. People understand culture as knowledge about what is real and how to live, and they measure its worth more by its pragmatic effects than by its philosophical coherence. Often, people assume and believe things that are logically contradictory, but rarely does that bother them as long as it all helps them get by in life. Furthermore, as much as culture can foster social solidarity, cultural differences also organize status distinctions and conflicts. Culture is the central medium by which social processes determine winners and losers. To understand American religion's demise, we need to attend to sociological issues of cultural identity, solidarity, conflict, competition, and transformation.

Another key distinction concerns different levels of people's conscious *awareness* of culture. Important here is the concept of "deep culture." Humans vary in how much of their culture they consciously reflect on. Some parts of culture occupy people's awareness only when they focus directly on them. Other parts people consider attentively only when circumstances force them to do so. Many other parts of culture, however, are so "obvious," so taken for granted, so "natural" that they rarely, if ever, are brought to mind.

"Deep culture" refers to knowledge that is so well established, widely shared, embedded in institutions, and taken for granted by nearly everyone that it need never come up for conscious inspection or affirmation.[11] In the United States, for example, the right of individual self-determination belongs to deep culture—being axiomatic, invisibly sacred—but the same does not in collectivist societies like China. Simply subjecting deep culture to questioning can be unnerving and threatening to the "existential security" that such culture normally provides. The obsolescence of American religion was in part the outcome of long-term shifts in deep culture.

People learn most of their basic culture knowledge and practices as children, adolescents, and emerging adults, and their cultural values and outlooks normally remain stable across their adult lives. Some individuals do change dramatically, but they are the exceptions that prove the rule. This means that *generations* of populations who come of age during the same times and experience the same historical events not only tend to share cultural sensibilities but also retain them through life. That leads us to expect that much historical cultural change occurs not within generations but between them. That is clearly true in our case of religious decline, as we see in the Chapter 1. To explain such changes sociologically, we need to examine the larger social transformations that drove key cultural shifts that impinged most upon younger generations. That is the strategy of this book.

Zeitgeist. I mentioned above that this book will explore the cultural zeitgeist that developed in recent decades to help explain religion's losses. "Zeitgeist" is a German-derived word that means "spirit of the age" or "times" (*geist*, spirit, like ghost + *zeit*, literally, time). Johns Hopkins University sociologist Monika Krause defines zeitgeists as "patterns in meaningful practices that are period-specific, cross over different areas of social life, and extend across geographical contexts."[12] Zeitgeists emerge and represent particular "stand-out" moments in history. They involve different institutional spheres of social life and groups of people. And they transcend specific locations and situations. We can analyze a zeitgeist, Krause writes, by investigating the formal properties of its particular time duration, the social scope of involvement or influence, the narrative course it follows, and the characteristic media and groups that "carry" it. I add that zeitgeists are also defined by specific embodying public figures and celebrities, crucial events, representative artistic and symbolic expressions, shared slogans, and other types of meaningful cultural markers present in real time (then) and in collective memory (later).[13]

Three examples of zeitgeists in American history that help to illustrate this are the Wild West, the Roaring Twenties, and the Sixties. Each of these readily evokes specific examples fitting the analytical categories above for anyone who was part of or knows about each period. The Roaring Twenties, for instance: the end of the First World War, economic boom, lavish parties, speakeasies, flappers and libertines, *The Great Gatsby*, bobbed hairdos, jazz, the Charleston, Art Deco, sexual license, organized crime, Coolidge, Hoover, moving pictures, the Golden Age of Radio, and the era's sudden collapse with the 1929 Black Tuesday crash of Wall Street. Readers can generate their own zeitgeist associations for the two other examples—which would no doubt include shared themes, images, events, symbols, slogans, and representatives for each. The point is not that any zeitgeist, whether experienced or remembered, fully describes most of what happened during its era. The Wild West was experienced very differently by Native Americans than it was by white settlers. And the Twenties were hardly Roaring for African Americans in the South. A zeitgeist rather *captures* and *represents* the defining *spirit* of an era—the dominant cultural "atmosphere" "in the air" of a particular period, which characterizes what the era was or is most definitively understood to be *about*. Zeitgeists are not about the typical experience of the average person during the era, but instead are the leading and most visible movements of people who are defining the cutting edge of cultural developments and the feeling of the age.

It must immediately be noted that social scientists and historians have for very long been averse—virtually allergic—to the concept of zeitgeist, so much so that the term is essentially obsolete in scholarship. One reason is that "zeitgeist" comes tainted by a genuinely problematic intellectual history shaped by thinkers like Georg W. F. Hegel and Karl Mannheim. Another is that it feels amorphous due to its evocation of metaphors like "spirit" and "atmosphere." How can we scientifically measure anything "in the air?" Is this not merely undisciplined amateur history-speak and simplistic pop cultural memory?

These objections can be answered. For starters, it is possible to reformulate the concept of zeitgeist to strip it of the problematic features of its intellectual legacy and make it a useful analytical category for contemporary social science. The work of Monika Krause mentioned above does just that, rehabilitating zeitgeist as a concept for analytical purposes so that the empirics of any given case, rather than a preconceived philosophy of history or tightly constructed social theory, drives its uses.[14] To discard the concept as useless because zeitgeists are amorphous and difficult to measure also exhibits a scientific positivism that we ought not to accept in the first place. Certain real features of human social life are simply less clear and measurable than others, yet these are often the most crucial. If there are such things as zeitgeists—as our phenomenological experiences of history tell us there are—we must do our best to study and understand them, however challenging that may be. Refusing concepts like zeitgeist, furthermore, seems to betray a "flat" view of history as merely so many chains of causal events and results. Judgments about the boundaries of historical eras and analyses of the significance of their key events, figures, symbols, sensibilities, and even *geists* require interpretation. But so does every other method and procedure in social science, however "objective" they may seem. I therefore proceed to use zeitgeist as a central analytical concept, leaving its validity to be judged by how illuminating it proves to be. For convenience, I will call the one we have recently been living through the "Millennial zeitgeist."

Generations. The story here is not about all Americans but primarily the experiences, interests, and identities of younger generations—of the coming-of-age teenagers, emerging adults, and younger adults who reached midlife in the 1990s and 2000s. Like zeitgeists and their historical eras, generations are culturally meaningful groupings that can be analytically useful ways to understand big social transformations.[15] They map especially well onto the religious changes of interest here. I deploy the conventional categories of Generation X and Millennials, bookended by Baby Boomers and Gen Zers. When it comes to religious obsolescence, Baby Boomers (born 1946–1964) are the backdrop scenery. The real action starts with Generation X (born 1965–1980) and takes off with Millennials (born 1981–1996). Gen X was the transitional hinge of cultural and religious change, breaking with the old order and signaling new directions. Millennials picked up that lead and substantially developed and advanced the new zeitgeist. Gen Z (born 1997–2012) is now carrying forward and working out the details of the new normal. Boomers helped prepare the ground for religion's growing obsolescence. But it was Americans in their teens, 20s, and 30s in the 1990s and 2000s who really made it happen.

Two Decades of Converging Perfect Storms

All of the evidence about traditional American religion's recent troubles points to two crucial decades of decisive change: the 1990s and 2000s. Little of the upheaval that was about to occur was evident before 1990. Fifteen or 20 years later, most everything about the new zeitgeist was evident and normalized. And everything since the late 2000s has essentially been extension, fallout, and mop-up. I can be even more precise. *The* pivotal year marking the launch of the new zeitgeist that remade religion was 1991. None of us knew that at the time. But, looking back, we can see that 1991 was *the* year the cultural tide turned on American religion's fortunes. Why and how so I explain in chapters ahead. And the year the momentous changes were completed? That is less clear, but I will say 2009. By that year, nearly all that mattered for our story—the causes of religion's obsolescence—had happened or at least been set in irreversible motion. Most by then had also become aware that things were not looking good for traditional religion.[16] So, nearly all of the important action actually happened during the two decades straddling the turn of this century. Or so I shall argue the evidence tells us.

Stepping back, as a prospective summary, my account here as a whole concerns big *cultural* transformations resulting from huge *historical* events and *institutional* changes driven by developments in technology, economics, politics, the media, education, business, social networks, law, marriage and family, and even warfare, all of which have played crucial though mostly unintended causal roles in driving religion into obsolescence. The reasons for these transformations were largely institutional. But the decisive changes affecting traditional religion were mediated through culture—across widespread, transformed assumptions, beliefs, values, norms, expectations, and aesthetics, as those shaped young people's life experiences, interests, identities, and commitments.

Those cultural transformations altered the sociocultural landscape that religion occupied, generating a new cultural zeitgeist that proved inhospitable to traditional religion. Religion became a species struggling mostly unsuccessfully to reproduce itself in a profoundly altered ecosystem featuring scarce resources and fierce competitors. Young people were coming of age in the face of new outlooks and opportunities for meeting their functional and existential needs. Religion's title to whatever piece of life's goods that it had once "owned" was disappearing. That spelled its obsolescence.

The Empirical Evidence

This book draws on a wide range of kinds of evidence to make its argument, summarized here and available in detail online.[17] First, the project team I led conducted 209 personal interviews with a diverse sample of

18-to-54-year-olds living in the United States. The vast majority of these interviews were conducted in 2022, sampled from a nationally representative survey fielded by AmeriSpeak of the National Opinion Research Center (NORC) at the University of Chicago. On that survey we asked a set of questions about respondents' religious histories and commitments that enabled us to target certain kinds of people for follow-up, in-depth interviews. Those included people who had declined religiously since their highly religious youth (called Decliners here), those who were raised religious and continued as adults to be religious (Maintainers), those who increased in religion since youth (Increasers), and those who had always been low and not religious (Nevers).[18] We also targeted "cultural creatives"—that is, those who worked in culture-producing occupations such as journalists, internet content creators, writers, and teachers. This produced interview data from respondents most relevant to our empirical and theoretical concerns yet drawn from a nationally representative probability sample of Americans. We also did pilot interviews in 2021 and 2022, designed to test the usefulness of our interview questions, which relied on convenience sampling and were conducted with mostly Millennials. These pilot interviews proved so interesting and useful that I include them in the larger interview dataset. Figure I.2 shows the locations of those we interviewed for this study.

Figure I.2 Locations of the 209 interviews conducted for this study.

In addition to the 209 interviews, we conducted four focus groups with an average of six participants in each. Focus group participants were mostly Millennials who had declined in religiousness since growing up, lived in Indiana and Michigan, and were recruited using online ads and indirect word of mouth. The focus groups, rather than asking participants to respond to verbal questions about their ideas and experiences, asked them simply to express and then explain their emotional reactions to a series of 50 visual images of American religious and non-religious people, social settings, and objects that we showed them without commentary. Assuming that people's relation to religion is based at least as much on affective feeling as conceptual beliefs, we wanted the focus groups to tap into emotional responses to visual representations rather than replies to verbal prompts. We recorded the focus group discussions digitally and in research notes, which we transcribed, and then systematically analyzed them together as a research team.

For data that could speak to historical changes in cultural discourses, I conducted multiple systematic searches of hundreds of keywords by individual years in book titles, online references, scholarly publications; various news, business, and political publications; television news coverage; and US newspapers going back to the early twentieth century. I first identified broad conceptual categories of theoretical and explanatory relevance potentially represented in these media. I then generated lists of every conceivably culturally relevant keyword or phrase for each of these categories. With the help of a digital data search expert, I systematically searched various digital corpuses of relevant bodies of data, counting per year the number of hits for each keyword or phrase. I aggregated those counts to sum the total number of hits for all keywords and phrases related to the broad conceptual categories across the years observed. The results are presented in figures and tables in many of the following chapters.

Fourth, after the main lines of argument for this book were developed and drafted, I conducted a second nationally representative survey on a host of beliefs and practices, religious and otherwise. The purpose of this survey was to assess popular views of many of the key issues and claims I raise in the chapters that follow. AmeriSpeak at NORC conducted this survey in November 2023, completing a sample of 2,009 US adults ages 18 to 77. I report results from the survey throughout the following chapters. Younger Gen Z respondents (ages 18–24) proved still too connected to their teenage years to offer valid comparisons with older generations on many of the questions, so I exclude all but the three oldest years of Gen Z (ages 25–27), which I merge with Millennials for analysis.[19]

Fifth, this book presents findings from my secondary analyses of multiple existing survey datasets, focusing especially on the General Social Survey (GSS). I also draw on many findings from the Pew Research Center, the Gallup Organization, and other reputable data sources. And I rely on the existing empirical research of countless colleagues and scholars whose names appear in the endnotes.

Finally, beginning with the planning phase of this project in 2021 and continuing thereafter, I engaged many conversations with a wide variety of persons who one way or another had their fingers on the pulse of American religion and possible cultural changes shaping it—mostly clergy and denominational leaders. These conversations were with Christians in mainline, evangelical, Black Protestant, and Catholic circles. They were meant to be sense-checking inquiries, not systematic data gathering and are not reported here except for occasional quotations. For the same reason, throughout this project, as opportunities presented themselves, I also struck up conversations about the issues in this book with various strangers and acquaintances under the age of 50. In many cases, what people had to say was striking, although, again, I systematically analyzed none and only mention a few in the chapters below. No single kind of data I bring to this book is conclusive, but altogether I believe they add up to evidence that makes a convincing case.

A few notes on my use of interview quotes in this book. First, while we sampled our in-depth interviews from a nationally representative survey, we intentionally oversampled those whose religiousness declined or were always low. Our sample of those types are thus representative of these categories of adult Americans, but our complete interview dataset overrepresents them. This means that the quotes in the following chapters are not a proportionate cross-section of all Americans but come especially from those who are less religious and often alienated from religion—exactly what we needed to answer the question of this book. Second, our interviews produced enough quotable evidence that, if included here, would inflate this book into a massive tome. In the interest of keeping this work a reasonable length, I limit interview quotes to only a handful per point they illustrate. The many more supporting quotes that could have also been included I gathered into a document that readers can download online to explore further the way the post-Boomers we interviewed talk about these matters.[20] The best way truly to grasp the character of the Millennial zeitgeist is to take the time to read those myriad interview quotes available online. Finally, I do not give demographic details (age, sex, state of residence, etc.) about each person quoted in this book despite gender and sexual identity figuring importantly in the argument. That is because those details about individual interview respondents—which in any case have to be general enough or altered to prevent deductive disclosure—are usually not crucial to the points they make regarding shared generational experiences of macro-cultural change.[21]

On Interviews, Culture, and Historical Causes

This is a work of historical cultural sociology. Its central question concerns how macro-cultural changes occurring across decades led to the demise of traditional religion. But how can personal interviews conducted in the early 2020s with younger generations provide evidence for an argument about culture preceding and including the 1990s and 2000s? Is there not a temporal disjuncture here? That crucial methodological question requires a response. The answer has three parts. First, interviews are only one piece of the larger assemblage of data supporting my argument, which I use primarily when they speak appropriately to specific points. Whenever possible I triangulate interview data with survey and public discourse data collected and published during the earlier periods in question. Personal retrospection is only one means I employ to understand the past.

Second, many (but not all) of the people we interviewed for this project lived through the key decades in question. They belong to the generations that were crucial in religion's obsolescence. Memories and retrospective accounts suffer known reliability problems, but they are far from worthless. Interpreted with appropriate caution, interviews can provide valuable evidence of people's lived experiences and outlooks and, indirectly, of cultural assumptions deemed widely acceptable. Third, interviews can provide valuable data not only for the things people remember and say, but also for what they do *not* say or remember and *how* they say what they do say. Delivery matters, not only content. Absences are just as real and telling as presences. Facial expressions, emotional reactions, inflections of speech, patterns of talk, and ignorance and neglect of certain topics and facts matter as much as words on transcription pages. Thus, my research team's recurring group analytical processing of interviews throughout the course of the project was just as valuable as our formal text analyses. Bottom line: while it would be foolish to rely on contemporary interviews alone to build an argument about historical cultural change, it would be equally unwise not to draw from interviews what useful evidence they have to offer.

Having said that, a few other key points need mentioning. While on an individual level people's reasons are important causes of their actions, the causes of social outcomes are more than just the sum of people's reasons.[22] Reasons and causes are related in human social life, but they are *not* identical. People are often not fully aware of or honest with themselves or others about why they do what they do. What they report to themselves and to researchers is often partial and potentially misleading. People are also usually only dimly aware of the larger sociological contexts and forces that shape those motivations. Yes, people lived through the end of the Cold War, 9/11, the invention of the internet, the Great Recession, and so on. But that does not mean they clearly perceived and understood how such events shaped their lives and choices, either at the time or afterward. If they did, we would not need the discipline of sociology—all we would need to understand and explain anything would be simply to ask the people who were involved. But we *do* need sociology to carefully and systematically fit together the pieces of the big picture that people normally don't see or understand. Even then, the task is immensely difficult and the result always incomplete. So, we can ask people why they left their religions, but that by itself cannot fully explain "the rise of the nones," for example. We need in addition to supplement this with richly informed sociological accounts of why those reasons would even be intelligible and motivating to those people in the first place.

This presents particular methodological challenges for macro-social analyses. In the best case, one hopes the influence of the contextualizing sociological forces show up in people's reports in a way that validates and illustrates the causal powers shaping their choices and actions. "Yes, when the internet was invented that affected me in ways A, B, and C such that I decided to do X and become Z." When that happens, people's accounts validate the macro-level arguments. But the limits of people's perceptions, recollections, interpretations, and articulations mean we are rarely capable of such analytical feats. Instead, we must grapple with gaps between the sociological forces that contextualize people's activities and whatever goes on in their thoughts, feelings, and desires that they can express in interviews. It usually sorts out quite imperfectly, but there is no way around the problem. Even so, what sociology can produce is immensely more illuminating than what only asking people yields.

In the following chapters, I attempt to bridge the gaps between big-picture sociological contexts and interview accounts in various ways. In the end, readers can judge whether they are convinced or not by the overall argument. Which leads to my final point: all of sociology is interpretive (and quantitative and qualitative). Every good sociological explanation describes qualities, counts quantities, and interprets them within some narrative in order to offer a satisfying explanation. A sociology missing any of those dimensions is impossible. This book is one interpretation of American religion's recent fate, one centered on the idea of obsolescence. I believe it offers a good and illuminating interpretation, providing insight into what is true about reality. But it is also incomplete and partial. There surely are other ways to narrate stories to capture important facts and features I have missed here. Still, every narration is accountable to the best available evidence. If I succeed, my account should also resonate with the personal experiences of readers who lived through the era I examine. If others disagree, I look forward to hearing their evidence and narratives. That is how good social science progresses.

Last Thoughts

For scholars, I hope this book makes a contribution not only to the sociology of religion but also to religious studies, cultural sociology, cultural studies, American studies, the history of religion, and beyond. I believe, with Monika Krause, that the concept of zeitgeist is worth retrieving for understanding time-specific cultural structures, and I hope my empirical use of it demonstrates its value for scholarship. I also hope the methods of quasi-Big Data collection used here contribute, however modestly, to developing the kind of methodological advances in different fields that some scholars have called for.[23] I wish, too, for this work to help strengthen the currently weak ties between sociology of religion and cultural sociology, which I think would benefit both.[24]

This book will also, I hope, speak to religious audiences. I trust its story will prove enlightening, even if disheartening. At a different level, I hope the sociological perspective here helps to counter two common but problematic tendencies I have observed in American religion, especially among Christians—what I call "theological idealism" and "program idealism." The first is the usually invisible assumption—perhaps particularly common among religious intellectuals, educators, authors, and some clergy—that, if only people could get their doctrinal and ethical *ideas* right, then they could (fill in the blank) do church correctly, make strong disciples, transform society, live faithfully, etc. The seasonal catalogues of religious publishing houses exemplify this theological idealism. The second is similar, though more common among pastors and other ministry people with boots on the ground: if only they could implement the right *programs*, then they could really (fill in the blank) keep our youth coming to church, make our message attractive, grow in numbers, evangelize our city, etc. Both are sociologically naïve.

Good ideas and programs matter for any institution. But neither operates in a vacuum. Without taking into account the larger social structures and cultural environments within which they operate, great ideas and programs themselves may accomplish little. Assuming, whether consciously or not, that simply getting the right ideas or programs will solve one's problems is short-sighted and often leads to disappointment. Contrasting with such idealisms, this book offers a sociological realism to help audiences better grasp the power of larger social, cultural, technological, economic, political, and other institutional contexts for shaping what ideas and programs likely can and cannot accomplish. The goal is not determinism or despair, but rather a more realistic awareness for readers, religious and not, of how the social world works and how powerful social and cultural structures are in forming human life. That awareness—"the sociological imagination"—promises to help us become clearer about the huge social and cultural forces that we all, in various ways, are up against and try to live through with grace—and hopefully some success.

I
SETTING THE STAGE

1
What Needs Explaining

The decline of traditional American religion has been well-documented. Many books, articles, and reports leave no doubt that a major shift has occurred. There is no need to rehash the details here. Still, a fundamental principle of social science is the need to "establish the phenomenon" before attempting to explain it.[1] So, while the rest of this book will focus on the *why*, we begin here with the *what*. What has happened to traditional American religion? What do things look like to religious leaders on the ground? The evidence offers multiple empirical indicators of a larger *latent* fact about traditional American religion: that it has not only suffered weakening and decline but also has become *obsolete*—at least among Americans under the age of 50, which is to say nearly all of America in the not-distant future.

US Religious Affiliation

How have Americans' religious affiliations changed? The General Social Survey (GSS)—one of the best national surveys of American adults, which has been around since the early 1970s—asks respondents whether they affiliate with a religion and, if so, how strongly. And when you look at all Americans together, you find a fairly steady rate of religious affiliation, leading, until recently, to a broad agreement that the United States is an unusually religious nation showing few signs of secularization.

In 2016, however, David Voas and Mark Chaves, sociologists at the University College London and Duke University, respectively, published an article in the *American Journal of Sociology* that gave a different view.[2] Instead of looking at the religious affiliation of all Americans combined, they sorted them into groups by decade of birth, from those born before 1915 to those born in 1994. Their analysis revealed a different picture: each younger group surveyed between 1974 and 2014 reported noticeably lower rates of "strong" or "somewhat strong" religious affiliation than the group that came before. There was a bump up in religious affiliation for all age groups in the

1980s, but the long-term trends were clear: younger Americans were less likely to be religiously affiliated. The closer to the end of the twentieth century Americans were born, the more likely they were to report either no religious affiliation or a "not very strong" one. That article more than any other, on top of two decades of my own research on the religious and spiritual lives of American Millennials, changed my thinking about the condition and likely future of American religion.[3]

I asked Voas and Chaves what they thought about updating their findings with more recent years of the GSS. They liked the idea, and, very kindly, David offered to do just that for me as a professional courtesy. Figure 1.1 presents findings from his updated analysis. In addition to adding the three latest waves of GSS data (2016, 2018, and 2021), this analysis differs in another respect: it recalculates age cohorts not by decade of birth but by generations.[4]

We see in Figure 1.1 different trend lines moving across the years 1972 to 2021, each denoting the percentage of a generation's strength of religious affiliation—measured as self-reported "strong" or "somewhat strong"

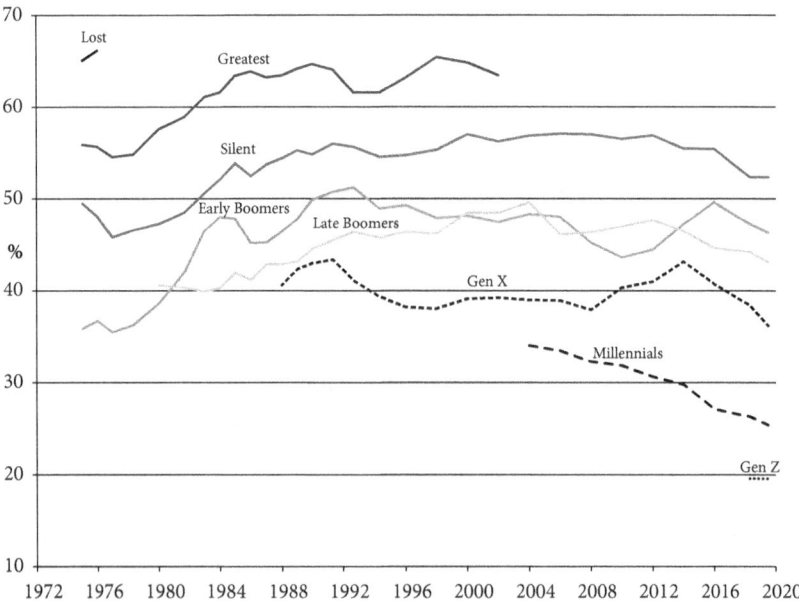

Figure 1.1 Strong or somewhat strong religious affiliation by generation, 1974–2021.

Source: General Social Survey, 1974–2021. Includes respondents ages 20–84 born in the United States. $N = 55,045$. Three-survey moving average.

affiliation with their religion.[5] Since Baby Boomers are a large generation spanning a long, culturally crucial period of time, I asked David Voas to split them in half into "early" and "late" Boomers. At the top left is a very short line representing the last living members of the "Lost Generation" (born 1833–1900) surveyed in 1972. Each line down represents a new, younger generation. At the bottom right are lines representing Millennials and a very short line for the youngest members of Generation Z (born 1997–2012), who started taking the GSS in 2021.

There are four key takeaways from these data. First, each successive generation born across the twentieth century was noticeably less strongly affiliated with religion than the next older generation. We can see a total decline among those reporting strong or somewhat strong religious affiliations, from roughly 65% reported by the Lost Generation down to about 20% by Generation Z. That is a huge decrease by generation for any social indicator.

Second, the historically predictable effect of young adults becoming more religious as they grow older stopped and was reversed after the Baby Boomers. In Figure 1.1, Boomers and older generations display an increase in strength of religious affiliation as they age.[6] That ended with Generation X, however: their strength of religious affiliation actually declined a little as they grew older. Millennials then reversed the traditional trend, becoming from the start less strongly religiously affiliated with every passing year. Before Generation X, religious organizations could expect some young people to strengthen their religious ties with age, often when they got married, had children, and settled into their local communities (increases among Gen Xers and older in Figure 1.1 also partly reflects a period effect of the 1980s, explained below). Generation X put an end to that, and Millennials shifted it into reverse by decreasing their religious affiliations the older they grew.

The third takeaway concerns historical timing: Figure 1.1 suggests that the parting of ways between Boomers and Generation X began at the start of the 1990s. When they first appeared in the survey in the late 1980s, Generation X was almost as strongly religiously affiliated as late Boomers. But the start of the 1990s sent the two in different directions. Boomers continued to increase in strength of religious affiliation, while Generation X declined. The growing gap between older and younger generations in the 1990s and 2000s is not huge but it is clear, and it fits other evidence that Generation X was the pivotal generation. This split—with Generation X and Millennials taking one path, older generations another—appears to have first opened up at the start of the 1990s.

Finally, a reasonable argument can be made that a "period effect" is also at work here. Namely, the conservative decade of the 1980s—the Reagan years, which touted a return to traditional virtues and religion—displays an increase in religious affiliation strength for Baby Boomer and older generations.[7] This apparent effect is not enormous and overlaps some with the aforementioned expected age effect for late Boomers. But by the 1980s, early Boomers and those of older generations had already done most of their marrying and having children, so their relatively more steeply increasing lines in the 1980s cannot be entirely explained by that age effect. That provides evidence, substantiated by more to come, for the argument that the 1980s put a temporary pause on cultural forces operating in the late 1960s and 1970s that were challenging traditional religion, which, after the 1980s, were restarted by Generation X and accelerated by Millennials.

US Religious Service Attendance

The GSS also asks American adults how frequently they attend religious services—a central feature of traditional religious practice. This allows for a similar analysis; namely, trends in religious attendance among different generations across time. Figure 1.2 shows an update of Voas and Chaves's 2016 analysis, showing those who attend services monthly or more often.

The story is similar. Regular service attendance has dropped among each younger generation of Americans born since 1900. In 1972, about six out of ten members of the Lost and Greatest generations reported attending religious services regularly; by 2021, only about one in four of the youngest generations reported the same—a 35% drop. The 1980s, however, show a temporary bump up in regular church attendance, especially for early Boomers and the Greatest Generation. Again, starting in the early 1990s, Generation X diverges from late Boomers in their respective trend lines. Millennials then take religious service attendance on a steep downhill run, and Generation Z picks up where they left off.

One additional observation: in the first half of the 2010s, the religious service attendance of not only Millennials but also of every living generation took a noticeable downward turn (the one exception being early Boomers, who had begun their longer-term decline in the early 1990s). The timing of the start of those downturns does not align precisely across the generations. But the larger trend is evident. By this time, the steep drop seen in

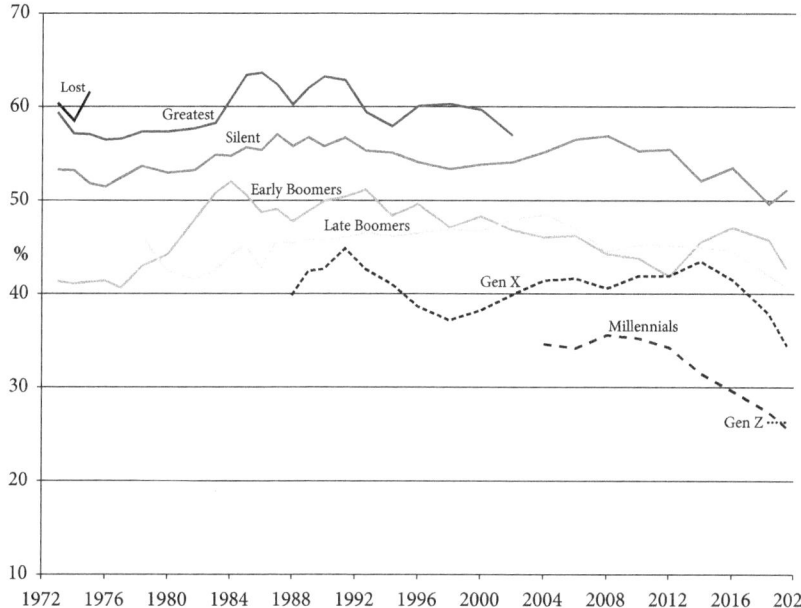

Figure 1.2 Religious service attendance monthly or more often by generation, 1972–2021.

Source: General Social Survey, 1972–2021. Includes respondents ages 20–84 born in the United States. N = 59,153. Three-survey moving average.

Millennials becomes closely paralleled by every other generation except early Boomers—the main difference being Millennials' lower starting baseline and the fact that they never experienced an increase as older generations had.

In short, regular attendance of religious services by adult Americans has been in long-term decline over at least the last half century, largely through a process of generational replacement. Rates of regular attendance were roughly stable across time within older generations until about 2010, but, from each generation to the next, the percentages of regularly attending Americans consistently dropped. Religious service attendance among the Boomer, Silent, and Greatest generations, and even the youngest members of Generation X, increased in the 1980s, but that was soon followed by a leveling off and eventual decline. At the start of the 1990s, Generation X also more clearly veered away from Boomers, with dipping attendance rates. Young adult Millennials continued that downward trend.[8] By roughly 2010, even older generations were attending religious services less regularly.

Average Age of Regular Religious Service Attenders

Another perspective on changes in religious service attendance can be found by computing the average age of regular attendees across time. Figure 1.3 presents the results of this calculation for adult Americans, again using GSS data collected from 1972 to 2021 (I show both mean and median averages, but the differences are negligible). "Regular" attendance here means attending two or three times a month or more often.

We see that the average age of regular religious service attenders in the United States increased appreciably across these years, especially after the early 2000s—though, again, with a quick dip in the early 1980s. In 1972, the average attendee by both measures was a bit over 47 years old. By 2021, the average age had risen to about 58, an increase of 11 years, or more than 20%. Furthermore, the COVID-19 pandemic artificially suppressed average age of attendees in 2021, since it disproportionately removed the most elderly religious attendees, lowering the final average age compared to what it would have been otherwise. The average age of clergy has risen as well, from 50 to 58, between 2000 and 2015.[9]

In short, the group of American adults who regularly attend religious services has gotten older in the past five decades, especially in the past 20 years. How can we explain that? One way is to note that Americans were living 5.9 years longer on average in 2021 than in 1972.[10] Some non-trivial part of the increase in Figure 1.3 is thus explained by an increased overall life

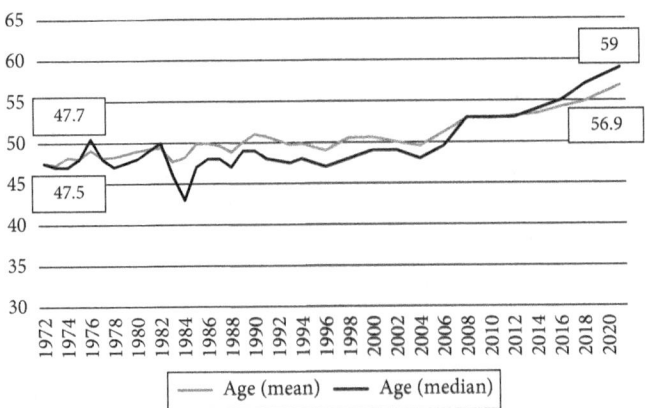

Figure 1.3 Average age of US regular religious service attenders by year, 1972–2021.

Source: General Social Survey, 1972–2021.

expectancy. However, increased life expectancy cannot be tipping the scales that much here because life expectancies and average ages of populations increase at different rates, the latter more slowly.[11] That means some other cause must explain part of the average age increase seen in Figure 1.3.[12] That answer is in Figure 1.2: younger Americans have been attending religious services at markedly lower and declining rates. The average age of those left attending services regularly has thus increased over time.

Knowing God Exists

Figure 1.4 repeats the same kind of analysis shown in Figures 1.1 and 1.2 but is focused on the number of adult Americans who report that they are certain that God exists. The GSS did not begin asking this question until 1988, but we can see the same pattern of religious decline by generation. Smaller percentages of each successive generation born since the early twentieth century profess that they know God exists. Older generations express more

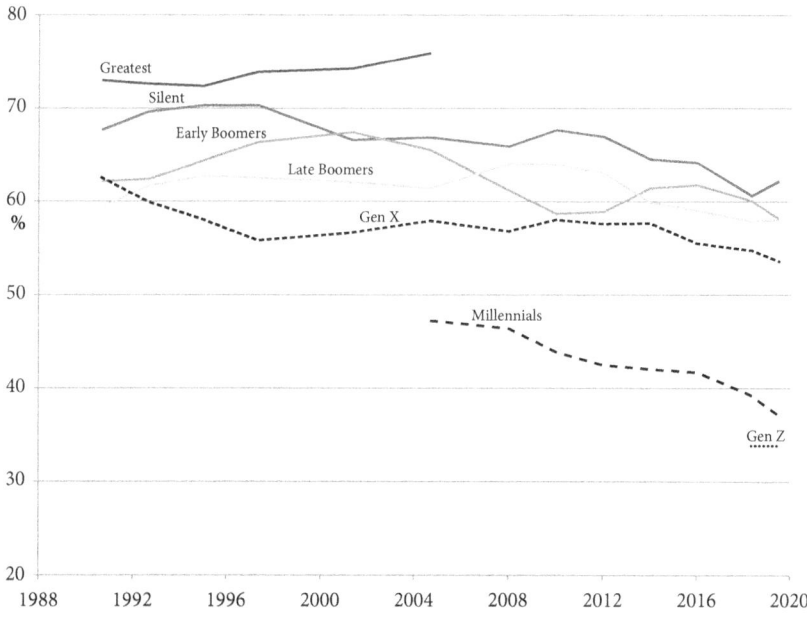

Figure 1.4 Knows God exists by generation, 1988–2021.
Source: General Social Survey, 1988–2021. Includes respondents ages 20–84 born in the United States. $N = 23{,}130$. Three-survey moving average.

certainty, younger generations less. Millennials especially express lower certainty about the existence of God and decline in their certainty over time at a faster rate than the rest. In 1988, nearly three-quarters of the Greatest Generation said they were certain God exists, an amount that increased some as they grew older. In 2021, only about one-third of Millennials reported the same, having dropped more than 10 percentage points from their baseline in only 16 years. Situated between those extremes, members of the Silent Generation, Baby Boomers, and Generation X all declined over time in their certainty about God's existence, with Generation X decreasing the most.

The Rise of "Not Religious" Americans

We turn next to the historic increase in numbers of not-religious Americans since the early 1990s, again using GSS data. Figure 1.5 shows two trend lines running from 1972 to 2021. One is the percentage of all adult Americans who report no religious affiliation; the other shows the same but is limited to 18-to-29-year-olds.[13] There we see low and stable numbers of all American adults (about 7%) and of 18- and 29-year-olds (about 12%) reporting no religious affiliation from 1972 until 1991. Little changed during that period. After

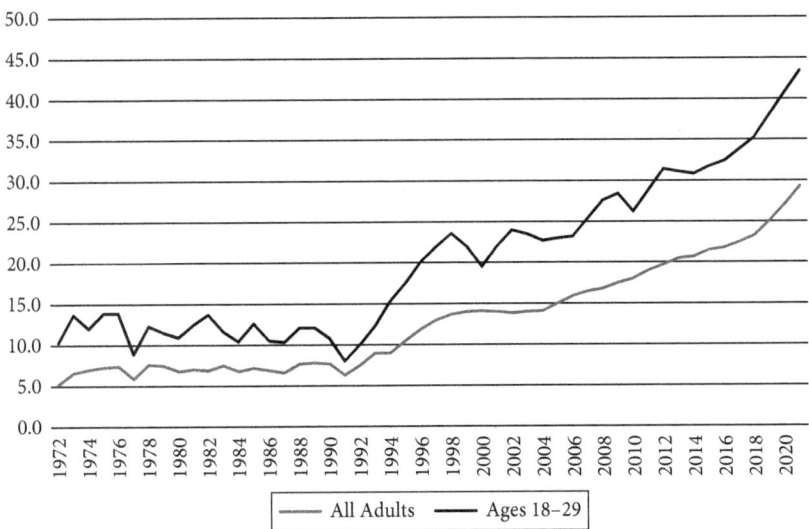

Figure 1.5 US adults self-identifying as "not religious," 1972–2021.
Source: General Social Survey, 1972–2021.
Note: Between-survey year mean values are imputed.

1991, however, those figures began to rise. The percent of not-religious adult Americans increased from 6.3% in 1991 to 29.3% in 2021, a growth of 4.7 times the baseline. For those ages 18–29, the growth was even more dramatic, from 7.9% to 43.4% in 2021, a number 5.5 times larger than the 1991 baseline.[14]

These numbers are staggering. "Few important social phenomena show such steady change over such a long time," observed Mike Hout, New York University sociologist, and Tom Smith, principal investigator of the GSS, in 2015. "We find no evidence of a slowdown," they added.[15] They were correct. The years since 2015 have shown no reduction in the growth of the number of self-identified not-religious Americans, especially among younger adults.

Identifying as "Spiritual but Not Religious"

While the share of Americans who claim no religious identity has clearly grown, there is another group that is more difficult to measure: the "spiritual but not religious." National surveys only began asking questions about this identity in 2005, and no survey has asked the same question about it consistently over time. We therefore lack trend data to measure its growth precisely. We do know from historical research on spirituality that popular interest in it is not new but has come and gone in waves.[16] The most recent wave rolled in at the start of the twenty-first century. Research in the Association for Religion Data Archives (ARDA) shows that, in the first two decades of this century, many national surveys asked whether people were "spiritual," with the question's wording differing among the surveys. Six of those surveys used question wordings that reliably speak to our interest here.[17] The results show that between 20.7% and 34.2% of Americans identified themselves with the label "spiritual but not religious," with the mean average for those five surveys being 25% claiming that identity. Based on these surveys, we can conclude that by the start of this century roughly one out of four American adults came to consider themselves "spiritual but not religious." That is a significant increase from earlier in the previous century. I explore this phenomenon in more depth in Chapter 7.

Church Closings

These declines in affiliation and attendance have, not surprisingly, had an impact on church growth. Research on Protestant congregation start-ups and closings—based on 34 denominations and groups that represent 60% of US Protestant churches—suggests that church closings overtook new church plantings in the latter 2010s.[18] In 2014, an estimated 4,000 new Protestant churches were planted, while 3,700 closed that year, resulting in a net gain of 300. In 2019, before COVID-19 spread in the United States, about 3,000 Protestant churches were started but 4,500 closed, resulting in a net loss of 1,500 in one year. Mainline and liberal Protestant churches were hardest hit, but white evangelical and Black Protestant churches have also been losing congregations.[19] In short, "church planting is slowing and the number of closures is growing," noted Ed Stetzer, executive director of the Wheaton College Billy Graham Center. Scott McConnell, executive director of Lifeway Research, which conducted the study noted above, observed that "over the last decade, most denominations have increased the attention they are giving to revive existing congregations that are struggling. This has been more than a fad. [It is] a response to a real, growing need to revitalize unhealthy congregations." Church-planting pastor and author Daniel Im commented, "Over the past few years, I've noticed a growing hesitancy to plant [new congregations], which is why these numbers don't surprise me. Starting a church from scratch is not as it used to be, especially with the rise in Boomer pastors retiring and needing to find a successor." More time and research are needed to confirm these trends. But considering that this loss began before the COVID-19 pandemic caused 20% of Americans to reduce their attendance and as younger generations increasingly replace older ones in the population, the number of Protestant churches should continue to decline.[20]

American Catholicism has also suffered the closing of thousands of parishes. The number of Catholic parishes in the United States in 1990 was 19,620. By 2022, more than 3,000 had closed or moved, and just 16,429 parishes remained, a 16.3% decline from the 1990 high.[21] Relatedly, the number of Catholic schools also declined. In 1990, there were 7,395 Catholic elementary schools operating in the United States. By 2022, that number dropped to 4,751, a 36% loss. In that same period, the number of Catholic secondary schools decreased by 11.3%. In addition, between 1990 and 2022, the number of Catholic infant baptisms declined by 56%, adult baptisms by 69%, first communions by 37%, and Catholic marriages by 70%.

According to the 2020 Faith Communities Today survey, the average size of US congregations also shrank significantly over the first two decades of this century. In 2000, the median number of attendees at a worship service was 137 people. By 2020, that number was reduced to 65—a 52% loss in size in 20 years. The percentage of all US religious congregations with worship service attendance of less than 100 grew from 45% to 65% in that same period. According to the report's metrics, two-thirds of congregations do not count as "spiritually vital." Most churches that were growing in size were those that were already large. Financial giving per capita declines with congregation size, so the overall amount of funding for all congregations has declined as well.[22]

These numbers help explain the surge in congregational closures, particularly among Christian churches. "There's a huge mismatch between small congregations and large properties," notes Richard Reinhard of the Niagara Consulting Group, which specializes in church building reuse and redevelopment. "Their real estate becomes too big and too expensive for them. In New York, San Francisco, Miami, developers are chomping at the bit to come in and get their hands on urban church properties and to turn them into luxury condos or . . . offices. In poorer communities and in rural communities, often churches just sit there and nothing happens to them."[23] Joel Belz of WORLD magazine put it this way: "Get ready, America . . . for the huge collapse from within that is soon to result in the locking of hundreds and then thousands of church doors across our country—all from the inside."[24]

Confidence in Religious Institutions

Another approach to assessing recent losses by traditional religion is to measure people's trust in traditional religion as an institution. Since the early 1970s, the Gallup Organization and the GSS have tracked Americans' confidence in various public institutions, including banks, newspapers, public schools, Congress, the military, television news, and the police. The decades-long trend is the same for 14 out of 15 institutions: declining confidence.[25] Americans have progressively lost confidence in almost every major social institution over the last half century. The only differences between the various institutions are the degrees of confidence expressed and the pace of the declines.[26] Among those institutions polled have been "organized religion" (GSS) and "the church or organized religion" (Gallup). Consistent with the larger trends, Americans over the past five decades expressed long-term declining confidence in religion, as shown in Figure 1.6.

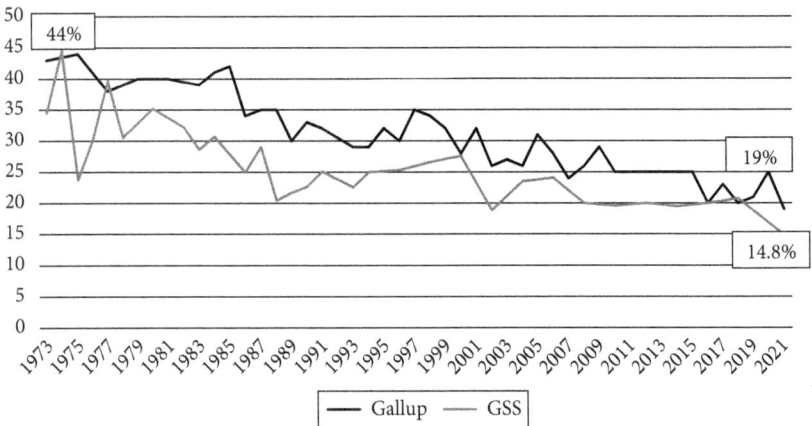

Figure 1.6 Percents US adults professing a great deal of confidence in organized religion, 1973–2021.
Source: General Social Survey, 1973–2021, Gallup 1973–2021.
Note: Between-survey year mean values are imputed.

In the early- to mid-1970s, about 44% of Americans professed a great deal of confidence in organized religion. By 2021, that number had dropped to 19% in the Gallup survey and below 15% in the GSS. These are massive decreases: between one-half and one-third of the baseline. Conversely, only 11% of Americans in 1973 reported to Gallup having "very little" or "no" confidence in religion; that increased to 31% in 2022.

Does this decline in confidence vary by age? Figure 1.7 shows the differences in trust in organized religion, as reported by GSS, separated into four distinct age groups. We can see that every age group declines in confidence in religion in roughly the same proportions. We also observe that the two younger age groups generally report lower absolute levels of trust than the two older groups, even as trust declined among all groups.[27] Trust in organized religion spiked at the start of the Jimmy Carter presidency and then dropped for most age groups by the end of his term. It jumped briefly again at the start of the conservative 1980s but then declined from there. By 2021, all age groups' levels of confidence in organized religion had been cut in half or more from their 1973 baselines. In sum, traditional religion has been losing ground among Americans, especially younger ones, no matter how you measure it: affiliation, practices, beliefs, identities, number of congregations, and confidence in religious organizations have all been declining.

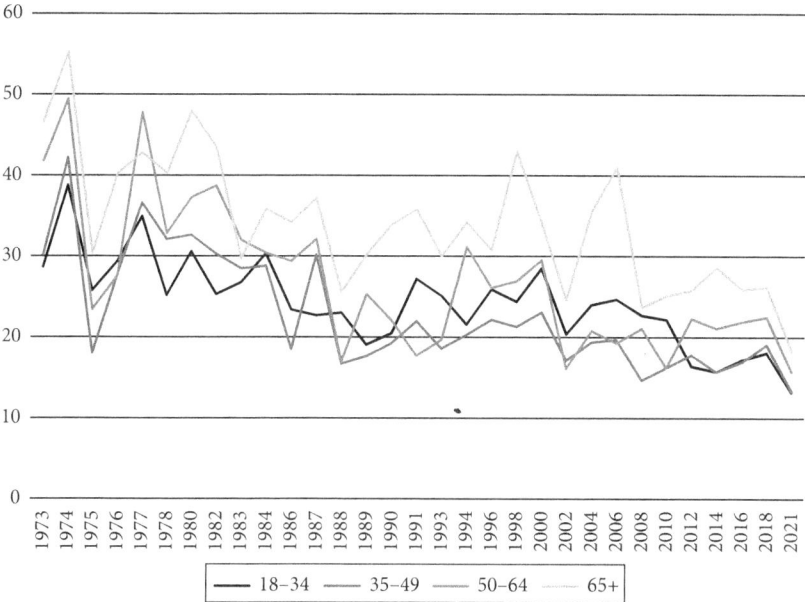

Figure 1.7 Professing a great deal of trust in organized religion, stratified by age groups, 1973–2021.

Source: General Social Survey, 1973–2021.

Note: Between-survey year mean values are imputed.

Ratings of Clergy Honesty and Ethical Standards

Americans' estimation of the ethics and ethics standards of US clergy has declined as well. For many years, Gallup has asked Americans to rate the moral integrity of people in many different occupations—from teachers to judges to car salespeople—with this question: "Please tell me how you would rate the honesty and ethical standards of people in these different fields—very high, high, average, low, or very low?" Figure 1.8 shows ratings of clergy from 1977 and 2021 for all Americans and those ages 18–34. In the mid-1980s, more than two-thirds of Americans believed that clergy had high or very high moral standards. By 2021, however, those ratings were cut by more than half, from 67% in 1985 to 32% in 2023.[28] The ratings by younger Americans, ages 18–34, fell even more sharply, from a high of 70% in 1985 to a mere 22% in 2021. The greatest declines occurred in the latter part of the 1980s, when sexual and financial scandals rocked prominent televangelists, and then again after the mid-2000s, when the widespread abuse of children by Catholic priests hit the news (discussed in detail in

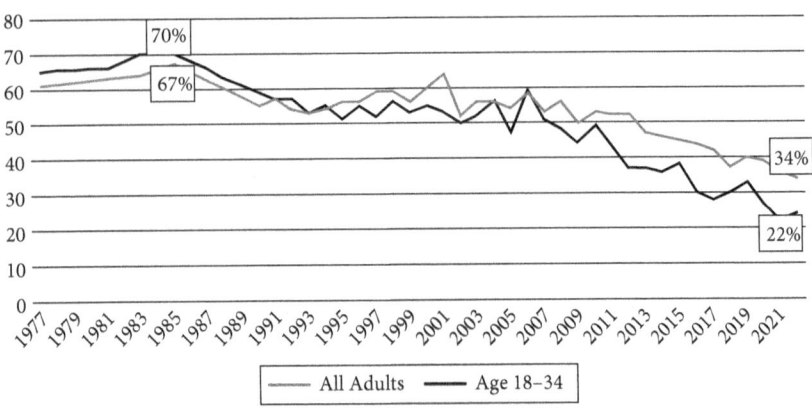

Figure 1.8 US clergy honesty and ethical standards rated high or very high by year (%).
Source: The Gallup Organization, 1977–2021.

Chapter 7). Thus, in the United States, the profession of religious leadership lost a moral luster it had long enjoyed. By the late 2000s, the majority of Americans no longer believed that clergy operated with very high standards of honesty and ethics.

Are Survey Measures of Religion Valid Indicators?

Some scholars, such as Nancy Ammerman, critique the kind of measures I have cited here. They argue that these kinds of surveys miss much of what is happening on the ground. These scholars contend that the sacred is in fact alive and well in the modern world but is often found outside of religious settings and cannot be readily captured by such standard religious measures.[29] I agree. In fact, this book's analysis illustrates those arguments well. While traditional religion has suffered undeniable losses, that is only part of the story—there is much more going on beneath the surface, a cultural "re-enchantment." In the following chapters, I will argue that this re-enchanted "more" relates directly to those losses. To understand the recent American religious experience, we will need to expand our field of vision and our analytical concepts well beyond those that can be measured by surveys. Still, my aim is to explain the decline of *traditional* religion. Doing so will require attending to all that Ammerman and similar critics emphasize. But for purposes of "establishing the phenomenon" the survey measures cited above are appropriate indicators of traditional religion's fate.

Dispatches from the Front by Religion Leaders

One way to get beyond survey data is to talk to people engaged in religious work on the ground. In an attempt to do just that, I spoke to a variety of pastors, seminary teachers, and other religious leaders. They were of different ages, genders, races, and religious traditions and were experienced in a wide range of religious work. Some were from relatively successful congregations and denominations, others not. Our conversations focused on their observations about changes in American culture and how they may have affected pastoral work. We talked about the ways in which the larger sociocultural environment may have changed over the decades and what impact on religion those changes might have had.

In these conversations, I cautioned against romanticizing the past, selective memory, rose-colored glasses, and threat-anxiety narratives sometimes used, consciously or not, to mobilize religious revitalization. I recount parts of some of these conversations here to add another view on the question of the growing losses and difficulties that traditional American religion has confronted in recent decades. The statistics above picture the world from a high altitude. The voices that follow give a sense of how those macro facts are refracted through the experiences of religious leaders in the trenches.

The universal perception among the people I consulted was that something big had definitely changed in the larger culture in recent decades and that this change has made religious work much more difficult. They offered different possible explanations for this change, but all were convinced—notwithstanding my cautions—that the world today is clearly different from the past they remembered in ways that made the work of religious ministry more challenging. One faculty member of a mainline Protestant seminary, for example, told me

> The world has changed, and it shows in expressions of the body, tattoos, piercings, sexual morality—bodies are indicators. Church pastors know that things have changed but they do not know how to deal with it, what to do about it. They themselves are often caught up in it—say, feel no need for piety, don't believe in sin anymore, are privately part of the new culture

themselves. Some pastors try creative ministry initiatives but usually it doesn't work. In an open cultural marketplace of "mindfulness" and social justice, pastors literally don't know how to share the gospel anymore, or what the church has to offer that is different. Some turn and blame their denominations for being out of date. I also know young adults well who were formed by Christianity and then decided they don't need it anymore. They think "works righteousness," meditation, diet, exercise, and sports will bring inner contentment. They're actually quite anxious, always looking to the internet for some answers or control in life. But they will not reconsider faith and church. They learned from the church, but now feel no need for it. The secular works for them, supposedly.

A pastor of a successful Black Protestant church described things in this way:

> How do you create sustainable outreach? Inviting college students to church today is like inviting them to outer space. The old vestiges are gone. Shiny digital devices are everywhere. Everyone has access to so many stories, narratives, information. It starts young, digital technology, kids now weigh all the possibilities against the gospel. You can't just tell people whatever in church and they believe it. Social media, Instagram, Snapchat, it absorbs attention, frames how they view the world, with social envy, fear of missing out, almost neurologically how to view the world. The gospel should be a worldview, but there are no shiny-button apps for the gospel. It's hard to ask people to turn away from things offered in this shiny bright world. There is a disconnect between the inherited church and the world in society, in music, dress, information. How do you even get youth now to take life's questions seriously? Can't download information they must believe. So, the question now is, how to get people to think about how they should even think itself?

A former pastor and now head of a Protestant church-leadership education program observed:

> Pastoring in the twentieth century was easier. I was one. I became a pastor at the end of a cultural era that supported "programmatic" church, where design and creativity happened at seminary or denominational headquarters then was pushed down to congregations for pastors to implement locally. That top-down model stopped working in the 1990s. It had

assumed a cultural homogeneity that was no longer there. Some tried to replicate Saddleback or Willow Creek. Disaster. Cultural diversity means pastoral and lay-leader work has become so much more complicated, you have to know how to read culture and pay close attention to context to be successful. Boomer churches were about homogeneity. But youth today live in highly diverse worlds—their friends, work, cultural diversity, with race and immigration. If they don't see that in church, nobody in their twenties will be there, they just will not be part of an isolated, homogeneous group. If Sunday morning feels different from day-to-day, they get suspicious. So, while older people wish to return to the past, youth want something different. Even seminary students don't want to go into established churches, they want to start their own with more diversity. Some young pastors innovate. But denominations are so focused on loss and consolidation that leadership doesn't support their creativity on the ground. The work now is both harder and more important. But not much in the culture helps to make things work. The seminary students I know are up for it, but the seminary itself is struggling to give the language to figure out how to move it forward. And pastors trying to deal with this are exhausted.

One thinker in a Catholic ministry-formation institute observed:

> There's a paradigm shift in habits and constructions of thought and behavior that is technology-driven, with social media platforms, digital devices. Yes, watered-down theology and distractions are corrosive to youth being engaged in the Christian story. Then institutions have lost a lot of trust and authority. Signing on to a parish to get fed isn't attractive. Self-actualization drives no felt need in people for religious institutions. Online are echo chambers, people may drift into religion, but not in the old ways. It's now loose associations of ideologically similar counterparts assembling in media-based tribes. It's very different. And now in a pandemic, the old ways people socialized, related, did community have been blown apart. Old parish and community cultures are blown to bits, not to mention people who have simply lost their faith. I see some good efforts to try to address these things, to find out what is missing in churches, to get to the root. But dealing with the digital world is also dividing parishes by age and opposing approach to new media. Even political divisions in national media news are divisive in parishes.

A mostly rural Black district conference leader in a mainline Protestant denomination reported that

> I see new complexities related to ministry. Before, church was the staple of communities in my area, not optional, so they put some fear into younger people. Now people are more aware, do their own research, don't need the church, feel they can have community on their own, not in a building. People now have ways to explore other faith traditions, not Christianity, and struggle to understand who God is and identify more as agnostic or atheists. The church has done a disservice to our witness too, with its own failings, creating a dark shadow over why anyone would want to be Christian, which affects foundational pillars of church work. People are ashamed, afraid to share their faith, keep it to themselves. We don't have adequate words for sharing faith, people do not share out loud, it's hidden, so then fewer others hear and know about it. Society as a whole has also contributed. Younger generations do not look to church as a primary place to be, don't value going to church except on holidays. They don't see how following Christ is a value-add to living lives. "Spiritual" is more popular, expressed in forms that don't require church. People do want community, to impact the world, that's still important. But not in church. Church now after COVID is like Netflix, you can binge watch on your schedule or tune it out. Why dress up and go Sunday morning when you can do what you want when you want? So the church needs to reimagine how to meet people where they are, not require Sunday mornings. But it's not clear we will do that.

More concisely, one pastor participant in an evangelical pastoral education class I monitored online observed simply, "There is nothing in the culture anymore that supports or reinforces what we are doing in Christian ministry."[30]

These observations and others reported to me suggest that a new cultural zeitgeist has emerged within which religious institutions are struggling to operate successfully. The winds have shifted, and it is no longer clear how best to sail. None of these observers provides a systematic analysis—they emphasize different features of the new context and specific difficulties it poses. Beyond the specific challenges, however, one detects a general groping in the dark for a clearer understanding of that bigger, inhospitable environment and what to do about it. Religious institutions lack any clear strategy or roadmap for renegotiating this new cultural terrain. These voices express not only loss but also being *at a loss*—the very kind of thing we would expect to hear from leaders whose institutions are suffering obsolescence.[31]

Conclusion

This chapter set out to establish an empirical fact; namely, that traditional American religion has in recent decades suffered major losses on multiple fronts, primarily among younger generations.[32] The evidence suggests that at least some of these losses built on longer-term trends, which appear to have paused in the 1980s, but which picked up again in the early 1990s and have accelerated since. Generation X was the pivot point that sent the culture off in new directions, forging an initial shift that Millennials self-assuredly embraced and have carried forward. Evidence suggests, too, that Boomers may be increasingly following the path first cleared by their children.

I take the multiple survey measures and reports of religious workers on the ground, discussed above, as indicators of a larger, latent cultural fact: that traditional religion in the United States has gone obsolete. Every indicator I have seen supports this interpretation. This is not just a story of declines in various sociological measures of religiousness: something bigger and more pervasive has occurred at the macro-cultural level. For younger generations especially, traditional religion has gone the way of the electric typewriter. Somewhere around the turn of this century, traditional religion shifted from being merely disfavored to being obsolete.

Do we have reason to believe that measurable religious decline indicates cultural obsolescence? We directly asked Americans their views on the matter. Table 1.1 shows the results of a question we asked on the 2023 Millennial Zeitgeist Survey about religion's relevance ("Which of the following comes closest to your view about the relevance of traditional religion in the US today?"). Cultural obsolescence, remember, involves much more than summations of survey opinions. But surveys can be useful indicators. Non-religious and less-religious Americans are the ones who have driven religious obsolescence. Regular religious service attenders, we can infer almost by definition, assume that religion is relevant. Table 1.1 thus presents findings both for "lower attenders" (those who attend religious services less frequently than once a month) and for the full sample. We see there that, among the 71% of Americans ages 25–77 who attend religious services less than once a month, 51% of Millennials report that they think US religion

Table 1.1 Views of Traditional US Religion's Relevance or Obsolescence by Generation

View of relevance of traditional US religion	Early Boomers	Later Boomers	Gen Xers	Millennials
Lower attenders				
Totally obsolete	11	9	11	25
Somewhat obsolete	26	28	34	26
Somewhat relevant	33	29	30	26
Highly relevant	22	23	11	8
Don't know	9	11	14	15
Full sample				
Totally obsolete	8	7	8	20
Somewhat obsolete	19	24	27	23
Somewhat relevant	28	28	29	27
Highly relevant	39	30	26	16
Don't know	6	11	11	14
TOTALS (unweighted *n*'s):	100 (*n* = 341)	100 (*n* = 358)	100 (*n* = 485)	100 (*n* = 677)

Source: Millennial Zeitgeist Survey, 2023 (*N* = 1,861).

Notes: Percents may not add to 100 due to rounding. Lower attenders attend religious services once a month or less often.

is obsolete (25+26%). Another 15% say they do not know, which suggests a disconnection from or lack of interest in the issue itself. About one-quarter grants that religion is somewhat relevant. Only 8% of lower-attending Millennials say that traditional religion is highly relevant—a minority that is highly disproportionately "born again" Protestants. (Exactly what this minority of respondents has in mind about religion being relevant we do not know. It is possible that some, likely not the "born again" group, are simply acknowledging that religion drives important political conflict—culture wars by the Christian Right and religious nationalists, for example. That, however, would not necessarily be an affirmation of the religion's value, since they may hate the religiously driven conflict that makes it socially relevant.) The bottom line is that two-thirds of the Millennial generation view religion as either obsolete or not a matter they have an opinion about, which is arguably an indirect expression of obsolescence.

As expected, older generations tend to view religion as more relevant than do Millennials, trending up from Gen Xers to Boomers. This means that, absent an unlikely future transformation in Millennials' views of religion, generational change will mean that more Americans will view religion as obsolete with each passing year. Also as expected, adding in the balance of survey respondents who attend religious services once a month or more often (the lower half of the table) increases reports of religion's relevance a little. The overall patterns are the same for the full sample as for the 71% of lower attenders, but the distributions shift a bit toward relevance. All of this comports with my argument about obsolescence: it does not mean total extinction or abandonment. Clearly some younger Americans still practice religion and view it as relevant. They are a distinct minority, however, whose share more in common with older generations than with their peers who are driving a different attitude about religion. Behind these basic survey numbers lie multiple layers of shared, influential cultural meanings, movements, and institutions—as we will see in the chapters that follow—that reinforce these trends. In short, for the majority of Millennials, religion has simply become obsolete. In the rest of this book, I will try to explain why and how that happened.

2

Religion Is Good When...

To understand why the social changes examined in the following chapters worked to make traditional religion obsolete, we must begin by understanding how Americans think about what religion is *good for*. Religious leaders may hope that people are religious because they believe the doctrines are true. Surely that's the case for some people. But Americans also value religion for reasons beyond theology—indeed, for reasons that are just as important, or even more important, to them than theology. Most Americans have a set of criteria for what proper religion should be and do, principles that make religion not just right but also good and useful. When they see religion validate those principles, they tend to affirm and support it. When they see religion violate those principles, they doubt, distance, and detach themselves. Explaining changes in Americans' interest in religion, therefore, requires understanding what Americans expect of religion and whether they see religion living up to those expectations.

In addition to the religious doctrines that Americans may or may not care about, they also evaluate religion by six imminent goods they believe it ought to deliver. People need not be consciously aware of these expectations and standards. Nobody articulates these assumed expectations systematically. But when people talk about why religion is good or bad, valuable or problematic, it becomes clear that these assumptions are running in the background of their minds. They help comprise the "cultural models" that govern what most Americans expect from religion and what they use to determine their evaluations of it.[1] These six goods are as follows.

1. **Morals**: Religion is good when it helps people to be good, moral, and nice and to make good choices in life—especially by teaching children the basics of ethics and decency.

Religion's primary job, in the minds of most Americans, is to make people good. Good people make life nicer for everyone and help society to function better. As one person told us bluntly, "A lot of religion is the practicality of how to get along with others so we can operate without killing each other, without disrupting the safety and security of people, so we can go about and be productive in some sense. Kind of offers an antidote to anarchy, I suppose."

Religion, most Americans assume, is at heart about teaching people to be moral and providing motivations to behave well. The Ten Commandments, Jesus's parable of the Good Samaritan, the command to love thy neighbor—all are tools for making people moral. As one person we interviewed told us, "Religion is one cultural tool useful for instilling values. If you look at the Golden Rule or other codification of kindness in various religions, you can see that is often a principle of religion, and religion can be a great tool for that." But the details do not matter much since most Americans consider all religions ultimately to offer essentially the same core moral teachings: be kind, forgive, do not steal or cheat, do not be mean or hurtful, do your best to be ethical and caring.[2] One of our interview subjects expressed this clearly: "Most religions are similar in style, basically the whole point in treating your neighbors as your brother, just being an overall good person, don't steal or harm, so on. A lot of religions are very similar. They have basic codes of conduct." Another put it more pithily: "Same stories, different deity."

Adults, most Americans think, may need some reminding about these moral teachings. But it is children who really need to learn basic morals because they are training for life and highly impressionable. Parents, most Americans believe, should be the primary moral teachers of children, but it can be smart for parents to draw on the aid of religious traditions to reinforce what they impart. Americans do not agree about children's innate morality. Some believe that children are naturally good but can benefit from having their innate moral decency reinforced by religion. Others think that children have both good and bad tendencies that can lead them down very different paths so they can definitely benefit from the positive ethical teachings of religion to steer them toward the correct path. Either way, if parents opt to draw on religious resources to help their children turn out to be good people, then religion is performing its proper function. As one person told us, "Growing up in the church, there were a lot of things I felt were really good teachings. Nowadays I completely disagree with the majority of it, but having the church as a child and it being a positive experience was a good way for me to tell good versus bad."

Sunday school, Bible school, Hebrew school, religious summer camps, religious day care, and hearing scripture read by clergy: these are valuable resources for early childhood moral education. For minority religious traditions with strong ethnic ties—such as Indian Hindus or Thai Buddhists—cultural clubs organized by temples also help to keep children tied to family identities and moral and cultural values. Teenage youth groups are also a good reinforcement of moral teachings for middle schoolers and, if parents can keep them attending that long, for high schoolers. Plus, these religious activities surround young people with peers from families who share their religious backgrounds and, presumably, moral ideals—thus reducing the time they might be exposed to less-positive influences.

Religion is also a good place for adults who have strayed from the path of moral living to get back on track. In the words of one interviewee, "I believe people can change, they just need to find some sort of guidance." That may involve attending a 12-step recovery group sponsored by a religious congregation. It may mean seeking healing and forgiveness in a religious counseling or support group. It might mean confession and guidance from clergy, elders, deacons, or other religious leaders. It could require becoming part of an "accountability group." Or it may simply be the renewed involvement in religion by adults who know in their heart that they need a life reset and could use the support of other good people. Whatever the circumstances and needs, the background assumption is that religion stands ready to help any person with the right intentions to acknowledge what is good and turn away from the bad.

Religion, according to this framework, is also expected to approach the teaching of moral goodness with persuasion, gentleness, and grace. Law enforcement, schools, justice systems, workplaces, and other secular social institutions cannot simply let all kinds of bad behavior go. They must be prepared to punish wrongdoing and failure as justice requires. American religion, however, is almost unique as an institution (families are the other example) in that people expect it to combine the serious promotion of good conduct with a generous acceptance of wrongdoing, at least when some version of confession and remorse is forthcoming. When someone violates a rule, members of the clergy, Bible study groups, and fellow believers should not behave like the police. Rather, people expect that, in religious contexts, people will deal with moral transgressions more gently. For Christians, for example, "God is gracious and forgives all transgressions," "Let the one who is without sin cast the first stone," and "Forgive us our trespasses as we forgive those who trespass against us" should be guiding principles. When that attitude is deployed as expected, most Americans approve.[3]

Two caveats. First, although most Americans see making people good as religion's primary purpose, few believe that religion holds a monopoly on training people in good morals. Many people and social institutions—families, parents, relatives, schools, teachers, sports teams, coaches, clubs, mentors, and more—teach and promote ethical living. That just happens to be one of religion's primary functions and values. Nearly all Americans say that the primary incubator for good values is the family and the primary teachers are parents. Religion, as most see it, is a more or less useful supplement. Some may want or need it, others might not. The choice is voluntary and depends on circumstances. To anticipate a key point that will emerge more fully below, this essentially means that, in the view of most Americans, the most important task religion specializes in—making people good—is not something that requires religion. That is, religion holds no "patent" on its most important "product," it enjoys no monopoly on the leading "service" it offers. By simple logic, then, most Americans see religion as a non-essential—an option, a supplement, a life accessory from which someone may or may not benefit. The position that religion holds in the larger field of social "goods and services," as many essentially see it, is clearly not strong.[4]

Second, nearly all Americans know that, realistically, not all religious people are good. Common is the assumption that, while in any given group or organization there will always be some bad apples, these need not spoil the whole barrel. Americans, in other words, do not expect perfection from religion. At the same time, most Americans also recognize that plenty of non-religious people are morally good. Religious and non-religious people and groups contain both good and bad. For many Americans, that itself does not condemn religion to irrelevance. Religion can still help many people to live good lives, even if some in religion are bad and religion is not required to be good. But this realistic recognition makes religion vulnerable in two ways. First, it adds weight to the idea that religion holds no monopoly or patent on its leading product. Second, there is a limit on the number of possible bad apples people will tolerate in the barrel. If religion ends up having too many bad people, then its reason for existing—and its credibility—is lost. Religion, in other words, faces a threshold for internal problems that, if crossed, discredits it. In some ways, most Americans, even if they are not personally religious, have big expectations of religion. And, as the saying goes, the bigger they are, the harder they fall. We will see the results of this framework of thinking engaging lived experience in the 1990s.

2. **Positive psychology**: Religion is good when it helps people cope with life, sustain a positive outlook, and feel calm, happy, affirmed, and encouraged.

A second good most Americans think religion can provide is emotional and psychological support.[5] When religion benefits people in these ways, nearly everyone has to commend it. If religion helps people cope, according to this view, it is hard to knock it. Life is difficult and gives people lots of reasons to feel anxious, frustrated, and discouraged. Nobody likes to feel this way, so if some people find ways to cope with life's difficulties in religion, then what's the problem? Many religious Americans tout this support as one of the benefits of having faith. Even most non-religious Americans acknowledge that religion offers this advantage and see it as good when it does. As one person told us, "Religion grounds people and gives something to turn to in difficult times of adversity. In moments of great loss, people often turn to religion, which is fantastic. The great losses I've experienced in life, I haven't felt the need to turn to religion, but I know that's not the same for everyone I love, they needed religion to get through it." To each their own, people say. Whatever floats your boat. You do you.

People rarely question *why* religion may make people feel better. Many anti-religious people might say that you should not rely on imaginary beings, superstitions, and other irrationalities to cope with life. Better to be realistic and depend on more intellectually honest sources of mental and emotional well-being. But that critique is a minority position. On the other end of the spectrum, a certain kind of highly religious American might say, "Darn right—people are not imagining a God or the power of prayer or the healing capacity of worship or the hope of heaven. All of those things are real and true, and that is exactly why they make believers happy and at peace." "If I'm going through a tough time, I just remind myself that I've been taking care of [by God] so far and will continue to be," one interviewee said. "Without faith, I would probably be bonkers." In the words of the old hymn, "It is well with my soul." But the most anti-religious and highly religious are outlier positions. Most Americans do not care for debates about theological metaphysics. The more pragmatic, majority sensibility holds that if it works, it's good.

This appreciation for religion's capacity to help people cope and feel positive works mostly in religion's favor. But it is can cut both ways. Not all parts of traditional religions make people feel good. Yes, religion should comfort the afflicted, but it should also afflict the comfortable. Christianity, for example, talks (or at least talked) about dying to oneself, enduring the dark night of the soul, tithing 10% of one's income, loving one's enemies, and the prospect of the rich burning in hell for ignoring the poor. Nonetheless, few Americans value religion for challenging them in ways that make them feel uncomfortable. The popular appreciation of religion for its positive emotional benefits must tempt some clergy to downplay the harder, more difficult, and demanding sides of their faiths. The American religious economy operates on voluntary adherence, attendance, and contributions by the faithful. So, for clergy, deciding how to present full and honest accounts of their traditions without alienating congregants can be a delicate matter. The supply side of religion must accommodate the demand side somewhat or many may walk out the door. And that can distort religious traditions. The so-called Beatitudes—which teach, "Blessed are the poor," "Blessed are those who mourn," "Blessed are those who suffer persecution"—can easily morph into, in the title of one former megachurch pastor's book, *The Be (Happy) Attitudes*.[6]

More germane to this book, plenty of Americans can and do decide that they are turned off by religion when it does not provide the expected psychological benefits. If religion is boring or confusing, why stick with it? If serious conflicts arise in one's congregation, why hang around? If getting involved only adds more stress to one's life, what's the point? Above all, if religion makes one feel guilty, goodbye. Guilt is bad. Religions, especially Catholicism and Judaism, have a lingering reputation for guilt. Life is hard enough without religion making its own people feel guilty. If that happens, religion becomes a liability, not an asset. That kind of religion is considered morbid, perhaps even pathological.[7] Better to do without it. That, at least, is the outlook of very many Americans who have left religion behind.

This positive psychology good of religion shows up in our interviews in these ways: "Any type of religion is good, is better than none. I don't care what it is. Having something that teaches a person to have faith in something beyond themselves gives them hope." "Finding peace is really important for a person because you really get to see people change." "Religion can provide people with a sense of purpose in life and comfort when encountering death. The idea that when you die you just cease to exist is kind of scary, so for some people, the idea of an afterlife could be a comforting way to approach life."

3. **Getting along**: Religion is good when it fosters community, social cooperation, peace, and harmony.

What is true at the psychological level is also true interpersonally and socially. Most Americans believe that religion should not only be making individuals more moral and positive, but it should also be building community and making the world a better place. "Religion is an important source of community and social cohesion, of moral teaching and personal identity," one interviewee told us, "it is good for society, it can create that community and cohesion." Since the world suffers loneliness and is riven with conflict and violence, another good thing religion can offer is to draw on whatever moral authority it has to promote community, benevolence, and peace. Americans believe that all religions at heart, when not corrupted, teach peace, love, and harmony. These are the rough societal equivalents of the morality religion is supposed to cultivate in children. Within families, similarly, if religion can provide a common identity and strengthening of relationships between family members without coercion, most Americans approve. Many parents value family solidarity and hope for it to continue after their children grow up and leave home. Some of them look to the religions in which they raise their children to provide the glue that holds families together.[8]

Similarly, most Americans are ready to grant religion their approval because of the community and belonging religion provides. Religious and nonreligious Americans know that local religious congregations are places where many find their second home, important friendships, and social support. Ask what is valuable about religion and many point to the community life, sharing, and learning together that religion affords. We heard that repeatedly in our interviews: "One good thing about religion is, if you're new to somewhere and want to go to church, you can find a church, do all the activities, meet all different people, and feel a part of that type of community," said one respondent. In the words of another: "I think the most appealing thing about religion is not the beliefs but the community: there's so many churches that bring people together, like a fish fry or a field trip, the camp for kids, things like that. Then if something happens to somebody in the church, they have other people that help out."

Previous studies have suggested that religion generated one-half of all the social capital in the United States, primarily through social ties in religious congregations.[9] Most Americans seems to value and want to be part of a warm, safe, supportive community, at least in theory. People know that churches, temples, synagogues, and mosques can and not infrequently do create that kind of desired community life. Religious Americans often extol their own congregations, expressing how much they value their community there. Most non-religious people who have no desire personally to belong to a religious congregation themselves appreciate that many others do and are happy for them.[10] Again, if it works for others and makes them content, more power to them.

But then comes the double-edged sword. Most Americans can also be suspicious of community. As much as community can be close, warm, and supportive, it can also be smothering and coercive. "Community," many worry, can be used as a nice word to cover for groupthink, invasions of privacy, and pressure to conform. Many Americans seem to suspect that something about religion makes religious communities especially susceptible to unhealthy forms of community. People's appreciation for religion can also backfire and turn people off when the conflict and feuding that religion is supposed to moderate is found within religious congregations or between religious people. Stories about political struggles dividing congregations and rumors about pious religious people who will not talk to each other are eye-rollers— and become justifications for avoiding religion altogether. Charity begins at home, as do peace, love, and harmony. Religion, people say, has to practice what it preaches in its own communities or it has no right to preach anything to anyone else. And when religious communities become exclusivist or exclusionary, people demand to know how religion can dare to promote social cooperation and harmony when it rejects certain people. Any religious group or person that is seen as judgmental, snobbish, or sectarian by implication violates the good it should be doing.[11] Once again, then, the positive potential of religion for helping people get along, of which Americans approve, comes with a shadow side that can potentially provoke their judgment and alienation.

When religion actively promotes social division, antagonism, or violence, that is seen as irredeemably wrong. Religious violence is perhaps the worst offense because it blatantly disobeys religion's own teachings of peace, love, and harmony. Not only does that make the world a worse place, it is also hypocritical. And promoting division, antagonism, and violence does not make many people feel emotionally positive.

American history shows that traditional religion can foster cooperation, peace, and community within and beyond religious groups—and that it has also sown division, conflict, and violence many times and in countless ways. When Americans in different situations have judged that religion was at least partly to blame for violence, that has prompted cooling attitudes toward religion. Louis Menand, for example, has argued that the religious fervor that helped inflame the American Civil War prompted intellectuals to conclude that religious certainty led to violence, which helped push the United States in secular directions in the later nineteenth century.[12] A similar shift, we will see, happened in the 1990s and 2000s as well.

4. **Modeling**: Religion is good when it provides societal role models for basic moral integrity, decency, and honesty—especially by religious leaders.

Religious Americans are proud when religious people, particularly from their own traditions and especially their religious leaders, demonstrate moral virtues publicly. As one believer told us, "My congregation really focuses on being that outward example of your inward faith." Even non-religious Americans can be pleased to see clergy speak and act in ways they consider virtuous. Many Americans look to religious leaders as vicarious carriers of society's moral values. Part of the "job" of clergy, in the minds of Americans, is not only to help individuals be good but also to be public models of goodness. Within their own religious communities, in public ceremonial events, and especially in the way they comport their personal lives, it somehow reassures Americans that a class of people exists out there who know, teach, practice, and demonstrate for others what moral virtues and integrity look like. Religious leaders essentially should be repositories of society's moral ideals and public representatives of the best of the culture. Many Americans thus suppose in the back of their minds that part of the occupational responsibility of religious leaders is not simply to lead their own religious communities, but also to represent their religions in public as models of their ideals for society.

This function is similar to what the sociologist Grace Davie describes as "vicarious religion."[13] Davie means that, while many people in her home country of the United Kingdom—and other parts of Europe—may not personally believe in and do not want to practice religion, they nevertheless still want and expect religion to continue to exist and carry out its activities. They would be very unhappy if, say, the Church of England just packed it in and closed up shop because of lack of support. No, Davie argues, even not-religious people—and many of them—want the church to go on functioning, to be ready to conduct baptisms and funerals when called upon, to represent the religious viewpoint in the House of Lords, to maintain in public the traditions and ideals that define their heritage. For example, when Princess Diana died in 1997, even the most non-religious of the British would have been shocked if she had been given a secular funeral. Everyone expected the Church of England to be at the ready to conduct a proper Anglican funeral in Westminster Abbey for such a solemn occasion. In such ways, Davie claims, religion serves a *vicarious* function for much of the (not very religious) population, representing and performing *for* them what they themselves do not. To American ears, this may sound like lazy duplicity. But, Davie replies, American religious individualism, voluntarism, and subjectivism—all profoundly influenced by popular evangelicalism—are very particularly American and not shared by, nor ought to be used as the standards to judge, religion in the rest of the world.

I suggest that something like vicarious religion functions in American culture as well. Religious Americans expect their own religious leaders to function as role models of ethics, virtue, and decency. So do most non-religious Americans.[14] Why should they be held to a higher standard, one might ask? Because they should practice what they preach, first, but also because part of their given occupation in society is to model and champion the best of what "we" consider good, right, and true, even if we consider their religious beliefs misguided.

As with the above standards, when this works well, religion benefits in the eyes of public opinion. But that opportunity to shine comes with a risk and a problem. The risk is the fact that religious leaders are humans and not angels and are therefore susceptible to stumbling and failing. When that happens, the price is high because, for most Americans, hypocrisy is one of the worst sins a religious person, much less public religious leader, can commit. If you climb onto or allow yourself to be put on a pedestal, the resulting fall might shatter you. The same does not apply to leaders in other fields. A married Wall Street banker caught with cocaine and prostitutes? Big deal, what did anyone expect? But a priest or rabbi or bishop or deacon? That's a different story.[15] Members of a fallen leader's religious community *may* be prepared to forgive them, but the American people are almost certainly not. That is the risk of religious role modeling.

Another problem also complicates these matters for even the most morally steadfast religious leaders. Over the past half century, Americans have become polarized about how to define what is good and true. In the 1950s, a religious leader could resolutely denounce godless communism or in the 1970s lead a coalition in the war against drugs, and nearly everyone would nod in approval. But in recent decades? Americans have become so divided about abortion, sexuality, race, immigration, gender, education, library books, and any other number of culture war conflicts that it is impossible for any leader to take a stand on any issue without provoking condemnation by those who disagree. To serve as a role model on behalf of any instance of "justice" or "equality" or even "truth" is automatically to be dragged into partisan warfare. What issues of moral integrity are safe for religious leaders to stand up for? Being nice? Honest? Sharing? Perhaps. But religious leaders then sound like they are teaching kindergarten.

The options for religious leaders trying to represent religion positively under those conditions are: try, fail, and be condemned; try and then succeed in making some faction happy and another furious; or give up. We know that in former eras of American history, such as the 1950s, religion enjoyed environments in which religious leaders could behave publicly in ways that reflected well on religion. Furthermore, even when they did not behave, there were fewer means for their duplicities and peccadillos to be exposed. But society has changed and, especially beginning in the 1990s, the "role model" standard for approbation began, with a good deal of "help" from religion itself, to work powerfully against traditional religion, as we will see below.

5. **Moderation**: Religion is good when it is moderate, not too weird, and certainly not fanatical or extremist.

For most Americans, if religion helps a person and serves society, that is fine, at least, and maybe great. But just don't take it too far. Don't overdo it. Don't be fanatical. Religion may be potentially good for some people when taken in moderation. But too much of it is scary, makes others uncomfortable, or leads to bad outcomes. In one interviewee's words, "I don't like when people take religion to extremes and convolute it into something it should never be. People use religion as a mask or excuse to be hateful or mean."

Simply *being* extremely religious can *itself* be a problem. There is just something wrong about it, most Americans think. That is what weird people do. "Evangelicals, they're a little kooky, in my opinion, just from what I've heard and seen. They're more of an extremist religion," one person told us. So religion may be acceptable, but only when it remains moderate, civil, and mostly private. Nearly all Americans believe this. Only the most zealous religious people would demur, seeing themselves not as weird but instead dedicated to the truth.

This realization first dawned on me while studying the religious and spiritual lives of American youth in the early 2000s. Conducting interviews with teenagers made plain that nearly all held in their minds a negative image of people who are "too religious," a phrase I heard repeatedly. For them, "too religious" peers were those who carried Bibles around school or had Jesus patches on their backpacks. That shared expectation of moderation shaped the way religious teenagers presented themselves. Nearly all sought to observe the unwritten rule that says whatever you're into is okay as long as you're not *too* into it by muting their own public religiousness.[16] The same emerged when I studied religious parents in the United States. Many hoped their children would grow up to be serious religious believers who practiced their family's faith with sincerity. But not many wanted their kids to become super-religious fanatics or anything. Moderation and civility were plenty good enough. As one interview subject stated plainly, "Do people need religion to learn morality? Yes, as long as it's not a radical, yes."

6. **National solidarity**: Religion is good when it strengthens America as a nation.

For a long time, religion was thought to be a source of American national identity and solidarity.[17] In a way, this was the national equivalent of religion's contribution to "getting along." In the colonial period, eight of the 13 original colonies had established state churches, intended in part to bind citizens together. Religious dissent, however, challenged those arrangements and, once the First Amendment was applied to the states, established churches became a thing of the past. Thereafter a powerful Protestant establishment arose through which "non-sectarian" Protestantism asserted itself as an informal religious cultural and political authority.[18] The intention was again to join the nation together in an unofficial cultural unity. That worked for those in power, but Catholics, Jews, Native Americans, and other minority religious groups were treated as second-class citizens or worse.

The Protestant establishment weakened in the early twentieth century, but, in its place, in time, a Cold War "Judeo-Christian" patriotism developed that again attempted to unify the nation. That era was a pinnacle of religion's ability to forge national identity and solidarity. In his book *God-Fearing and*

Free: A Spiritual History of America's Cold War, Jason Stephens argues that postwar religious and secular intellectuals fashioned a new national master narrative that enabled America to come to terms with a felt loss of innocence while also steeling itself for its epic struggle against communist totalitarianism.[19] The issues and debates among the intellectuals were complex. But at a popular level, the narrative was accessible: America, the land of religious freedom, stood against the atheist, Marxist-Leninist state communism of the Soviet bloc. In 1950, Pennsylvania Senator Edward Martin declared that "America must move forward with the atomic bomb in one hand and the cross in the other." President Dwight Eisenhower similarly championed the cause. As president-elect, Eisenhower declared, in 1952, that the American form of government was based on Judeo-Christian moral values.

> This is how they [the Founding Fathers in 1776] explained those [rights]: "We hold that all men are endowed by their Creator..." not by the accident of their birth, not by the color of their skins or by anything else, but "all men are endowed by their Creator." In other words, our form of government has no sense unless it is founded in a deeply felt religious faith, and I don't care what it is. With us of course it is the Judeo-Christian concept, but it must be a religion with all men created equal.[20]

Eisenhower confided the following to his close friend and guide, the Reverend Billy Graham: "I think one of the reasons I was elected was to help lead this country spiritually. We *need* a spiritual renewal."[21] Never one to miss an opportunity to evangelize, Graham publicly instructed, "If you would be a true patriot, then become a Christian. If you would be a loyal American, then become a loyal Christian."[22] Princeton historian Kevin Kruse writes, "Immediately after [taking] his oath, in his first official words as president, Eisenhower asked 125,000 Americans in attendance—and the estimated seventy million more watching on television—to bow their heads so that he might lead them in 'a little private prayer of my own' he had composed that morning." It began:

> Almighty God, as we stand here at this moment, my future associates in the Executive branch of Government join me in beseeching that Thou will make full and complete our dedication to the service of the people in this throng, and their fellow citizens everywhere.[23]

The new president's inaugural prayer was a public sensation, widely broadcast and reproduced. "An oilman from Shreveport, Louisiana, printed the prayer as a pamphlet, with the cover showing the smiling president on the left, the American flag on the right, and the cross directly above. At the bottom ran the oil-man's own prayer: 'God Save Our President Who Saved Our Country and Our World!' "[24] In the US Army during the 1950s, the *Chaplains' Character Guidance Manual* instructed that the world contained three kinds of nations: "demonic" (like the Soviet Union), "secular" (much of Europe), and "covenant" nations that recognized their dependence upon God (the United States).[25] In 1954, the US Congress added "under God" to the Pledge of Allegiance. In 1956, President Eisenhower signed into law "In God We Trust" as the official motto of the United States, an act that withstood legal challenges at the Supreme Court.

America had recovered from the war, the economic depression of the 1930s, and the "religious depression" of the 1920s and 1930s and enjoyed a new mission in solidarity, forged by a national religious identity and the fight against communism.[26] Church attendance swelled to an all-time high in the immediate postwar era. Historian Jonathan Herzog observes, in his book *The Spiritual-Industrial Complex: America's Religious Battle Against Communism in the Early Cold War*, that "during the early Cold War [Americans] came closer to consensus than at any other time in modern history" with regard to the question, "Does society need religion?"[27] This era's religious patriotism was not mainly the result of an organic upsurge in popular sentiment but was planned and promoted by American political, business, and religious elites.[28]

By all accounts, the 1960s and 1970s brought an end to Cold War patriotic religion and commenced a period of national self-doubt. But, by the late 1970s, the rise of public evangelicalism, the Religious Right, and Ronald Reagan introduced a short-lived revival of 1950s-style religiously infused patriotism. It was "Morning in America," and that new day was saturated once again with religious symbolism. Country music singer Lee Greenwood's 1984 hit, "God Bless the U.S.A.," reached number seven on the *Billboard* magazine "Hot Country Singles" chart and played at that year's Republican National Convention with President Reagan and First Lady Nancy Reagan present.

Religious liberals were aghast, but they were on the outs. Many young people found the Reagan Revolution inspiring and were proud again to be Americans, too. Whether or not they were personally very religious—Reagan was not particularly—the religious patriotism of the 1980s permeated the era and strengthened national solidarity once more. But this revival eventually ran out of steam in the 1990s. The world was on the cusp of massive transformations. In the following era, religion's ability to define, unify, and strengthen the nation was again seriously compromised. That brings us to the beginning of our story about religious obsolescence, which we pick up in the following chapters.

One point before proceeding: the people we interviewed had a hard time expressing this potential religious good. As we will see in Chapter 7, religion's capacity to serve as the basis of national solidarity had faded by the 2000s, so, by the time we conducted our interviews, it was difficult even to imagine. A few linked religion and American identity as a continuing part of deep culture:

> Moral guides in the US are closely linked with the American brand of Christianity, it's a big deal. I know there's so many different religions, but it's inescapable the way it informs how we think about punishment, wrongdoing, forgiveness, atonement—all are connected to that moral framework.

A (very) few other post-Boomers visualized this good by casting it in the nostalgic "lost Christian America" frame of the Christian Right.

> I don't like society becoming more secular because religion has been the foundation since our founding fathers. There were many things founded on God and "In God We Trust" is on our money. Generations before, there was a lot of the religion. Going secular is a big reason America is going to hell in a hand basket, why all this negativity and fighting. I don't like that they've taken prayer out of schools. We're headed for trouble, because if you don't teach people, they are supposed to learn it by osmosis? It's our job to carry those things on, and we've got a rude awakening if we don't change.

And,

> I hope we can go back to a more religious America that permeates society and government. Otherwise, it's pretty worrying to me. I don't think there's anything holding us together anymore. It makes me scared, as America has less of a foundation now, it's more shaky. I really am worried about the future. I wish I lived in the 1950s, where everyone was so united and proud of the country, unified, but I don't think anything's holding us anymore.

Such voices were very rare, however. Others, even those who were not unfriendly to religion, still did not suggest it as a possible basis of national solidarity.

> We don't need a lot of commonality, it's more that we're all Americans and all here to be free and live our lives freely. It would probably be beneficial to have a little more common ground across the board, but I don't know what that would look like exactly, without leaning into some weird nationalist like Hitler youth movement or something weird like that.

Religion's potential for promoting national solidarity stands out among the six potential goods reviewed here. While the others remain largely intact, most younger Americans had abandoned this one by the start of this century, when it became clear it was impossible (more on this in Chapter 7). Religion's inability to foster national solidarity was one of the causes of religion's obsolescence.

Conclusion

To grasp why and how a dominant religion fell into obsolescence at a point in time, it helps to understand what the majority of people thought makes religion good or useful in the first place. Naming those expectations up front shows why and how different kinds of changes would have made a majority conclude that religion is not good or useful anymore. The six goods that most Americans believe make religion potentially beneficial for people and society are all conditional: religion is good when it meets these expectations and bad when it doesn't. Readers would not be wrong to note that these popularly valued religious goods already partly deviate from what most religions traditionally understand themselves as most importantly offering, so these starting baselines of evaluation already reflect cultural slippage. But sociologically they are what matter for explaining religion's obsolescence. Most of these goods are culturally entrenched, but one (national solidarity) has largely disappeared this century due to cultural changes—both cause and effect of religion's obsolescence. But they were all operative in the period leading up to and into the 1990s and—insofar as they were, after 1991, violated in many ways—are helpful for explaining religion's fate.

3

Some Complex Ways Culture Changes

To help explain how traditional American religion became obsolete, it can be helpful to draw on existing models of how change happens from different areas of study. The decline of traditional American religion is a massive social change, the kind that doesn't happen often, and it can be difficult to wrap one's head around how such a massive change can occur. So, it may be helpful to draw analogies from how such change happens in other realms. Memorable images—like needles in haystacks or dropping the ball—appeal to our intuitive powers and can be useful in making sense of complex causal dynamics. Analogies should not be taken too far, of course, but they can provide useful insights. Here, I will introduce a few that seem particularly helpful in thinking about the decline of traditional American religion. I will refer back to these in the chapters ahead.

Population Ecology Species Decline

Why do the populations of some animal and plant species in ecological systems decline in number or go extinct? Why do the number of whales or bees or American chestnut trees dwindle in specific environments? Biologists, zoologists, botanists, and other scientists interested in population ecology show that most population decline can be explained by one or more of the following causes:

1. Pathogens, parasites, diseases
2. Invasive species
3. Habitat loss
4. Pollution
5. Overharvesting
6. Climate change

These causes of species decline should be clear enough. So should their relevance for the concern of this book. The "species" of American traditional religion has declined. What has caused that? What sort of "invasive species" might traditional religion have to contend with? What might be the analogue of a "pathogen, parasite, or disease" for a social institution like religion? What kind of "climate change" might make religion's cultural ecosystem uninhabitable? Sociocultural changes have put severe pressure on American religion. Analogies to population ecology can help us to understand how those changes have affected traditional religion.

Avalanche Science

An avalanche is a mass of material moving down a slope at high velocity. The material may be snow, ice, rock, mud, gravel, or some mixture of these. Avalanches start when some material on the upper slope breaks free from what was holding it in place and falls downhill, dislodging and accumulating material as it descends. A snow avalanche, for example, is usually caused by a combination of factors, including slope gradients, snowpack conditions, air temperatures, exposure to the sun, and vibrations from snowmobiles, construction work, and so on. Once they start, avalanches accelerate rapidly and expand in mass and volume as they accumulate snow and debris.

What might avalanches have in common with American religion's obsolescence? First, only particular combinations of conditions produce avalanches: the right combination of snowfall, terrain, weather, and so on. Otherwise, snow and ice will simply stay put on their slopes. Second, these major forces of nature are triggered by small disruptions. They may be melting pieces of ice falling from a cliff or the passing of a group on skis. But once the most vulnerable section of snow is dislodged, a massive slide of material quickly plows through everything in its path. Third, in the avalanche's track, masses of snow, ice, and other objects that were not on their own susceptible to plummeting downhill are, in a process of "entrainment," picked up and carried downward by the snow's force. The avalanche does not simply transport that added material. The material becomes part of the avalanche itself as the entire system grows in volume and mass.

Similar social forces have worked to make religion obsolete. A particular combination of conditions converged to make religion vulnerable. Some of the factors that triggered religion's eventual obsolescence were modest—not the kind of thing that would seem likely to set off an enormous transformation. And many people who might have been content with the status quo were swept up by the snowballing momentum already generated by others, further up the mountain, who were more ready for change. By making the initial break, these agents of change gathered up many more people who otherwise would likely have not contributed to religion's obsolescence.

One point just noted merits emphasis: that complex *combinations* of causes are often required to produce certain effects. It is not just avalanches: big changes in social life also often work this way. Multiple causes must converge at particular times under the right conditions to produce change.[1] Remove any one of these causes and the outcome will be different. Consider, for example, America's anti-establishment cultural revolution of the 1960s. No single cause produced it. Instead, a combination of causes converged with favorable timing—including the coming of age of the Baby Boom demographic bubble, US military losses in Vietnam, the civil rights movement of the 1950s and 1960s, swelling enrollments in colleges and universities, and the influence of artists like the Beatles and Bob Dylan and postwar "Beat Generation" authors—to produce a massive social change. The growing obsolescence of traditional American religion involves similar combinations of causes. No one cause was sufficient to produce the outcome; it took many interacting with each other.

Cultural Mismatch

"Cultural mismatch" is a theory that attempts to explain why some students do not perform as successfully as expected in school. The mismatch can be between teachers and students of different social classes and racial backgrounds. Or it can arise when first-generation college students attend universities dominated by students raised in families full of college-educated people. Such students often suffer lower well-being and poorer academic outcomes than peers with similar intellectual abilities who come from environments that are more similar to those of their schools. Many experience misunderstanding, frustration, and conflicts with their teachers. Others underperform or drop out. Some explanations for these outcomes focus on students' economic disadvantages or poor academic preparation, but those factors alone cannot explain the range of interpersonal confusions, discontent, and academic underperformance. To better explain those outcomes, scholars have proposed the idea of cultural mismatch.[2]

Cultural mismatch occurs when the culture of a school or program is quite different from the culture of a child's family, home, and neighborhood. Most American educational institutions assume and promote middle- and upper middle-class cultural norms of individualism, independence, self-direction, and self-promotion balanced with appropriate levels of orderliness, cooperation, and conformity. Those cultural values shape the instructors hired, programs offered, pedagogical practices, extracurricular activities, and other aspects of school culture. Meanwhile, students who come from dissimilar cultural backgrounds—with, say, working-class parents, close extended families, and more tolerance of "disorganization"—have been socialized into different cultural norms and operate in different comfort zones. An elementary school student, for instance, may have grown up in an urban, working-class family where yelling is a normal way to get adults' attention. But she is punished for such behavior in school, where teachers, who commute from the suburbs, expect everyone to sit quietly for hours and raise their hand to be called upon. A first-generation college student coming from a family environment that rewards unity, deference, and obedience will, starting on the first day of orientation, find themselves feeling disoriented by myriad facets of college life that emphasize independence, creativity, argument, and self-assertion—leading to self-doubt, anxiety, loneliness, alienation, and maybe depression, all of which adversely affect academic performance and social integration. The effects can be palpable, with some studies measuring higher levels of the stress hormone cortisol in culturally mismatched students.[3]

Three key points deserve mention. First, such difficulties encountered by students from under-represented groups mismatched to mainstream schools have little to do with their objective intellectual abilities, academic preparation, or emotional maturity. They may actually be stronger on those measures than their majority-group student peers. The difference in outcomes is caused instead by the cultural discrepancies between their family backgrounds and enforced school norms. Second, most culturally mismatched students have difficulty, especially in the midst of their struggles, understanding what is happening to them. They will feel frustration, doubt, and disappointment. But few will have the tools to grasp the real causes of their condition. So it is unrealistic to expect them to take stock of their reality, explain the reasons for their experiences, and come up with plans to overcome obstacles. Last, the incongruity problems of cultural mismatch not only cause emotional difficulties and lower grades, but also create barriers to academic performance that produce longer-term effects of structural social inequality and group segregation.

We can borrow the idea of cultural mismatch to help make sense of religion's obsolescence. Some accounts of American religion's adverse fate focus on the intellectual objections of non-religious people. People reject religion because they just cannot believe religious teachings, think science has the correct answers, and so on. Those objections are real and are part of the story. But another basic and powerful dynamic alienating especially younger generations from religion is a cultural mismatch. The post-1991 zeitgeist was rife with subtle but important cultural signals that just did not align, match up, or resonate culturally with traditional American religion. Conscious ideas and arguments may not matter as much as often-ineffable experiences, aesthetics, impressions, sensibilities, feelings, styles, tastes, gestures, and moods—things vastly harder to recognize, assess, articulate, and engage. What matters is not whether the idea of God is plausible. The issues, rather, thrash around the semiconscious subjectivities of young people who rove about their lives with fine-tuned antennae sensing whether or not things give off the right "vibe." Does it "resonate?" Does it give off "good energy?" Life in this dimension is sorted out in realms of tacit, intuitive, instinctive knowledge and response—always informed by the background zeitgeist. Cultural mismatch meant that, for most younger Americans, traditional religion did not resonate, so they discarded it.

Particulate Matter in the Atmosphere

The air we breathe contains invisible particles of matter that can have powerful effects on us. Many people, for example, suffer from allergies triggered by often imperceptible allergens, like pollen, dust, and mold spores. Such tiny stuff in the air has the power to make life miserable. Similarly, the exhaust pipes for burned fossil and biomass fuels—automobile tailpipes, power station smokestacks, woodstove chimneys—pump hundreds of different chemical particulates, gases, and liquid droplets into the air. Volcanoes also spew masses of ash, gases, and aerosols that are able to remain in the atmosphere for years and travel thousands of miles.[4] The air inside most buildings and households often contains many particulates from various sources.

When concentrated, some particulate matter creates a haze that reduces visibility. But normally it is invisible. According to the World Health

Organization, 99% of the world's population breathes air containing particulate pollutants exceeding healthy limits. But few of us realize it. Nevertheless, particulate matter irritates eyes, noses, and throats and gets into lungs, bloodstreams, and organs. The tinier the pollutant, the more easily and deeply it can enter a body. The health consequences are huge. Around the world, ambient and household particulate air pollution contributes to 6.7 million premature deaths annually from strokes, heart disease, obstructive pulmonary disease, and lung cancer.[5] Chronic but not fatal diseases are more widespread.

Something analogous works in cultural change. Like volcanoes, social, economic, political, and technological eruptions eject volumes of hot cultural matter into the atmosphere. Similarly, social movements, idea entrepreneurs, education reformers, and other sources pump loads of new ideas and discourses into the cultural environment. Populations close to these sources absorb them in high concentrations with clear effects. Those who are more distant have little clue about what is floating in the cultural air they breathe. But imperceptible does not mean trivial. The least obvious can prove the most influential over time. Cultural zeitgeists are unique atmospheres of ambient ideas, sensibilities, and practices created by the discharge of cultural particulate matter into the social environment—particular combinations of which coalesce with distinctive effects. This "spirit of the age" may feel intangible, but it is laden with real power to affect people's lives.

I do not mean to equate zeitgeists with pollution—the analogy breaks down there. What I do wish to suggest is this: social atmospheres are chock full of cultural "particulates" pumped into them by myriad sources. Most are invisible to the people breathing them in. But many people will nevertheless absorb enough floating cultural material to affect their outlooks, practices, and discourse, though they are often only vaguely aware that is happening. In certain circumstances, particular mixes of cultural particles fuse into distinct zeitgeists that can influence entire generations. That is what happened in American culture starting in the 1990s, one effect of which was to make traditional religion obsolete.

Delayed, Nonlinear Change

If you are going to persuasively explain a cause-and-effect relationship, it is important to get the timing right. If too much or too little time elapses between purported causes and effects, it can raise doubts about their connection. The candy you ate on Monday probably isn't the cause of your stomachache on Friday. Even so, sometimes forces act in the background long before their effects are triggered. An argument with your boss might be the result of a single remark, but it might also be the result of long-simmering resentment. So the question of timing can be tricky.

In this book's case, not all observed effects followed straightforwardly from their proposed causes. Most of the causes of American religion's obsolescence line up intuitively with their effects. But the consequences of others were delayed or uneven. Thinkers from various fields have developed models that explain such delayed and nonlinear effects. *Tipping points*, for example, are the critical moments when the addition of a few small changes to a developing or sustained condition causes a sudden and dramatic change to the whole system, usually leading to irreversible effects. Changes may at first be undetectable or slight until a tipping point is reached and the effects accelerate rapidly. The last little addition of cause tips the balance so that an entire system "topples" into a very different condition. *Threshold effects* are similar. These involve effects that are felt in small ways or not at all until a critical amount of what causes them is reached—after which, the results greatly increase in magnitude. For instance, a drug may have no intended effect until a specific dosage is reached, at which point its potency fully kicks in. Similar, too, is a *critical mass*: the minimum amount of some cause required to trigger or maintain a process that will lead to an outcome. This causal image derives from nuclear physics, in which a minimum amount of fissile material is needed to maintain a nuclear chain reaction. These ideas make sense of nonlinear changes that take place in irregularly spaced spurts of time, when, at key moments, change-effects activate, accelerate, or expand dramatically. They also account for qualitative transformations that sometimes emerge from crossing quantitative boundaries. In our task of explaining religion's obsolescence, they serve as analogies to help us comprehend how things that previously seemed normal and familiar quickly came to feel dated, alien, or irrelevant.

Another related analogy comes from the *punctuated equilibrium* theory of evolutionary change. Evolution scientists disagree about the timing and rates of evolution resulting from genetic mutations and natural selection. Some embrace the theory of "phyletic gradualism," which posits that species evolution occurs gradually over long periods of time. Others hypothesize a theory of "punctuated equilibrium," believing that evolutionary history consists of long stages of stability or stasis punctuated by rare bursts of dramatic change when new species split off.[6] I have no idea whether either of the two is correct. I simply want to borrow the idea of punctuated equilibrium as an analogy for uneven social change. Something like it can operate in human social life. Normally, social practices and institutions carry on with regularity and stability even when various forces of change press on them. But occasions periodically arise when disruptive causal forces destabilize normal life and produce rapid, dramatic changes. The story of this book is similar: major environmental changes suddenly punctuated traditional religion's comparatively stable equilibrium, splitting off new religion-like species that then competed against religion.

Adoption of Innovation

Innovations in technology, ideas, products, and practices do not automatically and evenly spread throughout populations. They must be adopted, embraced, and implemented by people. The processes involved can be complex. One explanation of how this works is Everett Rogers's "innovation adoption curve."[7] The idea is represented by a bell-shaped graph that divides populations into segments according to their readiness to adopt innovations. The highest middle point on the bell curve represents the majority of people who tend to wait a while before adopting innovations. The smaller tail end of the curve on the left represents the minority who adopt innovations early, and the opposite tail end on the right are those who are the last to adopt anything new. The idea is that innovations go through predictable phases of adoption by different types of people until the majority accepts them. This model segments a population into five types of adopters.

1. *Innovators*: Repeat risk-takers with social ties to other innovators and the appropriate resources and social statuses needed to absorb possible adoption failures
2. *Early Adopters*: More judicious adopters and opinion leaders who tend to enjoy better education and social status than the majority and are attuned to cultural trends
3. *Early Majority*: The large group of even more cautious people with social ties to early adopters, who wait to confirm that the early innovation proves worthwhile and kinks are worked out

4. *Late Majority*: People who generally tend to be doubtful of innovations, usually possessing lower social statuses and fewer financial resources
5. *Laggards*: People the most skeptical of change who value tradition, tend to be older, more socially isolated, and with low social statuses and financial means

Innovations are embraced first by the Innovators, then, unless they fail, soon after by Early Adopters. If innovations prove functional and valuable, the Early Majority may begin to buy in. The ultimate success of any innovation is determined by its capacity to move from Early Adopters to an embrace by the Early Majority, the most challenging transition in the process to achieve. If and once the Early Majority accepts an innovation, this means half of the population has adopted it and its final success is highly likely. What then remains is for the more risk-averse, skeptical, traditional, socially isolated, and poorer half of the population—the Late Majority and Laggards—to adopt the innovation, which most eventually will.

How does this help us? The obsolescence of religion required the adoption of innovative beliefs, discourses, and identities. Younger generations had to embrace ideas, attitudes, and practices that were different from those of older ones. Certain types of people first embraced elements of this new outlook, worked it out in their own lives, and so helped sustain and develop it. That in turn promoted the solidifying zeitgeist's influence over increasingly larger parts of the American population. By the 2000s, the Early Majority was absorbing it. This provides one way of understanding the developments of some such changes examined ahead.

Crowding Out

"Crowding out" refers, in economics, to increased government involvement in a part of an economy that causes decreased participation by other private and civil-society actors in that market. For example, a growing welfare state taking over increasingly large responsibilities for its citizens' health, childcare, and retirement needs crowds out other groups that also contribute to those needs, such as religious communities, extended families, private firms, and nonprofit organizations.[8] Usually such crowding out of others is not intended, but the effects are real nonetheless. More generally we can think of crowding out as the encroaching on and displacing of some actors in certain spheres of society by others whose activities become more demanding or attractive. In this book, we will see that American traditional religion's obsolescence resulted partly from it being simply crowded out of many people's lives by other demands and interests that developed over time for reasons not related to religion.

Professional Control over Expert Knowledge

University of Chicago sociologist Andrew Abbott published a book in 1988 that changed the way we think about professions.[9] Previous studies examined the rise of single professions through standard paths of "professionalization." Abbott told readers to think instead about professions competing against each other in shared ecological systems for recognition of their claims to exclusive jurisdiction over expert problem-solving knowledge. Professions, he said, are occupational groups that struggle to monopolize their "ownership" of fields by elbowing out rivals who claim to possess other knowledge about similar problems. They do so by seeking to win symbolic and material recognition from outsiders—lawmakers, regulators, insurers, public opinion—who can grant exclusive rights to control certain work activities. All of this plays out over time in processes of intergroup conflict in which contenders win, hold, or lose areas of control.

Why should professions be about struggle and conflict and not simply demonstrable competence? Because multiple occupation groups often claim to know how best to solve similar problems. For example, physicians, chiropractors, massage therapists, "alternative" medicine healers, and advocates of hallucinogenic drugs all claim to possess the expert knowledge needed to solve certain problems of bodily pain. That sets rival groups in structural competition to "own" the piece of "turf" they want to control. Their struggles involve not only making claims about the knowledge and skills required to solve problems but also claims defining the very nature of the problems to solve. Take depression, for instance: Should we think of it as a moral failure, a spiritual ill, the result of childhood developmental trauma, an imbalance of brain chemistry, or something else? Different occupational groups over time have proposed different ideas.[10] The group that succeeds in defining the problem on their terms will likely win monopoly authority over it. Thus, Abbott writes, "many occupations fight for turf, but only professions expand their cognitive domain by using abstract knowledge to annex new areas, to define them as their own proper work."[11]

This all develops dynamically over time because social and technological changes alter the conditions in which various occupation groups compete. Developments in society and technology create new problems, redefine old ones, and generate new forms of potentially expert knowledge. As a result, formerly dominant professions may weaken and have some or all of their turf annexed by rivals. Professions may migrate to new ecological problem-solving niches. And new groups may vie to control turf that existing professions monopolize. Professions thus arise, fail, succeed, dominate, and decline depending on changes in their ecological environments, on competitive forces, and on the evolving judgments of those who confer jurisdictional authority over work activities. Understood as "an interacting system, an ecology," Abbott observed, "a profession's success reflects as much the situations of its competitors and the system structure as it does the profession's own efforts."

How might Abbott's system of professions help us better understand American religion's obsolescence? Like the population ecology model above, it prompts us to broaden our focus beyond religion itself to examine the structure and makeup of the larger sociocultural environment and religion's niche within it. It prods us to consider, in the larger division of societal "labor," what problems, if any, religion has lost its monopoly on solving. To understand religion's losses, we should consider what specific expert knowledge and practices, if any, religion can lay persuasive claim to as its exclusive jurisdiction. Exactly what "turf" on the field of life does religion "own," and why may that have changed? Who among contending groups has been able to redefine life's problems in ways that persuade others that their knowledge and practices are preferable to religion's or make religion's irrelevant? Whose "expertise" has displaced religion's, and what social changes fostered their competitive advantage?

Conclusion

Most of this book's explanation of religion's obsolescence should be intuitively clear. But the story is complex and raises reasonable questions about timing, connections, and causal mechanisms. These causal models from diverse fields offer helpful analogies for our own analysis, hopefully also piquing and prepping readers' minds to delve into the heart of the story. That is where we will turn next.

II
PERFECT STORMS CONVERGING

4

Long-Term Social Trends

Common sense suggests that if you are looking to explain something, you shouldn't look far. If people are rioting in the streets, it is probably because the price of food just tripled. Most big social transformations, however, are not like that. Their roots extend further back in time. Focusing only on proximate causes misses crucial forces that made those later social changes possible.[1] To understand how history develops and how society and culture change, we need a longer-term perspective.

But not too long-term a perspective. Tracing the causes of historical change can devolve into an infinite regress. Every identifiable cause of anything in history was itself caused by prior causes. An exhaustive answer to this book's question might justifiably take us through the rise and triumph of therapeutic culture after Freud, Romanticism, the skeptical Enlightenment, the Protestant Reformation, the rise of late medieval nominalism and then all the way back to the emergence of monotheism in ancient Israel. A reasonable case can be made that American religion's recent obsolescence would not have occurred in the absence of those prior conditions.[2] But such distant historical causes must simply be acknowledged and taken for granted. Our purpose here is to explain the *relatively proximate* causes of religion's recent obsolescence.

This chapter and the next examine crucial trends that were under way well before American religion began its path to obsolescence in the 1990s and 2000s. The social changes recounted here concern not religion itself but culture and institutions more broadly. Some of these trends developed over such a long period of time that nearly everyone alive today takes them for granted. But they actually formed in the relatively recent past, and, without them, the fate of religion around the turn of the twenty-first century would have been different.

Higher Education for the Masses

For all of human history, until extremely recently, formal education was the privilege of tiny minorities of elites. The English word "school" descends etymologically from the Greek word for "leisure" (*skholē*) because in classical civilizations only a privileged few enjoyed the leisure to learn in the schools of the day. Almost everyone else worked as slaves or semi-free laborers. In the United States, right up through the Great Depression and World War II, attending college or university was the nearly exclusive privilege of men from WASP backgrounds.[3] It was not until the 1930s that a majority of American youth graduated from high school, much less college.[4]

After World War II, however, all that changed dramatically. In 1940, only 4–5% of American adults had completed college. The Servicemen's Readjustment Act of 1944, however—commonly known as the GI Bill—channeled large numbers of returning servicemen and women into higher education. That, the changing character of the US economy, college student exemption from the draft in the 1960s, and huge government subsidies for community colleges and state universities launched what would become a historically unprecedented increase in the number of Americans attending college (Figure 4.1).[5]

By 2020, nearly 40% of Americans held college degrees; another 12% had attended some college but not completed a degree.[6] Younger Americans were most likely to have experienced college: a 2018 survey showed that fully 66% of 25-to-30-year-olds had attended at least some college; 47% had earned at

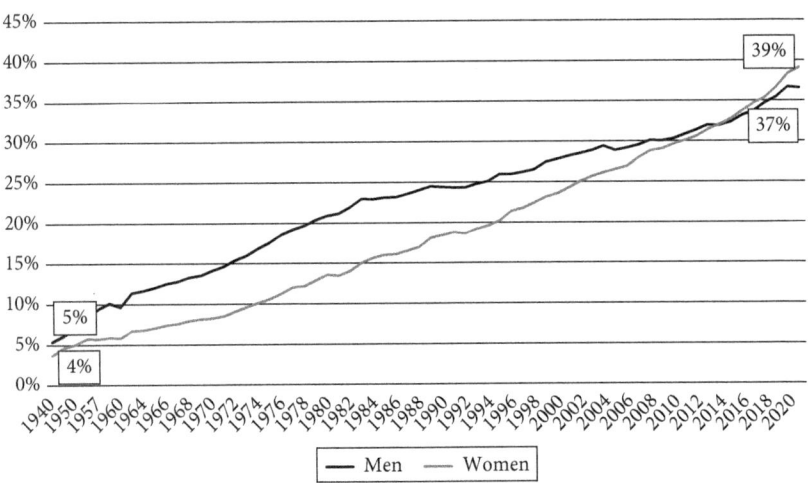

Figure 4.1 Completed four years of college in United States by year, 1940–2021 (%).
Source: US Census Bureau.

least an associate's degree.[7] In sum, by the mid-2020s, more than half of all Americans and even higher proportions of younger Americans had attended college. What only a few generations prior had been the exclusive advantage of privileged elites had become normal for children of the middle class and a possible route to upward mobility for those of the working class. As one person we interviewed observed, "For a good life you need education, you have to have it no matter what nowadays. You need some type of degree, of certification, because no one is going to be able to live a good life working at McDonald's."

Higher education for the masses could not, by itself, make religion go obsolete. Learning more per se does nothing necessarily to harm or promote religious faith and practice.[8] However, the massive postwar expansion of higher education did have two significant effects. First, it made possible and promoted a host of diverse *cultural* changes that more directly contributed to religion's obsolescence.[9] Few if any of those crucial cultural transformations could ever have happened had a huge chunk of American youth not gone to college. I will discuss this idea more below. For now, suffice it to say, the massive postwar expansion of American higher education was not the cause of religion's eventual obsolescence, but it was a necessary precondition.

Second, studies show that attending college during this period did tend to undermine American students' personal religiosity.[10] The American college student population as a whole tended to leave college less religious than it entered. The growth of higher education for many decades thus did exert some corrosive influences on religion in the United States. Until the 1990s, that is. Starting in the last decade of the previous century, going to college stopped having a negative influence on the religiousness of students.[11] Again, significant dynamics around culture and religion shifted in the 1990s. That change in the effects of higher education in the 1990s, however, does not contradict the thesis that religion's obsolescence started in that decade. It actually validates it, as we shall see.

Women Entering the Paid Workforce

At the same time that a growing share of Americans were attending college, a similar revolution was happening in the workforce. Between 1950 and 2000, the percentage of women ages 15 and older engaged in paid labor outside the home rose from 29% to 60%. For married women who lived with their spouses, the jump was from 28% to 62% from 1955 to 2000.[12]

How did this shift affect traditional religion? First, it reduced the pool of volunteer labor for religious congregations. Historically, men were more likely to hold formal authority in American traditional religions, while women performed much of the actual, local religious organizational work for free. The more time women spent on paid labor, the less time they had to devote to volunteer work in religious settings. Within American Catholicism, specifically, this same period witnessed huge losses in the number of priests and women religious, as we will see in the next chapter. With lay Catholic women entering the workforce in unprecedented numbers, there were many fewer left to fill the void of absent priests and women religious.

Furthermore, the growth of women in the paid labor force shaped the deinstitutionalization of marriage and family. Women could and did increasingly take care of themselves economically, reducing their dependence on traditional marriage and nuclear family households for their economic viability. Moreover, by the 1990s and 2000s, American work and parenting became much more demanding, crowding out religious participation for many (more on this in Chapter 6). The shift from single-breadwinner to two-income households decades earlier meant that many families saw few ways to negotiate increasingly demanding work and parenting expectations other than to reduce investments in "discretionary" activities, which is how many saw religion. And so many divested from religion. The big shift of US women into the paid workforce in the second half of the twentieth century did not directly harm religion. There is nothing intrinsically less religious about a woman who works. But a change of this magnitude is bound to have far-reaching consequences, and one of those is increased pressure on traditional religion.

The Deinstitutionalization of Marriage and Family

Traditional American religion has long been intimately connected with the "traditional" American family: two biological parents raising two or more children in one household, ideally with attendant support from grandparents and other extended family.[13] Viewed sociologically, this is clear: the programs, messages, schedules, and benefits of traditional religion primarily target and resonate best with married mothers and fathers raising kids. Whether this is intentional or not does not matter. It has long been true and remains so today.[14] The fact is that traditional religion is less effective and appealing to Americans in non-traditional, single-parent, and alternative family and nonfamily forms. Countless studies have shown that Americans who are divorced, single, cohabiting, childless, single parents, and in same-sex relationships are significantly less likely to be traditionally religious than are married adults with biological children.[15] The reasons for this are many and various. But the fact is undisputed. And it reinforces the first fact: traditional American religion plays to the strengths of traditional nuclear families.

Such a tight link between a certain kind of family life and religion makes it not much of an exaggeration to say that, as the traditional family American goes, so goes traditional religion. Demography may or may not be destiny, but, when it comes to American religion, family demography is extremely important. We therefore must understand the obsolescence of traditional American religion against the backdrop of huge changes in family culture, structures, and practices that unfolded over the preceding decades. Sociologists call this the "deinstitutionalization of marriage and family" because, with it, the traditional model loses its status as the institutionalized norm.[16] In essence, alternative family beliefs, forms, and practices have increasingly displaced the traditional American family.

Formal, legal marriage is the keystone of the traditional family model. Fewer marriages mean fewer such families. Between 1950 and 2021, the number of American adults (15 and older) who had never been married increased by roughly 50% (see Figure 4.2). In 1950, only one-fifth of women and one-quarter of men had never been married. Seven decades later, one-third of women and nearly 40% of men had never married. This increase was slow and steady over time but large nonetheless.[17]

At the same time, the way religion mattered for marriage was changing. Before 1960, for example, 81% of married Christians had spouses of the same religious tradition. Between 2010 and 2014, that number had dropped to 61%.[18] In some minority traditions, like American Judaism, the rates of religious intermarriage are very high.

One alternative to marriage is cohabitation: living together in the same household as romantic partners, not merely as roommates of convenience or friendship, for a short or long time, without legal formalization. Some cohabiting situations can and do develop into what by all appearances and practices is a traditional marriage and family life, without the paperwork.

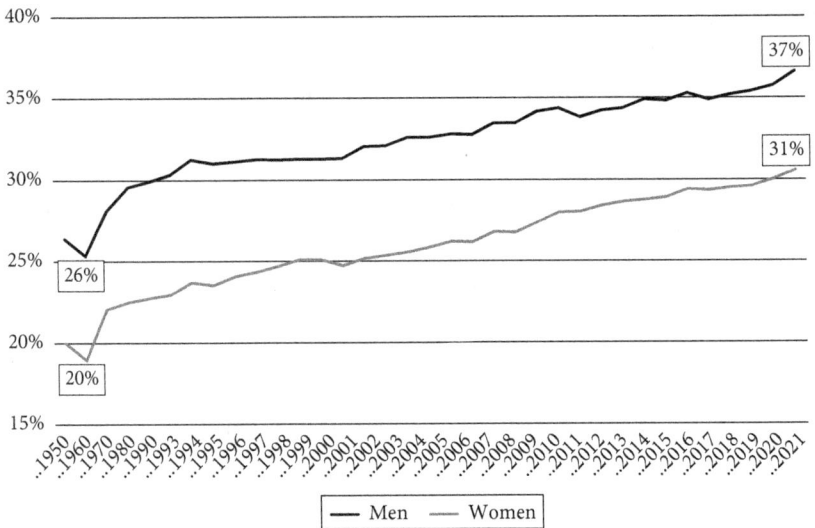

Figure 4.2 Never married US men and women 15 years old and older by year, 1950–2021 (%).

Source: US Census Bureau. *Note:* The decades 1950s–1980s are compressed in this chart on the left-hand side into the space of one year; single years are presented after 1993.

But, for the most part, cohabitation contravenes the norms of traditional marriage. It also violates many traditional religious teachings about family life and sexual ethics. An increase in cohabitation is therefore another indicator of the deinstitutionalization of marriage and family.

Between 1969 and 2021, there was a huge increase in the number of cohabiting households in the United States, both for all adults and for 25- to 34-year-olds specifically (in Figure 4.3, the scale for all adults is shown on the left side and for the younger age group on the right). In the late 1960s, cohabitation was practically nonexistent. Five decades later, however, 7% of all households and 17% of younger households featured cohabiting couples. By the mid-2010s, more American adults had cohabited at some time in their lives than had ever married—59% compared to 50%.[19] Cohabitation shifted over these years from being virtually unheard of to not uncommon and largely accepted by the cultural mainstream. At some point, most people stopped raising eyebrows at the notion. The vast majority of Americans now see cohabitation as acceptable even if the couple does not plan to marry.[20] Certain religious communities are the last strongholds of objections to "living in sin."

LONG-TERM SOCIAL TRENDS 79

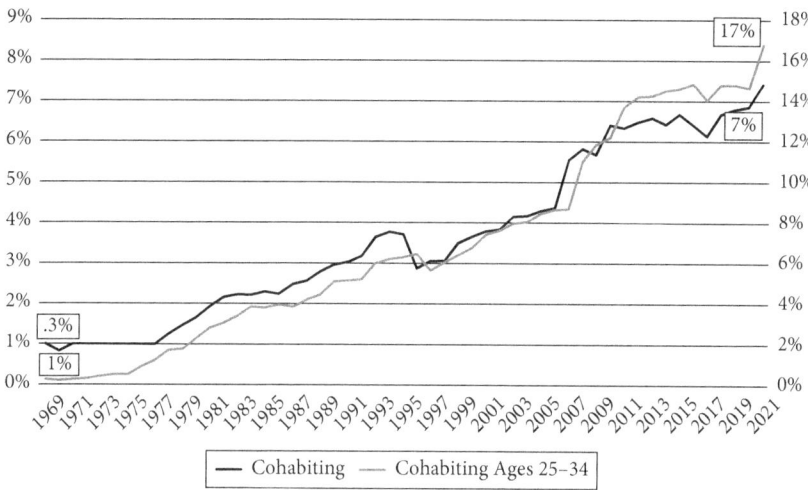

Figure 4.3 Cohabiting, all US households and by 25-to-34-year-olds, by year, 1969–2021 (%).
Source: US Census Bureau.

Another alternative to the traditional family is simply to live alone or with roommates or housemates to whom one is not related. Those households, too, have become more popular over time. Given how hypersocial humans are and the economic benefits of sharing household expenses, living alone is not an obviously natural choice. Yet, between 1969 and 2021, the percentage of US adults living alone doubled (Figure 4.4), and the percentage living with roommates or housemates in nonfamily households nearly doubled as well. In 2021, one-half of US adults lived in nonfamily households or alone.[21]

The traditional American family is not merely about marriage and household arrangements but also children. Two biological parents with children was once the norm. Parents divorcing and having children outside of marriage or choosing not to have children at all diverge from the traditional model. Everyone knows the US divorce rate is high: about 40–50% for first marriages and 60% for second marriages. That has led to a decline in two-parent households, including remarried parents, from 88% in 1960 to 70% in 2021 (the scale is shown on the left side of Figure 4.5). In an opposite trend, the percentage of US children living with a single parent—either through divorce or parents never marrying—increased nearly threefold, from 9% in 1960 to more than 26% in 2021 (the scale is shown on the right). This is far

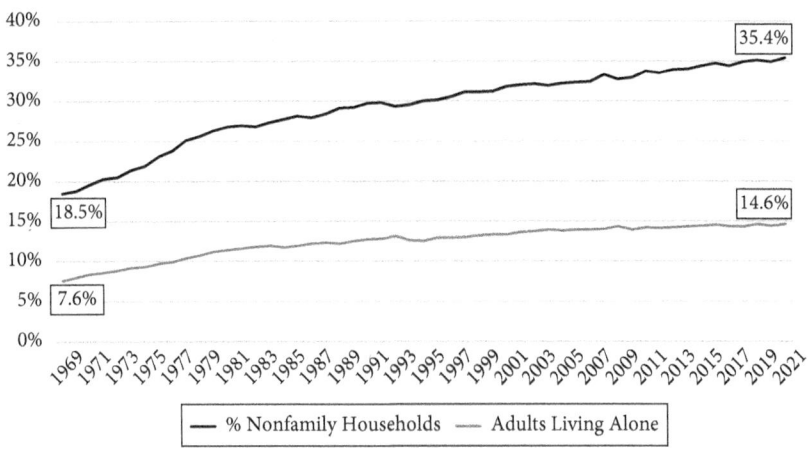

Figure 4.4 Percent of US adults living alone and in nonfamily households by year, 1969–2021.

Source: US Census Bureau.

Note: A "nonfamily" household consists of a one-person household (the resident living alone) or when a householder shares the residence exclusively with people to whom he or she is not related (i.e., roommates).

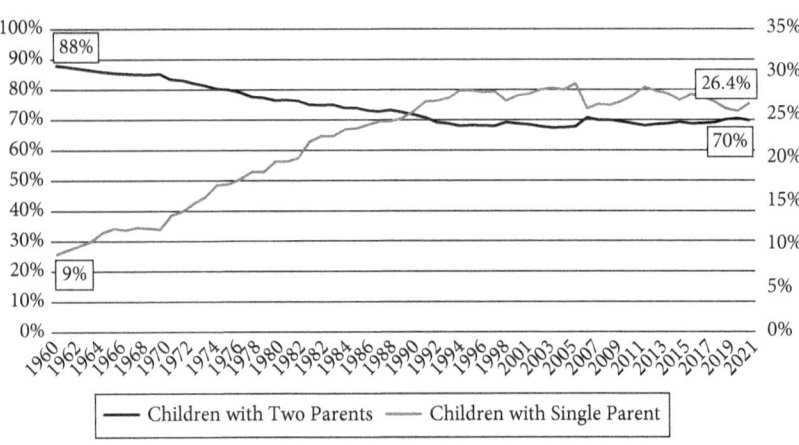

Figure 4.5 Percent of US children living with two parents and with a single parent by year, 1960–2021.

Source: US Census Bureau.

from a total rejection of traditional family norms. Still, it represents a significant shift in parenting structures for a sizeable minority of Americans, which prompted the eventual cultural normalizing of single parenthood among the cultural mainstream.[22]

Many Americans of course still do prize marriage.[23] Even so, another seemingly ordinary but in fact hugely important point about Americans who do marry is that they are waiting longer before tying the knot. In 1960, the average age of first marriage for women was a bit over 20 years old, and for men it was 22.8 years old (Figure 4.6). That provided only a few years after high school graduation to get a job or some college, choose a sweetheart, and settle down. Between then and 2020, Americans who eventually married added an average of eight additional years of waiting before finally walking down the aisle.

The reasons for these delays are many and complex, but their meaning and consequences are important.[24] As the saying goes, in earlier days young people got married and built a life together, whereas now they want first to build their own life and then maybe get married—or maybe not. Increasingly difficult economic circumstances and growing consumerist expectations contribute here, as do opportunities and imperatives in higher education noted above. But, in the end, delaying marriage indicates that the norms of traditional marriage have weakened somewhat in favor of other interests and goals.

We heard this in our interviews. One reported, "My father was married twice, and my mother three times. The fact that there were so many divorces between them definitely made me skeptical and definitely not inclined to

Figure 4.6 Average age of first marriage for US women and men by year, 1960–2021 (mean years of age).
Source: US Census Bureau.

rush to get married. It gave me the accurate impression that divorce is very common and it's not a pleasant thing." Another said, "The whole idea of marriage makes me personally feel I would be trapped, and I don't like the tethering. I don't need a piece of paper to tell me I love somebody. I don't need a husband to have a family. I'm good without all that." And, "My parents' generation waited less time before having kids. Once you have kids, it's easier to have community because things your kids are involved in, it gives you more sense of community hanging out with other young parents. Now people are waiting longer to have kids, maybe that's contributing to lack of community." Another put it bluntly:

> Traditional marriage and family is bullshit. I personally don't want to get married. I think to each its own. Some people, marriage is 'til death do them part. You can have common law. You got a live-in boyfriend, whatever. But personally I like my space.

The consequences for traditional religion are profound. American youth almost universally assume that practicing organized religion might be appropriate for adults but does not belong to the life-course script for youth after the age of, say, 15. One of the key markers of becoming a "real adult" is getting married.[25] Thus, by delaying marriage for the good part of a decade, twentysomethings exempt themselves from getting (re)involved in religion. They are not necessarily against religion, nor do they delay marriage to avoid religion. The demographic increase in age of first marriage in the context of certain cultural expectations and markers just produces that outcome without anyone having to think much about it.

Furthermore, the *specific time* of life when most of those who will eventually marry are delaying marriage is critical. Sociologists who study the life course show that life *transitions* are among the most consequential events in forming people into who they become in the long term.[26] According to the standard American life course script, the decade of one's 20s is typically, of all the decades, the one most densely packed with major transitions. The relative stability of life at home during elementary and secondary school is finished. Next comes a cascade of transitions concerning residential location, household arrangements, schooling, jobs and career, finances and budgeting, friendship networks, dating and romance, renegotiated relations with family of origin, political participation, and more. Many of these transitions also are not encountered only once but repeatedly.

Here is the point: the difference between getting married at age 21 versus 29—and thus the likelihood of settling down into established religion at the start or end of one's 20s—means the difference between navigating those crucial life transitions while involved in religion versus detached from it. In the former case, religion can help to shape how twentysomethings navigate those transitions and the choices, identities, and commitments that emerge from them. In the latter circumstance, religion is absent. In short, age of first marriage influences when, if ever, younger adults explore religion and maybe join religious congregations—such that the more they delay marriage, the more likely they also de facto delay potential religious (re)involvement, consequently removing religious influences from crucial transitions during one of the most important phases of life formation. The chances of a married couple being seriously religious at age 45 because they started thinking about religious involvement at age 25 are greater than that same couple who started thinking about religion at age 35 instead. Age of marriage is the crucial variable determining that difference.

In sum, by the 1990s, the deinstitutionalization of marriage and family in the United States had already significantly weakened one of the key structural factors that historically encouraged young adults to get (re)involved in traditional religion. Before we account for any other causal influence, religion was already appreciably disadvantaged by this single social change.

Declining Participation in Face-to-Face Membership Organizations

Americans' participation in most membership-based organizations involving face-to-face interactions declined over the decades leading up to the 1990s. According to the Social Capital Project's analyses of General Social Survey (GSS) data comparing organizational membership rates from 1974 to 2004, all kinds of organizations experienced losses over the 30-year period:[27]

- Fraternal: 52% loss
- Veterans: 42% loss
- Labor union: 41% loss
- Farm: 38% loss
- Greek: 24% loss

- School services: 18% loss
- Nationality based: 18% loss
- Political: 10% loss
- Sports: 5% loss
- Youth: 1% loss

Amid these declines in organizational membership rates, "church-related" organizations—which could include religious groups and associations in addition to traditional congregations—suffered a 25% loss.[28] Political scientist Robert Putnam has similarly shown declining trends in Americans' civic engagement over the decades after 1973. According to his analyses, for example, over this time period Americans became significantly less likely to attend a public meeting on town or school affairs, serve as an officer of a club or organization, or serve on a committee for a local organization.[29] Princeton sociologist Robert Wuthnow suggests understanding these changes not as decline but as reflecting more "porous" relationships reflecting a greater "psychological mobility" of young adults.[30] The post-Boomers we interviewed recognized these changes, telling us things like, "I don't feel I'm part of a community, maybe my strongest community now is just wherever I work. I sometimes volunteer, but I'm not that consistent with it—the only place I'm consistent is people I work around, relationships there. I do desire to be involved in some kind of community, but I'm not at the moment, it's just standing around at work." And,

> People in my generation don't have a sense of community. Older people, my parents, grandparents, they had community. That was a small town, and my mom still goes down to the library and meets up with a bunch of people and they do crafts and stuff. Then there was church for some people, different groups that hang out. But I live in the city now, and, for my age, we just don't do that.

And,

> A lot of people stick to themselves nowadays. I live in an apartment complex, and I barely know my neighbor. I don't know anyone, they move in and out so much. I don't think it's community, which to me means being involved in something. In my new career, I have a community of people there and I'll work with that. But no, I don't think there's a lot of community otherwise.

Nearly all of American religion is built on membership-based congregations involving in-person meetings for worship, prayer, education, and fellowship. When American religion entered the 1990s, a general drift away from that very kind of association was already well under way. The organizational form that made American religion was in general decline. We can think of that as a kind of habitat loss for religion as a species.

Triumphant Mass Consumerism

One of the ingredients that helped seal religion's fate in the 1990s and after was the intensification of mass consumerism as a way of life and shaper of identity. Some readers may fail to see a connection between Americans buying, consuming, and discarding lots of products and religion's obsolescence. But the connection exists. The emergence and proliferation of American mass consumerism is a subject one could spend many careers and countless publications exploring and explaining. For our purposes, I will limit myself to sketching the bare bones of the story. Essential to grasping the key ideas is realizing, first, how historically novel the consumerist way of life is and, second, how powerfully it forms identities, aspirations, and emotions. Both are difficult to appreciate when mass consumerism is all any of us among the living has ever known. But I am going to try to "make strange the familiar," as sociologists are fond of saying.

Viewed in long-term perspective, nearly all of human history has been spent in small bands of hunter-gatherer groups of about 30–40 people moving about in search of wild plants and animals to eat. Gathering and hunting food was life's main preoccupation, and possessions consisted of the necessities people could carry to new locations. Then, roughly 12,000 years ago (very recently in our species' long experience), humans learned to cultivate grains and domesticate animals, which enabled them to settle down in fixed locations. They began to live in agricultural societies, depending annually on the sun's energy to grow plants for humans and animals to eat. Those plants powered muscles that accomplished nearly all of the work that got done.[31] They burned tree and brush wood to make fires and harnessed a bit of water and wind power. Solar energy drove everything, through photosynthesis (plants and trees), evaporation (rain into rivers), and warming air masses (wind). The earth's climate during this period, the Holocene, was also unusually stable, facilitating humanity's agricultural success.[32]

Then, a mere few hundred years ago—the blink of an eye in the expanse of human history—everything changed. Humans discovered they could extract loads of a black material from the ground and burn it to power metal machines. That new energy source—coal—produced thousands of times more work than animal and human muscles ever could.[33] By the mid-nineteenth century, humans also discovered how systematically to drill, pump, and refine petroleum and natural gas to burn in powerful internal combustion engines. Discovering how to extract and burn fossil fuels was a power bonanza for human economic productivity. That derived from three facts. First, fossil fuels possess much greater energy densities than the biomasses that powered agricultural societies.[34] Second, fossil fuels are more concentrated in their recoverable locations and compact in burnable form than biomass—in short, easier to extract, store, and transport. Third, the kinds of engines that fossil fuels could power were more efficient and compact than the technologies of the agriculture era.[35]

That surge in concentrated energy supplies—first with coal but particularly with petroleum and natural gas—combined with new iron and steel machinery to escalate economic production dramatically, accelerating the Industrial Revolution and supercharging postwar capitalism.[36] The result was the increasingly efficient production of material goods in previously unimaginable quantities and quality.[37] America's big transition to coal power in the 1890s, and especially the addition of petroleum and natural gas in the 1930s, generated huge, unprecedented economic growth (Figure 4.7).

Until roughly the 1920s, American capitalism focused on production—on manufacturing products with increasing efficiency. That enterprise was a smashing success. Its achievement, however, created a problem: it produced a lot more stuff than populations had the capacity or mindset to buy. People's basic needs, material aspirations, and purchasing power remained modest. Fossil-fuel capitalism produced far beyond those limits. As a result, the system suffered recurrent cycles of overproduction, price collapses, business contractions, and worker layoffs, which only diminished aggregate purchasing power.[38] The instability of production-oriented capitalism was untenable. Threat of expansionist Russian bolshevism after 1918 and the Great Depression of the 1930s intensified the pressure to somehow stabilize capitalism. It became increasingly clear that rescuing capitalism would require making it attractive to wage laborers and not simply profitable for owners. President Franklin Roosevelt's New Deal legislation was one effort to do so.[39]

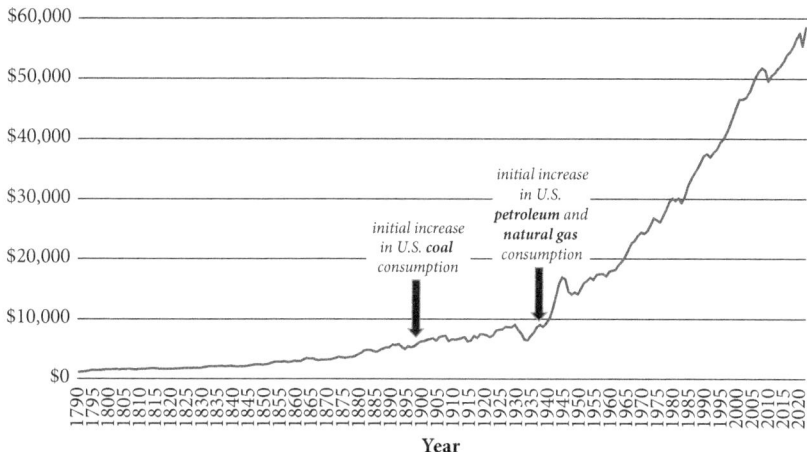

Figure 4.7 US real gross domestic product (GDP) per capita, 1790–2021 (standardized in 2012 dollars).
Source: Louise Johnson and Samuel Williamson (2023), "What Was the US GDP Then?" MeasuringWorth; Michael Mobilia and Owen Comstock (2019, July 1), "Petroleum, Natural Gas, and Coal Continue to Dominate US Energy Consumption," *Today in Energy*, US Energy Information Administration.

What helped capitalism thrive, however, was not so much a political breakthrough but an economic and cultural one. Namely, the invention and promotion of institutions, practices, and cultures of mass consumerism. The idea seemed perfect: balance capitalism's problem of massive overproduction with an equally massive increase in consumption. Soak up the supply, in other words, by motivating and facilitating greater demand. Producers would reap growing profits and consumers would enjoy material prosperity.[40]

The new mass-consumer capitalism triumphed but not automatically or naturally. It required difficult changes.[41] Employers needed to replace the nineteenth-century mentality of paying workers starvation wages with the counterintuitive idea of raising wages to create a population with real purchasing power.[42] The mass population, raised on the moral rectitude of thrift, sobriety, restraint, hard work, and delayed gratification, had to be re-educated to embrace limitless desires, continual accumulation, and the legitimacy of hedonic pleasure. Prospective consumers needed to abandon the prudent avoidance of debt as foolish and morally suspect, for example, and instead adopt "credit" and "installment buying" as endorsements of their personal financial reliability and as a reputable way to purchase goods without having to save for them. Shoppers had to be trained to buy products not first for their functional use value but for their status, identity, and emotional value. These and many related cultural and institutional transformations were required to make the new mass-consumer system work—assisted by the growth in urbanization, motion pictures, the romance ideal, upward mobility, and so on.[43]

Indispensable in this restructuring of capitalism and culture was the advertising industry, the evangelistic arm of capitalism deployed on apostolic mission. Until the late 1910s, advertising mostly consisted of detailed texts describing the features of products designed to convince customers of their usefulness for specific purposes. In those early days, the advertising profession viewed its mission as informing and "uplifting" society. The transition to mass consumerism, however, jettisoned that early method and mission.[44] Advertising's new job was to induce the masses to constantly buy products they did not need or perhaps even want. That required contriving novel strategies to generate new desires, cultivate discontent, and achieve the (temporary) satisfaction of those desires and the relief of that discontent through the continuous purchasing of products.[45] Advertising, for instance, induced consumers to worry about how others would see and judge them depending on whether they used a particular product or not. It taught people to associate material goods with desired traits of masculinity and femininity, success in romance, fulfilling friendships, and class sophistication. Advertising encouraged people to make choices based on feelings, insecurities, and impulse, not rational reflection or critical judgment.[46]

In its hugely successful campaign to sell ever-growing quantities of goods, the advertising industry transformed popular culture so that life was understood to be centrally about shopping for, buying, consuming, and discarding mass-manufactured products.[47] It vastly expanded what people considered basic necessities and raised expectations for the acquisition of money. Much of this is invisible to most post-Boomers, but some do express ideas like, "A big part of my shopping is the desire and need for more things. That's really hard because there are insidious ways they turn things you need to live into gratifying experiences. That's a very intentional process, and next thing you know, even the food you eat, clothes you wear, they become a very rewarding consumerist experiences." And, "My mom and grandfather, they're extremely driven, hardworking people, both very financially motivated as well. I'm more financially motivated than them. I have always grown up having a lot of nice things around me, but never feeling entitled, that I have to go out and get them myself. Being raised that way has made me want to have a certain type of job, a certain income, and certain types of material objects." And,

> I'm into things like anime and whatnot. My girlfriend and I just went to a store that sells that merchandise. It's expensive, all the options, and I'm stressed. I didn't get what I wanted but I still got to have my gratification buying something, that's pretty typical. Always susceptible to that deeper conditioning that makes you feel that way buying things. It creates a lot of tension and anxiety because it really reinforces how inescapable these things are, how it's like entrapment, imprisonment.

More fundamentally, this revolution redefined persons not primarily as citizens or Presbyterians or proud family farmers but as consumers: perpetually hungry creatures out to satiate their appetites through the acquisition of products purchased on the market. In short, American advertising successfully redefined a good life as the *goods* life and success as a steady upward march to ever greater material prosperity.[48] That marked a profound transformation of American deep culture away from agricultural-era visions and values.[49] Even very early on, increasing wealth began to corrode religions, and the cultural world it helped produce was mismatched with that of traditional religion.[50] Consumer capitalism was a kind of pollution threatening religion's survival. How that manifested itself in the 1990s is something we will examine more closely in Chapter 6.

Intensifying Expressive Individualism

One aspect of the cultural zeitgeist that helped make traditional religion obsolete was a particular view of the self, called "expressive individualism." This is the view that each individual possesses a unique inner self that needs to be discovered and authentically expressed, one that external authorities threaten to compromise and that, to realize authentically, individuals have to trust their subjective feelings and personal experiences as final authorities. Of course, this view was no invention of post-Boomers. Contemporary expressive individualism draws from many diverse cultural wellsprings.[51]

A major source of expressive individualism is an intense modern "inwardness." Philosopher Charles Taylor traces this back to St. Augustine of Hippo's belief that the intelligible, spiritual reality that provides order to the world and life is to be found not in the rational order of the cosmos or universal ideals, as earlier Greek philosophy had it, but by turning inward and tuning oneself to the light that God planted *within*. Augustine's *Confessions* models precisely that kind of difficult struggle to discover truth—or, rather, to stop evading it—through a reflective exploration of one's subjectivity. Another source of expressive individualism is the Western Enlightenment's emphasis on individual reason, rights, and self-determination. Rousseau's *Confessions* followed Augustine's in form but led the Frenchman not upward to God but inward to his irreducible subjective self.[52] Closely related to these Enlightenment emphases is the Western tradition of political liberalism's prioritizing of individual self-possession and autonomy. The American Revolution placed a particular American stamp on those convictions, insisting on political liberty, self-representation, and the inalienable right to pursue happiness.[53] "Don't tread on me!" and "Live free or die!," the rebelling colonists declared.[54] Such sentiments pushed many American religious traditions in democratic directions.[55]

Expressive individualism draws most directly on the Romantic movement of early nineteenth-century literature, art, and poetry, which rallied feeling, authenticity, particularity, and nature against the rationalism, regimentation, and machinery of then-emerging urban industrialism.[56] A related, though less familiar, influence is the cultural revolution of late eighteenth-century England, in which an earlier view of the self as fluid and flexible was replaced by a new, "modern" view assuming an essentialist concept of identity combined with psychological depth and interiority.[57] Representations of American expressive individualism included the 1920s bohemians and expatriates, 1940s hipsters, and 1950s beats. Those movements then fed into the 1960s counterculture's mix of liberation, rebellion, experimentation, "tuning in," free speech, etc.[58] In 1965, the rock band The Animals proclaimed "Baby! Baby! Remember! It's my life, and I'll do what I want. It's my mind, and I'll think what I want."[59] The 1970s spawned hosts of cultural movements propagating individual self-help and self-fulfillment, sometimes mingled with ideas from New Age philosophies and (Western reinterpretations of) recently arrived "Eastern" religions, such as Buddhism and Hinduism.

The 1980s throttled down those themes, largely replacing the discourse of expressive individualism with that of a *utilitarian* individualism more consonant with the "conservative" push for free markets, career success, and "traditional" virtues. When Hollywood villain Gordon Gekko claimed that

"Greed is good," he might have been expressing the slogan of the decade.[60] Even then, the capitalist mass consumerism celebrated during the Reagan era indirectly added weight of its own to expressive individualism. Neoliberal mass consumerism's insistence that people determine their own individual economic choices (the free market) and repudiate interference by overbearing state authorities (small government)—tweaks of classical economic and political liberal themes—underscored a culture of strong individualism and autonomy in ways that then mutated and were transplanted from utilitarian to expressive individualism in the following decades.

The 1980s, it turns out, were a minor pause in the advance of expressive individualism, which was too influential a current of modern Western culture for even the Reagan Revolution to squelch. As the 1980s passed into the 1990s, circumstances changed, and a resurgent expressive individualism revived among culturally creative youth—in part as a reaction against the conservative 1980s—and diffused to many Gen Xers and most Millennials. One did not need to be a card-carrying expressive individualist to be influenced by it since its many ideas and sensibilities had long been ejected into the atmosphere and floated around thickly as cultural particulate matter.[61] The vast majority of younger Americans, for example, have unconsciously embraced the central preoccupation of expressive individualism: personal *authenticity*.[62] To assess the extent of the popular embrace of expressive individualist values, we asked survey questions designed to measure agreement or disagreement with 12 distinct beliefs central to expressive individualism.

The clear majority of American adults of all generations agree with most of these expressive individualist beliefs. The three beliefs at the bottom of Table 4.1, which are strongly worded and involve some social-undesirability bias, attract only minority support, selecting out all but the hardest-core expressive individualists. Baby Boomers tend to agree with these beliefs more so than any other generation. The only exceptions are "I spend a great deal of time thinking about myself" and "People who perform their duty but remain unfulfilled have wasted their lives," where Millennials report greater agreement than Boomers. As expressive individualists, Millennials would seem to be not an aberration but a generation successfully socialized to embrace the values of their Boomer parents—despite their less promising economic prospects.

Expressive individualist beliefs are currently so widespread in American culture that it can be difficult to notice them. Here is how it showed up

Table 4.1 Agreement with Expressive Individualist Beliefs by Generation (%)

Indicators of expressive individualism	Early Boomers	Later Boomers	Gen Xers	Millennials
Agree: It is important to follow your heart and be true to yourself	92	85	87	80
Agree: Being authentic is more important than satisfying other people's expectations	92	90	82	79
Agree: It is important to reflect regularly on whether one is leading an authentic and fulfilling life	89	85	83	78
Agree: In a good community, everyone feels recognized and appreciated for who they truly are	82	80	77	76
Agree: People should be free to reinvent themselves to express who they really are inside	80	74	83	76
Agree: Nobody else knows what is good for you better than you yourself	79	77	75	64
Agree: Life is a journey about finding and expressing one's true self	77	75	78	74
Agree: People should not feel obligated to fulfill social commitments they did not choose	72	69	68	69
Agree: Individual freedom and emotional fulfillment are life's most important values	70	68	70	67
Agree: How a person feels is a better guide for how to live than reason or rules	42	40	39	39
Agree: I spend a great deal of time thinking about myself	33	34	39	53
Agree: People who perform their duty but remain unfulfilled have wasted their lives	22	25	31	34
TOTALS	100	100	100	100
Unweighted *n*'s	*n* = 341	*n* = 358	*n* = 485	*n* = 677

Source: Millennial Zeitgeist Survey, 2023 (*N* = 1,861). Percents may not add to 100 due to rounding. "Agree" means "strongly agree" and "somewhat agree" combined.

indirectly in our interviews: "I'd like to be into expression, being able to help other people express themselves and create a space for people to feel safe and evolved. In my early 20s, getting out of religion and living on my own, there was so much we didn't know, it was scary, I didn't have a support system and it took me a long time finding resources. So I would like to create a space where young people could look at what I did as a model, to show the many options and find the space to grow and figure out what you want to be, that would be ideal." And, "I'm not good at art but I have several friends who are, so I would like to go to an island with them and just paint and make movies, feature-length films, just trying to get across ideas and stuff through art. I might as well try to get famous if I'm gonna do art." And, "More young people have and experience autonomy from a younger age. My kids have the freedom to talk back to me in a way that certainly my parents would never have been able to talk back to their parents. They have more freedom to explore their own take on the world."

The obsolescence of traditional religion cannot be pinned on this factor alone. For one thing, the data in Table 4.1 tell us about 2023, not the 1990s or 2000s. For another, we do not see a major difference between older and younger generations that would explain religion's demise among post-Boomers particularly—not surprising, since this version of individualism has deep historical roots and flourished in the United States in the 1960s and 1970s, when many Boomers were young. Nonetheless, expressive individualism is a central element of the Millennial zeitgeist, as we will see especially in Chapter 9. It was one essential ingredient in a complex combination of factors that produced religion's obsolescence.

Empirical evidence supports that expectation. I created a single linear scale combining answers to the 12 statements in Table 4.1, then divided that scale into quartiles and plotted the answers against church attendance. Seventy-five percent of adults in the highest quartile of agreement to those statements attend religious services only once or twice a year or less, compared to 42% than those in the lowest quartile. Meanwhile, 38% of those in the lowest quartile of agreement attend religious service nearly every week or more often, compared to only 10% of those in the highest quartile. These differences remain statistically significant after controlling for age, education, income, sex, and race and ethnicity.[63] The causal directions may run both ways, but the association is strong, and the causal mechanism of cultural mismatch is evident.

From Materialist to Postmaterialist Culture

The twentieth century witnessed another fundamental cultural change, one that is related to the intensification of expressive individualism and had similarly large consequences for religion: a generational cultural shift from "materialist" to "postmaterialist" values. "Materialist" here means something different from the mass-consumer materialism described above: it is more about *scarcity* and *security* than consumption—for present purposes it might be better to think of these as "post-scarcity" values than postmaterialist. The late University of Michigan political scientist Ronald Inglehart first advanced this theory of materialist and postmaterialist culture in his 1977 book, *The Silent Revolution*.[64] The basic idea is that, as societies become more economically prosperous and physically secure, the values of their populations change to reflect those conditions. In social contexts of material scarcity and physical vulnerability, people prioritize the "materialist" values of material and physical *security*. As those societies become more economically prosperous and politically stable, people begin to take the attendant material and physical security for granted. They then prioritize "postmaterialist" (post-scarcity) values of individual autonomy and self-expression, which encourage interests in things like freedom of speech, environmentalism, and gender equality. The assumption is that only when people feel existentially confident about basic material security and bodily safety are they capable of desiring and appreciating "higher" values, such as individual self-direction and expression.[65] These values were manifest in our interviews in various ways, including talk such as this: "I would like to do something creative, if I could. I still don't know what this means. I'm trying to. I was just talking to my boyfriend about it last night. It's not about creating something to sell, necessarily. That'd be great if it sold, but just being creative." And,

> People just feel more spiritual. Organized religion is very constrictive. Modern-day teens or young people have so many other options, you can see the world on your phone and through experiences. For most young people it's about life experiences. My family and grandparents' generation were more about objects, because they came out of the Depression. They cared more about objects because they didn't have anything. They say, I want to give you this, I want to pass this down to you. But in this next generation, kids or young people don't care about things, they don't want material things. They want experiences, that's what they care about.

So when I think of organized religion, I think of a confined, constrictive institution, that is completely adverse, the opposite of what the majority of young people want. They want to be free, to be open. In an organized religious standpoint, you cannot be free and open. That's why there's more push toward spirituality and not organized religion.

Research, Inglehart noted, shows that people's basic life values are learned during childhood and adolescence and are largely settled by the time they reach adulthood. Growth in economic prosperity and physical security are also generally long-term social transformations. Therefore, societal shifts from materialist to postmaterialist cultures happen not within individual lives but through generational replacement. The social situations people encounter in their youth form their basic life values and alter little even when the society around them changes. Macro-cultural change still happens, though, because new generations who come of age in more economically and physically secure conditions adopt post-scarcity values, and eventually the materialist values and culture of older generations fade as people age and pass away.[66]

For example, those we call the Greatest and Silent Generations, who lived through the Great Depression and World War II, generally adhered to materialist values of security, order, and safety. The subsequent generation of Baby Boomers, however, who enjoyed postwar prosperity and general political stability, took security and safety as givens and instead adopted postmaterialist/post-scarcity values of individual autonomy, fulfillment, and self-expression. While Boomers were still young (the 1950s), materialist culture dominated society—think the Cold War, anti-communism, suburban materialism. When they reached late adolescence and young adulthood (the 1960s and early 1970s), the generations clashed over their different value systems—in conflicts over the Vietnam War, women's liberation, sexual freedom, student free speech, the counterculture, ecology, and so on. During the height and waning years of their power (the 1980s), older generations pushed back, reasserting materialist values—think the Reagan Revolution, the Religious Right, and the "return to traditional values, morality, and education." Finally, however, as the older generations aged out of institutional power and eventually passed on in the 1990s and after, the postmaterialist values of the younger generations became mainstream.

Inglehart spent his career marshalling survey findings and writing numerous books seeking to validate and develop this theory. Some find it persuasive, others not. In broad, descriptive outlines, I think Inglehart was mostly right. And Inglehart's idea of social context-driven generational shifts in basic values partly helps to explain religion's eventual obsolescence. In two books, he tried to apply his theory to explain religious secularization as a result of rising postmaterialism.[67] I think his claims about religion and secularization confuse enabling conditions, causes, and effects and are generally simplistic and over-argued.[68] Still, his larger theoretical model provides some insight when it comes to the question of this book. The obsolescence of religion that set in during the 1990s was the result of many complex cultural changes that occurred largely through generational replacement. Gen X was the hinge of history in this regard, Millennials pushed open a new cultural zeitgeist's door and stepped through, and Gen Z has inherited it as the new normal. The influence of postmaterialist/post-scarcity values was, we will see, a significant aspect of these transformations, contributing to the cultural mismatch between the emerging zeitgeist and traditional religion.

Rise of Emerging Adulthood

The demographic and cultural changes discussed above closely relate to another longer-term development in American culture that is crucial for our story here: the rise of emerging adulthood.[69] In the past half century, numerous macro social changes combined to create a new and genuinely distinct phase in the American life course. One of these factors we have already seen: the dramatic postwar growth of American higher education. In recent decades, increasing numbers of young people have chosen to spend four or more years in pursuit of their bachelor's degree in the hope of career success. Consequently, a large proportion of America's youth are no longer ending school and beginning jobs at age 18 but are extending their formal schooling well into their 20s. Those who aim to join America's professional and knowledge classes—precisely those who most powerfully shape US culture and society—are also continuing in graduate and professional school programs, sometimes into their 30s.

Another social change that helps to explain the rise of emerging adulthood is also something discussed above: the delay of marriage by American youth. For some decades after World War II, in the context of a booming industrial economy, many young people were anxious to get out of high school, marry, settle down, have children, and start long-term careers.[70] With the delay in age of first marriage, however, many young people spend almost a decade between high school graduation and marriage, enjoying unprecedented freedom as single people.[71]

Changes in the American and global economies that have undermined stable, life-long careers—more on this in Chapter 6—have also helped give rise to emerging adulthood. Solidly middle-class jobs have been replaced by work that offers less security, lower pay, and requires frequent new training and education. Young people since the 1980s, especially, have learned that they need to approach their careers with a variety of skills, maximal flexibility, and readiness to re-tool as needed. That itself pushed them toward extended schooling, delayed marriage, and, arguably, a general psychological tendency to postpone life commitments in order to maximize options and avoid dead ends.[72] No longer able, much less willing, to graduate from high school and take the factory or office job that their father or a friend arranged for them, many youth today spend 5 to 10 years experimenting with different job and career options before deciding on a long-term direction. Even then, that chosen option may not last or prove rewarding.

Moreover, and partly in response to the above, parents starting in the 1990s became increasingly willing to extend financial and other support to their children, well into their 20s and sometimes early 30s.[73] During the Great Recession that followed the financial crisis of 2008, many parents also allowed their grown-up children to return to living at home for free or at very low rents. These parental resources were intended to spare twentysomething children from failure economically and hopefully set them up for success. It also had the unintended consequence of enabling them to take a longer time to live in limbo before being forced to settle down into full adulthood, success or no success.

These and other social transformations have helped to dramatically alter the experience of most Americans roughly between the ages of 18 and 30. The transition to adulthood in recent decades, much research has shown, is more complex, disjointed, and confusing than it was in earlier times. The steps to and through schooling, first job, family formation, and parenthood—assuming these are even desired and feasible—are less well organized and coherent today than they were for generations past. At the same time, these years are marked by a historically unparalleled freedom to roam, experiment, maybe fail, learn, move on, and try something else.[74]

I find persuasive psychologist Jeffrey Arnett's argument that "emerging adulthood" is the most appropriate label for this new life-course phase.[75]

Rather than viewing these years as merely the last hurrah of adolescence or an early stage of real adulthood, it recognizes the unique characteristics of this novel stage of life. This phase typically involves intense identity exploration, instability, a focus on self, feeling in limbo or in transition or in-between, and a sense of possibilities, opportunities, and unparalleled hope. These are often accompanied by big doses of transience, confusion, anxiety, self-obsession, melodrama, conflict, disappointment, and sometimes emotional devastation.[76]

To grasp the significance of emerging adulthood, one needs to see that life stages are not immutable phases of human existence. Instead, they are cultural constructions that interact with biology and material production and so are shaped profoundly by the social and institutional conditions that generate and sustain them. "Teenagers" and "adolescence" were twentieth-century inventions, brought into being by changes in mass education, child labor laws, urbanization, suburbanization, mass consumerism, and the media. Similarly, this new, distinct, and important stage of emerging adulthood has been brought into existence by developments in American culture in recent decades. As a result, life for many between ages 18 and 30 years has morphed into a very different experience from that of previous generations.[77]

This has had huge consequences for young Americans' relationship to traditional religion. Emerging adulthood is in essence about *postponing settling down*—not as a matter of individual choice necessarily, but rather in response to powerful cultural life-course scripts that are generated by massive macro-institutional forces and reinforced by the pressure of tens of millions of peers following the same script. This typically means focusing more on oneself than on family or community, exploring various life possibilities rather than committing to one plan, transience instead of roots, and living in and enjoying the present more than investing in the long-term future. More than a few emerging adults in recent generations are not even confident there will be a long-term future, as we see below. Emerging adulthood also often, though not always, involves experimenting with drugs, alcohol, psychedelics, nonstop dating, travel, alternative sexual identities and practices, alternative subcultural networks (van life, rave culture, music genre scenes), and perhaps alternative spiritualties and religions. In emerging adult culture, as one navigates these experiences, the self is one's primary concern, personal authenticity is paramount, and subjective experience is authority.

In American culture, especially for younger generations, traditional religion is associated with the opposite of nearly all of that. Religion, in people's imaginations, is about settling down, family, community, commitment, belonging, history, eternity, tradition, roots, external authority, objective truth, self-disciple, sobriety, sexual self-control, ethical constancy, and service to others. The experience of emerging adulthood, then, is a major cultural mismatch with traditional religion. Almost nothing about emerging adulthood finds traditional religion appealing or relevant. As one Millennial explained,

> Studying and living religion takes a lot of time and commitment. It's a choice: Is that who I want to be or not? And when a choice involves living a life of chastity or moderation, in a college environment notorious for partying, indulgent drinking, drugs, sex, a lot of that is contrary to theocratic views in monotheistic religions. For young people, it's like, "Okay, which sounds more fun to me?" It's easy to conform to social pressures. And fewer people's friends are religious, and their families aren't involved.

The few aspects of traditional religion that in theory could be appealing—such as fulfilling emerging adults' common longing for stability and community—are nearly always overwhelmed by many features that are not. Emerging adulthood, which developed over recent decades, is thus a key driver of religious obsolescence among younger Americans.

Conclusion

Societies and cultures never turn on a dime. To understand the fate of American religion in the 1990s and after, we cannot simply focus on what happened in those particular years. Whatever transpired at that time occurred in a particular sociocultural context, one that was decades, sometimes centuries, in the making. Understanding religion's obsolescence thus requires not only identifying proximate causes but also the deeper historical shifts that made the effects of those causes possible. The large forces examined in this chapter—especially trends not obviously about religion—created the context for the momentous shifts of the 1990s. We turn next to explore developments in the decades prior to 1990 that more directly concern American religion.

5

The Developing Religious Environment

The large-scale social changes discussed in the previous chapter helped set the stage for American religion's obsolescence. But while those changes had enormous impacts on religion, they were not primarily changes *in* religion. What about long-term trends within the American religious landscape? We turn our attention to those now.

Mainline Protestant (Cultural Triumph and) Organizational Decline

Mainline Protestant denominations are some of the oldest and historically most influential branches of Christianity in the United States.[1] Many have existed since the colonial era, though the mainline really assumed its modern form early in the twentieth century, after fundamentalist and "modernist" churches and denominations went their separate ways. Mainline churches were the heart of the modernist camp. They tend to be moderate to progressive theologically, socially, and politically. Sometimes they are called "liberal" Protestant rather than mainline. In broad terms, they are normally contrasted with American evangelical, fundamentalist, Pentecostal, charismatic, and most historically Black churches. Interested in ecumenical relations, they affiliate with the National Council of Churches (rather than the National Association of Evangelicals) and the World Council of Churches. Mainline Protestant denominations together dominated American Protestantism for centuries, although their influence was always more institutional and cultural than numerical.[2]

After the decline of the old Protestant establishment that they informally ruled, the mainline reached a newfound strength in numbers and cultural influence in the postwar religious boom that peaked in the 1950s. But since the 1960s, it has suffered what has seemed like terminal decline. Sociologists have documented for many decades the shrinking of mainline Protestant churches (see Figure 5.1).[3] Between 1960 and 2010, the memberships of

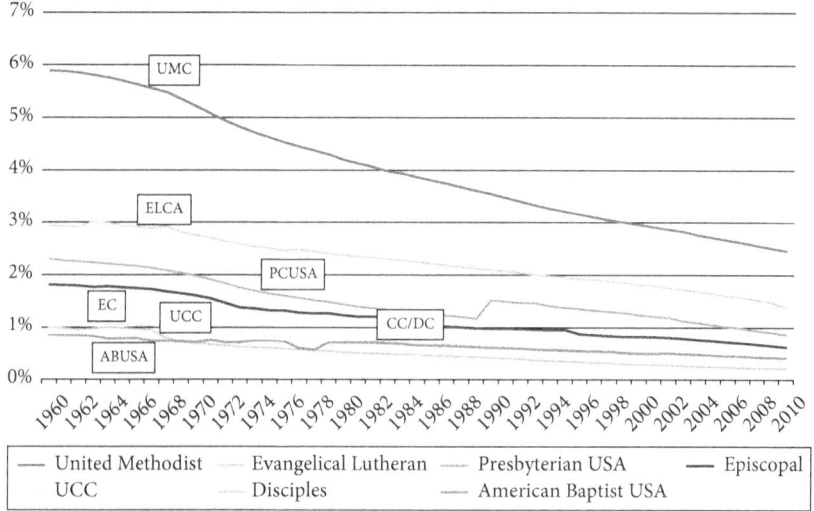

Figure 5.1 Mainline Protestant denominational memberships as percents of the US population, 1960–2010.

Source: Association of Religion Data Archives.

Note: Mean averages are imputed for occasional missing years. In cases of denominational mergers (e.g., UMC in 1968, ELCA in 1988), membership data on the combining denominations was used back to 1960.

these denominations as a percent of the total population declined from their 1960 baselines by these amounts:

- 79%: Christian Church (Disciples of Christ)
- 70%: United Church of Christ
- 65%: The Episcopal Church
- 62%: Presbyterian Church USA
- 58%: United Methodist Church
- 53%: Evangelical Lutheran Church in America
- 50%: American Baptist Churches USA

Sociologists and historians disagree about what exactly caused these declines. Some say the mainline became too theologically and socially liberal, others argue that mainliners suffered low fertility rates across the twentieth century because of their early adoption of birth control, and yet others point to the (urban) locations of mainline church buildings being mismatched to (suburban) populations, to low retention rates of children born into the mainline, and even to underperforming pastors.[4] Likely some combination of these and other factors were at work. What is clear is that the glory days of American mainline-liberal Protestantism had passed by the time the 1960s and 1970s arrived (see Figure 5.1).[5] Some rechristened the mainline the "sideline" or "oldline."[6]

Most observers have been so focused on membership statistics and loss of political influences, however, that they miss an insight: mainline Protestantism's organizational decline is in part arguably the consequence of the fact that it won a cultural victory. This is the argument of the late sociologist of religion Jay Demerath in a perceptive but underappreciated article, "Cultural Victory and Organizational Defeat in the Paradoxical Decline of Liberal Protestantism."[7] Demerath's argument is this: "Far from representing failure, the decline of Liberal Protestantism may actually stem from its success.... Liberal Protestants have lost structurally at the micro level precisely because they won culturally at the macro level."

What Demerath meant is that, over time, liberal Protestantism's core values—individualism, pluralism, emancipation, tolerance, free critical inquiry, and the authority of human experience—so permeated broader American culture that its own churches as organizations had difficulty surviving. One reason is that those liberal values have a tendency to undermine organizational vitality. Few robust organizations are built on foundations of strong individualism, autonomy, and free criticism. Furthermore, having succeeded in shaping mainstream culture, there was no longer anything distinctively useful about liberal churches. Liberal Protestantism increasingly seems redundant to the taken-for-granted mainstream that it helped create. Why keep meeting and mobilizing resources to promote what already dominates? In short, mainline Protestantism made itself superfluous through success.

If Demerath is right, those who remain mainline Protestant have more to be happy about than they realize: the breakdown of that tradition at one level is partly caused by a successful performance on a more important stage. By this logic, mainline Protestantism has paid the price in organizational strength for previously winning a bigger struggle over culture. Mainline Protestantism's impact on cultural discourse may be diffuse to the point of invisibility, but ideas and values are most powerful when they are so pervasive that they are invisible.[8]

What does this mean for our story? By the 1990s, mainline Protestantism was in no condition to deal with the emerging zeitgeist. Having suffered three decades of serious decline, mainline Protestantism lacked the discernment, energy, and dexterity to read and respond effectively to the signs of the times. While many, especially older, Americans still belonged to mainline churches, as an option for post-Boomer generations, mainline Protestantism had already gone obsolete before the 1990s.

Also, while in theory the moderate to liberal posture of mainline Protestantism should have made it more attractive to younger generations than more conservative religious traditions, in fact it was not. Mainline Protestant churches are among the least effective at both attracting new young people and retaining the youth raised in them.[9] Jay Demerath's interpretation of the mainline's decline helps make some sense of this. Individual autonomy, tolerance, pluralism, freedom from external authorities, the centrality of human experience, epistemological skepticism, and an aversion to anything "dogmatic" are routinely taken for granted by most younger Americans—even if the latter have no idea of the role mainline Protestantism played in disseminating those values to the broader culture. Post-Boomers may share many cultural values with this tradition, but they see no point to the religious part. What mainline Protestantism offers, beyond the general cultural values that it helped to propagate, are the particular church histories, liturgies, and theologies that make it a religious and not simply cultural organization. But few young Americans find much of interest or value in that. They seem irrelevant and dated.

Catholic Organizational Weakening

The American Roman Catholic Church also entered the 1990s an organizationally weakened and internally fissured Church. Like mainline Protestantism, Catholicism enjoyed a postwar boom in attendance and organizational strength. The number of clergy and religious (members of a religious order, like a monk or nun) was at an all-time high, parishes were growing, and Catholic schools were being built. But, in the late 1960s, those fortunes turned around.[10]

The signature Catholic event of the century was the Second Vatican Council of 1962 to 1965. Vatican II opened the Church up to a new appreciation for and dialogue with the modern world and to reforms within that many believed were needed.[11] While it reiterated traditional Catholic teachings on many central matters, Vatican II also promulgated numerous reforms for the Church, emphasizing the importance of the laity, the integrity of conscience, worship in the vernacular, ecumenical dialogue, and religious freedom and human rights. Protestantism had been at the heart of modernity from the start and so had centuries to gradually interpret and assimilate modern culture. Catholicism had generally resisted modernity, and its relative marginality in American culture during the late nineteenth and early twentieth centuries had served to shield the Church from many of the secularizing forces that influenced American Protestantism during that period.[12] Vatican II meant that American Catholics, many of whose leaders had previously worked to shut out, denounce, and resist modern culture, needed "in one frantic decade" to assimilate many features of modernity.[13] Starting in the early 1960s, "Catholicism . . . has really for the first time tried to absorb the effects of this whole vast modern development from the Enlightenment to the present in the short period between 1963 and 1973."[14] "The barriers against which the forces of change had been building up through the fifties gave way entirely," in historian Philip Gleason's words. "The results were so dramatic that they took even the proponents of reform by surprise."[15]

Instituting Vatican II on the ground proved an overwhelming challenge. After the Council ended, the American Church did a less than ideal job of instructing the faithful about its teachings and implications. Vatican II needed strong, clear transmission and interpretation by the bishops to the clergy, religious, and lay faithful. In retrospect, that did not seem to happen.[16] Most of the changes instituted by Vatican II were very popular among American Catholics. But significant uncertainty and misunderstanding also settled into Church life and culture, along with various kinds of experimentation and innovation. Looking back, many observers say that, at that crucial juncture, the American Church "dropped the ball" and as a result suffered harmful ambiguity, hesitation, misdirection, and, consequently, conflict.[17]

After Vatican II, many priests left their clerical roles, and a substantial number left the Church altogether. New vocations to the priesthood declined precipitously. Large numbers of women and men religious (nuns, monks, etc.) left their vowed religious lives, too. The number of priests and religious brothers and sisters in the American Church was never large historically. But the early twentieth century saw impressive growth in the number of priests and religious brothers and sisters, reaching a high-water mark at mid-century.[18] Starting in the 1960s, however, that trend dramatically reversed. Between 1965 and 1971, the American Catholic Church lost 10% of its priests. Between 1966 and 1969 alone, 3,413 priests left the priesthood and 4,322 women religious left religious life. In only 10 years, between 1967 and 1977, the number of enrolled Catholic seminarians was cut in half. In 1964, 47,500 American Catholic men were preparing for the priesthood, but, by 1984, that number had dropped to around 12,000—a 75% decline. During that same period, 241 Catholic seminaries closed their doors. Between 1945 and 1965, the number of vowed religious brothers had grown from 7,003 to 13,152 but then fell dramatically, declining 52% from 1965 to 1998.[19] Between 1965 and 2002 the population of women religious in the United States fell by nearly 60%. As a result, there were fewer priests, brothers, and sisters to serve parishioners. The number of American Catholic laypeople per Catholic priest, religious brother, and religious sister increased by 83%, 174%, and 163%, respectively, between 1965 and 1998.[20] Consequently, at a time when the Church was facing extraordinary new challenges in catechesis and faith formation, it was also suffering a dramatic reduction in the trained personnel necessary to conduct that work—as well as an added confusion and a crisis of confidence about what this decline in numbers meant.

The American Church also lacked the material resources to implement and pay for badly needed initiatives and programs. American Catholics are the least generous financial givers of all groups of American Christians. Studies consistently show that the vast majority of American Catholics give only a small amount of money to the Church and other causes—even after figuring in support for Catholic schools. For example, in 1960, American Catholics donated an average of 2.2% of their income, an amount well below the figure for most other American Christians and a number that has since declined. Between 1963 and 1983, American Catholics' financial contributions declined by *half*, from 2% to 1% of income.[21] This meant that dioceses, parishes, and other Catholic organizations usually lacked the material resources to build strong new programs after Vatican II.

All this had knock-on effects for Catholic primary and secondary schools. For generations, these had been staffed by priests and religious sisters and brothers who were committed to the Church, mostly well-trained in Church teachings, and relatively inexpensive to employ. By the mid-1900s, the American Catholic parochial school system had developed into an impressive and unique institution—there was nothing like it in scale and character in the rest of the world. As the changes described above unfolded, however, most Catholic schools, like parishes, suffered declining numbers of dedicated and affordable Church teachers and administrators. Between 1965 and 2002, the number of priests, sisters, and brothers teaching in Catholic schools declined from 114,000 to only 9,000—a 92% drop. Lay teachers and administrators filled the gap, often doing impressive work, but they were much more expensive to employ and changed the character of Catholic schooling.[22] The number of Catholic school students also dropped precipitously, from 4.2 million diocesan and parochial elementary school students in 1960 to 2.3 million in 1980—a 46% decline in 20 years.[23] The number of Catholic diocesan and parochial high school students declined by 21% between 1960 and 2001, from 520,128 to 375,125. Between 1964 and 1984, 40% of American Catholic high schools and 27% of Catholic elementary schools closed their doors.[24]

The year 1968 was an important turning point. That was when Pope Paul VI issued the papal encyclical *Humanae Vitae*, "On Human Life," a spiritual and theological reflection on human marriage and sexuality. The encyclical condemned the use of artificial contraception as contrary to God's design for human sexuality and marriage. The majority of American Catholics disagreed with that viewpoint, including many priests and some bishops. Many moderate Catholics in America were surprised and disappointed. Most liberals were stunned and appalled. Serious dissent arose, further unsettling the Church.

The encyclical also had momentous cultural consequences for Catholic laity. Rather than accepting its teachings as perhaps frustrating but authoritative, a majority of American Catholics decided the Church was wrong and that they would make their own moral decisions on the matter and use birth control if they so chose. With that, an epistemological rubicon was crossed where the Church's authority was concerned. For the first time, large numbers of American Catholics were, with seemingly clean consciences, assuming their own personal authority to judge the validity of the teachings of the Church and decide whether to follow its moral directives. Adhering to Church teachings had effectively become optional, and the authorized agent making the decisions had become the individual believer, not the Church. As one lay Catholic said: "I can't live with what the church says, y'know. I have to check my own self out with God."[25] Once that shift had been made, a whole range of beliefs and morals were put on the table for individual Catholics to choose for or against. By the 1980s, surveys showed that two-thirds of American Catholics said that individuals, not the Church, should make decisions about the morality of contraceptives. The reaction to *Humanae Vitae* had been a "declaration of independence" from the binding authority of papal teachings.[26]

American Catholicism became internally polarized. After Vatican II was announced in 1959, progressive elements in the American Church hoped that the institution would become a more genuinely democratic, inclusive, egalitarian, modernized institution. After the promulgation of the papal encyclical *Humanae Vitae* in 1968, however, and especially once the pontificate of Pope John Paul II began in 1978, many of the hopes of progressives and liberals were dashed. The practical reforms instituted following Vatican II were substantial but nothing like what liberal Catholics had anticipated and desired. Many in this generation of young, visionary, reformist, progressive Catholics soured or grew cynical.[27] Conservatives, for their part, fought with progressives about the changes afoot in the Church, which contributed to an increasingly polarized atmosphere.[28] These conflicts introduced a negative, acrimonious, divided element to the culture of the American Church that has lasted well into the twenty-first century.

The decades leading up to the 1990s, despite some positive developments, were hard times for the American Catholic Church. In the early 2000s, things would become unspeakably harder. But, even before then, American Catholics had become "a people adrift," and the Church as an institution had become seriously weakened and internally polarized compared to the pre-1960s era.[29] Like mainline Protestantism, American Catholicism had little capacity to comprehend and respond effectively to the cultural shifts that were to take place in the 1990s and after.

Moralizing of Religion, Downplaying Transcendence

At some time well before the 1990s, most Americans and some if not many religious institutions, too, it seems, came to view religion as essentially about making people morally good. Religion, in this view, is not primarily about divine worship, timeless truths, sacred historical traditions, eternal salvation, theological doctrines, or the like—except as they might inspire morality.[30] Rather, religion is an institution that exists to foster good behavior and life choices. This is why Americans approve of religion when it makes people good: it is doing its job well. The other stuff—prayer, worship, the sacred, salvation, rituals—are secondary trappings of religious particularities. Everybody's got some, but it's not what religion is most importantly about.[31]

This conception of religion would prove monumentally important in religion's obsolescence. But specifically how, when, why, and by whom religion became moralized in America has not been as directly and systematically researched as most of the other trends in this book. Nor is explaining that my purpose here. The social and intellectual sources of the American moralization of religion are surely many and complex. But one of its theological sources is clear. That is a certain stream of nineteenth-century Protestant theological liberalism.

The modernist and liberal theological project was to make Christianity compatible with modern assumptions and outlooks so that the "updated" religious faith could be plausible and reasonable to modern people. That usually required a "demythologizing" of traditional Christianity, reinterpreting the meanings of religious ideas in terms palatable to modern people. Miracles and demons, for example, had to be reinterpreted for scientific minds. One of the common moves that many liberal Protestants made was to reduce the Christian gospel to ethics. An illuminating example of this was the German Lutheran theologian and church historian Adolf von Harnack (1851–1930).

Harnack taught that Hellenistic philosophy and the distortions of early Christian writings had corrupted the original kernel of the Christian gospel. Enlightened moderns like himself and his audiences, he believed, however, could look back, strip away history's encrustations and myths, and rediscover the essence of the gospel.[32] What one discovers, Harnack said, is divinely inspired moral living. The modern gospel, he wrote, "has become spiritualised, and in the course of history it has learnt how to make a surer application of its ethical principles." Christianity, Harnack taught, is simply about the person Jesus Christ proclaiming the kingdom of God the Father, the "infinite value of the human soul," and the "higher righteousness" of the commandment to love. Creeds, councils, rituals, metaphysics, scholastic speculation, systematic theologies, ecclesiastical structures, rationalistic apologetics—all of those are confused historical accretions. They obscure the timeless heart of Christian truth.

Jesus Christ, Harnack said, revealed "the presence of the Eternal in time," raising up humanity's unlimited value from the indifferent order of nature. By experiencing and trusting God as a loving Father, humans learn they have an infinite value, a realization that enables them to live ethical lives intent on doing good by humbly loving their neighbors. Enacting this "supreme good" leads humans to a blessed and orderly life on earth. "Gentlemen, it is religion, the love of God and neighbor, which gives life a meaning," Harnack concluded. Religion as the morality of love represents "the forces and the standards which on the summits of our inner life shine out as our highest good, nay, as our real self." Consequently, humans need to be "earnest and courageous enough to accept them as the great Reality and direct our lives by them." In sum, Harnack declared, "Jesus combined religion and morality, and in this sense religion may be called the soul of morality, and morality the body of religion." In short, "the Gospel is a matter of ordinary morality."[33]

I am not suggesting that Harnack's reinterpretation of Christianity single-handedly moralized American religion. The liberal Protestantism he represented, however, contributed. Harnack was a key leader of the modernist movement in Western Christianity, which had an enormous influence on American liberal Protestantism. In my research interviews over decades, large swaths of Americans, both religious and not, talk as if they have read and absorbed Harnack and his colleagues: religion at heart is simple and has the ultimate practical aim of making people moral. Harnack's focus on the kingdom of God and the revelation of Jesus Christ has since mostly been subtracted, and the "supreme good" of humble love of neighbor has been moderated to the easier obligations to be kind, nice, and fair. But the underlying logic is otherwise the same. And it set religion up so that, when the larger cultural environment changed, it lost much of the "territory" over which it had once laid claim legitimately to control.

Which is to say: many, if not most, religious Americans would be comfortable with the brand of liberal faith described by Yale theologian H. Richard Niebuhr as being about "a God without wrath [who] brought men without sin into a kingdom without judgment through the ministrations of a Christ without a Cross."[34] They simply would have no idea about the genealogy of their taken-for-granted ideas. Still, when most Americans today talk about religion in interviews, they might just as well be paraphrasing liberal Protestant theologians from the nineteenth and early twentieth centuries. Adolf von Harnack, Albrecht Ritschl, Wilhelm Hermann, and Harry Emerson Fosdick would be proud. People today need not study liberal Protestant theology to be inducted into its worldview since it has become particulate matter in the cultural air that most Americans breathe.

This interpretation restates Jay Demerath's argument above. One-hundred-year-old liberal theologians have few explicit followers today. They are quaint and dated. Yet liberal theology does not need card-carrying disciples. The influence of these ideas has diffused so widely that they can disappear as intellectual figures and still claim triumph in their broader influence. The idea that religion is essentially morality can hardly be debated as a position since it is so routinely taken for granted as obvious reality. Only, today the message is not "Love because of the Kingdom of God the Father as Revealed in Jesus Christ" (Harnack)—not to mention "Sinners in the Hands of an Angry God" (Jonathan Edwards)—but "Life Is Hard but Try Your Best to Be Patient and Kind."

One way that liberals refashioned traditional religion to be palatable to modern minds was by downplaying if not eliminating from its discourse uncomfortable biblical ideas, such as divine judgment and hell. They also turned the focus of religion from eternity to life here and now. We can empirically, if imperfectly, observe this process in published religious discourse over time. The three largest Christian traditions in the United States—mainline Protestantism, evangelical Protestantism, and Roman Catholicism—have all published important periodicals over long periods. *The Christian Century*, published since the late nineteenth century, has been mainline Protestantism's flagship magazine for more than a century.[35] Evangelical Protestantism's version of the same is *Christianity Today*, published since 1956. Catholicism has not produced one leading national publication but numerous newspapers and magazines, both national and diocesan. One simply needs systematically to search such publications for keywords and phrases to see if they change in frequency of use or in meaning. I counted all of the times that certain keywords and phrases appeared in an article, review, or advertisement: heaven, hell, purgatory, eternity, eternal, afterlife, Judgment Day, paradise, transcendent, damnation, damned, soul saving, and saved or saving my/your/their/his/her soul or souls.[36] Here is what I found.

An initial examination of the *Christian Century*, first, made clear there simply was no need for an exhaustive search since there existed little variance to measure. A first and informal but close reading of the uses of my keywords revealed fairly frequent references to them in ways consistently suggesting the same meanings and attitudes across the decades. The *Christian Century* did reference ideas of transcendence and eternity often enough but nearly always to dismiss, denigrate, or otherwise marginalize serious belief in such matters. At times, the tone of such dismissals was respectful, but usually it was scoffing. "How could anyone anymore use the fear of hell to motivate faith?" "Rather than living for paradise, we should be working now to make the earth more like heaven." "Fundamentalists out to save souls ignore everything in the Bible that does not fit their hidebound doctrines." This attitude was consistent not only since 1945 but also from the publication's first years in the nineteenth century.

That is not surprising, given the fact that modernist-liberal American Protestantism has been battling fundamentalists for the soul of Christianity for more than a century. Well before the modernist-fundamentalist split, the mainline had abandoned its commitment to many of these eternal and transcendent concepts. Yet discourse in the *Christian Century* continued to employ these words and phrases in order to oppose them. The data from the key publication of this branch of American Protestantism thus revealed no significant change in the presence or meaning of references to transcendence and eternity. Because their meanings are consistently negative, precise counts of frequencies are not especially important for present purposes.

Christianity Today offers a different story. All issues of the magazine are archived, although only some in digitally searchable form; the rest were PDFs that had to be transformed into a searchable format. Figure 5.2 shows the number of occurrences of the keywords listed above for every issue from 1957 to 2022. The length of issues of *Christianity Today* changed significantly over time, so the numbers in Figure 5.2 are references per published page. Table 5.1 lists the total frequencies of all the terms (except purgatory) across all years, from most to least, those with a more obvious positive valence in italics and with a more negative in bold.

Findings presented in Figure 5.2 show a decrease in its use of language referencing eternal and transcendent themes between the mid-1960s and

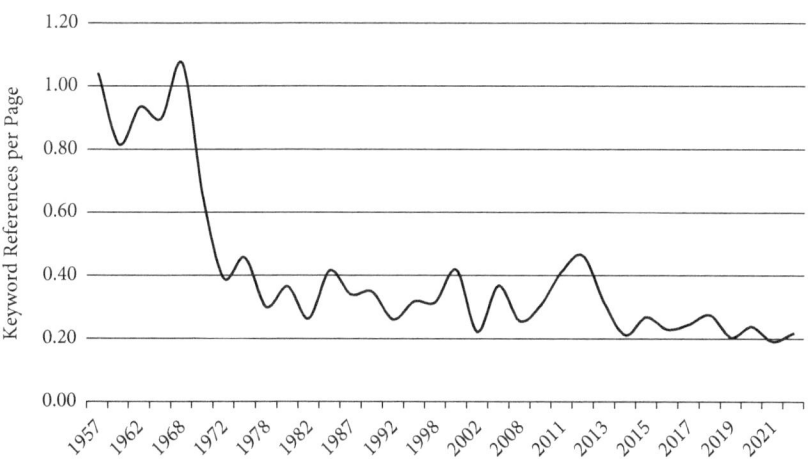

Figure 5.2 References to transcendent and eternity keywords in *Christianity Today*, 1957–2022.

Source: Christianity Today archives.

Table 5.1 Total Counts of Eternal and Transcendent Theme Keywords in *Christianity Today* (1957–2022)

Soul	3,918
Heaven	3,858
Judgment	2,856
Eternal	2,369
Hell	1,440
Eternity	919
Transcendent	461
Paradise	319
Afterlife	121
Damned	101
Judgment day	19

early 1980s. From the 1980s to 2022, the use of these terms remained fairly steady, with a modest decrease after 2014. The most striking way to read the figure is comparing start to finish, which shows a nontrivial decrease—dropping from one transcendent keyword per page to one every five pages, which is an 80% overall decline. Specific words matter, however. The biggest keyword losers here were "eternal," "heaven," "soul," and "judgment." "Eternity" declined in use as well, but less dramatically. The other keywords remained more stable in use—although their frequency in these pages is massively lower than the top six keywords, so they did not have much room to decline. Terms with a more negative valence (e.g., judgment) were not, however, more likely to be trimmed out than more positive terms (e.g., heaven). "Hell," for instance, was used not infrequently, and its usage did not change significantly over the decades. Altogether, this evidence indicates some downplaying of transcendent themes in *Christianity Today* over time—1968 through the 1970s being the most significant years.[37]

That leaves the discourse of American Catholics. I noted above that American Catholicism is not represented by one flagship publication but rather by a variety of Catholic magazines and newspapers published on and off over decades. Fortunately, many American Catholic publications have been digitized in the Catholic News Archives and are systematically searchable online by year.[38] Unfortunately, however, most publications are digitized for only some of the years of their publication. Eight different

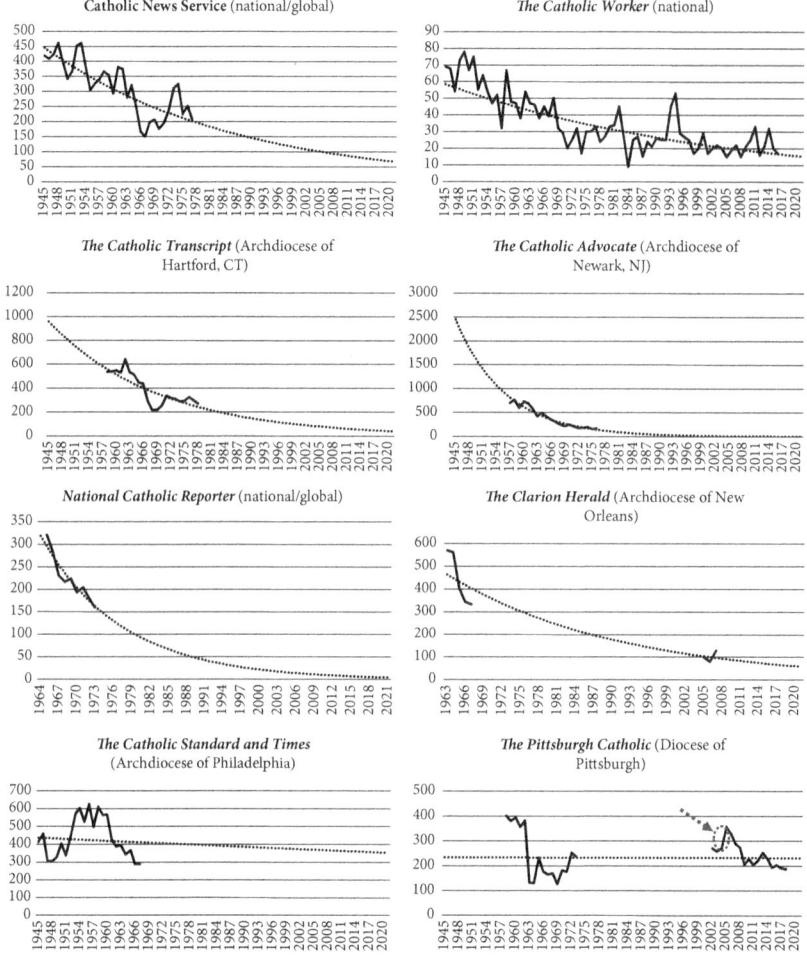

Figure 5.3 Counts of transcendent and eternity themes in articles, reviews, and advertisements of national and diocesan Catholic publications, 1945–2021.

Source: The Catholic News Archive Online.

Note: Thematic keywords searched were "Heaven," "Hell," "Purgatory," "Eternity," "Eternal," "Afterlife," "Judgment Day," "Paradise," "Transcendent," "Damnation," "Damned," "Saved or Saving My/Your/Their/His/Her Soul or Souls," "Soul Saving." Calculated exponential trend lines (dotted) are added.

Catholic publications, however, offered enough archived years to attempt an analysis.

Figure 5.3 shows the frequency of distinct references to my keywords and phrases for each publication, where digitized data exist, since 1945. A lot of data were missing. The thick lines represent counts for years with complete data. The thin, dotted curves are exponential trend lines statistically estimated from the data that do exist to the most likely projection of the observed trend for those years missing data. The evidence here is incomplete and so our conclusions must be tentative. Even so, Figure 5.3 does appear to reveal a general trend across the publications—namely, declines in the number of references to transcendent and eternal themes over the years at different periods of time. Projecting from available data, at least, it appears that American Catholics since 1945 talked and read less about transcendent and eternal themes as time passed. Stated differently, in the postwar era—especially the 1960s—American Catholicism downplayed one of the few things that, for better or worse, makes religion unique in the larger field of institutions and culture.

There are some important caveats here. First, this conclusion derives from a convenience sample of Catholic publications. They are diverse in type and scope but not representative of all Catholic publications, much less all Catholic discourse. Furthermore, nearly all of the cases are obviously missing significant chunks of data. In some instances, the observed data lines are short enough that drawing longer-term conclusions from them might feel like paleontologists reconstructing the entire skeleton of a large animal based on just a few unearthed bones and teeth. The exponential trend curves help in that task, but they could be empirically off. What makes the tentative conclusion worth considering, however, are the similar decline trends across all but one of the publications. No one or two instances can prove anything, but most of the cases producing downward trend lines would seem to tell us something. Quite likely, the available data suggest a real trend that did occur even during those years lacking data. That interpretation also fits everything else we know about American Catholicism during these decades.

Second, however, the last two publications in Figure 5.3 do not seem to fit the downward trends just mentioned. About *The Catholic Standard and Times*, one can at least see that references to transcendent and eternal themes bumped up at the zenith of the postwar Cold War-era religious revival and then proceeded to decline across the 1960s. That is too little evidence to lean much upon, but it does fit the larger Catholic story and the *Christianity Today* data just analyzed. The case of *The Pittsburgh Catholic* is trickier. We do see a major drop in transcendent and eternal references from 1957 to the 1960s. Even simply starting from the first data point and ending with the last would give us a significant decrease between the late 1950s and 2018. But that decline is complicated by a single bump up between 2002 and 2005 (spotlighted with a dotted circle marked by an arrow). So the calculated trend line is flat.³⁹ *The Pittsburgh Catholic* is thus an anomaly. One can still say that 6 or 7 out of 8 is not bad, and that American Catholicism is also too diverse for every case in a varied sample of publications to give the same results. I end with the same inference, then, hardly conclusive but at least highly suggestive: American Catholicism seems to have downplayed the transcendent and eternal in its discourse after 1945.

So far, we have focused on the "supply" side of religious discourse, which for my argument matters most. Before moving on, however, let us briefly examine the "demand" side of the issue in more recent years. In our 2023 Millennial Zeitgeist Survey, we asked two questions measuring American adults' interest in immanent versus transcendent concerns (see Table 5.2). Respondents do not agree in valuing immanent matters versus transcendent ones. Every generation, however, leans toward valuing immanence over transcendence. That leaning also increases noticeably with each younger generation. Only about half (52%) of early Boomers say life on earth, this world, today, and nature are more important to them than God, eternity,

Table 5.2 Immanent Versus Transcendent Interests by Generation (%)

	Early Boomers	Later Boomers	Gen Xers	Millennials
Which of the following is more important to you personally?				
Life on earth, this world, today, nature	52	55	60	64
God, eternity, heaven, a transcendent realm	49	45	41	37
I am more concerned with a good life here and now than what comes after death.				
Strongly agree	23	20	23	30
Somewhat agree	28	25	29	24
Somewhat disagree	19	26	20	18
Strongly disagree	27	23	19	16
Don't know	3	6	9	12
TOTALS (unweighted *n*'s):	100 (*n* = 341)	100 (*n* = 358)	100 (*n* = 485)	100 (*n* = 677)

Source: Millennial Zeitgeist Survey, 2023 (*N* = 1,861). Percents may not add to 100 due to rounding. "Don't know" answers to the first question are negligible so not reported.

heaven, and a transcendent realm. Nearly two-thirds of Millennials (64%) say the same.

The bottom half of Table 5.2 shows results on the same issue using a somewhat different question wording. There we see that respondents express diverse views about whether they are more concerned with a good life here and now or with what comes after death. With each new generation we observe a gradual shift toward an interest in life now. Millennials especially lean toward a concern with life here and now. A significant difference (besides "Don't know") concerns those who strongly disagree with the statement, those who are definitely more concerned with what comes after death, which declines from 27% to 16% from the oldest to youngest generation.

These differences may reflect an age effect (younger people of every generation being less concerned about death) or a generational effect (younger cohorts being less interested in life after death at whatever age than older ones) or some of both—we cannot tell from these data. What we can say, however, is that more than half of Millennials are more interested in their lives now than possible eternities. They are also noticeably more likely not to have an opinion on the matter. There is more than one way to interpret these findings. We should remember that a survey conducted in 2023 tells us nothing about historical processes at work during the 1990s and 2000s. One takeaway, however, is that well after traditional religion went obsolete, the US adult population still expresses a not-insignificant concern with things transcendent, although that decreases among younger people. I suggest that this interest helps fuel the rise in the popular re-enchanted embrace of "spirituality" and "occulture," which I discuss below. To the extent that traditional religion has over time downplayed transcendence, spirituality and occulture helped fill the vacuum.

Traditional religion's declining attention to matters of transcendence and eternity matters sociologically. When religion becomes a "concept," as Eisenhower put it, rather than one's identity, life, and salvation, it generates less commitment and investment. In this way, the moralizing of religion and its sidelining of transcendent themes are analogous to a disease sapping religion's strength as a species. Viewed in terms of Abbot's struggle among competing occupations to control as professions socially legitimate knowledge and problem-solving, downplaying transcendence has been a tactical error, making religion vulnerable to losing ground.

The Rise of Televangelism and the Religious Right

While American mainline Protestantism and Catholicism were suffering big losses in the 1960s and 1970s, American evangelicalism was growing ever stronger and more confident. The 1970s witnessed an astonishing "resurgence" of religion in public and political life all around the world, the most important expression of which in the United States was the resurgence of evangelicalism.[40] Especially as liberal Protestantism faded from view, evangelicalism rose—despite its own common perception of being marginalized and oppressed—to become the primary public face of "religion" in the United States.[41]

Some brief historical context will be helpful. In the four decades straddling the turn of the twentieth century, modernist and fundamentalist Protestants engaged in fierce struggles to control denominations, seminaries, and doctrine.[42] Most of those battles were settled by the end of the 1920s, and, while each side had won victories, the fundamentalists came out looking bad and beaten. Fundamentalist groups retreated from those theological and institutional wars into insular circles, focusing on policing boundaries and building separate institutions. The 1930s and wartime were a period of religious malaise in the United States generally. At war's end, however, a cadre of visionary young fundamentalists—including Billy Graham, Charles Fuller, and Carl Henry—launched a "neo-evangelical" movement to rehabilitate conservative Protestantism. They sought to leave behind fundamentalism's doctrinal and behavioral legalism and its obscurantism about science and higher education. Instead, they emphasized evangelism and making the traditional gospel and "biblical worldview" intellectually defensible. The old fundamentalists saw them—like the modernists before them—as liberalizing turncoats. The neo-evangelicals nonetheless managed to carve out a significant space in the American religious field, one situated between fundamentalists and liberals, and from there expanded their boundaries and territory.[43]

Many secular Americans assumed that American fundamentalists and evangelicals had disappeared after the 1920s since they were hardly visible in public life. When they did begin to reappear in the 1970s, most initially viewed them as backwater anti-moderns. In fact, entrepreneurial fundamentalists and evangelicals had since the 1920s been developing radio and later television programming that would appeal to large audiences and could support itself financially in the media market.[44] Their audiences were limited to their subculture and thus invisible to outsiders. But they were very large and made paid religious broadcasting financially viable.[45]

Mainline Protestant programming was also on the air, but its privileging proved fatal in time. Around 1928, the Federal Radio Commission began assigning stations to radio frequencies, forcing many independent religious radio stations to the margins. Soon both CBS and NBC stopped airing paid religious broadcasts. The Federal Council of Churches arranged to sponsor "mainline" broadcasts not considered "sectarian" with free airtime donated by major stations as a public service. Meanwhile, the fundamentalist broadcasters were forced to compete in the market by building distribution networks of myriad local stations that charged for airtime. In this way, they mastered the entrepreneurial production of programs that appealed to sizeable audiences willing to donate money to keep them on the air. Most popular was Charles and Grace Fuller's Old Fashioned Revival Hour, which was carried on the new Mutual Radio Network and, by the 1940s, had more listeners tuning in during Sunday evening prime time than the popular comedian Jack Benny. By the 1940s, in contrast, having never learned to compete in the media market with programming that was actually popular, most mainline Protestant productions went off the air when the networks pulled the plug on free public service programming. The original blessing of free airtime for mainline preachers proved a liability. Far from being anti-modern hillbillies, fundamentalists and evangelicals had become proficient at modern media technologies and markets while mainline media withered.[46]

Fundamentalist and evangelical radio programs began to switch to television broadcasting in 1949, starting with Jack Wyrtzen, Percy Crawford, and Rex Humbard. Oral Roberts began televising his evangelistic ministries in 1954. In 1961, Pat Robertson founded the first Christian television channel, the Christian Broadcasting Network, which began producing *The 700 Club* in 1966, hosted by Jim Bakker.[47] Billy Graham also launched major television evangelism crusades in the 1960s and 1970s. The spread of cable television in the 1970s and 1980s facilitated the proliferation of "televangelism" by popular hosts such as Oral Roberts, Jimmy Swaggart, Jim and Tammy Faye Bakker, Rex Humbard, Robert Schuller, James Robison, Jerry Falwell, and Pat Robertson.[48] By the 1980s, such programs were being broadcast on hundreds of channels and garnered tens of millions of viewers in the United States.[49] They were also broadcast in many scores of languages in more than 100 countries around the globe.[50] By the 1980s, mainstream America had become well aware of the televangelism industry, and the general reaction from those outside was incredulity and disparagement.

The Cold War boom in American religion spurred growth within evangelicalism as well as in mainline Protestantism and Catholicism. Evangelicals, however, remained mostly under the public's radar during that era—Billy Graham being one exception. The revolutions of the 1960s and widespread unease in the 1970s, however, "woke up" evangelicalism and moved it in new directions. The Eisenhower-era religious atmosphere had enabled many Americans, including most conservative Protestants, to suppose that the United States was not only founded as a Christian nation but also remained Christian in some general sense. The 1960s counterculture, sexual revolution, Vietnam War protests, the rise of the New Left, drug culture, and movements for women's liberation, student free speech, civil rights, and gay rights upended that easy supposition. The federal government's racial desegregation of the South and passage of the Civil Rights Acts of 1964 and 1968 also troubled many white evangelicals.[51] In the 1970s, the Vietnam quagmire, urban race riots, Watergate, *Roe v. Wade*, the OPEC oil embargo, rising divorce rates, spreading Soviet influence in the Third World, and the Iranian hostage crisis seemed to validate evangelical fears that America was crumbling because it had turned away from its Christian heritage.[52]

In 1979, Lynchburg, Virginia, Baptist minister Jerry Falwell Sr. and collaborators founded the Moral Majority. Its goal was to mobilize conservative Christians as a political force to counter what Falwell believed was national moral decay. Similar organizations also sprang up across the nation around this time, including American Christian Cause, Christian Voice, and the Christian Coalition. Falwell had previously been a fundamentalist who believed in saving souls, not political activism. But his distress over the state of the nation, which he believed to be founded on Christian principles yet secularizing and as a result degenerating, propelled him into politics.[53] Falwell, who had previously identified as a fundamentalist, began calling himself an evangelical, tapping into that movement's energy, and he led sectors of it into conservative political activism and a decades-long romance with the Republican Party. That movement, the so-called Christian Right (or Religious Right, as sometimes culturally conservative Jews and Mormons joined the cause), helped to elect multiple Republican presidents and proved influential in the politics of abortion, gay rights, education, drugs, school choice, and the state of Israel.[54] Christian Right organizations proliferated at the national, state, and local levels. Pat Robertson even campaigned, unsuccessfully, for the GOP nomination for president in 1988.

The rise of conservative Protestant televangelism in the media and the rise of the Christian Right in politics were distinct but overlapping and mutually reinforcing movements. The most prominent early leaders of the latter—Jerry Falwell and Pat Robertson—were already major players in the former. That gave them popular media platforms from which to launch and promote their political activities.[55]

Much more could be said about the Christian Right. For present purposes, however, what matters most for our question is the backlash. The rise of the Christian Right was shocking to many politically moderate and liberal Americans, to whom it seemed a regressive violation of the separation of church and state. Political activists bringing religious motivations and arguments into the sphere of public debate and policy was, to many, offensive and unacceptable. The liberal political tradition says that everyone is entitled to their personal religious beliefs, but they ought to be kept private, not brought into politics.[56] For many Americans, fairly or not, the Christian Right looked early on like a return to medieval theocracy and the religious wars of early modern Europe. In time, many realized it had mobilized a voting bloc big enough to become a power-player at all levels of politics.

These kinds of attitudes showed up in our focus groups when we asked participants to respond to photos of televangelists and Christian Right leaders. Here, for example, were the responses to an image of Jerry Falwell Sr. and Jr. together: "Hypocrite, don't like him," "It's a corporation, like they probably run like a big church," and, "I don't trust them, they look like politicians." In response to a photo of Pat Robertson in his prime, people said this: "Pat Robertson, no, I don't like him," "It's just another one you see when you wake up at night and he's on TV," "The 700 Club, it's just annoying to me," "He wants to use my money to buy himself a new watch," and, "Association of business and religion, which I feel is evil."

The backlash against the Christian Right, which I explore further in Chapter 8, turned out eventually to have sweeping consequences, alienating even previously religious Americans from traditional religion generally.[57] It was one of the crucial disturbances that triggered what would become a massive avalanche of cultural change. This was another irony: the movement to save Christian America for God ended up pushing many Americans away from Christianity, God, and the church.

The Spread of Eastern Religions and the New Age Movement

The 1960s in the United States saw a dramatic surge in interest in "Eastern" religions, like Hinduism, Buddhism, Jainism, and Sikhism. Westerners' curiosity about and explorations of Eastern religions had a long history, coming and going in waves.[58] The crucial event in the 1960s, however, was the passage of the US Immigration and Nationality Act of 1965. That Act reformed the previous immigration law, which had privileged western and northern European immigrants to foster US racial homogeneity. The new system opened up legal immigration from other parts of the world, notably, for our purposes, Asia. The years thereafter saw a dramatic increase in Asian immigrants to the United States, particularly on the West and East Coasts. The number of Asian immigrants to the United States in 2019 was 29 times greater than in 1960.[59] Many of those Asian immigrants naturally brought with them their religious practices and beliefs, thus exposing increasing numbers of Americans to them.[60]

The cultural consequences of the arrival of Eastern religions on American shores—along with related influences, such as the Beatles studying Transcendental Meditation with its founder, Maharishi Mahesh Yogi, in India—were profound. Some Americans studied and converted to traditional Eastern religions.[61] Members of the 1960s counterculture were often attracted to Eastern religions as a contrast to mainstream Western faiths.[62] Others began following gurus. Still other Americans became gurus and masters themselves.[63] Concepts from Eastern religions, like karma, were dislodged from their original meaning systems and popularized in the broader culture—as in, "Karma's a bitch" and "Karma will get you" (another example of cultural particulate matter diffusing in the atmosphere).[64] We will see in Chapter 9, in fact, that most adult Americans say they believe that the force of karma is real. Eastern religions also provided a wide palate of ideas and images that many spiritual entrepreneurs used to develop new religious philosophies and movements, usually called "cults" at that time. The New Age movement of the 1970s was particularly influenced by the reworking of Eastern religions.[65] Many of our interview respondents referenced "Eastern" religions in a positive light and professed more than a few ideas drawn from New Age thinking.

This American upsurge of interest in Eastern religions and the various offspring and hybrids it fostered was a hugely important development for the religious field prior to the 1990s, which helped prepare the way for the zeitgeist that emerged then and the accompanying obsolescence of traditional religion. Suddenly, there were several ancient religions and a number of new belief systems competing for the attention and affections of Americans.

The Ersatz "Warfare of Science and Religion" Narrative

One of the debates that bedevils American religion is the alleged inherent conflict between religion and science. The popular cultural assumption is that science and religion are two distinct claimants to trustworthy knowledge holding mutually exclusive and innately conflicting views from which only one—always science—can emerge as the winner. Nearly all Americans presuppose that science possesses proven facts, while religion requires leaps of faith. Science is based on empirical methods, religion on ancient books. Science is modern, open-minded, and leads to a brighter future, whereas religion is ancient, benighted, and burns people at the stake. Scientists agree about their established knowledge, while religious teachings are contradictory and irreconcilable. Science has given us electricity and antibiotics, while religion has produced the Dark Ages, the Crusades, and the Inquisition. The contrasts are clear, according to this narrative, and their implications are obvious.

It turns out, however, that this common view of science and religion is historically wrong. The idea that they are inherently incompatible kinds of truth claims ever battling for human allegiance turns out to be not a reflection of historical or logical reality but an ideological frame promoted by certain late-Victorian academics. Especially important were New York University chemist John William Draper who, in 1884, published his influential *History of the Conflict Between Religion and Science*; and Cornell University's first president, Andrew Dickson White, author of the much-read *A History of the Warfare of Science with Theology in Christendom*.[66] However, University of California sociologist Stephen Shapin noted in his landmark book, *The Scientific Revolution*, that "it has been a very long time since these ['warfare'] attitudes have been held by historians of science." Rather, the history of science reveals an "intimate connection between science and religion."[67] According to University of Wisconsin historians of science David Lindberg and Ronald Numbers, by the 1980s, we had seen "a developing consensus among scholars that Christianity and science had not [historically] been at war."[68]

Serious histories unbiased by the "warfare" frame have shown instead, for example, that the Catholic Church was in fact not a particular enemy of science and that most of the early leaders of the scientific revolution were theists, if not Christians, who viewed science and religious faith as compatible and mutually reinforcing.[69] They show that nineteenth-century Christians engaged evolutionary geology and biology not always antagonistically but by articulating a broad range of complex positions, including perspectives accommodating evolution.[70] The received "warfare" view of science and religion that we see was actually an ideological move of late-nineteenth-century activist secularizers, part of what I have elsewhere called a "secular revolution."[71] Far from being actual history, it was part of a struggle for social status and institutional control by secular activists, not an inherent logical conflict between faith and science.

The secular activists won, as public discourse and survey data attest. A national survey of 18-to-23-year-olds that I conducted in the early 2000s found that 70% of them agreed with the statement "The teachings of science and religion often ultimately conflict with each other." And 67% disagreed that "the findings of science and teachings of religion are entirely compatible with each other." As one recent interviewee told us, "Obviously, science is a big part of religion losing out. Science has had a huge impact on refuting a lot of the teachings about the universe." The majority also disagreed that some scientific discoveries had strengthened their religious faith.[72]

Why exactly the erroneous "warfare" view persists as gospel in the popular imagination long after historical scholarship repudiated it is itself a fascinating sociological puzzle, although beyond our capacity to explore here. What matters for present purposes are the practical effects that this popular frame has on American religion. Sociologists are fond of insisting that "if [people] define situations as real, they are real in their consequences."[73] The warfare narrative is very real in its consequences. "The older I got, seeing how the world works and science disproving [religious] stuff and the ability to think critically, religion all felt ridiculous," one interviewee told us. And, "I don't need religion in my life to tell me what to do. I can get rid of that. Science, that's the gold standard. Mainly because scientists are in it for the sake of science, they don't necessarily have an agenda. So science is good."

The militantly secular takeaway from the science versus religion narrative is that religion would best be suppressed and extinguished so that societies can be governed by rational, scientific knowledge instead of absurd superstitions. This outlook enjoyed an influential heyday for some years following September 11, 2001. Yet such militant secularism actually does not sit very well with most Gen Xers, Millennials, and Gen Zers. It sounds too similar to the overconfident religious zeal that makes religion so scary in the first place. Younger generations tend strongly toward relativism, tolerance, and avoiding being "judgy." They are also, as I discuss in subsequent chapters, generally not fond of interpersonal conflicts or systematic programs of ideological change. Furthermore, many younger Americans, even while assuming the superior authority of science over religion, maintain an openness to the idea that there may be more to reality going on "out there" than science can observe and explain. So extinguishing religions to produce a world of rational atheists is not an attractive prospect for many.

Instead, most Americans who are Generation X and younger resolve the uncomfortable science versus religion conflict in their heads. Science trumps religion when it comes to "real" knowledge, they believe. Religious truth claims are problematic, objectively considered. *However*, if religion works for some people, let it be. Religions can produce personally helpful and prosocial results. Why knock it? Religion can be very meaningful as part of a family heritage and personal value systems. As long as it is not damaging people, what is the harm? Everybody's place in life is arbitrarily determined by their random birth to whichever parents they got, anyway, so whatever anyone thinks is ultimately no more or less certain than anything else. Who can know what is ultimately true? Live and let live. Don't impose or harm. Don't judge. Including when it comes to religion.[74] (Unless when religion imposes, harms, or judges—then it deserves criticism.)

But that is getting ahead of the story. What matters most for now is this: the majority of Americans still assume the "deep culture" belief that science and religion have long been direct competitors over basic truth claims about reality and that, in any conflict between the two, science has always eventually won and will continue to win. That story took hold in the late nineteenth century and endures—despite plenty of scholarship to the contrary—in popular culture today.[75] In the struggle for control over legitimate knowledge and problem-solving, science has captured huge swaths of ground from religion. Circumstances in the 1990s and 2000s, however, further heightened the effects.

Declining Confidence in Organized Religion

In Chapter 1, I noted the long-term decline in Americans' confidence in organized religion—along with almost every other major public institution—measured by both Gallup and the General Social Survey since the 1970s (see Figures 1.6 and 1.7). That, I said, is one among many indicators of traditional religion's overall decline in strength and fall into obsolescence. Framed that way, the declining confidence in organized religion is an effect of other causes—which it is. But social trends occurring over long periods of time do not need exclusively to be either causes or effects. Social trends can be both causes *and* effects, brought on by earlier causes and creating new effects. So I return briefly here to the decline in public confidence in religion. Not only was it one indicator of the eventual larger cultural outcome of religious obsolescence. Along the way it also worked causally to help drag down the capacity of traditional religion to appeal to Americans, especially younger ones. It operated like an avalanche caused by an initial tremor that, through sheer gravity, became the cause of its own escalating size and velocity. Interacting with the many other forces and events described in these chapters, the declining confidence in religion hit a tipping point or critical mass and began itself to drive other changes toward religious obsolescence. In a way, this entire book is about declining confidence in religion—and many of the quotes from other chapters illustrate it—but these two summarize the matter for many post-Boomers: "When I hear the term 'traditional religion,' I think of control and misogyny, hypocrisy, pedophiles, nothing good, really," and "My feelings are not positive toward any type of institutional religion."

Obsolescence Postponed: Institutional Momentum and Diversion in the 1980s

Considering the trends described in this and the previous chapter, readers might justly wonder why it took until the 1990s for traditional religion to go obsolete. The combined forces we have examined here—the deinstitutionalization of marriage and family, the rise of emerging adulthood, the decline of face-to-face membership organizations, the rise of postmaterialist culture, the spread of mass consumerism, the intensification of expressive individualism, declining trust in organized religion, the believed trust of scientific over religious knowledge, the organizational decline of American mainline

Protestantism and Catholicism, the relegation of religion to custodian of morality, religion's own downplaying of eternal and transcendent themes, the backlash against televangelism and the Religious Right, and the cultural influences of Eastern religions—were all in place by the 1970s and seem like enough to trigger religion's demise. But that did not happen in the 1980s. Instead, religion actually appears to have enjoyed a slight bump in strength in that decade.

That, I suggest, was the result of two factors. The first is social or institutional momentum. Most of the trends discussed in this and the previous chapter had been developing for decades.[76] But traditional religion in the United States had centuries of historical forward movement. Even with religion's engines losing power and friction on the roadway increasing, so to speak, it is unrealistic to expect religion simply to have come to a stop. Most social structures are highly resilient and can withstand a lot of resistance.[77] Even with multiple social forces turning against religion by the late 1970s, the larger culture retained a broad, residual acceptance of received religion for delivering the kind of goods discussed in Chapter 2. It takes time for even powerful forces of social inertia, entropy, and friction to take down major institutional structures. Thus, even with all the trends we have seen so far stacked against traditional religion, it still had enough institutional momentum to keep working for a time.

Second, as mentioned above, the 1980s were a period that stood out from the two decades that preceded and followed it, countering or at least delaying some of the effects of the trends examined. National culture in the 1980s, as embodied in the Reagan Revolution, the increased intensity of the Cold War conflict, and the ascendant power of the Religious Right, accentuated a return to "conservative," traditional, and homespun family, religious, educational, and political values and virtues. That, at least, was the image. Conservative religion had a voice. Liberal and secular forces were knocked back on their heels. The gathering perfect storm of forces that would later cause religion's obsolescence decelerated for the decade. Longer-term trends and transformations were placed on temporary pause. The 1980s were the proverbial calm in the eye of the storm between the destructive winds of the 1960s and 1990s. In fact, many of the elements that would coalesce in the soon-to-emerge cultural zeitgeist were already developing below the visible surface during and partly as a reaction against the 1980s. But traditional religion's expiration date was extended to the last decade of the twentieth century.

Conclusion

The sociocultural conditions and forces that drove American traditional religion into obsolescence were a long time in the making. The causes of the losses that seemed suddenly to befall religion starting in the 1990s did not appear overnight. Nobody in the preceding decades foresaw the big picture that was developing or what the consequences might be for religion. As late as the twilight of the 1980s, it seemed that traditional religion was "back." That was an illusion, however. Once that decade had passed, many trending forces of the 1960s and 1970s gained new momentum. All it took then was an unpredictable set of further events to push religion into terminal decline. That is the story of the next two chapters.

6

The 1990s

Beginning of the End

By the start of the 1990s, American traditional religion was sociologically vulnerable. Over the course of the next 15 years, it would be battered into defeat. The engines of its demise came in many forms: technological, economic, demographic, and ideological. These were mostly not direct attacks—the consequences were largely unintended. Yet, by the end of the first decade of the twenty-first century, for the vast majority of younger Americans and a large number of older ones, religion had become obsolete.

End of the Cold War

In 1991, the world as we knew it fell apart. For decades, geopolitics had been defined by the conflict between Western democratic capitalism and Eastern communism. Then, suddenly, the Soviet Union collapsed and the Cold War was over.

A key feature of the Cold War was the United States' antagonism toward the state-sponsored Marxist-Leninist atheism of the Soviet Union.[1] America defined itself in opposition as a God-fearing nation that worshipped and relied upon the Almighty while maintaining religious freedom. American patriotism required belief in God—not necessarily for individuals personally but as a source of national identity.[2] Positing atheism as central to the communist enemy ensured religion a place of privilege in the collective American sense of self.

With the end of the Cold War, that place of privilege disappeared. The United States no longer faced a godless "evil empire" against which to define itself. The Berlin Wall had fallen, the Soviet Union dissolved, and, in 1992, Russia's new president, Boris Yeltsin, returned to church, professing that, after decades of atheism, he had become a believing orthodox Christian. Yeltsin pointed to a need for "reviving the people's spirituality and culture, achieving national unity and preserving civil peace in the country," so, he said, "I serve the Lord and the people."[3] Religious Americans had a huge cause to celebrate. President George H. W. Bush said, "The biggest thing that has happened in the world in my life, in our lives, is this: By the grace of God, America won the Cold War."[4] The future was now free from godless state ideologies (ignoring those of China and North Korea); God-fearing civilization had triumphed. President Bush proclaimed the blessings of a "Peace Dividend" and the coming of a New World Order.[5]

Bush was right. The United States was on the cusp of a new order. Yet it would turn out to be one that no longer required religion to shore up national identity. The victory over godless communism that America and the West had achieved "by the grace of God" would, ironically, result in an America with much less interest in God. The end of the Cold War was a jolt that helped to trigger the cultural avalanche that plowed over religion in the next two decades.

Ascendant Neoliberalism Capitalism

The defeat of communism paved the way for a new form of capitalism to sweep across the globe: neoliberalism. Understanding what that means requires a quick history. The "neo" in neoliberalism was an updating of the old liberalism that had governed industrial capitalism through the end of the 1920s. For centuries prior to liberal economics, economically nationalist governments played directive roles in managing national economic strategies, joint stock companies, imperialism, trade tariffs, and early colonial exploits. Eighteenth-century classical liberals, such as Adam Smith, argued persuasively for dramatically reduced government direction, and the English and American economies, among others, were run increasingly according to liberal laissez-faire principles, allowing entrepreneurs, businessmen, and industrial magnates to operate in free markets lightly governed by state regulations. Domineering "robber barons" of the Gilded Age—Mellon, Carnegie, Rockefeller, Morgan, Stanford, Vanderbilt, and Duke, to name a few—used their power to crush and buy out smaller competitors and build massive empires. Economies boomed, driven by the power of fossil fuels, but then also busted due to recurrent overproduction.

Progressive era leaders, such as Teddy Roosevelt, began to use the power of government to rein in and regulate that "Wild West" capitalism and restored market competition through "trust busting." The Great Depression of the 1930s put an end to economic liberalism; the theory was then replaced with "Keynesian" economics, named after the economist John Maynard Keynes. That approach encouraged government intervention to stimulate demand and stabilize the business cycle. The era through to the postwar years also saw the rise of welfare states in Europe and, to a lesser extent, the United States. That system flourished during the postwar economic boom. By the 1970s, however, Western economies were struggling—due partly to shocking oil price hikes—with "stagflation," a combination of slow economic growth and inflation. Complicating, too, were a host of political and military troubles during the Nixon and Carter presidencies. America seemed to be losing its grip. Popular discontent was mounting.

President Ronald Reagan rode into office in 1980 promising to revive the economy and rebuild national strength by rolling back the government economic interventions of the previous 50 years. Prime Minister Margaret Thatcher did much the same in the United Kingdom. A central piece of the Reagan-Thatcher revolution was neoliberal economic policy.[6] The idea was to return to the laissez-faire approach of free markets, free trade, lower taxes, privatization, competition, and smaller government. The revolution succeeded, at least partly, aided significantly by technologies of globalization that took off over the next decade. By the Clinton-Blair era of the 1990s, neoliberal capitalism was by appeal and imposition proliferating around the world—including, for a brief time, in post-Soviet Russia. Neoliberalism profoundly transformed American and global economics.[7]

"Neoliberalism" is often used by leftist critics as an all-purpose term of abuse when inveighing against "late modern" capitalism in general. But it refers to a specific strain of capitalism that has its own particular history. A small group of economists launched neoliberalism as an economic, political, and social project at the end of World War II. In the wake of the war's horrific devastation, they gathered at Switzerland's Mont Pelerin alpine resort, in April 1947, at the invitation of Austrian economist Friedrich Hayek. There they discussed how to create a prosperous, capitalist, globalized world that would avoid war and state despotism. That meeting led to the formation of the Mont Pelerin Society, which included the economists Friedrich Hayek, Milton Friedman, and James Buchanan. Over the next 30 years, their minority views incubated and developed, with the University of Chicago serving as the institutional home base.[8]

The first real government attempt to implement neoliberalism arrived with the US CIA-sponsored overthrow and killing of Chile's Marxist president, Salvador Allende, in September 1973. Allende was replaced by a US-backed authoritarian military dictator, Augusto Pinochet. The new president appointed a set of economists, known as the "Chicago Boys," to overhaul the Chilean economy along neoliberal lines. Chile's economy grew quickly at first.[9] That impressed Reagan and Thatcher, who, advised by other neoliberal and "supply side" economists, determined to push neoliberalism themselves.

The neoliberal policies that Reagan and Thatcher initiated, and that went global in the 1990s, opposed state intervention in economics and social issues, labor unions, overregulation of business, the nationalization of industries, and tariffs. They sought to minimize public service sectors in areas like healthcare, education, and utilities. They promoted free markets, privatization, deregulation, competition, efficiency, small government, offshoring, global trade, technology, and austerity programs for less powerful, "developing" nations.[10] Social problems should be addressed through civil society and volunteerism.[11] While championing economic "freedom," neoliberalism was also wary of robust democracy, fearing that popular people-power leads to distorted economies through legislated entitlements and regulations that bloat governments and break their budgets.[12]

The champions of neoliberalism were significantly—though not entirely—successful in remaking the world. They were effective enough, however, that the structures, rules, practices, and cultures that younger Gen Xers and all Millennials grew up in were profoundly different from those that Baby Boomers and older Americans had encountered.

Here we return to our story of religious obsolescence. To comprehend neoliberalism's real significance for our interests, we need to understand it as more than a set of economic policies. Neoliberal economics comes with huge mental, moral, and cultural corollaries.[13] Neoliberalism fosters a culture, a way of valuing, imagining, thinking, and judging. So what does this have to do with traditional religion in the 1990s and after? The answer is: plenty. Neoliberalism's causal influences, however, are not straightforward but indirect. They were achieved through the reshaping of the conditions of work and associated cultural dispositions.[14] That occurred in three crucial ways.

First, neoliberal capitalism in a competitive, globalized economy raised the bar for what it took to sustain a successful career in the 1990s and beyond. Gone were the days of a high school or college graduate holding a secure job for life with the same firm. Many previously well-paying blue- and white-collar jobs were outsourced to foreign countries with cheaper labor and fewer workers' rights.[15] Many permanent jobs were downsized into temporary positions without benefits. Labor unions had diminished in the 1970s, and they could not be counted on to protect workers from these trends. Pensions, retirement savings, and health insurance were privatized, and employers shifted the costs to their employees. Accelerating technological change made a range of old skills obsolete, demanding retraining or job loss.[16] Good jobs at the top grew fewer while less stable jobs increased at the bottom. "Precarity" became the new term describing the condition of many wage workers in the neoliberal order.[17]

For younger Gen Xers and Millennials entering the labor market, all of this demanded a new, intensified orientation to work and careers.[18] They had to choose careers that would grant financial security and began shifting to more "practical" educational paths.[19] They had to become more competitive. To keep their eyes on opportunities to upgrade, retrain, or earn another certification or degree. To network more actively in career circles. To work longer hours. To multitask to the limit. To think about work over weekends. To impress their bosses more than their colleagues did. To build their resumes. To look for openings for better jobs.[20] Those who did not would be left behind. And, with increasingly larger shares of a growing economic pie going to fewer high-skilled people at the top, getting left behind was a very real and unappealing possibility.[21]

The consequence for religion was that younger Gen Xers and Millennials had to invest much more time, attention, energy, and emotions into preparing for, launching, and developing what they hoped would be successful careers. This was especially true of college-educated and more socially integrated young adults who stood better chances at success: the same sort who historically were also more likely to join a religious congregation. "Your dream job is out there," one commentator observed, "so never stop hustling . . . it's a blueprint for spiritual and physical exhaustion."[22] Time, attention, energy, and emotional capacity are finite, so young adults had less of those available for thinking about, getting involved with, and practicing religion. Increasingly, weekends could not include a day of worship and rest because a pressing work deadline had to be met. Time that previously would have been available for reading scripture or praying was spent instead researching strategies for job advancement or writing graduate program applications. Better for the hyper-responsible post-Boomer to drop out of Bible study altogether than to show up late half the time because of unpredictable overtime work. In short, the job and career demands of neoliberal capitalism "crowded out" religion.

Many noted this shift in our interviews: "Unfortunately life is too busy to seek out communities of people," said one respondent. "People think they're living the American dream, but I think they're just slaves to work, tax, school, work, sleep—you're just a hamster on a wheel," said another. Another explained, "There's less value placed on religious communities now. We work way more than previous generations, so people probably don't want to spend their Sunday in Mass. People find their sense of community at other places." Again, "As my wife and I work more and have more responsibilities, we become more isolated, because we don't have the time or energy or desire to want to interact outside of work or home. We just don't have time, I don't have time to do anything other than home and work and kids—that's it. I deal with people in my profession, so I don't want to come home and deal with other people, I want to be left alone." Another confirmed: "Maturity, getting older, making decisions for ourselves, independence, having to pay for our own school or housing, made us think, 'Well, I don't have time to be praying' or 'I don't have time to go every Sunday to church, I have to study for this exam.' There's always something that came up, and you learned, 'Well, God is important, but let me just take care of these adult things I have to take care of.'"

My survey data back this up. The findings cannot tell us about the experience of post-Boomers in the 1990s and 2000s. But they can give some sense of what things look like in the aftermath of obsolescence. We see in Table 6.1 that post-Boomers express more financial stress and busyness than Boomers. More than half of Gen Xers and Millennials say financial risk drives them to work hard simply not to fall behind. Almost half of Millennials say they are too busy to get involved in local community organizations. And one out of three post-Boomers say life is too hectic and stressful to get involved in a local religious organization. This is not entirely surprising since, at the time of this survey, many Millennials and Gen Xers were in demanding careers and at crucial stages of family life. We cannot compare these findings with the same from a survey decades ago to assess change over time. We do know, however, that, starting in the 1990s, neoliberalism dramatically changed the nature of work and life in ways that are consistent with the data we see here. Many Millennials feel they are too busy and stressed to invest in local community organizations, including religious congregations.

Table 6.1 Time Stresses and Community Involvement by Generation (%)

	Early Boomers	Later Boomers	Gen Xers	Millennials
Agree: "I feel financially at risk, so I have to work hard not to fall behind."	31	44	54	59
Agree: "I am too busy to get involved in local community organizations."	25	38	41	47
Agree: "Even if I wanted to, life is too hectic and stressful to get involved in a local religious organization."	20	27	32	32
TOTALS (unweighted n's):	100 (n = 341)	100 (n = 358)	100 (n = 485)	100 (n = 677)

Source: Millennial Zeitgeist Survey, 2023 (N = 1,861). Percents may not add to 100 due to rounding. "Agree" means "strongly agree" and "somewhat agree" combined.

The second way neoliberalism undercut traditional religion was by requiring workers to become more mobile. The neoliberal workplace not only demanded that workers intensify investments in their jobs or fall behind. It also demanded greater mobility of every kind.[23] Neoliberalism is all about increasing fluidity, reducing transaction costs, specializing for efficiencies, and capitalizing on every competitive advantage. That often meant creating jobs, work tasks, and project teams that were flexible and adaptable. It required moving people around a lot—within offices, across teams, to different headquarters and plants, and sometimes to other countries. This was true especially for younger workers, whose positions were less settled and secure. Mergers and acquisitions, which neoliberalism encouraged, also involved plenty of downsizing and job shifting, which forced workers without warning to move within or between firms or be laid off.

The implicit social contract of mutual commitment between firms and workers under the old order fostered stability. Work may have been boring, but one could at least settle into it and into one's home, town, and neighborhood—and religious congregation. Neoliberalism's cancelation of that contract conveyed a clear message: always be ready to move, stay open to transition, never get locked in. That meant geographical mobility, which also had psychic consequences. Even if one liked one's job and it felt secure, it was still risky to relax. Things changed unpredictably and rapidly in the neoliberal order, and one might suddenly find oneself needing to move for any number of reasons. The contract could end soon, and who knows where the next will come from? So younger workers, especially, learned to stay mentally and emotionally prepared to transfer, to relocate, to jump to something different.

Mobility for work translated into transience as a state of mind. Post-Boomers became job nomads and career prospectors, both in spirit and reality.[24] As one interviewee said, "No strong community. I'm a nomad, I don't really have a strong sense of belonging because I've moved around a lot in my life, not small moves, but continent-changing moves. So I never felt I could adhere to any community strongly or belong to any particular group." Another told us: "Community is less for my generation than previous ones. People move from their home state or city, and there's less to draw people in without religion. People just don't have the social places to gather." Still another said:

> I'm open to the idea of a higher power, there's likely some sort of higher power or higher force. But I don't place myself squarely in an institutionalized religion you could label. I wouldn't say anything particularly turned me away besides the lack of time currently. And I've been moving around because of college, so it's been hard to identify and establish a community where I feel like I really belong and want to participate long term.

My 2023 Millennial Zeitgeist Survey found that, when asked if they have yet "settled down in life now by having a long-term job and stable place to live," 34% of Millennials (ages 25–42) reported either that they had not or did not know, which is reasonable to interpret as probably not. That compares to 18%, 15%, and 10% of the same for Gen Xers, Later Boomers, and Early Boomers, respectively. It makes sense that younger generations are less settled down than older ones. But the fact that one-third of younger adult Americans have not yet settled down makes it that much harder for traditional religion to recruit them to join and commit.

The same survey also asked respondents how many times they have moved their place of residence since they turned 18, which I standardized as median moves per decade.[25] Baby Boomers (early and later combined) reported moving an average of 1.28 times per decade, Gen Xers 1.71 times, and Millennials 2.94 times per decade. The average Millennial in a standardized comparison has moved almost two times more per decade than the average

Boomer. Residential moves disrupt the social ties of everyone in a mover's network and shape perceptions of the normalcy of transience. Also, only one move can potentially weaken any mover's ties to religious organizations. So, an average increase of 1.7 more moves per decade by the largest generation in US history can concatenate over time into larger social effects. In the context of the many other factors examined in these chapters, increased post-Boomer mobility contributed to the perfect storm that made religion obsolete.

What exactly does this have to do with younger Americans and religion in the 1990s and after? American traditional religion, as I have said, has long stood for and in practice actually required people to settle in, put down roots, join a congregation, invest in a community, and carry on a tradition. That way of life was well suited for agricultural societies needing central community gatherings and for urban and suburban societies with stable neighborhoods. It is not well suited to the neoliberal regime.[26] Americans who have moved are generally less likely to become involved in religious congregations than those who have stayed in place (the American South offering one exception at least in former decades).[27] Twentysomethings and thirtysomethings who are looking to move out and up, who are not sure what next year looks like, or who simply know they need to do whatever management asks are not good candidates for church or temple membership.[28] In short, the mental and physical transience that accompanies neoliberal capitalism is the enemy of stability, and traditional religion thrives under stable conditions.

The third way that neoliberalism challenged traditional religion was by cultivating a new cultural sensibility that is antithetical to most traditional religions. In a thousand and one ways, neoliberal capitalism socializes people to value autonomous individualism, continual innovation, material prosperity, market exchange relations, consumer satisfaction, endless competition, globalized cosmopolitanism, and the monetizing and marketizing of almost all aspects of life.[29] In the 1990s and 2000s, it was virtually impossible not to breathe in the ubiquitous spirit of neoliberalism, which had "polluted" the cultural atmosphere, making the survival of religion as a species more difficult. Many of these features were present in other forms of capitalism of former eras, but neoliberalism supercharged them, which had consequences for religion, as one post-Boomer explained.

> I don't think society becoming less religious is bad. But it is negative that we're replacing that with being busier. Religion integrated and gave us time

to pause and engage in rituals and socialize and relax. That's been filled with additional activities, reasons to spend more money, do more shopping, go more places. So there are negatives.

The underlying question is: What kind of cultural reality does neoliberalism create, and how do different institutions and systems help sustain it? In the neoliberal worldview, atomistic individuals negotiate social life as a marketplace in which each individual competes against and exchanges with others to achieve gains of wealth and status.[30] Money becomes the one common reference of value and relations since substantive values, virtues, and ends are seen as mere "preferences" that vary infinitely across individuals. Neoliberalism defines humans as fundamentally satisfaction-seeking consumers of acquired objects and experiences who pursue lifestyles of continual improvement though technological innovation and economic interactions.[31] To succeed is to win the competitive economic game.[32] As Jake Meador wrote in *The Atlantic*, the reason some leave religion is simply due to

> how American life works in the 21st century. [It] simply isn't set up to promote mutuality, care, or common life. Rather, it is designed to maximize individual accomplishment as defined by professional and financial success. Such a system leaves precious little time or energy for forms of community that don't contribute to one's professional life.[33]

This neoliberal conception is simply not compatible with those of American traditional religions—especially Christianity, Judaism, and Islam, which, despite their vast theological differences, would agree that the neoliberal view is not only wrong but also delusional.[34] For traditional American religions, humans are divinely dependent and socially interdependent creatures who inhabit a morally significant universe in which they are on a quest to realize, with divine aid, their spiritually and morally higher selves, the aim of which is to enjoy flourishing lives in communities of peace and love that reside under the governing care and judgment of God.[35] Even modernized versions of those religions—such as Reform Judaism and liberal Protestantism—would insist that human life, purpose, and destiny are infinitely more complex, noble, and profound than the self of neoliberalism, which exists as a mere efficient producer, rational exchanger, and desiring consumer.[36]

The point is this: the neoliberal idea of "true" and "good" human selves and those of traditional religions oppose each other in a zero-sum conflict. When one gains, the other loses. The more one is internalized, the more foreign the other becomes.[37] In the 1990s, neoliberal capitalism triumphed, restructuring institutions and reshaping cultures. People who came of age in this era were socialized into neoliberalism's pervasive cultural reality. You could try to resist it, but that was extremely difficult.[38] To generations of young people socialized into neoliberal capitalism's deep cultural categories and assumptions about "reality," traditional religion seemed foreign, antiquated, and weird. The cultural mismatch was immense. The climate change it provoked was hostile. Starting in the 1980s and hitting high gear in the 1990s, neoliberal culture just pushed traditional religion aside.

The Digital Revolution

The Digital Revolution does not need much explaining. In 1995, the internet had 16 million global users; by 2000, it was 350 million; and, by 2005, 1 billion people were using the internet. Handheld cellular mobile phones were first developed in the 1970s and 1980s, but 1991 saw the launch of second-generation cellular technology. Blackberries hit the market in 1999, and, in 2007, Steve Jobs announced the release of the first iPhone. Experimental social media platforms became available in the mid-1990s, internet chatrooms became popular in the late 1990s, followed in the early 2000s by the popular Friendster, Myspace, and Facebook. YouTube launched in 2005, Twitter in 2006, and Instagram in 2010.

Our interest here is the effects of digital media on culture and how it helped drive traditional religion into obsolescence for younger generations. Accumulated empirical evidence suggests conflicts between digital media use and religiousness. Conclusions from recent studies include these:

- "We find that internet use is associated with decreased probability of religious affiliation."
- "I find that internet use is associated with increases in being religiously unaffiliated and decreases in religious exclusivism."
- "Higher levels of internet use correspond with lower levels of prayer, reading sacred texts, attending religious services, and considering

religion personally important. Internet use also correlates positively with being an atheist and being religiously unaffiliated."[39]

But to get beyond correlations, we need better to understand causal mechanisms. How and why would digital technologies harm religion? The Digital Revolution was and is corrosive to religion in at least 10 distinct ways.

First, new digital media became a time and attention suck. With ever-new ways to spend time online—surfing the web, posting in chatrooms, creating and updating profiles, playing games, checking the news, sharing photos, consuming pornography, shopping online, or any number of other activities—people had less time for everything else. Some of these activities just replaced older ones—such as shopping online instead of driving to malls. But most activities were new additions to people's lives (surfing the web) or encouraged even more time spent on existing tasks (writing lots of texts and emails instead of a few handwritten letters). More than a few post-Boomers we interviewed reported stories similar to this: "I use social media addictively, and I try to limit it, because it's so easy to do that all the time, to continually doom scroll. It's very easy to doom scroll, so I have to actively try and cut it out of my life."

In 1995, 14% of Americans were online, a figure that rose to 21–23% in 1996 and 31–41% in 1998, depending on the survey. In 1999, American adults spent an average of 7 hours a week online, according to Harris Interactive. In 2000, Americans spent an average of 9.4 hours a week online, 3.3 of which were at home. By 2016, hours spent per week online had grown to 23.6, of which 17.6 were spent at home (not work or school). Additional hours spent online not at home, work, or school, such as at internet cafes, other people's homes, and libraries, grew from 0.3 in 2000 to 2.1 in 2016. In 2005, 72% of Americans said they surfed the web ("went online without a specific destination") often or sometimes; by 2016, that number had risen to 85%. Time spent by Americans on mobile devices has also increased steadily, from an average of 2 hours, 32 minutes in 2014 to nearly 4 hours in 2021. The age group that spends the most time online are 25-to-29-year-olds —37% of whom spent 16 or many more hours per week online in 2009. They are followed by 30-to-39-year-olds and 18-to-24-year-olds. In 2018, one out of four American adults reported being "almost constantly" online.[40]

In my 2023 Millennial Zeitgeist Survey, Millennials reported spending an average of 5 hours a day online, not counting work: 2.4 hours on social media and another 2.6 hours elsewhere on the internet. Gen Xers, by comparison, reported a sum of 3.7 hours per day online, Later Boomers 3 hours, and Early Boomers 3.3 hours per day.[41] These latter numbers refer to 2023, not the 1990s or 2000s. But they help to explain some of the experience of seeming lack of time reported in Table 6.1 that makes religious involvement feel impossible to many Millennials.

The negative opportunity costs for religion are obvious. Every extra hour of time spent on digital media is one less hour to spend on something else. Practicing religion is not the only place from which people could pull time and attention, but, given all of the other forces working against religion in the 1990s and after, it was an obvious one. For those already disinclined to continue practicing religion, telling oneself that "I am just too busy right now" would seem like a reasonable justification—even when the time crunch was caused by increased time spent looking at screens. In any case, screens won over religious meetings. Empirical evidence supports that expectation. In my 2023 Millennial Zeitgeist Survey, 62% of adults who spend 5 hours or more online per day attend religious services less than once a year (or never). For those who spend less than 2 hours per day, the number is 44%. At the other end of the spectrum, 20% of those who are online less than 2 hours a day attend religious services weekly, compared to only 5% of those online 5 or more hours a day. These differences remain statistically significant after controlling for age, education, income, sex, and race and ethnicity.[42] The causal directions here likely run both ways, but the association is strong and the competition for a finite amount of time and attention is unmistakable.

Second, digital media created new, alternative, flexible ways to find "community" that required fewer commitments. The Digital Revolution was truly revolutionary in connecting people instantaneously without them having to physically move. The landline telephone had been doing that for half a century. But digital technology's addition of visual images, instantaneous data transfers, and user mobility propelled social connections to unimaginable new levels. The network structure of the digital world also made it possible for users to connect to many others together in groups of shared interests. People's ideas of "friends" and "communities" changed. As interview respondents observed, "People may have the open-mindedness, but maybe are less authentic or something? It does seem less authentic because they have 20 times more friends because they are 20 times more connected." And, "On our phones, the internet, we're able to pick and choose who we want to hang out with, what information we want to see, what we want others to see about us, and who we want to have see that information; we're able to compartmentalize a lot." For these reasons, many observe that these new relationships fail to replace the older, in-person communities, reporting, for example, that "social media gives the appearance of having a social life without actually requiring you to go out and interact with anybody" and "I'm not super close with friends, I found myself feeling lonely, just struggling with a sense of connection. I wonder if a lot of people my age feel like that and it's not just me, because what social media has become for us, maybe it has made us feel more lonely."

In the pre-digital world, participating in one's communities normally required regularly meeting people in the same space. After the Digital Revolution, Americans could sit at home on their screens interacting with countless others whom they had never met but whom they considered friends. They also did not have to coordinate times to meet since one could login and catch up on conversation threads whenever it was convenient. Furthermore, such relationships were highly porous. One could easily join and then quit, post, or lurk. Digital platforms and profiles also made it simple to identify the exact people one wanted to talk to and ignore all others, which took 1970s and 1980s "lifestyle enclaves" to a whole new level.[43] Online communication also allowed anonymity and distance. People could behave in ways they never would in person—"flaming" strangers, creating fake identities, sharing rude photos, or simply deleting and blocking others. There was no need to deal with difficult people, as in face-to-face communities.[44] The autonomy, anonymity, flexibility, and convenience were astonishing.

The implications for traditional religion are clear. Most Americans think that one of religion's most important purposes is providing community. Online communities introduced entirely new ways to find connections, friends, support, and shared identities that were quicker, simpler, and more customizable than any real religious congregation. Boomers may have had their suspicions, but post-Boomers who grew up in this digital culture found this way of connecting easy and natural. Gen Zers cannot imagine life any other way. In short, the online communities created by the Digital Revolution matched a central function of traditional religion in ways that, for many, seemed preferable—even if in the longer run they proved disappointing. Like the electric typewriter meeting desktop computers, religion faced a new competitor that boasted huge comparative advantages. As one interview participant observed,

> We're all heavily inside technology and involved in video games, computers, Netflix, all that. I don't feel the sense of real community, it's been lost with

my generation. There're still people that do want to have community, connect with others, have a relationship. But it's lost its touch. Right now, our generation doesn't want to do that. They don't trust their neighbors. There's a sense of, you can only trust yourself or your family or your close friends. They don't want to reach out to others.

Third, the internet enhanced the capacity to expose and learn about the dark side of religion. Prior to the internet, there were surely plenty of religious wrongs, abuses, and scandals. But with more primitive communication technologies it was easier to keep them secret and contain damage. People who knew about sins being committed in religious groups had a harder time blowing whistles. The internet provided new ways for damaging information to spread quickly. That fed a growing popular demand for exposés and increased the public's willingness to believe them. The "spiral of silence" was broken.[45] Everyone became fair game. Outing the corrupt or adulterous pastor or pedophile priest became more feasible. The internet thus dramatically increased the public's exposure to stories about religious misdeeds and hypocrisies. As one interview participant noted, "It's easier for people now to see the ways religion falls short because the internet makes everything so accessible." And another: "We know more now, we know better. The good thing about the internet is that you can learn almost instantly about any news in the world, and obviously even though nothing is 100% truth, you can actually tell, because religion doesn't keep up with the times."

Fourth, the internet triggered a mindboggling explosion of information accessible to anyone with a few clicks of the keyboard. Before, people got information by talking to other people, looking in the library, taking in scheduled programs on radio or television, and subscribing to publications. Information flows were enormously slower and more limited, and the costs of searching were massively greater. That meant, in practice, that most people were much more constrained in what they knew and how much new information they were willing and able to find. The word "revolutionized" does not do justice to the ways internet search engines, especially Google, changed that. Gone were the days when people mostly knew mostly what family, school, friends, and television taught them; when, for example, people of faith knew that other religions, philosophies, and subcultures existed but did not really know too much about them. On the internet, anyone could easily find out seemingly everything about anything. With that, the range of potential new influences and authorities multiplied exponentially. This

THE 1990S: BEGINNING OF THE END   143

detonated an explosion of "cognitive pluralism" and openness to alternative possibilities.

Pluralism need not harm anyone's religious faith—especially if they have thought deeply about it. But many Americans have not thought that deeply, so learning about other belief systems—religious and otherwise—destabilized their religious beliefs. Before the internet, only the truly curious learned much about religions besides their own. It was possible, but it took real effort. Google eliminated that effort and shifted the burden instead onto anyone who wanted to remain sheltered from the onslaught of information. In that context, younger generations of curious Americans who swam in digital oceans were forced to address the relativizing implications of religious and philosophical differences. "What makes me think my religion is true and right when there are so many others who believe differently?" became a more intensely troubling question. Given the disorienting effects of popular postmodernism (more on this to come), the common imperative not to judge others, and the paradox of choice, many younger Americans answered the question by attenuating if not abandoning their religious faith.[46]

Fifth, the Digital Revolution offered readers a private realm in which to express, explore, and discuss their religious questions and doubts. The internet connected strangers with shared interests in anonymous settings. Early chatrooms and message boards allowed for the kinds of privacy in free expression and conversation unknown in the pre-internet world. Users could write their honest thoughts, feelings, and desires to strangers, anonymously. The true identities of anyone who asked hard questions, expressed serious doubts, or exposed clergy misdeeds did not need to be revealed. Anyone could hide behind the veil of digital secrecy and explore their curiosities, issues, interests, and fantasies with anonymous others. Anyone could, with minimal risk, look into ideas and interests that their religious communities might consider forbidden. Internet connections enabled everyone to listen to and ponder the views of others in unthreatening ways.[47] That privacy and anonymity dramatically expanded people's freedom to question and explore without having to fear the gaze of disapproving eyes or social sanctions. Again, the "spiral of silence" ended.[48] In short, the internet curtailed the ordinary means of social control that traditional religions used to keep people within the fold.

A sixth way that the Digital Revolution unintentionally undermined traditional religion was by assisting religious dissidents in finding each other and forming alternative, supportive groups and movements. Being a member of a small minority group in a large country can be isolating. There may be many thousands like you out there, but, because you are spread apart, others seem to barely exist. Prior to the internet, this was the condition of many Americans who held or dabbled with various minority religious, spiritual, and philosophical views—pagans, atheists, spiritualists, wiccans, and those with esoteric, alternative, and occult religious and spiritual ideas. Some may have belonged to formal organizations with membership lists, newsletters, and occasional meetings, but most would have remained disconnected and isolated.

Suddenly, the internet could connect these people with each other through chatrooms, web pages, and other digitally based "places" to meet. In a few years, Facebook groups and other social media networks formed. People with minority and alternative views suddenly got connected. They realized there were not as few of their type as it seemed. They found places of belonging that understood and affirmed them. They learned more about their interests from others in their new groups. They discovered more organizations, meetings, and festivals that they did not know existed. Self-confidence grew as they realized they were part of something bigger and as their groups gained in numbers and visibility. Their views were gradually destigmatized. Before the internet, being a pagan or witch would have seemed bizarre to many people. Soon it became simply one more identity with which the public was becoming more familiar and that some even thought might be cool. Before the internet, being a doubting Mormon was isolating. The Digital Revolution, however, made them realize that they were far from alone but shared an experience with countless others with similar stories.

For traditional religions that already enjoyed their own identities, organizations, networks, and communication channels, this meant more competition. Previously isolated dissidents now had the means to recruit, organize, and mobilize groups and movements to attract even more interest and change public opinion. Some people involved in traditional religion (or their children) could peel off and defect to different groups. Others who might have gotten involved in religion at a certain stage of life could instead explore a wider range of interesting alternatives. New curiosities were piqued, more options considered. The number of spiritual products on the easily available market had increased significantly. Like every other causal mechanism here, that did not alone put traditional religion down, but it did sap some of its strength and change the larger culture.

A seventh means by which the Digital Revolution made life more difficult for traditional religion was by shrinking people's attention spans and heightening expectations of being continually stimulated and entertained. Research shows that internet usage decreases people's capacity to focus their attention for lengths of time.[49] Some of our interview respondents notice this among their peers and younger generations. One said, "The reason for religion's decline is pretty basic: technology. Our focus is just gone. We just have so many things pulling on our attention and it's exhausting, it's just too much." Another reported, "Most people my age and younger don't actually pay attention to what's going on in the world in terms of politics, media, and things like that, unless it's keeping up with the Kardashians, which is annoying. I wish more would actually pay attention in the news and look at different sources to gather information." Online texts are short. Visual images dominate. Communications are abbreviated. Information, images, and game action come rapid-fire. Everything online is designed to grab attention, spark interest, get likes, generate clicks. Everything must be amusing, quirky, enticing, happy, titillating, enraging—or else it will be ignored.[50]

Traditional religion cannot compete. Worse, religion itself becomes inaccessible and impossible to people shorn of their capacities to sit in silence, live with mysteries, and wrestle with the meanings of ideas and arguments from ages past.[51] Traditional religion can sometimes be boring. That is part of the program. Religion is repetitive and cyclical. It repeats texts, practices, and rituals. It cycles back to the same sabbaths, holy days, and sacred seasons. It involves most of the same people, meeting after meeting. It does not exist to stimulate and amuse. It sets out with ancient texts and traditions to form and transform people across their lives and create distinctive communities. Traditional religion historically does not poll audiences about what they feel will make them happy and then cater to that. Religion tells people what it believes will foster their genuine, higher flourishing and calls them into ways of life that promote that. Traditional religion is an acquired taste that takes training and effort to understand, appreciate, and love. Digital media is an addictive drug offering quick dopamine-fueled euphoria followed by a craving for the next fix.[52]

An eighth influence of the Digital Revolution on religion concerns information and image stimulus overload. Human minds and emotions are not built to process torrents of data. But content creators design unremitting steams of information and images to seize people's attention—to entice, sell, provoke, and amuse.[53] As one post-Boomer we interviewed related:

> Good living for me would be having something I enjoy and the space to enjoy it, to be free to relax and enjoy it. I don't have that anymore. I used to read, but I've gotten overstimulated. I can't read a book without being distracted by my phone or something, I can't just sit down and read a book. So "happy" for me as an individual would be finding one thing that I can give my attention to and just relax and be at peace.

Eventually the overstimulation and information saturation become too much. Purportedly authoritative information that contradicts itself—a common feature of online discourse—exacerbates the overload. A stream of depressing news about which one can do nothing—another common feature—intensifies it. Overkill may occur in one sitting, build up over a span of time, or become a chronic condition. Sometimes people recognize it happening to them, but usually not. Either way, it takes a toll. Stress, fatigue, detachment, gloom, sleeplessness, withdrawal, and even further compulsive immersion in digital stimulation are some of the results.[54]

In theory, religion could serve as a refuge from this overload. Quiet prayer, contemplation, worship, centering, reading, meditation, singing, connecting to other humans in person, volunteering, sharing a meal—they might all help. But they are not where most overloaded Americans turn. Little in advertisement-driven, mass-consumerist culture encourages it. It doesn't really make anyone any money. Rather, the dominant message is to alleviate one's stress and distress—temporarily—by shopping for and buying new products.[55] Some American religions have tried to get hip to the culture, arguably compounding the overload with their own flashy worship teams and slick media shows. Instead of religion, most overloaded Americans turn to exercise, time in nature, yoga, meditation, and various forms of mindfulness and spirituality to cope.[56]

Ninth, and relatedly, the incoherent oceans of news, advice, and opinions has the effect of corroding trust in external authorities and relocating the seat of authority within each individual's self. The internet by design obliterated gatekeeper authorities. Its designers hoped that the web would radically democratize information-seeking and -sharing and so transform society to make it more equal, free, and participatory.[57] No more coteries of experts to control what gets said and what gets edited out. Online, anybody could say whatever they wanted for anyone else to read. Such direct communication between ordinary people would, internet pioneers hoped, produce more active, responsible, informed citizens. That vision, however, assumed that users would be committed to open-minded learning and reason, and giant corporations would not control and manipulate digital information. We have since learned better.

The internet offers much of genuine value, but it also produces mountains of misinformation and manipulation. Users looking to find definitive answers to their questions online must become their own gatekeepers. Sitting alone as they scroll, they have nobody to turn to for help discerning what to believe. Individual users are thus trained by the medium itself to become their own final authorities. Nobody has to teach this explicitly because the experience itself socializes users into the stance: distrust others' claims to knowledge, sort through the piles of conflicting information, and just decide for yourself. "Do your own research," as the saying goes. More generally, digital media "promote a meta-realism in which the world is a flexible space where reality can be created or manipulated."[58] What follows from there are post-fact, post-truth cultures and politics.[59] Thus, one interview participant observed:

> With social media, you're only consuming what others want you to consume, what they're willing to put out there. That by definition is going to be a redacted view of society, whether it's purposeful, whether they're ashamed of something they're not sharing, it just literally slipped their mind, or they just didn't think to mention it because who can detail their entire life in a paragraph on a website.

The internet encourages its users to treat all knowledge claims as mere opinion, to be suspicious of experts and external authorities, and to make oneself the final arbiter of truth. The more people internalize such dispositions, the less intelligible and appealing traditional religion will seem to them. Sacred scripture, history, tradition, ritual, sacraments, preaching, teaching, and divinity itself are simply folded into the thousands of hits on the list of Google returns. What to believe? Who can know? Only each individual authority for themselves.

The final way the Digital Revolution contributed to traditional religion's obsolescence was by radically transforming the basic structure of organizations and, as a result, the mental maps those models help shape. The pre-internet world was generally organized in centralized, top-down structures of command and control. The basic model was the same for everything from corporations (like General Motors) to clubs (like the Girl Scouts).

Centralized offices designed and controlled the organizational identities, product and program features, and strategies and decisions. Directives were sent down chains of command for implementation at lower levels. Information was gathered below and returned to the top for analysis. Communications ran from and to centralized hubs of authority and control. Work was carried out in brick-and-mortar facilities. Change required the cooperation of those at the top of the center.

The logic and functioning of the internet established a very different structural model: the network. Networks have few centers or heads. Participants are distributed across broad fields of relations. Networks shift form over time, depending on who is connected to whom in what configurations. Information can flow through multiple channels. Innovation and initiative can develop out of various nodes of the network. Authority is possible to designate and follow. But because control of information and resource flows is more diffuse, authoritative decisions and policies are more difficult to enforce. The possibilities for break-away network clusters are many. Bricks and mortar are unnecessary.[60]

Networks have not eliminated the old model. General Motors still has a central, physical office. But, as an organizational form, networks are a much better fit for digital interactions. They also facilitate efficiencies of process that serve neoliberalism. Furthermore, network structures transform people's cultural expectations of relations, work process, and behavior. People on whom the network vision has been imprinted, for instance, do not understand simply following directives from above. They recognize participating in groups that get tasks done. Implementing uniform plans makes little sense. Rather, collaborating with creative, skilled colleagues is effective and rewarding. In short, the network model of the Digital Revolution not only provides a new organizational structure but also cultivates and reinforces an instinctive way of thinking, imagining, and behaving.

Almost every traditional religion in the United States is organized on the pre-internet model of centralized, top-down administration. Consider any denomination. It has a centralized physical headquarters, designated leaders, and bureaucratic offices that produce standard educational curricula and publications. It has bylaws and rules of order, and it leads national gatherings. It controls its own seminaries and administers standards for the ordination of clergy. The planting of new and closing of dying congregations is likely centrally strategized. Significant innovations require approval from above.

Almost everyone meets in dedicated brick-and-mortar buildings. In the most general terms, most American religious denominations are oriented toward maintenance and control. Meanwhile, the internet, in conjunction with forces of globalization, is all about outward-facing creation and expansion.

Many younger Gen Xers and most Millennials and Gen Zers experience the standard model that organizes traditional religion as archaic, clunky, overbearing, weird, and frustrating. Such reactions are felt even before they are thought. Those negative evaluations are not a theoretical critique. They spring from experiences and expectations shaped by network models and practices made real by the Digital Revolution.[61] For younger Americans with jobs in network organizations, traditional religious structures feel alien. For those who work in old-model organizations, the last thing they want to join is a religion that operates like big corporate employers.[62] Their instinct is either to shake their heads and walk away or, if they care, to mobilize network resources to try end runs around established systems to do things better. Few centralized, top-down organizations, however, appreciate young innovators attempting end runs around their procedures and decisions. It rarely ends well.

Meanwhile, most of the newly emergent re-enchanted communities of alternative religions and spiritualties—not counting the relatively rare authoritarian cults—organize themselves as networks. They usually have fewer orthodoxies to guard and are more open to individual differences in belief and practices. Many have been organized by younger people whose brains are wired by and for networks. Individual entrepreneurs promoting alternative religious and spiritual beliefs also capitalized on digital technologies—desktops, laptops, printers, publishing software, blogs, self-publishing tools, Amazon, webinars, and so on—to communicate their ideas. Few of these groups take out mortgages to build their own physical spaces. Thus, completely apart from the actual content of any group's official beliefs, the mere feel of the spiritual and re-enchanted communities gives off good vibes for generations socialized by the internet. And vibes usually matter more to them than doctrines.

Each of these 10 causal mechanisms had some effect. Together—cumulatively, interactively, synergistically—they changed the world. And while early internet entrepreneurs did want to change the world, they weren't trying to destroy traditional American religion. That was mostly collateral damage.

Pop Postmodernism

In the 1990s, postmodernism and related theories swept through American universities. College students during this decade would have had difficulty getting through their four years of school without being exposed to some of the basic ideas from these theoretical programs. Postmodern thinkers did not generally set out to damage American religion. A few religious intellectuals even argued that they served the cause of religious faith.[63] When absorbed by people on the ground in what I call "pop postmodernism," however, these ideas proved powerfully corrosive to religion. A few different though similar schools of thought—postmodernism, social constructionism, and neopragmatism, which I parse out here—contributed to and reinforced pop postmodernism. Their importance for our purposes matters in their contribution to the popular versions that masses of ordinary young people took away from these high theories.

Interest in postmodernism among American academics increased significantly in the humanities in the 1980s. By the 1990s, it was all the rage. Postmodernism was always controversial, especially for natural scientists and many in the social sciences. But controversy drew attention, and, during the 1990s, postmodernism's critique of the modern seemed to many to have the upper hand. Those unpersuaded at least had to deal with it.

My interest here is not parsing out what postmodern theorists "really" said or meant. Our concern rather is grasping its popular reception and cultural influences: what we can call "popular postmodernism," or "pop pomo" for short. For American postsecondary students in the 1990s who were paying any attention, these are some basic postmodern ideas that might have impressed them:

- "Grand narratives" and "metanarratives" are no longer believable.
- No single reality exists that humans can "correctly" understand.
- The meanings originally intended by authors of texts are impossible to know.
- All identities and meanings are unstable, multiple, and fluid.
- Authorities, experts, and others with power should be critiqued and resisted.
- All knowledge is relativized by its place in culture, history, and social structure.

- Claims to objective, absolute, universal, or value-free truth or truths are erroneous.
- Consistency, coherence, logic, and unity are of dubious value.
- Truth claims are disguised quests for power and domination needing deconstruction.
- Always maintain a posture of skepticism, irony, and critical distance.

Students paying close attention might have absorbed these additional ideas:

- Things and people do not have essences that make them what they are.
- Modern progress and scientific triumph are illusions.
- Allegedly universal binary oppositions and fixed categories are invalid.
- Western males deploy rationality and reason as faux-universal stories to dominate others.
- One should treat society and nature like texts or discourses that lack objective truth.
- One must embrace multiplicity, eclecticism, rhetorical self-referentiality, and contradiction.

In retrospect, postmodernism turns out to have been a strange mixture of some valid, important critiques of modern pretensions and delusions, on the one hand, and an intoxicating brew of intellectual hyperbole, discursive silliness, and moral irresponsibility, on the other. It was neither all gold nor all dross, which made it both enticing and contentious—a good recipe for academic attention and influence. Postmodernism was also not merely an abstract intellectual discourse but also reflected and made a lot of sense in terms of real-world developments in society. It was plausible for sociological reasons.[64] Its combination of legitimate criticisms and impenetrable jargon shielded postmodernism from serious scrutiny long enough for it to have an enormous if diffuse impact on many educated Americans and in popular culture.

Is it possible to measure the growth of postmodernist discourse in public life? Can the claim that it had an "enormous impact" be quantified? Yes, somewhat, but only indirectly. No survey researchers in the 1990s asked university students, "How much have you been influenced by postmodernism?" or "Which of the following postmodernist ideas do you believe?" That would have been useless anyway. But we can at least measure changes in discourse

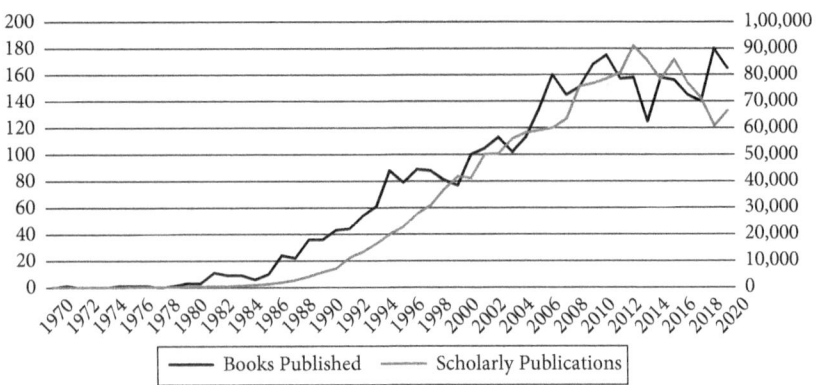

Figure 6.1 "Postmodernism" books and scholarly publications by year, 1970–2020.
Source: The Library of Congress, Google Books, Amazon.com.

about postmodernism across time to provide proxy measures of people's changes of exposure to postmodern ideas.

Figure 6.1 shows the number of scholarly books, articles, reviews, and related pieces about postmodernism published in the United States each year from 1970 to 2020—separating books (with number of titles on the left side) from other kinds of academic publications (with number of titles on the right). The numbers represent new publications per year, not cumulative totals. Figure 6.1 shows a trickle of scholarly publications on postmodernism in the 1980s, increasing with a major takeoff in the 1990s and continuing to a plateau after 2010. During the 1990s, articles lagged somewhat behind books in number but caught up by 2000. Until the late 1980s, fewer than 20 books on postmodernism were published each year. By the mid-1990s that number had more than quadrupled. By 2010, about 150 academic books per year were being published on postmodernism. In the mere 10 years after 1990, the number of non-book scholarly publications about postmodernism grew sevenfold, peaking in 2013 with 90,000 references. Clearly, postmodernism was a hot subject in American academia in the 1990s and well into the twenty-first century.

An alternative way to measure changes in scholarly interest in postmodernism is to count references over time to key postmodernist thinkers. Table 6.2 shows the number of hits returned by Google Scholar for five key leaders in postmodern thought, four of whom—Michel Foucault, Jacques Derrida, Jean Baudrillard, and Jean-François Lyotard—were intellectual leaders in

Table 6.2 References to Postmodernist Thinkers in Google Scholar by Decade

Decade	Foucault	Nietzsche	Derrida	Baudrillard	Lyotard
1970s	6,780	17,000	3,230	565	389
1980s	22,100	25,100	15,800	2,920	3,660
1990s	120,000	57,500	56,200	15,400	20,000
2000s	284,800	156,000	113,000	31,400	35,500
2010s	558,000	252,000	115,000	35,300	34,500

contemporary postmodernism, and one, Friedrich Nietzsche, being the movement's most important intellectual progenitor from the prior century. The results in Table 6.2 parallel those of Figure 6.1. References to these five postmodernist thinkers are substantial and increasing in the 1970s and 1980s. They explode in magnitude in the 1990s and after, during which these postmodernist luminaries were receiving tens and hundreds of thousands of references in scholarly works per decade.

Did postmodernism generate attention and discussion beyond scholarly circles? Figure 6.2 shows a similar trend occurring in non-scholarly media from 1991 to 2021. References to postmodernism in these media were few at the start of the 1990s but increased by nearly four times in only nine years, from 1991 to 2000. Starting in the early 2000s, media discourse about postmodernism declined but remained three times more frequent than the baseline year until the end of the 2010s. This fits the brief historical account above about postmodernism's rise. What matters for us is the fact that postmodern ideas occupied a heightened presence in public discourse for three decades.

Yet another way to measure broad cultural interest in postmodernism is by counting references to indicative keywords on Google across time. Figure 6.3 shows the yearly and cumulative number of mentions (with counts on the left and right, respectively) of postmodernism on the internet per year, from 1995 to 2020. We see there that internet discussions of things postmodern lagged behind scholarly interest by two decades. That makes sense since it would take time for an insurgent intellectual movement that started among French philosophers and literary critics to develop an influence among American university faculties and then, through them, their students and the public beyond. Even so, by 2010, the internet returned 300,000 hits on postmodernism. We are talking here about scales of tens of thousands, so the lower end of the curve still represents a huge number of hits.

154 PERFECT STORMS CONVERGING

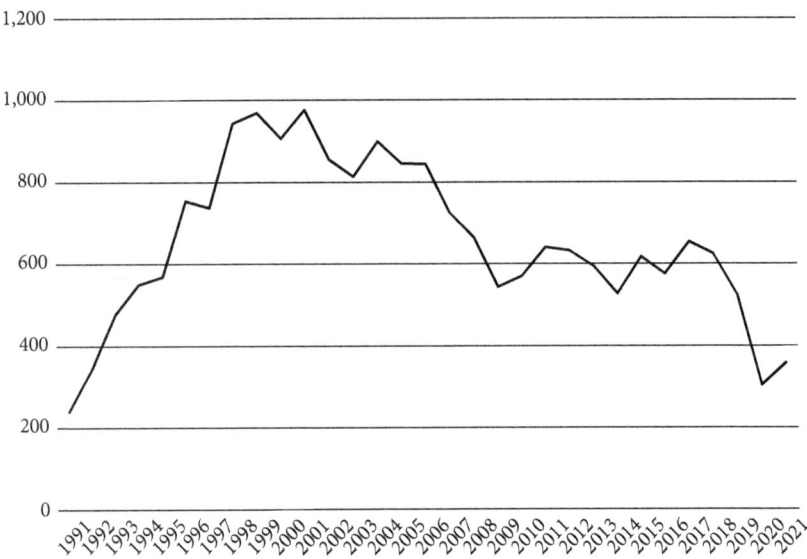

Figure 6.2 Media references to postmodernism by year, 1991–2021.
Source: Nexis Uni corpus.

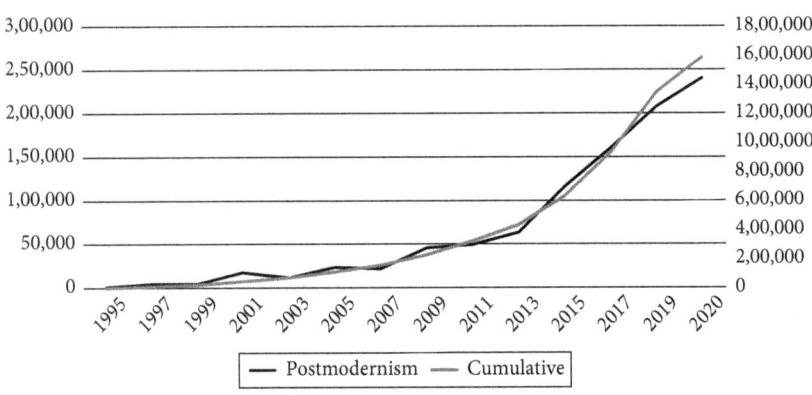

Figure 6.3 Google internet hits on "postmodernism" by year, 1995–2020.

(A crucial methodological point to note here about my use of internet counts in this book. Some readers may think to criticize these findings by pointing out that the growth in internet hits observed in Figure 6.3 and other figures to follow mirrors the massive increase of all internet websites from 1995 to 2020. That observation is correct but, for present purposes, also irrelevant. The point is not that public interest in postmodernism grew faster than the internet itself, which would have been nearly impossible for anything to have done. My point is rather that the exploding internet provided one important means by which popular interest in postmodernism was expressed and promulgated. Using the other measures above, I demonstrate major real growth in public attention of postmodernism and related terms in media references, books published, and scholarly publications [Figures 6.1, 6.2, 6.4, 6.6, 6.7]. There is no question that public discourse about postmodernism and related ideas increased during the period in question. Measures of that growth on the internet at the time simply indicate the massively increased availability of references to it on that hugely important communications media. And, as search engine technologies grew more sophisticated, potential interest in or exposure to postmodernism and related matters would not have gotten lost in the cacophony of overall internet growth about all possible topics—since users were not consuming representative samples of all internet content—but would have generated more relevant hits for any users surfing the web. Furthermore, not all topics produced hits growing in proportion to the internet's expansion; some, as we see in Chapter 7, were much delayed. Demonstrable growth in online discourse about postmodernism and other subjects examined below thus provides us one indirect but valid measure among others of the supply of postmodern ideas in public culture.)

This evidence suggests that postmodernist ideas landed on American shores in the 1980s, proliferated in academic and other circles in the 1990s, and diffused in more popular discourse in the second decade of the 2000s. From there we can infer that those ideas influenced the scholarship, careers, and students of a generation of American academics in higher education and eventually filtered out into many streams of popular culture. That makes it unsurprising that vulgarized expressions of postmodernist ideas showed up routinely in my interviews with youth and emerging adults in the 2000s and 2010s.[65]

A different but related academic theory and perspective that had similar unintended consequences for religion was social constructionism, sometimes also referred to as "social constructivism." The core idea of social constructionism is that the categories, definitions, and meanings of everything in human cultural life are not inherent but are constructed through social interactions and embedded in social structures and institutions, into which successive generations are socialized to take as simple reality. The most important text promoting social constructionism was Peter Berger and Thomas

Luckmann's 1967 gem *The Social Construction of Reality: A Treatise in the Sociology of Knowledge*.[66]

Social constructionism of all varieties has been popular in the discipline of sociology since the publication of Berger and Luckmann's landmark 1967 book. Over time, its appeal gradually spread to other disciplines and eventually beyond higher education. By the 1990s, social constructionism had come under the influence of postmodernism and various movements to "de-essentialize" components of structured inequalities (race, ethnicity, gender, sexuality, etc.). Often the social constructionism that emanated from academia and was absorbed into the broader culture slipped without much reflection from reasonable realist into radical anti-realist versions. The claim that everything that seems to exist is merely a human social construction, so that "reality" has no objective grounding, was not uncommon. People, it seemed, had created everything and could recreate anything with enough courage and willpower. The inevitable result was the cognitive and moral relativism of all human knowledge and ethics. Few bothered to consider at first how intellectually and morally self-defeating that is—that if everything is relative, then we possess no standard by which to decide that any idea or ethic is better than another, in which case all that remain are desire and power. Some in time walked back and qualified their claims. But the practical upshot was to vaccinate many young minds against confidence in the objective existence of anything.

As with postmodernism, it is not possible to measure directly the influence of social constructionism over time. More modest gauges will have to suffice. Figure 6.4 depicts the number of books and scholarly publications published on social constructionism each year between 1970 and 2020. As with the figures above, we see an increase in these publications in the 1980s, noticeable growth in the 1990s, and major increases after 2000. Social constructionism was, like postmodernism, a growth industry in American higher education—although the less steep line shows it was not as trendy a sensation as postmodernism during the same years.

Figure 6.5 shows the number of hits for Google searches of social constructionist keywords between 1995 and 2020. The pattern is similar to that for postmodernism in Figure 6.3: modest growth in references until the early 2000s, after which the increase in mentions accelerates. In 2000, the internet contained few references to social constructionism; 15 and 20 years later, Google would return 150,000 and 375,000 hits, respectively, on the term. (The same reply to the critical question about the increase in

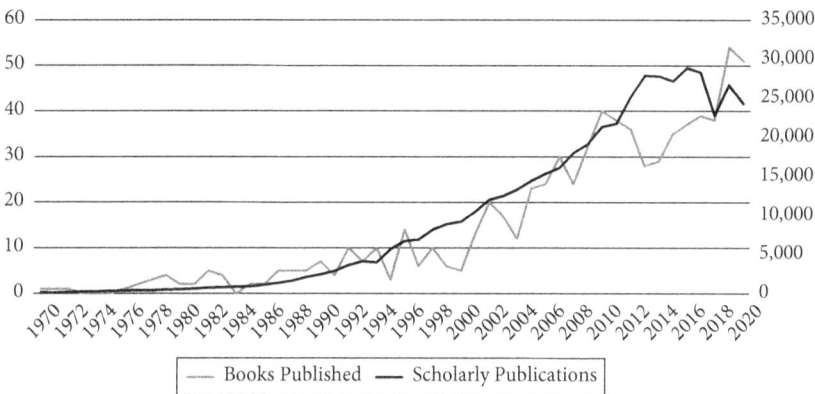

Figure 6.4 Social constructionism books and scholarly publications by year, 1970–2020.
Source: The Library of Congress, Google Books, Amazon.com, Google Scholar.

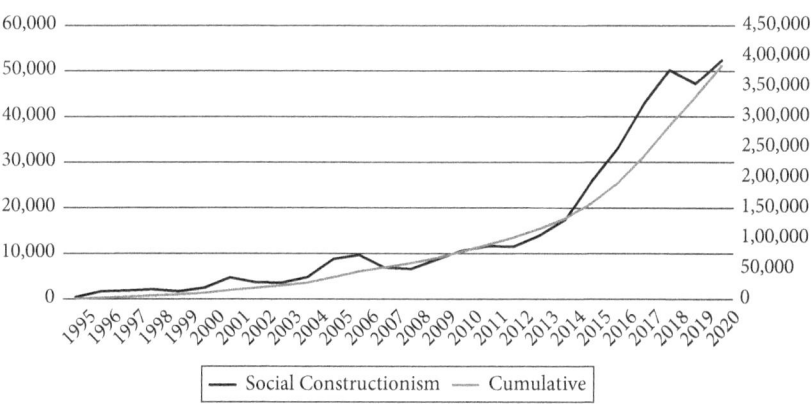

Figure 6.5 Google internet hits on "social constructionism" by year, 1995–2020.

hits mirroring the increase in websites addressed above applies here.) As with the other causal factors described in this book, the influence of social constructionism on young people's views of traditional religion by itself was no doubt modest. Again, what mattered was the cumulative, interactive, and synergistic effect of all of these factors together. The typical takeaways that ordinary Americans got from social constructionism, whether consciously or by osmosis, reinforced pop postmodernism.

A third intellectual influence worth mentioning also began in the 1980s and took off in the 1990s. That was the neopragmatism of American philosopher Richard Rorty.[67] In 1979, Rorty published his influential book *Philosophy and the Mirror of Nature*.[68] It received mixed reviews at first, but with time his influence grew. Human knowledge, Rorty argued, is not a matter of ideas and language reflecting like a mirror the way things are in the external world. Humans enjoy no unmediated access to that world. And language exists and operates as an entirely different sort of thing than objective reality. Knowledge and reality are essentially incommensurate.

Furthermore, "facts" are not objectively given by the world but are actively created by human interpretations. Human knowledge is constituted through language. And because language is inescapably historically and culturally situated, so then is all human knowledge. Universal rationality is hopeless. "Truth" is merely an honorary title people give to claims that work for them and that they wish to make stick with others. "Advances" in knowledge in reality are like the somewhat arbitrary "paradigm shifts" described by Thomas Kuhn in *The Structure of Scientific Revolutions*.[69] Lacking positive, external, self-evident foundations for justified knowledge, humans need to learn to redefine "truth" as beliefs that prove *useful*—therein lies the pragmatism. Having learned this, people need to live with an attitude of "irony," that is, a detachment from their beliefs resulting from the knowledge that they lack grounding. Live by them provisionally—what other choice does anyone have?—but do not take them too seriously.

Rorty was intentionally provocative, and his arguments were controversial among analytic philosophers. But his works were widely discussed and broadly influential.[70] His arguments made an especially enormous impression on scholars in the humanities, many of whom were also in the throes of postmodernism. Rorty's arguments resonated with postmodernist sensibilities, and some argue that he helped shape some postmodern thinkers. How widespread, then, was Rorty's influence? As above, that is not possible to measure directly. Counting references to "Richard Rorty" on Google and Google Scholar, however, is at least suggestive. Figure 6.6 shows counts by year of the number of books and scholarly publications on neopragmatism issued between 1970 and 2020 (with book counts on the left and scholarly publications on the right). Similar to the figures above, publishing interest in neopragmatism began to stir in the 1980s, took off in the 1990s, and boomed in the 2000s and after. Note that these counts are new titles per year, meaning that their cumulative numbers over time— available in Barnes & Noble and libraries and eventually on Amazon—would add up to much larger numbers.

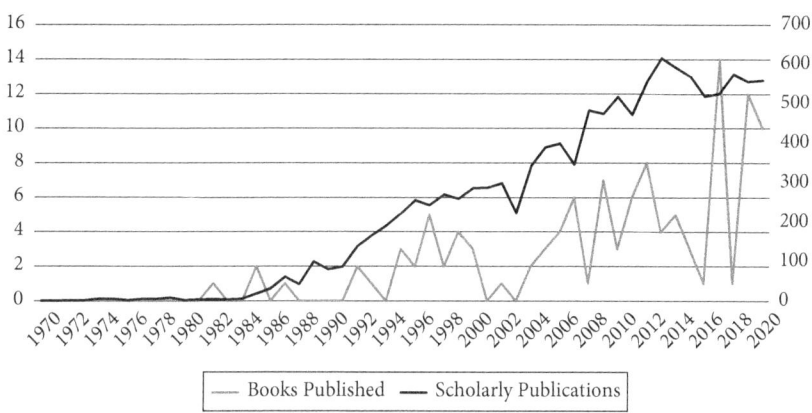

Figure 6.6 "Neopragmatism" books and scholarly publications by year, 1970–2020.
Source: The Library of Congress, Google Books, Amazon.com, Google Scholar.

Table 6.3 References to Neopragmatist Philosopher Richard Rorty in Google and Google Scholar by Decade

Decade	Google	Google Scholar
1970s	0	1,370
1980s	6	7,380
1990s	138	24,700
2000s	1,540	37,600
2010s	6,320	33,800

As to references to Rorty specifically, Table 6.3 shows total counts per decade of references to him by name, from the 1970s to the 2010s. There we see a similar growth pattern. The first decade after the publication of Rorty's seminal 1979 book shows a significant bump in Google Scholar references. While the relative rate of growth slows in the 1990s and after, in absolute numbers, Rorty gains immense attention. Google also shows significant increases of references to Rorty on the internet in the twenty-first century. In comparative terms (see Table 6.2), Rorty is no Foucault, but he definitely plays in the league of the postmodernists Baudrillard and Lyotard and had a significant influence on thinking about religion.[71]

As we saw with the discredited warfare of science and religion narrative, what happens in real scholarship can sound very different from what trickles down from it to the ground. Popular interpretations of big ideas are bowdlerized versions of the originals, and these often-inaccurate versions end up becoming more culturally important than the original ideas themselves. They pervade cultural atmospheres like barely visible particulate matter put out by smokestacks and tailpipes. Tracing out the many ways that movements like postmodernism diffuse into culture is an important task but beyond my capacity here. Simply observing that these movements, in fact, did, here is the question that matters: What did members of Gen X and Millennials actually pick up and take away from the postmodernist, social constructionist, and neopragmatist ideas to which they may have been exposed directly or indirectly in the 1990s? In what form did their ideas filter out and take shape in popular beliefs and discourse? Something like this:

- Beware of people who claim to know truth, they are either naïve or manipulative.
- Beware of comprehensive interpretations of life and the world, they're out to control you.
- Realize that whatever you believe is human-made, biographically biased, culturally relative.
- "Knowledge" and "convictions" are nothing more than individual subjective opinions.
- Nothing applies to everybody, there are no universals or absolutes.
- It's impossible for anyone with one view to judge the views of others who are different.
- Thinking that beliefs should fit together coherently is overrated, contradictions are fine.
- How you "feel" subjectively is as good a guide for choosing how to live as anything else.
- You must believe and join some things, but never with too much certainty or investment.

When my colleagues and I interviewed many hundreds of Millennial teenagers across the United States in 2003, 2005, 2008, and 2013, these ideas were commonly expressed. They were also, even for the minority who resisted them, the cultural ocean in which every last one swam. Already by the early 2000s, it did not take a college philosophy degree to have absorbed these ideas as the obvious truth. Middle schoolers and high schoolers expressed them routinely and freely. They were just the way it was. When, in 2021 and 2022, my colleagues and I interviewed 209 older Gen Xers, Millennials, and Gen Zers around the country and ran focus groups with the same populations, these were also the operative background assumptions governing most of what they had to say. As presuppositions they were largely invisible to those who voiced them. A small sample sounded like this: "Truths about reality or morality, it's whatever people believe. It depends on culture and their traditions," and "I am the biggest social constructionist of all time. So, yes, I think people are taught their morals throughout their lives—morals that are advantageous to the people who are teaching them the morals," and "Make your reality what you want." The consistency with which this dominant view was expressed was impressive: "Moral truths are more relative than anything. Not harming others would be pretty universal, but even within different people and cultures that would differ. So, it would all be relative." "It's really an individual process, what we perceive as truth and how we navigate knowing it or trying to obtain it. I don't even know, I can't even guess what somebody else's reality is, what their previous experience is that brought them to this point." "Life is ambiguous and everybody has their own science to back up their own believing." And, "I think truth is 100% subjective. I don't think there's any real objective truth that we can know. My experience is my experience, and I can't know anything about another experience other than what I'm experiencing."

A few post-Boomers did express concern about postmodern relativism, such as:

> Religion's decline is bad. Time will tell, but it doesn't feel right to me. We're missing lot of crucial elements of culture nowadays. We're slipping into this postmodern everything-is-relative, every-experience-is-truth, every-morality-is-based-on-how-you-perceive-it, so there is no actual objective good or truth or reality, and that's just not practical. Music is a good analogy because it operates with a clear set of rules: there's 12 notes, a certain amount of rhythmic points within a bar. You have boundaries, and when you have them you can play with boundaries and make meaning out of what would just be chaos on a page. But postmodernism says we'll get rid of the 12 notes, of the bar line, like none of it actually exists, you're just pretending it to exist. Regardless of whether or not that's true, throwing out the bar lines and 12 notes, you're not going to make something better, you're just going to drown in chaos because there is nothing to put the world back

in order. That's a really serious force to play with. People don't realize how deeply the need of boundaries goes in culture. It's a very deep human need.

But such expressions of concern were rare.

To see whether pop postmodernist ideas retain their influence decades later, my 2023 Millennial Zeitgeist Survey asked whether respondents agreed with questions about relativism and objective life meaning (see Table 6.4). These findings do not measure beliefs in the 1990s but how the zeitgeist that emerged then shaped beliefs decades later, including those of some Boomers. The first two rows show the percent of each generation that agrees with the morally relativistic statements. Substantial minorities of each generation do, although younger generations are more likely to agree with these ideas than are older ones. The bottom half of the table shows results by generation about

Table 6.4 Beliefs About Moral Skepticism and Relativism and the Meaning and Purpose of Life by Generation (%)

	Early Boomers	Later Boomers	Gen Xers	Millennials
Agree: "The world is always changing and we should adjust our views of what is morally right and wrong to reflect those changes."	42	44	48	53
Agree: "Morality is relative, there are no definite rights and wrongs for everybody."	35	33	36	40
Which comes closest to what you believe about the meaning and purpose of life?				
Life has no larger meaning or purpose.	2	5	4	8
The meaning and purpose of life is whatever individuals make for themselves.	42	46	45	49
Life has an objective meaning and purpose beyond what individuals may choose or think.	46	38	37	30
Not Sure	10	12	14	14
TOTALS	100	100	100	100
(unweighted *n*'s):	(*n* = 341)	(*n* = 358)	(*n* = 485)	(*n* = 677)

Source: Millennial Zeitgeist Survey, 2023 (*N* = 1,861). Percentages may not add to 100 due to rounding. "Agree" means "strongly agree" and "somewhat agree" combined.

the meaning and purpose of life. Again, while only a minority of any generation believes that life has an objective meaning and purpose, Millennials are the least likely to believe that. Only 30% of Millennials believe that "life has an objective meaning and purpose beyond what individuals may choose or think." The balance of 70% who do not affirm that believe that life has no larger meaning or purpose (8%) say that individuals have to make their own meaning and purpose for themselves (49%), or they are not sure (14%). Millennials are thus the generation least likely to affirm that life has an objective meaning and purpose.

Back to the big picture: How did all of the above affect the status of traditional religion among younger generations in the 1990s and beyond? Mostly, religion just made little sense. It didn't fit. The glitch was not so much that the doctrines and rituals were implausible. Nor was the problem that religion was irrelevant for modern people (religion could be helpful ethically, psychologically, and relationally for some people). It was more that the deep cultural assumptions necessary to take religion seriously on its own terms were no longer available to younger generations.[72] At its very worst, religion was a sham that duped gullible people into believing nonsense and giving away their money. But, for most, religion was a fine and maybe even nice thing that one could choose to do if it helped, but for the most part should not be taken too seriously or invested in too much. Of course, a relatively few committed religious young people closely adhered to their traditions. But, for most, religion didn't fit on cognitive maps. It was culturally mismatched.[73]

Multicultural Education

Multicultural education began to appear in primary, middle, and secondary schools around the country in the 1990s.[74] The intellectual roots of what became multicultural education go back to the early twentieth century. The Black civil rights movements of the 1950s and 1960s sparked an interest in inclusive educational curricula. Social movements in the 1960s and 1970s promoting feminism, gay rights, the elimination of poverty, and other causes agitated for educational reforms to take diversity seriously.[75] By the 1980s, progressive scholars in many university schools of education—mostly Baby Boomers who had lived through the protests of previous decades—advanced influential critiques of existing monocultural curricula and called for reforms. The 1980s also saw major political campaigns opposing multicultural education.[76] Nonetheless, growing agreement by education theorists and many state education administrators led to the systematic revision of widely used textbooks and curricular materials. Multicultural education was then systematically rolled out in districts, schools, and classrooms during the 1990s, in most public and many private schools. Most Millennials were raised on multiculturalism for most of their schooling.[77]

The multicultural approach was translated from the original ideas of thinkers in university education schools to textbooks and teaching materials suitable for children and teenagers. Nearly one-quarter of a million teachers across the nation had to be trained in the purposes, goals, and methods of the new curricula and texts. Success in those trainings assumed that the trainers leading them were well-informed and competent. Teachers in classrooms then had to make the new program work with their students. No doubt some of those teachers were ready, willing, and able, but others were dubious and muddled themselves. The implementation process, then, was something like the "telephone game" played by countless people working through multiple levels of bureaucracy. By many accounts, the multicultural education movement was a success. But multiculturalism is an issue as complex as it is important. By the time it filtered down to children, its ideas could often be compressed into a few simplistic takeaways:

1. Everything on offer is acceptable (except intolerance).
2. No belief or community is better than another.
3. It is wrong to judge anything culturally different.

While many students came away with skills for living justly and kindly in a pluralistic society, they also may have ended up thinking they needed to accept a kind of relativism that would make it hard to believe strongly in any particular ideas.[78] Once again, one did not have to consciously affirm this ideology since its real influence floated like invisible particles in the cultural atmosphere. When carefully considered, multiculturalism and traditional religion are compatible if not mutually supportive. But a generation of people becoming relativists about human knowledge, beliefs, and morality is not good for traditional religion. With a planned curriculum and progression of textbooks deployed for at least 12 years of schooling, multiculturalism's lessons usually trumped traditional religion in the minds of growing Millennials.

Millennial Geographical Mobility to Cities

Neoliberal capitalism, as previously mentioned, required workers to be more itinerant mentally and geographically, and Gen Xers and Millennials turned out to be highly geographically mobile, even more so than the quite mobile Baby Boomers before them.[79] Millennials were the most nomadic of those three generations. The post-Boomers we interviewed recognized this, reporting, "My generation, especially the middle to upper class that went to college, were more likely to move away. The people I'm aware of, most of us moved away from where we're from, so it's harder to find community when you do that, especially when finding a church is not a given," and "The people I grew up with, everyone moved away. I ended up moving away and when you move away and you don't know people, it's really hard to feel a part of community." Earlier generations of Americans tended to move out of small- and medium-sized towns and into big cities as young adults, and then moved out to the suburbs when they married and had children. Millennials and Gen Xers, too, moved into city centers as they came of age, especially those with college degrees. Each did so in larger numbers than previous generations. Because their transitions to full adulthood were delayed by various factors, which extended their time as emerging adults, Millennials especially also tended to remain living in big city centers longer than previous generations. The 1990s, then, was a period of peak mobility for Gen Xers and older Millennials, uprooting especially the former from their places of origin and transplanting them to new locations, particularly city centers.

Americans who relocate are less likely to be religiously involved than those who stay in place, despite feeling a sense of lost community. In addition, exactly where Millennials moved to and lived could have negatively affected their religious involvements. The US Religion Census's Religious Congregations and Membership Study, 2010 (Metro Area File), compiled data on the number of religious adherents and rate of adherence for 236 religious groups in US metropolitan areas. I combined that dataset with US Census Bureau data on the metropolitan areas with the highest in-migration rates (between 1995 and 2000) and largest total populations (in 2000) of single, college-educated 25-to-29-year-olds. For each of the metro areas with the highest migration and population rates, I calculated their percentage differences from the national average rate of religious adherents. Drawing on several sources, we can see how well migration correlates with religious adherence (see Table 6.5).[80] Metropolitan areas with the highest

Table 6.5 Religious Adherence Rates of US Metro Areas Popular with Single, Educated, Young Adults

16 US metro areas with highest in-migration rates (>20%) of single, college-educated 25-to-29-year-olds, 1995–2000 (in order of percent differences, not migration rank)	Difference from US national average (48.2%) of religious adherence (2010)
Dallas-Fort Worth-Arlington, TX	7.1%
Charlotte-Gastonia-Rock Hill, NC-SC	3.5%
Atlanta-Sandy Springs-Marietta, GA	1.5%
Wenatchee-East Wenatchee, WA	−4.0%
Boise City-Nampa, ID	−6.0%
Gainesville, FL	−6.9%
Mount Vernon-Anacortes, WA	−8.5%
Denver-Aurora-Broomfield, CO	−10.4%
San Francisco-Oakland-Fremont, CA	−10.4%
Phoenix-Mesa-Glendale, AZ	−10.7%
Las Vegas-Paradise, NV	−12.5%
Seattle-Tacoma-Bellevue, WA	−12.6%
Naples-Macro Island, FL	−13.7%
Portland-South Portland-Biddeford, ME	−19.2%
Carson City, NV	−21.2%
Bend, OR	−22.7%
	Mean: 48.2% (standard deviation: 11.97%)

Source: US Religion Census Religious Congregations and Membership Study, 2010 (Metro Area File), US Census.

1995–2000 in-migration rates of single, college-educated, 25-to-29-year-olds—Gen Xers—tended to have lower religious adherence rates than the national average. Thirteen of the 16 metro areas fell below the national average. More than half of all were metro areas that had 10–22% lower religious adherence rates than the US average. In short, the places where mobile Gen Xers lived in greatest concentrations in the late 1990s were not so religious.

We can look more broadly at the US metro areas with the largest populations of single, college-educated, 25-to-29-year-olds in 2000—at the time a mix of Millennials and Gen Xers—without regard to migration (see Table 6.6). Half of the metro areas with higher concentrations of young people had both

Table 6.6 Religious Adherence Rates of US Metro Areas with High Populations of Single, Educated, Young Adults

16 US metro areas with largest populations (>256,000) of single, college-educated 23-to-39-year-olds, 2010 (in order of percent differences, not population rank)	Difference from US national average (48.2%) of religious adherence (2010)
Chicago-Joliet-Naperville, IL-IN-WI	8.9%
Boston-Cambridge-Quincy, MA-NH	8.5%
New York-Northern New Jersey-Long Island, NY-NJ-PA	7.4%
Dallas-Fort-Worth-Arlington, TX	7.1%
Houston-Sugar Land-Baytown, TX	6.9%
Philadelphia-Camden-Wilmington, PA-NJ-DE-MD	6.4%
Minneapolis-St. Paul-Bloomington, MN-WI	3.8%
Los Angeles-Long Beach-Santa Ana, CA	3.2%
Cleveland-Elyria-Mentor, OH	3.0%
Atlanta-Sandy Springs-Marietta, GA	1.5%
Detroit-Warren-Livonia, MI	−3.6%
Washington-Arlington-Alexandria, DC-VA-MD-WV	−3.7%
Wenatchee-East Wenatchee, WA	−4.0%
San Diego-Carlsbad-San Marcos, CA	−4.3%
Miami-Fort Lauderdale-Pompano Beach, FL	−10.2%
Denver-Aurora-Bloomfield, CO	−10.4%
San Francisco-Oakland-Fermont, CA	−10.4%
Phoenix-Mesa-Glendale, AZ	−10.7%
Seattle-Tacoma-Bellevue, WA	−12.6%
Portland-South Portland-Bidderford, ME	−19.2%
	Mean: 48.2% (standard deviation: 11.97%)

Source: US Religion Census Religious Congregations and Membership Study, 2010 (Metro Area File), US Census.

above-average rates of religious adherence, the other half was below average. Still, the overall differences lean in the direction of lower-than-average religious adherence rates, with differences greater on the low end (−19.2%) than the higher end (8.9%). Furthermore, the higher-than-average numbers for Chicago, Boston, New York, and Philadelphia are skewed by their sizeable nominal-but-not-practicing Catholic populations. In both tables, the least religious cities are in western states, Maine, and Florida; the most religious are in the South, the Midwest, Northeast, and Texas.

168 PERFECT STORMS CONVERGING

These findings are not strong enough to be more than suggestive. But the sociologically credible idea they suggest is that the increased geographical mobility of post-Boomer generations helped diminish their religiousness, however modestly, by two means: first, by the disruption of their prior social networks, and second, by their moving to somewhat less religious destinations, especially when heading west. Added to that is the fact that post-Boomers, whether moving or not, concentrate in cities with lower-than-average religious adherence rates.

The Rise of Intensive Parenting

Another 1990s development in the sphere of family that inadvertently contributed to traditional religion's demise was the rise of "intensive parenting." Shifting expectations around "good" parenting increased the time, energy, money, and attention expended on raising children. For kids it meant lives that were busier and booked up by parents who were highly involved in their schedules and activities.[81] The *non*-intensive-parenting model, by contrast, expected decent parents to ensure their children were safe, fed, cleaned-up, and made it to school. Children should know they were loved, then allowed free time and independence to live their own lives, play outside, and learn life lessons. In this version, parents provide safe and healthy contexts and children do the growing up.

For various reasons—including intensified competition to succeed in the new neoliberal capitalist order—a cultural trend spread in the 1990s telling parents that the old model was not good enough.[82] Children needed more direction, assistance, and training. Good parents had to get more involved with their kids and spend more time, money, and energy on them to make sure they were raised properly.[83] The job of parenting intensified. Parents were expected to provide rich and diverse learning experiences that would prepare their children for successful careers and relationships. Parents needed to devote a lot of time to reading, playing, and talking with their children to stimulate and monitor their developmental progress. Ideally, parents would get their toddlers working on "early learning" computer software and play "learning" audio programs for their babies in cribs and bouncy seats. They needed to get more involved in their children's homework and school projects to guarantee they were completed correctly. College planning started early. Any advantage in learning would be worth the investment. Those, at least, were the normative ideals, which may have started in upper-middle class families but, in the 1990s, began to pervade middle-class culture.

From very early on, parents strategically had to arrange regular play dates with the "right" peers to influence their children's developing friendship networks. Most importantly, good parents were expected to enroll their children in a variety of stimulating and time-consuming extracurricular activities. It was no longer enough to pick up kids from their after-school field hockey or wrestling practice or to buy them their trumpet or clarinet in seventh grade when everyone was told to pick an instrument to learn. Intensive parenting required signing up children for a medley of art, music, or drama classes. It meant getting kids involved in organized competitive sports and, when they showed an interest and aptitude for one of them, sending them to skills camps and eventually having them try out for traveling teams. Intensive parenting involved researching the right summer camps for children, hiring tutors to fix slipping grades, planning memorable birthday parties, and taking children to museums to build their cultural capital. All of this was needed to increase children's chances of admission to better colleges and, if things went well, perhaps earn them a scholarship. It would turn them into more interesting, well-rounded people better prepared for more rewarding and successful marriages and careers.[84]

Many parents threw themselves into intensive parenting with the best of intentions. Emerging parenting chatrooms, mommy bloggers, and parenting advice books promoted the ideal. And growing industries of intensive-parenting products and activities—after-school enrichment programs, day camps, tutoring centers, sports camps, learning software, music teachers, and educational toy suppliers—not only assisted parents but also helped create a culture that pressured them to capitalize on all the opportunities that might help give their kids any possible advantage in the increasingly competitive game of life.[85]

The consequences for traditional religion were plain: more crowding out. The non-intensive-parenting model provided time, energy, and attention to take children to church, temple, or synagogue, Sunday school or Hebrew school, and maybe youth group. Spending those few hours a week was, for many, part of providing their kids a safe, healthy, clean environment in which to grow up. Rarely, however, did the activities demanded by intensive parenting involve *religious* classes, training, and camps. Those did not help with college admissions, scholarships, and careers. So the season of traveling soccer for Jennifer meant missing church and youth group for weeks.

Michael's weekend camping trip with friends was a reasonable substitute for Sunday school. Running from one after-school activity to the next left both dad and Amanda too worn out to make it to confirmation class Wednesday night. Christopher's pile of homework that mom needed to assist with kept them up late most weeknights, so by weekends both needed a break to relax. All this was bad enough for households with two parents; single parents had it worse.[86]

How could religion respond to this development? Tell people that being a good parent was not important? Although much intensive parenting went overboard, the activities it obliged seemed generally good. Religion had no plausible way to question, critique, or push back on its demands.[87] To suggest that religious meetings and activities might be more important than traveling baseball or art camp would sound petty. All anyone in religious communities could say was, "Hey, we missed you. Hope things are okay."

"Not Religious" as an Acceptable Identity Option

The dramatic rise in Americans identifying as religious "nones" starting in 1991 is an *indicator* of a much larger *outcome* that this book seeks to explain (see Figure 1.5). But that change also played a role in helping to *cause* that larger outcome. Here is a case where an initial effect—the rise of the religious nones—becomes a cause of its own escalation and more besides. When increasing numbers of Americans began describing themselves as "not religious" in the early 1990s, that sparked an interest among religion observers, which they reported, and it began to gain public attention (see Figure 6.7 for references to "religious nones" in a broad range of media). The more people learned that others were already embracing a non-religious identity, the more that became a plausible option for them, too. Had the number of US religious nones not begun to grow but remained at its long-standing 7%, many who eventually did declare themselves "not religious" would have stuck with whatever label they were using before. The first five years of "not religious" adopters, however, when reported in the media, were enough to make that identity more visible and acceptable. If nothing succeeds like success, then nothing helped the "not religious" category to grow like that category growing.

It does not appear that the rapid increase in not-religious Americans after 1991 at first involved dramatic transformations of existing beliefs and

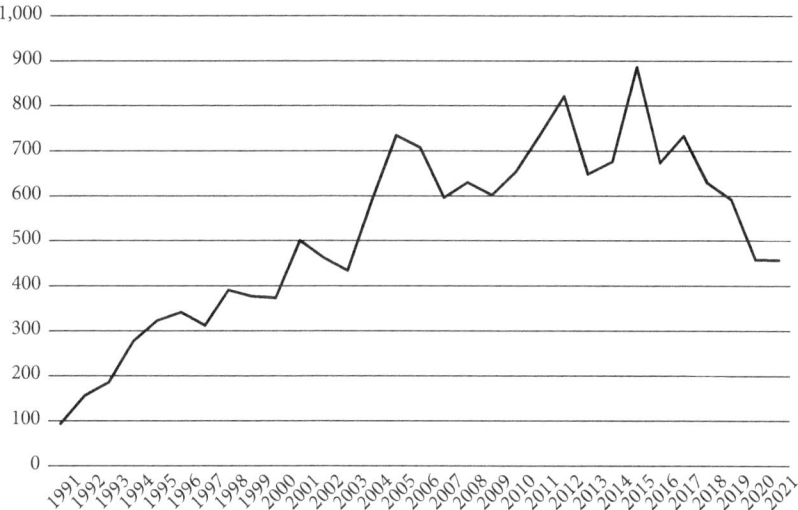

Figure 6.7 Media references to "religious nones" by year, 1991–2021.
Source: Nexis Uni corpus. (References to "ex-atheist" and "ex-agnostic" in the same corpus totaled to only 15 during 1991–2021.)

practices. Many who "became" not religious were already religiously marginal and so already "at risk" of switching out.[88] Until the early to mid-1990s, however, declaring oneself "not religious" was associated in many minds with hard-core atheism and therefore was not a culturally popular option. The growing numbers of people identifying as nones increased its broader acceptability, lowering barriers for others to join in. The more people joined, the further the growth trend continued, opening the option for ever-more religiously diverse types of people. In short, once the first switchers got the ball rolling, it became for a time a semi–self-perpetuating process, whereby a previously moderately deviant identity transformed into an acceptable and eventually cool and popular identity. Non-religion was like a continually growing snowball or avalanche speeding downhill, growing ever larger along the way.

I do not mean that not-religious Americans adopted that identity through a herd mentality or by being passively swept into a cultural current by forces of social gravity. No, people who switched into the "no religion" identity had their own real reasons for doing so. They were the agents of their actions. Nevertheless, people act in social contexts and take into account cultural meanings and practical consequences. The sudden increase in and reporting on religious "nones" after 1991 altered the cultural context and the consequences for becoming a "none," opening up new opportunities in ways that made sense to many Americans. It also prompted new discussions in which people could own and consider possible doubts about their religious identifications. The results are history.

Conclusion

The 1990s were the tipping point for traditional religion. Structural weaknesses existed and had been worsening for decades before. But the end of the Cold War, the spread of neoliberal capitalism, and the effects of the Digital Revolution together changed macro-social conditions drastically. Simplified versions of postmodernist and multicultural education were then injected into that context, spreading notions of truth, knowledge, and authority that seriously undercut what most traditional religion presupposed. Younger Americans were also increasingly mobile geographically and transient psychologically, which postponed their settling into life situations that might have encouraged religious (re)involvement. Those who had moved into positions long associated with increased religious (re)involvement—becoming parents of children—were under new intensive-parenting pressures to invest more in activities and programs for their children that competed against religious participation.

The social and cultural conditions that had previously sustained American religion were eroding dramatically. The number, mass, and complexity of forces working against religion were multiplying. Those things that made religion sensible and valuable were fading, especially for younger generations. Looking back, we can see now that 1991 launched a new cultural zeitgeist that had little use for religion. That was the beginning of the end. Nobody had planned it, but American religion was going obsolete. In the following decade, "going" became "gone."

7

The 2000s

Obsolescence Assured

By the end of the 1990s, a series of sociological trends were converging to erode the ground on which American traditional religion stood. In the 2000s, the foundation began to crumble. At the time, the conditions were unclear and confusing, and their ultimate effects uncertain. In retrospect, we see that religion's demise was overdetermined. Forces that had been building for decades reached full strength in the 2000s. Religion's obsolescence was assured.

September 11, 2001

If the end of the Cold War was a defining historic moment of the twentieth century, September 11 (9/11) was the same for the start of the twenty-first. A mere 10 years after the announcement of a New World Order and a "Peace Dividend," the United States was thrown into a war on terror. The terrorist attacks on September 11 changed the direction of history. Other commentators have told that story. Our purpose is to focus on its consequences for traditional religion.

At first glance, one might puzzle over how foreign terrorist attacks planned in Afghanistan could have any effect on the Catholic church on Maple Street, the Jewish synagogue on Sixth Avenue, the AME church on Green Lane. But September 11 had profound effects, none of which for religion was salutary.

The most important of the consequences was a reversal in Americans' ideas and feelings about "religion." As we saw earlier, most Americans consider religion "good" when it makes people moral and nice, helps them to feel positive and happy, promotes cooperation and peace, models moral integrity and decency, and is moderate, not extreme. September 11 violated each of those tenets in traumatic ways. While the grievances and interests that motivated the terrorist attacks were complex, a certain version of religion, a particular extremist interpretation of Islam, was at the center. President George W. Bush did his sincere best at the time to convince Americans that al Qaeda did not represent Islam. "The face of terror is not the true faith of Islam," he insisted.[1]

But the trauma was so profound and the role of religion in it so apparent that there was little anyone could say that would have put al Qaeda into proper perspective and shielded "religion" from the damaging associations that would stick to it in the era afterward. Anti-Muslim sentiment spread immediately. Broader anti-religious arguments followed. Rational minds might have been able to distinguish the guilty from the innocent where religious beliefs and believers were concerned. But most Americans were in no frame of mind to sustain careful distinctions. Public discourse about "religion" began to take a darker tone. Table 7.1 schematizes this by contrasting the old, positive cultural associations with "religion" against the post-9/11 bad associations.

Detailing the complex processes by which September 11 and its aftermath shifted Americans' ideas about religion would require an entire book. For our purposes, it is sufficient to observe that the shift happened. One way it

Table 7.1 American Cultural Associations with "Religion" Before and After September 11

Pre-9/11 Positive Associations	Post-9/11 damaging associations
Eisenhower Cold War Era	Fanatical
National unity for victory	Violent
Anti-communist Americanism	Extremist
Freedom, conscience, democracy	Murderous
Good citizenship	Radical
	Terrorist
Reagan Revival Era	Zealous
National strength	Fundamentalist
Family values	Hateful
Wholesome virtues	Suicidal
Optimism	Sectarian
	Bigoted
Good Religion in the American Imaginary	Heartless
Promotes morality and niceness	Aggressive
Helps to feel positive, happy, calm	Armed
Promotes cooperation, peace, harmony	Dangerous
Builds national solidarity	Irrational
Models integrity, decency, honesty	Destabilizing
Is moderate, not extreme	Ruthless
	Foreign

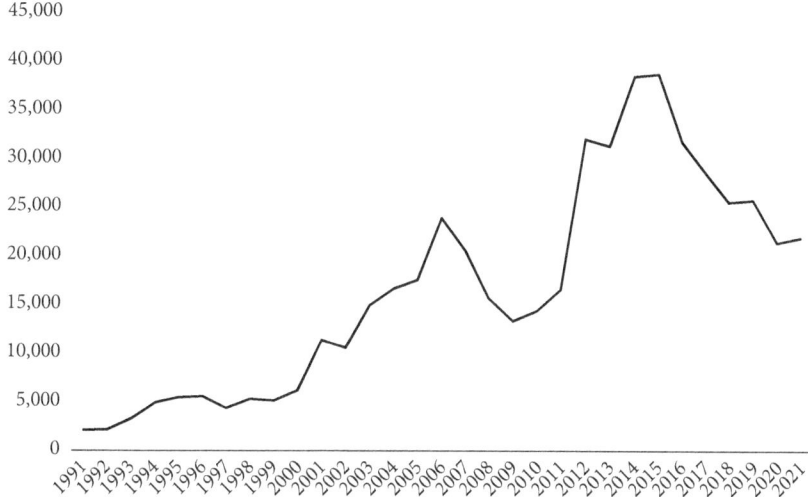

Figure 7.1 Media references to religious violence by year, 1991–2021.
Source: Nexis Uni corpus.

happened was through the news media. While the media had discussed religious violence before, after September 11, coverage of this topic increased multiple times over. In the corpus of media sources I analyzed, the number of references directly linking "religion" and "violence" jumped from 5,000 per year before 9/11 to five and eventually eight times that number in following years (See Figure 7.1).

By September 2001, many Americans had started to look askance at religion. Some individuals may have wished to maintain positive views of religion. But the cultural tide on religion was turning rapidly. No individuals who wished to stand their ground could stop such a current. A new zeitgeist in which religion was suspect was emerging.

Figure 7.2 depicts changes in television news reports on religious violence and on the 9/11 mastermind, Osama bin Laden. Once again, we see upward spikes after the terrorist attacks and during the ensuing war on terror.[2] Americans who watched television news during these years were thus constantly reminded of religion's association with violence and terror, and this tainted religion.

I deliberately use the word "association" here. The most powerful "logics" of the human mind work not through rational reasoning but by linking distinct ideas and objects, often metaphorically and analogically.[3] The idea or

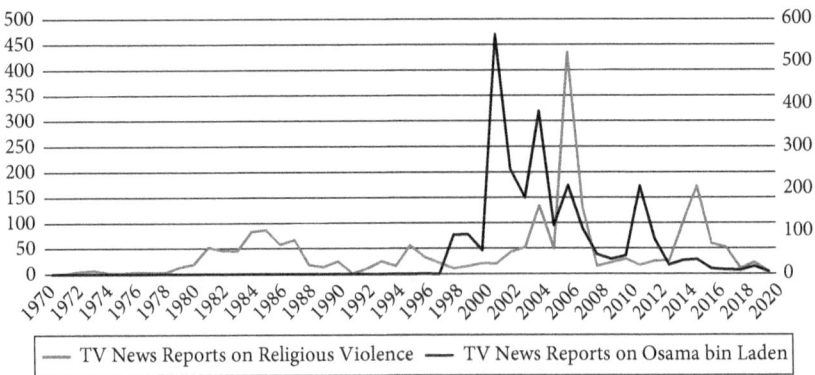

Figure 7.2 Network television news reports on "religious violence" and "Osama bin Laden" by year, 1970–2020.
Source: The Vanderbilt Television News Archives.

image of "religion" becoming polluted by September 11 did not require a majority of people to consciously think, "Now I see religion as violent and so I feel more negative about it."[4] That proposition would be rationally contestable. All that was needed was a constant association of "religion" with "violence"—and *those* being associated in visual memory with the explosive fireballs blowing out of the World Trade Center towers. That is how cultural meanings often shift—less through conscious belief formation, more through the repetition of concepts and images that evoke powerful emotions.

The number of books (scholarly and popular) and scholarly publications (such as journal articles and reviews) about religious violence grew dramatically between 2001 and 2020 (see Figure 7.3). Between 1970 and September 11, one could have been immersed in the areas of these publications and had little idea that religion and violence had anything to do with each other.[5] The terrorist attacks changed all that, after which there was a 15-year upsurge in publications linking religion and violence.[6] Media and television news coverage was reinforced in bookstores, libraries, and universities.

Similar themes took longer to show up on the internet, a lag we observed in previous chapters. Nevertheless, by the late 2000s, references to the specific terms "religious hate" and "religious violence" also began to increase online, as shown in Figure 7.4. The more people got online, the more they discussed these topics, which did not help religion's image in the public sphere. It did not take explicit arguments to damage religion in the public imagination—although those were coming, too, as we will see. It only took

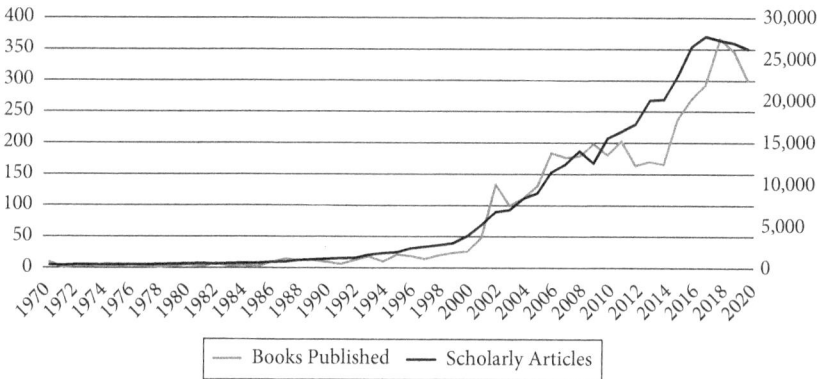

Figure 7.3 "Religious violence" books and scholarly publications by year, 1970–2020.
Source: The Library of Congress, Google Books, Amazon.com, Google Scholar.

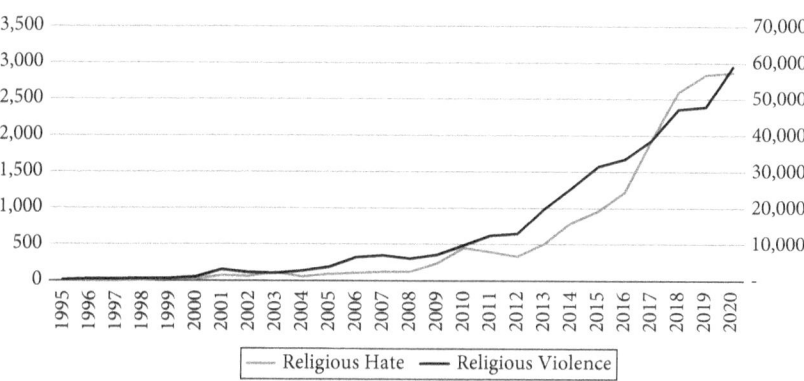

Figure 7.4 Google internet hits on "religious hate" and "religious violence" by year, 1995–2020.

streams of discourse associating religion with negative images and ideas. That discourse flowed unremittingly after September 11.

Younger generations of Americans who did not have earlier decades of more positive views of religion to draw on were the most shaped by these developments. In the end, "religion," whether or not it had anything to do with the terror attacks, had picked up—like burrs attaching to clothes as one walks through a field—a collection of damaging cultural associations. In the context of the myriad corrosive forces examined in this book and in the absence of countervailing forces, they proved a major liability. Shifting metaphors, we can think of September 11 in terms of population ecology's species decline as triggering a major climate change that made religion's environment much more difficult to survive in.

The New Atheism

Not all the reputational damage that religion suffered after September 11 was inadvertent. A group of aggressively anti-religious intellectuals, dubbed the New Atheists by journalist Gary Wolf, actively sought to damage religion.[7] I have emphasized throughout this book the unplanned and unintended nature of the sociological forces that caused religion's demise. The New Atheism is a notable exception. The leaders of this intellectual movement—including Sam Harris, Richard Dawkins, Christopher Hitchens, and Daniel Dennett—intentionally sought to drive religion to extinction. They gained huge attention, stirred controversy, and influenced many Americans. Atheism has been around for as long as theism, but it has taken different postures in different contexts. Sometimes atheism is simply the professed intellectual belief that no god exists. Other times it appealed for tolerance toward unbelievers. The New Atheism of the 2000s was more antagonistic and criticized religion as irrational, unscientific, and socially pernicious.[8]

September 11 was the trigger. The neuroscientist Sam Harris, following a time of "grief and stupefaction" after the terrorist attacks, penned *The End of Faith: Religion, Terror, and the Future of Reason*, published in 2004.[9] Harris then followed with a 2006 book, *Letter to a Christian Nation*, which aimed "to demolish the intellectual and moral pretensions of Christianity in its most committed forms." It shot to number seven on the *New York Times* bestseller list. In 2006, Oxford University biologist Richard Dawkins published *The God Delusion*, whose title says it all. Within nine weeks, it reached number four on the *New York Times* hardcover nonfiction bestseller list and remained on the list for 51 weeks. That same year, Tufts University philosopher Daniel Dennett published *Breaking the Spell: Religion as a Natural Phenomenon*, arguing that religion should be subjected to scientific analysis to understand its true nature.[10] It, too, became a *New York Times* bestseller. In 2007, Christopher Hitchen published *God Is Not Great: How Religion Poisons Everything*, charging organized religion with being "violent, irrational, intolerant, allied to racism, tribalism, and bigotry, invested in

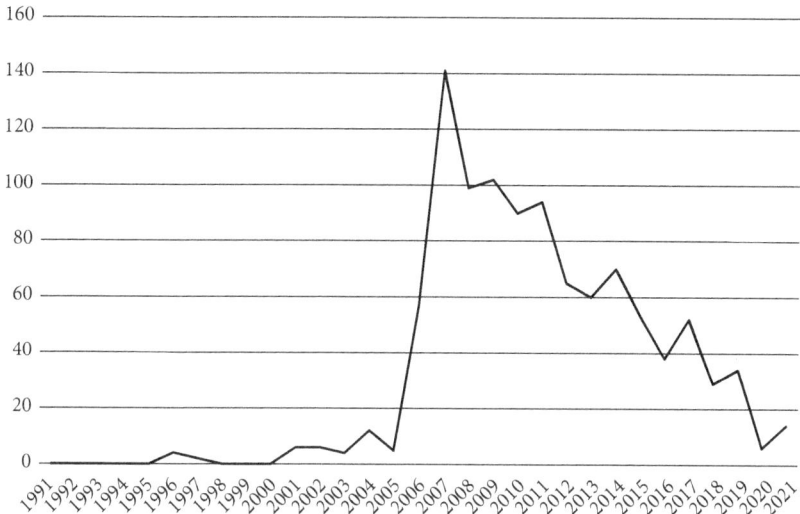

Figure 7.5 Media references to the new atheism by year, 1991–2021.
Source: Nexis Uni corpus.

ignorance and hostile to free inquiry, contemptuous of women and coercive toward children." Within three weeks it was number one on the *New York Times* bestseller list.

The new atheists generated massive attention and controversy among journalists, commentators, and critics. Dawkins, Harris, and Hitchens were labeled "the unholy trinity."[11] They plus Dennett became popularly known as the "Four Horsemen of the Non-Apocalypse." Others called them "evangelical atheists." *Rolling Stone* magazine crowned Harris the first "Hot Atheist."[12] Many friendly thinkers endorsed their works. Hostile intellectuals savaged their arguments as ignorant and simplistic.[13] One understated retrospective noted simply that "New Atheism's arguments were never very sophisticated or historically informed."[14] In less than 10 years, the New Atheism movement ran out of steam.[15] But, during its brief time in the spotlight, it inflicted real damage on American religion.

We can indirectly measure the extent of New Atheism's attention in public culture through the attention various media paid it. References to New Atheism jumped after the publication of Harris's *The End of Faith* and only decreased over the next 15 years (see Figure 7.5). The same is true for the number of new books and scholarly publications produced on New Atheism between 1970 and 2020 (see Figure 7.6).[16]

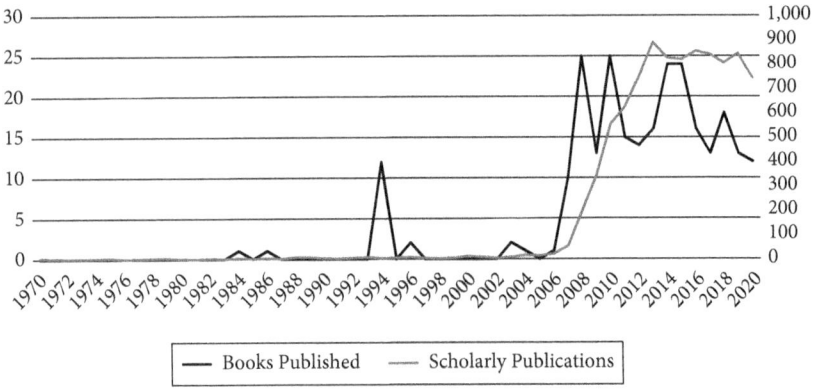

Figure 7.6 "New atheism" books and scholarly publications by year, 1970–2020.
Source: The Library of Congress, Google Books, Amazon.com, Google Scholar.

Table 7.2 References to New Atheist Advocates in Google Scholar by Decade

Decade	Dawkins	Dennett	Hitchens	Harris
1980s	95	74	28	0
1990s	682	466	77	0
2000s	4,500	2,160	1,030	686
2010s	13,800	5,590	4,940	3,320

Source: Google Scholar.

Google Scholar can also track the rising popularity of the four leading New Atheists (see Table 7.2).[17] All but the younger Harris had some scholarly references listed online before the 2000s.[18] Their roles in the New Atheist movement propelled them to remarkable levels of attention after September 11.

By the launch of the New Atheist movement, the internet had grown sufficiently popular that it did not take long for the movement to accumulate thousands of mentions online. Figure 7.7 presents the number of Google returns on related terms, per year and cumulatively. Within 10 years of the publication of Dawkins's *God Delusion* and Dennett's *Breaking the Spell*, a Google search on New Atheism returned 70,000 hits. Viewed in long

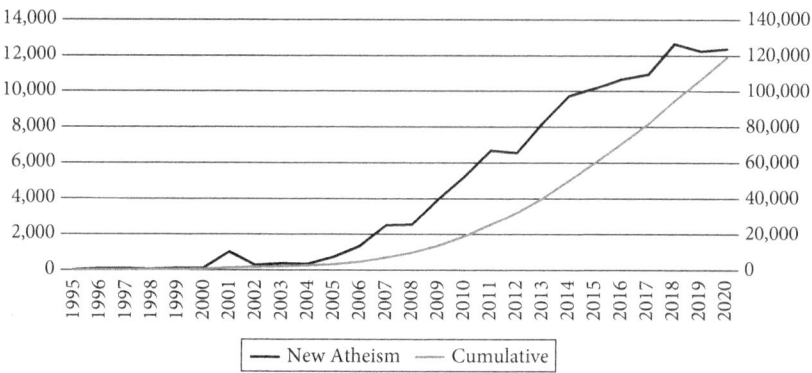

Figure 7.7 Google internet hits on "new atheism" by year, 1995–2020.

historical terms, the New Atheism was a flash in the pan. But that flash in its time was incendiary.

Without the attacks of September 11, the New Atheism would likely have not had much influence. But with the disappearance of Cold War America's need for an Almighty-honoring national identity and the dark cultural associations cast on religion by the shadow of September 11, the New Atheism was able to gain a hearing from people newly open to critical views on religion.

How did the New Atheism contribute to American traditional religion's obsolescence? One thing it did not do was convince many religiously committed Americans to become atheists. If anything, it provoked a major critical response by religious apologists from many traditions, who produced a small library of books and articles that picked the Four Horsemen apart for the flaws in their arguments—which, most religion scholars at the time agreed, were many. But the loyalty of highly religiously committed Americans was not at stake here, any more than the dedication of already hard-core atheists. Who really mattered were the majority of Americans in the middle, those who had no strong feelings about religion one way or the other. These were the "swing voters," so to speak, enough of whom the New Atheism helped pull away from moderate, nominal, and passive support for religion.

Overall, the New Atheism had five distinct effects. First, it energized the already anti-religious minority, emboldening increasingly outspoken critiques and solidifying their identity through the backing of bestselling intellectuals taken seriously by the media. Second, it provided convincing references and justifications to those who already felt negatively toward religion but had not known how to express their criticisms. For these, the Four Horsemen functioned as "vicarious thinkers" who figured out why religion was bad so that they did not have to on their own. Third, the New Atheists convinced some readers who were religiously ambivalent before September 11 that religion really is bad and ideally should just go away. These were the "swing voters." All of that reinforced the negative associations with religion. In these ways, the New Atheism was another jolt in public culture that helped trigger what became an avalanche of cultural change that eventually buried religion.

The fourth and fifth effects are less about influencing individuals and more about altering the cultural environment. Even for Americans who were not up to speed on the New Atheism, those ideas had still become particulate matter floating in the cultural atmosphere, which could affect everyone breathing it, whether they knew it or not. The New Atheism was also an ideological pathogen for religion. It literally attacked and tried to kill religion. Thus, fourth, the New Atheism "controversialized" religion in new ways. It redefined traditional religion as a matter for debate. It forced a contest, an argument, a conflict. It made religion fight back. Since one of the characteristics of "good" religion in Americans' minds is that it promotes peace and harmony, the mere fact of religion scuffling as a contestant in a controversial, public dispute disadvantaged it. Sometimes mere accusations of crimes damage reputations, regardless of how true or false they may be. Last, the New Atheism partially swung the burden of proof onto religion to demonstrate its goodness. By shifting the default position closer to its perspective, the New Atheism made it harder for people to assume religion is more good than bad. It created a new cultural atmosphere in which religion was the accused, on the defensive—one in which Hitchens's extreme claim that "religion poisons everything" and Dawkins's suggestion that religion is the "root of all evil" had sensitized even those it did not fully convince to the darker sides of belief.[19] All of that was reflected in some of our research interviews, for example:

> When I started researching religion, the first person I read a lot of was Richard Dawkins. He's well known as a vocal atheist. Through him, I discovered others. Daniel Dennett is one, Sam Harris another. I don't really know many philosophers, but they have a lot of interesting thoughts and books, and I subscribe to some of their ideas for sure.

Another said,

> I listened to a musician who was a Christian artist for a long time but then fell away from the faith and became an atheist. His album was like, "okay I'm an atheist now" kind of thing, just documented his fall from Christendom and things religious, and he makes a lot of really good points in that album. The first time I heard that I definitely did not have a developed enough worldview to incorporate those challenges. It was just like, "This guy actually has it right," and Christianity is a total sham. It's just something we buy and sell, just a function of our brains making meaning out of experience where there isn't necessarily anything. That was a good three years of my life when I just completely rejected Christianity. That record then introduced me to more atheist writers, I got into Richard Dawkins for a while and there's a lot of really good atheist critiques of religion.

And another,

> I follow someone by the name of Sam Harris—he is an atheist, but he also believes in a capacity for human beings to have experiences similar to Jesus or the Buddha. A lot of people believe that comes from a god or a higher power. But he believes you don't need those external sources to develop the qualities of love, compassion, kindness, wisdom. You can get that outside of religion. At this point in life, I would say I believe more in Buddha than the God of Christianity. I would say I believe in a higher power, considering Buddha a higher power.

A Third Sexual Revolution

The 2000s saw a major transformation in sexual culture—something like a third sexual revolution—that contributed to religion's obsolescence. Historians locate the first American sexual revolution in the 1920s, when soldiers who had experienced more freedom while serving in Europe returned from World War I. This, combined with the growing rejection of Victorian moral sensibilities, the expanded privacy afforded by the increased use of automobiles, the spread of movies and advertising culture, and the influence of Freudian psychology, led to a major increase in sex before marriage and more libertine attitudes in urbane circles. The second American sexual revolution occurred in the latter 1960s and 1970s, resulting from the Boomers coming of age, the massive expansion of higher education, and the invention of the birth control pill. That revolution involved further increases in sex outside of marriage, the growing acceptance of casual sex, a reimagined view of women as sexually empowered and liberated, and a new public interest in people experimenting with "open marriage" and the "swinger lifestyle."[20]

We can summarize the features of the third sexual revolution, which began in the late 1990s, with three D's: diversification, democratization, and "de-shaming" of previously objectionable sexual behaviors and identities. Larger swaths of especially younger Americans became more familiar with a greater variety of sexual behaviors and relationships, resulting in the more widespread experimentation by ordinary people with sexual behaviors previously considered deviant. An added feature was a greater tolerance of ambiguity in intimate relationships. Millennials especially decided that close relationships did not have to be neatly classified as "friends," "dating," "engaged," or the like. Life and experiences were more fluid and flexible than those categories allowed.

One expression of these changes was the blurring of the boundaries between sexual relationships and friendships. For many decades, being "just friends" meant not being romantically or physically involved, close perhaps, but platonically. So clear was that meaning that it was a standard way to break up with a boyfriend or girlfriend: "Can we just be friends?" The 2000s popularized new types of relationships that mixed friendships or acquaintanceships with intimate sexual relations. What was novel was not the sex being casual—nothing new there—but that it was with someone with whom one had an ongoing non-romantic relationship rather than someone one expected never to see again.[21]

The paradigmatic example of this new kind of relationship was "friends with benefits." The first pop culture use of this term was Alanis Morissette's 1995 track, "Head Over Feet," in which she sang, "You're my best friend, best friend with benefits." The singer and "best friend" in that song, however, were in a romantic relationship. In late 1999, an Oregon University student group used the phrase as the title of a play they performed. By the 2000s, use of the term spread, with its meaning shifting to refer simply to two friends who hook up without the usual complications of romance and commitment. By 2011, Hollywood caught on and released two friends-with-benefits romantic comedy films, *Friends with Benefits* and *No Strings Attached*, which further popularized the concept.

A related term, "booty call," referred to a phone call or message with a friend or acquaintance arranging a time and place for casual sex, and to the person to whom the call is made (e.g., "she's my booty call"). The phrase's origins are murky, but "Booty Call" first appears as the title of a track on the 1993 album of the hip-hop duo, Duice, followed by the Da Ko Boyz 1994 song, "Da Booty Call." In 1997, the romantic comedy film *Booty Call* hit theaters. By the late 1990s, the expression was referenced on various popular television programs. It, too, proliferated in popular use in the 2000s.[22] Other phrases that emerged in this era referring to similar relationships were "fuck buddy" and "no strings attached."

Another aspect of this third sexual revolution was the growing awareness and acceptance as normal of sexual encounters and relationships involving more than two partners. Humans have engaged in various kinds of multipartner, non-monogamous sexual behavior throughout history. What changed in the 2000s was the democratization and normalization of these types of sexual behavior. They morphed from being culturally out of the mainstream to being almost culturally institutionalized, complete with their own identities, vocabularies, variations, communities, and ethics. One version of this was *polyamory*, or people engaging in multiple, romantic, usually sexual relationships requiring the consent of all those involved. A lexicon developed: polyfidelity, polysexual, poly family, polyamorous, and so on. Another version was ethical or consensual non-monogamy—a general term for relationships in which all partners gave clear consent to engage in romantic, intimate, or sexual relationships with multiple people.

The swinger lifestyle of the 1970s also re-emerged in new forms, the most familiar one being open marriage. This re-emergence gave rise to the term "monogamish," that is, relationships that are romantically mostly monogamous but also allow for some agreed-upon outside sexual relationships. This larger environment generated many other approaches to multipartner and casual sexuality. They included "relationship anarchy" (fluid relationships with no defined rules), "unicorns" (single bisexual females who have intimate relations with couples, who are called "unicorn hunters"), and "situationships" (casual intimate relationships lacking definition, expectations, and norms due in part to the fear that clarity might make things awkward). Figure 7.8 depicts the complex possibilities of sexual relationships that emerged in the 2000s in a graphic created by Franklin Veaux, a polyamory advocate.

The era also gave rise to related urban legends bordering on moral panics. For example, in her 2002 book *Epidemic: How Teen Sex Is Killing Our Kids*,

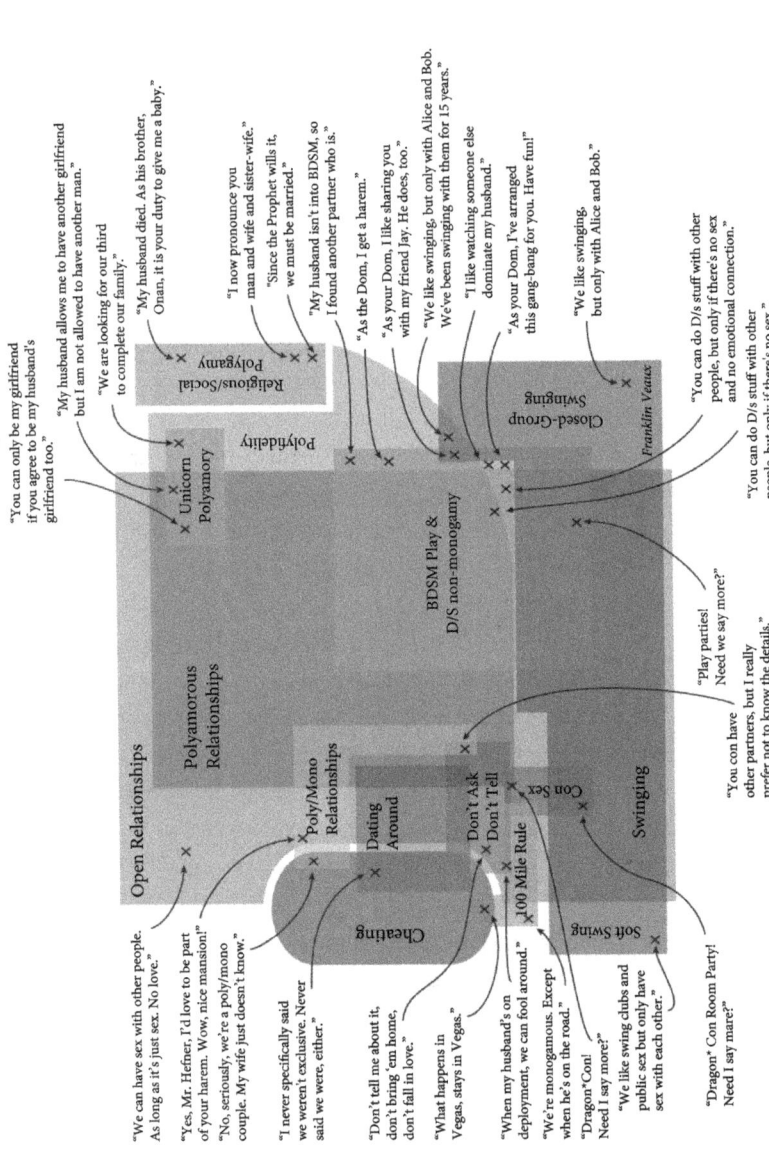

Figure 7.8 The complex configurations of third sexual revolution relationship types.
Credit: Franklin Veaux.

the Christian pediatrician Meg Meeker described the "rainbow party." This was a gathering where middle and high school girls wore differing shades of lipstick and took turns giving boys oral sex in sequence, leaving multicolored bands on their penises, resembling a rainbow. That idea was the focus of an Oprah Winfrey Show in 2003, "Is Your Child Leading a Double Life?," and the subject of a 2005 young adult novel called *Rainbow Party* that was met with much consternation.[23] Rainbow parties turned out to be mostly fiction. Even as mere urban legends, however, they reflected something of the era's larger cultural changes in the air.

"Hooking up" was another part of this 2000s sexual revolution. Hookups were not invented in the 1990s; they happened in practice long before they had a name.[24] But, by the 1990s, that term became the common way to describe casual intimacies between strangers and acquaintances that were becoming normal among young Americans, especially college students.[25] Indeed, a defining and alluring characteristic of hooking up was that it was intentionally ambiguous. Nobody knew exactly what it meant. Hooking up might involve making out with a stranger for 10 minutes in the hallway of a party before returning to one's buddies. It might mean having sexual intercourse with someone you met in class. To tell your friends that you hooked up with someone the night before afforded the pleasure of both revealing and keeping a secret, of confessing to having been "naughty" without saying exactly how naughty one was. Many emerging adults who engaged in hookup culture in fact had bad experiences.[26] By the late 1990s, though, it had become the new norm.

Yet another expression of this revolution in sexual mores was the "sex positive" movement. As the name suggests, it promoted every expression of consensual sex as a natural and healthy part of human experience, affirming sexual pleasure for its own sake and encouraging sexual experimentation and responsibility. The movement sought to eradicate society's negative and shameful judgments and feelings about sex, freeing people from embarrassment and guilt. It opposed "prude-shaming," "slut-shaming," and "kink-shaming" of all kinds while supporting, among other things, sex-workers' rights, legal public female toplessness, and comprehensive positive sex education for youth.[27] The phrase "sex-positive" was first used in the late 1990s, associated with the founding of the Center for Sex and Culture in San Francisco and the Center for Sex Positive Culture in Seattle. The movement promoted its beliefs online, through social media, YouTube, festivals, dance parties, education centers, and more.

The third sexual revolution included widespread efforts to "de-shame" previously embarrassing and shameful sexual topics. Condemning "slut shaming" was only one part of this. College women who hooked up and stayed overnight somewhere other than their own residence had notoriously dreaded the "walk of shame" back to their dorms the following morning. The new sexual culture insisted that they had nothing to be ashamed of and should walk in public with self-confidence. Similarly, regularly viewing pornography, masturbating, using sex toys, and sharing nude photos of oneself became part of normal, open life for many. Ordinary emerging adults went into business with webcams at home, performing sex shows for viewers paying with credit cards to watch. Young women became older wealthy men's "sugar babies" to help pay their bills and did not mind telling friends. Sexting—sending nude photos to others—became a phenomenon despite the risks of public exposure. Unknown numbers of young women answered Craigslist "Hot Girls Wanted" ads for a shot to have sex on camera in the hope of becoming porn stars.[28] Participants in consensual erotic practices and role-plays entailing bondage, dominance, submission, discipline, sadomasochism, and sexual fetishes came out, confidently owning their sexual proclivities. Kink went mainstream. The point is not that most Americans suddenly embraced sexual positivity. The point is that there was a drastic decrease in the number of sexual activities or attitudes considered shameful by the broader culture. "On 1950s television, married couples like the Ricardos and Nelsons had separate beds; on 1990s television, shows such as *Friends* and *Sex and the City* featured unmarried women casually discussing their sexual escapades."[29]

Media references to many of these terms increased across the 1990s and 2000s (see Figure 7.9). "Hooking up" is separated out from the other terms in Figure 7.9 because of its longer use in time and relatively greater reference frequency—combining them in one line would have muddled the findings. The term "hooking up" (counts indexed on the right side) appears to have been in use prior to 1991—getting about 500 references that year. The number of references to hooking up increased further during the 1990s and 2000s. The other terms that belonged to this third sexual revolution—"friends with benefits," "polyamory," "ethical non-monogamy," and so on (counts indexed on the left) were also referenced in the 1990s but increased in the 2000s, especially in that decade's latter years and into the 2010s. Combined, we see more than two decades of increased media discourse around liberalizing sexual practices.

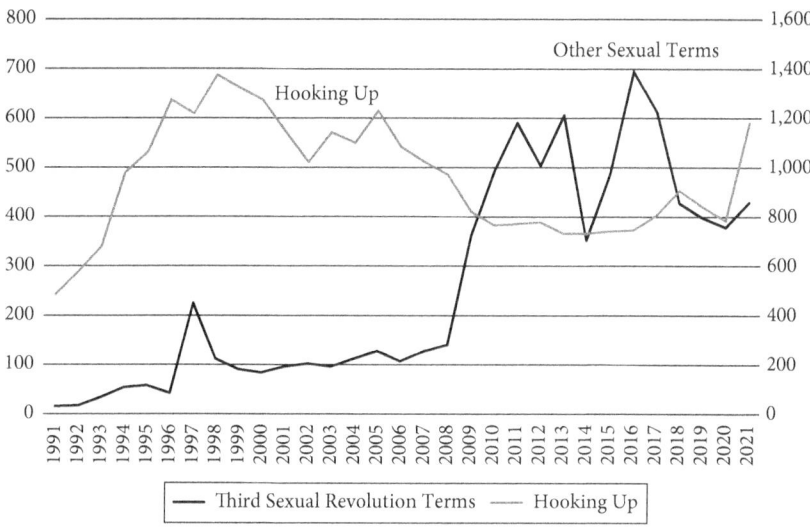

Figure 7.9 Media references to hooking up and Third sexual revolution terms, 1991–2021.
Source: Nexus Uni corpus

We can see the same patterns in internet search terms between 1995 and 2010. Certain terms, such as "hooking up" and "sugar baby" were not possible to search because they scooped up too many references not related to sex—such as instructions for hooking up electrical systems and "Sugar Baby" watermelons. The search terms in Table 7.3 are those unambiguously related to sex. What we see is a gradual increase in number of Google hits in the 1990s as the early internet grew, followed by major increases in the 2000s, as the internet proliferated and as this sexual revolution spread culturally. Remember that these numbers are distinct Google hits added each year, which accumulated into the total numbers listed at the bottom of the table. The 2010s saw an additional explosion of these terms on the internet.[30] The generations who came of age in the digital era and spent the most time of all Americans surfing the web were much more likely to be exposed to the ideas and images of the new sexual culture.

(I remind readers of the methodological point made in the previous chapter about the use of internet counts as data for my argument: the observation that much of the increase here mirrors the growth of all internet websites during this time may be correct but is also, for present purposes, irrelevant. Again, the point is not that internet references to these terms grew

Table 7.3 Number of Google Hits per Year on Select Third Sexual Revolution Terms (1995–2010)

Year	Open relationships	Polyamory	Friends with benefits	Fuck buddy	Sexting	Sex Toys	MILF
1995	22	11	11	8	20	331	3,900
1996	77	23	360	16	292	4,350	13,800
1997	124	22	115	13	575	4,790	15,100
1998	104	82	480	22	610	5,990	17,400
1999	180	202	212	28	638	11,100	23,100
2000	246	192	394	27	1,420	14,000	42,200
2001	635	926	631	649	5,610	47,000	107,000
2002	397	534	765	432	3,100	65,400	70,200
2003	395	555	765	432	3,100	41,800	61,700
2004	504	567	753	417	1,460	37,800	72,100
2005	896	475	1,240	841	2,870	52,900	155,000
2006	1,630	2,110	2,100	1,510	5,360	70,900	213,000
2007	1,920	2,030	2,530	2,140	30,300	80,500	2,110,000
2008	3,270	3,450	2,520	2,050	42,000	82,400	4,700,000
2009	5,100	5,890	6,670	3,920	43,600	124,000	7,930,000
2010	6,380	5,750	16,500	25,000	49,800	244,000	19,800,000
Totals	21,880	22,819	36,131	37,577	190,655	887,261	35,334,500

faster than the internet itself, but rather that the exploding internet provided a crucial means by which interest in the new sexual culture was expressed and promulgated.)

What were the causes of this sexual revolution? Most are familiar. The Digital Revolution takes much of the credit. Digital cameras made it easy and inexpensive to produce pornography. The internet made it easy to distribute and profit from porn. Cell phones made it easy to share sexual images and links. The online world also dramatically increased the public visibility of "alternative" sexual subcultures and practices. With the internet and cell phones came online dating and hookup websites and apps—the timing of the launch of those having influence on sexual attitudes and mores are shown in Table 7.4.

The book publishing industry also cashed in on popular demand generated by the third sexual revolution. In the neoliberal order, when the market indicates a demand, producers deliver a supply—and, it turns out,

Table 7.4 Launch Years of Culture Influencing Dating and Hookup Websites and Apps

1996	Adult Friend Finder
1999	Gaydar
2002	Ashley Madison
2002	Date Hookup
2002	Dudesnude
2003	PlentyofFish
2004	Secret Benefits
2004	Sugar Daddy for Me
2004	OkCupid
2006	Seeking Arrangement
2006	Badoo
2007	What's Your Price
2007	Zoosk
2009	Grindr
2009	Elite Singles
2012	Tinder
2012	Hinge
2013	Her
2015	Pure

increases in supplies, under the visible hand of advertising, also generate new demands. For one example, the emergence of consensual non-monogamy was cultivated by books like *The Ethical Slut: A Guide to Infinite Sexual Possibilities* (1997), *Opening Up: A Guide to Creating and Sustaining Open Relationships* (2008), *Sex at Dawn* (2010), and *More Than Two: A Practical Guide to Ethical Polyamory* (2014).[31]

Another influence arousing and guiding the sexual revolution of the 2000s, one having less to do with digital technologies and market opportunities, was third-wave feminism. That movement launched in the early 1990s, influenced in part by poststructuralist readings of gender, especially Judith Butler's *Gender Trouble* (1990), and a feminist punk subculture in the Pacific Northwest. Led by Gen Xers, third-wave feminism emphasized diversity, individuality, and sex positivity. It taught young women to "not be inhibited by traditional norms of sexuality that stigmatize female sexual experimentation in non-committed relationships [or] ... by a sense that one form of sexual practice is more 'feminist' than another."[32] In comparison to earlier waves of feminism, it viewed itself as more sexually evolved and expressive. Third-wave feminism also rejected the labeling of young women engaging in casual sexual relationships as "sluts." This movement's influence on the larger developing sexual culture was not overwhelming, but it was significant.

To assess the impact and staying power of this third sexual revolution, the 2023 Millennial Zeitgeist Survey asked six questions about related beliefs (see Table 7.5). We see that between roughly 50% and 70% of Americans in every surveyed generation affirm beliefs stemming from the third sexual revolution. Differences between generations are minor.

Table 7.5 Third Sexual Revolution Beliefs by Generation (%)

	Early Boomers	Later Boomers	Gen Xers	Millennials
Agree: Individuals should be able to choose their own sexual and gender identities without social pressures or laws interfering.	60	56	58	59
Agree: Mature adults watching pornography for pleasure and stimulation is perfectly okay.	55	54	59	61
Disagree: Heterosexual marriage is the only morally acceptable place for sex.	60 (disagree)	49 (disagree)	53 (disagree)	58 (disagree)
Agree: Casual sex between friends or acquaintances (i.e., "friends with benefits," "booty calls," "hooking up") is okay if it is consensual and safe.	59	57	66	62
Agree: American adults having consensual sexual relationships with more than one other person (i.e., in polyamory, ethical non-monogamy, swinging) is their business, which other people should not judge.	62	65	71	66
Agree: Traditional religious teachings about sex and gender oppress LGBTQ+ people.	54	55	53	51
TOTALS (unweighted *n*'s):	100 (*n* = 341)	100 (*n* = 358)	100 (*n* = 485)	100 (*n* = 677)

American adults in all generations have embraced the ethics of the third sexual revolution.

Post-Boomers' embrace of this sexual revolution showed up in most of our interviews, with people saying things like, "I don't buy the idea that there's only one person you will be married to. Polyamory doesn't work for me, but if it works for other people, rock on, you're consenting adults. Do whatever works for you," and "Sex is ultimately a very innate, carnal, primal thing in all humans, and because of how complex we are it can manifest itself in many different ways. People like different things, they have different preferences, wants, and desires, and that should be okay," and "Hooking up culture, it's perfectly fine. Just to be safe, condoms, get tested. Traditional sexual morality, it's unrealistic," and "Sex is great. Almost everybody fucks." Many viewed the new sexual ethic as healthy.

> I don't think there's much wrong with pornography and sex in our culture. Opening that conversation is important because it helps teach people what you are comfortable with and being able to articulate that. Having questions, being curious, learning that, as long as it's involving consensual adults, you're not breaking laws or anything. Just the openness and talking about it or if you enjoy it.

And that typically was contrasted with traditional sexual mores.

> I don't think hooking up, porn, sex in the media is bad. Especially younger people are wanting to explore and push boundaries, to learn new things and explore and find out different ways of thinking. The cookie-cutter norm traditional religion and traditional society has pushed on us, it's not right.

Another agreed:

> Traditional views are unrealistic. It's up to the individual. If someone feels it works for them and it's what they want, there's nothing wrong. If you want to be polyamorous, there's nothing necessarily wrong either way. It's just different choices in life.

How did these changing cultural attitudes, identities, and behaviors regarding sex affect post-Boomers' views of religion?[33] As far as most post-Boomers are concerned, traditional religion teaches two things about sex: there should be no sex outside of marriage, and same-sex relationships are immoral. That view is a bit simplistic. But that was how most post-Boomers understood it, which is what matters for the present explanation. Except for a minority of highly committed religious post-Boomers who understood and adhered to their traditions' teachings, most saw these religious teachings on sex as at least outdated and more likely ridiculous. People just are going to have sex outside of marriage, the thinking went, and there is nothing wrong with that. And queer people just are that way, and there is nothing wrong with them. Evangelical purity campaigns like "True Love Waits" (about which more in the next chapter) looked preposterous in comparison. More cultural mismatch.

If the first two sexual revolutions were about liberation, the third added to that a loss of innocence and boundaries, with the unchecked commodification of sex and treatment of persons as bodies to be consumed and, in some cases, violated at will.[34] For traditional religion, the new sexual culture both polluted its ecological environment and changed its climate, increasing the levels of toxicity and stress, which weakened its capacity as a species to reproduce and survive. The world that surrounded post-Boomers by the 2000s was no longer debating the morality of "sex before marriage" but exploring porn websites, friends with benefits, ethical non-monogamy, webcam sex, polyamory, fuck buddies, "dick pic" sexting, sugar baby–sugar daddy relationships, LUG (lesbian until graduation), Girls Gone Wild, "Free the Nipple" campaigns, BDSM kink, and the disowning of shame over masturbation, fetishes, and serial hookups. Hooking up was old news. In the 2000s, the news was that young women knew not to feel bad about it in the least. In such a context, religion was something from the Dark Ages. For issues, experiences, and identities as hugely important as sex and sexuality, religion was "behind the times." It was not even worth thinking about, much less arguing with. The attitude of many talking about religion and sex in our interviews was a bemused perplexity. For the minority of post-Boomers who wished to resist the new sexual culture, it was difficult to escape from breathing in at least some of the cultural particulate matter it ejected into the common atmosphere.

LGBTQ+ Mainstreamed

Another important sociocultural transformation of the 2000s was the increased public visibility and mainstream acceptance of those who were

LGBTQ+. The struggle for gay rights was decades in the making. It matured and came to a head in the 1990s, and it tipped the popular-opinion and legal scales in the 2000s. The full story is long and complex.[35] A few historical highlights will suffice for our purposes. In the 1990s, the majority of Americans still opposed same-sex marriage. Non-straight groups had wrestled for a few decades with inclusive but meaningful terms of identity. Gay became "gay and lesbian." Bisexual was then added. In the 1990s, the acronyms GLBT and LGBT became more common. In the 2000s, LGBT became preferred over GLBT to give lesbians greater visibility.[36] Around that term rallied many forces to change culture and law on sexual and gender identity in the United States.

In addition to steadily growing movement activism, news events forced the question for the American public. In 1993, a trans man, Brandon Teena, was gang raped and murdered in Nebraska by two young men. In 1994, the Clinton administration established "Don't ask, don't tell" as the official US policy on military service for non-heterosexual people; it remained in effect until 2011. LGBT History Month in the United States first occurred in 1994. In 1997, popular television personality Ellen DeGeneres came out as lesbian on her sitcom, which was the first US television show featuring a lesbian or gay lead character (the following year the show was cancelled.) In 1998, two young men brutally beat a gay Wyoming college student, Matthew Shepard, tied him to a fence, and left him strung there overnight. Shepard died six days later. In 2003, the US Supreme Court overturned state sodomy laws, proclaiming rights to privacy and decriminalizing homosexual behavior. In 2004, Massachusetts became the first US state to legally recognize same-sex marriage, followed by other states in subsequent years. In 2009, President Obama signed the Matthew Shepard Hate Crimes and Prevention Act into law, expanding the 1969 US federal hate crime law to include crimes motivated by a victim's actual or perceived sexual orientation or gender identity, making it the first federal law legally protecting transgender people.

Media references to LGBTQ issues increased during the 1990s and surged in the early 2000s (see Figure 7.10). The spike in 2004 is driven mostly by widespread and heated debates over same-sex marriage laws and ballot referenda. Media references declined after that but then increased even further in the 2010s. The pattern is smoother for books published (Table 7.6), with major growth ramping up in the 1990s and after.

Scholarly publications on LGBTQ issues (see Figure 7.11) lagged behind public media coverage but still increased steadily throughout the 2000s—by

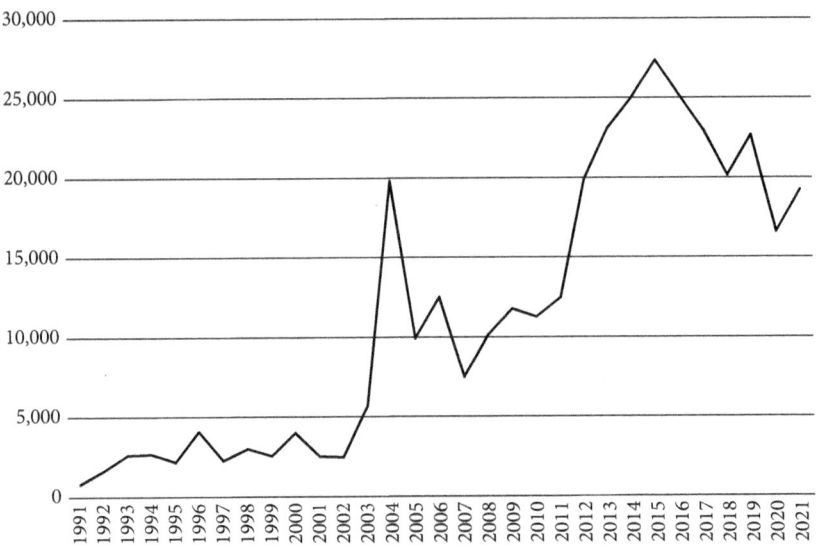

Figure 7.10 Media references to LGBTQ issues by year, 1991–2021.
Source: Nexis Uni corpus.

Table 7.6 Books with LGBTQ+ Topics in Titles or Subtitles, Published by Decade

Decade	Google Books
1970s	28
1980s	56
1990s	139
2000s	248
2010s	805

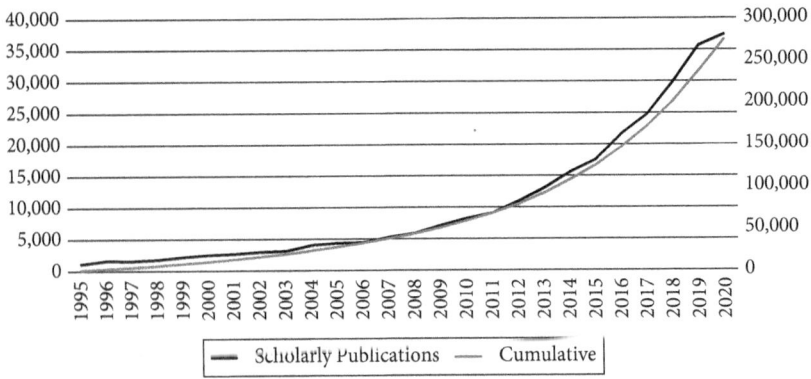

Figure 7.11 Scholarly publications on LGBTQ themes by year, 1995–2020.
Source: Google Scholar

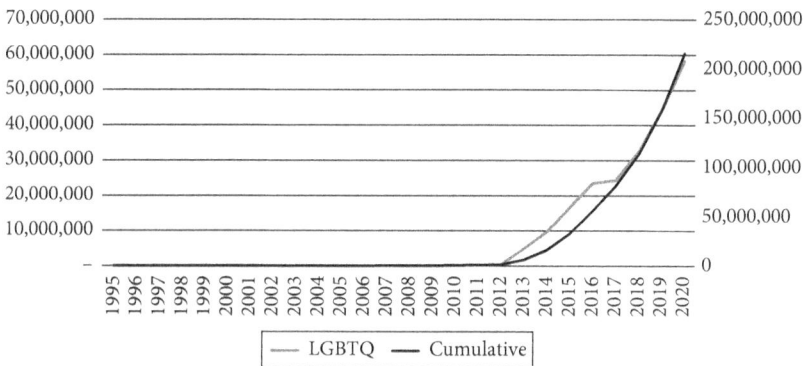

Figure 7.12 Google internet hits on "LGBTQ" themes by year, 1995–2020.

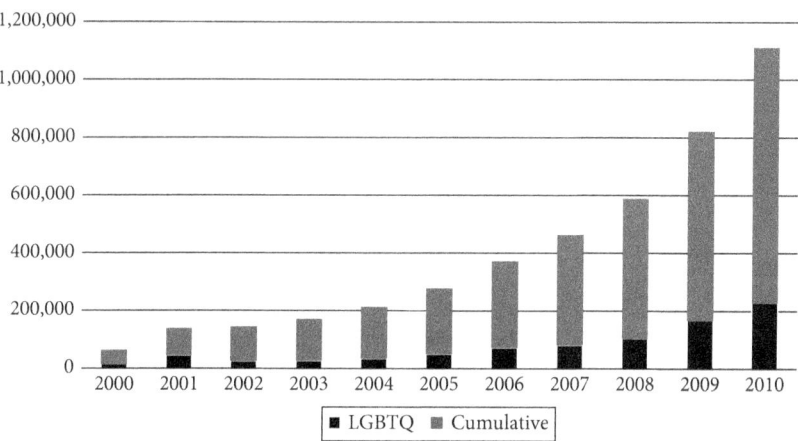

Figure 7.13 Internet hits on LGBTQ themes by year, 2000–2010.

the mid-2000s accumulating to 40,000 references. Hits on LGBTQ+ related keyword searches on Google (see Figure 7.12) appear to show an even longer lag in increases, seemingly not growing until 2012. That, however, is an illusion of scale. It results from the eventual mammoth number of Google hits reached by 2020 (more than 200 million), which, when fit into a single graphic, visually drives down the relatively "smaller" number of hits during the 2000s, which were growing to more than 1 million. We can get a more accurate picture of the growth of yearly and cumulative internet hits on LGBTQ+ themes by zooming in on the 2000s (see Figure 7.13). In sum, interest in LGBTQ+ concerns grew dramatically across many forms of media in the 1900s and 2000s, both reflecting and driving heightened cultural awareness and public debate about the place of LGBTQ+ people in American society.

Associated with that activism and those events and debates was a sea change in public opinion and law in the 2000s. US public opinion on the moral acceptability of same-sex relationships changed dramatically in the twenty-first century (see Figure 7.14). What we see is a dramatic reversal of Americans' opinions in a short time. In 2001, the belief that gay and lesbian relationships are not morally acceptable led the opposite by 13 percentage points—53% to 40%. Seven years later, in 2008, public opinion was split at 48% even. By the end of the decade, the belief that gay and lesbian relationships are morally acceptable became the majority and, in the years following, continued to increase. By 2015, 63% of Americans said "morally acceptable"; by 2022, 71% said the same (not depicted here). In one key decade, American public opinion on same-sex morality shifted greatly, changing the majority view from unacceptable to acceptable. Those who continued to believe same-sex relationships were morally wrong were, by 2009, the minority, with the tide of public opinion flowing strongly against them.

The same reversal of public opinion also occurred with the question of legal same-sex marriage. Every year, Gallup asked, "Do you think marriages between same-sex couples should or should not be recognized by the law as valid, with the same rights as traditional marriages?" In 1996, only 27% of Americans said same-sex marriages should be valid, while 68% said they should not. Over the following eight years, that 41% gap closed steadily to a 13% difference in 2004. It remained stable until 2009, closed entirely in 2011, and then reversed. By 2016, 61% of Americans said same-sex marriage should be valid, while only 37% said they should not. A graph of these numbers would look like the same kind of stretched X of crossing trend lines we see in Figure 7.14.[37] Millennials were at the vanguard of public opinion. In 2001, 18-to-34-year-olds were 25% more likely to say same-sex relationships are morally acceptable than were those 55 and older. Those age disparities in opinion remained stable for more than a decade. In all but one survey year during the 2000s, a majority of 18-to-34-year-olds approved of same-sex relationships, while a majority of those 55 or older did not arrive there until 2013. By that year, 74% of 18–to 34-year-olds approved same-sex relationships; by 2021, that number had reached 84%.[38] Millennials were "the first to be wholly exposed to this new shift in thinking [the public acceptance of same-sex marriage and LGBT issues]. For Millennials, it has always been a normal way of life, and being gay, lesbian, bi-sexual, or transgender [was] believed to be just a part of who the individual is."[39]

When colleagues and I interviewed many hundreds of US teenage Millennials in 2003, 2005, and 2008, the viewpoint expressed by the vast

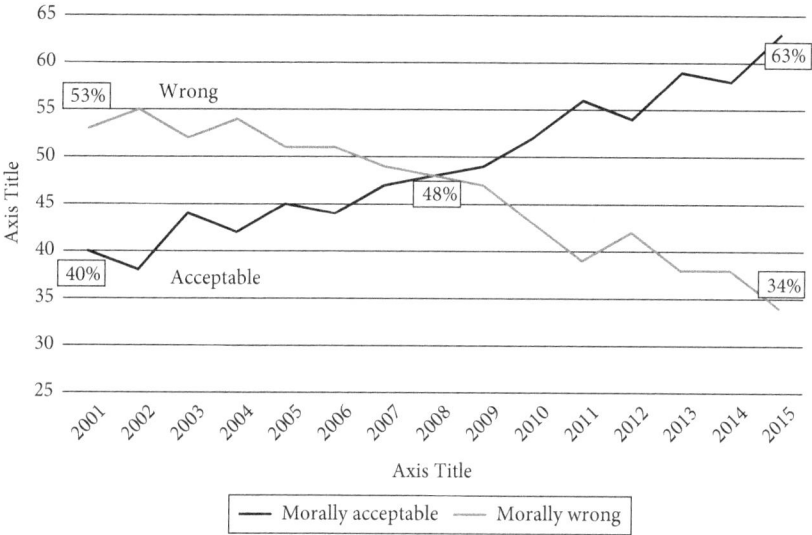

Figure 7.14 US public opinion on the moral acceptability of gay and lesbian relationships, 2001–2015 (%).
Source: The Gallup Organization.
Note: Responses to the survey question, "Are gay or lesbian relationships morally acceptable?"

majority on this subject was, "What's the big deal? People can do whatever they want."[40] Millennials were "early adopters" of this tolerant attitude. One 2022 interviewee told us, "I love to believe what's happened in history is for the better. We've made good progress on LGBTQ+ issues and the feminist front in the last 20 years. That feels like progress to me, there's been a lot of wonderful change." Another said,

> Baby Boomers were all very traditional and wanted things done a certain way. A lot of Gen Xers started pushing diversity. The whole LGBTQ+ thing started to become more accepted by younger people, less so by older. So there was a lot of breaking traditional values and progressing.

And another said,

> If you're gay and want to get married, I don't care as long as you're happy. A couple of my good friends are gay, they're married, and they're cool. Sure, whatever, gay marriage, I'm totally fine with it if that's what makes you happy. If that's what you want to do, totally fine. People who say gay marriage is bad, that's a very old-fashioned way of thinking.

How did this mainstreaming of LGBTQ+ identities in the 2000s affect younger generations' views of traditional religion? As we saw in the previous section on sexual mores, young Americans believe traditional religion teaches that same-sex relationships, not to mention bisexuality and transsexuality, are morally unacceptable. That was correct about most US religious traditions and denominations. So here, as before, on an issue of massive public if not personal importance in the 2000s, young generations of Americans saw religion as outdated and behind the times.[41] Worse, many believed religion was unjustly contributing to—if not leading the charge on—the systematic oppression of whole classes of people who simply wanted to be able to love who they loved. That, too, violated entries on the short list of things religion could do to count as good. In interviews, this was a key talking point for explaining why, among other reasons, Millennials had little interest in affiliating with religion: "People are getting more accepting of others. The gay issue is really big, the transgender issue, people trying to end sexism, which a lot of traditional religions support. A lot of people are turning against religions because they want to be more accepting of different people." More pointedly: "The most disturbing thing about religion these days are young children committing suicide because they're Christians or whatever, and classmates are picking on them because they're gay. It just doesn't make sense to me, no sense whatsoever. Religion is behind all of this, rather than just accepting people for who and what they are—who cares?" Another told us,

> The new younger generation is very free with who they are. There were kids who were transgender or gender-fluid when I was in high school, but it wasn't acceptable. That's not the case with young people now. Because of that and the rules of some religious institutions, they don't fit so they are not drawn to it. We didn't have a choice, we didn't know any different. They have a choice now, and if it doesn't feel good, they don't want to be a part of it.

Religious Pluralism and National Identity

The US Immigration Act of 1965 eliminated the quotas linking immigration to national origins, as we noted in Chapter 5, and launched a process of American religious diversification. Over the following decades, immigrants from all regions of the world came to the United States, bringing with them their religions, which often were not "Judeo-Christian." After enough growth, religious minorities achieved a significant presence in America, and scholars started noticing. The end of the Cold War, as we also saw, removed the need to emphasize the nation's shared religious solidarity. Public discussion about America growing religiously diverse increased in the 1990s and continued in the 2000s. In 2001, Harvard professor of religion Diana Eck published what for our purposes was a landmark book: *A New Religious America: How a "Christian Country" Has Become the World's Most Religiously Diverse Nation*.[42] It was, the book jacket stated, an "eye-opening guide to the religious realities of America today."

> Muslims, Buddhists, Hindus, Sikhs, Jains, Zoroastrians, and new varieties of Jews and Catholics have arrived from every part of the globe, radically altering the religious landscape of the United States. Members of the world's religions live not just on the other side of the world but in our neighborhoods; Hindu children go to school with Jewish children; Muslims, Buddhists, and Sikhs work side-by-side with Protestants and Catholics. This new religious diversity is now a Main Street phenomenon.

Publishers Weekly wrote that Eck's book details the "explosion of Muslim, Hindu and Buddhist communities in America" and "delivers a stunning tour de force that may forever change the way Americans claim to be 'one nation, under God.'"[43] More than a few religion scholars thought Eck's claim that "the United States is the most religiously diverse nation in the world" was overstated. But it did point to something real and important. Other authors followed with similar publications in the succeeding years, with titles such as *America and the Challenges of Religious Diversity*, *What It Means to Be American: Attitudes Towards Increasing Diversity in America Ten Years After 9/11*, *America's Changing Religious Identity*, and *Out of Many Faiths: Religious Diversity and the American Promise*.[44] *America's Changing Religious Identity* expressed the common theme.

> The American religious landscape is undergoing a dramatic transformation. White Christians, once the dominant religious group in the US, now account for fewer than half of all adults living in the country. Today, fewer than half of all states are majority white Christian. . . . The American religious landscape has undergone dramatic changes in the last decade

and is more diverse today than at any time since modern sociological measurements began.

This heightened interest in US religious diversity was not a mere academic affair. Media attention to religious pluralism ramped up at the start of the 1990s, sustained itself across the decade, and increased even more during the 2000s and after (see Figure 7.15).

Google likewise shows a bump in internet references and book titles related to "religious diversity" and "religious pluralism" during the 1990s and a continued growth in the 2000s (Figure 7.16). Millennials did not have to read Diana Eck's book, in other words, to be exposed to the idea that America was becoming much more religiously diverse. It was playing on the era's cultural airwaves.

Millennials had good reason to understand heightened religious pluralism. They lived diversity. Theirs was the most racially and ethnically diverse generation the United States had ever seen. In 2002, 39% of Millennials were racial and ethnic minorities. That compares to only 30% of Gen Xers and 18% of Baby Boomers when they were 6–21 years old. Gen Z, following Millennials, was even more diverse.[45] Every day in school, on athletic fields, and with their peers in public, post-Boomer generations lived with diversity.

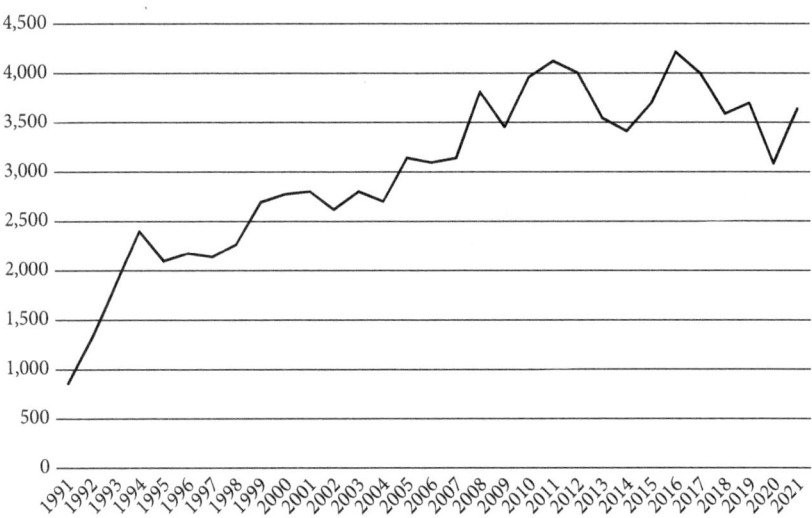

Figure 7.15 Media references to religious pluralism by year, 1991–2021.
Source: Nexis Uni corpus.

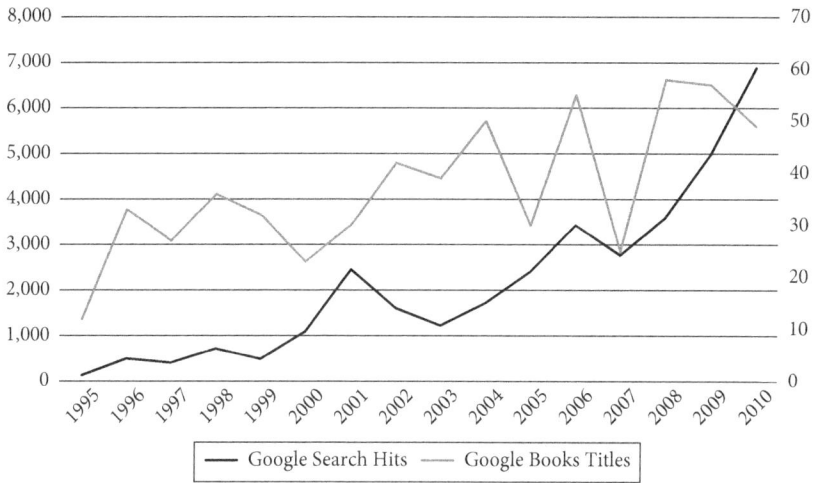

Figure 7.16 Number of Google hits and Google books titles on religious diversity and pluralism, 1995–2010.
Source: Google, Google Books.

Pluralism was existentially real and natural for them. The idea that the United States was becoming highly religiously diverse to them made obvious sense.

How did this growing realization affect younger generations' relations with traditional religion? Decades of immigration had not only diversified but also helped bolster religious life in the United States. On average, at the end of the twentieth century, individuals who had immigrated were more religious than non-immigrant Americans.[46] American religion benefited demographically from the new immigration. Heightened public attention to America's growing religious pluralism, however, also worked culturally against American traditional religion in at least three ways.

First, younger generations became culturally sensitized to America's "explosion" of religious diversity, which contributed to their downplaying of religious particularity and embrace of epistemological relativism. Their lived realities of racial, ethnic, and religious pluralism comported with the popular postmodernism they had picked up in classrooms and broader public discourse. Millennials especially drew the obvious conclusion: all religions are just human constructions, historically and culturally relative, with no one being better or more valid than any other. The clear adjunct conclusion was that since no one should ever offend anyone else or create any conflict in pluralistic spaces, everyone should make a concerted effort to downplay their own religious particularities so as not to cause friction with others.[47] What the valuable awareness of real religious diversity unintentionally led to, in short, was this tacit rule: find a least common denominator way to interact across differences and adhere to it.

That explains why, when colleagues and I interviewed hundreds of Millennials in the 2000s, exceedingly few Christians among them mentioned "Jesus." That, despite our two-hour interviews being primarily about their religious and spiritual lives. Talking about "God" was safe. But "Jesus" was too particular and potentially offensive to mention, so he rarely showed up.[48] For traditional religions to flourish in pluralistic societies, everyone involved needs to learn how to maintain and express their own particulars with the right balance of self-confidence, humility, and respect for differences. That is a lesson younger Americans did not learn. For them, to respect others meant curtailing if not abandoning one's own serious beliefs and practices.

Second, the more society's growing racial and ethnic diversity became normal to post-Boomers, the more abnormal the demographics of most traditional religious congregations felt to them. American religion has long been highly segregated by race and ethnicity, reflecting legacies of Jim Crow segregation and nativist hostility to new immigrants.[49] Aside from experiments in multiracial congregations and some Pentecostal churches, this remained true into the twenty-first century.[50] The normal experience of increasing numbers of post-Boomers, by contrast, involved life and relationships with people of various races, ethnicities, and religious backgrounds. That was their daily existential reality. Walking through the doors of a typical American religious congregation, however, would place them in a visibly homogenous group of people. The effect? Recall the words of the former pastor quoted in Chapter 1 about Boomer churches being about homogeneity and youth living in highly diverse world: "If they don't see [diversity] in church, nobody in their 20s will be there, they just will not be part of an isolated, homogeneous group." Post-Boomers recognizing this would not require a conscious analysis. The simple "vibe" of group sameness would be strong enough to turn many post-Boomers away. The typical congregational demographics would also add evidence supporting their common view that religion is badly "behind the times."

A third way that America's real and publicized religious pluralism pushed younger generations away from traditional religion was by disqualifying religion as a potential contributing basis for national identity. Every nation needs some larger ideal and image, often with sacred qualities, to provide shared identity and cohesion.[51] The United States long drew on biblical imagery to construct its national identity.[52] By the 2000s, most young people would have found that unacceptable.

The elephant-in-the-room question was: What, if anything, holds the United States together? What is the basis of national identity and solidarity in the new millennium?[53] The answers were far from obvious. In theory, religion might have contributed, in some reconfigured narrative about mutual respect and concord in a pluralistic world. That, however, would have taken visionary political, religious, and cultural leadership that did not emerge. The Christian Right was continuing its belligerent attacks on a new social order in a culture war it could neither entirely win nor lose. The New Atheists wished to make religion extinct. American politics was polarizing. American religions were navigating their own internal battles over denominational policies and scandals around sex, gender, money, and more. In that context, the news that America had become the most religiously diverse nation on earth did not sound for Millennials the major chord of harmony-in-difference but more dissonant notes of fracture, breakup, and disintegration.

Survey data corroborate the inability of religion to serve, as it had in the past, as an ongoing basis for national identity. The Pew Research Center asked questions in 2016, 2020, and 2022 about factors that people in the United States believe "are important for being truly American."[54] Unfortunately, these survey data do not go back far enough in time to trace changes over decades. Furthermore, the question does not ask about religion generally but "Christianity" specifically. Pew asked about only two of the factors in 2022, hence the single bars, and asked about one of the factors in only two years, hence the double bars (see Figure 7.17). Despite some spottiness in the data, we can draw three conclusions.

First, religion (being a Christian) was the least likely of all the factors said to be important for being authentically American. Generational differences on this point were hefty: fully 44% of respondents ages 50 and older in 2016 said being a Christian is "very important" to being truly American, while only 18% of those under age 35 said the same.[55] Second, across the years surveyed, fewer and fewer respondents said that any of the factors asked about were important for being truly American—reflecting a growing uncertainty about exactly what does or should hold Americans together. Putting those first two points together, we also observe a major decline in the public's belief that religion is important for being a good American, decreasing from

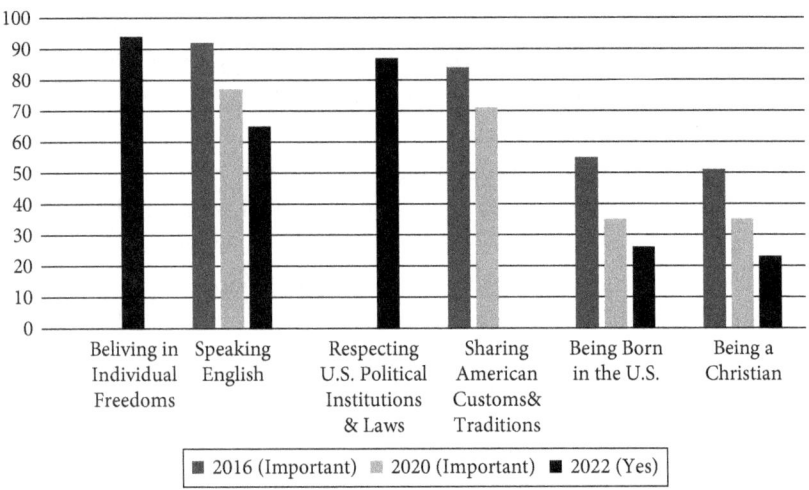

Figure 7.17 Factors important for being truly American, 2016, 2020, 2022.
Source: Pew Research Center.
Note: "Important" combines "very" and "somewhat important"; "Yes" as opposed to "no" and no answer.

51% saying "yes" in 2016 to only 23% by 2022—a 55% decline from the baseline in six years. Third, the factor that scored the highest in 2022 does not lend support to traditional religion. "Believing in individual freedom" (94% said "yes" in 2022) is not about any shared substantive culture but instead a broad allowance for differences. "Respecting US political institutions and laws" entails somewhat more substantive commitments, yet references a politically liberal system that accentuates individualism, downplays collective identities, and emphasizes procedural rights over substantive goods. If those are the most important features of being a good American, then religion's position remains tenuous.

My own Millennial Zeitgeist Survey of 2023 asked respondents whether they agreed or disagreed with the statement, "Religion is a 'glue' that can help hold American society together today." Only 37% of Millennials agreed with this statement, while 29% strongly disagreed. Theirs is the least likely generation to believe in religion as a basis for national solidarity: 50% of Gen X respondents agreed with the statement while 20% strongly disagreed; 52% of later Boomers agreed and 17% strongly disagreed. And 60% of early Boomers agreed while 13% strongly disagreed. Millennials stand out for having decided that religious pluralism and other factors make the idea that religion could serve as a basis of national solidarity impossible. Issues of national identity and solidarity were not easy ones for post-Boomers to discuss in our interviews, but a few did offer their thoughts, for example:

> The problem we have as a country now is people think we're one religion and we're not. I don't understand how they don't remember we took in people from all over the world. That's the whole basis of America. And now we're restricting and saying we need to think with just one mind, that we're only Christian when there's Islam, Jewish, all sorts of people out there. Do your own thing with your people if you believe it and need to practice the rituals, go for it. But it's people who don't let others be who bother me, as extreme as bombing mosques. Just because they don't agree in how they think.

Another said,

> As a Christian, religion's decline is sad to me. I want everybody to meet and love Jesus. But I also understand that we're not the Christian nation we originally were and that people are able to have other beliefs. And that's okay.

Another explored the issue with this admittedly wishful thinking:

> Is it important that all Americans share something together? Yeah. I think we need to figure out a religion that everybody can join, or maybe make up a new one. In my mind I wish we could all come up with a new religion that fits everybody under one umbrella. Let's add everybody up and everybody's got in, one place where we all can come together where everybody's God is displayed, and we share, respect, and listen to them, listen to us, listen to everybody. Maybe we can come together that way. But that's never going to happen.

Except for those miniscule few post-Boomers studying Emile Durkheim and Robert Bellah in graduate school, young Americans in the 2000s were not thinking at this level of abstraction. Still, many were tuned in to the world around them. And people can intuitively sense at inexpressible levels of awareness what is going on out there and what it probably means. For the young, America's growing religious diversity meant this: traditional religion had even one less contribution to make to life and society than in former days. An extra nail in traditional American religion's coffin.

Identity Politics and the Sacralizing of Partisan Politics

The growth of identity politics also pushed against traditional religion, crowding it out. This is a huge topic unto itself, the basic story of which is already familiar.[56] For present purposes, suffice it to say that, especially during our two crucial decades, US political power, groups, and struggles shifted increasingly away from traditional material and security policies and instead into the recognition, validation, and demands of various subgroup identities.[57] As race, ethnicity, sexual orientation, gender, and other particular statuses came increasingly to define salient group memberships and personal and social identities, older religious markers—such as Protestant versus Catholic, Episcopalian versus Pentecostal—receded in importance. Being a person of color, gay, disabled, a feminist, Southern, white, and so on eclipsed religious affiliation in meaning. Exceptions included cases in which religion was tightly bound to ethnicity—for example, the recent rise of white Christian nationalism. But generally, most Americans' particular faith or denomination lost the status significance, emotional resonance, and political implications it would have had earlier in history.

That was the first step toward the sidelining of religion by politics. The second was that American politics itself became increasingly invested with quasi-religious importance. Politics became sacralized on both the right and the left.[58] For increasing numbers of Americans, political party faction became one's tribe, ideology became dogma, political personalities like prophets, campaign rallies resembled revival services—all seeking the "salvation" of America from whoever was the diabolical adversary. The intolerance and narrow-mindedness for which the New Atheists had damned religion increasingly showed up in the ostensibly secular realm of politics. Political struggle took on a quasi-religious fervor and, for those participating, a quasi-religious identity. The more this sacralization of politics occurred, the more American identities migrated from spaces of traditional sacredness, such as religion, to this other realm.[59]

Crucibles of Despair: The War on Terror, Political Polarization, Global Warming

The first decade of the twenty-first century was a time of growing dread for young Americans. While the 1990s certainly had problems, they seemed in retrospect a time of happy progress. Democratic capitalism beat totalitarian communism, personal computers were getting cheaper and more powerful every year, global economies were flourishing, Bill Clinton was puffing on cigars on the golf course. It was almost the Roaring Twenties again in high-tech form. In his campaign at the end of that era, presidential candidate George W. Bush promised to be a "compassionate conservative" who focused on issues like education and access to home ownership.

Then came September 11. The attacks themselves angered and frightened Americans, and reaction to the attacks sent the United States down a very dark road. If any one moment defines this era, it may be this: President George W. Bush, landing a fighter jet on an aircraft carrier, standing under a "Mission Accomplished" banner, and proclaiming that "major combat operations in Iraq have ended; in the battle of Iraq, the United States and our allies have prevailed." The war in Iraq would drag on for another eight years. When President Bush gave that speech, 104 American soldiers had died in the war. Before combat operations really ended in 2011, another 3,320 Americans had been killed and 31,900 wounded or maimed. Altogether, about half a million combatants and civilians died in the Iraq war, including journalists, aid workers, and private contractors.

After justifying the invasion on the grounds that Iraq had weapons of mass destruction and was prepared to use them, the United States found no such weapons. Saddam Hussein had no ties to al Qaeda, despite US government officials' claims. The White House, it turned out, had lied to start the Iraq war. And the disasters kept coming. The Abu Ghraib prison disgrace. Guantanamo Bay. Waterboarding. Anthrax attacks. Domestic surveillance. Post-invasion insurgencies. Suicide bombings. Improvised explosive devices. 1,558 limb amputations for US soldiers. Kidnappings, mutilations, beheadings. Civilian murders. The "Surge." A destroyed economy. 1.7 million internal refugees. A barely functional new Iraqi regime installed. The 20 years of war in Afghanistan. Taliban insurgencies. Human shields. Recurring massacres. Millions more refugees. Wikileaks. Torture as official US policy. The rise of the Islamic State. Mass beheadings broadcast on video. A sudden exit from Afghanistan by the US military and immediate takeover by the Taliban.

The total price tag to Americans for the war on terror? Eight trillion dollars and 900,000 total deaths.[60] All this was reported in depressing detail every day for years on end.

Meanwhile, Americans and their political leaders were not pulling together to fight a good fight but breaking apart in polarized conflict.[61] Having learned a sanitized version of US history and politics in elementary school, Millennials grew up into a poisonous political world. Hanging chads. Red versus Blue. "Gotcha" politics. Demonizing opponents. Political violence. Culture wars. Other news took the mood from bad to worse. The Dot.com bubble. Skyrocketing federal debt. Hurricanes Katrina and Rita. Proliferating computer hacks, worms, viruses, and breaches. Eliot Spitzer. Enron. WorldCom. Bernie Madoff. The financial meltdown of 2008–2009. The Great Recession. Mass shootings.

If military and domestic problems were not enough, the world in the 2000s provided plenty more to depress Millennials. Global recession. Olympics scandals. The Catholic sexual abuse and cover-up scandal. North Korea going nuclear. Israel and Palestine's continued bloodbath. Darfur. The Indonesian tsunami. SARS and swine flu. Australia on fire. Terrorist bombings. Civil wars and drug wars. And the constant stream of bad news from Iraq and Afghanistan.

These were not the happiest times to be coming of age. It was not only that bad things were happening, but also that society's political and business leaders were lying, cheating, stealing, and profiting in ways that made Watergate, the Clinton–Lewinsky affair, and the savings and loan crisis seem like preschool playtime.[62] Some religious leaders were not behaving any better. It was not merely depressing. For youth especially, it was seriously demoralizing.

Added to all those issues that caused anxiety and depression among Millennials was global warming and climate change. Over the course of the 2000s, global warming science grew more sophisticated, producing more—and more reliable—material about planetary overheating and climate change. Every new year seemed to be the warmest year on record. Forecasts of climate change's destruction were becoming frighteningly clearer. Al Gore, having barely lost the 2000 election to George W. Bush, was touring the country with his documentary, *An Inconvenient Truth* (2006), warning about global warming. Real, scary signs of climate change were materializing. Meanwhile, carbon industries were funding climate denial campaigns. Republican leaders who had previously expressed concern about global warming recanted and became agnostics and deniers. Imperatives of immediate economic growth continually eclipsed efforts to address the looming climate catastrophe.

Millennials were much more likely to believe in global warming than the Boomers who actually had the power to do something about it. Millennials felt powerless and knew they would suffer much more than those Boomers who would be gone before all hell broke loose. The accumulating facts induced fright, anger, grief, and depression. Clinicians were soon naming new mental health syndromes, such as "climate grief," "eco anxiety," "environmental nihilism," to be spreading among American youth. For Millennials, the bleak idea was beginning to sink in that, realistically, they might not have any real future. Karla Vermeulen, professor of psychology at SUNY New Paltz, calls Millennials "Generation Disaster."[63]

Such concerns and anxieties have continued in the years since. We asked participants in the Millennial Zeitgeist Survey 2023 "How much, if any, do climate change and global warming make you think or feel the following?" Sixty percent of Millennials said that "a huge amount" or "a lot" (as opposed to "some," "very little," or "none at all") of "Humans have failed to take care of the planet," while 47% believe that "humans, animals, and the planet will be badly threatened in coming years." An astounding 33% of Millennials believe that "Humanity is doomed," while 28% report that they feel a huge amount or a lot of "sadness, fear, anxiety, or anger over the climate crisis." And 19% say they think that "a huge amount" or "a lot" of "Young people should consider not having children because their future will be bad." On every question, Millennials report the greatest concern and anxiety about environmental degradation and the climate crisis (Table 7.7).[64]

What does all this darkness, anxiety, and despair have to do with traditional religion? At least two things, I suggest. The first is that it has contributed to younger generations' distrust of authorities, including religious authorities. As we saw in previous chapters, a lack of confidence in American institutions and their leaders was already running in the background.[65] That was not a Millennial innovation but a fact of American life. But post-Boomers who watched as their leaders regularly skirted and violated morals and laws were driven to particular cynicism and contempt. The fact that most leaders were willing to destroy the future of the planet, humanity, and nature for their own short-term profit and power, for example, was mind-boggling and heart-breaking to many younger Americans. Had religious leaders stood out as clear exceptions, standing up for what was right at their own personal expense, that might have made a difference.

Second, the decade's darkness, anxiety, and despair created a mood that was culturally mismatched with traditional religion. This effect was

Table 7.7 Environmental and Climate-Change Concern and Anxiety Reported by Generation (%)

How much, if any, do climate change and global warming make you think or feel the following?	Early Boomers	Later Boomers	Gen Xers	Millennials
Humans have failed to take care of the planet.				
A huge amount	19	19	30	31
A lot	29	29	21	29
Humans, animals, and the planet will be badly threatened in coming years.				
A huge amount	15	16	20	23
A lot	26	20	24	24
Humanity is doomed.				
A huge amount	2	5	10	11
A lot	10	10	17	22
I feel sadness, fear, anxiety, or anger over the climate crisis.				
A huge amount	7	7	8	11
A lot	17	15	12	17
Young people should consider not having children because their future will be bad.				
A huge amount	2	3	5	8
A lot	2	4	9	11
TOTALS	100	100	100	100
(unweighted *n*'s):	(*n* = 341)	(*n* = 358)	(*n* = 485)	(*n* = 677)

Source: Millennial Zeitgeist Survey, 2023 (*N* = 1,861). Percents may not add to 100 due to rounding. Answer categories were a huge amount, a lot, some, very little, none at all.

more amorphous than leadership distrust but equally consequential. In Americans' minds, religion is not about anxiety, despair, depression, and nihilism. It preaches faith, hope, salvation, growth. It is about love, kindness, joy, and doing good. It means dressing up nicely, smiling, being cheerful and happy. In another place and time, religion might have appealed as a respite from the darkness. But what Millennials took to be religion's sunny orientation seemed to many of them so distant from the realities of the world that it felt inauthentic. Religion's faith and hope could not overcome cynicism and despair. It actually seemed rather to belong to the entire fabric of Boomer counterfeit reality and dissembling tactics that had created the mess of a world so bleak.[66] Millennials did not think all this out consciously and systematically, of course, and could not well or fully articulate what they felt. But it was clear from what they said in interviews and reading between the lines how things looked to them. One, for instance, said,

> Pre-9/11 things were different. There was a lot of hope. People didn't just have crushing panic attacks every day of their lives for no reason. The world was a lot lighter. Our country, the general feeling was just so much lighter. Bill Clinton was getting blowjobs. Like, who cares? That's not bad compared to all the horrible, egregious corruption, the billionaires, everyone targeted by corporation ads. There was none of that. We didn't even have social media. I didn't have a cell phone until I was 25. So it was very light, a lightness to that pre-9/11, pre-social media that doesn't exist anymore. I felt good. I felt "I can go to college and do whatever I want and save the world." I might have some loans, but I'll pay them off, no big deal. Now that's devastating for students.

Another told us,

> It's been a hell of a ride because 9/11 and the Iraq war had no connection, but Bush forced them together. That was a low point. Then we had the high point of Obama, and some things got changed but a lot didn't. We thought he was a transformational figure but. . . . So disenchantment, loss of hope, thinking about my lack of efficacy in the world. Growing up I was told, "you've got to protect the environment, make the world a better place." But it's just a downward slope of disenchantment seeing how the world works, that I have almost no influence and no one does. The people in power don't really care about the environment or about world peace. Then it went to an even lower low with Trump.

And still another,

> There's just cynicism growing. Young people look at the world and think we got the short end of the stick, so we don't trust the people before us. They basically set us up for failure, so are the ones who have to fix whatever problems are going on. That's where the cynicism comes from. And the more cynicism there is, the more people want to be independent and

just don't trust religious people anymore. They think they don't need them or that they understand religion as their own person, individually, without needing anyone else. That's what's happening.

What many post-Boomers wanted to hear was someone telling the unvarnished truth, sitting with them in the darkness without an easy answer, validating their incredulity, anxiety, and grief. As some said in interviews, "I would rather live with authentic depression than fake happiness." What Millennials mostly saw from religion was overly cheerful megachurch evangelicals. Right-wing political activists tearing the world further apart. Muslims trying to avoid being assaulted by Islamophobes. Clergy captive to the demands of powerful Boomer congregants. "Biblical" obsessions with homosexuality and abortion. Inane television preachers. Do-gooder volunteers thinking they had "done their part" by handing out turkeys to poor people once a year at Thanksgiving. And continual revelations about clergy pedophiles and church cover-ups.

Of all the institutions in the United States that possessed the internal resources to take seriously Millennials' darkness, despondency, and semi-suppressed anger, it should have been religion. Who else owns the language of and has spent countless millennia wrestling with evil, depravity, brokenness, damnation, suffering, redemption, hope against hope, and a meaning to life beyond the horizons of the present? American religion by the end of the twentieth century, however, had become defined as the place specializing in making people good, nice, and happy. "Religion is for good people," or even "goodie-goodies," as some said in interviews. So, as the world in the 2000s grew more grim, religion was not the place post-Boomers expected to look to make sense of their dread, gloom, and demoralization. Instead, some only hoped they as individuals would somehow manage to rise above the general disorder they saw around them.[67] Religion may have had a chance to connect, but it missed by a mile.

The Disappearing American Dream

In the 2000s, younger Americans suffered a major economic shock accompanied by a big cultural disappointment: their declining economic prospects and diminishing chance of achieving the traditional "American Dream." The 1990s had seen the longest phase of economic growth in

American history. Even so, economic inequalities between the wealthiest few and the majority of Americans had been growing since the 1980s. Then, in 2001, the Dot.com bubble burst when the exuberantly overvalued stock prices of the first wave of internet companies crashed. The technology-heavy NASDAQ lost 78% of its value, eventually taking more than 15 years to recover those losses. Half of all tech startups failed. The crash wiped out $5 trillion in market capitalization, tarnished the internet's original luster, and spotlighted the insecurities of the new internet economy. Months later, the terrorist attacks of September 11 tipped the US economy into a recession. Unemployment reached 5.5%, and gross domestic product (GDP) fell by 0.95%. Gen Xers, 21–36 years old at the time, were the hardest hit. *BusinessWeek* reported in 2002 that "many Gen Xers have now been flushed out of their first-, second-, and third-choice careers—and dumped firmly on the path of downward mobility."[68] Millennials, who at the time were children, teenagers, and just starting college or work, looked on with apprehension.

Seven years later, the subprime mortgage crisis and collapse of the housing bubble triggered the Great Recession, the longest and deepest economic downturn since the Great Depression. Real GDP declined more than 4%, and unemployment peaked at 10%. Stock markets tumbled, major financial companies headed into bankruptcy, and a global financial crisis and recession ensued. The recession badly damaged the finances of vast numbers of Americans. Almost 9 million jobs disappeared. US households lost roughly $19 trillion in net worth. About 10 million Americans lost their homes through foreclosure. Meanwhile, the federal government provided $700 billion to save banks and corporations deemed "too big to fail." Many important economic indicators did not return to pre-recession levels for almost a decade.

Millennials were teenagers and emerging adults at the time and suffered acutely. Unemployment for those ages 16–24 reached a high of 19%.[69] Furthermore, upon graduation, about two-thirds of 2008 college graduates held student loan debt, with average debt among those two-thirds at $23,200, a large increase over the decade before. "Just when college grads thought they'd be starting their careers and laying the foundation for their eventual retirements, the crisis pulled the rug out from under their feet."[70] Adding injury to injury, just when Millennials were finally beginning to recover from the huge setback after 2008, the massive economic downturn from the COVID-19 pandemic hit them extra hard again.

The long-term, negative impact of the Great Recession on Millennials is well known.[71] Bodies of research produced disheartening headlines, such as, "Millennials Are the Unluckiest Generation in US History," "How the Last 20 Years of Economic Turmoil Broke Millennials," "Millennials Are the New Lost Generation," and "Millennials Are Screwed: Why Millennials Are Facing the Scariest Financial Future of Any Generation Since the Great Depression."[72] Millennials realized they would be the first American generation to fare worse economically than their parents. Expectations of home ownership, new car purchases, savings cushions, and eventual comfortable retirements seemed increasingly unrealistic. Achieving the American Dream felt like a prospect once offered and then pulled away. "Millennials were honed [in the 1990s] ... into machines of self-optimization ... only to have the economy blow up their dreams."[73] At first, most Millennials hoped they would somehow survive unscathed.[74] But, as the truth sank in, the mood became a cocktail of alarm, anger, and despondency.[75] One interviewee told us, "For most Millennials, the American Dream has proven to be a false promise." For another, "it feels like an American nightmare because it just doesn't seem like the dream is reachable." Another sank further into despair:

> I've become a lot more pessimistic about the American Dream in general, cause now it's just like, how am I going to survive until I die? [Interviewer: What were your earlier ideas of the American Dream?] Nonexistent—it was something reserved for our parents but nothing for our generation. When I was little, it didn't feel that way, but once I got older it was like they all climbed their way up and found what they needed, and then kicked the ladder out from under them for the next generations.

For some, the loss of the American Dream and traditional values was explicitly linked.

> The American Dream idea of having a house and a couple of kids was completely unrealistic to believe. Most people my age are like, "We're probably never going to own a house or pay off our student loans. We're not going to be able to do things our parents did when they were our age." And if it doesn't seem possible, it isn't appealing. It's just been an unveiling and tarnished like, our parents weren't really in love, they just stayed married because they felt they had to. Like the horrors of the American housewife and everything. I think more and more independence, freedom, cultural

exchanges are pointing toward different values. This is a generation of redefinition. I'm Muslim, comfortably, I'm not the typical image of what you'd expect. But I exist, it's possible for me to exist. And there are others like me, I have other queer, brown, radical friends. But there's no way for me to follow a more traditional model because I don't exist in it. But we know people like us exist and think the same way. So it ruins the illusion held by traditional values that certain alternatives aren't possible.

Millennials echoed those outlooks in my 2023 Millennial Zeitgeist Survey, which asked about the statement, "I have as good a chance of achieving the 'American Dream' as previous generations."[76] The overall pattern of responses shows a clear decline in confidence about achieving the American Dream across generations (see Table 7.8). Millennials are especially pessimistic: 53% of them disagreed with the statement, and another 9% said they were not sure. Only 13% strongly agreed with the idea that their chances of realizing the American Dream were as good as that of previous generations.

The consequences of this experience for Millennials were many. The economic calamities caused them to delay marrying and starting families. Settling down into full adulthood on mainstream terms turned out for many to be economically impossible. Those determined to enjoy career success despite the bleak economic environment had to devote even more time, attention, and energy to their educations and jobs than the neoliberal intensification of work in the 1990s had already demanded. Others who despaired of career

Table 7.8 Perceived Chances of Achieving the "American Dream" by Generation (%)

I have as good a chance of achieving the "American Dream" as previous generations.	Early Boomers	Later Boomers	Gen Xers	Millennials
Strongly agree	29	25	25	13
Somewhat agree	51	46	37	25
Somewhat disagree	11	15	14	28
Strongly disagree	5	9	16	25
Not sure	3	6	8	9
TOTALS (unweighted n's):	100 ($n = 341$)	100 ($n = 358$)	100 ($n = 485$)	100 ($n = 677$)

Source: Millennial Zeitgeist Survey, 2023 ($N = 1,861$). Percents may not add to 100 due to rounding.

success decided that work would not be what gave meaning to their lives.[77] Many felt betrayed by greedy, dishonest business and political leaders more concerned with taking care of the richest 1% than anyone else. Essentially nobody who helped cause the subprime mortgage crisis and financial meltdown was held responsible—instead they walked away with multimillion-dollar bonuses while millions of ordinary Americans everywhere had their lives ruined. That was hard to stomach. And if it was true that the financial meltdown was simply the unfortunate result of complicated processes involving no bad actors, that meant that the entire system was more fragile and untrustworthy than anyone had known. In time, these developments fueled a new generational war: that of resentful Millennials against entitled Boomers. All of this further eroded already weakening confidence and trust in societal leaders and authorities and prevented young people from making commitments to the larger social system.[78] The less people feel an ownership stake in their society, the less fair society seems and the fewer opportunities they see for the redress of wrongs, the fewer investments they make in its institutions. Having seen their futures compromised by impersonal systems and unaccountable persons, many Millennials began to divest emotionally and aspirationally from the mainstream way of life. The more dismal the future looked, the more they focused on living in the moment and finding alternative sources of meaning.

These dynamics reinforced forces that were already pulling younger generations away from traditional religion. The cultural mood badly mismatched the presumed spirit of traditional religion. Religion, they believed, was for families with children, for good and happy people, for those invested in their local communities. All very nice for old people who were consuming their harvest of the postwar economic boom. Millennials, however, felt alienated in ways that carried over into their feelings about religion.

Good Without God

Religion's competitive advantage in helping people to be morally good began to slip further in the 2000s, when non-religious advocates began pressing the claim that anyone can be "good without God." This was not a new idea. The common cultural assumption that religion's job was to teach and encourage moral behavior had been, at least since the 1960s, routinely accompanied by the recognition that many other institutions and people performed that task, too: family, teachers, youth clubs, coaches, and so on. As such, religion had no unique part to play in the production of a decent society. It had to share that function with other producers in the societal division of labor. Still, many Americans believed religion did have a special role in promoting morality, that the God factor made a difference. Other, especially less religious, Americans believed otherwise. But the issue was not a point of major contention.

In the late 2000s and after, however, the question of the value of religion in moral education came into sharp focus. Increasing numbers of non-religious Americans had been growing dissatisfied with the implication that they and their children might somehow be morally disadvantaged. The zeitgeist's prohibition against judging others who are different disallowed the suggestion that religious people might somehow be better at morality. Too, increasing numbers who identified as "spiritual" (see below) believed that authentic spirituality led to better living than did old-fashioned religion. The question of whether society needed religion to promote morality began to shift from private opinion to a public debate.

Some religious apologists in the 1990s had publicly defended the necessity of theism for rational moral commitment.[79] Dissenters pushed back. A spate of books hit the market in the late 2000s and into the 2010s—after the New Atheists had made their mark—arguing against the necessity of God and religion to be morally good. Their titles included

- *Can We Be Good Without God?* (2000)
- *Good Without God: What a Billion Nonreligious People Do Believe* (2009)
- *Morality Without God?* (2009)
- *Is Goodness Without God Good Enough?* (2009)
- *The Moral Landscape: How Science Can Determine Human Values* (2010)
- *The Ethical Project* (2011)
- *Good Without God* (2012)
- *Atheist Mind, Humanist Heart: Rewriting the Ten Commandments for the Twenty-First Century* (2014)
- *Living the Secular Life: New Answers to Old Questions* (2014)
- *The Necessity of Secularism: Why God Can't Tell Us* (2014)
- *Living a Good Life Without Religion* (2014)
- *Grace Without God: The Search for Meaning, Purpose, and Belonging in a Secular Age* (2016)[80]

It took some time for the "Good Without God" campaign to make its mark on the internet. Google searches on that exact phrase return only a handful of hits in the 1990s and mere hundreds in the 2000s. In the early 2010s, however, those numbers increased to the thousands. The book by Harvard University's humanist chaplain Greg Epstein, *Good Without God: What a Billion Nonreligious People Do Believe* (2009), was the key catalyst of the debate.[81] On the internet, where images and sound bites overwhelmed textual arguments, memes often made points more sharply than reasoned claims. Figure 7.18 depicts one meme representing the spirit of the increasingly assertive good-without-God position.

The idea that one could be moral without God enjoyed a commonsense advantage: ordinary observation revealed that there were many seemingly ethical non-religious people and some not very good religious people. By contrast, the contentions that morality required belief in God depended on more complex, philosophical arguments, like a "moral bank account" view of culture in history.[82] Given the zeitgeist, such more complex arguments were sometimes received as condemnations of non-religious people as immoral and special pleading on behalf of religion. Complicating the argument for theists was the growing movement of Americans who believed they could have God (or gods, the goddess, or other versions of divinity) without the trappings of organized religion. A "personal relationship with God" was all many post-Boomers said they needed to be good (as described in Chapter 8). Furthermore, by the 2000s, the bar on what counted as morally good was set not too high. Many teenagers I interviewed in the 2000s defined bad people

Figure 7.18 Internet meme mocking the belief that morality depends on God.

as "murderers, bank robbers, and rapists"—suggesting that only hardened criminals would not qualify as good. Morality meant not hurting others: "Just don't be a dick." More rigorous moral demands that in the past might have sent people seeking divine help—like loving one's enemies, giving liberally to the poor, praying for those who hate you, forgiving without measure—were not on the cultural radar. That lower bar also made it easier not to need God to be good.

The debate over morality's dependence on God helped shift public opinion in the "no" direction—a trend that continued up to the time of this writing. In 2002, 40% of all American adults took the view that "it is not necessary to believe in God in order to be moral and have good values."[83] In the next five years, that number inched up a bit. By 2011, the good-without-God view had grown to 49%, and, by 2017, again to 56%. In 2022, the percentage of Americans reporting that good morals and values do not depend on God had jumped again to 65%. In two decades, *one-quarter* of American adults had changed their thinking to agree with the good-without-God view. An innovative view that previously was accepted only by early adopters had gone mainstream and was embraced by two-thirds of Americans.

Some of this shift was the result of generational replacement since younger generations were significantly more likely than older to think God was not necessary for morality.[84] For instance, in 2002, 63% of 18-to-29-year-olds said "it is not necessary to believe in God in order to be moral and have good values," while 56% of 30-to-49-year-olds, 49% of 50-to-64-year-olds, and only 38% of those 65 years old and older said the same—a 25% gap between the youngest and oldest age categories. The percentage difference in 2017 between the youngest and oldest age groups was 26%.[85] These differences are mostly cohort effects, not age effects, meaning that as younger Americans replace older ones over time, increasing numbers of Americans will believe people can be good without God.

The insistence that people can be moral without religion was one of the most pervasive in our interviews. A small sample: "I found comfort going to church and learning things, but it's not spiritually supportive of me anymore. I don't think you need religion to be a good person. Having religion or a belief in a higher power can be helpful to one's mental health and well-being, but it's not necessary to be a good person," and "For anyone who is okay conforming to religion or if they're just lost, religion definitely can guide them. If you're not one of those people, you can tap into your feelings or intuition to know how to navigate life on your own without that compass," and

"No, I don't think people need religion to be moral. There are people with moral values who are not religious, they might not have the same morals as religious people or dictated by different religions, but that doesn't stop them from being moral. They could've have learned it from somewhere else." For some, the idea that God is needed to make one moral pushes them away from religion.

> I feel annoyed by the Ten Commandments when a religious person tells me I have to follow these. Because I don't have religion, yet I probably knew most of the commandments just because I'm a good person. I don't need them to know that. I know not to steal. I also feel annoyed because I don't write my rules for my kids on the wall.

This shift in public belief was not entirely happenstance—it resulted partly from good-without-God advocates actively championing that view. Seen through the theory lens of Abbot's competitive system of professions (see Chapter 3), non-religious challengers made a determined and successful effort to wrest control of cultural territory over which religion had previously established some claim to legitimate jurisdiction. Their purpose was to undercut religion and strengthen the legitimacy of secular ethics. Even then, major populations do not so dramatically change their views in a social vacuum or merely because of the publication of some books. The host of larger forces and events described in these pages set a particular sociocultural context that both motivated those good-without-God advocates to press their cause and made their arguments persuasive to many others. With the loss of its position as an important moral educator, religion was left with much less to offer Americans. Some parents with children and other adults still opted to tap into religion for moral instruction and support. But the proportion of younger generations who were forming nuclear families who might feel that need was shrinking. And the proportion of those who believed religion was advantageous for that purpose was also dwindling. The math did not work in religion's favor.

We interviewed numerous parents who had been raised in a religion, fell away from faith as they grew up, but then later decided to become involved in a religious congregation mostly for the sake of their children. Their explanations? "Even though it's not really important to me now, I have to admit it was good for me to be exposed to that as a child, and I guess I want the same for my kids." That may not be a pastor's or rabbi's preferred answer, but it is better than nothing. This dynamic, however, depends on marginally religious parents actually having had that positive experience as a child in a church, synagogue, or temple to remember. As fewer Americans have felt the need to access religion for the moral education of their children, fewer of those children will have that experience to remember and perhaps want for their own kids.

"Spiritual but Not Religious"

During the 2000s, a new counter-religious identity emerged that began to attract even more Americans: "spiritual but not religious," or just plain "spiritual," with the "not-religious" part implied. Interest in people identifying as "spiritual" took off in the 2010s. But that built on a start developed in the 2000s, especially in the second half of the decade. The "spiritual" label appealed to people who wanted to distance themselves from traditional religion but did not feel comfortable thinking of themselves as straight-up secular. "Spiritual" signaled that, even though you were not religious, you still cared about the inner life of the soul and perhaps even believed in some higher power or energy that might possibly be "out there" or "in here" within the human self. It provided a place to escape from organized religion that did not land people in a barren, meaningless existence, but instead something that felt deeper, richer, more alive. "Spiritual" had the great advantage of leaving behind all of the historical, doctrinal, and organizational baggage of traditional religion. Yet to claim the spiritual identity was a positive affirmation. One *was* something, unlike the negative meanings of atheist (not a theist), agnostic (do not know), and secularist (not governed by the sacred).

Exactly how many spiritual-but-not-religious Americans there were in the 2000s is unclear. The meaning of the term itself was nascent and unstable. Scholars, who were struggling to figure out the term's meaning and how best to study it, asked differently worded versions of survey questions, and these differences in wording affected answers.[86] For instance, the 2005 Faith and Family in America Survey asked: "Which of the following comes closest to describing your beliefs—you are religious, you are spiritual but not religious, or you are neither?" Thirty-four percent of respondents answered "spiritual but not religious."[87] The General Social Survey (GSS) has asked two separate questions: "To what extent do you consider yourself a religious person?," and "To what extent do you consider yourself a spiritual person?"[88] In 2006 and

2008, 26% of GSS respondents said they were more spiritual than religious; by 2010, the number grew to 29%.[89] The early statistics were somewhat confusing. And probably more than a few "spiritual" Americans at the time were uncertain themselves. But the picture has since become clearer. In 2017, a Pew Research Center report showed that 27% of Americans were "spiritual but not religious." That identity was growing evenly across men and women, white individuals and people of color, Democrats and Republicans.[90] What is now clear is that something new was afoot that a substantial minority of especially young Americans found appealing.[91] And whatever else it was, it was "not religious."

Media, scholarly, and internet attention to the developing "spiritual" trend lagged behind Americans' identification with the term on the ground. Media references to the term increased in the 2000s (see Figure 7.19), but the absolute numbers are not large. The same is true of books and scholarly publications on "spiritual but not religious" (see Figure 7.20). Google internet hits on the phrase (Figure 7.21) likewise begin to grow in the 2000s but not at the pace we might have expected until the 2010s. By 2010, cumulative hits only numbered around 2,000.

Many of the post-Boomers we interviewed described their shift from being religious to being spiritual and their greater satisfaction with their spirituality: "People refer to 'spirituality' now. Religion is a negative connotation for me. I think spirituality is more what I'm in line with at this point in my life," one told us. Another said that "Americans are becoming less religious,

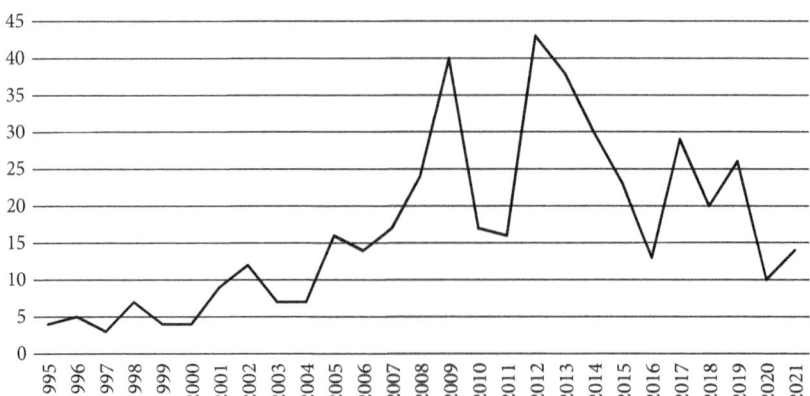

Figure 7.19 Media references to "spiritual but not religious," 1995–2021.
Source: Nexus Uni corpus

THE 2000S: OBSOLESCENCE ASSURED   225

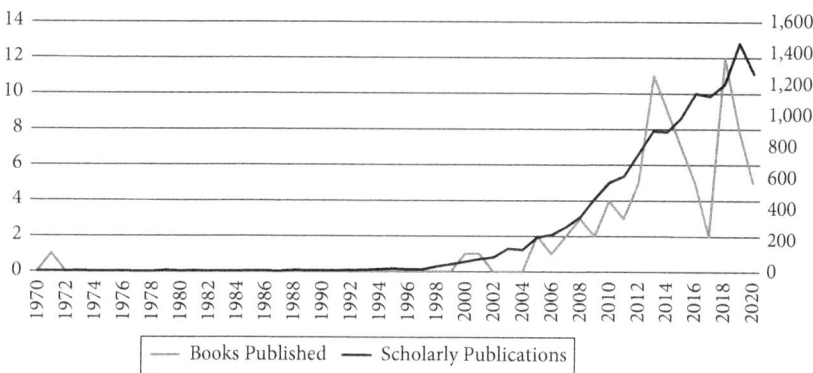

Figure 7.20 "Spiritual but not religious" books and scholarly publications by year, 1970–2020.
Source: The Library of Congress, Google Books, Amazon.com, Google Scholar.

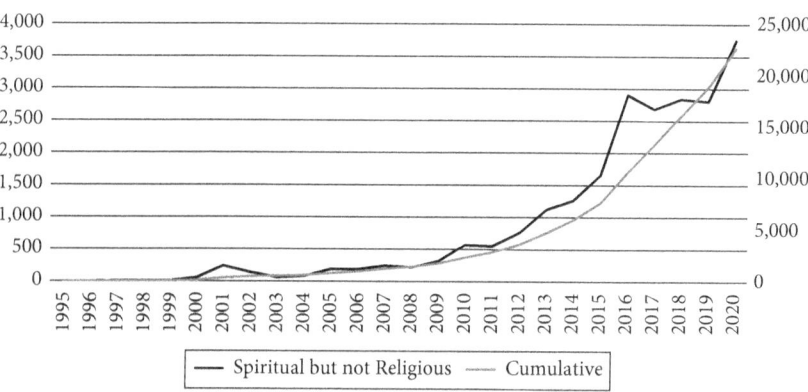

Figure 7.21 Google internet hits on "spiritual but not religious" by year, 1995–2020.

but not less spiritual. People are always gonna crave guidance or a higher power, and people are just more open-minded about different ways to fill that void. The big-box religions just aren't appealing, so they're looking in different areas to fulfill their needs." Another clarified:

> I'm not into religion that much. I'm into spirituality. Religion in my opinion is man-written rules about spirituality. I learned from a young age differences between different religions. To me spirituality is different, and I can find it if I go to temple or with my friends to other places of worship, I can find that same feeling.

And yet another:

> I started realizing there's a lot more to the spiritual side of things that aren't necessarily religious, like being spiritual without being religious. That was where I started to believe you don't necessarily have to believe in God, you can just enjoy life for what it is, seeing birth, life, death, and how that cycle is repeated. There's more to enjoying life than just finding answers, like learning how to just live.

What matters most for our story is that, in addition to the new survey-answer category of "not religious" (the "nones") marking out a growing space for itself on the American non- and post-religious identity field, another, related identity had also entered and was staking out its own expanding space, too.[92] The competition for religion got even bigger. Whereas "religion" picked up a host of negative associations after September 11, "spirituality" created a new option for a quasi-religious affiliation that benefits from an array of positive vibes. The innovation adoption of the acronym "SBNR" as a new religious identity proceeded rapidly from early adopters into the early majority population. It spread diffusely throughout the culture like particulate matter. It was not quite the dawning of the Age of Aquarius. But it helped secure religion's relegation to obsolescence.[93]

The Continued Rise of the Religious "Nones"

A dramatic increase in the number of Americans declaring themselves "not religious" began, as we have seen, in 1991 (see Figure 5.4). That growth in the religious "nones" continued throughout the 2000s (see Figure 1.5). As it did, writers and commentators began paying increased attention, giving the phenomenon more public visibility, helping to make it a consideration for additional prospective "nones." The number of books published on the topic showed a significant increase in the 2000s (see Figure 7.22). Scholarly publications, which usually lag behind popular discussions, did not pick up until the following decade. Figure 7.23 shows internet references to the rise of the non-religious from 1995 to 2020, both by year (hit counts indexed on the left) and cumulatively (on the right). There we see an increase of nearly 20,000 hits during the 2000s, which then takes off enormously the following decade.

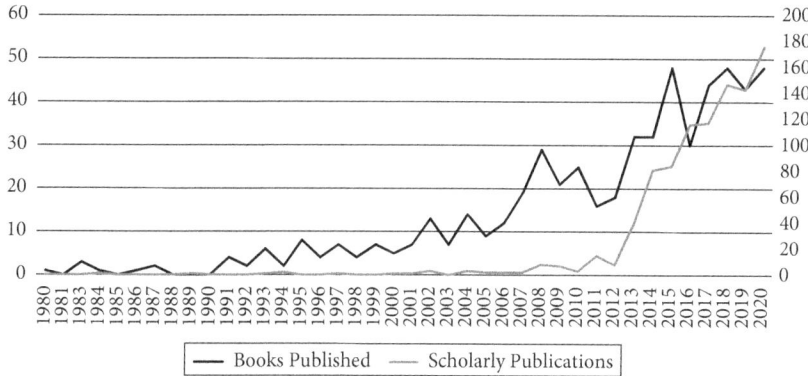

Figure 7.22 "Rise of the non-religious" books and scholarly publications by year, 1980–2020.
Source: The Library of Congress, Google Books, Amazon.com, Google Scholar.

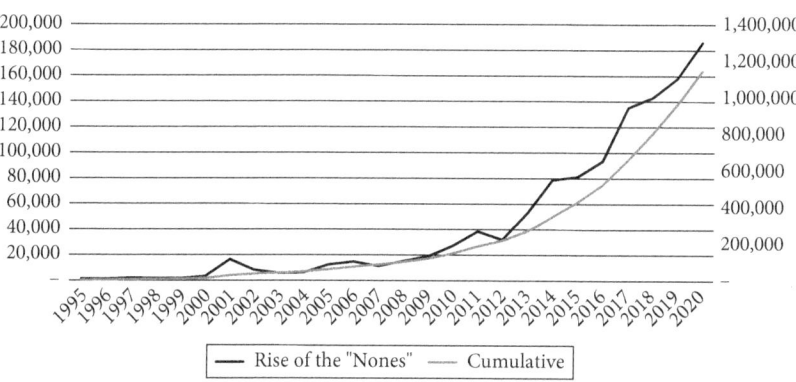

Figure 7.23 Google internet hits on the "rise of the non-religious" by year, 1995–2020.

One question to ask of my analysis is whether perhaps the public focus on Americans leaving religion (Figures 5.4, 7.20, and 7.21) was perhaps matched by another emphasis on abandoning religious unbelief and becoming religious, thus offsetting the cultural impact of the rise of the "nones." To test that idea, I compared the number of internet hits on "ex-religious" with the same for "ex-atheist." Figure 7.24 shows the results. We see clearly there that internet references to departures from religion outstripped those to departures from atheism, especially in the 2010s. The latter did not balance out the

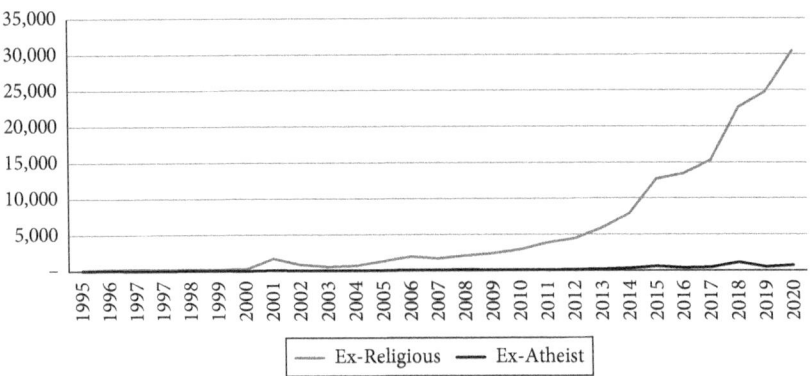

Figure 7.24 Google internet hits on "ex-religious" and "ex-atheist" by year, 1995–2020.

former in public discourse because it was not doing so in real life. Massively, more Americans were exiting religion than joining it.

With the unrelenting growth of religious "nones" in the 2000s, the snowballing or bandwagon effects I described in the previous chapter continued unabated. Religious nones begat more religious nones.[94]

Conclusion

Most of the social forces that rendered traditional religion obsolete arose outside of and appeared to have nothing to do with religion—the New Atheism and the "Good Without God" movement being the two exceptions here. At the time their ramifications for religion were not particularly clear, nor were the most effective possible responses to them. Religious actors also had little capacity to prevent or control them.

A complete account of religion's obsolescence cannot leave matters there, however. Other developments and events within religion itself were also crucial in its demise.

8
Religious Self-Destructions

By the beginning of the new millennium, traditional American religion had been battered from all sides by large-scale social forces and was badly injured. But what finally did it in was a series of self-inflicted wounds. American evangelicalism played an especially important role in that, primarily because, by that time, it had risen to become the dominant American religion in cultural attention and influence and so held an outsized importance in the cultural imagination. In the minds of many, this prominence made evangelicalism stand in for "religion" broadly, such that problems within evangelicalism in particular became problems for "religion" generally. Evangelicalism thus plays a leading role in this chapter.

Religious Scandals

Beginning in the late 1980s, scores of public scandals rocked religious communities as religious leaders were exposed for having committed various sexual, financial, and other wrongdoings. For more than two decades, scandals touched almost every religious tradition in the United States, demoralizing the faithful and disgracing leaders. Many were very high-profile, others more regional and local. An important characteristic of these scandals was the seemingly continual stream of revelations that gave rise to them. As soon as anyone thought they could believe the bad news was finally halted, another story broke, adding to the litany of dishonor and outrage. The moral and legal breaches were so recurrent they began to seem systemic.[1]

Scandalous behavior by religious figures is nothing new. But three factors increased the number and impact of public revelations of religious transgressions. First, the rise of digital recording technologies and the internet made uncovering and publicizing religious misbehaviors much easier. Second, the media stopped steering clear of coverage of religious wrongs, growing increasingly bold in reporting religious misconduct. Third, the public visibility of certain religious figures and their sanctimonious claims to righteousness invited antagonists to look actively for ways to take them down.

Whatever the causes, the cultural consequences for the American public, especially younger generations, were the same: massive damage. The scandals violated most of the virtues believed to make religion good. They demonstrated that religion did not make people moral, did not help its own leaders cope with life's challenges and temptations, did not promote social peace and harmony, and did not model virtuous behavior for others. In most cases, religious leaders not only did wrong, they also irreparably harmed innocent others. The scandals just ruined religion's credibility.

The biggest and most protracted religious atrocities of this period occurred within the Roman Catholic Church, where it was revealed that priests had sexually abused minors and that the Church had covered it up. Numerous seemingly disconnected cases of allegations, revelations, inquiries, hearings, confessions, verdicts, and apologies over the abuse of children by Catholic priests in many countries around the world had surfaced for some decades before the scandal blew wide open. Until the early 2000s, the handling of allegations of sexual abuse was mostly left up to individual bishops, not the Vatican or national associations. The issue of child sexual abuse by US Catholic clergy became public in 1985, after a priest in Louisiana pled guilty to 11 counts of molestation of boys. The media, the public, and some scholars then began to pay increased attention to such allegations during the latter 1980s and the 1990s.[2] An investigation by reporters from *The Boston Globe* in 2002 broke open the case in the United States and led to widespread media reporting on the issue.[3] Not only were a growing number of priests found to have sexually abused minors for decades—most in the 1960s and 1970s—but a pattern also emerged of Church leaders covering up those cases. Further reporting by *The Dallas Morning News* revealed, contrary to denials by Church officials, that Catholic authorities had moved many hundreds of accused priests to other parishes, dioceses, and countries, where they were allowed to minister unsupervised in settings involving minors. In a few hundred such cases, leaders clearly sought to evade law enforcement.[4] Church leaders were found to have failed to report crimes by clergy to the police and to have resisted cooperation with legal investigations.[5] Coverage of those wrongdoings emboldened other victims of abuse to come forward with allegations of abuse, generating more lawsuits and criminal investigations.[6]

The United States has among the highest number of cases of accused priests in the world. An early 2000s study commissioned by the US bishops reported that more than 10,500 individual victims of sexual abuse credibly accused nearly 4,400 US Catholic priests and deacons in active ministry.[7] A grand jury in Pennsylvania, in 2018, issued an 884-page report stating that more than 300 priests in most of the Catholic dioceses in Pennsylvania sexually abused more than 1,000 children, adding that there "were likely to be thousands more" victims.[8] The report said that Church officials followed a "playbook for concealing the truth" and minimized the abuse with phrases such as "inappropriate contact" rather than "rape." Because of the time that had elapsed since the abuses, only two priests in the state faced criminal charges. Josh Shapiro, the state attorney general, said, "They protected their institution at all costs. As the grand jury found, the church showed a complete disdain for victims."[9]

Popes apologized. The Vatican was occasionally defensive.[10] Several bishops and hundreds of priests resigned or were laicized. Almost all avoided legal consequences. Catholic laity pushed for reforms.[11] Some were enacted, but many were not. Plaintiffs filed thousands of civil lawsuits against the Church, which paid out more than $3 billion in settlements. Numerous Catholic dioceses filed for bankruptcy.[12] The scandal, after breaking open in 2002, saw national news coverage of it continue regularly for more than two decades. As of this writing, new revelations of past abuses and charges of ongoing abuse surface regularly.[13]

Other high-profile religious scandals over the 1990s and 2000s involved prominent Protestant leaders, especially in white evangelical and Pentecostal circles. Research shows that sexual abuse occurred no less in Protestant churches than in Catholic parishes and seminaries.[14] Again, as the cases continued to pile up, the explanation that these were just a few isolated incidents became increasingly difficult to defend. The power and status of religious leadership seemed to lend itself to the temptation to lead a double life. Some of the more notorious cases of white Protestant scandals—those that showed up in national news and with which readers may be familiar—are itemized in Table 8.1.[15] Every scandal listed here and others besides were covered in the national news, providing plenty of opportunity for Americans to see religion's dirty laundry aired.

The white conservative Protestant scandals just kept coming. For example, a damning 2022 report from a seven-month independent investigation into how the Southern Baptist Convention (SBC)—the largest Protestant denomination in the United States—handled allegations of pastoral sexual abuses revealed that denominational leaders had been keeping

Table 8.1 Major US Conservative Protestant Leader Scandals (1985–2017)

Year	Leader	Scandal	Consequences
1985–1986	Peter Popoff, televangelist, faith healer, prosperity preacher	Exposed for burglarizing his own offices to explain missing funds raised to send Bibles to the Soviet Union	Declining ratings and donations, ministry bankruptcy, debt of $1.5 million
		Exposed for using a concealed earpiece to receive radio messages from his wife, who gave him information about audience members during religious services while falsely claiming in "miraculous healing sermons" that God revealed this information to him so that Popoff could cure them through faith healing	Comeback in late 1990s targeting Black television audiences, in mid-2000s selling healing "Miracle Spring Water" in paid television infomercials
Subject of satire in multiple media
1987–1989	Jim Bakker, host of PTL Club televangelism ministry	Payoff of $279,000 to church secretary, Jessica Hahn, to silence accusations of his drugging and raping her, 1980	Resigned from PTL, taken over by Jerry Falwell Sr.
Dismissed from Assemblies of God ministry
		Used $350,000 raised on the air to fund overseas missions, instead used to pay for part his Christian theme park, Heritage USA	Found guilty of 24 felony counts of mail fraud, wire fraud, and conspiracy, sentenced to 45 years and $500,000 fine
		Misused $1.3 million of funds raised on the air for personal benefit, 1980–1983	
		Embezzled $3.4 million of Heritage USA funds as a "bonus," 1987	
		Allegations of homosexual and bisexual activities, 1988	
1988, 1991	Jimmy Swaggart, televangelist, musician	Exposed in 1988 meeting a prostitute, Debra Murphree, in Louisiana motel, as a retaliation by defrocked preacher, Marvin Gorman, whom Swaggart had accused of multiple adulterous affairs	Gave a tearful "I have sinned" message on live television, apologizing to his family, congregation, TV audience, and God
Suspended and defrocked from ministry by Assemblies of God
		Exposed in 1991, in California, with a prostitute, Rosemary Garcia, whom he picked up in his car to have sex	Subject of satire in multiple media

Table 8.1 Continued

Year	Leader	Scandal	Consequences
1991	Robert Tilton, televangelist, prosperity preacher	Exposed by ABC News for throwing away "Success-N-Life" viewer prayer requests without reading or praying for them, keeping the accompanying money sent to the ministry, totaling to an estimated $80 million a year	Television ministry cancelled 1993, multiple fraud lawsuits by several ministry donors Revived ministry in late-1990s, grossing $24 million a year Subject of satire in multiple media
1992	Michael Warnke, evangelist, Christian comedian	Exposed after gaining national fame for false claims about being a Christian convert from and an expert on Satanism, earned graduate degrees, number of times wounded in Vietnam, drug dealing, alcoholism, sexual orgies, and ministry financial needs	Record contract cancelled, ministry shut down
1992, 2001, 2007	Earl Paulk, megachurch pastor, Cathedral at Chapel Hill	Exposed for multiple counts of child molestation, adultery, and incestuous abuse	Died of cancer during court trials
1994	Paul Jennings Hill, former Presbyterian (OPC, PCA) pastor	Murdered abortion doctor John Britton and his bodyguard, James Barrett, outside abortion clinic with a 12-gauge pump-action shotgun fired at close range	Found guilty of first-degree premeditated murder, executed by lethal injection in 2003
1996, 2021	Kent Hovind, fundamentalist evangelist, Young Earth creationist advocate, conspiracy theorist, tax protester	Found guilty of not paying federal taxes, 1996 Arrested for assault, battery, and burglary in an incident with a ministry secretary, 2002 58 felony convictions for failing to pay taxes, obstructing federal agents, and structuring cash transactions, 2006 Convicted of domestic violence against his estranged wife, 2021	Charges dropped Sentenced to 10 years in prison and $600,000 to be paid in restitution Sentenced to one year in jail, fined $500, ordered to pay restitution for medical expenses
1998	Bob Moorehead, pastor, Overlake Christian Church	Exposed for multiple sexual assaults on young men in his church congregation, masturbating in a public bathroom	Investigated by church leadership, resigned pastoral position

(*continued*)

Table 8.1 Continued

Year	Leader	Scandal	Consequences
1999	Gerald Payne, Greater Ministries International, evangelical financial investor	Exposed for running a Ponzi scheme in an affinity fraud taking almost $500 million from 18,000 investors, promising 200% returns in 17 months based on promises in the Bible, all money lost	Leaders sentenced to 12–27 years in prison
1999	Baptist Foundation of Arizona, Southern Baptist investment firm	Bankruptcy due to affinity investment fraud including Ponzi schemes and cooking books, leaving a $460 million investors' liability	Eight participants found guilty in criminal trial, multiple prison sentences, and fines of $159 million
2006	Ted Haggard, president, National Association of Evangelicals, church pastor, informal advisor to President George W. Bush	Exposed by a male prostitute and masseur, Mike Jones, for paid sex in a hotel and for purchasing and using crystal methamphetamine. Exposed in 2009 for an "inappropriate relationship" with a young man who attended his church in 2006	Fired from head pastor of his church. Resigned from the National Association of Evangelicals
2006	Lonnie Latham, senior pastor, South Tulsa Baptist Church	Arrested for propositioning a plainclothes police officer for oral sex in an area known for cruising related to male prostitution, claimed to be ministering to police but later admitted guilt	Resigned from pastorate, executive committee of the Southern Baptist Convention, and as the recording secretary of the Southern Baptist General Convention of Oklahoma, found not guilty in court for reasons of evidence
2009	Tony Alamo, founder Tony Alamo Christian Ministries	Convicted of 10 counts of child rape and transporting minors across state lines for sex	Sentenced to 175 years in prison, 27 ministry properties forfeited to pay $2.5 million in restitution to victims
2010	George Reckers, psychologist, Southern Baptist minister, board member, Family Research Council, anti-gay lobbyist	Exposed for hiring a 20-year-old "rent boy" through Rentboy.com website as a companion on a 10-day European vacation, accused of involving sexual massages and nude photos	Resigned as officer and scientific advisor of National Association for Research & Therapy of Homosexuality

RELIGIOUS SELF-DESTRUCTIONS   235

Table 8.1 Continued

Year	Leader	Scandal	Consequences
2010	Marcus Lamb, televangelist, prosperity preacher, CEO, Daystar Television Network, COVID-19 vaccine denier	Exposed for extramarital affairs when three Daystar employee women asked for $7.5 million in exchange for silence on the matter	Affairs publicly disclosed on television, no criminal charges filed, civil suits and countersuits filed but later dropped
		Later exposed by an *Inside Edition* investigation for purchasing a 14-seat Gulfstream V aircraft worth $9 million for family vacations, using $3.9 million received by Daystar from US government COVID-19 "Paycheck Protection Program"	Paid back funds with interest
2011	Trinity Baptist Church, Chuck Phelps, Concord, NH	Senior pastor, Chuck Phelps, covered up the rape of a 15-year-old babysitter, Tina Anderson, by a church member, Earnest Willis, which resulted in a pregnancy, by forcing Anderson to "confess her sin" to the congregation, sending her to a Baptist family in Colorado during her pregnancy, and pressuring her to give her child up for adoption	Featured in an ABC TV *20/20* program on religious abuse
			Willis found guilty of four counts of forcible rape and felonious sexual assault, and sentenced to 15–30 years in prison
2014	Bill Gothard, founder of the Institute in Basic Life Principles (IBLP), Basic Youth Conflicts	Accused by 34 women of sexual harassment and molestation, with some incidents allegedly occurring when the victims were minors	Barred from serving in any counseling, leadership, or board role in IBLP
2014	Mark Driscoll, megachurch pastor, Mars Hill Church	Accused of plagiarism, psychological abuse, manipulating book sales numbers, bullying, misogyny, public vulgarity	Removed from pastoral leadership positions
			Book sales suspended
2014, 2017	Bob Coy, founding pastor, Calvary Chapel Fort Lauderdale	Exposed for committing adultery and a pornography addiction	Resigned his pastorate, divorced, submitted to a "restoration process"
		Accused of sexually molesting a 4-year-old girl, continuing to her teenage years	Report unproven, charges never filed

(*continued*)

Table 8.1 Continued

Year	Leader	Scandal	Consequences
2015, 2021	Josh Duggar, reality television personality, conservative Christian values advocate	Exposed for molesting five underage girls, including four siblings, when he was aged 14–15 Exposed by data breach for subscribing to Ashley Madison marital affairs dating website, then admitting to watching internet pornography and being unfaithful to his wife Found guilty of receiving and possessing child pornography	*19 Kids and Counting* TV show cancelled Voluntarily checked into an addiction rehabilitation center Sentenced to 12 years in prison
2017	Ravi Zacharias, founder, Ravi Zacharias International Ministries, apologist	Exposed by multiple sources of serious sexual abuse, misconduct, and predation, mostly posthumously Exposed for misrepresenting his experiences at University of Cambridge and the University of Oxford	Widely denounced, all related organizations removed his name, all authored books discontinued

Sources: Select religious scandals covered by *The New York Times*, *The Chicago Tribune*, and *The Los Angeles Times*, *The Seattle Times*, *Time*, and *Newsweek* magazines.

a confidential list of alleged abusers in a 205-page database, covering 2000 to 2019, which included more than 700 cases. The investigation's final report stated that survivors who reported abuses "met, time and time again, with resistance, stonewalling, and even outright hostility" from the denomination's highest leadership, which was "singularly focused on avoiding liability for the SBC."[16] This was the same denomination that urged Millennial youth in the 1990s to take pledges to protect their sexual purity by remaining virgins until marriage.

Scandals erupted in other religious traditions, too. For example, in 1998, federal prosecutors indicted Henry Lyons, the former president of the National Baptist Convention, the largest predominantly Black denomination in the United States, for fraud, extortion, money laundering, conspiracy, and tax evasion. After agreeing to a plea bargain, Lyons was sentenced in 1999 to more than five years in jail for misappropriating more than $4 million. In 2008, Walter Ronnie Sailor Jr., pastor of Greater New Light Missionary Baptist Church, resigned after a government sting operation caught him laundering money that he believed were proceeds from the sale of cocaine, which he then tried to cover up, laundering $250,000 through false loans using church property as collateral. Sailor pled guilty and was sentenced to five years imprisonment. In 2010, Eddie Long, senior pastor of the Georgia megachurch New Birth Missionary Baptist Church, was accused by five men in his congregation of using his pastoral influence to coerce them into sexual relationships with him, compensating the men from the church's payroll; buying them cars, gifts, and overseas trips; and using scripture to justify their sexual activities. Long refused to address the allegations directly. Lawsuits and countersuits ensued, all of which were settled out of court.[17]

Mainline Protestants were not spared. In 1999, Harvard Divinity School dean Ronald Thiemann resigned from office after a computer technician found thousands of pornographic images on his university-owned personal use computer. In 2001, respected University of Minnesota New Testament scholar and Episcopal priest Richard Pervo was arrested when investigators found thousands of images of child pornography on his university work computer. Pervo pled guilty to counts of possession and distribution of child pornography, was sentenced to one year in a state workhouse and eight years of probation, and resigned his university post. Ellen Cooke was convicted in 1996 of embezzling more than $1.5 million from the national offices of the Episcopal Church while serving as treasurer and for tax evasion.[18]

American Jewish communities also produced their share of scandals. Fred Neulander, for instance, a Reform Jewish rabbi from New Jersey, was convicted in 1994 of hiring two hit men to murder his wife, during which time he was also involved in an affair with a married Philadelphia radio personality. The trial was broadcast on live television and became a media spectacle. Neulander was sentenced to 30 years in prison. In 2000, Orthodox rabbi and Yeshiva high school principal Baruch Lanner resigned after being exposed for physically, sexually, and emotionally abusing scores of teenagers, male and female, for decades. Lanner was convicted in 2002 of abusing two teenage girls in his school and sentenced to seven years in prison. The case was covered by the *New York Times* and multiple Jewish publications. Over the next decade a number of other Jewish leaders would make similar headlines for financial and sexual scandals. Milton Balkany, member of the Orthodox community, was exposed for misappropriation of charitable funds in 2003, as well as hedge fund extortion, blackmail, wire fraud, and making false statements in 2010. An Orthodox rabbi, Joel Yehuda Kolko, was charged with sexually abusing two six-year-olds and forcing an adult former student to touch him during a school visit. Baltimore rabbi, Menachem Youlus, was arrested for mail fraud and wire fraud for falsely claiming that, as a "Jewish Indiana Jones," he had rescued Holocaust-era Torah scrolls from Eastern Europe, which he sold at inflated prices. Washington, DC, rabbi Barry Freundel was arrested and convicted for committing 52 counts of voyeurism of women in a *mikveh* (a Jewish ritual bath), sentenced to 6.5 years in prison, fined $13,000, and forced to settle a class action lawsuit for $14.25 million. The New York "Divorce Coercion Gang" was a Haredi Jewish group, nine of whom were arrested in 2013 for kidnapping and sometimes torturing Jewish men in the New York City area to force them to grant their wives religious divorces.

Fundamentalist Church of Latter Day Saints (LDS, Mormon) leaders contributed as well. Ervil LeBaron, for instance, was the leader of a schismatic, polygamous LDS group who had married 13 women. He was apprehended in Mexico, in 1979, for ordering the murders of numerous rivals. LeBaron was sentenced to life in prison, from which, before committing suicide, he directed more murders—all of which was covered in multiple nonfiction books, a number of television series, and a documentary film. In 1989, the leader of a schismatic LDS sect in Ohio, Jeffrey Lundgren, orchestrated the murder of a family of five, was arrested, and executed, with many of his co-conspirators receiving long prison sentences. The affair was covered in the press and in two books. In the mid-2000s, Warren Jeffs, leader of another schismatic, polygamous group in Utah, was arrested for multiple counts of child sexual assault, incest, sexual conduct with minors, rape as an accomplice, and sentenced to life in prison. That story was written about in many books and covered in numerous documentaries, including a Netflix series. Warren Jeffs was replaced in leadership after his arrest by Wendell Loy Nielsen, who was then indicted on three counts of bigamy, having allegedly married a total of 34 women besides his legal wife and marrying girls as young as 12 years. Nielsen was convicted in 2012, sentenced to 10 years in prison, and ordered to pay a $30,000 fine.[19]

Other bizarre cases of killings and abductions by religious people reinforced the impression that religion was more interested in creating evil rather than saving people from it. These include Andrea Yates, who, in 2001, drowned her five children in order, she said, "to save them from eternal hell," a discourse she learned from her devout evangelical husband. There was Eric Rudolf, the Olympic Park bomber, whose domestic terrorism during the 1996 Atlanta Olympics killed two and injured more than 100 people.

Rudolf told police that his bombings were motivated by religious opposition to abortion and "the homosexual agenda," quoting Bible passages to justify his actions and saying, "I was born a Catholic, and with forgiveness I hope to die one." They also include Brian Mitchell, who, in 2002, abducted 14-year-old Elizabeth Smart at knifepoint from her home in Salt Lake City and held her in captivity for nine months before she was discovered and rescued. Mitchell had formerly been a member of the LDS Church before he was excommunicated for claiming to be a prophet who received divine visions, after which he dressed like Jesus and panhandled on city streets. Many of these perpetrators clearly suffer from mental illnesses, so religion cannot be blamed directly for their crimes. But their connection to religion inevitably strengthened the association in the public's mind between religion and fanaticism.

The most infamous and widely covered event linking religion, madness, and deadly violence during this period was the 51-day siege by federal agents of David Koresh's Branch Davidian compound in Waco, Texas, in 1993. In an initial failed federal assault on the compound, four agents of the Bureau of Alcohol, Tobacco, and Firearms (ATF) and six Branch Davidians died in exchanges of gunfire. Seven weeks later, during a second federal assault using tear gas and mechanized battering rams, the compound was set ablaze. How the fire started remains in dispute. The extended standoff gave the media ample opportunity to report details of the case. Koresh, we learned, had been a born-again Christian in the Southern Baptist Church and later joined his mother's denomination, the Seventh-Day Adventist Church. He moved to Waco in 1981 and joined the Branch Davidians, a splinter group. After years of disputes and internal power struggles among leaders, claims to divine revelations, and violent conflicts, Koresh came to lead the group and own the compound where they lived. He changed his birth name, Vernon Howell, to David Koresh, after Israel's greatest king (David) and the Persian king Cyrus the Great (Koresh in Hebrew), who set the captive Israelites free, thus "professing himself to be the spiritual descendant of King David, a messianic figure carrying out a divinely commissioned errand."[20] Subsequent allegations of child abuse, statutory rape, and firearms violations brought federal agents to investigate, and the world watched on live television as federal agents attacked and the inferno consumed those barricaded inside. Koresh, 14 other adults, and five children died of gunshot wounds, and one three-year-old died of stab wounds to the chest. The entire catastrophe underscored the dangers not only of government mishandlings of deviant groups but also, more broadly, religion's capacity—if not propensity—to produce frightening, fanatical, and deadly ideas.[21]

Other cases of religious scandals continued to stagger the public. Jean Vanier, for example, was the beloved Catholic founder of L'Arche, an international network of communities for people with developmental disabilities, and an influential author. After his death in 2019, it came out that Vanier had engaged in "manipulative and emotionally abusive" sexual relations with six women in France between 1970 and 2005. In 2023, a second report said that Vanier had initiated sexual acts or intimate gestures—such as caressing breasts or kissing mouths without consent—with 25 different women. Those who knew Vanier, who had devoted his life to living with and caring for the disabled, or had been inspired by his writings could hardly believe the news. Another shocking scandal concerned the Mennonite theologian John Howard Yoder, probably the most influential pacifist Anabaptist thinker since the Reformation. Rumors that Yoder had sexually harassed, abused, and assaulted women had circulated in Christian orbits for decades, and Yoder was finally publicly confronted in 1992. Yoder submitted to the discipline of his church conference but also suggested that he was innocent and the victim of a conspiracy. He died in 1997. Eventually, it came out that Yoder had sexually abused more than 100 women during the 1970s and 1980s, and that leaders at the seminary where Yoder taught knew about his abuses but did not act on them properly.[22] The contrast between Yoder's compelling call for Christian nonviolence and his practice of sexual abuse was stunning. Americans less enamored with religion generally did not find it surprising, given the prior decades of accumulating reports about scandals from seemingly all religious quarters.

One of the most astonishing scandals worth mentioning because of its connection to the Christian Right, although it falls past the two decades of our focus, was the downfall of Jerry Falwell Jr., the son of the founder of the Moral Majority in the 1970s and president of the conservative evangelical Liberty University, which his father had founded and built into a major enterprise. From at least 2012 to 2014 and perhaps until 2018, Falwell's wife, Becki, had a sexual affair with a twentysomething pool boy, Giancarlo Granda, who worked at a luxury hotel in Miami Beach. Falwell allegedly not only knew of the affair but also approved of it and, by some accounts, enjoyed watching his wife having sex with Granda. Falwell allegedly boasted in work circles about his own sexual prowess and shared with certain male friends somewhat salacious photographs of his wife—which he later asked

RELIGIOUS SELF-DESTRUCTIONS   241

Michael Cohen (who was also Donald Trump's "fixer") to find and dispose of. In 2020, the pool boy, in possession of damning audiotapes, emails, and texts, attempted to blackmail Falwell and his wife for a pile of money, threatening to expose the affair. They refused payment, the affair went public, and Falwell and his wife made an open statement admitting to parts of the matter. Compromising photographs then began circulating publicly, including one of Falwell with a younger woman not his wife, both in states of partial undress. Falwell resigned his post as president of Liberty University. Lawsuits and countersuits followed. Falwell's career ended not simply in disgrace but in a manner that exemplified behaviors normalized by the third sexual revolution.[23]

The continuing list of religious public scandals during the 1990s and 2000s and beyond is very long and not necessary to continue to detail. They include additional religious leaders from Willow Creek Church, non-denominational churches, Jehovah's Witness, Black Islam, Wicca, prosperity preachers, Baptist denominations, Hindu movements, the Nation of Islam, and various new religious movements. Some of the names of the ignominious, which may be familiar to some readers, include Bill Hybels, Gilbert Bilezikian, Matthew Hale, Larry Lea, Khalid Abdul Muhammad, John Paulk, Walter Fauntroy, Kirtanananda Swami, Dwight York, Yusuf Bey, Terry Hornbuckle, Bernie Ward, Creflo Dollar, Coy Prevette, Barry Minkow, David Justin Freeman, Kenny Klein, Brother Stair, and Keith Raniere.

These are individual cases of religious scandals reported in the national news. Just how prevalent were discussions of religious scandals in the US media? Figure 8.1 shows total counts of references to keywords concerning religious scandals in the large corpus of media. There we see a moderate number of references to religious scandals in the 1990s, which peaked whenever new major revelations occurred. The numbers jump with *The Boston Globe* reporting on the Catholic priest abuse and cover-up scandal in 2002. During the 2000s, the number of media references to religious scandals doubled, with peaks at new revelations jumping much higher. The point here, however, is not to explain individual spikes and drops in numbers, but rather to demonstrate extensive media attention to religious scandals and its growth during the 2000s.

Figure 8.2 shows the number of internet hits returned by Google searches on the four key phrases "priest abuse," "clergy abuse," "church scandal," and "religious scandal" from 1995 to 2022. Between 1995 and 1999, those phrases showed up on the internet 162 times. By the end of 2009, their cumulative

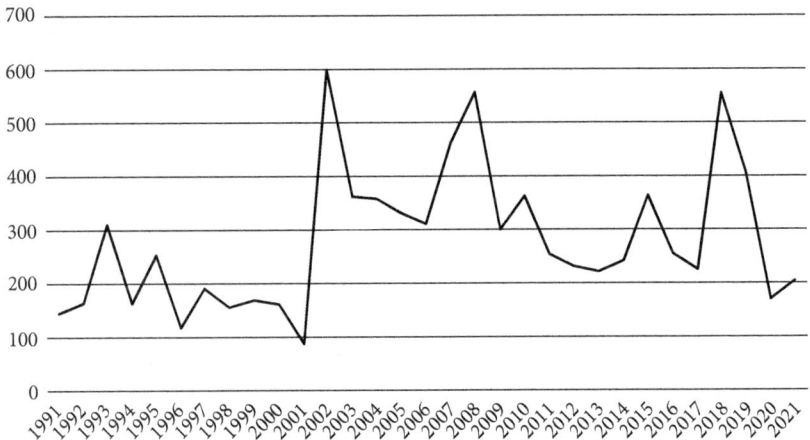

Figure 8.1 Media references to religious scandals by year, 1991–2021.
Source: Nexis Uni corpus.

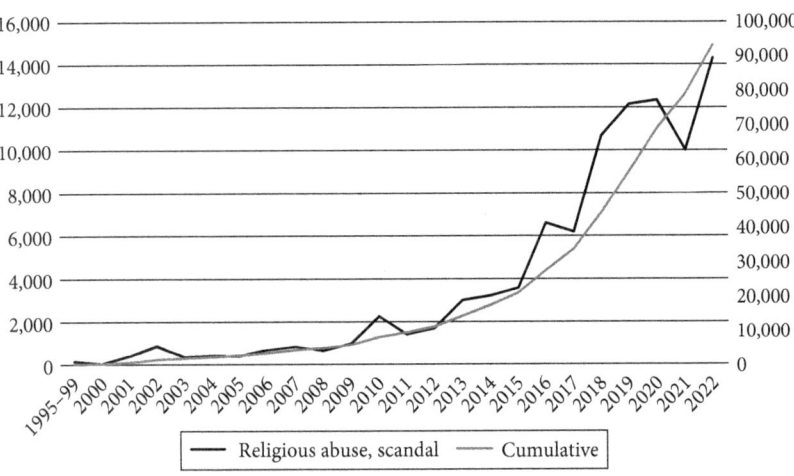

Figure 8.2 Google internet hits on religious abuse and scandal keywords.
Source: Google searches on "priest abuse," "clergy abuse," "church scandal," "religious scandal."

hits added to 5,766, and, by 2019, 46,499 hits. The cumulative total by 2022 was 93,135 hits on those four key phrases. This figure of internet coverage of religious scandals in the 1990s and 2000s appears dwarfed by the surge in mentions after 2015, but the absolute count in our two key decades still numbers in the thousands. Anyone reading internet news and discussions in the 2000s would easily have come across information about religious scandals.

The Digital Revolution again played an important role in these larger dynamics. (Lest readers suspect that the linguistic promiscuity of the internet would return large numbers of hits on searches of just about any keywords, I also for comparison searched for hits on "non-religious scandal," "ex-religious scandal," "atheist scandal," "secularism scandal," "freethinker scandal," "apostate scandal," and those same six modifiers combined with "abuse." That returned a mere 22 hits for all of 1995–2022. Meaning that, for every one internet mention of an explicitly non-religious abuse or scandal, Google returned 4,233 mentions of religious abuse or scandal.) Of course, the internet provided thousands of discussions of scandalous abuses in schools, colleges, youth organizations, workplaces, and so on. But it was impossible to isolate specifically not-religious hits because many of the incidents discussed involved schools, clubs, and other settings that were religious. This does not mean that the internet discriminated against religion by underreporting non-religious abuses and scandals, simply that religious abuses and scandals were highly visibly present on the internet during the crucial decades in question. What we can say is that the technological capacity and cultural stomach for exposing scandalous behaviors had increased.

How did this "interminable parade of institutional failures" contribute to traditional religion's obsolescence?[24] I noted above that the scandals violated most of the reasons that Americans think religion can be good. Not only did they fail to demonstrate the potential value and virtues of religion, they also proved the very opposite. They gave the lie to the idea that religion specializes in making people good. Religious scandals contributed to the shift toward negative associations attached to "religion" after September 11. They validated charges of hypocrisy against religion—one of the most damning critiques in Americans' minds. They gave lethal ammunition to the New Atheists. The continual stream of revelations of wrongdoings suggested the possibility that religion had somehow become more corrupt in recent times.[25] It added weight to the pile of depressing news that emotionally burdened (especially young) people in the 2000s and made it increasingly hard for people to trust American leaders and institutions. Religious scandals were not the straw but the log that broke the camel's back.

References to religious scandals peppered our interviews with post-Millennials, usually unprompted, as passing remarks accompanied by eyerolls and head shakes. A few offered a bit more than an eyeroll, with comments like, "One evangelical comes to mind unfortunately who had some massive scandals going on, which just made me think, okay, well, there's another guy who says he is so religious but he's behaving badly behind the scenes." Not all mentions of religious scandals came from the national news; some were respondents' personal experiences.

> I worked at the church camp surrounded by people I thought believed in the same thing. Then it turned into sexual harassment or abuse at camp for me, personally. That has been so hard for me to overcome, growing up and seeing, hearing all about that. That was a turning point for me. Then going to college and hearing about XYZ in the Bible. When I got out of college, I was like, "Okay, I'm questioning basically everything I was taught."

Most post-Boomers commented on religious scandals they had heard about online and in the news.

> Information is much more available, more easily these days. Back in the day, we may not have known what was going on in different institutions, but now we know the Southern Baptist Convention finally admitted all the sexual abuse and harassment. Everybody knew what was going on, but they were able to hide it and keep it in the shadows. In my generation and the next, it's much easier to call out the hypocrisy that absolutely turns off most people.

Few knew details but most had a general idea about the scandals, which definitely turns them off to religion: "People have lost trust in religious institutions because of sex and financial scandals. It's like, if they're not following it in the Vatican, why should I follow it here?" Others connected religious scandals to a broader loss of trust in institutions. One told us, "People start to see how a lot of religious institutions are corrupt, like you only have to look at the Catholic Church's handling of pedophile priests. Young people in particular feel disillusioned with the power structures around them in general and translate that into religion. Then they say, 'I'm not part of anything, I'm spiritual, I think there is something out there.'" Another said, "The controversy in the Catholic Church affected a lot of people personally. You read it, and why do you want to be part of it? When Volkswagen years ago was lying about their emissions, I didn't want to buy a Volkswagen, so why would I want to be a part of a church doing all these terrible things?"

Most Americans can understand the transgressions of individuals. Nobody is perfect, we think, and a few people are wicked. But institutional evasions and whitewashings look insidiously systemic. It can appear that people in power are more concerned with protecting organizational reputations than real people. That kind of cover-up is, to many Americans, totally unacceptable. Moreover, had these scandals been few and far between, they could have been dismissed as isolated incidents. But scandals during this time seemed to come at a rapid-fire pace and with an almost predictable regularity. That suggested that these were not merely occasional slipups but something systemic. Either religion attracted fools and frauds for leaders, or it produced them. And the religious followers who believed them and gave them money were either stupid or gullible. Either way, on both counts, something was quite wrong with religion, it seemed.[26] All of that combined to damage religion's credibility for most, especially younger, Americans. In a 2020 national survey conducted by the Pew Research Center, of the 53% of Americans who said that Christianity's influence in the United States is decreasing, 58% of them said that "misconduct by Christian leaders" is a "major cause" of that decline, and an additional 34% said it was a "minor cause." Meaning, 49% of all Americans believed that misconduct by Christian leaders has helped cause Christianity's declining influence.[27]

Beyond the question of religion's general credibility, much about these religious scandals seemed to validate the assumptions and outlooks of some other movements that were undermining traditional religion. Consider the third sexual revolution and the movement for LGBTQ+ rights discussed in Chapter 7. Some features of the religious scandals seemed implicitly to validate their outlooks. Anti-gay religious campaigners meeting furtively with male prostitutes. Conservative activists consuming pornography. Married pastors having affairs with church employees. Celibate clergy lusting after minors. One argument of conservative religious leaders who opposed sexual revolutions and LGBTQ+ movements was that sex does not define who and what a person is and that sexually "sinful lifestyles" can be resisted with God's help. But hypocritical scandalous behaviors suggested the opposite. Sometimes the aftermath of scandals also revealed the subtle triumph of sexual revolution. Disgraced evangelical pastor and leader Ted Haggard, for instance, conceded in a 2011 interview published in *GQ* magazine, "I think that probably, if I were 21 in this society, I would identify myself as a bisexual."[28] Honest and no doubt true. Culturally speaking, however, that admission itself compromises the deeper heteronormative assumptions on which many religious opponents of the acceptance of LGBTQ+ people stood. If Haggard could be that candid in those terms, they why shouldn't every Millennial swimming in the currents of the third sexual revolution do as they desired?[29] And, if so, why pay any attention to outdated religious teachings about sex?

A similar logic applies to religion's financial scandals and neoliberal capitalist culture. Religion can preach all it wants about seeking God, truth, heaven, justice, and spiritual growth more than worldly Mammon. But, in the eyes of young Americans, far too many preachers embezzling church funds or scamming ordinary donors of their hard-earned money invalidates all that sermonizing. It doesn't matter that many other religious leaders are financially honorable. People do not make the news for being honest. In the context of a globalizing society and world that everywhere, in every way, says that money, careers, markets, assets, competition, and profits are all that really matter, repeated religious financial scandals do nothing but validate that neoliberal capitalist cultural worldview.

The generational discrepancies between the people involved in the scandals described above and the Millennials hearing about them would also not have been lost on Millennials. The majority of those caught in the scandals named above were Baby Boomers, 30% were Silent Generation, and 5% Greatest Generation—meaning 90% of the subjects of the religion scandals were "old people." Only 6.7% were Gen X and 3.3% Millennials. This was, of course, mathematically inevitable given the time period and the age at which institutional leaders are capable of getting into such publicly significant trouble. But the consequence for Millennials was the same: it associated organized religion and religious failures with older people whom they saw handing them a generally screwed-up world. Few points of contact or empathy existed.

On the 2023 Millennial Zeitgeist Survey we asked: "Which of the following do you think is more true about the religious scandals over sex and money in the news in recent decades?" The two answer options were: "The scandals are caused by a few 'bad apples' among otherwise mostly good religious leaders," and "The scandals show that something about religion makes religious leaders tend toward bad behavior." We see in Table 8.2 that a majority of Baby Boomers are more willing to give the benefit of the doubt to the "bad apples" interpretation. But that sympathy erodes with Gen Xers and declines to only 30% among Millennials. The idea that "something about religion makes leaders tend toward bad behavior" was chosen by 35% of Millennials; 36% said they did not know either way. Compared to older generations, Millennials proved by far the least sympathetic to religion when it

Table 8.2 Interpretations of Religious Scandals by Generation (%)

Which of the following do you think is more true about the religious scandals over sex and money in the news in recent decades?	Early Boomers	Later Boomers	Gen Xers	Millennials
The scandals are caused by a few "bad apples" among otherwise mostly good religious leaders.	61	53	46	30
The scandals show that something about religion makes religious leaders tend toward bad behavior.	17	25	28	35
Don't know	22	22	26	36
TOTALS	100	100	100	100
(unweighted *n*'s):	(*n* = 341)	(*n* = 358)	(*n* = 485)	(*n* = 677)

Source: Millennial Zeitgeist Survey, 2023 (*N* = 1,861). Percents may not add to 100 due to rounding.

comes to religious scandals and the most ready to believe that the scandals reveal something nefarious about religion itself.

Imagine getting together a roomful of experts on American religion and culture and asking them to come up with a plan to wreck American traditional religion as efficiently as possible. What would they recommend? One of the best ideas they could propose would be to set up a steady stream of prominent religious leaders being caught engaging in a variety of sexual and financial scandals that would be publicized widely in multiple media. Scandals involving behaviors that directly contradict the public teachings of those leaders would be great because hypocrisy is repulsive. Scandals that take advantage of and harm minors and honest, ordinary Americans are even better—outrage is powerful. Scandals that implicate not only individuals but also organizations are the best—these play on Americans' distrust of institutions and leave no plausible excuses. The roomful of experts who came up with that idea would have earned their consulting fees plus a hefty bonus. But it did not take that hypothetical roomful of experts concocting a diabolical plan to ruin American religion. American religion did it to itself. More precisely, a very small group of religious leaders did—and very effectively.[30]

Emphasis on "very small." To keep matters in perspective we must remind ourselves that the vast majority of US clergy and other leaders are not and have never been engaged in scandalous sexual, financial, or violent misdeeds. Studies show, for instance, that even at the height of American

Catholic priest abuse in the 1960s and 1970s, only a fraction—about 4%—of all priests committed these wrongs.[31] The great majority were practicing their vocations faithfully. Furthermore, adults in schools, youth organizations, businesses, sports, and other non-religious institutions commit sexual abuse and financial improprieties at no lower rates than religious leaders. But it only takes a few to ruin things for everyone else. Recent years have made this lesson clear: good leaders can accomplish truly valuable and important things with a great deal of effort, while bad leaders can wreck it all quickly and easily. Even the word "bad" here fails to capture the complexities of scandal dynamics. Some religious leaders caught in wrongdoings were truly sick and evil. Others had no personal religious commitments but were happy to exploit religion for their scheming ends. Still others were sincerely religious but also mere vulnerable humans compromised by powerful temptations—and their supervisors often failed as much as they did. In any case, preventing problematic leaders from inflicting such damage requires leadership from institutions that are strong and robust under stress. What the previous chapters have shown, however, is that, by the 1990s, American religion was anything but that. So the damage was immense.

Evangelical Mission Drift

After World War II, the American neo-evangelical movement set out to rebuild a "gospel-centered" Christianity from the ruins of a fundamentalism wrecked by the modernist-fundamentalist battles of the 1920s.[32] Its leaders wished to salvage what they believed was good in broad, mid-nineteenth-century American evangelicalism—the biblical gospel of salvation in Jesus Christ. Postwar neo-evangelicalism was determined to avoid both modernism's theological liberalism and fundamentalism's sectarianism, anti-intellectualism, and legalism. The relaunched evangelical movement set for itself two central goals. One was to evangelize the United States and the world by spreading the gospel. The second was to engage secular culture with compelling ideas, arguments, and challenges grounded in a biblical worldview.[33] Success would be measured by two standards: winning people to Christ and offering a Christian account of reality that was intellectually respectable and compelling. Billy Graham exemplified the first mission, pragmatically cooperating with even mainline Protestant churches and on principled grounds resisting pressures for racial segregation in the interest of the gospel.³⁴ Carl F. H. Henry exemplified the second mission by critiquing both liberalism and fundamentalism, building multiple evangelical institutions, and producing galvanizing intellectual work in doctrine, philosophy, and ethics that attempted to "remake the modern mind."³⁵

Evangelicalism remained focused on those two goals from the mid-1940s to the mid-1970s. Then, in the late 1970s, it gave way to what organizational sociologists call "mission drift." The upheavals and revolutions of the 1960s and 1970s had introduced the fearful notion that "the culture" was not actually being won for Christ but was in fact sliding away into secularism, hedonism, and godless humanism. The pivotal figure cutting evangelicalism loose from its founding mission was Francis Schaeffer, a Reformed Presbyterian pastor and theologian from the Philadelphia area. After a decade pastoring in the United States, Schaeffer and his wife, Edith, herself a prolific author, moved to the Swiss Alps and founded a community called L'Abri—French for "the shelter"—that offered philosophy seminars and a spiritual community. In the following years, thousands of young people visited L'Abri, where they soaked up the Schaeffers' hospitality and Francis's philosophical defenses of Christianity and reflections on art, ecology, and spirituality. Schaeffer's earlier writings directly followed the second goal set by American neo-evangelicalism—namely, trying to advance a respectable and defensible Christian philosophical account of reality.

In the 1970s, however, Schaeffer took a political turn, having become convinced that "secular humanism" was taking over Western culture and institutions, as evidenced by its acceptance of abortion and euthanasia and what he saw as the rise of an elite authoritarian state. The result would eventually lead to social chaos and breakdown. He argued this in his sweeping 1976 book, *How Should We Then Live: The Rise and Decline of Western Thought and Culture*, which was followed by *Whatever Happened to the Human Race?* (1979, coauthored with C. Everett Koop, the two-term US surgeon general in the Reagan administration) and *A Christian Manifesto* (1980). His central message was that the Judeo-Christian worldview had cultivated true humanism in the West and that its disappearance would inevitably lead to social breakdown and barbarism, the early signs of which Schaeffer said were already appearing. In response, Christians needed "to change the course of history by returning to biblical Truth and by allowing Christ to be Lord in all of life."³⁶

Schaeffer's message struck a hypersensitive nerve in US evangelicalism. He traveled and spoke to many American evangelical groups. *How Should*

We Then Live? was made into a five-hour film series, the production of which was bankrolled by wealthy American evangelicals. The series "became a sensation among evangelicals, drawing audiences of up to five thousand in the churches that screened it. The accompanying book was a best-seller in the evangelical market," selling 40,000 copies in the first three months.[37] Historian Michael Hamilton said this of Schaeffer: "Perhaps no intellectual save C. S. Lewis affected the thinking of evangelicals more profoundly; perhaps no leader of the period save Billy Graham left a deeper stamp on the movement as a whole."[38] Many televangelists, like Jerry Falwell and Pat Robertson, incorporated Schaeffer's analysis into their televised messages. Nearly every leader of what soon emerged as the Christian Right credited Schaeffer's works for helping to mobilize their concern and commitment.

My purpose here is not to evaluate the merits of Schaeffer's thinking nor the theological validity of conservative Christian political activism. Our question concerns how these transformations in American evangelicalism eventually contributed to making American religion obsolete. The answers, to which I have alluded in prior chapters, are these. First, a segment of the American population that was friendly to religion but also believed religion should not get directly involved in partisan politics was appalled by the rising power of the Christian Right. This segment of the population essentially decided that if that was where American religion was going, they wanted no part of it. These people, who might have been nominally religious, distanced themselves from the Christian Right by starting to identify as "not religious"—triggering the "rise of the nones" avalanche that subsequently swept up many others in its path. This initial reaction might have been expected, but the larger and longer consequences were unintended and ironic. The premise of the Moral "Majority" was that most Americans would agree with Falwell's politics. Some did, but not, it turned out, the majority they had assumed. And some of those who did not agree helped to start a movement that backfired not only on Falwell but also on evangelicalism as a whole and eventually all of religion.

American evangelicalism's turn from its original missions of evangelization and intellectual influence and toward political power generated a defensive backlash from a broad array of Americans who otherwise had been willing to coexist and possibly even converse with conservative religion. Evangelicals like Billy Graham and Carl Henry had worked to build ties with people despite differences, to create favorable conditions for Christian proclamation and persuasion. Evangelicalism's political turn, by contrast, fostered antagonism, alienation, and demonization. The most visible face of what was then becoming the new mainstream American religion was not standing at the door like Jesus, knocking and waiting to see if it opened. It was a righteous police force bashing down the door to set things right. This helped create a larger sociocultural-political dynamic of hostility, coercion, and polarization that only grew worse with time. Combined with the many other forces discussed in previous chapters, this decisively turned off many younger Americans—including evangelicals—not only to conservative Protestantism but also to religion in general.[39]

Second, the American conservative political establishment's eagerness to capitalize on evangelicalism's political mobilization gave the latter a seat at the table in Washington. Unlike the fundamentalists of the first two decades of the twentieth century who were treated as hillbillies, obscurantists, and pariahs, late-twentieth-century evangelicals saw their leaders treated as important players in the White House and Congress. That was a heady experience for a demographic that Washington, Hollywood, and Madison Avenue barely knew existed until the late 1970s. With Republican electoral successes, evangelicals rose from being displaced outsiders to part of The Establishment. For many, especially older, evangelicals, that welcome felt good, deserved, and satisfying. But for many younger Americans, this assimilation into establishment politics only reinforced the view of religion as part of a larger institutional order run by older people—one that was not to be trusted.

Third, evangelicalism's political turn rebranded the entire religious tradition as a right-wing bloc in the Republican Party coalition. American evangelical history is in fact composed of a hugely diverse heritage of social and political positions and movements, including progressive and even radical ones.[40] In the 1970s, evangelicalism also experienced a temporary but major opening to countercultural and progressive social and political ideas.[41] The 1980s, however, obliterated that. What developed in the popular mind, whether justified or not, was the notion that evangelical = conservative = Republican. Very many evangelicals actually opposed the Christian Right for various reasons, but their voices were drowned out in the tumult. This political turn rebranded evangelicalism as essentially religiously driven conservative politics. And it occurred in a culture of long-term declining confidence in most social institutions, especially political ones, and decreasing trust in religious institutions and religious leaders' ethics. The main effect of evangelical political successes among most ordinary Americans, especially among younger generations, was to foster distance and mistrust.

Fourth, the evangelical political turn in the late 1970s profoundly altered the character and posture of evangelicalism itself. Both early- and mid-nineteenth-century American evangelicalism and postwar neo-evangelicalism conveyed a general spirit of confidence, openness, and optimism about the future. Insecurities lurked beneath the surface but did not dominate. Francis Schaeffer's message, which helped reshape evangelicalism's central narrative and reset its agenda, brought those insecurities to the surface and nurtured them in unkinder directions. Evangelicals increasingly adopted the role of the victim of cultural persecution by their newly discovered nemesis, secular humanism. They cast themselves as the last-ditch hope to save America and Western civilization from a destructive adversary. Evangelical culture thus became increasingly self-protective, reactive, and conspiratorial, ready to condemn those who would deny what they believed was the Truth. Evangelicalism's story was no longer that God in the person of Jesus Christ loves all of us sinners and wants us to embrace him and be changed into the person he created us to be. That pitch was replaced by a script that painted unbelievers as secularists out to destroy not just evangelicals themselves but also all of the liberty and prosperity that the Christian faith had supposedly provided Americans.[42] Evangelicalism, in other words, had reverted to the same defensive, reactive, victimized spirit of the old fundamentalist movement that people like Billy Graham and Carl Henry had worked so hard to banish.[43]

Fast forward to the 1990s. Gen Xers are teenagers and young adults, and older Millennials are starting to come of age. They did not experience the 1950s, 1960s, and 1970s as their Boomer parents had. They have not lost a bygone Christian America. They are infinitely more likely to know about Britney Spears than Billy Graham. They have grown up in a world where diversity has always been a fact of life. Intelligent people, they believe, know that truth and morality are relative and know to beware of people who claim otherwise. Most have absorbed an ethos of expressive individualism, a desire to succeed, and a general distrust of authorities. Democratic neoliberal capitalism has won the day. New digital technologies are beginning to come online. The economy is humming. Then along comes these old super-religious white guys yammering about George Washington praying at Valley Forge, the evils of feminists and abortion and gays, and the perils of secular humanism.[44] They might as well be from outer space. And we are supposed to accept the religion behind their archaic politics? Whatever. Goodbye.[45]

Findings from my Millennial Zeitgeist Survey confirm this interpretation. In it we asked, "How do conservative Christian groups organizing political power (the 'Christian Right') make you feel about American religion generally?" (see Table 8.3). The majority of Millennials (56%) said it turns them off to religion, while 36% said it doesn't affect their view of religion either way—an indicator of apathy about religion generally. Only 8% of Millennials said Christian Right activism attracts them to religion. Millennials have become the most hostile of the surveyed generations to conservative Christian political activism.

These attitudes manifested themselves in our interviews as well, for example: "The religious right has been so strongly associated with zealots with draconian or closed-minded type views of how people should behave, very puritanical and often demonizing. That's a huge turn off for me." Similarly, another told us, "A lot of religion comes off as just angry, and the rise of the evangelical church, especially as it relates to politics, it's extreme. It's no different than sharia law, what some of these guys are saying. So when younger generations hear that, they're like, 'Oh, my God, religion is for the fanatical' or 'It's just old-school.'" Others emphasized the disconnect between what "good" religion does and what they saw happening: "Christianity and religion more broadly have been branded the wrong way. It's become part of a political viewpoint rather than a knowledge-seeking or communal struggling." And, "It's best for religion to be independent of politics. Religions will have their feelings on certain policy issues, but in the end should avoid taking strong stances because at the end of day we are all God's children and

Table 8.3 Reaction to the Christian Right by Generation (%)

How do conservative Christian groups organizing political power (the "Christian Right") make you feel about American religion generally?	Early Boomers	Later Boomers	Gen Xers	Millennials
It turns me off to religion.	36	41	43	56
It attracts me to religion.	7	7	6	8
It neither turns me off nor attracts me.	58	52	51	36
TOTALS (unweighted *n*'s):	100 (*n* = 341)	100 (*n* = 358)	100 (*n* = 485)	100 (*n* = 677)

Source: Millennial Zeitgeist Survey, 2023 (*N* = 1,861). Percents may not add to 100 due to rounding.

should all love one another and not be divisive. So religion's role in politics shouldn't be very involved because it's just creating divisiveness."

Some readers will object that I am conflating American evangelicalism with the Christian Right, which, although they overlap, are not the same. That is correct, but for this analysis also irrelevant. What matters here is not what actually happened. What matters is how people understood things at the time. Few Americans, even religious ones, and especially Millennials, are well versed in fine distinctions concerning religion. Most operate with very basic categories typically picked up from the media, which itself is rarely sophisticated about religion.[46] Evangelicalism has no central authority or official representatives or spokespeople. It is a decentralized patchwork of various traditions with strong populist and entrepreneurial tendencies. This means that whichever leader can talk loudest and longest into the microphone and attract the most media attention ends up being the de facto face of evangelicalism. That frustrates evangelicals who do not like what the loudmouths are saying, but it is built into the tradition itself. So, with the rise of the Christian Right, when the noisiest and most "newsworthy" evangelicals at the microphone were "Take Back America for God" political activists, the entire evangelical tradition became for most outsiders represented by Falwell, Robertson, and their ilk.[47] Only later did it become clear the extent to which their *actual* legacy was to "Push Americans Away from the Church."

To be clear, I am not claiming that, had evangelicalism stayed on course with the postwar movement's dual mission of evangelism and intellectual and cultural engagement, traditional religion would not have gone obsolete. I suspect that would have made a modest difference, all else being equal. But history only happens one way, and such counterfactuals are ultimately imponderable. Evangelical mission drift was only one part of much larger, more complex dynamics of combinational causes. But it was an important part of the mix.

Evangelical Me-and-God Spirituality

Evangelicalism, it turns out, taught Americans to be hyper-individualistic in their approach to God and spirituality in ways that also badly backfired. In interviews with post-Boomer Americans, I was astonished to hear a classic American evangelical phrase invoked repeatedly to explain why they think nobody needs a religious congregation to be religious or spiritual. All that mattered, many said, was "having a personal relationship with God." When asked whether they think being part of a religious congregation is important or necessary for being a good follower of a religion, a very common answer was, "No, I have my own personal relationship with God, I don't need an organization," or "As long as someone has a personal relationship with God, institutions are not the point."

American evangelicalism does not own the expression "personal relationship with God." But, for decades, it was a crucial refrain employed in evangelism and apologetics to press people to make serious Christian commitments, to personalize their faith and not simply be nominal Christians. To mere churchgoers, evangelicals replied, "Going to church does not make anyone a Christian any more than sitting in a garage makes you an automobile—you need to have a personal relationship with God." To others who said they believed in God, evangelicals pressed, "Great, but just believing is not enough, you need to have a personal relationship with Jesus." Evangelical ex-Catholics might commonly testify, "I used to just go to Mass and do the rituals, but then I became a Christian and I love my personal relationship with God." The mantra "have a personal relationship with God" was in postwar evangelicalism almost as essential as "Jesus died on the cross for my sins."

J. I. Packer's 1973 book, *Knowing God*, is a classic of evangelical popular theology. It has sold more than 1million copies, has been published in 13 languages, and was ranked 5 on *Christianity Today*'s list of "Top 50 Books That Have Shaped Evangelicals."[48] Packer's book continually stressed God's personal nature, insisting that learning about God is not merely an intellectual exercise but a means to develop a deeper relationship with God. Ranked number 1 on the same *Christianity Today* list is Rosalind Rinker's 1959 classic, *Prayer: Conversing with God*, another bestseller.[49] Rinker, a "writer, missionary, and dedicated evangelical worker," taught readers that "prayer is a dialogue between two persons who love each other." God is someone with whom Christians can and need to have a close personal relationship. The list of evangelical books, articles, evangelistic tracts, films, sermons, and website pieces that emphasize the same message are legion. The phrase "personal relationship with God" is one every evangelical has heard since childhood or their conversion. Google searches on "evangelical personal relationship with God" and "with Jesus" as of this writing return 9,750,000 and 5,230,000 results, respectively.

American evangelicals leveraged this phrase for decades to attract potential converts with the prospect of intimately knowing their "personal Lord and Savior." It also set evangelicalism apart from other traditions—especially Catholicism and much of mainline Protestantism—that did not employ this language. It set an internal standard for evangelicals that promoted a strong devotional life of scripture study and prayer. And it served as a constant reminder that evangelical faith is not about organized "churchianity" but individually knowing, loving, and following God. Culturally, the phrase resonated deeply with American individualism, subjectivism, and esteeming interpersonal relations over institutional concerns.

Importantly, however, American evangelicals *never* meant the phrase "personal relationship with God" to imply that a believer who enjoyed such a relationship did not need a church. Relating to God personally was the essential heart of Christian faith, but everyone still also needed to be active in a local church (or at least a para-church ministry) to help cultivate that relationship and express it properly in the world, as commanded by the Bible. Billy Graham crusades, for instance, did not simply ask people to pray "the sinner's prayer" of repentance and trust in Jesus, but immediately moved to connect converts with area churches.

Here, however, we stumble on another unanticipated and ironic consequence of religious developments. American evangelicals have been incredibly successful in communicating the discourse of "having a personal relationship with God." All kinds of Americans with different backgrounds and relations to religion now use that phrase fluently—except with purposes different from, often opposite to, the way evangelicals intended. The first use by many younger Americans, as mentioned above, is to explain why they do not need to participate in any religious organization to be whatever religiously or spiritually they are. They have a *personal* relationship with God. That is what is meaningful. Why complicate that by getting tangled up with some institution? "I feel like I have a relationship with God," many post-Boomers said, "but I don't need to go to church to see God, I don't need to go sit in a Catholic Mass to hear things I don't understand."

The second way that many contemporary Americans' use of this phrase backfired on its original evangelical intentions was by its authorizing each individual to decide their own view of who or what "God" is. In evangelical parlance, the God with whom one might have a personal relationship is always and only "the God of the Bible." God is not something people sort out as fitting or workable for themselves based on their experiences. God just *is*, the eternal "I am," and as revealed in the historical divine-human person of Jesus Christ, the Way, the Truth, and the Life. But that is not what it means to the countless Americans who confidently reference their own personal relationship with God. Their God or gods need not be defined by the Bible. The being or power or energy with whom or which they have a "personal relationship" could be any number of different entities. In principle, for them, the Bible is merely one resource among many that individuals might choose to draw on to form ideas of the divine. But it certainly need not be authoritative or exclusive. Syncretism, personal "insight," evolutionary development, individual experience, and more besides can play a role in helping define who or what God or god or the divine is for any given person. That is about as far from evangelical sensibilities as one can get.

This ironic migration of "personal relationship with God" from evangelicalism to individualistic spirituality is emblematic of a larger unintended evangelical influence on American culture that also contributed to tradition religion's obsolescence—namely, the valorization of individual subjectivity as the seat of authenticity and authority. One hallmark of American evangelicalism is its denigration of religious practices that it views as dry, formal, ritualistic, rationalistic, scholastic, uninspired, external, or rote. Each believer's spiritual life needs to be alive, genuine, dynamic, personal, warm, moving, and experienced in heart and soul. Spiritual renewal, devotion, and growth help create an intimate interior experience of God and self. Evangelicals cannot be just interested in a ministry; they have to "have a heart for" it. It is not enough simply to recite a creed or sing hymns or praise songs, one needs to *really feel* it inside, the more intensely the better. The historical influences of pietism, the Second Great Awakening, and frontier revivalism on evangelicalism in this way have remained powerful, as have those of the more recent charismatic movement.

The underlying cultural structure is that subjective individual experience is the litmus test of authentic faith, authoritatively confirming and expressing what is spiritually true for each believer. Historically, for most of evangelicalism, individual experience was always to be guided by the teachings of the Bible as interpreted by one's pastor and denomination. In recent decades, though, many American evangelicals have been reading the Bible and asking, "What do these verses mean *to me?*"[50] As evangelicalism displaced mainline Protestantism as America's dominant form of religion, this kind of religious individualism spread into the broader culture.[51] That opened the door to alternative spiritualities that adopted that same evangelical subjectivism and discourse. Evangelicalism provided the cultural template for authorizing and authenticating a cultural turn that superseded evangelicalism. By then, there was no arguing with inner personal experience. Once again, this was unintended but real in consequence nonetheless.

In some ways, what happened to evangelicalism parallels what happened to mainline Protestantism: cultural success leading to organizational decline (see Chapter 5). Evangelicalism spread the word about having a personal relationship with God. Here was a case of a religious tradition ejecting a particular discourse into the larger cultural atmosphere like the particulate matter ejected by a volcano. But people adopted and deployed that very discourse for their own purposes—namely, to relieve themselves of an obligation to follow any particular teachings about who or what God is or to participate in any religious congregation. If evangelicals bear any blame for this, it is because they resorted to simplistic sound bites to communicate their message. Their pragmatic style and schooling in media-savvy communications—get out the message in a slogan that does not overcomplicate matters—were instrumental in their success. But simple slogans are also easy to adapt for different purposes. Evangelicalism's "me-and-God" mentality has thus been turned against not only evangelicalism but also traditional religion generally.

Evangelical Biblicist Foundationalist Epistemology

A few other features of American evangelicalism help to explain religion's eventual obsolescence. The first concerns epistemology, or how we know what we know. Many people think of evangelicalism as conservative and traditional. Evangelicalism itself lays claim to continuity with the long historical Christian tradition, going back to the early church and rejuvenated by the Reformation. But evangelicalism is also profoundly modern. Protestantism inaugurated and shaped early European modernity. Evangelicalism's roots in American puritanism, pietism, and revivalism sink no deeper than the seventeenth and eighteenth centuries. American evangelicalism has (until very recently) treated medieval and post-patristic Christianity as a black hole of Roman Catholic corruption. Evangelicalism lacks an appreciation of the religious authority of tradition and history. And it accesses "the early church" primarily through biblical texts. In this sense, it is not unfair to say that evangelicalism is bound by—even captive to—modernity. A crucial way this mattered was its unacknowledged embrace of strong modern foundationalist epistemologies in the form of infallible and inerrant theories of scripture.

Strong foundationalism is the especially modern epistemic project of identifying some indubitable foundation—what philosophers call "non-inferential" beliefs—on which to build reliable knowledge. Such an irrefutable foundation, if identified, would provide the basis on which valid inferences could produce other beliefs that rational persons would have to accept as true. The problem of identifying a strong non-inferential foundation goes back at least to Aristotle. But moderns have been especially fixated with discovering such a foundation because the core project of modernity itself is about reconstituting social order on the basis of universal secular reason rather than revelation, tradition, divinity, or cosmic order. The latter are considered no longer things about which most people can agree and therefore no longer a basis on which to build society. Modernity has thus been about the effort to come up with a secular foundation on which to build social order.

American evangelicalism, being essentially modern, embraced the need for such a strong foundation but tried to Christianize it. For evangelicals, the true foundation of human knowledge is the Bible. Because God is the source and measure of all truth, because God does not mislead or lie, and because the Bible is God's revelation of his word to humans, the Bible is an unerring foundation for knowledge. This move both affirmed modern ideas about justified knowledge and retained the basis of Christian authority—or so it seemed. Many nineteenth-century evangelicals actually embraced a "two books" doctrine, according to which God reveals himself both in "the book of nature" and "the book of scripture," which were believed to be compatible and complementary. But, as Darwinism and other scientific developments pushed people away from the idea that nature reveals the design and purposes of God, evangelical thinkers tended to talk less about the book of nature. What was left, then, was the Bible.

After the modernist–fundamentalist splits, the postwar neo-evangelicals retained the central belief in scripture as the proper, strong foundation of knowledge. Some evangelical apologists supplemented scripture with rational evidentialist arguments. One example was Josh McDowell's influential 1972 book, *Evidence That Demands a Verdict*, which marshalled historical and legal attestations—like archeological discoveries—to "prove" the authenticity of the Bible and divinity of Christ. Seeking to chart a reasonable, middle-way course, evangelicals were castigated by surviving fundamentalists for supposedly compromising biblical authority, while liberals dismissed their theories of scripture as patently naïve. Within evangelicalism, hair-splitting conflicts also developed over the nature of biblical inspiration, authority, and trustworthiness—driven by the dual and sometimes tension-fraught quests both to sustain conservative Christian orthodoxy and advance intellectually respectable scholarship. These internal struggles came to a head with the 1978 publication of *The Battle for the Bible*, in which its author, the influential evangelical thinker Harold Lindsell, went to the mat for the doctrine of "total inerrancy."

But a funny thing happened then on the way to establishing biblical authority: the argument collapsed under the weight of perceived philosophical failures of the larger modern approach to which it had hitched its wagon. By the 1990s, it appeared the modern quest for a philosophical foundation had failed, and we had entered the *post*modern era, in which there is no such thing as universal truth (as described in Chapter 6). Evangelicalism, having bet all of its chips on the biblical foundation of truth, discovered that the casino had terminated all games and rewritten the house rules. Whichever theory of scriptural inerrancy or infallibility that evangelicals championed was suddenly irrelevant. Its basic strategy of realizing truth was passé. The question of which account of biblical authority was correct no longer mattered because indubitable truth no longer mattered, being considered impossible.

For decades, Billy Graham had built his case for Christian conversion on this incessantly repeated phrase: "The Bible says..." For those who believed in the Bible, the phrase served as an authority that compelled countless people to walk down the aisle to give their lives to Christ. By the time Millennials came along, however, the issue was not whether one believed the Bible or interpreted it correctly. The reality, it seemed, was that Truth was a fiction, indubitable foundations were a mirage, universal reason was a scam. The problem for evangelicalism after postmodernism was thus not that its claims were false, but that the entire way it went about thinking about making claims was outdated and misguided.

Very few post-Boomers we interviewed discussed these ideas directly, but you can hear them in the assumptions behind what they said. One person told us, for example: "Christian book authors project their ideology onto a topic, then pull scripture out of context for support. But to act like it's one way and only one way turns a lot of people off in my generation. The only way that works is if you stay so cut off from the real world and just have your echo chamber, and that was me for years, but not now." In the words of another, "Religion has become a defined answer rather than a process, which is ultimately less appealing, unless you're already checking all the boxes with a particular view." Some embraced pop postmodern ideas pretty directly: "The idea of multiple truths is a thing, people are not interested in being told what is true." Others were more focused on the Bible, specifically.

> It's a crazy world that we make social and political decisions based off the Bible. I'm sure the Bible had good intentions, but the Bible wasn't written by God but by men of the majority of their time. This isn't the word of God, it's the word of men who had their own agenda, then someone compiled it together for a very specific purpose. But people act like it's the end-all, be-all without understanding.

That kind of thinking extended into ideas about religion as a whole.

> A lot of churches act like they have all the answers to life. I don't believe the Bible gives all the answers, every single detail. But preachers talk about what God thinks about dating, going to the movies, birth control or abortion, whatever the hot-button issue—things that aren't even in the Bible. Then you get out in the world and actually start meeting minorities, people with nontraditional lives, who didn't have parents, really messed up life, you start to realize, wait, things are not so simple. You start listening to what's said in church and realize this is not important, this is just a guy with a Bible, not somebody who's informed about any of this.

Evangelicalism thus found itself in an impossible position. It had painted itself into a corner from which there was no exit. Backpedaling on the Bible as the source of ultimate truth was impossible. Continuing to insist on the Bible as the infallible word of God had become culturally incomprehensible. Shifting Christian authority from scripture to the "inner testimony of the Holy Spirit" entailed capitulating to individualistic subjectivism that would worry even hard-core Pentecostals. Accommodating the postmodern condition meant abandoning the rational persuasiveness of the gospel for the consolation prize of Christianity as just another narrative and language game that anyone might choose or not choose to incorporate into their fluidly morphing selfhoods. In the 2000s, the "emerging church movement" arose in progressive wings of American evangelicalism that called for evangelicals to engage postmodern culture constructively. Suffice it for our purposes to say that, after this movement's controversies with the old guard died down, its profitable impact on mainstream evangelicalism was slight.[52] If anything, it generated a biblicist backlash.

The evangelical highway to Truth turned out to be a culturally epistemic dead end. Knowing that the strong postmodernist program was impossible, academic philosophy developed more sophisticated arguments in defense of more moderate or "soft" versions of foundationalism—some of which included belief in God as properly basic.[53] However, similar to the chasm between what historians of science know and what the general public "knows" about the seemingly inevitable warfare between science and religion, almost nothing of sophisticated moderate foundationalism has trickled down to ordinary people. As far as deep culture goes, postmodernism remains massively more influential than reasonable philosophical epistemologies. So, in the end, as far as most Millennials were concerned, some evangelical youth groups might be cool for teens to attend for a while, and if evangelical Christianity helped some people to cope with life, then fine. Otherwise, it did not seem on its face culturally credible.

Evangelical Purity Campaigns

In the early 1990s, a new and highly visible movement emerged within American evangelicalism that eventually became known as "purity culture." What "purity" meant was abstinence before marriage, especially for girls. The relevant cultural environment was the closing of the allegedly virtues-oriented, "conservative" 1980s, continuing fear over the AIDS epidemic, the explosion of pornography available in VHS format, and the first inklings of what the Digital Revolution might bring for sexual culture. In this context, movement leaders promoted modest dress, virginity pledges, the rejection of dating, and purity ceremonies.

Advocates of purity culture claimed that the practice of dating encouraged sexual temptation and that the multiple breakups involved in dating were "practice for divorce." Dating therefore should be refused in favor of traditional models of courtship leading to marriage.[54] Purity activists instructed girls and young women to dress and act modestly to avoid tempting young men. To have sex before marriage, they said, was like becoming a chewed-up piece of gum: already used and slimy, and so nothing anybody would want.

Purity was a broad category. It meant not only abstaining from sexual intercourse before marriage but also from "sexual thoughts, sexual touching, pornography, and actions that are known to lead to sexual arousal."[55]

Numerous campaigns developed to promote purity culture and lifestyles, including True Love Waits (TLW), launched by Southern Baptists in 1993, and the Silver Ring Thing (SRT), founded in 1995 by a pastor named Denny Pattyn. Typically, religious youth would take a vow of sexual abstinence until marriage—a virginity pledge—and mark this vow by wearing purity rings, chastity rings, or "promise rings." The TLW pledge stated, "Believing that true love waits, I make a commitment to God, myself, my family, my friends, my future mate and my future children to be sexually abstinent from this day until the day I enter a biblical marriage relationship." The SRT described itself as "a unique para-church youth ministry that promotes the message of abstinence until marriage." Its mission was "to motivate, educate, support and transform generations of young people to embrace a lifestyle of Christ-centered sexual abstinence until marriage." Its longer-term vision was "to create a culture shift in America where abstinence becomes the norm again rather than the exception."

The movement organized Christian hip-hop and rock concerts to promote purity among teens, distributing pledge cards to audience members and encouraging them to sign. Multiple other religious denominations and traditions, including a sector of Catholicism, joined the movement. The SRT received more than $1 million in grants under the George W. Bush administration for promoting abstinence-based sex education.[56] In the first year of the TLW campaign, more than 100,000 youth signed the pledge. By 2003, a reported 2.5 million US youth had pledged to remain sexually abstinent until marriage.[57] The purity culture movement also included more locally and regionally organized "purity balls"—dance formals attended by teenage daughters and their fathers, where the girls would publicly make virginity pledges and fathers promised to protect their girls' physical, mental, and spiritual purity.[58]

While purity culture concentrated primarily on girls and young women, a male analogue focused on "resisting sexual temptation," an obligation for both unmarried and married men. Boys and men did not have to take pledges, wear rings, attend formal dances with parents, or dress modestly. Their task was to read a key text, *Every Man's Battle: Winning the War on Sexual Temptation One Victory at a Time*, and then learn resolutely to discipline their eyes and minds.[59] With secular culture offering countless sexual temptations for men, the book offered hope: "Thankfully, [it is] not impossible to rise above them. Shattering the perception that men are unable to control their thoughts and roving eyes, *Every Man's Battle* shares the stories of dozens who have escaped the trap of sexual immorality and presents a practical, detailed plan for any man who desires sexual purity." Much of the book's appeal was its frank acknowldgment that Christian men in fact lust—and worse. The huge success of the book also spawned the publisher's marketing of a small library of workbooks, companions, and scriptures for every young man, married man, son, woman, young woman, single woman, and more. While men of all ages knew, to their relief, that every other man shared the same temptations and sins, the pressure remained on for them never to look at potentially sexually tempting images or women or to entertain such in their thoughts.

By the end of the 2000s, the purity culture movement was kaput. Research showed that it had highly uneven effects on sexual behaviors and sexually transmitted diseases (STDs).[60] But what matters most for our purposes is the backlash it generated among those—including some purity culture advocates—who had trusted it and felt wounded, regretful, and angry. Unsurprisingly, non-evangelical critics published numerous condemnations, including Jessica Valenti's 2009 book, *The Purity Myth: How America's Obsession with Virginity Is Hurting Young Women*.[61] What mattered more, however, was the reaction by many from within evangelicalism. As the generation of evangelical youth influenced by purity culture moved through emerging adulthood and sometimes into marriage, many began publicly voicing online and in print that their participation in purity culture had badly damaged them emotionally, relationally, and sexually. These early criticisms of purity culture emboldened others to share similar grievances. An anti–purity-culture movement began to form that lambasted the manipulation, shame, repression, behaviorism, legalism, and misogyny that produced damaging effects that often lasted into adulthood and marriage.

Perhaps the starkest representations of the backlash against purity culture involved Joshua Harris, the author of one of the movement's most influential books, *I Kissed Dating Goodbye*, published in 1997.[62] Purity culture advocates and followers celebrated Harris's book, while many non-Christians and some Christians roundly criticized it. Ten years after its first publication, Harris noted publicly that many readers were applying his message with a rigid legalism he did not like. By 2016, Harris showed signs that he was beginning to reconsider some of his book's basic arguments. In 2018, Harris publicly apologized to many who had been harmed by the influence of his book and asked his publisher to discontinue it. He then began working with a religious film company on a documentary, *I Survived I Kissed Dating Goodbye*. In 2019, Harris revealed on Instagram that he and his wife were separating as a result of "significant changes [that] have taken place in both of us." Shortly thereafter, he announced that he no longer considered himself a Christian. Harris's film company cancelled distribution of the *I Survived* film.[63] The transformation was telling and representative of larger dynamics underway.

By 2019, a deluge of books began hitting the market, usually authored by women who had suffered from purity culture, with titles like

- *Pure: Inside the Evangelical Movement That Shamed a Generation of Young Women and How I Broke Free*
- *#ChurchToo: How Purity Culture Upholds Abuse and How to Find Healing*
- *Shameless: A Case for Not Feeling Bad About Feeling Good (About Sex)*
- *Beyond Shame: Creating a Healthy Sex Life on Your Own Terms*
- *You Are Your Own: A Reckoning with the Religious Trauma of Evangelical Christianity*
- *On Her Knees: Memoir of a Prayerful Jezebel*
- *Wayward: A Memoir of Spiritual Warfare and Sexual Purity*
- *Talking Back to Purity Culture: Rediscovering Faithful Christian Sexuality*
- *She Deserves Better: Raising Girls to Resist Toxic Teachings on Sex, Self, and Speaking Up*[64]

Some of these authors had found ways to retain their Christian faith in some form, usually as ex-evangelicals, despite the damage done to them by purity culture. Others had totally turned their backs on Christianity and urged others to follow them. In addition to books, countless essays and articles online, in print, and on podcasts lambasted purity culture, with titles such as

- "Tainted Love: Reckoning with the Damage of Purity Culture"
- "Shame and Regret: How Evangelical Purity Culture Failed a Generation"
- "Why Purity Culture Is Toxic: A Female Perspective"
- "Why I Won't Raise My Children in the Purity Culture That Raised Me"[65]

Some also wrote about how purity culture damaged young men as well.[66] Social media played a key role in spurring and communicating these grievances.

The traumas resulting from purity culture and church abuse scandals gave rise to a recovery movement focused on "spiritual abuse," "toxic religion," and healing from "religious trauma syndrome," as well as on escaping conservative Protestantism altogether.[67] There were new therapy centers, institutes, and trainings, such as the Religious Trauma Institute, a certification program in religious trauma studies, and the Reclamation Collective: Holding Space for Folks Navigating Religious Trauma, Spiritual Abuse, and Adverse Religious Experiences.[68] A Google search on "purity culture damage" at the time of this writing returns 16,900,000 results. In short, the blowback against the evangelical purity culture of the 1990s and 2000s was and is widespread and intense.

The negative fallout from the purity culture movement contributed to the growing obsolescence of traditional religion in at least two ways. First, countless numbers of Millennial evangelicals, especially women, grew up deciding that the religion of their youth was a source of manipulation, shame, repression, sexual double standards, obsessions with virginity, negative views of bodies, and idolized views of marriage that were distorted and damaging. Such realizations dissolved whatever glue of affection might otherwise have bonded them to their religion. Since they had been so committed to purity as youth, they would have been the most likely to remain committed as young adults had they not become thus alienated. Instead, many joined the "exvangelical" movement.[69] Many went on to explore their sexuality in ways evangelicalism would disapprove of. Purity culture being so interwoven with the Christianity that they knew meant for them that rejecting the former often required abandoning the latter as well. Since American women tend to remain more religious than American men and can often bring husbands and children back with them to religion, the gendered nature of this particular alienation was especially significant for religion's demise.

A few of our interview respondents negatively spoke openly about this.

> Sex in the media is good. That's different from how I grew up in "purity culture." I don't know where that comes from, but it definitely had harmful effects. I definitely had to work through some shame stuff I shouldn't have felt. Sex is a natural part of life. The more open we are, the more people can

feel comfortable figuring themselves out and not have all this shame coloring their worldview.

Another told us,

> Our country's beginnings as a Puritan society perpetuate this idea of sexual purity or prudishness. But in our day and age, with access to information, that can be harmful rather than truthful and honest about different bodies, consensual sexual interests, relationships. Hiding it says it doesn't exist, when we know it does. Who are we protecting? It's more harmful to be lying and hiding these things rather than understanding them and making our own decisions. So it's great to move in the direction of open honesty, access to education and knowledge, rather than saying it's taboo and we don't do this here.

Second, the purity culture movement further alienated numerous nonevangelical Americans from religion. Many adults in mental health fields, for example, came to learn that evangelicalism had damaged a significant part of an entire generation of young women with what seemed to them to be a strange ideology. Purity culture helped to create a new array of pathologies—spiritual abuse, religious trauma, toxic faith, adverse religious experiences—from which many young people needed to be healed. This added weight to the negative associations attached to religion by September 11 and the New Atheists. Part of the blowback against purity culture also included attention to the problem of hypermasculinity in evangelical culture. By the end of the 2010s, American evangelicalism had long been struggling to come to terms with difficulties around both right-wing politics and race.[70] The fallout from the purity movement highlighted another skeleton in the closet: evangelicalism's history of male-dominated, muscular, female-submissive, "spiritually badass," masculine culture.[71] Public criticisms of evangelicalism from within and without began cutting increasingly deeper.[72]

Denominational Culture Wars

Americans believe that religion should help people get along in peace and community. Relationships, organizations, cities, and nations suffer persistent conflict. One potential value that religion brings to the world, Americans assume, is to help alleviate human struggles and promote harmony. As the culture wars of recent decades raged, many Americans discovered not only that the country is at war over a set of "lifestyle" issues in politics and culture but that most American religious denominations are too. Religion, they realized, often does not offer a refuge from caustic public conflicts, but instead reproduces and perpetuates them. Americans of all generations participate in culture wars, both religious and otherwise. But for the many post-Boomers who prioritize a "live and let live" ethic, denominational fights—added to all of the other factors examined in these chapters—are yet another reason to steer clear of religion.

The religious battles are continuous, contentious, and visible. The US press loves to cover religious people fighting, and the internet helps spread reporting by both journalists and partisans. Southern Baptists in the 1980s modeled how one bloc in a denomination could mobilize to take over the reins of power and oust its rivals. In that case, Boomer and Silent generation fundamentalists took on the denomination's moderates and won.[73] Following suit, activists in many major US denominations launched movements to advance their causes.

Those causes have often mirrored larger cultural battles: women's ordination, the blessing of same-sex marriages, abortion, and the ordination of gays and lesbians to the clergy. Various denominations have also fought internally over views on racial equality, capital punishment, stem cell research, divorce, assisted suicide, climate change, separation of church and state, relations with other churches, gun control, welcoming transgender and gender non-conforming people, the Israel–Palestinian conflict, and more. Conservative denominations have tussled over some of those issues, especially women's ordination, but also biblical inerrancy, evolution, the reality and value of charismatic gifts like "speaking in tongues," and how to deal with heterodox teachers. Many congregations in both mainline and conservative Protestantism have also for decades been embroiled in what has become known as "The Worship Wars," that is, conflicts between those who prefer traditional styles of music and liturgy versus advocates of more "contemporary" praise and worship music, dance, and so forth. For their part, American Catholics have been in conflict for decades over the liturgy, women's ordination, LGBTQ+ issues, abortion, lay governance, and reforms related to the clerical abuse scandal. When internal cultural wars finally drive major denominations to formal splits—as with the Episcopal Church in 2009 and the United Methodist Church in 2023—there inevitably follow years of legal wrangling between congregations, bishops, denominations, and other power-players over who gets to keep the church buildings and other assets. It can appear that nothing but money and power are at stake. As one post-Boomer we interviewed reported, "My denomination has a divide over the LGBTQ+ community that's been hard for me personally, because I believe God loves all and it doesn't really matter who you love or who you are. Maybe the US is a little more progressive than other parts of the world, but it has made a divide in my religion."

Another, from another point of view, said,

> Morality has gone out the window over the past 20 years. We get accepting of gay marriage, then people start saying we should allow it in church, and churches were like, no. I could see the point, but then that comes to division like, How come we can't get married in traditional Christian church? How come we don't allow my friends to do that? This has become heavily political in denominations with division, people get confused and it becomes overwhelming because it's like, What denomination should I go to? I'm a conservative, and it is overwhelming and complicated because I feel if I go to the wrong church, I won't be accepted. Everything is so politicized, churches are politicized, like if you're conservative or liberal, you have to go to a certain denomination. If you behave some way on gay marriage or fill in the blank, sex before marriage, multiple marriages, then you can still go to heaven, but if you don't get baptized, you go to hell. It's overwhelming for our generation, that's what chased us away from religion.

Not all Americans pay attention to these denominational culture wars. But those who do quickly learn that these religious groups are not simply collections of believers who share similar creeds and convictions. They are bureaucratic institutions—an immediate red flag for those who distrust organizations—with complex administrative structures. To outsiders, they can seem like thinly sacralized versions of secular government and politics—run, some cynics may suspect, by people who do not have what it takes to win in "the real world" so instead play at being big fish in the small pond of religion. Furthermore, journalism reporting on denominational battles employs the same language of "rifts," "divisions," "impasses," and "standoffs" that news coverage of Washington politics uses.[74] That can be a big turn-off for many Americans, especially younger generations already suspicious of religion.

Some post-Boomers have been at the forefront of denominational culture wars since the 1990s. But, as with national political cultural wars, the activists are a minority. Most post-Boomers did not see the importance of religious denominations in the first place. Those with minimal personal investment in culture war issues readily concluded that religious groups are no different from secular ones. It is all about ideologies, power, status, money, and winning. Many post-Boomers who really did care about issues like women's rights, LGBTQ+ people, and abortion wondered why religion is "so far behind the times" to be still fighting over those controversies. At a psycho-emotional level, large numbers of Millennials (and now Gen Zers) were struggling with anxiety and despair about their careers, debt, healthcare, economic prospects, relationships, and the earth's environmental future. Then they hear news reports about denominational battles, maneuverings, and divisions over issues they either don't care about or think should have been settled long ago. Why would they want to be part of religion? They already have enough tension, uncertainty, and anxiety in their lives, thank you.

My 2023 Millennial Zeitgeist Survey attempted to assess Americans' views about denominational culture wars. Since relatively few people are directly involved in these conflicts, for most this is something they might only know about through news headlines or hearsay. The survey asked respondents, "If you heard about religious denominations fighting over 'culture wars' issues like gender and LGBTQ inclusion, which of the following would you more likely think?" One answer framed the issue in the positive light of religion trying to do good: "It is good that religious people strive to sort out what they believe to be right and true." The alternative was, "Religion is as polarized as everything else, so it can't bring love and peace to the world." Table 8.4 shows the results. Respondents are fairly evenly split about whether denominational conflicts reflect something good or bad about religion. But the trend across generations moves in a negative direction. More than half of Millennials said it showed religion being just as polarized as everything else.[75]

These battles loomed relatively small in the public imagination—their effect pales in comparison with that of religious scandals, for example—but, even if modest, they were a real and contributing factor to religious obsolescence.

Table 8.4 Interpreting the Meaning of Denominational Culture Wars by Generation (%)

If you heard about religious denominations fighting over "culture wars" issues like gender and LGBTQ inclusion, which of the following would you more likely think?	Early Boomers	Later Boomers	Gen Xers	Millennials
Religion is as polarized as everything else, so it can't bring love and peace to the world.	40	42	49	52
It is good that religious people strive to sort out what they believe to be right and true.	60	58	52	48
TOTALS (unweighted *n*'s):	100 (*n* = 341)	100 (*n* = 358)	100 (*n* = 485)	100 (*n* = 677)

Source: Millennial Zeitgeist Survey, 2023 (*N* = 1,861). Percents may not add to 100 due to rounding.

Religion as a Tool for Social Control

One of the most offensive parts of traditional religion for post-Boomers is their perception that people use religion as an implement to control other people. We will discuss this again soon, but it merits brief mention here. Given what post-Boomers believe about individual uniqueness, autonomy, and authenticity—examined more in the next chapter—institutional religion's tendency to regulate, control, and dictate what people think, believe, and do is seen as a form of abuse. If religion has any value in the world, post-Boomers think, it is through promoting goodness, happiness, and freedom. Legalistic rules, guilt trips, demanding dogmas, threats of punishment, manipulation, and the like greatly disturb younger Americans.

Interview participants had plenty to say about this. One told us, "When religion tells you what you can and can't do with your body or your family, or who you love or who you like, it's insane." These rules were often backed up by threats of punishment. As another related, "I've heard so many sermons saying, do this and do this and do this and you'll go to heaven, and then if you mess up, you're going to burn in eternity forever. Makes me feel sick to my stomach, but I know people that believe that." Another felt similarly, "The Ten Commandments scare me because, growing up, I always thought if you didn't follow every single one, it's an automatic life sentence to hell. That was not said explicitly, necessarily, but because they brought it up so much, like the Ten Commandments, you have to do these." And sometimes, those punishments came in this world, not the hereafter: "I went to a Christian college where you have to go to chapel a certain number of times per semester, you're forced to go or else you get punished. I was like, you're forcing us to go to chapel? No."

Yet another told us,

> Pictures of Jesus make me feel annoyed, like, Jesus is waiting for the hammer to fall again. Like, okay, if I screw up I'm not going to heaven, but if I ask for forgiveness, then I'm going to heaven. What if I screw up and don't have a chance to ask forgiveness? I don't go heaven? It's just pressure, pressure.

These kinds of experiences made more than a few younger Americans conclude, as one told us, "I don't think religion offers moral guidance. Religion just manipulates people." Nobody seemed to notice that religious control is an inherent risk, perhaps even an inevitable dark mutation of Americans' shared expectation that religion exists to make people be good. Some post-Boomers believe this is inherent to religion itself, others that it is mostly a tendency of fundamentalist, sectarian, and hierarchical religious groups. In this larger cultural context, either view provides yet another way that religion contributed to its own demise.

Congregational Stalwart Power-Hoarding Boomers

Finally, to the micro level. In many religious congregations, older members often want to hold on to positions of power and visibility well beyond the point where it would be good for the congregations for them to step down. This is understandable. People who have invested so much of their lives, money, and emotions in congregations wish to continue to influence them in what they think are good directions. Generational leadership transitions are a challenge for many nonprofit organizations that depend on volunteerism. As a general rule, humans tend to prefer to hold on to power rather than give it up. For many older people, stepping down from roles long held can be fraught with larger, troubling meanings about growing old, being sidelined, and mortality. Serving just one more term on the board of elders, vestry, or pastoral search committee defers those issues. In dysfunctional congregations, some people actually believe they are entitled to run things because their grandfather or great aunt so-and-so was such-and-such and did this and that. Heaven help clergy who attempt to assist the rise of new generations of leaders with new ideas while older stalwarts remain around to grumble, resist, or leave.

This challenge is a byproduct of what is actually a great strength of American religious congregations—namely, they are the last few remaining public institutions not rigidly segregated by age. Many American institutions function with de facto and sometimes official groupings by age—schools with grade levels being a prime example. US religious congregations are nearly unique in the larger institutional environment, providing natural settings for intergenerational interactions, if not always participation in leadership. They aim to be genuinely holistic communities of different kinds of people gathered around specific faiths or traditions. When they function well, such settings can be sociologically very good for the people involved. But congregations can also face problems around power and influence associated with age.

When it comes to the issue of power hoarding by congregational stalwarts, the consequences for younger generations are often not good for the whole. For those congregations fortunate enough to have people of younger generations who want to get involved—beyond changing diapers in nurseries—power hoarding leaves few vacancies in positions in which rising younger members may contribute their talents and learn new skills and responsibilities for the future. We examined in Chapter 6 how the "network" sensibilities and mental maps regarding organizational structure and process of younger people raised in the digital age can clash with those who grew up in earlier, hierarchical, top-down eras and systems. Those differences are difficult enough to try to manage when brought together. But when participatory, network-oriented younger people find older members blocking their contributions, they are likely to say, "Okay, fine, we'll go someplace else that works better for us." Likely those other places will not be religious organizations.

I had a revealing conversation with a Gen X pastor of a mainline Protestant congregation in the suburbs of a big East Coast city. He described the challenges in dealing in his congregation with what I am calling generational power hoarding.

> We have younger families with kids who live nearby because of good public schools. But many of our members are still stuck in a twentieth-century

model of church. I have a colleague in his seventies who says Boomers back in the day commonly moved into church leadership roles in their thirties. Now those very same people are still running things in church! We have to make room for new leaders. But Boomers are having a hard time letting go, even when they don't want to do the work.

Why, I asked, do they want to hang on? "For Boomers," he explained, "it's more about identity and being valued as a member of a community, like, 'If I don't chair a committee, then who am I?' It's partly about power and control, but under that is identity insecurity. The world is so different across generations and changing so quickly, it can be hard for them." I asked him to elaborate.

> Boomers definitely have a different, slower way of doing things. Younger people are used to collaboration tools, moving things quickly, getting a lot done. Things move lots faster for youth with way different styles. It gets painful. Organizational style is a huge issue for attracting younger generations. If you look, society has major professional leaders in their thirties. I am not going to ask young lawyers in my church to do fall clean-up duty! The church needs to change organizational cultures in a way that fits younger generations' life experiences. So I'm trying to approach volunteering as talent recruitment and placement.

He continued to emphasize the differences in life experience across generations. "Youth who are overeducated and underemployed and trying to start careers are in vastly different worlds than Boomers, who lived through the largest economic boom in the history of the world. The younger ones have a hard time connecting. Their default is not to go to a 'house of worship' to learn about religion but instead to go to TED Talks and YouTube." So how, I asked, is trying to change the culture of his congregation going? "It's a lot of work transitioning leadership to younger people," he said. "But the pace of social change is accelerating, and we need people in church who know the speed that the world works in. The old style just does not work, and we need to figure this out because we are headed toward a cliff."

This pastor is fortunate to have the problem of figuring out how to move younger members into leadership roles in his Boomer-dominated congregation. Unlike many US congregations, his actually includes interested Millennials who want to get involved. The situation he describes at the micro level of his church, however, elucidates larger dynamics at work in religious congregations around the country, especially since the 1990s. The life experiences, tempos, and work styles of Millennials are very different from those of Baby Boomers. Yet another cultural mismatch. Intergenerational voluntary teamwork can be difficult enough under favorable conditions. But when congregational stalwarts resist passing on batons of leadership and initiative to rising generations—assuming there even are any around who want them—not many of the latter are going to wait around until the old folks die so they can eventually have their turn. That, as this pastor observed, "just does not work."

Conclusion

American traditional religion found itself at the start of this millennium facing a broad social, economic, technological, political, and cultural environment that threatened its relevance, plausibility, and appeal among most post-Boomer Americans. Almost all of those forces were unplanned and unintended for that effect. Nevertheless, they drove religion toward obsolescence. To make matters worse, some religious leaders and organizational cultures did traditional religion no favors. It was almost as if the myriad sociocultural forces pressuring traditional religion from the outside drove some religious leaders to do things on the inside that were ill-advised, sometimes unconscionable. Some might say that, in these decades, religion strangled itself by its own hand. Many religious people and institutions may have been doing countless good, worthwhile, and admirable things. But those did not and do not attract attention. The goods in religion in the 1990s and 2000s were overwhelmed by a collective of injurious forces that led post-Boomers to turn their backs on religion. Not that they sat down and weighed the pros and cons—this shift transpired at the level of intuitive personal experience shaped by the pervasive public culture. That, it turns out, was a culture in which religion was going obsolete.

III
THE AFTERMATH

9
Contours of the Millennial Zeitgeist

I have throughout this book referred to a distinctive cultural zeitgeist that emerged in the 1990s and developed through the 2000s. This was the atmosphere in which traditional religion fell into obsolescence. The zeitgeist was both a cause of that obsolescence and in part a result of it—the two were mutually reinforcing. My story thus far has concerned macro-historical causal events, innovations, and trends. We now turn to explore the cultural outcome of those developments—the zeitgeist itself. What *was* the spirit of the age in the 1990s and 2000s? And why and how did it edge religion into the margins of life?

Zeitgeists are harder to describe than, say, voting patterns or church attendance rates. They are cultural atmospheres, moods of an era, feelings in the air. Still, zeitgeists are real and can powerfully shape people who live through them. This chapter takes multiple approaches to describe the character of the zeitgeist. Fragmentation and incoherence were essential features of the zeitgeist itself that show up here in my descriptions of the era. I start by setting a big-picture context sketching the dominant tones of the historically relevant decades. I then spell out central cultural themes that gave the zeitgeist its particular personality. Following that, I venture an analysis of the zeitgeist's formal properties, in which I hope most readers can locate their own lives and experiences. The chapter then takes another stab at capturing the attitude of the age in the form of advice that a hypothetical zeitgeist veteran might give a novice. Readers are then invited to watch three music videos from the era that exemplify the mood of the zeitgeist and its contrast with traditional religion. All of that seeks to capture a sense of the public culture side of the zeitgeist. What follows then—an outline of the cultural model underlying the zeitgeist—reflects more the personal culture side of the zeitgeist.

The overall intention here is not to provide a comprehensive depiction of the zeitgeist for its own sake but to make clearer how the cultural atmosphere of the era undid religion. Working through these different ways of approaching the zeitgeist, readers should focus on the following

280 THE AFTERMATH

questions: How would one expect traditional religion to fare in such a cultural atmosphere? How does the picture of reality embodied in that spirit of the age resonate or not with the picture offered by religion? How would religion appear to young Americans who soaked in the zeitgeist's concerns, moods, and sensibilities?

The Cultural Tenor of Successive Decades

First, some big-picture context. We might say that the "long 1950s," which encompassed 1946 to 1959, was a time of *anxious normalcy*. The era was dominated by the postwar economic boom, suburbanization, Eisenhower conservativism, organizational conformity, corporate gray suits, Main Street window-shopping, Doris Day and Jimmy Stewart and John Wayne, and the "traditional" nuclear family. But it also included the Cold War, the specter of nuclear annihilation, an emerging civil rights movement, Brando and Elvis, teenage mania, and the Beat Generation on the margins. Conventionality suppressing disquiet was an ideal environment for the era's mainstream religious boom.[1]

The 1960s, entailing 1960 to 1971, was a season of *troubled optimism*. It was the time of Baby Boomers coming of age, JFK, the Peace Corps, Apollo on the moon, the Great Society, MLK Jr., Freedom Summer, the Age of Aquarius, the Pill, sexual liberation, Greenwich Village, the Summer of Love, Woodstock, "turning East," the free speech movement, hippies and yippies, as well as weed and acid, the Beatles, Joplin, Dylan, the Stones, *The Graduate*, *Easy Rider*, *Dr. Strangelove*, the Cuban missile crisis, Vietnam, Kent State, Altamont, race riots, the Chicago DNC, and repeated political assassinations. The hopes of youth in the face of establishment repression created a time of questioning religion's relevance and experimenting with new alternatives.

The 1970s, considered as 1972 to 1979, was a period of *shaken anxiety*. Nixon, Vietnam, more race riots, Bye-Bye Miss American Pie, the war on drugs, Watergate, impeachment, OPEC oil embargos, the energy crisis, stagflation, Three Mile Island, Jimmy Carter, Soviet aggressions, the Iranian hostage crisis, astronomical interest rates, superpower slippage, Jonestown, the divorce revolution, the Me Generation, New Age preachers, disco, underground punk, arena rock, Jackson Browne, Led Zeppelin, Aerosmith, Black Sabbath, *The Godfather*, *Taxi Driver*, *Alien*, *Jaws*, and *Apocalypse Now*.

The pervasive unease and bleakness combined with mainline Protestant and Catholic decline engendered religious anxieties and new evangelical mobilizations.

The 1980s was a phase of *hopeful rebirth*. It was "Morning in America" with Ronald Reagan, the "Teflon president," the Iran hostage "October Surprise," renewed Cold War fortitude, neoliberalism's rollout, tax cuts, unions crushed, liberalism retreating, Grenada invaded, standing up to the Sandinistas, Oliver North, cable TV and VCRs, MTV, the Walkman emerging, *Top Gun*, *Rambo I*, *II*, and *III*, *Rocky III* and *IV*, *Karate Kid*, *Tootsie*, big-hair rock bands, patriotic televangelists, and the Moral Majority, Family Research Council, and Christian Coalition. Still, underground punk, No Nukes protests, Iran-Contra, Gen X *Breakfast Club* attitudes, the spawning of Goth, and the breakout of religious sex and financial scandals signaled that the optimistic rebirth could not last forever. Nonetheless, for a time, conservative religion at least seemed on a rebound.

The 1990s, considered from the revolutions of 1989 until 2001, swept in with immense transformations in a spirit of *boundary-breaking exhilaration*. The decade had its troubles. But they were overshadowed by the relief and promise of the Soviet Union's collapse, the end of the Cold War, the New World Order, the Peace Dividend, neoliberalism's triumph, unrestrained globalization, "Third Way" politics, Clinton-Blair grins, the prevailing of democratic capitalism, the successful and televised Gulf War, global prosperity, Nelson Mandela, NAFTA, a federal budget surplus, *Titanic*, *Pretty Woman*, *The Lion King*, *Sister Act*, *Saving Private Ryan*, *Toy Story*, ubiquitous sitcom TV, Japanese anime, proliferating McMansions, gene therapy trials, Viagra, Furbies, Pokémon, medical cannabis legalized in California, the birth of the internet, the "information superhighway," Dot.com euphoria, the invention of dating apps, the ubiquitous Walkman, and the spread of cordless phones, video games, pagers, portable CD players, and desktop computers. Even the Monica Lewinsky scandal, the Columbine school massacre, Hurricane Andrew, Jeffrey Dahmer, war in the Balkans, ethnic cleansing, repeated terrorist bombings, the assassination of Yitzhak Rabin, deepening domestic political incivility, and growing conflicts over church and state could not deflate the good times. Meanwhile, beneath the happy surface, a weird and darker underculture was growing in *Twin Peaks*, *The X-Files*, *Pulp Fiction*, *Fight Club*, *Fargo*, *Edward Scissorhands*, *The Blair Witch Project*, *The Matrix*, *Jurassic Park*, *Armageddon*, *The Silence of the Lambs*, grunge and indie rock, gangsta rap, raves, Goth subculture, emo, and myriad postmodern miens. This was the beginning of the end of traditional religion, although at the time that was impossible to detect.

The 2000s, then, were times of *depressing gloom*. September 11, Bush II, the war on terror, invasion of Iraq, White House lies, Abu Ghraib, the Dot.com bubble burst, Silicon Valley surveillance, revenge porn, the spread of antidepressants, growing obesity and diabetes, the space shuttle *Columbia* disaster, the 2008 financial meltdown, the Great Recession, growing economic precarity, the rise of the China superpower, deadly European heatwaves, Australia on fire, *An Inconvenient Truth*, intensifying domestic political nastiness, and Catholic priest abuse and cover-up scandals. Dark movies were ubiquitous, *The Departed, Memento, The Dark Knight, No Country for Old Men, Mystic River, There Will Be Blood, Inglorious Basterds, Lost in Translation, Kill Bill, Black Hawk Down* among them. Many enjoyed iPods, GPS navigation, digital cameras, the internet, social media, iPhones, flat panel displays, television and movie streaming, and apps for everything. But digital life's dark side was also showing its malignant face.

The realities of these decades were, of course, more complicated. But reality is not what matters most when it comes to cultural representations, either lived or remembered. More important are the events, figures, symbols, slogans, sensibilities, and artistic expressions that represent periods of time. These, I suggest, were those that capture the public mood of these decades as Americans experienced them at the time and made sense of them in retrospect.

An important observation: while the two decades flanking the turn of our century were crucial in religion's obsolescence, they embodied different moods. The 1990s were overall upbeat and exciting. The 2000s were somber and hard. The spirit of the age across both decades was one single zeitgeist, with continuities of underlying assumptions, interests, and responses. Yet its tenor shifted from the 1990s to the 2000s. If we want to attach labels (like "The Roaring Twenties" or "The Wild West") we might differentiate "The Unbounded Nineties" from "The Gloomy 2000s." I am less concerned with labels, however, than with the recognition that this era's one zeitgeist underwent an internal swing from one feeling to another. That down-spirited shift—like that of the late 1960s into the 1970s—itself contributed to religion's obsolescence. In the first phase of the zeitgeist, things seemed so good that people found themselves wondering why anyone would need religion. In the second, reality seemed so bleak that religion's proffered hope and comfort seemed superficial and unrealistic.

Thematic Tones of the Age

Can we say more about the tone or feel of the zeitgeist that spanned the 1990s and 2000s? What follows enumerates core cultural themes and sensibilities that helped define its spirit. No such tally can be systematic or coherent since cultures are generally not coherent systems. These features and feelings arose from a variety of sources—most described in previous chapters—and were expressed in disparate ways. Some fit one decade better than the other. Together they name central contours and feelings of the era. The times felt

- Connected: Networked, global, open, plugged in, roving, appropriating
- Virtual: Digitized, simulated, on screen, transcending face-to-face, blurring lines between reality and images
- Competitive: Intensified competition for unequal economic prosperity, middle classes losing ground, a growing precariat
- Unregulated: Liquidated elite standards, gatekeeper authorities broken down, popular antinomianism (resistance to established rules), the "democratization of genius"[2]
- Entertained: Amused, distracted, mass spectacle, over-the-top performance, global sporting events, aspirations of luxury and carnival for all
- Hypersexualized: Continually pushing the envelope on nudity, body displays, sex, kink
- Unbounded: Guardrails down, free exploration, unbalanced, fluid, lacking fixed groundings
- Shameless: Embarrassment eroded, privacy lost, the previously behind-closed-doors exposed to the masses
- Relativist: Against judging, tolerant, acceptance of difference, multiculturalist, "You do you"
- Dark: Grim, somber, extinguished innocence, raw knowledge of harsh reality
- Defeated: Disappointed, lowered expectations, letdown, progress for the privileged only
- Moronic: Male "mooks" doing reckless stunts on camara for attention and laughs, comedy of idiots, "bloopers," "fails," funniest videos morphing toward FailArmy
- Floating: Insensible to tradition, lost connection to history, presentism, a novel world unfolding, the "End of History," the future unimaginable

- Fluid: Liquid experience, flux, reinventing body and identity makeovers, flexible personhoods, gender mutability, body piercings, tattoos, fluorescent hair
- Conflicted: Escalating political, religious, cultural wars accompanied by the avoidance of interpersonal conflict, Rodney King, South Central LA, O. J. Simpson, rising polarization
- Re-enchanted: Revived fascination with the paranormal, supernatural, mysterious, occult, monstrous, magical, fantastic, pagan

The question, again: How would or could traditional religion fit into an era defined by such feelings and moods?

Toward a Formal Analytics of the Millennial Zeitgeist

Next follows an examination of formal analytical dimensions of the zeitgeist by means of concepts noted in the Introduction.

Time Duration

The zeitgeist broke out in 1991 and lasted through the 2000s. "Broke out" acknowledges that many of its cultural roots in various subcultures and movements had developed over preceding decades and, some, even centuries. 1991, however, was the year it all started coming together to express and shape post-Boomer culture on a macro level. Whether and when the zeitgeist has ended is more difficult to judge this close to the era. By my reckoning, as of this writing, Gen Z has made no significant breaks from the post-Boomer cultural sensibility but is continuing to work out the implications of the inherited culture.

Why was 1991 the starting year? The impact of the end of the Cold War on the fate of American religion was huge but was not the only portentous event of 1991. The following belong to the mix of happenings that year that proved to be turning points in the direction of the emerging zeitgeist:

- The first uptick in Americans identifying as religious "nones."
- The launch of the World Wide Web (WWW) and first web page going live.

- The launch of America Online (AOL).
- The rollout of second-generation cellular phone technology.
- The Dow Jones Industrial Average closing above 3,000 for the first time in history.
- The Seattle-based grunge band Nirvana releasing its album *Nevermind*, selling 11 million copies and terminating the reign of 1970s–1980s synth pop and big-hair glam rock.
- Hip-hop breaking into the mainstream.
- Multiple important occulture role-play games (RPGs) launched, including *Vampire: The Masquerade*, *Kult*, *Dark Conspiracy*, and *Tales from the Floating Vagabond*.
- UVA sociologist, James D. Hunter, publishing *Culture Wars: The Struggle to Define America*.
- Supreme Court nominee Clarence Thomas accused by Anita Thomas of sexual harassment (Thomas is confirmed nevertheless).

In addition, these 1991 events contributed indirectly in various ways to the feel of the coming new era:

- Los Angeles Lakers's Magic Johnson announces he has HIV.
- The Tailhook scandal exposes sexual assaults on 83 women at a US Navy association meeting in Las Vegas.
- Operation Desert Storm is a huge US military success broadcast daily on television.
- South African apartheid is legally repealed.
- Boris Yeltsin is elected president of Russia.
- President Bush makes unilateral reductions in nuclear weapons; Russia responds in kind.
- *Seinfeld*, the "show about nothing," begins its second-season climb in ratings to rank number 1.
- *Sonic the Hedgehog* video game is released, selling 2 million copies.

Spatial and Social Scope

This dimension concerns a zeitgeist's reach across geographical and social space. Where and among whom was it important? Following John Hopkins University sociologist Monika Kraus, we need not assume that a zeitgeist unites an era as an integrated cultural whole.[3] In the United States, the Millennial zeitgeist originated in East and West Coast urban areas and spread out from there through many media. Its primary "carriers" were post-Boomers. Cable television, franchised pop culture retailers (like Abercrombie & Fitch and Urban Outfitters), the internet, and eventually smart phones spread the zeitgeist nearly everywhere. Its intellectual sources—postmodernism, multiculturalism, and so on—trickled down from universities and colleges. Its pop culture contents were mostly creations of marginalized young people, like rap and hip-hop artists from New York and Los Angeles and alienated Seattle-area grunge rockers. More privileged adolescents—white suburban teenagers who emulated urban Black youth culture, wore grunge flannel shirts and combat boots and assumed Goth and emo attitudes—proved fertile grounds for its flourishing.

Few American religious communities remained untouched by the zeitgeist. The pervasive cultural power of the spirit of the age overwhelmed any potential zeitgeist-resistant religious influences on post-Boomers. If anything, religious youth programs and styles often incorporated its trappings—Exhibit A being the then-ubiquitous hip, chill youth group leader sporting a soul-patch, torn R. E. M. tee shirt, and flipped-back baseball cap. Truly immune populations tended to be exceptionally religiously sheltered—serving on Church of Latter Day Saints (LDS, Mormon) missions, attending fundamentalist colleges, and so on. Baby Boomers, despite having earlier prepared much of the ideological groundwork for the zeitgeist, often treated Gen Xers and Millennials as bewildering and sometimes deficient—they usually kept their distance until some began to buy in during the latter 2000s and 2010s. Except in some pockets, the Millennial zeitgeist was eventually pervasive.

Narrative Course

The question here concerns how the zeitgeist's scope evolved over time. As earlier chapters argued, we can trace some of its cultural threads back to various pioneers and movements for decades and centuries. Many key themes first became established in Boomer popular culture in the 1960s and 1970s. After the inhibiting 1980s suppressed their development, the floodgates began opening in 1991. The host of forces and events described in the previous five chapters brought on the zeitgeist rapidly. Its initial adverse effects on traditional religion were already evident in the 1990s, as we

CONTOURS OF THE MILLENNIAL ZEITGEIST   287

saw in Chapter 1. Empirical indicators and my own reading of the times suggest that the zeitgeist has continued as the dominant spirit of the 2010s and beyond, transmuted in some ways but also intensified among Generation Z. When and how the Millennial zeitgeist will morph into something clearly different, as of this writing, remains to be seen.

Characteristic "Carrying" Groups and Media

The zeitgeist was, I have said, birthed and carried by post-Boomers—first developed and trialed by Gen Xers, then expanded and amplified full-blown by Millennials.[4] Culturally and economically alienated, though not necessarily disadvantaged, youth were early adopters and promoters. Key initial launching and carrying media were cable television, proliferating independent record labels, and the subcultural infrastructures of role-play games, like Dungeons & Dragons and *Vampire: The Masquerade*. MTV was an especially important early promoter and carrier. In time, the internet and digital-related technologies took over previous leaders as the dominant media carriers of the zeitgeist. Culturally attuned Gen Xers and older Millennials developed most of the creative initiatives and content, while Silent Generation and Boomer capitalists owned and reaped profits from the key firms and industries. Multiple musical movements and genres—post-punk, pop punk, grunge, emo, death metal, extreme metal, hardcore, indie rock, gangsta rap, industrial—helped lead the way in setting influential aesthetics and manners. As the zeitgeist expanded its influence, new populations, like white and Asian suburban teenagers and college students, became additional carrier groups.

Crucial Events

Much of this book has been spent explaining the events that produced and defined the Millennial zeitgeist, a few of which I mention here. Key events on the bright face of the zeitgeist include the end of the Cold War, the public introduction to the internet, neocapitalist global prosperity, and possibly the 1997 Kyoto Protocol on climate change. For post-Boomers, the initially happiest part of the era was all the shiny, new technology. On the dark side, major events include the South Central Los Angeles riots of

1992, the Columbine High School massacre, the Oklahoma City bombing, the murder of Matthew Shepard, the O. J. Simpson "trial of the century," the Y2K scare, September 11, the Dot.com bubble burst, and Hurricane Katrina. Emblematic of and contributing to the zeitgeist's bleakness was the suicide of Nirvana's Kurt Cobain in 1994.

Embodying Public Figures and Celebrities

The complexity and longevity of the Millennial zeitgeist means it includes countless public figures and celebrities who embodied and promoted it in various ways. That overwhelming number of personas is itself an indicative feature of the zeitgeist, signaling the centrality in it of unending superstars, personalities, artists, controversialists, bands, entertainers, and other celebrities. Their dominant presence conveys how essential media technology was for enabling the zeitgeist and the critical role that the consumption of entertainment, fame, attractiveness, and competition played in its ethos. I could list pages of public personas who figured in creating and defining the spirit of this age, but space limitations curb my enumeration to a short list of representatives. Selection for focus here is a tricky matter since influence on and representation of the zeitgeist are not the same as most popular or highest earning. Any short list is bound to be debatable. My choices are based primarily on how these figures shaped and embodied the zeitgeist in the 1990s and 2000s in ways that affected traditional religion. Gen Xers include

- Kurt Cobain
- Jessica Simpson
- Tupac Shakur
- Charlie Sheen
- Kim Kardashian
- Monica Lewinski
- Oprah Winfrey[5]
- Sergey Brin
- Pamela Anderson
- Eminem
- Jennifer Aniston
- Leonardo DiCaprio
- Snoop Dogg
- Sarah Jessica Parker
- Billy Joe Armstrong
- Snooki
- Paris Hilton
- Winona Ryder
- Sinéad O'Connor
- Black Eyed Peas
- River Phoenix
- Kanye West
- Robert Downey Jr.
- Alanis Morissette

- The Notorious B.I.G
- Jennifer Love Hewitt
- R. Kelly
- Nelly
- Elliott Smith
- Jennifer Lopez
- Julia Roberts
- 50 Cent
- Pete Wentz
- Puffy Daddy
- Jay-Z

Millennial-generation public figures and celebrities of the zeitgeist important in the 1990s and 2000s include

- Britney Spears
- Beyoncé
- Justin Bieber
- Miley Cyrus
- Mark Zuckerberg
- Kelly Clarkson
- No Doubt
- Katy Perry
- The Killers
- Hilary Duff
- Kristen Stewart
- Robert Pattinson
- Lady Gaga
- Amy Winehouse
- Brendon Urie
- Taylor Swift
- Justin Timberlake
- The Olsen Twins

Assuming that the religious and spiritual lives of these public figures and celebrities might signal what is normal or cool to post-Boomers, we systematically analyzed available online information on the topic for all of the names listed above. The results obviously cannot reveal what actually goes on in the minds, hearts, and practices of these people, only what the public can learn about them from internet searches. Eighty-one percent of those named above were raised in some religious context—which is not surprising, especially for American singers who often first learn music and performance in religious congregations. Nineteen percent were not raised religious. Of the 81% raised religious, 36% appear to have remained religious or returned to religion during their years of fame—often after periods away from faith while struggling with addictions or other problems. Pamela Anderson, for example—whose stolen sex tape helped launch the VHS pornography revolution—says she grew up wanting to become a nun and still incorporates religion into her daily life: "I have my prayers I say in the morning. I have to do my routine, my Hail Marys, my little thing with my little Mary sculpture."[6] Kanye West and Justin Bieber are also both famously Christian. Of those raised in a religion, 64% dropped out as young adults—with 40% of them appearing to have become not religious and 24% professing to be "spiritual but not religious." Of the 19% of the group not raised in a religion, all but two remained not religious during their years of fame—the exceptions being Eminem and 50 Cent, who came to profess the importance of spirituality and a higher power.

The most publicly accessible signals about religion that these biographies communicate come in the form of quips that many provide in interviews, nearly all of which—even from those who remain religious—express iconic zeitgeist themes. Oprah Winfrey, for instance, who sometimes attends an evangelical church in Dallas, Texas, famously said, "I have church with myself. I have church walking down the street. I believe in the God force that lives inside all of us, and once you tap into that, you can do anything." Jennifer Aniston, who for some time attended the Greek Orthodox Church yet keeps her religious views private, said in an interview, "I don't have a religion. I believe in a God. I don't know what it looks like, but it's MY God, my interpretation of the supernatural." Julia Roberts, whose father was Baptist and mother was Catholic, was raised Catholic but later converted to Hinduism for "spiritual satisfaction," she said, because the "spirituality in it transcends many barriers of mere religion." Snoop Dog, who was raised Baptist, later reported to be a member of the Nation of Islam and then a convert to Rastafarianism, has said that all religions are the same, being about "God-fearing people" believing that "love is love." He says religion is very personal and should not be pushed on people. Robert Downey Jr., whose father was Jewish and mother Catholic, has described himself as "Jewish Buddhist," consulted astrologers, had interest in Hare Krishna, and practiced Catholicism while in prison, eventually calling himself part of the "Spiritual Green Party."[7]

Symbolic and Artistic Expressions

The most important symbolic expression of the early zeitgeist was MTV. If any single event could be taken as emblematic of the tone of the zeitgeist's middle period, it might be the release of the Pamela Anderson–Tommy Lee sex tape. The cell phone selfie was the archetypical symbolic expression of the latter zeitgeist. Other important expressions came in television and movies, with these providing a partial list of what could be a very full inventory: *The Simpsons, Beavis and Butt-Head, Sex and the City, Seinfeld, Friends, Beverly Hills, 90210, Baywatch, Dawson's Creek,* the *Twilight* saga, the *Austin Powers* movies, *Basic Instinct, Striptease, Dumb and Dumber, Jerry Springer, American Idol, Road Rules, Celebrity Deathmatch, Undressed, MTV Cribs, The Swan, Pimp My Car, The CollegeHumor Show, Newlyweds: Nick and Jessica, Punk'd, Jersey Shore, What Not to Wear, The Real Housewives of Orange County,* and *Date My Mom*. Important zeitgeist books include the Harry Potter series, *Eat Pray Love,* the *Goosebumps* series, *Chicken Soup for the Soul, The Da Vinci Code,* and *The Hunger Games* trilogy. Musical movements that shaped the zeitgeist were grunge, hip-hop, indie rock, alternative, industrial rock, skate punk, ska, metal, electronic dance music, Britpop, and teen pop. Myriad subgenres of metal developed, including industrial, stoner, speed, sludge, thrash, black, Viking, doom, and death metal. Significant stage musicals include *Rent, Wicked, High School Musical, Dear Evan Hansen, Spamalot,* and *American Idiot*. "High art" expressions of the zeitgeist would include Robert Mapplethorpe's *The Perfect Moment* photography exhibit tour of 1989–1990, and Andres Serrano's 1987 *Immersion (Piss Christ)*, which created controversy for two decades. Those familiar with the items on these lists should understand the cultural mismatches between almost all of them and the beliefs and sensibilities of traditional religion.

Styles of Attire and Presentation of Self

This enormous topic I must keep brief. 1990s styles emphasized minimalist, casual, and sometimes unkempt looks, and tattoos and body piercings grew more popular. The 2000s were an eclectic mash-up of global styles, ethnic designs, and the looks of retro movements and music subcultures. The zeitgeist reveled in the multiplicity of options of attire that expressed unique personal identities—although, ironically, most were trends and fads modeled after television, movie, and music stars. With globalized clothes production pushing fast fashion, apparel identity makeovers were easy and quick. Certain of the fluctuating styles and trends during these two decades were especially relevant for our purposes, including the following:

> *Grunge*: Pacific Northwest plaid flannel shirts, casual and untucked, ripped and faded jeans, band logo tee-shirts, all worn loosely with

combat boots, simple jewelry, and bold makeup—ideally bought cheap at a thrift store.

Hip-hop: Urban sportswear, including baseball caps, droopy pants, basketball shorts, tracksuits, hoodies, and bling. Retro gangster influences included double-breasted suits, silk shirts, bowler hats, and gator-skin shoes.

Streetwear: Distressed skinny jeans, baggy shirts, tracksuits, hoodies, thrift-shop graphic tee-shirts.

Hipster: Vintage clothes, alternative fashions, or a combination of clashing fashions, including skinny jeans, knit beanies, lumberjack beards, elaborate moustaches, thick-rimmed or no-lens glasses.

Goth: Tight pants, leather skirts, frilly shirts, velvet blazers, black leather trench coats, antique corsets, fetish attire, lace gloves, winkle-picker shoes, black demonia boots, long black hair, facial piercings.

Punk and Skater: Ripped jeans, black leather jackets, checked shirts, studded belts, bright spiky hair, choker necklaces, fingerless fashion gloves, Vans shoes, chained wallets.

1960s Bohemian: Low-rise jeans, capris, dresses over jeans, cowl-neck shirts, peasant shirts, cropped jackets, chunky belts, aviator sunglasses, jelly bracelets, ballet flats, platform boots.

Rave clubwear: Bell-bottoms pants, neoprene jackets, tight nylon shirts and quilted vests, studded belts, platform shoes, faux fur jackets, scarves, and bags, fluffy neon boots, bright phat pants, brightly dyed hair, dreadlocks, tattoos, piercings, wristbands and collars, whistles, pacifiers, white gloves, glow sticks, feather boas.

Indie sleaze: Reacting to the Great Recession, cheap, torn, skinny jeans, high-top Converse sneakers, studded platform lace-up boots, tennis skirts, shimmering leggings, sheer tops, ballet flats, leather jackets, fedoras, shutter shades, no-lens glasses, chunky jewelry, chokers, layered necklaces, and smudged eye makeup.

As different as these styles were, they shared the avant-garde intention of resisting and critiquing social conventionality. They demonstrated disdain for mainstream norms, certifying wearers as alienated, offbeat originals. They announced authenticity, validating wearers' unspoken claims of having come from the hood, the tenement, the working class, the disaffected and the oppressed. Many merged a playful, childlike dressing-up fun with an intimidating "fuck you" attitude toward outsiders. They both seized and scorned ordinary onlookers' attention.

Their ensembles often reflected the postmodern sensibility of eclecticism and disharmony. They embodied creativity, estrangement, dissent—and, some said, a particular narcissism. In principle, a religion could embrace and make welcome the sensibilities embodied in these styles. Christianity's founder, for example, was notorious for hanging out with marginal and questionable types. But American traditional religion at the turn of the century was not well positioned to make alienated and anti-conventional youth feel welcomed. Post-Boomers viewed religion as something for good people, and little in the zeitgeist aspired to be good.

Common Slogans

The spirit of the age showed in the era's slang: "Whatever," "don't judge me," "no duh," "you do you," "take a chill pill," "as if!," "let's get crunk," "bros over hoes," "bae," "biatch," "dope," "sick," "buff," "shook," "7-up yours," "that's hot," "talk to the hand, 'cos the face ain't listening," "meh," "going postal," "bling bling," "peace out." The self-assurance, indifference, sarcasm, cliquishness, and trash talk this slang expressed fit poorly with life in traditional religion. Revealing, too, were the era's ubiquitous advertising jingles and brand slogans: "Obey your thirst," "Hungry why wait?," "Do what feels right," "Think different," "Do it your way," "I want my baby back ribs," "Gotta have my Pops," "Have you had your fun today?," "I don't wanna grow up, I'm a Toys R Us kid," "Because you're worth it," "Expect more, pay less," "Be all that you can be," "Where's the beef?," "Once you pop, you can't stop," "Double your pleasure, double your fun," "Just do it," "Live beyond expectations," "Drive your ambition," "Maybe she's born with it, maybe it's Maybelline," "Every kiss begins with Kay," "Have a Coke and smile," "Good food, good life," "Life tastes good," "Open happiness." Unrelenting were the dogmas of consumer entitlement, impulsiveness, competition, the right to self-indulgence, and consumption = happiness. Some slogans commodified eternity through jewelry: "A diamond is forever." Chapter 4 examined the cultural consequences of mass-consumer capitalism. The zeitgeist expressed those consequences. The more consumerism's narratives shaped the values, aspirations, and identities of young Americans, the more alien and mismatched traditional religious narratives felt.

A Caveat

To be clear, I am not claiming that every cultural phenomenon in the 1990s and 2000s belonged to the Millennial zeitgeist. The items named above are a select inventory of cultural expressions that more clearly expressed the zeitgeist. But the zeitgeist stood out among and against other cultural expressions of the era. Some differences were generational: the Millennial zeitgeist was a post-Boomer thing; older Americans had other cultural interests—including upscaling their lifestyles, rollerblading and cycling, and perhaps religion. Gen Xers and Millennials were also part of other cultural streams not clearly part of the zeitgeist discussed here. Important younger public figures who were not particularly part of the Millennial zeitgeist included Whitney Houston, Tiger Woods, Sandra Bullock, and Tom Cruise. Big movies like *Forrest Gump*, *Schindler's List*, *Beauty and the Beast*, and *Pride and Prejudice* and television shows like *ER*, *Coach*, and *NCIS* were all popular during this period but not part of the zeitgeist. Common slang used well outside the zeitgeist included "my bad" and "coolness." In clothing fashion, more mainstream styles besides standard work attire for professionals were casual khakis with white tee-shirts, midi-length dresses, overalls, and UGGs. The era also saw the Kate Middleton look and an elegant Hollywood star mien—also not part of the zeitgeist. The point here is that not everything in these two decades was zeitgeisty. So the Millennial zeitgeist was not the only movement and feeling in post-Boomer culture during this time. It was, however, the definite cultural center of gravity and the most important cultural reality for understanding traditional religion's obsolescence.

The Defining Grunge Rock (and Mismatched Christian Counterparts)

Yet another way to get a feel for the zeitgeist is to study its defining music. Musical influences in the 1990s and 2000s were complicated. For our purposes, we can focus on of the pivotal song that ended the era of big-hair glam rock and helped launch the Millennial zeitgeist: the grunge band Nirvana's 1991 smash hit "Smells Like Teen Spirit." No single song can capture the attitude of an entire era, but if any song could, this would be it. "Smells" hit a cultural nerve and came to be considered by critics as one of the most influential songs in rock history.[8] One out of 10 of the post-Boomers we interviewed named Nirvana as an influence in their life.

Here is the exercise for readers. Search YouTube for "Nirvana – Smells like Teen Spirit" and click on the "Official Music Video" version that should appear at the top. Watch it once through, taking note of the lyrics, images, and mood. Remember that whatever Nirvana was "trying" to say is less important than the impact it had on audiences, its "performative effect." What would this hit video have impressed upon the youth audiences? What sensibilities, outlook, attitude would it have evoked, encouraged, promoted? What do the lyric contents, tone, style, performers, and "plot" communicate? Then watch the video again, noticing the mélange of smoky gloom; boredom; alienation; sarcasm; lyrical contradiction; references to danger, denial, and self-denigration; frenzied breakdown; expressive physicality; "scarlet letter" Anarchy symbols on cheerleaders; the low-status janitor caught up in the vibe; and a school principal bound with a dunce cap. The final, epitomizing words: "Whatever, nevermind."

Consider then how American traditional religion might have related to this music. What of interest and relevance might a pastor or rabbi have had to say to the millions of Gen Xers for whom this song and video struck home? What, if any, points of connection might have existed between traditional religion and grunge? Very few to none, I suggest—as the years after 1991 proved.

To drive home the point of cultural mismatch, next listen for comparison to the YouTube videos of the number 1 song on the Contemporary Christian Music (CCM) chart that same year, 1991: Wayne Watson's "Home Free."[9] Much of this soft pop tune sounds like elevator music. The lyrics address human grief and suffering, but the proposed solution is that "eventually, at the ultimate healing, we will be home free" in heaven. In short: pie in the sky, by and by. The recommended prayer in the face of suffering? "Not mine, but your will be done"—that is, submission like Jesus to death on a cross, though sung in a velvety soothing voice. Our interest here is not theological validity but cultural understanding. Consider the countless American Gen X youth for whom "Smells Like Teen Spirit" resounded like a thunderclap in 1991. Imagine what Watson's "Home Free" would represent to them. Softness, comfort, and an easy otherworldly evasion of grief in the present— for mothers, husbands, and wives (older people) who are named in the song as those who suffer. The cultural dissonance was huge.

For good measure, finally, watch the YouTube video of the number 1 tune on the CCM chart for 1992 (when "Smells Like Teen Spirit" was rocketing to platinum on the charts), the mullet-sporting, vocal quartet, 4Him's song, "Basics of Life."[10] Here, mimicking the discourse of the Christian Right, we hear a lament about the loss of cultural "virtues" and "morals" that in days past "governed our lives." The lyrics warn a "new day has dawned" in which truth is lost, right and wrong confused, God denied, and faith placed instead in human reason and meditation. The bad is represented (in black-and-white visuals) as somber blue-collar people smoking in a gritty grill café and a cantankerous woman fighting with her exasperated man in front of their upset child. The good is depicted (in color) as happy, harmonious, white, middle-class families riding horses together on sunlit farm pastures.[11] A pretty, white clapboard, country church backgrounds the confession, "I still believe in the old rugged cross" (referencing a popular church hymn written in 1912). Race shows up in all important actors being white, and Black individuals as grinning backup musicians. All the romance depicted is of heterosexual Boomer and Silent Generation couples. Thus, as the Millennial zeitgeist rose on the national scene, the top Christian music of 1992 conveyed a misty nostalgia for a bygone, white, bourgeois social order and religious governance of life. The contrast with Nirvana's mega-hit could not have been starker. Gen Xers (and, soon, Millennials) were not buying the religious thing at all.[12]

The Zeitgeist in Expert Advice

The spirits of zeitgeists are often best conveyed through fiction—*The Great Gatsby* being one example. Sociology is not fiction. I offer, however, one last approach to describing the Millennial zeitgeist in quasi-fictional form, that is, the hypothetical advice that I imagine an experienced participant in the zeitgeist might give a newcomer, as follows:

> Listen, life is short, then it's over. Boom. It can be a bitch or a beach. Make the most of it while you can. Don't waste your youth. Figure out who you are and don't let anybody tell you different. Find your journey and go for it. No limits. No regrets. The opportunities are amazing. The world is an infinite shopping trip, dance party, job promotion, hookup, whatever you want. You might even get lucky and make real money. In any case, expect to get cynical pretty quick, then just have a good satirical smirk. You gotta

be smart cause the world is mean, competition is crazy, people get hurt. It sucks. Don't be that victim or loser. Watch out for scams and manipulators. Don't get stuck. Keep moving forward. Be true to yourself. Enjoy your family and friends. Don't screw others. Don't try to change anyone. Live and let live. Sure, the world is a train wreck and the future is probably shit. Just live in the moment. Try to make a difference if you want, but don't be naïve. It's all a big game. Nobody's got the answers. Reality is weirder than authorities know or will say—don't be surprised to find out there is more going on out there than science or the government will admit. Believe your gut. Play life on your terms. Take care of yourself. Find some inner peace that works for you. Don't get too serious. Chill. Enjoy the show. It's all good. Even when it's not.

Note that this advice says nothing critical about religion—an absence that itself is telling. Why talk about something irrelevant? If any reader suspects or hopes that absence might be a mere oversight, they should consider how traditional religion would fit into this advice's larger picture of reality and life. Is there a place? The only related room is for individual "spirituality," for inner peace or other esoteric, re-enchanted, or non-traditional ideas that keep life interesting.

An Analytical Model of Zeitgeist Cultural Assumptions

Finally, I shift to develop an "analytical model" of the cultural beliefs underlying the zeitgeist, one based on the kind developed by cognitive anthropologists.[13] An analytical model in this approach is a reconstruction in condensed, organized, propositional forms of people's operating cultural models—that is, their shared, subjective, cognitive assumptions and beliefs. The *cultural* models are the real, operative background beliefs people actually hold and use to make sense of life. *Analytical* models are the propositional reconstructions of those cultural models that scholars of culture formulate. This is done through a careful, systematic analysis of extended discourse—in this case, of our in-depth interviews and focus groups with post-Boomers. People's cognitions are organized in "schemas" that are neither systematically ordered nor entirely random but are instead variably coherent and structured. They often cluster together into what we call *cultural models*. Behind and beneath what people are able to explain in interviews lay complex networks of assumptions and beliefs that inform what they do say. *Analytical* models organize and systematically structure the assumptions and beliefs of those cultural models for others to understand.

How does it work? Researchers do not have direct access to people's minds. Nor can people simply sit down and tell you about all of their assumptions and beliefs, many of which are too obvious or opaque to state. People intuitively know a lot more than they can directly tell. How then can we identify their operative cognitive beliefs? The answer is through careful analysis of people's discourse. Get people to talk a lot and from different perspectives about a subject of interest, closely study what they say and how they say it, and develop from that a systematic analysis of the cognitive assumptions and beliefs people hold. This method "brings to the surface" suppositions about which they may not even be consciously reflective.[14] This requires not only taking at face value what people say on the "surface" but also listening and interpreting what their discourse reveals.[15] We can then reconstruct those cognitive assumptions and beliefs in simplified, propositional forms. When done well, those analytical models "ring true"—which is to say, people should be able to recognize themselves in the reconstructed beliefs. In short, analytical models present in *condensed propositional form* the kinds of statements that people *would* make about their cultural cognitions *if they were fully self-aware, honest, and articulate* about their true assumptions and beliefs organized in their cultural models.[16]

What then are the underlying assumptions and beliefs that define the Millennial zeitgeist? Some of what follows we heard already in the previous historical chapters—which make sense, since that social history produced these ideas. Some of these also have roots far preceding the zeitgeist—for example, in the cultural revolutions of the 1960s, which rebooted in the 1990s. We find more than a few logical tensions or contradictions here, which is common in culture. Altogether, these underlying beliefs offer another way to understand the zeitgeist that pushed traditional religion into obsolescence.[17] The first 20 concern beliefs about life in general, while the second set of 14 are about religion specifically.[18]

1. *Each individual possesses a distinctive, essential selfhood that they need to discover, cultivate, realize, and express.* No two people are alike. Everyone has a particular package of beliefs, interests, and activities that fits their authentic personality and life.

In our interviews with post-Boomers, they continually said things like, "I think truth about reality or morality is different for everybody, everybody's is different," and "I'm still on that journey of figuring out what is my best self." The idea seemed almost scripted: "Everyone has their own individual meaning of what life is." "Individuals should follow their own thoughts and ideas, because not every individual is the same." "What a good life is could be so different for everyone." So as a result: "Trust your own personal beliefs. I don't think anybody can really tell you."

2. *Neglecting one's unique selfhood is irresponsible.* Discovering, cultivating, realizing, and expressing one's essential selfhood is one of life's most important tasks. Failing to do so for reasons within one's control is not only regrettable but also wrong.

This assumption was expressed in a variety of ways. Some spoke of self-actualization: "My view is mainly to progress in the sense of trying to achieve self-actualization and making the most of your life here." Others, of self-improvement and personal growth: "Now that I'm happy with my body after all of these years, I'm looking to the future, like okay, what's next? What else is there to improve?," and "I'm constantly trying to improve and be better. The moment you stop or think you know it all or you're good, that's when you stop growing. It's so important to continually try to improve and be better, so I try to keep that at the forefront of my mind. We're never gonna be perfect, but just striving in that direction is important." Central to all expressions of this assumption is the idea of remaining true to one's unique selfhood.

> If people wanna have a good life, they should build a foundation on their core values, take the time to sit down and reflect, pray if that's their thing, or meditate on what is the most important thing to them. They should write those things down and make sure they stay true to themselves. Like your own personal mission statement—what's the most important thing to me in my life? Then anything they do, any choice they make should be centered around what is most important to them and build toward that. To build a good life, you need goals and a plan for the things you want out of life, what's important to you, and then go and execute.

3. *Distinctively unique selves should be expected to change over time.* Little in life is fixed or stable enough for people to count on across an entire lifetime.

Flexibility of selfhood thus prevents selfhood essentialism from constraining options of evolving identities.

A common idea we heard in interviews was, "I don't really think there is much of an ultimate purpose or meaning, other than whatever you decide you want your life to be. That's the jazz of it: you get to improvise and decide for yourself what the meaning is." And,

> Given that we live in this interdependent world and everything is constantly changing, there is no permanence to be had. I'm aging. I mean nothing, nothing is permanent, not in me, not in you, not in the world. Everything is constantly in flux. So we've got to learn to be okay with this, how to let go. That's my philosophy of life.

The result is a continual impermanence of one's self existing in tension with the notion that everyone has one's unique essential selfhood.

> Be open to it evolving and changing over time. My best life now is completely different from what my best life would have been two years ago. I could not have imagined myself then being where I'm at now. It's important to accept change as not always a bad thing. Then just taking my situation every day, and expanding it to every week, every month, every year. What are my goals? Are they realistic? Are they anything exciting for life? If not, I need to change them.

4. *Authentic selves are continually at risk of being denied, twisted, or repressed by the combined energies of two powerfully alienating forces*:
   (a) the *external* forces of organized conformism, including parents, school, religion, workplace, peers, and media; and
   (b) the *internal* forces of *mental self-falsification*, such as insecurity, doubt, fear, self-judging, emotional dysfunction, and laziness.

Post-Boomers expressed the need to protect their distinctive selves against inauthenticity in a variety of ways, such as, "We need to stop listening to the outside world and go to our own self, to get toyed with yourself and your own being," and "I find it easy to look at other people's lives and think I want that or it looks nice. But really I am trying to learn how to find what's best for me now." The external social world does not care about one's good: "What makes for a good life? Work–life balance. Definitely. Don't kill yourself. Because the company is a machine. You've got to think of that and remember you're not." The threat is ever present:

> How do you figure out your purpose in life if you're living up to society's standards all the time? If you live in a world where you're taught to think one way, how do you find your purpose in that? How can you find out individually who you are if you're continuously being told you have to be a certain way, you can't do this, you can't do that?

Individuals must learn to resist those alienating forces, to actively fight against them:

> My philosophy of life: don't let society change who you are, don't ever let them change your heart. Because life itself is constantly a challenge. Just don't let it change you. All the institutions failed. I used to think that our leaders were like sacred, but they're not, they just commit improprieties.

The goal is to prevent one's "best self" from being compromised: "Even a year ago I was not in a good place, being overstressed, not sleeping enough, undereating, it was not good. So that sparked my whole taking seriously being my best self, versus like Instagram's best self."

5. *Growing up means "becoming one's own" person.* That requires breaking from forces that prevent you from becoming your authentic self, both external and internal. Each growing self must be prepared to veer from the past and reinvent itself.

The danger is accepting "someone else's reality" instead of the "reality you want": "A good life is just always being curious and finding what makes you happy, and not wishing your life away, not dreaming that someone else's reality would be your own. Make your reality what you want." Religion in particular needs to be questioned as possibly compromising one's own reality: "My family's religion was a tradition I grew up doing. But, as I got older, I realized that's the way that my parents perceived it, but not the same way I perceived it." And,

> The Catholic Church had a huge, negative influence on me. My parents were very religious and pro-life, and they took us children every year to the March on Washington. But as I grew up and developed my own opinions,

mine are very different now. That experience taught me civic duty, that you can protest. But as I got older and learned how to think for myself, I went the other way, made my own decisions, opened my mind, and said "no." There was no way the universe could be explained by one religion created by men, it seems so much bigger than that. My religious upbringing definitely had a negative effect, well, maybe some positive, because it did get me to think about things, even if it set me on a different course.

6. *To discover one's "true self," individuals must rely on their own subjective intuitive responses to their personal experiences.* One gains self-knowledge *internally*. Each individual is their *own* sole authority. (That said, one may voluntarily choose input and validation from certain outsiders, like therapists and life coaches.)[19]

Individual subjectivism is the zeitgeist's practical epistemology: "Individuals should trust their own stuff to decide how to live. There are influences out there, but you have to follow your own instinct and what you want." The external world provides information, but individuals choose what to do with it: "External things can inform, but I don't feel they have any sort of authority. No one has authority over anybody's life other than themselves." Behind this assumption is a distrust in the possibility of objective truth and value.

> You will find some light or guidance inside you that will take you there. Everything is subjective, no objective truths, it depends on how you were raised, the place you were born, your generation. Everything is subjective to them. History shows so many different approaches to life and culture, how to live and be better. So it depends on every single individual to find out what's the best way for them in this world.

Cultural and religious traditions can never override subjective experience: "If religion says gender equality is not true, people in my generation are more apt to choose their personal experience of truth over societal religious traditions. They say, 'I'm rejecting, I don't want those traditions because they don't align with my experience of the truth.'" In rare cases, this subjectivism can return post-Boomers to religion.

> I came back to religion because living life as an atheist is terrible. It was miserable, I couldn't go on, I got to a point where I was so unhappy. Regardless

whether you want to make an objective truth claim, there's no better claim than lived experience. And if the experience of me being an atheist is miserable, I don't want that. I would rather put my faith in something that brings me joy and meaning. It's really just as simple as that.

Even then, what drives the process is not conviction about objective truth but the pragmatic individual, subjective feeling consequences of believing or not. For most post-Boomers, that means leaving religion when it does not vibe.

7. *"Enlightened" individuals can scavenge alienating society for resources for self-realization.* These may include
   (a) targeted *experiences* of world- and self-discovery, such as meetup groups, workshops, and planned encounters, like Burning Man or wilderness trips; and
   (b) enriching *information* and self-education, such as self-help books, seminars, and YouTube programs.

All such resources, however, must be *voluntary*, *porous*, and *flexible*, never constraining or uniform.

The external, social, institutional world is not totally bad, because it contains resources that individuals can use to inform and develop their authentic selves. For some, that involves therapy: "I am living more for myself now, paying more attention to myself. That's a Gen X thing. It took us a while to get to that, but we're doing therapy now and we're taking care of ourselves." For others, it is reading: "I figure out the meaning or purpose of life by reading. I do my thing and reading is it. Reading is where I look for things that inspire or for answers to the question, maybe astrophysics or philosophy or something." Science can be another societal source of information for figuring out one's own life: "I feel individuals should trust their own beliefs, but, at the same time, it doesn't hurt to be educated to help make decisions as well, like having an idea about science and things like that." Post-Boomers also use the internet and social media as resources to sort out their own interests, including religion and spirituality.

> YouTube is excellent for learning about spirituality and religion. I go there to learn about religion as history, watch talks, listen to podcasts. I even listen to audio religious texts. Recently I listened to a book in the Bible

called Proverbs, which was interesting. That's probably the only book in the Bible I've ever enjoyed. That was cool. Yeah, the internet, Wikipedia. I'll go on there and look up stuff about religion all the time.

Personal experiences at organized events and festivals are another way to pursue the discovery and expression of one's true self, as noted here about the Burning Man festival in Nevada: "Burning Man to me means freedom, and freedom is very good. That's what I get from it because you're going out and finding your own person and experiencing life to its fullest."

8. *A good person living a good life is happy with themselves, cares for and enjoys their loved ones, and should be decent to other people they encounter.* It is good to enjoy what you do for a living, but it is not the highest value. Work is ultimately just a means to providing the basics of life. Real meaning and happiness come from relationships, experiences, and satisfaction with oneself. "Social ethics" are interpersonal and minimal, not institutional.[20] A really good person may go the extra mile to make the world "a better place" even for strangers, but that is not necessary.

The post-Boomers we interviewed were nearly unanimous about this vision of the good, saying things like, "A good life is just being happy with the people around you, your family, being able to pay bills and have a little money to spend on me. I'm satisfied, it doesn't have to be that much, but as long as my bills are taken care of and my family around me is happy, that's amazing." And,

> I'm living a good life, yeah. Good life is the self, really. I'm here. I'm happy. I'm taking care of myself. I'm good. I've gotten this far. I have a good life because I'm happy. That's rare. I don't see happy in a lot of other people. I wish I did, but things are hard and life sucks. But that doesn't make life not good.

Living a good life as a good person in the zeitgeist is not about selfish, me-first egoism. People should ideally be decent to each other interpersonally, though not necessarily for transcendent reasons: "Our greater purpose is to live lives of joy and happiness but also to do good things, like being kind, creating community, taking care of the people who need it. So culturally and individually, sure, there's a purpose, but in a cosmic religious way, no." The good in life is found in the immanent realm.

> A good life is having basic needs met, health, food, shelter, access to nature and community based on caring for all those things. Functioning so each human interaction can fulfill whatever potential they're seeking, whatever that means for them. Material stuff is not necessary for a good life. It's nice, it's great. You want to have a nice house and nice car, nice things. But family, good relationships with people, that's important for sure.

The recurrent tension between being good to oneself and good to others requires balancing competing interests.

> My philosophy of life? Don't be a jerk. Try to achieve a balance between enjoying the limited time I have for life and doing right by others. Don't make yourself miserable out of guilt, doing everything you possibly can to help other people at your own expense. But don't be a selfish, self-centered jerk. Try to find a balance, to look out for number one to a certain point and look out for others to a certain point.

In the end, being good with oneself is non-negotiable: "What makes a good life is being able to get up in the morning and look at the mirror and love the person you're seeing there."

9. Social institutions are inherently impersonal, which is bad, and tend strongly to be corrupted by money and power, which is worse. Most institutions, however originally well-intentioned, end up serving their leaders, not the regular people they profess to help. Institutions therefore deserve to be approached with suspicion. (For that matter, most *people* also deserve suspicion until they prove trustworthy.) Nobody may force other individuals out of bad institutions if they choose them, but it is fair to criticize those people and their institutions.

Distrust of social institutions, religious and otherwise, was ubiquitous in our interviews, in which people commonly said things like, "I feel very suspicious, very suspicious of institutions, especially where they're hierarchal. Hierarchy counts [negatively] a whole lot." Sometimes that suspicion turned to disgust: "I immediately feel icky, gross, when I think of institutional religion. The first thing I think is powerful people as a way to control others, to harm others, to get rich, to make themselves better and harming a lot of people along the way." These criticisms had a strong individualist streak: "I think individuals should run their own lives. I don't trust big corporations, it's all about money with them. If you let a corporation or a government decide, there's always some shady things going on in the background, so I think it's better for the individual to find their own way." Something about simply being organized tends to corruption:

> The whole point of spirituality is to be individual. Once it becomes a group process, you find the risk of being tainted by the organization itself. The whole point is to give you inner meaning on your own. Organizations hurt more than help. It is beneficial to keep it as an individual process, just because when you try to organize it, you run the risk of it being tainted by somebody else's energy.

Many say that institutions, religious and otherwise, distort morality: "Not being in organized religion anymore, I don't feel like I've lost my moral compass. I actually feel in some ways maybe it's become stronger." Even allegedly good institutions require suspicion: "I want to be positive but anything that involves donation to charity, I always think it's a scam." This general distrust can and maybe should also be applied to dealings with individuals: "Lots of people are looking at what's in it for them, unfortunately, so I always think when I first meet someone, they're probably an asshole, until they prove me otherwise. I don't think the other way, that you're probably a great person until you do something negative. You prove to me you're a good person first before I trust you." All of this reinforces the beliefs that individuals need to protect and direct themselves: "You can't trust institutions, they're grasping at straws, they don't know themselves. Who are they to tell me how to live my life, you know? Excuse me."

10. *The right of any person or institution to authority or respect must be earned—no social role or position entitles you to it.* The default position is skepticism, while any trust and deference must be demonstrably deserved. Generally, of all institutions, science has earned the most right to respect.

Few we interviewed expressed this in precise terms, but this assumption was implicit in much of what they did say, such as, "I'm leery of any particular institution dictating how people should live. Some institutions should have authority over certain things, like the scientific community saying people should get vaccinated, it should have that authority and people should do that because vaccines help people. But I wouldn't be happy with a religious institution or a famous teacher having authority over the way I live, so it depends on the particular institution and the way their authority is used."

A sort of folk empiricism prevailed: "Maybe the economy or science could be authorities in life. We should listen to science that has been proven and make decisions based on that, not anything else. People should make their decisions and live their lives around things that can be proven through education and research." And, even while many are skeptical of government, they still mostly believe in democracy: "To some degree science and political systems are authorities for me, but you still got to take everything with a grain of salt and you can't take all of it 100%, you've got to remain a little bit skeptical. We as a society have our government, and we all signed a social contract to adhere to it, and I feel that is the right way to do things, democracy. That's probably the best option now."

11. *Any person or institution's claim to possess truth is indefensible and unacceptable.* Such claims reveal arrogance, judgmentalism, and perhaps power-grabbing. Truth is relative to cultures, history, and persons. Everyone should distrust claims to comprehensive or universal "truths."

Some of this comes from the demand to respect everyone's personal uniqueness and autonomy: "I hate when somebody tries to push their stuff on me, so I refused to push my stuff on them. I believe what I believe, and, if you want to know that, I'll be happy to share. But people shouldn't ram their stuff down your throat, it should be up to the individual, and I never want it to be a 'mine's better than yours' type of deal." In other cases, it seems to stem more from the influence of pop postmodernism: "I'm hesitant and critical about teachings just told to me as absolute truth, that this is how it is. Seeing other viewpoints, there are other sides to this story, so we don't need to say this is the one and only way. That led me to this higher ... like ... disconnect with my original traditions." Nearly any comprehensive truth claim can annoy post-Boomers, but religious ones are especially galling: "I get frustrated because Christians will shove it down your throat and make you feel like you are less than them because you believe different. They throw scripture at you 100%, like that just proves it. They may believe that, but others don't believe in Jesus, so why?" In another person's words:

> When somebody tries to preach to me, I get upset. Don't try to tell me how to live my life when at one point in time, you were no better. Don't try to run my life. I am who I am. I look at life totally different than some people, my beliefs are different. It's me, myself that has to learn from my mistakes, and I don't need somebody else telling me.

And, "for me with religion, if that's your thing, cool, whatever, just don't try and shove it down my throat." This "shove down throat" image is routinely associated with religious people directly expressing their beliefs. For many, it is not only uncomfortable but also feels like violence.

12. *The sheer amount of information and options available on everything is overwhelming.*

The internet, social media, advertising, media streaming, and consumer products are cognitively and emotionally overloading. It is good and may be necessary to keep up with everything going on, but it is also exhausting.

Post-Boomers said things like, "We are living in a more and more complicated world, and there is so much information out there. We are easily influenced by peer pressure because the information we have is so readily available. First, we have difficulty distinguishing what information is correct and what's incorrect, and, second, because there's so much information, we do not have time to really look into and try to understand it." Feeling overwhelmed with often-negative information also decreases trust in institutions.

> My generation is just more cynical, critical of all institutions, not just religious ones. Before the internet, you were not constantly getting bombarded with media about all the terrible things happening in the world. There were not 20 different cable news networks all screaming about how evil the other person is. Things objectively were worse in the past. But all we get bombarded with now is hate and how terrible things are, and that causes people to be cynical, against all institutions.

Many post-Boomers are aware of this difficulty but do not feel empowered to do anything about it. For example: "With the big shift in technology, with religion, there's just too much going on. Always just another thing. I wonder what's going to happen because I don't think we can go on much longer like this. The fragmentation of our attention and the way it overwhelms, it's not good for us, not feeding us well."

13. *Younger generations face diminished economic opportunities. Their chances of achieving the American Dream are slim.* Boomers were lucky. Post-Boomers are screwed. The options for post-Boomers now are either (a) invest intensely in *career* competition (the "hustle culture" described below)

and hope to achieve, (b) find *alternative* life goals and meanings (van life, nature, the esoteric), or (c) embrace an *oppositional* identity (punk, Goth, grunge, emo, burnout, biker communities, etc.). This may be aided by drugs, alcohol, antidepressants, or other means of coping.

Many post-Boomers expressed awareness of their declining economic prospects: "The news makes me sad and disappointed because, in my lifetime, the news was sometimes positive, but the majority now is not, and that has gotten worse over time. So having that dream of being an adult on your own, married, having a house, it disappoints me, because especially knowing the economy situation and how bad politics are in this country, not to mention global warming, it made me kind of not want to be an adult." Some felt they had been sold a bill of goods: "I had pretty big dreams for myself, and my family encouraged me to shoot for the stars and nothing could stop me if I pushed myself. Growing up I had no limits on what I thought I could do. It really wasn't until I got older and actually experienced tussles that I realized maybe I can't do that." Many we interviewed expressed a learned contentment with involuntarily downsized lifestyles: "I feel the American Dream is irrelevant to someone like me because I'm happier just living day to day with more modest things in life without struggling financially," and "I'm very content with my family in a little house, we don't have everything we need, but it's absolutely near and dear to me. It's not about commercial successes being rich and famous, it's about the little things in life. To me, the American Dream is having the ability to accomplish stuff without society trying to hinder you." Others aspire partly to drop out of the mainstream.

> If I was financially secure, I would get a half-acre of land, start homesteading, growing my own food, have a smaller eco-footprint, recycle, making new uses of old things. Maybe play a lot more video games, probably smoke a lot more weed. I was pretty bored in life, so I tried growing vegetables this year. I really enjoy it, was really fun learning about plants. Right now I'm growing tomatoes and peppers. It's really fulfilling. I love animals, too. My girlfriend and I got an Airbnb at this farm town and there was goats and chickens, and it was so big and really quiet. I was like, "man, I really like this, I could definitely see myself doing this."

14. *Hope can be hard to come by.* Economic, political, environmental, financial, career, family, relationship, and other problems make a bright future hard to envision. Just getting through the day can be a struggle.

Not many post-Boomers we interviewed were hopeful about the future. They said things like, "Society and the world? I'm not particularly hopeful. I think society and the world as a whole will continue to slowly disintegrate until the conclusion, I think we are going to continue to go downhill." For some, that pessimism shaded into despair: "I want to feel hopeful but I am absolutely terrified. I don't even know if I want to have children because I'm so scared of what it's even going to look like in 10 years, let alone 40. I don't know, it's really, really scary to think about—I want to have hope for us, but it's not really there," and "I'm so pessimistic about the world. I think humans are the worst and the planet is going to kill us off soon." The gloom that settled in during the 2000s has not dissipated. For some, the despondency is material.

> I would like to have the things I need without having to worry. But right now, I'm worried that I have almost no money to my name until next week's payday, which is tough. I'm not going to a food shelter, but if something pops up, like my phone dies, I have no way. I got $8 in the bank. That's where I worry. If something big comes up, I can't do a goddamn thing about it.

For others, the despondency is more existential.

> I have no idea what life's purpose is. It feels like it's just to work and die. You work, do school, do your regular job schedule, then you die. I guess you're supposed to procreate, too, but it seems like a big joke because I don't know what the whole point of life is. I feel like you've got to find small things you enjoy, that bring you light in this dark world. I guess that's the purpose of life, to find small things you enjoy and find joy in. I don't know.

Underlying much of the hopelessness is a belief that powerful people and institutions do not care about them: "Not hopeful. There are those in power who don't want what's best for the people. That sums it up."

15. *"Hustle culture" is unavoidable.* Life is an endless stream of hurrying, multitasking, performing, advancing, and pleasing others. Even becoming one's "best self" is an item to tick off a list. Everyone is forced to maximize the utility of time with productive payoffs.

Post-Boomers wish for lives without stress, rush, and hassle. But that is hard to find. Instead, they say, "We live in a society where we're all just zombies, just nine to five, something happens and we're like, oh, that happened, oh well, keep going. Years from now we won't have any history," and "My version of a happy life is just being stress-free. There's always going to be some stress, but I had a lot of stress as a young adult, I was stressing everything, work, school, finances, family drama." For those still hoping to realize the American Dream, that means more hustling now.

> How much money can I make? Am I capable of making more money? Are there more opportunities I'm not exploring? Other than when you're working all the time and don't have an opportunity to enjoy anything because you're busy working and taking care of kids all the time. Things like that, those would be part of that American Dream I'm still trying to obtain.

For some, simply managing the imperative to hustle is an ongoing job itself.

> If I am working too much and not enjoying life, can't read the books that I want, can't spend time with my partner, can't go to the beach because I'm so tired or working, then I need to read just something. Adjust my schedule to get out of the house more, treat myself to peace, to have energy to go to the beach, just being aware of it. It's super easy for me to get caught up and feel tired working all the time. I've noticed I have a tendency to forget that work is not life, it's a job to make ends meet and attain goals, not all of my life, just one aspect. It's big, which is why it's important to enjoy where you work or at least find some sort of fulfillment, at least just not hate your job.

Feeling this stress affects people's attention to spiritual practices.

> "Spiritual" for me has taken a back seat at this time. I haven't completely lost it, but I don't meditate as much as I used to. I should. It'd be good for me. But I'm still overwhelmed with my current situation and just trying to take care of my family's physical needs first.

16. *Experiences of sacredness are to be found in the immanent world—* in concerts, nature, dance, drugs, sports, family, clubbing, unexplained coincidences, serendipitous moments of joy. The here and now is what

is real. Those who are attuned to it may find uplifting, even transcendent experiences.

Religions may grow and decline, but people and societies never lose some sense of sacred objects and values. In the Millennial zeitgeist, the sacred has migrated away from divine and transcendent realms to experiences, objects, and relationships in the immanent world. The most common profession we heard is that nature is sacred: "Dawn and dusk, the sunset and sunrise are really sacred. Those are always really special moments, they always feel like really magical moments," and "Seeing all of the stars on a moonless night and realizing just how small we are as individuals and how small this planet is, that is such a precious, privileged moment," and "Nature can be very spiritual, I just love being out in nature, the calmness. Sometimes I go camping out with alligators, yes, that's good. But for the most part I think being in nature and spending time with the earth is sacred." For others, art is sacred: "Music is sacred, that's a good one. Nature is an excellent one, too. Nature is beautiful and sacred and should be cherished," and "Human endeavors, especially artistic endeavors, are sacred in the sense that they're something that one person can create and share with another person. The conversation between people through art or creative writing, I find that sort of relationship to be sacred in the same way that maybe somebody else sees religion being sacred to them." For some, the sacred includes the experience of sex and drugs.

> Sex, of course sex is a sacred part of being a human being. Also exploring your own consciousness, even if you use drugs and psychedelics, that's sacred to yourself. Something that brings me spiritual peace is when I—this sounds so cheesy, so feel free to judge me—but when I smoke weed, I breathe it in and take a second to feel myself, and then blow it back out. That's a sort of sacred act for me, too.

Another said,

> Medicine journeys are very sacred. I've been getting into psychedelic mushrooms, and those experiences of altered consciousness feel very close to the planet. That feels sacred to me. This is very powerful medicine that needs to be respected. It's very close to truth. So those are a sacred time, sacred medicine. I think anything that feels really powerful, with a lot of life force behind it, anything could be sacred. It's all about the intention.

For yet others, more prosaic practices prove to be sacred: "I like to take care of my lawn and garden, that's almost sacred. It's an important hobby of mine that I dedicate a lot of time and energy to, my garden and my lawn." One person we interviewed offered this culturally perceptive observation: "I think what's sacred is everyone's right to self-autonomy, being able to decide what one wants in life, essentially freedom, that's sacred." Nearly all post-Boomers take these views as common sense. On rare occasions, someone connects the common search for sacredness and transcendence in the immanent world with the demise of traditional religion, with critiques like this:

> Religion's decline is worrisome because I don't see anything else replacing it. People have less direction in life, so they start chasing only after short-term, wonderful, super-high, awesome experiences that get them going emotionally or leave them with really cool highs. But if you're constantly pursuing only short-term gratifications, you'll never be satisfied 'cause you're always just looking for the next big high, what's gonna be awesome.

17. *The possibility of a historical tradition guiding one's life is nearly inconceivable.* At most, "tradition" means family holiday customs, such as Christmas tree decorating or Thanksgiving dinners. Positive, formative, substantive, moral continuity of identities and practices across generations are almost unimaginable.

In our interviews, we asked these questions:

- Is there anything in your life that makes you feel connected to something bigger than just your individual life—like a larger tradition, heritage, movement, or cause?
- When you hear the word "historical tradition," what does it make you think of? What images come to mind?
- Would you say there are any external institutions or traditions that you think should have authority for living life? That should be trusted and relied on to know how to live?

Most respondents struggled to answer. Many could not understand what we were asking about. Some partly understood but could not think of any answers. We heard a lot of this: "Historical tradition, I can't think of anything right now. I don't have any general associations with the word. For me, not much traditional, to be honest," and "Aside from the song in 'Fiddler on the

Roof,' nothing in particular. I think of family traditions, we have a few we've kept over the years, like going to the beach every summer." Sometimes there was a vague negative cast to the answers: "When I hear the word 'historical tradition,' I think of the museum. Just old things, very old things." Some associated historical traditions with acting mindlessly: "Thinking of family traditions, we do things and we don't know why we do them, just because we were told to do them, you know, generational rituals that were passed down." Others noted the power in certain traditions to do harm.

> Ceremony, ritual, tradition, they strike me like they could be bad. Power, ceremonies that use shows of power and status, yes. That don't feel good. They feel cold, empty, like a show. You know what I'm saying? But there's other ceremonial things and ritualistic things that are happy, like family reunions, stuff like that.

Nearly all emotional associations with traditions were negative. "'Historical tradition,' I unfortunately think of slavery. I think of pilgrims and puritanical pressure to conform," and "Tradition makes me think of staying stuck or trying to even regress to an earlier state. When I think of that, it becomes negative, like you're halting progress because of you want things to stay the same." Nearly everyone says that being subject to the influence of traditions should be a matter of individual choice: "People should just follow their own individual traditions and how to live. I don't think there's any certain ones set in stone people should have to follow." The rare post-Boomer expressed a vague longing for the rootedness that the word "tradition" evoked in them: "Gosh, I actually wish I had some traditions, wish I knew more about where my family's from, where they came from. I wish I had some, honestly, something like that with my family, traditions handed down. I wish we had, but we don't got none of that." But the majority would not have objected to the quip one respondent shared: "There's a meme that says 'tradition is just peer pressure from dead people.' I think that's more or less on the note."

18. *It is natural to crave strong relationships and community, but that desire is counteracted by not knowing what those look like or how to find them and by busyness, hesitations to commit, and negative past experiences.* It is better to maintain one's autonomy, safety, and options, even at the cost of some loneliness.

Many post-Boomers have friends and family ties. But many also long for something more: to belong to real communities. We were not expecting in interviews to hear as much of this as we did: "I don't have much community. It's something I'm striving for, wanting a strong sense of community somewhere, whether at work or an activity or the neighborhood. I've never had a strong sense of community anywhere, and it's something I long for," and "I really haven't been part of a community. I have family, coworkers, but I really don't have many friends. I try to keep my circle small because there ain't that many people you can trust nowadays, as people want to get the upper hand on you." This reflects trends we noted in previous chapters: increased geographic mobility, declining participation in voluntary organizations, the demands of neoliberalism, the fakeness of social media, living with growing gloom and despair, distrust of institutions, and political polarization (by the time of our interviews, it also indicated the lasting effects of COVID-19). The lack of community is also a result of religion's obsolescence.[21] Genuine community requires webs of relationships in geographical proximity, which many do not enjoy.

> I miss a sense of community. I wish I was closer to my mom. I wish I had a close group of friends because most of my good friends don't live locally, so that makes it difficult. Some of them are an hour away or a country away, and I wish I had them right here where I could walk next door and be best friends with my neighbor or that I would meet somebody once a week for lunch or something like that. But I don't have that.

The isolation feeds on itself: "I don't really have faith in anyone or anything," one post-Boomer told us, "I'm out looking at everything from a distance, concerned, wondering how it's going to turn on me or not be in my favor."

19. *Saying or implying to another adult what they should believe, do, or be is wrong. Some suspect that even doing so to one's child may be wrong.* Do not judge others. People will of course judge others in their minds, but they should keep that to themselves and later maybe share it with friends. Anyone may offer other people what they think *if* they express interest, but you may not impose without invitation. (Except to insist that nobody may impose anything on others.)

These feelings expressed another nearly universal sentiment: "Don't tell me how to live my life. My life is my life," and "Being a good person means don't judge people. That's being a good person." Respecting other people means leaving them alone: "Just let people be. If they believe, if they don't, that's their choice, their life." This means religions must not proclaim their messages too confidently: "The church can teach this and that, but I am still going to decide for myself how I wanted to live and be." This can extend even to teaching children.

> The one thing I can't stand is people indoctrinating their kids. You're putting kids in church from the time they can't even walk to when they either rebel or continue with it on their own. That's not allowing them the opportunity to decide for themselves if they want to believe it or not. In a way you're grooming them, just like grooming somebody to do something terrible.

Some report that "I'd probably let my kids make their own choice about religion, what they want to be in life, kind of figure out life themselves. If they said, hey, I want to go to church, I would take them. But I wouldn't force it on them, because it got forced on me as a kid."

20. *Interpersonal and political conflicts are bad and to be avoided.* Everyone should just live and let live. Don't hurt others. Don't judge others. Everyone should just do their own thing, chill, and be happy.

Most post-Boomers are tired of conflicts, wars, and drama. Their general spirit is, "Let's not fight, no need to fight, whatever, I'll cater to whatever needs you need, if it's got anything to do with us getting along," and "Just live your life and let other people live their life as well, don't try to tell people how they're supposed to live. Just let everybody live as they want, no judgment, no arguments." This means learning to let other people do what you believe is wrong: "It's corny, but my philosophy of life is live and let live. If somebody's living a certain way that we think is immoral or inappropriate, look the other way and keep living your life. It's not going to kill you to do that and you avoid a lot more conflicts." Judgementalism is the worst sin: "Too many people judge too many others, and you shouldn't judge, like the old saying: you shouldn't judge a book by its cover. We're lucky for having freedoms and liberties but have to understand there are other people who live differently, and we need to be able to accept that." This rule applies not only to religious people but also to atheists and everyone in between: "I have always said people are allowed to have their own opinions, I'm non-confrontational.

Some militant atheists obviously feel strongly about what they're fighting for. If they're doing it in a peaceful manner, I don't have no problem with it, as long as they're not doing something stupid, just let them do their thing."

21. *Life is short so enjoy it to the fullest.* Develop a healthy "fear of missing out" (FOMO), even if it is stressful and tiring.

This belief is simple and widespread: "You only live once, so might as well do what you want. I'm always saying 'YOLO.' You only live once, so might as well go on that vacation, eat that cake." Eternity is not really a consideration: "We are put on earth, we live just to die, we're not eternal. Basically morality: there's earthly life, I'm not going to be here forever. So make the best of you as you can." The sentiment is not always pure hedonism. People should think about the effects of their actions: "YOLO. Just living your truth and doing what makes you feel good, as long as you understand that some things have consequences and you're ready to accept those, do what you want." But you shouldn't worry about what other people think: "Live a good life while you can. Do the things you have been wanting to do and don't really worry about what anyone else thinks about how you live your life. I think you'd have a pretty good time."

We can now turn to those beliefs that concern religion specifically:

22. *Religion is a personal "opinion" of individual choice—whether religion is true or false is not at issue.*

This is rarely stated outright, but is implicit in much of what people say, such as, "I mainly believe in people believing whatever they wish, and support them in whatever," and "I'm super into people finding their own experience of truth and just flipping that out. You can't look down on people who are spiritual but not religious. That person is never going to fight a war over their religion because they're open to many different perspectives." In this view, every individual possesses her own truth: "Live the way you want to live and don't let people tell you how to live your life because, at the end of the day, it's your life, your truth, your happiness that's on the line. Not someone else's happiness and truth." This approach can soften criticisms of religion: "In general, I am against institutionalized religion, but not necessarily religion as a whole. I like free thought in religion, to have a discussion about what means the most to different people, as opposed to just sitting and being told what something means." Viewing religion as personal opinion can also cause religious people to keep to themselves: "I don't push my faith on others. It helps me and other people I know. But I also know it's not for everybody." Religion then is essentially a matter of consumer choice.

> I'm indifferent on religion. Religion and spirituality are such personal things. If others don't have it, I don't judge or think of them any less. I might be curious if they think we live, we die, that's it? I struggle there's not something more. But again, it's such a personal thing. Nowadays, religion is not how I live my life or raise my kids. But if that's someone's choice, that is their prerogative, they're free to make that choice.

23. *Anybody can believe anything they want, if it "works for them"—the only requirement is that they don't bother anyone else with it.* Religious beliefs are personal, even private affairs to be kept internally. Friends may share their beliefs with each other as matters of mutual curiosity or interest. Everyone then is obliged to respect others. Never should anyone imply that their religious beliefs are right for others.

This follows consistently from a number of prior assumptions and is clearly and consistently expressed. This is often conveyed in positive terms: "Yeah, whatever works for you. I can't judge people for how they choose to handle their spiritual life. Whatever works for them and whatever works for me." But sometimes it takes on a more negative cast: "Someone trying to force their thoughts on people, I don't like that. I feel everybody should arrive at their ideas however they arrive, whatever works for him may not work for me, you know?" The drawing of clear identity and belief boundaries here is key.

> Religion has no place in my life. But I have Muslim or Christian friends, some of whom practice what their religion tells them. But it's for them. I don't talk about my beliefs. I do, but I don't press it, don't force. They talk, too, like, "This is my religion, my spirituality, it's for me."

Some are extremely insistent on everyone respecting those boundaries.

> Don't be a dick and don't bother people. Don't shove your beliefs in people's faces and say I have a right to do this. You don't. You can believe what you want. You can be gay, blue, queer. I don't give a crap. I don't care if you're into Trump. Just don't jam it in my face because you think you have the right. Do your thing by yourself or with your people and stay out of my face. I'm not interested. Leave me the fuck alone. If I'm interested, I'll ask.

Otherwise, don't knock on my door. I don't want your pamphlet. Don't leave fliers on my car. Leave me alone.

24. *People expressing their beliefs about religion in public, among strangers, is annoying, probably even offensive.* This is true of both religious beliefs and strong atheist beliefs. Keep it to yourself. Everyone has the right not to have to hear what others believe. Proactive public proselytizing is distasteful at best, crossing a line of civility.

About this, most post-Boomers are adamant. For example: "Mormon missionaries are like car salesmen. I'm not going to buy something just because you have me in the parking lot. I'm going to buy what I want to buy, and when I'm ready I'll get somebody." This rule holds for all beliefs related to religion, including atheism: "An atheist demonstrating in public is like people who push the Bible, he's just pushing the opposite. Why can't you just live your religion yourself? If people want to believe in God, let them believe, but don't stand there and put it in the face that there's no God." This even applies to less indirect expressions of belief.

> Religious bumper stickers? Thumbs way down. Way down. Because just shut up. Get the stickers off your car. I will know your beliefs based on how you treat other people. Same with anti-religious stickers. I hate them both.

And, "The Ten Commandments in public spaces feels judgmental to me, like people proving you are doing something wrong according to their religion. Like, we get it, we don't need a gallows out there. It just feels judgmental."

25. *It is not necessary to be well-informed about religion to criticize and dismiss it.* No obligation exists actually to know historical and doctrinal facts. Stereotypes, hearsay, anecdotes, and internet memes are good enough "facts" with which to disparage and dismiss religion.

This does not need much explaining. The interview quotes speak for themselves:

- "The Bible makes my eyes roll. I've never read it, actually, I know it's hard to read."
- "I think the first commandment is a lie because it says thou shall not put any other gods before me. But then you pray to Jesus. [*Interviewer: Well, Jesus is part of the holy trinity according to . . .*] I mean if there's a God,

- that's God, you know, Jesus is supposed to be his son, you know what I mean? So I don't believe anything."
- "God is supposed to be a jealous God? I wasn't brought up to be jealous, I didn't grow up where my father was jealous and insecure of my mother. So I think it's pure insanity, religion and all, it's pure insanity."
- "I don't understand the whole Jesus on the cross thing, I never have understood how it makes sense. I mean in the end God sacrificed his son for us, but why? I wouldn't sacrifice my child for anybody."
- "Literally in the Bible it says Jesus was basically black. But in every place, what do you see?: the white Jesus with beautiful white skin. This man is living out in the wilderness, he would be sunburned to a crisp, it's just not possible."
- "Christians follow the law and don't think morally about the things they're doing. People who follow the Holy Bible. I don't know. That's what I read."
- "Take a look around the world at countries that have high levels of religiosity, it's not necessarily good. Hitler's Germany was full of people who were very religious and look what happened."
- "I think it's a complete joke that Catholics have to pay for forgiveness. I definitely think they're more greedy than your average Christian."
- "I don't know much about Catholic, but it's kind of a weird, with the outfits the priests wear and the whole thing with the smoke. I don't get all that. I've been to some Catholic weddings or baptisms, and I don't get the whole ceremony."
- "Honestly, I think evangelicalism is nuts. I don't know why people are attracted to that, how they find themselves there. I think we would be better without it, but I don't know enough about it."

26. *Religion's job is to help some people "be good" and to provide community. But religion is not necessary for either.* Some people may need religion for morality and community. But still, some religious people are not good and abuse others in their communities. And lots of non-religious people are good and can find community elsewhere. Since religion's main "specialties" are available elsewhere, religion is essentially a "lifestyle accessory" that people can adopt for their own personal reasons.

By now this theme should be familiar. "It depends. Religion can give people moral compasses, and it can also corrupt people's moral compasses, too," and "Religion isn't necessary for people to live moral lives. It can help some people become better and live lives worth living, absolutely, no question, religion can be a way moral education can occur. But I don't think religion is required for moral education." The instrumentalized view of religion here as a societal "tool" of socialization and social control is clear.

> Some people need religion, that set of guardrails, and some need more guardrails than others. But not everybody needs religion. It's one of the tools that can be used by society to teach. Most religions have the same tenets: don't kill, don't steal, broad similarities. So, it's one of the tools that society can use, but not necessarily the only or even the best tool.

27. *If religion has value, it is immanent and instrumental.* Religion can be useful for psychological coping, community, learning ethics, and so on. But it is not something a normal person looks to for transcendent truths or values, such as divine revelation, salvation, or heaven.

This theme, too, should be familiar by now. When people see value in religion, that value accrues in the here and now. "There's definitely value in religion. We need to think that life has a purpose, so that's one role of religion, is to structure what we think that purposes is, and so the value. We need a cognitive framework to structure our lives and our societies, religion is part of that structure." Sometimes that value is very pedestrian.

> Appealing things about religion are just the community aspect—it's a free place to go, to blow out a candle, or sing or pray. Sometimes that's the only venue you can get that kind of stuff in a community. I also got some free dance classes out of it. Other people do choir, that's free, that's all cool.

"My religious background has given me stability and structure in life, long-term perspective, and helps me to know what I'm working toward." Or, "You got to send your kid to camp, so why not vacation Bible school? It's an available summer camp among all the other camps. You need to fill your summer, so send the children to vacation Bible school."

Often the value is therapeutic. Even in religious settings, sometimes the actual religious content can be difficult to discern: "I'm currently a part of a Bible study that meets once a month. It's not often we actually get into the Bible, it's more talking about personal issues, so we don't get to the Bible very often in our Bible study." And, "I don't think religion offers anything unique, but it does offer a game plan, let's say, a fine cursory moral grounding to operate in the world. Society needs to operate, good, here's the basic plan."

28. *Getting involved in organized religion is not necessary or even advisable because*
   (a) *anyone interested can have a "personal relationship with God" on their own, and*
   (b) *social institutions can be dangerous.*

Religion is a double-edged sword—it can do some good but also great harm. Some individuals may need or benefit from participation in religious congregations, but they need to be careful not to be manipulated or abused.[22]

This view we discussed above, but it merits underscoring here as part of the zeitgeist's cultural structure. People told us, "I don't believe in religion. I believe in a relationship, my relationship with God, without saying I'm that religious." And,

> For me, religion is within the person. I love that my mom goes to church, but I don't need to be in church, in the building to be religious. It's more of a cult setting in some of those situations, those huge churches that broadcast TV shows. I can sit at my home and read scripture or pray, can sit in my car and do it anywhere. I hear "organized" or "institutionalized," it's an insane-asylum type of thing.

Even churchgoers say this: "You don't have to physically go to a building to praise God, you can pray at home. I just go because I get satisfaction out of it."

29. *If traditional religion wants to attract people, it bears the burden of innovating and marketing itself.* Boomers enjoyed "seeker churches." Everyone is a discriminating consumer in competitive marketplaces. "Here we are now, entertain us," as Nirvana said. It is not people's task to get religion or find God, but religion's obligation to "keep up with the times" and appeal to prospective believers, if it wants to try—although that is likely a doomed pursuit.

Again, few post-Boomers expressed this assumption explicitly, but it was implied in much of their talk: "Religion is losing out honestly because it hasn't evolved, they're still teaching the same things they have for hundreds of years, while people are evolving. There's different ways of looking at things, and religions haven't learned to adapt. If you want to appeal to young people, you need to be on their level and learn what's important to them, instead of trying to teach them stuff that's outdated and old and not relevant." And,

> How relevant are the Ten Commandments as moral standards for today? Thou shalt not have other gods before me? Well, to each their own. Thou shall not kill. Yes, we all agree, don't kill. Shall not commit adultery? How realistic is that if adultery is defined as any form of non-monogamous, non-married sex? Not relevant. Thou shall not lie. Well, white lies can be really useful sometimes. Some say Christianity has good morals for teaching children, but they also say things like save sex 'til marriage, which is really unrealistic and creates weird, unhealthy taboos around sexuality.

This is directly connected to a lack of faith in institutions: "Millennials and Gen Z are very anti-institution in general, and view religion as an old-fashioned organization. A lot of values of super-religious people aren't progressive. Younger generations are more progressive in how they live and want to create change."

30. *Hypocrisy is damning.* The more righteous anyone purports to be, the more scrutiny they require and the more condemnation they deserve if they fail to live up.

Post-Boomers frequently said things like: "I've had very bad experiences with Catholicism, like being told I should not exist because my dad is atheist and stuff. Small town, it's just eye-rolling for me. A lot of hypocrisy," and "Growing up, Sunday was more about getting dressed up to show to church. The focus wasn't about what we're going to learn, who we are going to connect with, but about how we're going to look when we get there and talking to you afterward. That was the main focus, really just showing up and showing face." Post-Boomers often express suspicion of seemingly joyful religious worship: "My reaction to charismatic praise people is it's disingenuous. Are they pretending to be that into it, or are that many people really feeling this moved? That's my first reaction." Perceived hypocrisy is toxic for religion.

> I hate religion so much. Some of the messages are good but the delivery is not. I don't need religion: we just need good influences and examples to be taught morality. And they can be taught outside the church, by the right

people. The last time I attended a service, I walked out because I could not stand being in church. It's filled with hypocrites and preachers and priests living double lives.

31. *It is normal in any religious life to experience much fluidity and drift in and out.* Steady, long-term commitments, memberships, and spiritual practices are unusual. Recurrent reorientations to spirituality and religion for those involved are (as in most of the rest of life) common.

The religious careers and spiritual journeys of post-Boomers often involve a lot of change: "I've come from religion to all the way away, and now coming back to it, to where I do kind of believe." "I read through the whole Bible three years ago, wanted to do that as I was older because I grew up in church. I left church, went back to church, left church again. And now I'm at a point in my life where it's just, I believe in God, but don't do church." "I'm still figuring it all out, I've gone through waves. I'm more spiritual right now than a few years ago when I experienced loss in my life and I just didn't believe in any higher power at all. I didn't think there was anything that could be a higher power, but now I'm coming back around to it." And, "People are changing, young people change their views all the time. It's inevitable, change, new discoveries are made. If an ancient religion is found that might align with someone's beliefs nowadays, they might follow that religion, it might be resurfaced." Those religious journeys mirror other, similar changes in other aspects of life.

> In my twenties, I met a girl and definitely leaned away from Christianity and my political views changed. I was right-wing before, very traditional American Christian conservative, even slightly racist as a child. I felt people who were different were lesser than me. That had a lot to do with my upbringing and being in the church. Then getting into my twenties, I became agnostic, don't think there is no God or anything, I just don't know. Then as I aged, I believe Christianity is the main one for me because that's what I grew up in. Then I start seeing how evil I believe it is, no different than lobbying for politicians. So then I go 100% atheist for a little while, like there is absolutely no God, how could he allow children to have cancer and stuff like that? But I get kind of angsty about it. Then more recently I'm at this point where it's not a truth for me, but that doesn't mean it isn't for someone else. So I'm not going to say there is not a greater power out there, a God or what have you.

This religious fluidity can also show up even in the careers of clergy.

> I became an ordained minister and then walked away from it. I didn't want to be a hypocrite. I smoked a lot of marijuana and can't go there on Sunday and tell them in the pews not to drink and not to smoke marijuana when I was doing it myself. I figured that was hypocritical of me to criticize somebody else for something I was doing at the same time. Ministers try to believe in doing right. I don't try to judge anybody.

32. *"Mainstream" and familiar religious things are less interesting and valuable than alternative, novel, fringe beliefs or those of historically oppressed peoples.* Baptist, Catholic, Presbyterian, Methodist are boring, too common and ordinary to be appealing or significant. Eastern, native, magical, esoteric religions, and maybe Judaism and Islam are probably pretty cool.

This "double standard" about categories of religion—mainstream versus alternative, "Western" versus "Eastern"—was common and blatant in post-Boomer talk, although few seemed to recognize it. In contrast to the negativity around familiar American religions, they often said things like this:

- "I think the Native American ceremonies are beautiful."
- "Pagan religion is based on nature, so it brings me a lot of calm thinking about nature."
- "Chakras feels peaceful, like yoga feels peaceful. The idea of mindfulness is very needed in society, to have time to be still and put the mind at ease and not racing. It could do a lot of good."
- "I wish I knew more about Buddhism. I know one Buddhist. It seems like such a harmonious way to go about things, and if you need instructions, need community, and you find it there and it works, why not?"

At times, some talked like apologists for religions that were not their own.

> In a college sociology class, I did a study of Wiccans, went to a meeting to see what they do. I learned they believe whatever they do comes back to them 10 times. So if they do bad, it comes back 10 times worse. They believe in the earth and nature. That's the witchcraft stuff, it's all about nature, and witchcraft is supposed to make good things happen, not bad things. Because if they do something bad to you, it's gonna hurt them a lot worse. If I had to go to a religion, I would definitely go there.

33. *Syncretism is perfectly legitimate.* Beliefs, symbols, interests, sensibilities, icons, and practices need not cohere or be internally consistent. Nobody needs to inhabit only one tradition or belief system. That is restrictive. Concerns with coherence and consistency are probably authoritarian and totalizing. Explore, tinker, combine, destabilize, be quirky, surprise, be a bricoleur—whatever you like.

Post-Boomers who are not totally hostile to religion and spirituality often take an eclectic approach to their beliefs and practices. One told us, "Every religion contains some sort of wisdom I can take something out of, which I'm currently doing, and it's influencing me because I believe it has a lot to do with mental health, too. I think that peace between all these other people, all these wisdoms, you see people going through the same struggles you do. So maybe you can find peace in what they found peace in, just keep trying and keep moving." Another: "You don't have to find happiness only in religion. And you can take pieces of other religions. People are making their own 'religions' by meshing all the religions and finding their own peace and harmony with that." Such views are available in print: "I read a book that said if you could take at least one piece from different religions or cultures and learn it, that is what was meant to be." Some are putting it into organizational practice.

> I went to an experimental church of all different types of religions coming together, it had rituals that incorporated all different religions. It was like our own made-up ritual, which was very lovely, very positive. It was just reaching out to any god out there. We made it our own, and it seemed like we were a family.

Some religious parents are teaching syncretism to their children.

> My children and their friends are very much in the same mindset as me, where they take from religion what they want to take. There is more exposure to difference, like we have friends who are half Jewish and half Catholic, and we celebrate Hanukkah and Christmas. My children are lucky because growing up they've been exposed to other religions that have all this beautiful stuff to offer. You don't have to be just one or the other, you take what you want. Today that's a real thing, just take what you want. It's less "I need to be part of this church" and more that "I need to be part of this circle of humans." I think religions are going to meld eventually.

34. *The old, modern doctrines of scientistic materialism, naturalism, and empiricism may very well be inadequate.* Some kind of "spiritual" realm, "something bigger" that science cannot access or explain, may exist or probably exists "out there." Nobody really knows. But nobody knows otherwise. It is best to be open-minded. Atheists who are certain that no god exists are just as rigid as religious people who are certain their god exists. Don't be so sure. Dogma is a problem. Mystery and ambiguity are cool.

This captures the spirit of this view:

> Birth and death are all I can really be sure about. That doesn't preclude the possibility or probability of there being more. There's tons of stuff in the natural world we don't know shit about. We didn't really know about electricity or x-rays or microwaves. Now we know about that. So who knows what's really out there? Shit, you can't know, you don't know.

That opens up a lot of possibilities that previous American generations would have considered fringe. Sometimes those are liberal borrowings from other traditions, including Eastern religions: "Karma and reincarnation, we don't have any proof that either of those exists from a scientific standpoint. But people swear it's a real thing"; or Native American or African ones: "I believe we are surrounded by spirits of ancestors, beings that were here before us. I feel they influence and are surrounding us. Just that relationship with the past is really important and real, in that sense it's a sacred bond." Others are more idiosyncratic and personal: "I believe we all are intertwined with imaginary lines to every person on the planet, and we influence each other with our decisions and feelings and things we say and do."

Often these ideas are grounded in some kind of experience: "Sometime a higher being, that spirituality may be reaching out to you. There's been moments in my life where in dreams, I don't know how to explain it, there's a state you can get in and see or feel something right that moment, you feel one with the world and with yourself, like you're part of a plan and everything makes sense." Another person told us: "I have this weird feeling like there's definitely people who have died who have given me signs, things that give the feeling like they're there, in songs or in animals. That makes the hair on my arms stand up when these things happen." Sometimes this openness to mysteries feeds on uncertainty.

> God is somewhere outside of our universe. That's where things get crazy, because it sounds very sci-fi and really cool. But there's so much we haven't

explored as far as space or the universe or anything. And just maybe one of those things we haven't explored just happens to be there somewhere. Maybe, that's the thing for me, it's always just a maybe. And that says that I can't have a definitive answer.

Other times, spiritual beliefs come across with certitude.

> I believe we live life every day in some strange way, shape, or form. I don't know if it's coincidental, I don't think so, but I've had some mysterious things happen to me and came out absolutely blessed. I believe that's a destiny. We're always on the journey until the end, and my spirit doesn't die here. Long after I'm gone, it's going to continue on. Life has been too great for it not to be.

In this regard, while the Millennial zeitgeist has made traditional religion obsolete, it has *not* been a triumph for naturalistic secularism—contrary to the claims of standard secularization theorists. Something more complex is going on.

35. *The options are no longer simply religion or secularity.* There are other possibilities for anyone interested in alternative forms of enchantment, magic, the paranormal, paganism, the occult, and a buffet of spiritual (but not religious) beliefs and practices.

Beyond traditionally religious and seriously secularist minorities of post-Boomers, a wide space is open in which many are exploring alternative sacred beliefs and practices and re-enchanted cultures. Here are the kinds of things they say:

- "New Age, Wicca, witchcraft, new religious movements. Love them."
- "I do believe in psychics and mediums, as a spiritual person, I definitely believe in that. Not ghosts, but spirits, yeah, I believe in that stuff."
- "Auras, I do believe people that can carry a certain energy to them, that's why when you talk to a person, you feel comfortable with them or uncomfortable. That's kind of like the spiritual aspect of auras."

Some people have clearly thought extensively about this.

> From a spiritual perspective, we're here to learn. We are the divine. The divine is within us and without us. We are the divine and the divine is all

around us. We are the universe manifested in a certain way, trying to experience earth, life. If you think about it, religion is all the same energy, all the universe, just without the control aspect of religion.

And others have been longtime practitioners.

Paganism has been my life for as long as I can remember. Not so much the magic, but polytheism, believing that the world was created by people-gods like me. They may be immortal, but they make mistakes, fight among themselves, have emotions, are not just in the abyss, they have honor, just like I do. And the more time moves forward, when the day of reckoning comes, those with higher honor will move forward, too.

The spiritual testimonies some give are enthusiastic.

Chakras makes me feel whole. I believe in chakras, it's very important. It makes me feel whole and calm. I guess the embodiment of the whole thing, it's bringing your entire body together as a whole. So instead of reaching out to a God, you're reaching into yourself.

Or,

If you get into meditation, you can really get in there and become part of the collective consciousness. It's almost a power and, without having anything else to compared to, feels like the force. It's something everybody has and is capable of, you can connect with people and with moments. It's hard to explain, but if you are into meditation, you might understand what I'm saying. It's a oneness feeling that gives this understanding of a god-connection or goddess or call it what you want but you feel connected in that way to this higher, great mystery.

Even people who do not personally follow these alternatives are often happy to endorse them: "People that practice magic, that's awesome if that's your truth, what you love, that's great. A lot of these other religions, they do no harm to others, and that's one of the biggest things, doing no harm to others, then you're okay." This can include parents:

My daughter loves crystals and stuff like that. She likes something, and it hurts my wallet. We went to some festival not long ago and she bought all kinds of stuff from a booth. If she likes that stuff, I have no problem with it. She rubs a long crystal, she holds it and rubs it. She said it's good energy. I'm like, okay, whatever you're into.

Almost none of the post-Boomers we interviewed criticized these views as commonly and harshly as they did traditional religion.

What can we make of all this?

I am not suggesting that these propositionally rendered beliefs comprise an internally coherent cultural system. Nor am I saying these propositions summarize every important dimension of post-Boomer culture. Our focus is on those parts most relevant to younger Americans' view of religion. The argument, rather, is just this. These 35 beliefs, taken together as a loose network of ideas, are not only intelligible when viewed in context of the historical developments and social structures that fostered and reinforce them, they also lead to an obvious conclusion about traditional religion. Namely, that religion is obsolete—redundant and unnecessary at best, outdated, discredited, and damaging at worst. That is what the majority of younger Americans decided in the 1990s and 2000s. That is what explains the major religious losses described in Chapter 1. Given everything discussed here against the backdrop of all we examined in preceding chapters, it is difficult to imagine how traditional religion could have remained vibrant, relevant, and attractive to most younger Americans. It can sometimes seem remarkable, in fact, that any younger Americans remain religious at all.

The Reality of Re-Enchantment

The last four propositions point to something very important. Traditional religion going obsolete does not mean Americans have lost interest in things supernatural, enchanted, or quasi-religious. Far from it. Neither does it mean most Americans have embraced secularism, naturalism, scientism, and atheism. Those appear to most post-Boomers too empty and dreary to be engaging. Instead, the received binary opposition of religion versus atheism has given way to the rise of two alternatives: the first we can call "spirituality," and the second I will call "occulture."[23] Together they present movements best understood as *the re-enchantment of American culture.*

My 2023 Millennial Zeitgeist Survey demonstrates Americans' beliefs in the reality of a raft of paranormal, magical, occultic, and New Age ideas.[24]

CONTOURS OF THE MILLENNIAL ZEITGEIST 331

The question was posed this way: "Of the following things that some people believe in, which would you say you believe are actually real?" The phrase "actually real" was intended to get respondents to think about the *actual existence* of these things. Respondents were given five options to choose from: "I definitely believe," "I maybe believe but am not sure," "I do not believe," "I do not believe and I find it ridiculous that anyone believes this," and "I don't know." That wider spread of possible responses better captures the way different people actually think about such matters and so provides greater insight into the nuances about such ideas among people on the ground. Table 9.1 shows the percentage of people who definitely believe or possibly believe in the listed ideas.

First, we see that large numbers of American adults not only do not dismiss most of the spiritual, paranormal, magical, occultic, esoteric, and New Age ideas in the table but also that sizeable minorities report "definitely" believing them and larger minorities "maybe" believe them. American religion may have become obsolete, but most Americans have not become naturalistic secularists. Many have instead become re-enchanted through spirituality and occulture. It is normal in examining such tables to focus immediately on comparisons of differences between groups. But the place to start is absolute percentages within categories. Thus, 40–45% of Americans between the ages of 25 and 68 say they definitely believe in the reality of karma, and another 30% also might. Continuing down the list, a *majority* of Americans 25–68 definitely or maybe believe in *half* of the ideas in Table 9.1. Substantial minorities of especially post-Boomers also believe in the rest of the list. Even considering the three least-believed ideas, 33% of Millennials nonetheless report definitely or maybe believing in bigfoot, 25% in werewolves, and 19% in vampires. Those are considerable numbers for such heretofore exotic beliefs.

Some readers may be tempted to discount this as survey respondents just joking around, but close attention to what has been developing in the culture over the past decades would commend taking these responses seriously. Spirituality and occulture have been growing in major ways. In the past, when news stories occasionally reported the number of Americans who believe in astrology, for example, the amused responses were often something like, "How can people be so ridiculous?" My thesis here, to the contrary, is that, in the Millennial zeitgeist, such beliefs are not fringe silliness but part of bigger, significant cultural movements deserving serious attention.

Table 9.1 American Adults' Belief in Non-Naturalistic Phenomena by Generation (%)

Of the following things that some people believe in, which would you say you believe are actually real?	Early Boomers	Later Boomers	Gen Xers	Millennials
Karma (a universal force repaying good and bad)				
I definitely believe	20	41	45	40
I maybe believe but am not sure	39	31	29	27
Demons or evil spirits active in the world today				
I definitely believe	35	41	44	37
I maybe believe but am not sure	23	23	26	24
Angels active in the world today				
I definitely believe	40	51	47	35
I maybe believe but am not sure	28	23	22	23
UFOs, aliens that visit earth, unidentified aerial phenomenon (UAPs)				
I definitely believe	20	28	23	33
I maybe believe but am not sure	35	34	39	30
The ability to project positive and negative energies outside oneself				
I definitely believe	20	26	35	32
I maybe believe but am not sure	34	34	33	31
Nature spirits or spiritual energies in nature				
I definitely believe	18	24	25	29
I maybe believe but am not sure	32	36	36	30
Miraculous healings				
I definitely believe	39	43	39	28
I maybe believe but am not sure	37	26	28	29
Ghosts that haunt people or houses				
I definitely believe	12	19	26	27
I maybe believe but am not sure	34	33	34	30
Psychic abilities, ESP, empath powers, a "sixth sense"				
I definitely believe	23	29	31	26
I maybe believe but am not sure	47	35	36	32
Family members who are dead visiting or communicating with you or living relatives				
I definitely believe	15	26	30	24
I maybe believe but am not sure	35	30	29	31

Table 9.1 Continued

Of the following things that some people believe in, which would you say you believe are actually real?	Early Boomers	Later Boomers	Gen Xers	Millennials
Auras or chakras (energy centers of the body)				
I definitely believe	15	15	20	20
I maybe believe but am not sure	28	36	33	33
Reincarnation (having lived past lives and reborn into this world)				
I definitely believe	10	16	19	18
I maybe believe but am not sure	30	29	33	33
Making desires come true by mentally visualizing them ("manifesting" through "the law of attraction")				
I definitely believe	10	15	19	18
I maybe believe but am not sure	29	31	32	31
Good luck charms, symbols, or numbers				
I definitely believe	6	12	19	18
I maybe believe but am not sure	26	36	37	30
Communication with the dead who are not family members				
I definitely believe	7	11	16	18
I maybe believe but am not sure	16	26	36	27
Spirits channeled in living people's bodies				
I definitely believe	9	11	15	18
I maybe believe but am not sure	19	29	37	30
Astrology (the belief that celestial bodies affect human affairs)				
I definitely believe	12	14	14	17
I maybe believe but am not sure	25	32	31	25
Tarot cards for fortune-telling				
I definitely believe	5	9	11	16
I maybe believe but am not sure	17	20	23	21
Certain objects having spiritual powers (e.g., crystals, pyramids)				
I definitely believe	6	9	17	14
I maybe believe but am not sure	21	26	26	25
The ability to see into the past or future				
I definitely believe	9	14	16	15
I maybe believe but am not sure	36	39	32	33

(*continued*)

Table 9.1 Continued

Of the following things that some people believe in, which would you say you believe are actually real?	Early Boomers	Later Boomers	Gen Xers	Millennials
The ability to cast real magic spells or curses (not stage performance magic)				
I definitely believe	3	13	13	14
I maybe believe but am not sure	19	23	25	20
Reiki healing (transferring universal energy by laying on hands)				
I definitely believe	13	13	15	11
I maybe believe but am not sure	30	31	33	30
Bigfoot				
I definitely believe	4	6	8	10
I maybe believe but am not sure	25	27	25	23
Werewolves				
I definitely believe	5	3	6	9
I maybe believe but am not sure	11	9	13	16
Vampires				
I definitely believe	3	2	5	7
I maybe believe but am not sure	7	9	13	12
TOTALS (unweighted n's):	100 ($n = 341$)	100 ($n = 358$)	100 ($n = 485$)	100 ($n = 677$)

Source: Millennial Zeitgeist Survey, 2023 ($N = 1,861$). Percents may not add to 100 due to rounding. Answer categories were "a huge amount," "a lot," "some," "very little," "none at all."

Second, Table 9.1 reveals a pattern of belief in these ideas being more widespread among younger generations than older. Early Boomers are the least open to any of these ideas. Gen X usually reports the highest levels of definite and possible belief in them, often more so than Millennials. The only exceptions are communicating with the dead, channeling spirits, astrology, tarot cards, magic spells and curses, bigfoot, werewolves, and vampires—in which Millennials believe most, by a few points. These modest differences may be a cohort effect of Gen Xers being truly the most "into" these ideas, with Millennials being a bit more skeptical. Or it may be an age effect of Millennials needing more life experience and greater exposure to "alternative" parts of culture before being prepared to declare their belief in these ideas, which more eventually will. Time will tell. Having noted those differences, however, Gen X and Millennials look sufficiently similar overall that the inclusive label "post-Boomer" works well here.

Another observation: in two cases, Later Boomers report higher levels of credence than Gen Xers: belief in angels and miraculous healings. Not coincidentally, these are the two from the list that also belong to parts of traditional religion. They are also the two ideas about which Millennials show the greatest drop in definite belief relative to Gen Xers. Late Boomer belief in these two and Millennials' relative distance from them may both come in part from their possible associations with traditional religious outlooks. In sum, in keeping with my argument about the zeitgeist, belief in these supernatural, enchanted, magical, esoteric, occultic, and sometimes dark ideas had, by 2023, become astonishingly common and generally more widespread among post-Boomers than older generations.

Although the re-enchantment story has not played a major part in the preceding chapters, and although I cannot fit a robust analysis of the re-enchantment of American culture into this volume, grasping the point here about spirituality and occulture is absolutely essential to understanding this book's argument. Religion did not become obsolete because secularity won the day. *Religion lost out in good measure because alternatives that are actually more like religion than secularism emerged as cultural options that proved attractive to many post-Boomers.* These ideas and interests replaced religion more easily than secularism could. Traditional religion has to compete against spirituality and occulture. But so does secularism. Nobody of a secularist persuasion could come away from Table 9.1 thinking their viewpoint has emerged victorious. If anything, while occulture and spirituality represent functional *replacements* for traditional religion, they are outright *rejections* of core premises of secularism. The jury is still out, it would seem, on whether replacement or rejection is the more threatening possibility for traditional religion. In any case, this development substantiates my argument that the decline of traditional religion does not count as support for secularization theory. In this multiposition field, religion can lose without secularism winning. The implications are huge.

In brief, one key takeaway about the Millennial zeitgeist is this: through immense, tectonic shifts in global and national sociocultural orders, the terrain on which religion and secularism have long contended as binary rivals has undergone upheaval and reconfiguration. New players have gained in numbers and influence. The cultural landscape has become more complex and, for religion, more challenging than before. Understanding the big picture adequately requires recognizing the larger significance of this rise of spirituality and occulture.

Conclusion: Why the Zeitgeist Made Religion Obsolete

So what exactly about the Millennial zeitgeist rendered traditional religion obsolete? Why the cultural mismatch? I close this chapter drawing together much of the above into this analytical summary. In heart and soul, as a matter of deep culture, the Millennial zeitgeist was (and seems to remain):

- *Immanent*: Focused on the here and now, not the transcendent or otherworldly
- *Individualistic*: Envisioning society as a collection of atomistic, choice-making selves
- *Anti-institutional*: Avoiding structured social groups and institutions
- *Presentist*: Captive to the contemporary, unmoored from history and tradition
- *Relativist*: Viewing knowledge, truth, and ethics as opinions dependent on perspectives
- *Distrustful*: Suspicious of most people's and organization's motives and agendas
- *Subjectivist*: Assuming interior feelings and experience to be the best guides for living
- *Anti-authority*: Hostile to structured social roles of influence and power
- *Fluid*: Expecting change, instability, revision, mobility
- *Multicultural*: Comfortable with sociocultural diversity, dubious of homogenous groups
- *Minimalist*: Preferring to strip away unnecessary systems, particularities, creeds
- *Transgressive*: Breaking down received boundaries, norms, categories, decorum
- *Pornographic*: Inundated by images of nudity, sex, and violence of all sorts in most media
- *Jaded*: Bored by hype and defeated by disappointment, scandals, and dim futures
- *Consumerist*: Conceiving the good life as continually acquiring new experiences and products
- *Entertained*: Soaking up relentless stimulation, amusement, performance, spectacle
- *Re-enchanted*: Open to believing "weird" stuff that enlightened modernity had suppressed

Of course not every post-Boomer was or is all of these things. We are not talking about individuals here but the macro-cultural mood of generations. The zeitgeist shaped many individual Gen Xers and nearly all Millennials but in different ways, in various degrees, in diverse settings. Furthermore, again, the zeitgeist did not push most post-Boomers into hard-core secularism. Some did become naturalistic, scientistic atheists. But even more moved into the alternative camps of spirituality and occulture. By the turn of the twenty-first century, the main options were not the simple binaries of religious and secular. The re-enchantment of culture opened up plenty of space for those wanting to leave traditional religion yet not wishing to become fully secularized. That, too, presented even more challenges for traditional religion.

Lest anyone take any of this to be Millennial bashing, I repeat that this zeitgeist is not the novel creation of an aberrant generation. It is the natural outcome of the social, institutional, technological, and cultural conditions in which post-Boomers were socialized. Older generations were the ones that created and fostered those conditions, among whom the owners of its technology and culture industries profited spectacularly. Post-Boomers were raised by Boomer parents who instilled in them most of the values and attitudes that their children, under different technological and social conditions, pushed to new limits. As D. H. Lawrence observed, "It is a curious thing, but the ideas of one generation become the instincts of the next."[25] Gen Xers and Millennials coming of age simply tried to make sense of the world they were handed. The zeitgeist was the meaning they made of it, a cultural bricolage pieced together from materials at hand in a way that seemed to them sensible and resonant. It was not a rebellion against an alienating system in need of change—that was the Baby Boomers' story. It was a functional adaptation to a seductive-yet-wounding system against which protest seemed futile and exit impossible. Some readers may love the zeitgeist. But if any critique is justified, therefore, sociological realism tells us to direct it not at "kids these days" but at the larger social system that helped create those kids.

Let us return then to the questions posed at the start of this chapter. How would we expect traditional religion to fare in such a cultural atmosphere? How does the picture of reality embodied in this zeitgeist resonate or not with the picture offered by traditional religion? How would religion appear to young Americans who soaked in the zeitgeist's concerns, moods, and sensibilities? The answer is that traditional religion's picture of reality did not resonate with most of those who soaked up the zeitgeist. American religion's demise has not been due to its farfetched belief contents—as most atheists and some secularization theorists would have it—but because of its own fossilized cultural forms that it was unable to shake. Religion in the Millennial zeitgeist felt alien and disconnected from what mattered in life—in short, badly culturally mismatched. The vibes were off.

10

Through the Exit Doors

As traditional American religion became obsolete for post-Boomers, many no longer had any use for it, and it faded from their lives. We return now to this basic consequence of religion's obsolescence: the mass exodus of post-Boomers from traditional religion. Why did so many leave the religions of their youth? This chapter draws on our interviews with post-Boomers to answer this question. Most of this book has explored the larger sociological forces that have led to religion's obsolescence. The following pages elucidate how many post-Boomers experienced and responded to those forces.

Of course, the reasons people give for their actions will never provide a complete explanation. People have blind spots and often lack perspective on the consequences of massive social changes. So we should not expect the interview responses below to map perfectly onto larger societal trends. Nonetheless, hearing what people say about religion—especially attending to the voices of the many who grew up in a religion and later left it behind—provides a window into the ways they experienced and make sense of the large social and cultural conditions that shaped their lives, which can contribute to a fuller understanding of religion's demise.

This chapter begins by examining what members of the younger generations said turns them off about religion and why they left the faiths of their youth. It also considers the perspectives of younger Americans who didn't leave religion altogether but became less religious. The chapter then turns to examine three important minority American religions—Judaism, Black Protestantism, and Mormonism—that offer important lessons about religious obsolescence. Attending to these smaller traditions matters not simply for representing religious minority voices, but because each is a theoretically important case that provides insight into how the macro-sociological forces described in the preceding chapters work out in particular religious contexts.

340   THE AFTERMATH

Religious Turn-Offs

What do post-Boomers dislike about religion? We asked our interview respondents what, if anything, about religion turned them off, what they thought was bad or problematic. Most of them had plenty of criticisms to voice (Table 10.1). I studied their answers to this question systematically and, through a multiple iteration process of thematic grouping, sorted respondents' answers into general categories. I also separated respondents into religious types according to their different life experiences with religion.[1] Respondents often offered multipart answers that contributed to more than one category. The numbers should be interpreted as the percentage of interviewees of each religious type who mentioned that category of answer. The columns are not expected to add to 100.[2]

Religious Decliners—those who became less religious over the course of their lives—have more critical things to say about religion than those who have always been religiously marginal (*Nevers*). However, those who remained religious (*Still Religious*) or became more religious (*Increasers*) have plenty of criticisms of religion, too. Post-Boomers, even religious ones, have a lot to say about what turns them off about religion. One of the most common critiques of religion is the harm it causes people. Whatever good they acknowledge religion may do for humans, the majority of most post-Boomers also say that religion is a source of violence, suffering, oppression, destruction, war, and division. Some of this critique focused on the exclusion of those who are LGBTQ+ or on religion's mistreatment of women. One, for instance, related,

> As a divorced woman living in the South, what place do I really have in the Catholic Church today? I've had increasing issue over time with women not having equal opportunity, and, of course, being divorced doesn't jive. So yes, as of today, my own religion doesn't make a place I am comfortable. So where do I turn? I'm smart enough to just sit tight and try to be a good person on my own.

Others pointed to religion's role in propagating and propping up racism, slavery, and colonialism. Most who made this larger criticism, however, just said generally that religion is guilty of harming people through social injustice, oppression, and violence. Sometimes this was expressed in sweeping historical generalizations, like this:

Table 10.1 Religious Turn-Offs for Post-Boomer Americans (%)

Bad and criticized features of traditional religion mentioned	Decliners (N = 135)	Still Religious (N = 34)	Increased (N = 20)	Low Stable + NR (N = 17)
Harm: Causes violence, suffering, oppression, destruction, war, division	77	59	40	47
Of which specifically anti-LGBTQ	14	3	15	6
Of which specifically anti-female, misogynous	12	3	–	6
Of which specifically justifying racism, slavery, colonialism	4	3	–	6
Social control: Tool of manipulation, conformity, imposition	50	6	5	–
Exclusivity: Overly narrow, strict, demanding, superior	46	65	60	41
Leaders: Clergy misuse of power, corruption, priest sex abuse	33	29	10	18
Money: All about money, greed, like a business, swindling people	23	15	–	12
Politicized: Right-wing politics, violates separation of church and state	17	18	–	18
Coercion: Forced, especially on children, aggression, proselytizing	17	–	15	12
Outdated: Old doctrines and ethics not keeping with the times	17	3	–	–
Hypocrisy: Religious people don't live what they preach	14	24	5	–
Ritualism: Role, formal, mindless, boring, flat	8	14	15	12
Rigidity: Organizational inflexibility, too structured, hierarchy, buildings	8	3	25	–
Weirdness: Just being weird, following dumb ideas	8	–	–	24
Hell: Preaching threats of damnation, fire, and brimstone	5	3	–	6
Founding falsehoods: Religious base is all myth, lies, errors	4	–	–	–
Fashion show: Church about looks, comparing appearances	5	9	–	–

(*continued*)

Table 10.1 Continued

Bad and criticized features of traditional religion mentioned	Decliners ($N=135$)	Still Religious ($N=34$)	Increased ($N=20$)	Low Stable + NR ($N=17$)
Irrational: Disregards science, proof, facts, logic	4	–	–	18
Devalues good works: Grace and forgiveness demotivate being good	3	–	–	–
Cliquish: Unfriendly groups in churches	2	–	–	–
Diversity: Too much disagreement, divisions between religious	0.8	–	10	12
Demanding: Expects too much commitment, time, energy, involvement	0.8			6
Eco-blind: Ignores environmental problems, sustainability issues	0.8	–	–	–
Discomfort: Individuals can feel awkward, have bad feelings	0.8	6	–	6
Unanswered prayers: God doesn't answer	–	–	–	6
Excused bad behavior: In name of forgiveness, grave	–	6	–	6
False doctrines: Erroneous teachings, lead people astray	–	3	5	6
Too easy: Gets watered down, simplified, commercialized	–	–	5	6

My dad told me early and often that more people have died in the name of religion than any other cause, and it's just so true. A lot of the evil in the world is because of ideals espoused by people's interpretation of religion. No religion out there is inherently evil, and a lot of good people are doing good things in the name of religion. But there are a lot of bad people doing bad things in the name of their religion, too.

Another said,

I believe religion has done more to damage the human race than anything else on this planet. The Christian message has been preached for

2,000 years, and we're no better off because of it. For so many people, religions corrupt their minds. I'm just not a fan.

Others spoke in much more personal terms.

> Sunday school made me anxious because when the sermon would come up, I would go with the other kids to children's church and I'd get bullied. Bullied as a kid in the children's church. So it makes me anxious. Go figure.

Some turned the ideals of religion against their experience of the realities of traditional religion. One, for instance, recalled, "I remember one of my youth pastors telling me, 'Sometimes you just need to stop thinking,' to which I was like, 'Okay, I don't think Jesus would tell me that.'" Another said,

> My daughter used to love going to church. Now I have to convince her to go because she feels like what goes on there is not what God wants. I've always taught her Jesus loves everybody and you should love like Jesus does. But at church they teach a lot of "don't do this or that," "don't hang out with the wrong people, gay friends," whatever, and she doesn't agree with that. She thinks God wants us to be loving. Plus, they've had issues not being able to keep a youth group leader. So a lot of that has turned her off.

Half of the Decliners objected to religion because they see it as a tool of social control, manipulation, and enforced conformity. As one observed, "Organized religion to me is a confined, constrictive institution and completely adverse, the exact opposite of what most young people want. They want to be free, to be open." Few of the other religious types mentioned this objection. The most common turn-off among the more religious types (Still Religious and Increasers) was religion's capacity for exclusivity: being too narrow, strict, demanding, and superior in attitude. Large percentages of the less religious types agreed but voiced this critique about 20% less often than the more religious. From there, the criticisms become less common. One-third of Decliners and fewer of the other types mentioned misbehavior by religious leaders. Non-trivial minorities of all but the Increasers said that religion is often too concerned with money, can be greedy, out for profit, and sometimes cheat people. Almost one in five of all but the Increasers objected to religion becoming politicized by getting involved in right-wing politics.

From there, the turn-offs of religion start to vary more widely across religious types. Somewhat lower numbers of three of the types said that religion sometimes distastefully coerces vulnerable people by forcing beliefs on children or too heavy-handedly proselytizing others. Then 17% of Decliners (but almost none of the others) charged religion with being outdated, holding on to beliefs that are out of touch with the times. The Still Religious were the most likely to object to hypocrisy in religion—that people do not practice what they preach. Some even saw this in religious practices per se, as in this report:

> I went to a Baptist college, where I got invited to a concert where everybody around me was doing the "raise and praise" performative thing [raising hands in worship]. It's attention-seeking, they want to put on display how much they're into it. My feelings were not good, it was fake, false. It's like the act of going out of your way to do it. It felt competitive.

Minorities of the two more religious types also emphasized the problem of religion being too formal, boring, mindless, rote, and ritualistic. For instance: "I just feel bored with the whole thing because my grandfather is a Southern Baptist minister, so I've heard the same sermon over and over. I just remember sitting in the hallways, like, okay, when can I leave?" One in four of the religious Increasers complained about religion's organizational rigidity, hierarchy, and inflexibility. One in four of the Nevers (but few of the others) said that religion can just get weird and follows what they think are dumb or objectionable ideas. Turning the typical meaning of Jesus's crucifixion on its head, for example, one voiced this objection:

> The Jesus story, why would you want to tell your kids about somebody being murdered to save them, and then showing them pictures or even a movie with that much gore? I mean, I understand that children aren't always going to be innocent, the world is a dark place. But I don't want to subject my children to that, it's super gruesome. I feel sad because I shouldn't need the image to show me how bad this man was beaten to save me from my sins.

The remaining 15 turn-offs were voiced by much smaller minorities of respondents. One exception is the nearly one in five of the Nevers who noted religion's irrationality in ignoring science, facts, proof, and logic.

The *tone* of these answers in interviews differed by religious types. Religious Decliners tended to speak in tones of dismissive condemnation. They were critical and done with it all. The tone of those who had increased religiously exhibited more frustration over religion's bad features. They were aggravated that the religion they had come to value was self-destructive. The tone of the Maintainer types, by comparison, reflected a more theoretical awareness of how bad religion can be and of problems they had heard or experienced, but this was typically coupled with a stronger appreciation for religion's good features. Finally, the Nevers generally reflected a more detached spirit overall since religion is not central to their existence. The intensity with which the post-Boomers we interviewed expressed their feelings also varied. For some, it was simply "thanks but no thanks." Others were positively bitter: "Everything that I've been taught and told was a lie."

What do we learn from these findings? The main feature of religion that younger Americans of all religious types say turns them off concerns its misuse of influence and power to violate people's autonomy, integrity, and well-being. Religion does people harm physically, materially, socially, and mentally, they say, and damages, coerces, and excludes certain people in ways that negates its legitimacy. For some, these are intrinsic religious propensities, for others, the unfortunate behaviors of a minority. Some of these wrongs are said to be caused by religious leaders, others by religious cultures per se. Some we interviewed added other lesser criticisms: irrationality, weirdness, cliquishness, unanswered prayers. But the core objections to religion that turn off most American post-Boomers center on the multiple kinds of harm it has done or does to people.

Explanations for Leaving Religion

Of the 209 Americans ages 18–54 whom we interviewed for this project, 135 were religious Decliners—people who had grown up highly religious or whose families were highly religious but who, by the time they completed the national survey from which we sampled them, identified as having little or no religion. We spent a good part of our interviews asking them to tell us their life stories. We made sure to find out the occasions when and reasons why they left the religions of their youth. We did not directly ask, "So, why did you drop your religion?" but gleaned reasons from their larger life histories. That

Table 10.2 Reasons Given for Leaving Childhood Religion as Teenagers or Adults

Reasons given	Number of cases
Religion is not about institutions but a personal matter	66
Religion is a personal journey, became "spiritual"	58
Just drifted away, apathy	46
Life obligations got in the way	33
Left religion after high school or beginning of college	32
Religious hypocrites	28
No one religion is true, so cannot commit to one	19
Religious institutions are corrupt and greedy	18
Religious institutions are anti-LGBTQ+	17
Religious institutions seek power and are manipulative	16
Death of a loved one	15
Morality does not need religion	11
Negative interaction with clergy or fellow congregants	11
Sex scandals	11
The problem of evil, explaining bad in the world	10
Alternate philosophies and logic make more sense	9
COVID-19 disrupted attendance	6
Unanswered prayers	6
Religion getting involved in politics	5
Religion is bad for society	5
Total Decliner Interviews	135

Source: LZ interviews of Decliners, 2021, 2022.

approach provided a fuller sense of who these people were, avoided coming off as interrogating, and placed their explanations for leaving religion in an illuminating narrative context.[3] We studied their life stories closely and sorted their reasons for distancing from religion into thematic categories (see Table 10.2). Some reasons are clearer and more explanatory than others. As noted above, we need not take these as the "real" or only reasons for religious disaffiliation. Most are part of larger causal processes. Even so, they tell us much of value about the sense that ex-religious people make of religion and the kinds of justifications they have for disaffiliating.

The most frequent explanation (66 out of 135 cases, 49%) is that religion is a personal matter, not about social institutions. This is actually not much of a causal explanation since it tells us little about how or why these people came to this view. But it discloses a cultural assumption that is a key part of the zeitgeist driving religion's obsolescence: whatever religion is, it is not something institutional. In this view, any individual can be as little or much personally religious as they wish without any connection to a religious congregation or denomination. In fact, institutional religion will likely distort religion's true essence. Genuine religion is properly a personal, individual, perhaps private matter—meaning, by implication, that these people believe religion may have some value but religious institutions do not. So, in whatever way these 66 people think about it specifically, institutional religion compelled them to distance themselves from religion.

The second most common reason (43%) is closely related: that religion is a personal journey, not a matter of organized affiliation or participation. Many people who mentioned this also said they had become "spiritual but not religious." For many, this is an inverted way to say the same thing as the first reason: that one can subtract the institution and retain the essence of religion by following an individual life journey, which is often understood in terms of personal spirituality. This again gives no information about how and why people came to this belief. But it provides the justifying account for their leaving traditional religion and reveals a cultural assumption seen as legitimate. Between these first two explanations, the vast majority of Decliners shed light on why they left religion: they believe religious institutions are at best superfluous and at worst dangerous. One, for example, expressed, "Just seeing a denominational headquarters makes me feel angry. I feel angry because I didn't know that church had headquarters, I never realized how much money was involved. I mean, they have headquarters, there has to be a lot of money going on." So whatever form of (quasi-)religion or spirituality they are practicing, they think it can be a personal matter that does not require being part of a group. Here Americans' distrust of social institutions and their deployment of the classic evangelical discourse of "personal relationship with God" reveal their influences.

Decliners' next three most mentioned reasons cluster into the larger experience of just passively drifting away: apathy, life obligations, busyness, life-course transitions, and sidetracking journeys caused them to fade out of religion. There was no decisive or purposeful break, just a gradual wandering off. These kinds of answers sounded like this: "Religion is one of those things for me I have a lot of apathy towards I just don't care. Like, do you believe if there's a God or not? I don't know, I don't care—I used to think about it a lot when I was younger, but now I just don't care." Another told us,

> I don't not believe in God, but I'm not gonna sit here and preach his existence. I wouldn't be opposed to starting to go to church again, but it's also not like I'm going to seek out the opportunity to go. I feel like I'm just indifferent toward it. I don't know, it's not something super important to me right now.

The next five reasons also group into a larger type offering negative critiques of religion, many of which we saw in Table 10.2: hypocrisy, false claims to truth, corruption, greed, rejection of those who are LGBTQ+, power-grabbing, manipulation, negative interactions with clergy and other laypeople, sex abuse scandals, and religion being bad for society generally.[4] Many we interviewed discussed this in very personal terms, including wrongs they observed religion visiting on their parents long ago, for example:

> My dad went to a Catholic school, was an altar boy, for him the Catholic Church was a big part of life. Then he was excommunicated because he got divorced. That was a huge deal. After that, he saw religion in a totally different light. He couldn't believe that suddenly he was basically not seen by the Catholic Church any more, after he had been there for so many years, just because of something like that. Divorce is horrible but it's not a sin. But religion, not moving or adapting with the times, gets set in stone like, "This is right, this is wrong, no matter what." It doesn't need to. Nothing is black and white.

And another recounted,

> My church growing up, there was too many contradictions for me. My dad was trying to be a deacon for like 70 years, and they were like, "Okay, brother we'll get back to you," you know what I mean? It was just very misleading. And visiting church leaders asking for money, we have to pay them for being here? Like, no, it's not okay.

That people do not need religion to be moral—a reason stated by 11 Decliners—is also a form of criticism of religion, although it overlaps with the anti-institutional sentiment above, too. Last, smaller number of Decliners cite existential and intellectual reasons for leaving religion. These include the death of a loved one, evil and suffering in the world, various philosophical problems, logical or scientific disproof, and unanswered prayers. One, for instance, said,

> Another reason Christianity makes me angry is all the bad stuff that goes on in the world, why can't that be stopped? If Jesus died on cross to stop sin, then why are little babies being murdered? If God's that powerful and all knowing, why are you letting this happen? It's just not understanding why he would let that happen if he's the way I've always understood, loving and caring. If he is, why are people dying such horrible deaths, you know, you have all the power in the world, why can't you stop it from happening?

Another objected with this logic: "The fact that there's so many different translations and versions of the Bible gives people the idea that if there's so much conflict within it, then how can there be any truth to it?"

The boundaries between most of these explanations are not sharp. Many likely overlap and relate to others—for instance, getting a bad vibe from a pastor could have caused someone to stop going to church, which in turn could have fostered a spiritual-but-not-religious identity and a belief that one does not need religion to be moral. Altogether, these explanations provide a good sense of how post-Boomers who left the strong religions of their youth understand their reasons and highlight central cultural structures behind religious obsolescence. We can interpret all this in more than one way. But one basic conclusion seems justified: in the cultural zeitgeist that emerged after 1991, many post-Boomers came to see traditional religion as some combination of issues extraneous to what really matters, not particularly worth hanging on to, and guilty of many wrongs. Religion had become superfluous, disposable, and morally objectionable—and therefore obsolete.

Comparing Other Accounts of Disaffiliation

We are not the first to have asked ex-religious Americans why they left the religions of their youth. In 2015, the Pew Research Center asked more than 900 survey respondents who had disaffiliated from religion to explain in their own words why they no longer identified with religion. Their answers coalesced around certain common themes.[5] I was curious whether my own

Table 10.3 Why Religious "Nones" Left Their Religions of Youth

Reasons for becoming not religious	%
Just doesn't believe	40
Negative feelings about and critiques of religion	18
Personal choice	16
Different personal religious and spiritual views	10
Failed search for religion	4
Philosophical objections	4
Practical difficulties of participating	3
Not raised very religious	2
Social disconnection, lack of ties	1
Don't know, can't explain	1

Source: 2015 Pew survey follow-up to the 2014 Pew Research Center Religious Landscape Survey ($N = 925$).

categorizing of the original verbatim answers would lead to results similar to those in the initial report, and Pew generously granted me access to them, which I re-categorized. Each response fits into one category of answer, so the reported percentages (when not rounded) add to 100.

My results, reported in Table 10.3, proved similar to Pew's original findings but were somewhat more complex. Comparing the 2015 Pew results with those from our interviews reported in Table 10.2 is a bit challenging because some of the answer categories do not match up. For example, the Pew answer "Just Doesn't Believe" doesn't neatly match any of the categories above. Much of this difference could be due to the different methods of data collection used. We gleaned our reasons from in-depth interviews, while Pew's came from an open-ended survey question given online and over the telephone, and both of those tend to produce more abbreviated responses. In addition, our Decliners grew up in highly religious contexts, whereas Pew's respondents were simply raised in some religion.

The Pew results are illuminating nonetheless and roughly parallel those from our interviews. Interpreted broadly, a large share of the Pew respondents say they just no longer believe. This could mean they stopped believing in God, in institutional religion, or in the doctrinal systems of their original denominations. We know, however, that only a minority of American religious "nones" are declared atheists, so many of these stopped believing in something about religion other than the existence of God. Almost one in five attribute their disaffiliation to grievances they held against religion. More than one in six said it was simply their personal choice, which does not explain much, other than implicitly revealing the assumption that individuals are the seat of final authority and that religion sometimes functions as a "personal identity accessory."[6] One out of ten said different religious or spiritual views kept them away from religion, suggesting they embraced some kind of spirituality or other quasi-religious views that did not fit traditional religion. A few said they unsuccessfully tried to find a religion that worked for them or had practical difficulties practicing religion. Less than 1 in 20 pointed to philosophical objections to religion (although, again, some of the "just doesn't believe" group may fall into this category but simply did not spell out the reasons why they no longer believe). The big-picture takeaway? Large numbers of post-Boomers no longer believe that anyone needs a social institution to be a spiritual or moral person, and religion is seen not as a force for good in the world but instead as a source of harm, discrimination, manipulation, exclusion, and control.

New York Times writer Jessica Grose published a piece in April 2023, "Lots of Americans Are Losing Their Religion. Have You?" In it, she invited readers to share with her their stories of religious disaffiliation. She received more than 7,000 responses. In studying them, Grose noticed three major trends in disaffiliated people's stories, which she categorized this way:

- *Seekers*: Those who had switched religious affiliation more than once but still might have some religious connections
- *Skeptics*: Those who had an abrupt break from the church of their youth, after which they became atheists or agnostics
- *Slow Faders*: Others who drifted away from religion fairly late in life, whose religious disaffiliation took time

Seekers "don't want to lose that transcendent feeling," Grose observed, but they could not find transcendence in traditional religion. They also cited problems with religion, such as authoritarian leaders, sexual repression, unanswered prayers, and conservative politicization. So they looked elsewhere: to spirituality, Buddhism, Islam, nature, and so on. Skeptics were often raised in conservative religions but, in their teenage and young adult years, began to believe that what they had been taught was false. So they left. Slow Faders were life-long, family-tied religious practitioners until some major life change—retirement, the death of a loved one, a political realignment—triggered long-simmering, previously unvoiced doubts that grew too loud to ignore.[7]

Grose's journalistic opt-in results do not reflect a representative sample of Americans but are instructive nevertheless. Many ex-religious Americans who did not find transcendence and spirituality in traditional religion still look for it elsewhere. Another group reacted against the (especially conservative) religious teachings they believed as children by dumping the entire package as adults. Another cluster had long-standing connections to religion sustained by family and community ties, but these broke down later in life after unsettling life transitions turned preexisting modest doubts into major problems with beliefs and then disaffiliation.[8] In sum, again, we find from Grose's open-ended method of collecting narratives that Americans' growing disaffiliation from religion involves combinations of people not finding institutional religion helpful or necessary and an incapacity to believe some traditional religious teachings—often prompted by growing up into a more complicated and skeptical culture or some major disrupting life event. We can best understand the growing influence of these dynamics, I suggest, as resulting from the causal forces and events described in the preceding chapters and the cultural zeitgeist that emerged from them.

Three Important Minority Traditions

This book's macro, historical-cultural approach has mostly treated "post-Boomers," "Millennials," and the like as a single group similarly influenced by shared macro forces and events. Sociologists specialize in generalizations. At the same time, this macro approach tends to fly at too high an altitude to see variations in how those causal factors influence diverse religious and demographic types of Americans differently—which they sometimes do. We need in-depth, fine-grained explorations of how younger generations from religious traditions experienced and responded to the big changes described in the preceding chapters. That is beyond the purview of this book and deserving of more dedicated, in-depth studies. That said, I would be remiss not to mention three particularly important traditions that appear to counter historical expectations on the question of disaffiliating from religion. These are not merely interesting religious traditions to zoom in on—they are theoretically important cases to examine.

This book's Appendix explores the statistics of non-religious Americans. Two groups in Figure A.1 there diverge conspicuously from the general trend of Millennials becoming non-religious at quite higher rates than previous generations: those who were raised Jewish and Mormon. What jumps out is that Millennials raised Jewish were *less* likely than Gen Xers raised Jewish to identify as not religious (17.8% compared to 18.6%). What is remarkable about the Millennials raised Mormon is they were much *more* likely as adults to identify as not-religious (47.6%, a more than doubling of the Gen X figure of 21.4%) than Millennials raised in every other religious tradition. In addition, we see that Black Protestant Millennials are less likely to identify as "nones" than are Millennials of any other religious tradition analyzed. These findings are significant because, until recently, research showed that Mormon youth were the least likely to disaffiliate, while Jewish youth have been experiencing high rates of intermarriage and cultural assimilation, which has contributed to overall Jewish population decline in the United States. Those stories no longer appear to be true. The Black Protestant case is more in keeping with expectations but also raises new questions. Other scholars have already noted these changes but, given how they counter conventional wisdom, they are worth underscoring here.

Jewish Millennials

Leaders of American Judaism have long been concerned about threatening declines in Jewish religious and cultural practices and in the Jewish population itself. These concerns arose from growing rates of intermarriage and increased cultural assimilation. In 1964, *Look* magazine famously ran a cover story on "The Vanishing American Jew." Since then, surveys of the American Jewish population and other research have raised concerns about the fate of Judaism in the United States. Some continue to express great anxiety. City College of New York sociologist William Helmheich, for example, said in 2017, "However you play with the numbers, the outlook ... for the Jewish community ... doesn't look good. ... In truth, Jews are disappearing as a people."[9] My own research on Millennials in the 2000s showed that Jewish teenagers scored low on many religiousness measures and that only 61% of teenagers ages 13–17 who identified as Jewish did so five years later at ages 18–23.[10]

More recent investigations, however, suggest that Jewish Millennials—including those raised in religiously intermarried households—may be displaying a greater readiness than older generations to continue identifying as Jewish and to engage in some Jewish religious observances. One study revealed that Millennial children of Jewish intermarriage were more likely than in previous generations to be raised Jewish, to identify as Jewish in adulthood, not to identify with another religion, and to attend Passover seders and Jewish worship services.[11] Another study showed that Jewish young adult Millennials in the United States are more likely than older Jews to view their Jewishness as a matter of religion and not merely culture or ethnicity. An American Jewish Committee survey of US Jewish Millennials found that fully 33% said that what best describes their connection to Judaism is "Judaism is a religion, a faith," instead of the options stating that Judaism is a "culture, a cultural identity," "an ethnicity," or "a nationality."[12] A 2017 report on Jewish Millennials based on focus groups and a national survey shows that, despite the majority having only one Jewish parent, US Jewish Millennials highly value their Jewish identity, place great importance on their religious identity, are interested in religion, and often express their religiousness in traditional and formal ways. Jewish Millennials in the United States are also more likely than those of older generations to have a traditional idea of God, attend religious services more frequently, pray or meditate more often, believe in some form of life after death, and be comfortable conversing with others about different spiritual views.[13] That report summarized its findings this way:

> Even as American Millennial Jews insist on the elasticity of identity and spirituality . . . they are also unique in the extent to which they bounce back to familiar indicators and behaviors when embodying their own Jewishness. . . . [Focus group quotes] attest to this proclivity: "There's something to be said for a continuing tradition. I respect that." "If you don't put in the work, the relationship dies." "You have to maintain those traditions and pass them on to the next [generation].". . . Millennial Jews in America present quite a paradox. . . . They are free-thinking and flexible in their spiritual and religious identity, yet they gravitate toward formal customs and ancient expressions of faith. . . . They reject rigid or traditional definitions of what it means to be Jewish but—more than any other generation—still consider their Jewish identity to be very important to them. . . . The most concrete trait about this generation is open-mindedness. . . . But . . . their

heritage and the belonging it provides still inevitably and deeply affect their beliefs, in a way that contrasts with the average American Millennial.[14]

My modest result in the Appendix—that Millennials raised Jewish were slightly less likely than Gen Xers raised Jewish to identify as not religious—fits well with these recent assessments.

If this proves true over time, this Jewish Millennial counter-trend is important and instructive. That is because the likely causes of this outcome were intentional interventions. In 1990, the National Jewish Population Survey released a report on the state of Jewish demographics that hit like a bombshell. Among its numerous concerning statistics: the intermarriage rate of American Jews was 52%, a number that "clearly inaugurated the present era of intense concern about Jewish continuity."[15] In response, a large number of Jewish organizations committed to unprecedented fundraising campaigns to finance an array of new programs to better educate and socialize Jewish youth—including Hillel and Chabad University campus organizations, Israel heritage trips, and other Jewish learning initiatives. Among them was the heritage tourism program Birthright Israel, launched in 1999, which has sent more than 800,000 young American Jews to visit Israel.[16] Some American Jewish communities, beginning in the 1980s and into the 1990s, also decided to open up communal practices to be more inclusive and welcoming of religiously intermarried parents and their children.[17] By many accounts, the internet has also enabled many young Jews who have dispersed across the country to stay connected to Jewish communities, events, and friends. These programs and policies, many observers suggest, seem to have succeeded in moving the needle on the retention rates of American Jewish Millennials.[18] If so, in a society in which nearly all trends have run in the opposite direction, that is a huge accomplishment. Observers of American Judaism still disagree about the condition and likely future of the Jewish community.[19] But some recent evidence seems to offer American Judaism a ray of hope in otherwise gloomy times for religion.[20]

Other religious traditions may find this story intriguing and consider whether they might attempt similar efforts. The general principle—that major financial investments into smart, innovative initiatives that better religiously educate and socialize youth can make a difference—might be transferrable. Still, American Judaism enjoys some distinctive and complex features not shared by many other American traditions. One is that it is not only a religion but for many also an ethnicity, a culture, even a nationality. That may help it counter causal mechanisms of secularization differently than, say, Methodism or Lutheranism.[21] Another is that many in American Judaism view Israel as a physical, national homeland that is historically important and geopolitically insecure, visits to which by Jewish youth seem to have made real differences in their identifications and commitments.[22] American Catholics might have some approximation in Rome, but the relevant historical circumstances and other factors are different. One suspects that Presbyterians sending their youth on heritage tours (to where? Geneva? Westminster Abbey?) would not have quite the same impact as does Birthright Israel.[23] American Jews—by virtue of their history, minority status, and relatively greater wealth and political influence—also face particular vulnerabilities and enjoy particular protections in American culture. On the one hand, their long history of persecution and the Holocaust still affects Jews today in ways that the persecution of, say, Baptists in England and colonial Massachusetts do not shape US Baptists. On the other hand, anti-Semitism, which has seen a resurgence, is more closely monitored than anti-Catholicism or anti-Mormonism. It also tends to draw the US Jewish community more closely together, making Jewish identity more salient.[24] Various other religious traditions may thus draw useful lessons from the apparently partly successful efforts of Jewish organizations to counter the identity-corrosive effects of Jewish intermarriage. But they will not be directly translatable; they would require a great deal of tradition-appropriate adaptation. In any event, the case of Jewish Millennials stands out as an important episode countering the dominant trend.

Black Protestant Millennials

The story of Black Protestant Millennials is somewhat less complicated but no less important than that of post-Boomer Jews. Two key facts deserve note. First, of all major religious traditions, Black Protestantism is the most likely to retain its Millennials. Black Protestant Millennials remain the most religiously affiliated, believing, and practicing and the least likely to have become religious "nones" (Appendix Figure A.1). This suggests the possibility of somewhat successful resistance—under the right conditions, at least for the present—to the forces of religious obsolescence that have debilitated most other traditions. Numerous scholars have highlighted the crucial role the church has played in sustaining Black communities for generations.[25] The American Black experience of slavery, repression, violence, and discrimination has made the Black church crucial to survival, solidarity, and advancement.[26] The racial specificity of the Black church gives it an identity reinforcement not entirely unlike "ethnic" Judaism. Those and other dynamics continue to influence Black American youth, as evident in the relatively greater religiousness of post-Boomer Black Americans.[27]

The Black post-Boomers we interviewed were much more likely than their peers to express warm nostalgia for the religious worlds in which they were raised—even when that felt like a world they could not inhabit now. For example:

> I just remember the smell as one of those things that evokes the memory of religion done right. My grandmother went to a very small church in a white building, didn't have any flourishes, it was clean, and I remember the smell of this church and my grandmother wearing a bleached white dress to usher in this church. There was a sense of revelry and respect for this bombastic man who led this church. He made me as a little girl feel something when he spoke. And when they had community events, the local homeless guy could walk up and get a meal and not be made to feel any kind of way. People would come to my grandmother's house when she was sick to bring her food. I recall the little wicker collection plate would come around with even pennies in it. I remember seeing the pastor outside of church driving around, he would stop and say hello and it felt like community. Vacation Bible school was very important, kids who went could get a meal and juice. I remember events where we brought clothes and furniture and they would give it to other people, there was cooked dinner, it felt like community. To me that's religion done right, done well. Just the smell is the most powerful memory.

Another said,

> When I was younger, at home, I used to sing in the church choir, and they called me out as a lead singer because the person was sick one time and they knew I knew the song. I was probably 12 or 13. I sung that song and something took over me, I just had no control over anything, and we thought that's what religion was. It was a very peaceful, happy type of feeling and I never felt that again in my life.

And,

> I was extremely close to my grandmother, so she taught me a lot about the faith. I would also go to church with my father occasionally. I was very observant as a kid. When I went to churches with my father, I would observe everything and take it in, and it just didn't leave an impression in my heart as my grandmother's, hers left more of an impression on me, I felt that group of people lived a little more according to the Bible standards.

Compared to white post-Boomers, who often expressed alienation and anger about religious organizations, religiously uninvolved Black youth were also more likely to report they were not attending church because they believed they were not living properly Christian lives and did not want to be hypocrites. The man quoted above who attended church with his grandmother and father, for instance, said that he struggles with reconciling being gay and his religious faith.

> I would like to get myself back on track spiritually, but right now I'm just chilling. I don't want to be phony, being honest is the biggest thing for me, even more important than church. I feel like God knows, I can go to church every Sunday if I want, but if I'm doing things God wouldn't necessarily accept, then who am I doing it for? For Him or for the people there? If for people there, that defeats the purpose. So I would like to get myself back on track, but I'm also not going to be phony and act like I'm not living or talking or acting a certain way. Chilling is the best way of putting it, but I can't chill too long because that's not a good option.

Another told us,

> I was more involved but then slowed down and got to zero. I would like to get back involved. I got to figure out the best way of doing it not being phony because it's very important to me to not live one way and then go to church on Sundays and act in another way. People that do that, they're not doing it for God, because God knows regardless. He knows what you're doing, and you're not doing Him a favor by going to His meetings or services one day a week and then six days a week living like a heathen.

Still another explained,

> I had a great understanding of my religion, I memorized the verses, read the Bible, knew it all. So especially going to college and partying, drinking, I know I'm not supposed to drink in my religion. So why am I going to continue to go to church and put on this religious show that I'm talking versus doing? I know later that night I'm going to go out and break a bunch of rules we have in religion. Talk about heaven or hell, we should be strict on those things, and I'm not going to be what they call a lukewarm Christian. Being in the middle is the worst place. So either I'm going all in or I just won't. That's why I stopped, because I'm not going to stop drinking, so why am I going to go to church and put myself through that? I'll just go do my own thing.

The hypocrisy of others in church, while an issue for nearly everyone, seemed to be an even bigger concern among Black post-Boomers than their peers. The one quoted above who sang in his church choir reported this:

> As I got older, I felt I didn't want to be involved with churches. Don't get me wrong, I spent a lot of time in churches, that's what made me this way. I learned I have to be in a church to seek faith, God, I get it. That's why God's people gather. But I learned I have my faith wherever I'm at, whether or not I'm at church. Then learning that's not why everyone is there was a big deterrent for me, to not only question faith but stirred my feelings about faith, because you get all these people that talk about faith and none of them faithful. Even in my family, some have the voice of angels but yet the actions are a whole different story than words. They're not living the right way themselves, but they're telling you how to live. And that goes for Catholics, Baptists, everywhere, and it does get me mad. So yeah, that was my big turn.

This distancing from church despite frequent warm memories points to a second larger fact: Black Millennials and Gen Zers appear to be showing signs of moving in religiously disaffected directions similar to their peers in many other religious traditions. The religious "advantage" the Black church enjoys with its youth may be starting to slip. Recall the observations of the Black church pastor quoted in Chapter 1: "Inviting college students to church today is like inviting them to outer space. The old vestiges are gone." Looking ahead to the Appendix, note the increased slope of the curve in Figure A.1 from Black Protestant Gen Xers to Millennials in identifying as not religious. A Pew Research Center report on religious Black Americans shows that 49% of Black Millennials seldom or never attend church, compared to 26% and 31% of Black Silent Generation and Boomers, respectively. Among those who do attend religious services, Black post-Boomers are also more likely than their elders to attend white and multiracial religious congregations.[28] Conflicts between church teachings and those identifying as LGBTQ+ also alienate some Black Millennials.[29]

At the same time, scholars point out that Black youth often relate to and practice religion in ways different from dominant white religious patterns, which may mean that decreases in survey numbers are less informative.[30] As much uncertainty exists about the fate of the post-Boomer Black church as that of American Judaism. But nobody should expect that Black youth are immune from the massive forces of cultural change described in the preceding chapters. Many Black church leaders have noticed generational shifts that trouble them and are attempting to respond constructively.[31] Time will tell whether efforts like theirs are able successfully to resist the zeitgeist's influence of religious obsolescence.

Mormon Millennials

Mormonism is legendary for its impressive retention rates among young people. Studies I conducted in the 2000s found unusual success in fostering high levels of religious adherence and practice among Millennial Mormon (Church of Latter Day Saints; LDS) teenagers.[32] But, I have since realized, focusing on LDS teenagers can be misleading. Most American youth who pull away from their family's religion typically do so during their late teenage years. Not so for Mormons. Most who leave the LDS church do so in their later 20s, after a longer process of questioning and separation. That is because exiting Mormonism usually means not simply leaving an organization but abandoning a central, core personal identity.[33] So, while Mormon retention looked solid in the early 2000s, in the years since, as Millennial Mormons moved through emerging adulthood, they began exiting the LDS church in dramatic, unprecedented numbers.

Studies produce different statistics, but they all point in the same direction. The Pew Research Center reported that, in 2007, Mormons enjoyed a strong overall retention rate of 70%. By 2014, however, that retention rate had dropped to 64% for all generations and 62% for Millennials. That is the optimistic reading. The General Social Survey, by comparison, shows a 46% retention rate for Mormon Millennials, compared to a 75% rate for Silent Generation Mormons, 72% for Boomers, and 63% for Gen Xers. Jana Riess's 2016 "Next Mormon Survey" showed the "activity rate" (regularly participating in church services) of Mormon Millennials to be 46%.[34] That the LDS Millennial regular participation rate has fallen below 50% reveals a huge drop compared to previous generations.

A combination of factors explains this LDS Millennial exodus.[35] Some Millennials leave Mormonism over what they see as patriarchy, sexism, heterosexism, racism, the marginalizing of single adults, and sexual repression in the church. Others lose faith in the reliability of the historical accounts of the church's founding, are scandalized by the polygamous practices of its founders, or are put off by the frequency of changes in official church teachings. Some report they simply feel judged, misunderstood, and forced to conform. Others find Mormon history and practices—such as secret temple ceremonies—wacky or cultish. Still others point to archaeological, linguistic, and genetic evidence discrediting the Book of Mormon. According to Riess's research, ex-Mormons of different generations offer varying reasons for their leaving the church. The top 10 reasons that Millennials disaffiliate are because they

1. Feel judged and misunderstood
2. Do not trust their church leadership [tied for first]
3. Have issues with the church's treatment of those who are LGBTQ
4. Cannot reconcile their personal values with church teachings
5. Just drift away
6. Stop believing the LDS was the one true church
7. Have problem with the Book of Mormon
8. Engage in behaviors deemed sinful by the church
9. Resist the church's stress on conformity [tied for eighth]
10. Dislike how women are treated in the church[36]

Most of these reflect the same critical themes in Tables 10.1 and 10.2. One particular factor in LDS disaffiliation, however, is that Mormonism, unlike mainline Protestantism and Catholicism, makes little room for moderately involved adherents. Mormonism is a high-demand faith that expects everyone to be "all in." Multiple mechanisms ensure that sporadic and half-hearted Mormonism is not an option. That is historically a sociological strength of the tradition. However, this can backfire. Mormons who find they cannot be fully devoted face only one alternative: to leave entirely. More than half of LDS Millennials have taken that path, becoming "exmo's" and "postmo's."

The internet has greatly facilitated Millennial Mormon disaffiliation. For many who grew up firmly within a Mormon social world, the internet offered an eye-opening exposure to religious, cultural, and ethical differences that undermined their religious confidence. The internet also expedited the widespread sharing of exit stories from thousands who left Mormonism. Websites with names like exmormon.org, postmormon.org, and quitmormon.org are available to help anyone leave the church.[37] The internet is also a major source of information that is critical—and for some damning—of the LDS church. In 2017, for instance, an anti-LDS WikiLeaks-type website, MormonLeaks, uploaded a cache of embarrassing LDS church documents, including financial records, internal memos, and a PowerPoint presentation on "issues and concerns leading people away from the gospel." The church sued and had the documents removed, but not before others already copied and spread them around the internet.[38] In a separate incident, a Mormon whistleblower exposed that the LDS church had accumulated a $100 billion investment fund, built from ordinary members' tithes, and allegedly used false statements, systematic accounting fraud, and violations of federal law to conceal its existence.[39] This kind of thing might have been revealed in prior eras, but the internet made the exposure exponentially faster and wider reaching.

The internet also provides ready-made communities of ex-Mormons for new leavers to join. Doubting and ex-Mormons "use the internet as their sanctuary, engaging in a ritual of sharing that binds them in a spiritual community, despite their disavowal of faith."[40] So, "for people who have left recently, there is a built-in community waiting to receive them."[41] One former Brigham Young University student observed, "Gen Z is probably the first generation in Mormonism to have access to others to validate what they are going through. . . . If you have doubts about the church, you can always find a community [on TikTok]." Another said, "Previous generations are told to obey, and I believe we have a new generation that is choosing to reflect on what they feel is right rather than what they are told is right. [Gen Z] is finally getting accurate information and choosing for themselves." Whereas previously, said this student, "a Mormon in Salt Lake in the 1970s would have to go to a scary bookshop to get some forbidden book about the truth of [church founder] Joseph Smith."[42]

Compared to defectors from other American religions, ex-LDS Millennials appear to sustain greater animosity toward the religion they left. The LDS church's deep penetration into their personal lives growing up combined with its "love it or leave it" standards can generate powerful feelings of anger and resentment when they finally exit. Some become "career apostates," spending years publishing anti-Mormon books and essays.[43] Many accuse the church of "stealing" from them the ability to think freely and the possibility of having healthy views of sexuality and their own bodies.[44] Common among ex-Mormons are narratives of "cultural estrangement" and breaking "out of captivity" that emphasize the need for long-term "recovery" and the reconstruction of basic identities in the face of what scholars call "world collapse."[45] In online forums about why Millennials leave the LDS church, ex-Mormons write, for example, "Who wants to listen to old dudes drone on about a kiddie-raping sex cult from the 1800s and pretend they were geniuses who saw angels?" And, "The church is boring as hell, meaningless in the face of modern norms, and everyone's eyes are open to reality now," and "Their truth claims are garbage—no, the Book of Mormon is not factual [but] made up by JS or a conspirator."[46] Exiting the LDS church also often involves traumatizing blowback from family members disappointed and hurt by the their loved one's decision to defect.[47] All this helps explain the large number of vibrant ex-Mormon groups offering support, advice, and resources to prospective and new disaffiliates. It also portends that few alienated Mormon Millennials will likely return to the LDS church in the future.

Stepping back, it is clear, in the words of scholar Matthew Bowman, that the LDS church "is not able to sustain the sort of intense, demanding community that Mormons who grew up in Utah in the middle of the 20th century took for granted."[48] Mormon Millennials have been shaped by the same zeitgeist engendered by the macro forces and events this book has described. Thus, what not long ago was called "the fastest growing religion in the world" is now grappling with mass defections by its Millennials.

Conclusion

The story of this chapter—and this book—is a dismal one for traditional religion. The long-term macro transformations, the Millennial zeitgeist, and religious obsolescence have led to throngs of post-Boomers exiting traditional religion. Next, we step back and consider again in conclusion some big-picture implications of the larger story.

Conclusion

This book is a lesson in sociological realism. What can we learn?

For starters, we can learn to take the long view. Significant social transformations do not happen overnight. They do not necessarily come with advance warning, either. What can appear to be dramatic transformations are usually the result of trends, events, and forces long in the making. Pressures and contradictions take time to build. Forces of continuity resist change for significant stretches. Big shifts can be under way for long periods without apparent consequences until they reach a tipping point or critical mass, when everything changes. Particulate matter in the atmosphere is invisible yet accumulates in bodies over time to the point where it causes disease and death. Innovations may seem to appeal only to early adopters until, quite rapidly, they become commonplace. Understanding important social changes, then, requires not focusing only on the events immediately preceding them but also on more complicated, long-term causal forces.

Another lesson is the need to take socially dominant institutions seriously for understanding cultural change. How people think and talk at any given time cannot be taken as the proximate drivers of historical development. Discourse does not itself create institutional reality, and people merely talking differently rarely changes much.[1] Cultural ideas have the causal power at times to shift the directions of history, as Max Weber argued. But cultural ideas and their discourses are not free-floating or self-directing. They are the products of social institutions and technology regimes operating in specific historical, material circumstances. In every epoch, to modify Karl Marx, the ruling ideas are those that resonate with and reinforce the ruling, or at least ascendent, social institutions. To understand the obsolescence of traditional religion, we must comprehend the governing institutions of that era. We need to think in terms of institutional plate tectonics, not summations of individuals' neurologically grounded capacities to believe in God.

The governing institutions most relevant for the demise of American traditional religion were globalized neoliberal mass-consumer capitalism; its media and communications arm in cable television, the internet, social media, and smart phones; and its proselytizing arm in the advertising and marketing industries; along with growing universities and colleges; immigration policy; and the war on terror (which started as a mission and became a kind of institution). Those helped reshape other key institutions, cultures, and practices, including marriage and family, work and careers, sex and gender, life aspirations, ideas about knowledge and truth, post-scarcity values, expressive individualism, parenting practices, responses to social pluralism, identity politics, and more.

American traditional religions, for their part, did little to respond well to these transformations. By the 1970s, parts of conservative Protestantism were reacting by mobilizing political power to try to reverse the tides. Other parts tried to adapt with television ministries, seeker churches, mega congregations, charismatic praise worship, postmodern theologies, and so on. That worked well enough for Baby Boomers and some Gen Xers through the 1980s. But it stopped working when Millennials came of age. The cultural impacts of the governing social institutions hit tipping points for post-Boomers. Prompted in part by religion's own multiple transgressions and missteps, some Gen Xers and many Millennials adapted themselves to this new environment by ditching religion. In their eyes, religion offered nothing essential and came with major liabilities. Even so, to return to the centrality of institutions, every such individual experience and choice about religion still took place within and was profoundly influenced by the ruling institutions of the social environment.

For these reasons, to make good sense of traditional religion's obsolescence, we cannot take as adequate explanations ex-religious people's professed reasons for identifying as religious "nones" and "spiritual but not religious." They tell us some important things, but hardly everything—and very little about the broader conditions under which those people found beliefs and identities plausible and attractive or not. People are rarely fully aware and articulate when it comes to themselves and the larger forces that impinge on their experiences. It takes systematic, disciplined inquiry into self and society to achieve that. Stage, scenery, script, and lighting are just as important as action and spoken lines.

For these reasons, too, it will not suffice simply to believe that American traditional religion was done in by anti-religious activists operating in the time preceding its obsolescence. Some such campaigners were involved, but they played small roles compared to the convergence of accumulating macro-sociological storms that beset religion, not to mention the incalculable damage that some religious leaders themselves inflicted on their own religions. Activist atheists have modest reasons to crow, and religious people have little reason to blame their adversaries. Religious actors were more destructive to religion than militant atheists—in fact, they handed the atheists much fodder for their incriminating indictments.

Such sociological realism has implications for understanding everyday lives. Religious leaders, for example, may, to employ another metaphor, be swimming furiously in their work to achieve their goals, but if they are unknowingly swimming in a particular context, against a cultural gulf stream current, it may appear they are making headway as water rushes past but, in fact, may be getting nowhere or even being swept backward. In my observation, many who care about a declining American religion, especially clergy, take their struggles too personally. They also often believe that the right ideas and programs can turn things around—the "theological idealism" and "program idealism" I mentioned in the Introduction[2]—and can feel they are to blame when they don't. Sociological realism instead summons everyone to appreciate the force of big-picture social contexts on our personal experiences and to realistically face the limits and opportunities in moving forward.

Damned If It Do, Damned If It Don't

Part of religion's slide into obsolescence involved finding itself caught in complicated webs of no-win situations. When religion seriously accommodated pluralism, it became milquetoast. When it proclaimed a distinctive message, it was narrow-minded. Granting that people could be good without God was self-degrading. But insisting that people need God if they are to be good was arrogant and hurtful. When religion taught traditional sexual and family morality, it was archaic and unrealistic. When liberal religious denominations welcomed most types of relationships and expressions of sexuality, there was nothing distinctive to attract adherents. When religion embraced the role of mere keeper-of-moralism, it ended up having nothing of unique interest to say. When it proclaimed its theology as distinctively true—perhaps insisting that "being a good person" actually has little to do with what faith is really about—that was exclusivist and judgmental. Religious leaders and followers who were genuinely upright confirmed that religion is only for especially good people, not "real" humans. When religious leaders committed the same sins as everyone else, they were horrible hypocrites. Liturgical religions with formal styles were stuffy, rote, outdated—pipe organs and hymnbooks were the Dark Ages. But when pastors tried Jimmy Buffet–style guises or sported the Gen X hipster look, that was pandering—their Fender guitars and charismatic praise-fests were fake performances and parodies of "real" entertainment. Religion was in postmodern culture viewed as just another language game amid a cacophony of narratives and myths. Simultaneously, religion was presumed to be the inevitable loser to science, its obvious epistemic superior, which somehow rose above postmodern deconstruction. When religion offered post-Boomers the kind of strong communities they said they yearned for, they kept their distance because real community could limit one's autonomy and options. When religion attempted means of engagement with minimal community obligations, that felt impersonal. When religions met face-to-face during regularly scheduled services, that was too demanding for busy people's lives. When they gathered online or through other media, that was too electronically mediated and anonymous. Name the issue, religion lost no matter what.

The point is not that religion deserves a pity party, but that obsolescence brings with it multiple conundrums for those not ready to just give up. Once deep culture becomes structured in certain ways, it can be nearly impossible for culturally mismatched traditions and institutions to find spaces in which they make any sense. Once certain concatenations of events and social forces gain momentum, doors begin to shut on possible constructive responses. When religion gets crowded out by other imperatives, it becomes easily dismissed or excused away no matter what form it takes. American religion faced repeated no-win situations not because the "nones" were being vindictive or irrational but because deep culture worked to limit religion's realistic options.

Not by Secularization Alone

This book's story also presents an empirical challenge to traditional secularization theory, which holds that, as societies become more modern and developed, they will become more secular. While traditional religion has declined in the United States, it has not been replaced by sheer secularism. Religious obsolescence in the United States has not meant the disappearance of the sacred, spiritual, magical, enchanted, supernatural, occult, ecstatic, or divine. They remain alive and well. The sacred and ecstatic have migrated to new locations. The spiritual is reconstituted in new forms. Old divinities are replaced with new and sometimes even older ones. One has to crawl under a rock to escape popular interest in spirituality, magic, and occulture. But to see that, one needs to discard certain theoretical blinders. The cultural field of play today is not a binary one on which two teams face off and battle for supremacy. The field is occupied by many competitors playing different games, some clusters of which do not even look like teams. Far from religion's growing obsolescence entailing the triumph of secularity, then, the American experience demonstrates instead the relocating and morphing of religionish things to nontraditional sites and expressions.

While some of the causes of religious obsolescence explained in this book were secularizing forces, many others were pressures from competing alternative religions and quasi-religions and spiritualities. American society has indeed become more secular in some ways. But it has also become re-enchanted by spirituality and occulture in other ways that belie any inexorable march to secularity. Max Weber would smile wryly about American religion helping to dig its own grave. But he would be confounded by the reversal of disenchantment in contemporary American culture. And while these other forms of enchantment compete with religion, they outright reject a secularist cosmology. The American case thus disappoints skeptical Enlightenment hopes for the arrival of a rational, scientific, secular social order—and its academic counterpart, secularization theory.

Secularization theory is not flat wrong, which helps explain its longevity. But it is part blind and untenably overachieving. An adequate sociology of religion requires more complex, nuanced, and context-dependent theoretical accounts. Traditional secularization theory, far from being "beyond doubt," needs to be revised as not a master narrative of modernity but instead as one set of causal mechanisms that sometimes but not always or in the same ways tend to move some societies in secular directions.[3] Secularization happens. But so do a lot of other processes, including ones that perpetuate and strengthen the sacred, spiritual, enchanted, magical, supernatural, occult, ecstatic, and divine in modern life—even if outside the structures of traditional religion.

And the Future?

I was, while working on this book project, often asked whether religions don't simply run through cycles of strength and decline. Might we expect a religious revival sometime in the future? The answer is: such foreseeable cycles do not exist, neo-positivist wishful thinking notwithstanding. History and social life are too particular and volatile for such things. More generally, we should take seriously the droll saying, "It is difficult to make predictions, especially about the future." Some may hope that a post–Gen Z generation will in time revive traditional religion. But, at present, nothing on the sociological horizon indicates this as likely. Quite the opposite. Nothing in the 2010s or early 2020s fundamentally reversed any of the big forces of change let loose in the 1990s and 2000s. If anything, they have intensified. American traditional religion is, for post-Boomers, now culturally polluted, and that contamination cannot be quickly and easily cleaned up. At some point, the decline of religion will have to plateau, if for no other reason than that fewer religious people will be left to leave. But leveling off is not revival. History suggests that colossal socioeconomic disruptions—like a major global economic depression or societal breakdown due to global overheating and climate change—would likely incite popular (if short-lived) enthusiasm for different religions. But precedent also says to expect them to be apocalyptic, sectarian, and cultish, not traditional.

Beyond that, I can only offer a final bit of empirical evidence from my Millennial Zeitgeist Survey. The data do not yield a reliable forecast but do provide glimpses of generational differences that can inform thinking about the near term. First, our survey asked respondents to choose which of the following best describes their upbringing:

- I was raised in a strongly religious household.
- I was raised in a moderately religious household.
- I was raised in a weakly religious household.
- I was not raised in a religious household, but one that was open to spiritual things.
- I was not raised in a religious nor spiritual household.
- Don't know.

Their answers show that each successive generation from Boomers to Millennials was raised in a slightly less strongly religious household. Twenty-three percent of Boomers, 21% of Gen Xers, and 20% of Millennials said they were raised in a strongly religious household. Similar modest declines are evident for those raised in moderately religious households. Trends moved in opposite directions for those raised in not-religious households open to spiritual things (5% Boomers, 5% Gen Xers, 10% Millennials) and in households that were neither religious nor spiritual (8% Boomers, 10% Gen Xers, 14% Millennials). Millennials and Gen Xers were also 16 times more likely than Boomers to say "Don't know," which tells us about religious apathy and illiteracy. We know that the strongest statistical association with being religious as an adult is having been raised religiously as a child. Parents are usually the most important influence shaping the religious lives of American youth.[4] The kinds of religious families in which our survey respondents were raised is also strongly associated with their current frequency of religious service attendance. This means that—in the absence of some unexpected event or force that overrides these powerful dynamics—the decline in younger generations being raised in strongly religious households offers no sociological reason to believe that traditional religion will somehow bounce back from obsolescence to a new vigor.

We also directly asked respondents in our survey whether they thought that, in the next five years, they would become more religious, less religious, or stay about the same religiously. Most said they expected to stay the same: 65% of Boomers and 58% each of Gen Xers and Millennials. Since younger generations are as a baseline already less religious than older ones, this means that, if they stick to their expectations, they will remain at those lower levels of religiousness. Five percent of Boomers said they would become less religious, compared to 8% of Gen Xers and 10% of Millennials who said the same. As to becoming more religious, 24% of Boomers, 26% of Gen Xers, and 21% of Millennials said they thought they would. And, again, the younger the generation, the more likely to answer "Don't know."

Predictions such as these are of course not necessarily reliable. For example, in a national study I conducted in 2005, 53% of Millennials said that they expected to be attending religious services when they were 30 years old, but, in 2023, only 21% of Millennials were attending religious services twice a month or more often. Young emerging adult Millennials grossly overestimated how religious they would be two decades into the future.[5] In short, the vast majority of Americans are not expecting to become any more religious in coming years. And the minority of post-Boomers who do think they may become more religious are starting from relatively lower levels of religiousness. Even if they do become more religious, that might only move them into the "somewhat" religious range, hardly enough to return American traditional religion to anything like its former glory. In short, the best guess about what the coming decades may look like for traditional religion is what recent decades have actually looked like, only more so.

Less difficult than predicting religion's future is anticipating some of the likely social consequences of religion's obsolescence. Observers have already noted an increase in Americans' feelings of isolation and loneliness, which can be attributed to many factors, including decreased participation in religious congregations. Social capital and trust in the United States will likely grow thinner as the consequences of religion's obsolescence play out, not generally in ways most consider good for people and societies. In the past, religion has served as a key resource for many people's mental and emotional coping, meaning-making, and social support—even if for some others "religious trauma" and "spiritual abuse" have been damaging. So we should not be surprised if religious obsolescence leads to increased mental health problems—which is already reported to be happening in "epidemic" proportions among younger generations. Sociologists have demonstrated that religion has numerous prosocial effects, so other socially deleterious results will also likely follow the declining vitality of American religion. Having said that, it would be futile for "society" to try to bolster traditional religion just to sustain these benefits. Embracing such instrumentalist ways of legitimizing itself is part of what set religion up for obsolescence in the first place.

Forecasting the future is not in the sociologist's job description. History is full of surprises. But nothing on the sociological radar screen suggests anything but the continued obsolescence of traditional religion in the coming years, along with the growing influences of re-enchanted spirituality and occulture. Religion will not go extinct. But it will likely remain a marginalized species in an unfavorable American sociocultural ecosystem.

Among the more unlikely but not impossible of history's surprises would be if American traditional religions turned their difficult predicament into an opportunity for self-critical soul-searching. What, finally, are they trying to do and why? What are essential to their traditions' core identities and missions—without which they would not be themselves—versus cultural positions that may seem non-negotiable but are actually liabilities? Viewed sociologically, scrambling to keep the status quo intact while still somehow becoming more "relevant"—especially according to standards of relevance defined not by the religious traditions themselves—is a losing proposition. So are defensive retrenchments and the staking of "faithfulness" on the fighting of culture wars, not to mention religious nationalism. And simply "liberalizing" traditional religion does not have an impressive track record of success.

Present conditions would seem instead to commend a more brutally honest "Come to Jesus" (if I may) confrontation with the extent of traditional religion's current predicament. As James Baldwin once observed, "Not everything that is faced can be changed, but nothing can be changed until it is faced." What might come of such deep soul-searching is anyone's guess. Any kind of major transformation would be risky, would certainly produce further numerical losses in the short term, and might very well fail. Still, to borrow from a biblical parable, perhaps a season has come for traditional religion's remaining seeds to fall into the ground and appear to die so that some much more fruitful life might be born.

APPENDIX

The Changing Social Locations of Religious Nones, 1970s–2010s

This book discussed social forces that pushed Americans away from religion and to the non-religious identities that many adopted. To substantiate certain claims made earlier and to fill out our understanding of changes in the social locations of not-religious Americans over time, I analyzed General Social Survey (GSS) data from 1972 to 2021 to identify characteristics of religious "nones." The population examined is all non-institutionalized adult Americans older than age 18. Table A.1 shows simple descriptive percentages for US adults identifying as not religious across these five decades.

We see in Table A.1 that males are more likely than females to identify as religious "nones," although that difference gradually diminished across the decades. Women in America have been becoming increasingly non-religious over time. Older Americans have been becoming increasingly non-religious as well—until the 2010s, at least. This is the logical result of some combination of existing non-religious Americans growing older and perhaps already older Americans becoming not religious. Since the median age increases across the first three observed decades are less than 10 years, they are being moderated by continual streams of young religious nones joining the ranks and perhaps a few older previous nones subsequently reidentifying as religious. By the 2010s, huge numbers of non-religious Millennials had moved into adulthood and, adding their extra-large proportions of non-religious identities, reversed the aging trend to bring the median age of religious nones down by six years from the decade before.

Across these decades, not-religious American adults become proportionately less white (decreasing from 91% to 78%) as a result of the marked increase in Hispanic and Asian, as well as other races and ethnicities (from 1% to 10%). The proportion of Black nones grew modestly from the 1970s to the 1980s (from 8% to 12%), after which the numbers level off. Differences in education remain fairly stable until the 2010s, when those with bachelor and graduate degrees increase their shares of non-religious identities. During the 1990s and 2000s, less educated Americans became a modestly larger part of the not-religious population, but then shrunk back to their original numbers relative to the growth of the more highly educated. That does not necessarily mean the less educated returned to religion but likely that the more educated became not religious at faster rates. Finally, across these decades, residents of the South and Mountain states increased their representations among the non-religious, while the proportion of Northeasterners and West Coasters dropped some. Those living in the Midwest maintained a steady one-quarter share of American nones.

I also ran logistic regression models using the same GSS data. The dependent variable is identifying as not religious versus selecting any other religious identity. All models include all of the variables presented in tables, except for geographical region—for which the region lived in as an adult variable replaces the region lived in at age 16 variable.

Table A.1 Demographic Distribution of US Non-Religious Adults by Decade, 1970s–2010s (%)

	1970s	1980s	1990s	2000s	2010s
Male	62	59	57	56	53
Age (median)	30	33	36	46	40
Race/ethnicity					
White	91	85	84	81	78
Black	8	12	9	10	12
Hispanic, Asian, other	1	4	7	9	10
Educational degree					
Post-grad degree	8	9	9	11	15
BA degree	17	17	18	18	23
High school degree	47	45	51	50	45
Region raised in					
Northeast	23	21	19	18	17
Midwest	25	26	23	25	24
South	20	22	24	27	28
Mountain	6	6	10	10	11
West Coast	26	25	25	21	20

Source: General Social Survey, 1972–2021.

Statistically insignificant results are marked "ns" for not significant. Table A.2 shows results by decade, in the order the variables are discussed.

First, we see that residential mobility is positively associated with identifying as not religious. For every decade until the end of the 2000s, Americans who had moved out of the state they grew up in were significantly more likely to be not religious than those who did not move. This adds evidence validating the negative relationship between mobility and religiousness noted in Chapter 6. Second, results confirm the argument in Chapter 4 about the relationship between the deinstitutionalization of marriage and family and decreased religiousness. Americans who grew up with two parents are in every decade significantly less likely to be not religious than those raised by one or no parent. In addition, those who as adults were never married, divorced, or separated were significantly more likely than married Americans to identify as not religious. These results are net of each other and the other variables included in the models, including age differences.

Third, results confirm the argument in Chapter 4 about the influence of the expansion of higher education on religion. During the 1970s and 1980s, Americans who had earned a bachelor's degree were more likely than those who had not to identify as not religious. In the 1990s and 2000s, however, that significant association disappeared, though it curiously reappeared in the 2010s. Going to college had a negative relationship with religious identity for two decades, but stopped in the 1990s, as previous studies have found. Graduate education is consistently more strongly associated with identifying as not religious across all the decades.

Table A.2 Demographics of Being Not Religious as an Adult, Comparison by Decade, 1970s–2010s (odds ratios)

	1970s	1980s	1990s	2000s	2010s
Mobility since teenager (comparison: Not Moved)					
Moved in same state	ns	ns	1.28	ns	ns
Moved to different state	1.45	1.4	1.44	1.40	ns
Grew up with two parents	0.73	0.76	0.81	0.72	0.77
Marital status (comparison: Married/Widowed)					
Never married	2.50	1.70	1.85	1.95	1.91
Divorced or Separated	1.79	1.89	1.83	1.55	1.50
Education (comparison: Less than BA)					
Bachelors	1.74	1.36	ns	ns	1.21
Postgrad	1.93	1.70	1.25	1.53	1.35
Older age	0.98	0.97	0.98	0.98	0.98
Male	1.99	2.03	1.86	1.66	1.56
Race (comparison: White)					
Black	ns	ns	ns	0.66	0.73
Hispanic, Asian, other	ns	ns	ns	0.63	0.60
Grew up in (comparison: Farm or Rural)					
Small town	ns	ns	ns	1.18	ns
Medium size city	1.32	1.39	ns	ns	ns
Suburb of big city	1.41	1.50	1.44	1.39	1.25
Big city	1.45	1.42	1.23	1.34	1.21
Religion raised in (comparison: No Religion)					
Black Protestant	0.14	0.07	0.05	0.08	0.12
White conservative protestant	0.17	0.08	0.09	0.11	0.13
Mainline protestant	0.17	0.09	0.11	0.13	0.20
Catholic or Orthodox	0.15	0.08	0.10	0.10	0.17
Jewish	0.19	0.08	0.08	0.09	0.11
Mormon	0.08	0.09	0.09	0.21	0.27
Other religion	0.24	0.15	0.29	0.36	0.45
Region lived as teenager (comparison: Northeast)					
South	0.66	0.63	0.71	0.67	0.74
Midwest	ns	ns	ns	ns	ns

(*continued*)

Table A.2 Continued

	1970s	1980s	1990s	2000s	2010s
Mountain	ns	ns	1.42	ns	1.28
West Coast	1.70	1.47	1.47	1.30	1.43
Region lived in as adult (comparison: Northeast)					
South	0.67	0.66	0.68	0.63	0.72
Midwest	ns	ns	ns	ns	ns
Mountain	1.51	ns	1.35	ns	1.32
West Coast	1.82	1.55	1.55	1.37	1.50

Source: General Social Survey, 1972–2021.

Other results are worth noting. Younger Americans in all decades are unsurprisingly more likely to identify as religious nones. Each additional older year of life decreased the odds of an American adult being non-religious by 2% (calculated as 1 minus .98). Males are more likely than females to be not religious as adults, although that difference diminishes in strength from the 1980s on, as Table A.1 also showed. Racial and ethnic minorities in the 2000s and after were significantly less likely than white individuals to identify as not religious, even though greater proportions of racial and ethnic minorities identified as non-religious over time (Table A.1). Also, Americans who grew up in larger population centers during whichever decade they were children were more likely to identify as not religious as adults than were those who grew up on farms or in other rural settings. Significant differences for growing up in small town and medium-sized cities are few and spotty.

Americans who were raised in any religious contexts (during whichever decade they were children and teenagers[1]) are consistently more likely to remain religious as adults compared to those raised not religious. That is not surprising. This difference was somewhat less pronounced in the 1970s but grew stronger in the 1980s and 1990s. This "protective" (or, depending on one's view of religion, "impeding") association of being raised in a religion against becoming not religious as an adult weakened somewhat in the 2010s for all religious traditions but most noticeably for those raised in other religions, Mormonism, mainline Protestantism, and Catholicism. This is consistent with the idea that cultural changes by this time—the emergence of a new zeitgeist—made growing up to become a religious "none" relatively more likely for those raised religiously in especially these traditions than for the same in previous decades. The protective effect (assuming causality here) of being raised religious diminished after the 2000s. Again, these results are statistically significant after controlling for the differences made by all of the other variables presented in the table.

Finally, geographic region matters. For all decades, having lived in the South as a teenager (compared to the Northeast) diminishes the odds of being not religious as an adult, while having lived on the West Coast as a teenager (compared to the Northeast) increases the odds. Having lived in Mountain states as a teenager increases the odds for the 1990s and 2010s but not the other decades. The results show no differences

APPENDIX 379

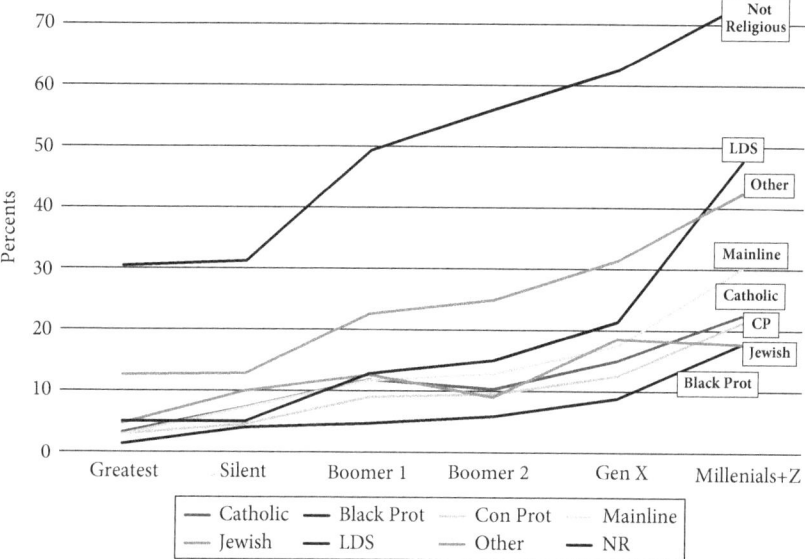

Figure A.1 Percent adult non-religious by religious tradition at age 16 and generation.
Source: General Social Survey, 1973–2018.

between living during the teenage years in the Midwest and the Northeast.[2] Results for residential region of adult respondents are similar: compared to Americans living in the Northeast, those who live as adults in the South have lower odds and those on the West Coast have higher odds of identifying as not religious, net of the other variables in the model.

I used the same data to compare differences in generations of Americans raised in each religious tradition becoming non-religious as adults at the time they took the GSS survey.[3] This tells us how each religious tradition fared across generations in losing youth affiliated with them as teenagers to adult non-religious identities. Because of relatively small sample sizes of GSS Generation Z respondents, I combined them with the Millennials category. The results of that analysis are presented graphically in Figure A.1 and as percentages in Table A.3.

Figure A.1 shows that every religious tradition examined became increasingly less able, with each successive generation across time, to retain those who were raised in them, especially with the youngest generations (except for Jewish Millennials, as discussed in Chapter 10). The slopes inch gradually up through the younger Boomer generation. Those raised Black Protestant are least likely to become non-religious as adults, conservative Protestants and Jewish the next least, Catholics the next, and so on. Adults in the United States who, at age 16, affiliated with other religions tended during most but not all of the generations to switch to non-religious identities at higher rates than the other religious traditions.

What stands out in Figure A.1 is the suddenly steep slope up for LDS respondents between Generation X and the Millennials. Until the younger Boomer generation, the line

Table A.3 Percent Non-Religious as Adults by Generation and Religious Tradition at Age 16

Generation	Catholic	Black Prot	Con Prot	Mainline	Jewish	LDS	Other	NR
Greatest	3.2	1.3	2.9	2.8	4.7	5	12.6	30.4
Silent	7.3	4	4.5	7.2	10	5	12.8	31.2
Boomer 1	11.8	4.7	9	11.7	12.6	12.8	22.6	49.3
Boomer 2	10.3	5.9	9.5	12.8	9	15	24.9	56.1
Gen X	15	8.8	12.5	17.4	18.6	21.4	31.4	62.6
Millennials + Z	22.4	17.7	21.25	30.1	17.8	47.6	42.4	73.5

Source: General Social Survey, 1973–2018.

for LDS respondents mixes in with the rest of the pack in relatively low defections to becoming religious "nones" as adults. LDS younger Boomers and Gen Xers, however, begin to diverge upwardly from mainline Protestants. Everything changed when the Millennial generation shows up, when the increase in leaving the LDS church and becoming not religious spikes up with the steepest slope in the figure, surpassing those raised in other religions. In numbers (Table A.3), 21.4% of Gen Xers who affiliated as LDS at age 16 later as adults identified as "nones," while among Millennials, the percent jumps to 47.6%. That major increase for LDS Millennials is a remarkable finding. Previous studies showed that the LDS church enjoyed high retention rates of its youth.[4] These more recent GSS data, however, reveal a huge change in LDS retention rates for Millennials. The Millennial generation in general, from all religious traditions, has become less religious at higher rates than previous generations. But LDS Millennials appear to have been leading the pack in defecting to adult non-religious identities, outpacing even Millennials raised in other religions. Something big has been going on with LDS Millennials, as discussed in Chapter 10.[5]

Another observation. While every religious tradition examined here lost growing shares of their youth with each successive generation, the "non-religious" group improved its retention rate over time (the top trend line). That is, the non-religious grew increasingly successful with succeeding generations at retaining its youth. Stated conversely, religious traditions became less successful at recruiting them away from being not religious. GSS "nones" who reported being not religious at age 16 increased from just above 30% among the Greatest and Silent Generations to 49% and 56% among older and younger Boomers, respectively. Those numbers then rose to 62.6% among Gen Xers and 73.5% among Millennials.

I attribute the relatively low retention rate of the oldest two generations in significant part to the postwar, religion-venerating culture of the Cold War, which I've described in earlier chapters. It simply would have been easier for members of the Greatest and Silent Generations to join some religion during the two decades between 1945 and 1965 (as did my own non-religious Silent Generation parents in 1961, for instance, when I was a baby). As older Baby Boomers came of age in the mid-1960s, however, although the Cold War was still very much on, the larger culture was changing dramatically. Given the many sociological transformations described in this book, becoming religious would have been increasingly less appealing to Boomers and subsequent generations raised in non-religious households. That produced the clearly upward slope in the non-religious line that we see in Figure A.1. The great majority of Generation X and Millennials raised as "nones" were happy as adults to remain not religious.

To explore further with multivariate analyses, I ran a logistic regression model to compare the odds of each generation by religion-at-age-16 category being non-religious as adults, using older Baby Boomer mainline Protestants as a middle-of-the-road comparison group. The model statistically controlled for respondents' sex, education, race and ethnicity, marital status, number of parents raised by, religion of the country lived in at age 16, urban–rural environment at age 16, and residential mobility as an adult. I dropped respondents who reported being non-religious at age 16 from the analysis since the religious categories compared to them are predictably much less likely to be non-religious as adults. Table A.4 presents the results.

There we observe a general pattern across generations consistent with the previous figure and table. Older generations are less likely to be non-religious as adults and recent generations are more likely. Compared to older Baby Boomer mainline Protestants, across almost every religious tradition in which respondents were raised (reported as adults having been at age 16), those from older generations (the Greatest and Silent Generations) are less likely to be not religious as adults. The few exceptions are those whose differences are not significant (ns)—Silent Generation Jewish, Greatest Generation LDS, and Greatest and Silent Generation other religions. Older Boomers raised in only two religious traditions were significantly different from older Boomer mainline Protestants. Black Protestant older Boomers were less likely than the comparison to be non-religious as adults (odds ratio .56), and older Boomers in other religions at age 16 were more likely (odds ratio 1.68). Difference between younger Boomers in other religious traditions and mainline Protestant older Boomers were generally not significant, except for Black Protestant younger Boomers being less likely (.63) and other religions (1.96) being more likely to be not religious as adults.

Younger generations are, again, where things get interesting. Members of Gen X who at age 16 were Catholic, Black Protestant, and conservative Protestant are not significantly more likely to be non-religious as adults than older Boomer mainline Protestants. Members of Gen X who at age 16 were mainline Protestant, Jewish, LDS, and other religions are significantly more likely, compared to the same. The highest odds ratios in those comparisons are with other religions (2.57) and Jewish (2.48). Finally, for every religious group at age 16, Millennials (with a few Gen Zers added) are significantly more likely than older Boomer mainline Protestants to report on their GSS survey that they are not religious. The odds ratios estimating those differences increase in order from reporting at age 16 being Catholic (1.67), conservative Protestant (1.68), Black Protestant (1.82), mainline Protestant (2.38), other religion (3.32), LDS (5.03), and Jewish (5.23). The remarkably high odds ratio here for LDS Millennials confirms the findings of the previous table and figure and the discussion of them in Chapter 10.

To conclude, many Americans affiliated with religious traditions as teenagers dropped those religious connections as adults. The more recently they were born, the more likely they would be as adults to have become non-religious. The most important generation that dramatically accelerated these trends was Millennials. And that brings us back to the 1990s and 2000s and the big story of this book.

Table A.4 Odds of Being Non-Religious as an Adult, by Generations and Religious Tradition Raised In

Generation of religious tradition at age 16	Odds ratios of being non-religious as an adult (compared to older Baby Boomers raised mainline Protestant)	Dummy variable sample size
Catholic		
Greatest	.31	2,426
Silent	.65	3,486
Older Boomers	Ns	3,432
Younger Boomers	.79	3,881
Generation X	Ns	3,513
Millennials + Generation Z	1.67	1,290
Black Protestant		
Greatest	.22	1,043
Silent	.55	1,354
Older Boomers	.56	1,170
Younger Boomers	.63	1,295
Generation X	Ns	1,028
Millennials + Generation Z	1.82	401
Conservative Protestant		
Greatest	.37	2,727
Silent	.47	3,536
Older Boomers	Ns	2,758
Younger Boomers	Ns	2,867
Generation X	Ns	2,685
Millennials + Generation Z	1.68	1,079
Mainline Protestant		
Greatest	.30	3,750
Silent	.66	3,551
Older Boomers	REFERENCE	2,682
Younger Boomers	Ns	2,389
Generation X	1.32	1,464
Millennials + Generation Z	2.38	408
Jewish		
Greatest	.42	299
Silent	Ns	315
Older Boomers	Ns	258

Table A.4 Continued

Generation of religious tradition at age 16	Odds ratios of being non-religious as an adult (compared to older Baby Boomers raised mainline Protestant)	Dummy variable sample size
Younger Boomers	Ns	223
Generation X	2.48	191
Millennials + Generation Z	5.23	102
Latter Day Saints		
Greatest	Ns	79
Silent	.36	140
Older Boomers	Ns	108
Younger Boomers	Ns	160
Generation X	1.51	158
Millennials + Generation Z	5.03	63
Other Religions		
Greatest	Ns	163
Silent	Ns	234
Older Boomers	1.68	229
Younger Boomers	1.96	349
Generation X	2.57	470
Millennials + Generation Z	3.32	194

Source: General Social Survey, 1973–2018. Note: Controlling for sex, education, race/ethnicity, marital status, number of parents raised by, religion of the country at age 16, urban–rural environment at age 16, and residential mobility as an adult. Respondents not religious at age 16 are omitted from the analysis.

Notes

Introduction

1. Jay Wexler (2019), *Our Non-Christian Nation: How Atheists, Satanists, Pagans, and Others Are Demanding Their Rightful Place in Public Life*, Redwood Press.
2. For example, Phil Zuckerman (2012), *Faith No More: Why People Reject Religion*, Oxford University Press. Although Zuckerman eventually rightly notes that the "reasons [people give] are not necessarily [the actual] causes" for their rejecting religion (163–166). See also Michael Lipka (2016, August 24), "Why America's 'Nones' Left Religion Behind," Pew Research Center (https://www.pewresearch.org/short-reads/2016/08/24/why-americas-nones-left-religion-behind/); George Barna and David Kinnaman (2014), *Churchless*, Tyndale; Ryan Cragun and Jesse Smith (2024), *Goodbye Religion: The Causes and Consequences of Secularization*, NYU Press.
3. J. Paul Nyquist and Carson Nyquist (2013), *The Post-Church Christian*, Moody; James Emery White (2014), *The Rise of the Nones*, Baker; David Kinnaman (2007), *UnChristian*, Baker; Robert McCarty and John Vitek (2017), *Going, Going, Gone: The Dynamics of Disaffiliation in Youth Catholics*, Saint Mary's Press; Russell Moore (2023), *Losing Our Religion*, Sentinel.
4. For example, Derek Thompson (2019, September 26), "Three Decades Ago, America Lost Its Religion. Why?" *The Atlantic*; Bob Smietana (2022), *Reorganized Religion: The Reshaping of the American Church and Why It Matters*, Worthy.
5. For example, Ronald Inglehart (2021), *Religion's Sudden Decline: What's Causing It and What's Coming Next?*, Oxford University Press; Ryan Burge (2021), *The Nones: Where They Came from, Who They Are, and Where They Are Going*, Fortress Press, 35–67; Joel Thiessen and Sara Wilkins-LaFlamme (2020), *None of the Above*, New York University Press, 27–55. Some scholarly works on the subject are not concerned with explaining the cause of religious losses but instead their consequences: for example, David Campbell, Geoffrey Layman, and John Green (2021), *Secular Surge: A New Fault Line in American Politics*, Cambridge University Press.
6. Simply being old and ordinary, however, does not make obsolescence, as David Edgerton demonstrates in *The Shock of the Old* (2006), Oxford University Press.
7. Christian Smith (ed.) (2003), *The Secular Revolution*, University of California Press.
8. The following draws on Peter Berger and Thomas Luckmann (1967), *The Social Construction of Reality*, Anchor; Alfred Schutz (1967), *Phenomenology of the Social World*, Northwestern University Press; Clifford Geertz (1966), *The Interpretation of Cultures*, Hutchison, 87–125; Margaret Archer (2008), *Culture and Agency*, Cambridge University Press; Anthony Giddens (1986), *The Constitution of Society*, University of California Press; Pierre Bourdieu (1977), *Outline of a Theory of Practice*, Cambridge University Press; Christian Smith (2015), *To Flourish or Destruct*, University of Chicago Press; and, broadly, the work of Charles Sanders Peirce.
9. Embodied knowledge, some of which is "muscle memory," includes things like knowing how to ride a bike, drive a car, swim, type on a keyboard, and play piano.
10. Ann Swidler and Jorge Arditi (1994), "The New Sociology of Knowledge," *Annual Review of Sociology* 20: 305–329.
11. See James D. Hunter (2024), *Democracy and Solidarity*, Yale University Press.
12. Monika Krause, (2019), "What Is Zeitgeist? Examining Period-Specific Cultural Patterns," *Poetics* 76: 1–10.
13. A closely related concept is Raymond Williams's idea of "structures of feeling." See Williams (1977), *Marxism and Literature*, Oxford University Press, 128–135; Devika Sharma and Frederik Tygstrup (2015), *Structures of Feeling*, DeGruyter; Craig Calhoun (ed.), (2002), "Structures of Feeling," in *Dictionary of the Social Sciences*, Oxford University Press, 469. Max Weber's concept of "ethos" is arguably similar.
14. Krause, for example, grounds zeitgeists in the activity of human practices and material structures, not a spectral, history-driving Spirit; removes from zeitgeist the idea that only one can exist at any given time, thus opening up the potential for a pluralism of overlapping zeitgeists defining different aspects of social life in coinciding eras; acknowledges that some people living through any zeitgeist may remain oblivious to its importance and immune to its influences;

notes that a zeitgeist need not pervade a whole society at any given time; and loosens the strict connection between zeitgeists and generations, recognizing that a zeitgeist may link more than one generation at any given time and may outlast its originally defining generation.
15. Bobby Duffy (2021), *Generations*, Atlantic Books; Jean Twenge (2023), *Generations*, Atria Books.
16. To be clear, I do not mean that the Millennial zeitgeist was ended in 2019 but that the dynamics bringing it into being were essentially accomplished.
17. Online *Methodological Appendix*, https://global.oup.com/us/companion.websites/9780197800737/appendix/.
18. Note that many "Maintainers" went through phases of lower religiousness in the course of their lives but were raised highly religious and were so at the time of our interviews; "Nevers" (a simplified term used for convenience) includes both always non-religious and low-religious people.
19. College-age Gen Zers threw off analyses in later chapters about residential mobility and settling down in life, for example.
20. Extended interview quotes, https://global.oup.com/us/companion.websites/9780197800737/appendix/.
21. The quotes are also edited, per standard social research practices, to eliminate filler and confusing and extraneous words and phrases that muddy the speaker's primary intended meanings.
22. Christian Smith (2015), *To Flourish or Destruct: A Personalist Theory of Human Goods, Motivations, Failure, and Evil*, University of Chicago Press.
23. For example, Christopher Bail (2014), "The Cultural Environment: Measuring Culture with Big Data," *Theory and Society* 43: 465–482.
24. Penny Edgell (2012), "A Cultural Sociology of Religion," *Annual Review of Sociology* 38: 247–265.

Chapter 1

1. Robert K. Merton (1987), "Three Fragments from a Sociologist's Notebooks: Establishing the Phenomenon, Specified Ignorance, and Strategic Research Materials," *Annual Review of Sociology* 13: 1–29.
2. David Voas and Mark Chaves, "Is the United States a Counterexample to the Secularization Thesis?" *American Journal of Sociology*, 121: 1517–1556.
3. In the National Study of Youth and Religion (NSYR).
4. Generations are defined by years of birth as follows: Lost (1883–1900), Greatest (1901–1926), Silent (1927–1945), Early Boomers (1946–1955), Late Boomers (1956–1964), Generation X (1965–1980), Millennials (1981–1996), Generation Z (1997–2012). Other details: the sample is weighted using the following variables: for years prior to 2000, wtssall; for 2000 and 2002, wtssps; for 2004 through 2021, wtssnrps. Black oversamples from 1982 and 1987 are excluded. Sample sizes in the notes for Figures 1.3, 1.4, and 1.6 are unweighted counts. Values for generation by survey year are used only when based on counts of 100 or more. The moving average is based on three surveys, except for the final survey year when it is calculated from the last two surveys, or, similarly, for the first point in a series if the generation appears after the beginning of the period shown. Exceptions are made for the Lost Generation, where a threshold of 50 is used, and Gen Z, where the counts for 2018 and 2021 are pooled. The short line segments on the graphs should be interpreted as point estimates (of the end and the beginning respectively) for these two generations. From 1977 onward, only respondents who were born in the United States are included in order to remove the effect of more highly religious immigrants; for earlier years, and where data on nativity are missing, being resident in the United States at age 16 is used as a proxy. The GSS Codebook for 2021 includes the following caveat: "To safeguard the health of staff and respondents during the COVID-19 pandemic, the 2021 GSS data collection used a mail-to-web methodology instead of its traditional in-person interviews. Research and interpretation done using the data should take extra care to ensure the analysis reflects actual changes in public opinion and is not unduly influenced by the change in data collection methods." A case has been made that highly religious individuals are under-represented in the 2021 survey. Average levels of religiosity are indeed lower than in previous years. That said, these indicators also declined in 2016 and 2018. We will have to wait for later waves to judge the impact of the data collection mode on the 2021 results. Note that the trend lines up to 2016 in the graphs are unaffected by values for 2021 (points shown for 2016 are an average of values from 2014, 2016, and 2018).
5. The usual question on strength of affiliation, upon confirming some religious affiliation, was, "Would you call yourself a strong X or a not very strong X?" The response "somewhat strong"

was not offered by the interviewer as an option but was coded if volunteered by the respondent. In 2021, one version of the internet-based web survey (completed by half of the sample) included "somewhat strong" as an answer option; the other half were forced to choose between "strong" and "not very strong." Although more respondents choose "somewhat strong" when it is offered explicitly, the net effect of the experiment might have been to depress the total for strong/somewhat strong affiliation, given that half the sample was not allowed the "somewhat" option.
6. The youngest ages of the Greatest and Silent Generations are cut off here, but their overall trend in older years parallels those of Boomers and suggests a consistent pattern.
7. I will use the term "conservative" as it is commonly referenced in American public discourse, even though most so-called conservatives in the United States are actually some version of classical liberals or libertarians, whose economic programs tend to degrade rather than conserve traditional moral cultures, not to mention the planet's life-support ecosystem. See Christopher Lasch (1986), "What's Wrong with the Right?" *Tikkun* 1: 23–29; Lasch (1986), "Why the Left Has No Future," *Tikkun* 1: 92–97; Robert Nisbet (2012, July 15), "Conservatives and Libertarians: Uneasy Cousins," *The Imaginative Conservative*; and Jeremy Seabrook (1995), "Values for Money," *New Statesman & Society* 8: 18–20.
8. Also see Daniel Cox, Kelsey Hammond, and Kyle Gray (2023), "Generation Z and the Transformation of American Adolescence," Survey Center on American Life, 4.
9. Scott Thuma (2021), *Twenty Years of Congregational Change*, Hartford Institute for Religious Research, 19.
10. According to the Center for Disease Control's National Center for Health Statistics, the average life expectancy of men and women (combined) in 1972 was 71.2 years, which by 2001 had increased to 76.1 years. Elizabeth Arias, Betzaida Tejada-Vera, Kenneth Kochanek, and Farida Ahmad (2022), "Provisional Life Expectancy Estimates for 2021," *Vital Statistics Rapid Release Report* No. 23.
11. That is because an increased life expectancy extends the number of years at the high end of populations by that full value, while all of the others in the population with ages below the earlier life-expectancy baseline continue mathematically to hold down the average age of the population.
12. Religious Americans tend to live longer than the non-religious, but I know of no evidence showing that this differential changed during the years under consideration (i.e., an increase in the longer years that religious Americans live), so that cannot provide an explanation.
13. GSS 1972–2018 data analyses were weighted using wtssall; 2021 data were weighted using wtssps.
14. GSS 2021 numbers should be interpreted with caution, given COVID-19 and other possible data comparability questions, until future survey surveys can put them into perspective. Taking a more methodologically conservative approach by using GSS 2018 as our end date instead of 2021, we still see that, between 1991 and 2018, the percent of not-religious adult Americans had almost quadrupled, increasing from 6.3% to 23.4%; among those ages 18–29 during the same period, the percentages increased from 7.9% to 35.2%, more than quadrupling in size.
15. General Social Survey (2015, March 10), "Fewer Americans Affiliate with Organized Religion," *GSS Press Summary*, 1, 2.
16. For example, Leigh Eric Schmidt (2005), *Restless Souls: The Making of American Spirituality*, HarperSanFrancisco; Courtney Bender (2010), *The New Metaphysicals: Spirituality and the American Religious Imagination*, University of Chicago Press.
17. Those are the Faith and Family in America 2005, GSS 2008, the National Election Study 2012 and 2016, the Chapman Survey of American Fears 2014, and GSS 2018.
18. Aaron Earls (2021, May 25), "Protestant Church Closures Outpace Openings in U.S.," Lifeway Research. Numbers from studied denominations are extrapolated to all Protestant churches.
19. Yusuf Ransome, Insang Song, Linh Pham, and Camille Busette (2022, May 3), "Churches Are Closing in Predominantly Black Communities," The Brookings Institution; Martyn Whittock (2021, July 18), "The Strange Decline of US Evangelicalism," *Christianity Today*; Aaron Blake (2021, July 8), "The Rapid Decline of White Evangelical America," *Washington Post*.
20. Justin Nortey and Michael Rotolo (2023, March 28), "How the Pandemic Has Affected Attendance at U.S. Religious Services," Pew Research Center; Cheryl Bacon (2022, March 30), "Church Closing Trend Began Before Covid-19," *The Christian Chronicle*.
21. Center for Applied Research in the Apostolate. Frequently Requested Statistics. Parishes.
22. Among entire religious traditions, worship service attendance only increased among Muslim, Baha'i, and Jewish congregations; see Thuma, "Twenty Years."

23. Scott Neuman (2023, May 17), "The Faithful See Both Crisis and Opportunity as Churches Close Across the Country," NPR.
24. Joel Belz (2022, December 22), "A Tidal Wave of Church Closings," WORLD.
25. The one exception being the military. Gallup asked about 15 institutions, GSS about 13.
26. Tom W. Smith and Jaesok Son (2013), "Trends in Public Attitudes About Confidence in Institutions," NORC at the University of Chicago; Gallup (2022), "Confidence in Institutions."
27. Political scientist Ryan Burge has analyzed the GSS data by the generational categories I use in this book, not by general age cohort. His results show that, after the Silent Generation, the rates of declining confidence accelerate for each new generation, starting with Boomers, increasing with Gen X, and dropping off precipitously among Millennials; see Burge (2021), "Trust Is Waning in One Key Area," *Goo*.
28. Megan Brenan and Jeffrey Jones (2024, January 22), "Ethics Ratings of Nearly All Professions Down in U.S.," Gallup..
29. Nancy Ammerman (2006), *Everyday Religion*, Oxford University Press; Ammerman (2013), *Sacred Stories, Spiritual Tribes*, Oxford University Press; Ammerman (2021), *Studying Lived Religion*, New York University Press.
30. These voices represent parts of mainstream American religion. Traditional religious groups that serve more recent immigrant groups—such as Islamic, Hindu, and Buddhist communities—face even more complicated challenges due to complex ethnic, generational, and cultural differences that must be negotiated, described astutely by Nicolette Manglos-Weber (2020), "The New Immigrants and Religious Parenting," in Christian Smith and Amy Adamczyk, *Handing Down the Faith*, Oxford University Press, 117–160.
31. With hard career consequences for some: Todd Ferguson and Josh Packard (2022), *Stuck: Why Clergy Are Alienated from Their Calling, Congregation, and Career*, Fortress Press.
32. For one general summary focused on Christianity, see Pew Research Center (2019, October 17), "In U.S., Decline of Christianity Continues at Rapid Pace,"

Chapter 2

1. For details on what I base my arguments on in this chapter, see the relevant section of the online Methodological Appendix at https://global.oup.com/us/companion.websites/9780197800737/appendix/. See also Christian Smith, Bridget Ritz, and Michael Rotolo (2019), *Religious Parenting*, Princeton University Press, chapter 5.
2. This almost universal assumption relates directly to what in previous writings I have called "moralistic therapeutic deism" as the actual, functional, de facto religion of most Americans, both youth and adults; seeChristian Smith and Melinda Denton (2005), *Soul Searching*, Oxford University Press, chapter 4. I conceptually distinguish mora*lity* from mora*lism*. Mora*lity* concerns codes of conduct or standards of virtue distinguishing good from bad, right from wrong character, behavior, desires, attitudes, etc. Morality is not arbitrary but derives from some relatively coherent philosophy, narrative, or belief system that provides intelligible explanations and justifications of those codes or standards. With morality, the imperative (what one ought to do) follows from the indicative (the way things are) and so makes reasonable sense in some larger picture of reality. Mora*lism*, by contrast, involves efforts to instruct or demand of oneself and other people to behave in ways one considers correct or righteous, often with a strict, critical, opinionated attitude. Moralistic attitudes and behaviors are often loosely coupled with, if not entirely disconnected from, larger philosophies, narratives, and belief systems that would explain and justify their demands, often operating as free-floating assertions relying more on pressure than persuasion to induce expected behavior. Viewed through the lens of the population ecology species decline model (Chapter 3), moralistic therapeutic deism can be seen analogically as parasitical on traditional religion, which I already suggested in Smith and Denton, *Soul Searching*, 166.
3. For readers familiar with sociological theory, it is almost as if Americans operate with a structural-functionalist view of society as expressed by mid-twentieth-century theorist Talcott Parsons—namely, that society is comprised of a set of social institutions, each of which having a specific functional role to play to maintain the order and well-being of the whole. Religion is one of those institutions whose primary functional role is to help regulate social behavior but in so doing must employ a particular cultural posture of grace, understanding, and forgiveness.
4. The term "field" in this book roughly follows Pierre Bourdieu (1993), *The Field of Cultural Production*, Columbia University Press; and Neil Fligstein and Doug McAdam (2012), *A Theory of Fields*, Oxford University Press.

5. This valuing of positive psychology also connects to the therapeutic aspect of the moralistic therapeutic deism noted in Note 2. Also see Donald Meyer (1980), *The Positive Thinkers: Religion as Pop Psychology from Mary Baker Eddy to Oral Roberts*, Pantheon.
6. See Robert Schuller (1987), *The Be (Happy) Attitudes: 8 Positive Attitudes That Can Transform Your Life*, Bantam (which enjoys a 4.6 out of 5 stars rating by Amazon readers), and myriad similar books by popular clergy on Amazon, including by Joel and Victoria Osteen.
7. Here we notice a tension between the first two valued traits of religion—teaching people to be morally good and not making them feel guilty—which can put religion into a bind. How to teach moral right from wrong to people who do not always do right without addressing the doing wrong and what it means and why it is bad? Moral education can presumably proceed without centering guilt. But nearly everyone believes that when someone does something genuinely wrong, their conscience ought to feel bad about it. Those who don't we call sociopaths. One way to undo this bind is simply to preach moral virtues and not get into how anyone actually lives. Just put it out there and let people do with it what they wish. Another way to relax this tension is by setting the bar for "moral" and "good" low enough that it is not hard to succeed. As numerous Millennial teenagers told me in research interviews in the early 2000s, "Just don't be an asshole, that's all" and "As long as you're not a murderer, bank robber, or rapist, you're good." But, it seems to me, this tension is never entirely resolved.
8. Smith et al., *Religious Parenting*, chapter 3.
9. Robert Putnam (2000), *Bowling Alone*, Simon and Schuster.
10. Rachel Martin (2023, September 10), "The Search for a Church That Isn't a Church," *All Things Considered*, NPR; Jessica Grose (2023, June 28), "What Churches Offer That 'Nones' Still Long For," *New York Times*.
11. Satirically portrayed by *Saturday Night Live*'s sanctimonious Enid Strict, "The Church Lady" (appearing 1986–1990, 1996, 2000, 2011, and 2016).
12. Luis Menand (2002), *The Metaphysical Club*, Farrar, Straus and Giroux.
13. Grace Davie (2007), "Vicarious Religion," in Nancy Ammerman (ed.), *Everyday Religion*, Oxford University Press, 21–35; Davie (2010), "Vicarious Religion: A Response," *Journal of Contemporary Religion* 25: 261–266; Davie (2006), "Is Europe an Exceptional Case?," *The Hedgehog Review* 7: 23–34.
14. In that sense, Americans treat religious leaders like the "totems" Emile Durkheim theorizes in *Elementary Forms of Religious Life* (1996), Karen Fields (ed.), The Free Press.
15. See, for example, the 2009 HBO documentary, *The Trials of Ted Haggard* (Alexandra Pelosi, director).
16. Immoderation and incivility are not universally bad, apparently, but primarily when it comes to religion. Extreme sports, in which people risk life and limb, might be all the rage. Someone being obsessively fanatical about "their" sports team may be amusing. And teenagers (and adults, for that matter) can pressure, intimidate, even bully each other when it comes to all manner of things—the wrong clothes, the wrong friends, the wrong haircut, sharing homework, sexting, hooking up, sometimes nothing at all. But religion must be temperate to be acceptable.
17. Beyond the thousands of specific denominations and organizations, American civil religion has also been central in defining national identity. Robert Bellah (1967), "Civil Religion in America," *Daedalus* 96: 1–21.
18. Robert Handy (1984), *A Christian America: Protestant Hopes and Historical Realities*, Oxford University Press.
19. Jason Stephens (2010), *God-Fearing and Free: A Spiritual History of America's Cold War*, Harvard University Press.
20. Patrick Henry (1981), "'And I Don't Care What It Is': The Tradition-History of a Civil Religion Proof-Text," *Journal of the American Academy of Religion* XLIX: 35–47.
21. Kevin Kruse (2015), *One Nation Under God: How Corporate America Invented Christian America*, Basic Books, ix. Emphasis in the original.
22. Quoted in James Farrell (1997), *The Spirit of the Sixties*, Routledge, 40.
23. Kruse, *One Nation*, x.
24. Ibid., xi.
25. Jonathan Herzog (2011), *The Spiritual-Industrial Complex: America's Religious Battle Against Communism in the Early Cold War*, Oxford University Press, 3.
26. Robert Handy (1968), *The American Religious Depression, 1925–1935*, Fortress Press; William Inboden (2008), *Religion and American Foreign Policy, 1945–1960: The Soul of Containment*, Cambridge University Press; T. Jeremy Gunn (2009), *Spiritual Weapons: The Cold War and the*

Forging of an American National Religion, Praeger; Diane Kirby (ed.) (2003), *Religion and the Cold War*, Palgrave Macmillan; David Foglesong (2007), *The American Mission and the "Evil" Empire*, Cambridge University Press.
27. Herzog, *Spiritual-Industrial Complex*, 9; Elaine Tyler May (1988), *Homeward Bound: American Families in the Cold War Era*, Basic Books, 25–26.
28. Herzog, *Spiritual-Industrial Complex*; Kruse, *One Nation*; Stephens, *God-Fearing*.

Chapter 3

1. Multiple linear and categorical regression, the core of variables sociology, attempts to isolate the *independent* effects of different variables, which has its place, but whose logic contrasts with the combinational model described here.
2. See Nicole Stephens, Hazel Markus, and L. Taylor Phillips (2014), "Social Class Culture Cycles," *Annual Review of Psychology* 65: 611–634; Nicole Stephens, Stephanie Fryberg, Hazel Markus, Camille Johnson, and Rebecca Covarrubias (2012), "Unseen Disadvantage," *Journal of Personality and Social Psychology* 102(6): 1178–1197; Nicole Stephens, Sarah Townsend, and Andrea Dittmann (2019), "Social-Class Disparities in Higher Education and Professional Workplaces," *Current Directions in Psychological Science* 28(1): 67–73; L. Taylor Phillips, Nicole Stephens, Sarah Townsend, and Sébastien Goudeau (2020), "Access Is Not Enough," *Journal of Personality and Social Psychology* 119(5): 1–20.
3. Nicole Stephens, Sarah Townsend, Hazel Markus, and L. Taylor Phillips (2012), "A Cultural Mismatch: Independent Cultural Norms Produce Greater Increases in Cortisol and More Negative Emotions Among First-Generation College Students," *Journal of Experimental Social Psychology* 48(6): 389–1393. All of this compounds the challenges of other adjustments in food preferences, clothing styles, media consumption, speech dialects, and recreational activities, not to mention the missing of loved ones and friends back home.
4. Sara George (2014, December), "Volcanic Pollution," *International Pollution Issues*; Tyler Vanzo (2021, April 6), "How Do Volcanoes Affect Air Quality?" *Smart Air*.
5. World Health Organization (WHO) (2022, December), "Household Air Pollution," *Fact Sheet*.
6. Niles Eldredge and Stephen Gould (1972), "Punctuated Equilibria: An Alternative to Phyletic Gradualism," in Thomas Schopf (ed.), *Models in Paleobiology*, Freeman Cooper, 82–115.. Thomas Kuhn argued something similar about how science progresses through abrupt paradigm shifts instead of slow, steady accumulations of findings and gradual improvements of scientific theories; see Kuhn (1962), *The Structure of Scientific Revolutions*, University of Chicago Press.
7. Everett Rogers (1962), *Diffusion of Innovations*, Free Press.
8. Olivier Blanchard (2008), "Crowding Out," in *The New Palgrave Dictionary of Economics*, Palgrave Macmillan.
9. Andrew Abbott (1988), *The System of Professions: An Essay on the Division of Expert Labor*, University of Chicago Press. Quotes are from pp. 33, 102.
10. Note that even to name it as "*clinical* depression" or "major depressive mood disorder" is already to privilege one profession's conceptualization of the problem over others. Some former views of depression, by contrast, explained it as the result of an imbalance of humors causing "melancholia" (Ancient Greek: *melas*, "black" and *kholé*, "bile"), slow blood circulation, or internal moral conflicts.
11. Some professional and quasi-professional groups manage to negotiate arrangements of symbiotic cooperation. Rather than one of them going for winner-take-all control, they divide up sub-parcels of turf for collective benefit. For example, when it comes to the problem of selling and buying homes, real estate agents, mortgage companies, title companies, and insurance firms have negotiated a cooperative system for shared benefit—also cutting in property appraisers, home inspectors, pest exterminators, and repair contractors for small slices of the profits as useful subsidiary problem-solvers.

Chapter 4

1. See Gabriel Abend's distinguishing between factors that *cause* outcomes versus those that make outcomes *possible*: Abend (2020), "Making Things Possible," *Sociological Methods and Research* 51: 1–40.
2. For example, Philip Rieff (1966), *The Triumph of the Therapeutic*, Harper & Row; Roger Lundin (2005), *From Nature to Experience*, Rowman and Littlefield; James Byrne (1997), *Religion and the Enlightenment*, Westminster-John Knox; Jeffrey Stout (1981), *The Flight from Authority*,

University of Notre Dame Press; Brad Gregory (2015), *The Unintended Reformation*, Harvard University Press; Heiko Oberman (2012), *The Harvest of Medieval Theology*, Baker Books; William Placher (1996), *The Domestication of Transcendence*, Westminster-John Knox; Peter Berger (1967/1990), *The Sacred Canopy*, Anchor.
3. Julie Reuben (1996), *The Making of the Modern University*, University of Chicago Press; George Marsden (1996), *The Soul of the American University*, Oxford University Press.
4. Fewer than one in five 15-to-18-year-olds attended high school in 1910, and only 9% of all American 18-year-olds had graduated high school then; see Claudia Goldin and Lawrence Katz (2008), *The Race Between Education and Technology*, Harvard University Press, 195.
5. John Thelin (2019), *A History of American Higher Education*, Johns Hopkins University Press.
6. NSCRC (2023), *Some College, No Credential Student Outcomes*, National Student Clearinghouse Research Center.
7. US Census Bureau, "Educational Attainment in the United States: 2018."
8. See John Evans (2022), "Inquiry, Not Science, as the Source of Secularization in Higher Education," *Sociology of Religion* 83:102–129.
9. Claude Fischer and Michael Hout (2006), *Century of Difference*, Russel Sage; Robert Wuthnow (1990), *The Restructuring of American Religion*, Princeton University Press.
10. For example, Kenneth Feldman and Theodore Newcombe (1969), *The Impact of College on Students*, Jossey-Bass.
11. See, for example, Damon Mayrl and Jeremy Uecker (2012), "Higher Education and Religious Liberalization Among Young Adults," *Social Forces* 90: 181–208; Jeremy Uecker, Mark Regnerus, and Margaret Vaaler (2007), "Losing My Religion," *Social Forces* 85: 1667–1692; Jonathan Hill (2011), "Faith and Understanding," *Journal for the Scientific Study of Religion* 50: 533–551; Damon Mayrl and Freeden Oeur (2009),"Religion and Higher Education," *Journal for the Scientific Study of Religion* 48: 260–275; Philip Schwadel (2014), "Birth Cohort Changes in the Association Between College Education and Religious Non-Affiliation," *Social Forces* 93: 93: 719–746; Jennifer Lindholm, Alexander Astin, and Helen Astin (2010), *Cultivating the Spirit*, Jossey-Bass; Tim Clydesdale (2007), *The First Year Out*, University of Chicago Press; Harold Hartley (2004), "How College Affects Students' Religious Faith and Practice," *College Student Affairs Journal* 23: 111–129; Philip Schwedel (2017), "The Positives and Negatives of Higher Education," *Journal for the Scientific Study of Religion* 56: 869–885; Philip Schwadel (2016), "Does Higher Education Cause Religious Decline?" *Sociological Quarterly* 57: 759–786.
12. Esteban Ortiz-Ospina and Sandra Tzvetkova (2017, October 16), "Working Women," Our World in Data; Mitra Toossi (2002, May), "A Century of Change: The U.S. Labor Force, 1950–2050," *Monthly Labor Review* 125: 15–28; Kristie Engemann and Michael Owyang (2006), "Social Changes Lead Married Women into Labor Force," *The Regional Economist*, 10–11.
13. "Traditional" is in quotes here, it being as much a nostalgic cultural imaginary as the actual historical experience of the vast majority of Americans—see, for example, Stephanie Coontz (2016), *The Way We Never Were: American Families and the Nostalgia Trap*, Basic Books. American families have changed of late, but that does not mean that previously the "traditional" family was everybody's reality.
14. Penny Edgell (2005), *Religion and Family in a Changing Society*, Princeton University Press; Christian Smith, Bridget Ritz, and Michael Rotolo (2019), *Religious Parenting*, Princeton University Press.
15. For instance, Wuthnow (2007), *After the Baby Boomers*, Princeton University Press, chapter 3.
16. Andrew Cherlin (2004), "The Deinstitutionalization of American Marriage," *Journal of Marriage and Family*, 848–861; Andrew Cherlin (2020), "Degrees of Change," *Journal of Marriage and Family*, 62–80; Fischer and Hout, *Century of Difference*.
17. The apparent jump between 1960 and 1990 is due to the first four decades being spatially compressed in Figure 4.2.
18. Carlyle Murphy (2015, June 2), "Interfaith Marriage Is Common in U.S., Particularly Among the Recently Wed," Pew Research Center. .
19. Nikki Graf (2019), "Key Findings on Marriage and Cohabitation in the U.S," Pew Research Center.
20. Ibid.
21. Eric Klinenberg (2013), *Going Solo*, Penguin.
22. Social class, race, and ethnicity matter here, with countless sociological studies revealing the complexities of these matters as more than simply changes in cultural norms—for

example, Kathryn Edin and Maria Kefalas (2011), *Promises I Can Keep: Why Poor Women Put Motherhood Before Marriage*, University of California Press.
23. In fact, one of the causes of rising divorce rates since the turn of the twentieth century is arguably not the devaluation of marriage, as moralizing pundits have claimed, but a widespread growing demand for truly happy companionate marriages and increasing expectations of what marriage ought to provide spouses—see Elaine Tyler May's fascinating 1983 historical study, *Great Expectations: Marriage and Divorce in Post-Victorian America*, University of Chicago Press.
24. It means in part that many people want to experience more of "life" before settling down, want to finish an advanced graduate degree, do not see what "just a piece of paper" will add to an existing relationship, want to become more financially secure before making a commitment, are still uncertain about who to marry, do not feel mature enough to become someone's spouse and maybe a parent, and are loathe to risk becoming another divorce casualty adding to the countless numbers they saw and maybe suffered growing up. Ibid. Graf, "Key Findings"; Cherlin, "Degrees of Change."
25. Americans have culturally defined "full adulthood" as having accomplished new family formation, the end of schooling, a stable career job, financial independence, and a place to live that is a stable home.
26. Glen Elder (1985), *Life Course Dynamics: Trajectories and Transitions*, Cornell University Press; Barbara Stauber, Andreas Walther, and Richard A. Settersten (2022), *Doing Transitions in the Life Course*, Springer; Marini Margaret (1984), "The Order of Events in the Transition to Adulthood," *Sociology of Education* 57: 63–84.
27. Not absolute membership numbers.
28. Reported by the US Congress Joint Economic Committee (2019), "The Space Between," https://www.jec.senate.gov/public/index.cfm/republicans/analysis?ID=78A35E07-4C86-44A2-8480-BE0DB8CB104E. Membership rates in only professional, literary and arts, hobby, and service organizations increased over the same period, however, by 17%, 14%, 8%, and 7% each, respectively, significantly smaller numbers than the observed decreases.
29. Robert Putnam (2000), *Bowling Alone*, Simon and Schuster; also see Sherry Turkle (2017), *Alone Together*, Basic Books.
30. Wuthnow, *After the Baby Boomers*, 37–42.
31. Alfred Crosby (2007), *Children of the Sun*, W. W. Norton.
32. Vaclav Smil (2017), *Energy and Civilization*, MIT Press.
33. Ancient Chinese, Roman, and other civilizations mined, collected, and used small amounts of accessible coal, bitumen, and crude petroleum for various purposes. The modern game-changer was the invention in the eighteenth century of the steam engine, powered by coal, increasingly efficient models of which could pump water from deeper and more extensive mines, theretofore flooded, and thereby massively increase the supply of coal.
34. Ian Hore-Lacy (2006), *Nuclear Energy in the 21st Century*, Academic Press, 9; The Engineering Toolbox (n.d.), "Fossil and Alternative Fuels, https://www.engineeringtoolbox.com/fossil-fuels-energy-content-d_1298.html; Vaclav Smil (2022), *How the World Really Works*, Viking, 13–43.
35. Vaclav Smil (2021), *Grand Transitions*, Oxford University Press, 114–151.
36. Andreas Malm (2016), *Fossil Capital*, Verso; Tim DiMuzio (2015), *Carbon Capitalism*, Rowman and Littlefield.
37. J. R. McNeill and Peter Engelke (2014), *The Great Acceleration*, Harvard University Press.
38. Richard Vague (2021), *An Illustrated Business History of the United States*, University of Pennsylvania Press, 105–193.
39. Jonathan Levy (2021), *Ages of American Capitalism*, Random House.
40. Cesare Silla (2018), *The Rise of Consumer Capitalism in America*, Routledge; Nicholas Holm (2023), *Advertising and Consumer Society*, Routledge.
41. Roland Marchand (1998), *Creating the Corporate Soul*, University of California Press.
42. In fact, increased workers' wages in this era were generally not the result of enlightened employers strategizing the benefit to long-term profits, but rather of labor union agitation—which some employers met with violent suppression (unions not being legal until the 1935 National Labor Relations Act)—and government legislation, especially after the 1938 Fair Labor Standards Act, which established the right to a minimum wage. Nonetheless, eventually most owners and employers came to accept the value and necessity of paying workers enough to keep the American consumption-driven economy functioning well.
43. Pamela Walker Laird (1998), *Advertising Progress*, Johns Hopkins University Press.

44. Roland Marchand (1985), *Advertising the American Dream*, University of California Press.
45. Stewart Ewen (2001), *Captains of Consciousness: Advertising and the Social Roots of the Consumer Culture*, Basic Books; Stewart Ewen (1982), *Channels of Desire*, McGraw-Hill.
46. Stephen Fox (1997), *The Mirror Makers: A History of American Advertising*, University of Illinois Press; Tom Reichert (2003), *The Erotic History of Advertising*, Prometheus; Juliann Sivulka (2011), *Soap, Sex, and Cigarettes: A Cultural History of American Advertising*, Cengage Learning; Sivulka (2001), *Stronger Than Dirt: A Cultural History of Advertising Personal Hygiene in America*, Humanities Press.
47. Brian Moeran and Timothy de Waal Malefyt (eds.) (2003), *Advertising Cultures*, Routledge.
48. Gregory, *Unintended Reformation*, chapter 5; Jackson Lears (1995), *Fables of Abundance: A Cultural History of Advertising in America*, Basic Books.
49. Robert Bellah (1983, August 23), "Is Capitalism Compatible with 'Traditional Morality?'" http://www.robertbellah.com/lectures_2.htm.; John Judis (1999, April 26), "Value-free: How Capitalism Redefines Morality," *The New Republic*; Peter Mundy (2023), *Sacred Consumption*, Lexington Books; Arthur Berger (2020), *Ads, Fads, and Consumer Culture*, Rowman and Littlefield.
50. For example, Curtis Johnson (2021), *The Power of Mammon: The Market, Secularization, and New York Baptists, 1790–1922*, University of Tennessee Press.
51. Robert Bellah and Richard Madsen (eds.) (1987), *Individualism and Commitment in American Life*, HarperCollins; Carl Trueman (2020), *The Rise and Triumph of the Modern Self*, Crossway.
52. Ann Hartle (1983), *The Modern Self in Rousseau's Confessions*, University of Notre Dame Press.
53. Stephanie Walls (2015), *Individualism in the United States*, Bloomsbury Academic.
54. The latter penned by a Continental Army veteran, General John Stark, later in life.
55. Nathan Hatch (1989), *The Democratization of American Christianity*, Yale University Press.
56. Andrea Wulf (2022), *Magnificent Rebels: The First Romantics and the Invention of the Self*, Knopf; Gerald N. Izenberg (1992), *Impossible Individuality: Romanticism, Revolution, and the Origins of Modern Selfhood*, Princeton University Press.
57. Dror Wahrman (2004), *The Making of the Modern Self*, Yale University Press.
58. Damon Bach (2020), *The American Counterculture*, University Press of Kansas.
59. An attitude repeated in countless songs, such as Pink Floyd's 1979, "Another Brick in the Wall," Bon Jovi's "It's My Life" (2000), and the Beastie Boys' 1986 hit, "(You Gotta) Fight for Your Right (To Party!)"—the latter actually originally intended as an ironic parody of "rebellious" fraternity party culture, but which most fans, under sway of the dominant cultural paradigm, instead took as a straight rallying cry demanding partying rights; see Joe Taysom (2020, December 30), "The Reason Why the Beastie Boys Hated One of Their Biggest Tracks," *Far Out*, https://faroutmagazine.co.uk/beastie-boys-hate-fight-for-your-right/.
60. As proclaimed by Gekko in the 1987 film *Wall Street*.
61. See Ulrich Beck and Elisabeth Beck-Gernsheim (2002), *Individualization*, Sage.
62. Charles Guignon (2004), *On Being Authentic*, Routledge; Charles Lindholm (2008), *Culture and Authenticity*, Blackwell.
63. Regression results not shown here.
64. Ronald Inglehart (1977), *The Silent Revolution*, Princeton University Press.
65. Ronald Inglehart (1989), *Culture Shift in Advanced Industrial Society*, Princeton University Press.
66. Ronald Inglehart (2018), *Cultural Evolution*, Cambridge University Press.
67. Ronald Inglehart (2012), *Religion's Sudden Decline: What's Causing It, and What Comes Next?* Oxford University Press. Pippa Norris and Ronald Inglehart (2011), *Sacred and Secular: Religion and Politics Worldwide*, Cambridge University Press.
68. Inglehart's historical timing is also not right. Baby Boomers were the generation that rejected their parents' materialist values in favor of postmaterialist ones, according to Inglehart. Yet obsolescence did not befall religion until the arrival of a new cultural zeitgeist with the coming of age of Millennials, not Boomers. My account of religious obsolescence therefore needs to explain this discrepancy in historical timing, which the following chapters do.
69. Jeffrey Arnett (2006), "Emerging Adulthood," in Jeffrey Arnett and Jennifer Tanner (eds.), *Emerging Adults in America*, American Psychological Association, 3–19..
70. Young Americans in the nineteenth and early twentieth centuries, when society was more rural and agricultural, also married later in life than they did in the 1950s and 1960s. But macrosociocultural contexts matter for the significance of age of first marriage, such that major changes in the larger culture and social order in late twentieth-century America make the

experience of emerging adulthood very different from the young adulthood of a century and more ago.
71. The "total experience" of emerging adulthood (including the capacity to recover from mistakes) requires significant financial resources, making it more accessible to middle- and upper middle-class youth than those from poor and working classes. Nevertheless, the emerging adult lifestyle operates as an ideal cultural model to pursue, when possible, even for most of those lacking the means to experience it fully.
72. Those with bleaker economic prospects still tend to aspire to ideal emerging adult lifestyles, even if they cannot afford to achieve them.
73. According to one solid estimate from the early 2000s, American parents spend an average of $38,340 per child (equivalent to about $68,500 in 2023) in total material assistance (cash, housing, educational expenses, food, etc.) over the 17-year period between ages 18 and 34. Robert Schoeni and Karen Ross (2005), "Material Assistance from Families During the Transition to Adulthood," in Richard Settersten, Frank Furstenberg, and Rubén Rumbaut (eds.), *On the Frontiers of Adulthood*, University of Chicago Press, 396–416. Also see Beth Klongpayaba (2023, March 22), "Forty-Five Percent of Parents Still Cover Costs of Their Adult Children," Savings.com.
74. Christian Smith, with Patricia Snell (2009), *Souls in Transition*, Oxford University Press; Christian Smith, with Kari Christoffersen, Hilary Davidson, and Patricia Snell Herzog (2011), *Lost in Transition*, Oxford University Press.
75. Jeffrey Arnett (2004), *Emerging Adulthood*, Oxford University Press.
76. Shmuel Shulman (2023), *A New Lens on Emerging Adulthood: Fluidity as the Path to Settling Down*, Oxford University Press.
77. Alan Reifman (2022), *Journeys Through Emerging Adulthood*, Routledge.

Chapter 5

1. These are usually considered to include the American Baptist Churches USA, the Christian Church (Disciples of Christ), the Episcopal Church, the Evangelical Lutheran Church in America, the Presbyterian Church (USA), the United Church of Christ, and the United Methodist Church. Some scholars also include the smaller Reformed Church in America, the Church of the Brethren, and the Moravian Church in North America. See Jason Lantzer (2012), *Mainline Christianity*, New York University Press.
2. Robert Handy (1984), *A Christian America: Protestant Hopes and Historical Realities*, Oxford University Press.
3. Most discussions focus only on declining membership numbers, yet, across the same decades, the US population was also growing, making the mainline's losses even more acute.
4. For example, John Marcum (2017),"W(h)ither the Mainline?" *Review of Religious Research* 59: 119–134; Michael Hout, Andrew Greeley, and Melissa Wilde (2001), "The Demographic Imperative in Religious Change in the United States," *American Journal of Sociology* 107: 468–500; James Hudnut-Beumler and Mark Silk (eds.) (2018), *The Future of Mainline Protestantism in America*, Columbia University Press; Dean Kelley (1972), *Why Conservative Churches Are Growing*, Harper & Row; William Hutchison, Catherine Albanese, and Max Stackhouse (2018), "Forum: The Decline of Mainline Religion in American Culture," *Religion and American Culture* 1: 313–353; Dean Hoge, Benton Johnson, and Donald Luidens (1994), *Vanishing Boundaries*, Westminster/John Knox Press; Keith Wulff (2011), "Are Pastors the Cause of the Loss of Church Membership?" *Review of Religious Research*, 1–53, 1–7.
5. Mark Chaves (2017), *American Religion*, Princeton University Press, chapter 7.
6. K. L. Billingsley (1990), *From Mainline to Sideline*, Ethics and Public Policy Center; David Roozen (2004), *Oldline Protestantism*, Hartford Institute for Religion Research Working Paper.
7. Jay Demerath (1995), "Cultural Victory and Organizational Defeat in the Paradoxical Decline of Liberal Protestantism," *Journal for the Scientific Study of Religion* 34: 458–469.
8. Some sociologists suggest an even more nuanced picture is warranted: Robert Wuthnow and John Evans (eds.) (2002), *The Quiet Hand of God*, University of California Press.
9. Christian Smith and Melinda Denton (2005), *Soul Searching*, Oxford University Press, 36; Christian Smith, with Patricia Snell (2009), *Souls in Transition*, Oxford University Press, chapter 4.
10. Christian Smith, Kyle Longest, Jonathan Hill, and Kari Christoffersen (2014), *Young Catholic America*, Oxford University Press, chapter 1.
11. Mark Massa (2010), *The American Catholic Revolution*, Oxford University Press; John O'Malley (2008), *What Happened at Vatican II*, Harvard University Press; Helen Rose Ebaugh (1991),

Vatican II and U.S. Catholicism, JAI Press; Colleen McDannell (2011), *The Spirit of Vatican II*, Basic Books; Joseph Gremillion (1985), *Church and Culture Since Vatican II*, University of Notre Dame Press; John O'Malley, Joseph Komonchak, Stephen Schloesser, Neil Ormerod, and David Schultenover (2007), *Vatican II*, Continuum; Joseph Chinnici (2003), "The Reception of Vatican II in the United States," *Theological Studies* 64: 461–494; Adrian Hastings (ed.) (1991), *Modern Catholicism*, Oxford University Press; Ladislas Orsy (2009), *Receiving the Council*, Liturgical Press; Philip Gleason (1995), *Contending with Modernity*, Oxford University Press; Timothy Kelly (2009), *The Transformation of American Catholicism*, University of Notre Dame Press.
12. Massa, *The American Catholic Revolution*, 7–8; Christian Smith (ed.) (2003), *The Secular Revolution*, University of California Press; George Marsden (2006), *Fundamentalism and American Culture*, Oxford University Press.
13. Thomas Woods (2004), *The Church Confronts Modernity*, Columbia University Press; William Halsey (1980), *The Survival of American Innocence*, University of Notre Dame Press; Langdon Gilkey (1975), *Catholicism Confronts Modernity*, Seabury.
14. Gilkey, *Catholicism*, 34–35; Massa, *The American Catholic Revolution*.
15. Gleason, *Contending with Modernity*, 304.
16. Jay P. Dolan (1985), *The American Catholic Experience*, Doubleday, 430; Joseph Komonchak (1995), "Interpreting the Council," in Mary Jo Weaver and Scott Appleby (eds.), *Being Right*, Indiana University Press, 17–36; Scott Appleby (2007), "Decline or Relocation?," in Leslie Tentler (ed.), *The Church Confronts Modernity*, Catholic University of America Press, 208–236.
17. Audra Duganzic (2024), "Polarization and the Production and Reception of Liturgical Change in the U.S. Catholic Church After Vatican II," Sociology doctoral dissertation, University of Notre Dame.
18. Brian Froehle and Mary Gautier (2000), *Catholicism USA: A Portrait of the Catholic Church in the United States*, Orbis Books, 128–133; Dennis Castillo (1992), "The Origin of the Priest Shortage," *America* 167: 302–304.
19. Froehle and Gautier, *Catholicism USA*, 128.
20. Dolan, *American Catholic*, 436–438; James O'Toole (2008), *The Faithful: A History of Catholics in America*, Harvard University Press, 237; Froehle and Gautier, *Catholicism USA*, 109–123, 128; Richard Schoenherr and Lawrence Youth (1993), *Full Pews and Empty Altars*, University of Wisconsin Press; Margaret Mary Modde, "Departures from Religious Institutions," *New Catholic Encyclopedia* 570–571; James Hennesey (1981), *American Catholics*, Oxford University Press, 329–330; Peter Steinfels (2003), *A People Adrift*, Simon and Schuster, 29, 30; Richard Schoenherr (2004), *Goodbye Father*, Oxford University Press; Ann Carey (1997), *Sisters in Crisis*, Our Sunday Visitor.
21. Christian Smith and Michael Emerson, with Patricia Snell (2008), *Passing the Plate*, Oxford University Press; Andrew Greeley (1989), *Religious Change in America*, Harvard University Press, 67–74; Charles Zech (2000), *Why Catholics Don't Give*, Our Sunday Visitor.
22. Joseph Harris (1996), *The Cost of Catholic Parishes and Schools*, Sheed and Ward; Steinfels, *A People Adrift*, 212; James Youniss and John Convey (eds.) (2000), *Catholic Schools at the Crossroads*, Teachers College Press.
23. James Davidson (2005), *Catholicism in Motion*, Liguori Press, 76.
24. Dolan, *American Catholic*, 442; Hennesey, *American Catholics* 323–324; Davidson, *Catholicism in Motion*, 76; Andrew Greeley et al. (1976), *Catholic Schools in a Declining Church*, Sheed and Ward.
25. Quoted in Bruce Schulman (2001), *The Seventies*, Da Capo Press, 100.
26. See Philip Hammond (1992), *Religion and Personal Autonomy*, University of South Carolina Press.
27. Daniel Callahan (1965), *Generation of the Third Eye*, Sheed and Ward; Eugene Kennedy (2001), *The Unhealed Wound: The Church and Human Sexuality*, St. Martin's Press.
28. Mary Ellen Konieczny (2013), *The Spirit's Tether: Family, Work, and Religion Among American Catholics*, Oxford University Press; Mary Ellen Konieczny, Charles Camosy, and Tricia Bruce (2016), *Polarization in the US Catholic Church*, Liturgical Press.
29. Steinfels, *A People Adrift*.
30. See Chapter 2, note 2 for the distinction between mora*lity* and mora*lism*.
31. Smith and Denton, *Soul Searching*, 251, 286; Christian Smith and Amy Adamczyk (2021), *Handing Down the Faith*, Oxford University Press, 191–216.
32. This, ironically, is the conventional method that many conservative Protestants use to try to discover *the* truly "biblical" Christian faith, church form, and life—namely (try to) strip from

the "early church" experience all subsequent (except usually their own) history as corruption of the pure, original, authentic truth (Christian Smith [2012], *The Bible Made Impossible*, Brazos Press).

33. Adolf von Harnack (1908), *What Is Christianity?* Putnam's Sons. Quotes in this and the previous paragraph are from pages 40, 41, 143, 144.
34. H. Richard Niebuhr (1937), *The Kingdom of God in America*, Harper, 193.
35. For general context, see Keith Meador (2003), "'My Own Salvation': The *Christian Century* and Psychology's Secularizing of American Protestantism," in Smith, *The Secular Revolution*, chapter 6.
36. Against the potential critical argument that the number of keyword references counted should be divided by the number of pages or words published per year by each publication, I reply that, since the issue is simply the varying presence of certain themes in Catholic published discourse as an indicator of Catholic interest in and readiness to deal with those themes, of both the publishers and readers, then simple total use of and exposure to those keywords is a reasonable measure.
37. The meaning and usage of terms can change over time, complicating this kind of analysis, although that factor is less concerning when it comes to terms with historically deep meanings, like "hell" and "Judgment Day."
38. https://thecatholicnewsarchive.org/.
39. I spot-checked to see if this blip is explained by possible discussions, post-September 11, 2001, about death and the afterlife, but that does not appear to be so.
40. David Frum (2000), *How We Got Here—The 70s*, Basic Books, 147–158; Schulman, *The Seventies*, 92–96.
41. See Christian Smith et al. (1998), *American Evangelicalism*, University of Chicago Press.
42. Marsden, *Fundamentalism*; Frances Fitzgerald (2017), *The Evangelicals*, Simon and Schuster.
43. Smith et al., *American Evangelicalism*.
44. Catholicism was also present on radio and later television broadcasting, especially with the programs of Bishop Fulton Sheen in the 1950s and 1960s, but with much less significance for the fate of religion in the 1990s, so is not discussed here. See Christopher Lynch (2021), *Selling Catholicism*, University Press of Kentucky.
45. Michael Pohlman (2021), *Broadcasting the Faith*, Wipf and Stock; Kirk Farney (2022), *Ministers of a New Medium*, IVP.
46. Joel Carpenter (1997.), *Revive Us Again*, Oxford University Press, 131, 238–239; Dennis Voskuil (1990), "The Power of the Air: Evangelicals and the Rise of Religious Broadcasting," in Quentin Schultze (ed.), *American Evangelicals and the Mass Media*, Eerdmans, 69–95; Quentin Schultze (1988), "Evangelical Radio and the Rise of the Electronic Church," *Journal of Broadcasting and Electronic Media* 32: 289–306; David Clary (2022), *Soul Winners*, Prometheus.
47. Named for a 1962 telethon edition of the program that successfully raised $10 per month in pledges from 700 viewer "members," which enabled the show to pay its operating budget of $700 per month.
48. Jeffrey Hadden and Charles Swann (1981), *Prime Time Preachers*, Addison-Wesley; Steve Bruce (2020), *Pray TV*, Routledge; J. Gordon Melton, Phillip Lucas, and Jon Stone (1997), *Prime-Time Religion*, Oryx Press.
49. R. Frankl and Jeffrey Hadden (1987), "A Critical Review of the Religion and Television Research Report," *Review of Religious Research* 29: 111–124.
50. Marla Frederick (2015), *Colored Television*, Stanford University Press.
51. Randall Balmer (2021), *Bad Faith*, Eerdmans; Anthea Butler (2021), *White Evangelical Racism*, University of North Carolina Press.
52. J. Brooks Flippen (2011), *Jimmy Carter, the Politics of Family, and the Rise of the Religious Right*, University of Georgia Press; Kevin Kruse and Julian Zelizer (2019), *Fault Lines*, Norton.
53. David Farber (2004), "The Torch Has Fallen," in Beth Bailey and David Farber (eds.). *America in the 70s*, University Press of Kansas, 22–25.
54. Among the immense scholarly literature on the Christian Right, see Daniel Williams (2012), *God's Own Party*, Oxford University Press; Darren Dochuk (2010), *From Bible Belt to Sunbelt*, Norton.
55. Terry Heaton (2019), *The Gospel of Self: How Jesus Joined the GOP*, OR Books.
56. Jessica Grose (2023, May 10), "Christianity's Got a Branding Problem," *New York Times*.
57. Ruth Braustein (2021), "A Theory of Political Backlash: Assessing the Religious Right's Effects on the Religious Field," *Sociology of Religion* 83: 293–323.

58. Jenny Rose (2020), *Between Boston and Bombay*, Palgrave Macmillan; Thomas Tweed and Stephen Prothero (1998), *Asian Religions in America*, Oxford University Press; Gurinder Singh Mann, Paul Numrich, and Raymond Williams (2007), *Buddhists, Hindus and Sikhs in America*, Oxford University Press; Arthur Versluis (1993), *American Transcendentalism and Asian Religions*, Oxford University Press; William Garlington (2008), *The Baha'i Faith in America*, Rowman and Littlefield; Pankaj Jain (2019), *Dharma in America*, Routledge.
59. Mary Hanna and Jeanne Batalova (2021), "Immigrants from Asia in the United States," *Migration Information Source*, Migration Policy Institute.
60. Harvey Cox (1977), *Turning East*, Simon and Schuster.
61. What makes an Eastern religion "traditional," especially after having been transplanted to the United States, is a thorny matter; here, I simply mean attempting to remain true to the practices and beliefs understood to have started in their countries of origin rather than being intentionally modified.
62. James Farrell (1997), *The Spirit of the Sixties*, Routledge, 208.
63. Thomas A. Forsthoefel (ed.) (2005), *Gurus in America*, SUNY Press; Ann Gleig (ed.) (2014), *Homegrown Gurus*, SUNY Press.
64. Smith, with Snell, *Souls in Transition*, 20, 47–48, 160, 173.
65. Beth Bailey and David Farber (2004), "Introduction," in Bailey and Farber (eds.), *America in the 70s*, University Press of Kansas, 6–7; Frum, *How We Got Here*, 144–146; Schulman, *The Seventies*, 92–101.
66. Also see Maynard Shipley (1927), *The War on Modern Science*, Alfred Knopf.
67. Steven Shapin (1996), *The Scientific Revolution*, University of Chicago Press, 195. Also see David Livingstone (1987), *Darwin's Forgotten Defenders*, Eerdmans; James Moore (1979), *The Post-Darwinian Controversies*, Cambridge University Press. University of Pennsylvania sociologist Randall Collins states succinctly: "Science is theologically neutral" (1998), *The Sociology of Philosophies*, Harvard University Press, 571.
68. David Lindberg and Ronald Numbers (1986), *God and Nature*, University of California Press, 6.
69. Shapin, *Scientific Revolution*: "There is no longer any sustainable and interesting sense in which it can be said that the Catholic Church was 'unscientific' or even unambiguously opposed to 'the new science'" (p. 198). "In speaking about the purposes of changing natural knowledge in the seventeenth century, it is obligatory to treat its uses in supporting and extending broadly religious aims. There was no such thing as a necessary seventeenth-century conflict between science and religion" (p. 136).
70. Lindberg and Numbers, *God and Nature*: "Reconcilers experienced little difficulty accommodating the testimony of the rocks. When conflict occurred, it was not along a simple line separating scientists and clerics.... The issues raised by Darwin ... provoked widespread controversy ... but the conflicts surrounding Darwin were far more complex than the science-versus-religion formula suggests" (pp. 13–14). Also see Hunter Dupree (1986), "Christianity and the Scientific Community in the Age of Darwin," in David Lindberg and Ronald Numbers (eds.), *God and Nature*, University of California Press. 351–368.
71. Smith, *The Secular Revolution*.
72. Smith, with Snell, *Souls in Transition*, 139.
73. The "Thomas theorem," first expressed in W. I. Thomas and Dorothy Thomas (1928), *The Child in America*, Knopf.
74. Kyle Longest and Jeremy Uecker (2021), "It All Depends on How You Want to Believe," *Review of Religious Research* 63: 1–21.
75. This irony—that most Americans are confident that science enjoys a long history of disproving religion despite historical science disproving that very view as erroneous—illustrates the sociological insight that largely a-rational and irrational structures of cultural belief usually more powerfully shape people's outlooks and experiences than do rational reflection and scientific facts.
76. Robert Wuthnow (1988), *The Restructuring of American Religion: Society and Faith Since World War II*, Princeton University Press; Patrick McNamara (1992), *Conscience First, Tradition Second*, SUNY Press. Wade Clark Roof and William McKinney (1987), *American Mainline Religion*, Rutgers University Press, chapter 2; Robert Wuthnow (1998), *After Heaven*, University of California Press; Wade Clark Roof (1993), *A Generation of Seekers*, Harper Collins; Dean Hoge, Benton Johnson, and Donald Luidens (1994), *Vanishing Boundaries*, Westminster/John Knox; Philip Hammond (1992), *Religion and Personal Autonomy*, University of South Carolina Press.
77. Christian Smith (2010), "The Personal Sources of Social Structures," in *What Is a Person?*, University of Chicago Press, chapter 6..

Chapter 6

1. Damon Murray and Stephen Sorrell (eds.) (2019), *Godless Utopia*, Fuel Publishing; Paul Froese (2008), *The Plot to Kill God*, University of California Press.
2. See Chapter 2; Stevens, 2010; Jonathan Herzog (2011), Oxford University Press; Kevin Kruse (2015), *One Nation Under God: How Corporate America Invented Christian America*, Basic Books
3. Yeltsin added: "I came here [to church] to undergo a cleansing"; "I am acquiring a different world outlook which is probably connected with my psychological state and the situation in society"; "[my frequent church attendance is] normal—I don't believe it should be made a special point of"; "in church I feel I become cleaner.... It is difficult to explain this state, but for me it has become necessary and not only from my personal and spiritual point of view"; "[I was] born into a farmer's family, my great-grandfathers and grandfathers, my parents were believers. I have something in my genes—love of the land and a natural faith"; "[I feel] the need to support the church, and that means all kinds of denominations—I have respect for all of them. In order to give support to believers, we help religion, and we have programs to rehabilitate and build new churches, mosques, Buddhist temples, synagogues and so forth," Michael Parks (1992, June 15), "Yeltsin Sheds Atheism, Gets Religion Again," *Los Angeles Times*.
4. Quoted in Stephen Ambrose and Douglas Brinkley (2011), *Rise to Globalism*, Penguin Books.
5. President George W. H. Bush (1991, September 27), "U.S.-Soviet Nuclear Forces Reduction," C-SPAN; Meena Bose and Rosanna Perotti (2002), *From Cold War to New World Order*, Praeger.
6. Neoliberal economic, political, and social theory should not be confused with the "neoconservative" or "neocon" movement in the United States in the 1980s. These were somewhat related but distinct ideologies and interests that came together for political reasons after the 1970s. The original neoliberal vision was to avoid another war through widespread prosperity provided by free-market capitalism, thus centering economics. Neocons were more focused on maintaining national power in changing geopolitical contexts through military might and, if necessary, by waging war, thus subordinating economics to realpolitik power.
7. American neoliberalism would dominate for nearly three decades, until it hit two huge snags. The first was the catastrophic financial meltdown of early 2008 and the resulting Great Recession. That forced Federal Reserve chairman Alan Greenspan to confess publicly that he was mistaken in his neoliberal belief that enlightened self-interest would make the deregulation of financial markets succeed. "Those of us who have looked to the self-interest of lending institutions to protect shareholder's equity—myself especially—are in a state of shocked disbelief," Greenspan admitted in a 2008 congressional hearing, stating that he had been "partially" wrong to believe that complex trading instruments did not need government oversight. Congressman Henry Waxman asked Greenspan, "You found your view of the world, your ideology, was not right, it was not working?" He replied, "Absolutely, precisely.... You know, that's precisely the reason I was shocked." Neoliberalism's second snag was President Donald Trump's (2016–2020) populist program of economic nationalism, under the influence of his then-advisor Steve Bannon and similar thinkers, including provoked trade wars with China, which pulled the United States back from neoliberal free trade and internationalism generally. Trump's "America First" was a slogan that better fit sixteenth-century European mercantilism and interwar isolationism than any liberal or neoliberal era. As of this writing, neoliberalism's future is uncertain. See Wendy Brown (2019), *In the Ruins of Neoliberalism*, Columbia University Press.
8. Philip Mirowski and Dieter Plehwe (eds.) (2015), *The Road from Mont Pèlerin: The Making of the Neoliberal Thought Collective*, Harvard University Press; Daniel Jones (2014), *Masters of the Universe: Hayek, Friedman, and the Birth of Neoliberal Politics*, Princeton University Press; David Harvey (2005), *A Brief History of Neoliberalism*, Oxford University Press; Jamie Peck (2010), *Constructions of Neoliberal Reason*, Oxford University Press.
9. In retrospect, exactly how much credit neoliberal policies deserve for the "Chilean economic miracle" is debatable. For example, Ricardo French-Davis (2010), *Economic Reforms in Chile*, Palgrave Macmillan, 3–43; Donald Richards (1997), "Review: The Political Economy of the Chilean Miracle," *Latin American Research Review* 32: 139–159; James Cypher (2004, September/October), "Is Chile a Neoliberal Success?" *Dollars & Sense*.
10. Dictated and managed, ironically, by the supernational governing agencies the World Bank and the International Monetary Fund.
11. As represented, for instance, in George W. H. Bush's "Thousand Points of Light" 1988 presidential campaign slogan and his son's later "faith-based initiatives" programs. Melinda Cooper (2019), *Family Values: Between Neoliberalism and the New Social Conservatism*, Zone Books.

See Milton Friedman (1970, September 13), "The Social Responsibility of Business Is to Increase Its Profits," *New York Times Magazine*, 28–35.
12. Wendy Brown (2015), *Undoing the Demos*, Zone Books; Pierre Dardot and Christian Laval (2017), *The New Way of the World*, Verso. The general suspicion of democracy has a long pedigree, going back to Plato.
13. Ross Abbinnett (2022), *The Neoliberal Imagination*, Routledge; Robert Chernomas, Ian Hudson, and Mark Hudson (2019), *Neoliberal Lives*, Manchester University Press; Patricia Ventura (2012), *Neoliberal Culture*, Routledge.
14. Gary Gerstle (2022), *The Rise and Fall of the Neoliberal Order*, Oxford University Press.
15. Ruth Milkman (1997), *Farewell to the Factory*, University of California Press.
16. Bonnie Urciuoli (2008), "Skills and Selves in the New Workplace," *American Ethnologist* 35: 211–228; Marc Zao-Sanders and Kelly Palmer (2019, September 26), "Why Even New Grads Need to Reskill for the Future," *Harvard Business Review*.
17. Arne Kalleberg (2011), *Good Jobs, Bad Jobs: The Rise of Polarized and Precarious Employment Systems in the United States*, Russel Sage; Guy Standing (2011), *The Precariat*, Bloomsbury; Isabell Lorey (2015), *State of Insecurity: Government of the Precarious*, Verso.
18. Andrew Ross (2010), *Nice Work If You Can Get It: Life and Labor in Precarious Times*, New York University Press.
19. Comparing choices of college majors is illuminating: in 1970–1971, US colleges and universities conferred 31 times more bachelor's degrees in business, management, and marketing than in theology and religious vocations; by 1985–1986, that number had grown to 43 times more, by 1990–1991 to 52 times more, and, by 2019–2020, to 56 times more business than theology degrees. US Department of Education, National Center for Education Statistics, table 322.10: Bachelor's Degrees Conferred by Postsecondary Institutions, by Field of Study: Selected years, 1970–71 through 2019–20.
20. Malcolm Harris (2017), *Kids These Days*, Little, Brown.
21. Juliet Schor (1992), *The Overworked American*, Basic Books; Arne Kalleberg (2009), "Precarious Work, Insecure Workers," *American Sociological Review* 74: 1–22.
22. Steven Greenhouse (2008), *The Big Squeeze*, Knopf; Arne Kalleberg (2013), "Globalization and Precarious Work," *Contemporary Sociology* 42: 700–706.
23. Stephen Barley and Gideon Kunda (2004), *Gurus, Hired Guns and Warm Bodies*, Princeton University Press; Maya Manzi, Diana Ojeda, and Roberta Hawkins (2019), "Enough Wandering Around!" *The Professional Geographer* 71: 355–363.
24. Byung-Chul Han observes, "Twenty-first century society is no longer a [Foucauldian] disciplinary society, but rather an achievement society.... Its inhabitants are ... 'achievement-subjects.' They are entrepreneurs of themselves.... The imperative to achieve [is] the new commandment of late-modern society.... The human being as a whole [is] ... becoming a performance-machine.... One exploits oneself.... As its flipside, the society of achievement and activeness is generating excessive tiredness and exhaustion" (2015), *The Burnout Society*, Stanford University Press, 8, 10, 19, 30.
25. Age affects the amount of time for opportunities to move, so I divided reported number of moves by age (minus 18) and multiplied that figure by 10 to calculate number of moves per decade.
26. See Anthony Elliott and John Urry (2010), *Mobile Lives*, International Library of Sociology.
27. Michael Welch and John Baltzell (1984), "Geographic Mobility, Social Integration, and Church Attendance," *Journal for the Scientific Study of Religion* 23: 75–91; Reginald Bibby (1997), "Going, Going, Gone: The Impact of Geographical Mobility on Religious Involvement," *Review of Religious Research* 38: 289–307; Christian Smith, David Sikkink, and Jason Bailey (1998), "Devotion in Dixie and Beyond," *Journal for the Scientific Study of Religion* 37: 494–506.
28. Derek Thompson (2019, February 24), "Workism Is Making Americans Miserable: For the College Educated Elite, Work Has Morphed Into a Religious Identity," *The Atlantic*.
29. Richard Sennett (1998), *The Corrosion of Character: The Personal Consequences of Work in the New Capitalism*, Norton; Ilana Gershon. "Neoliberal Agency," *Current Anthropology* 52: 537–555; Nikolas Rose (1999), *Governing the Soul*, Free Association Press.
30. J. McGuigan (2014), "The Neoliberal Self," *Culture Unbound* 6: 223–240; Katharyne Mitchell (2003), "Educating the National Citizen in Neoliberal Times," *Transactions* 28: 387–403; Jeremy Gilbert (ed.) (2016), *Neoliberal Culture*, Lawrence & Wishart; Mary Wrenn and William Waller (2017), "Care and the Neoliberal Individual," *Journal of Economic Issues* 201: 495–502; Thomas Teo (2018), "*Homo Neoliberalus*," *Theory & Psychology* 28: 581–599; Elizabeth Houghton (2019), "Becoming a Neoliberal Subject," *Ephemera* 19: 615–629.

31. Matthew McDonald, Stephen Wearing, and Jess Ponting (2013), "Narcissism and Neo-Liberalism: Work, Leisure, and Alienation in an Era of Consumption," *Society and Leisure* 30: 489–510; Hanna-Mari Ikonen and Minna Nikunen (2019), "Young Adults and the Tuning of the Entrepreneurial Mindset in Neoliberal Capitalism," *Journal of Youth Studies* 22: 824–838. Han again: "The late-modern achievement-subject does not pursue works of duty. Its maxims are not obedience, law, and the fulfillment of obligation, but rather freedom, pleasure, and inclination.... It expects the profits of enjoyment from work" (*The Burnout Society,* 38).
32. Adam Kotsko (2018), *Neoliberalism's Demons,* Stanford University Press.
33. Jake Meador (2023, July 29), "The Misunderstood Reason Millions of Americans Stopped Going to Church," *The Atlantic.*
34. Rodney Clapp (2021), *Naming Neoliberalism,* Fortress Press; Paul Babie and Michael Trainor (2019), *Neoliberalism and the Biblical Voice,* Routledge; Kevin Hargaden (2018), *Theological Ethics in a Neoliberal Age,* Cascade Books.

    Matthew Eggemeier and Peter Fritz (2020), *Send Lazarus,* Fordham University Press; Matthew Eggemeier (2020), *Against Empire,* Cascade Books, 14–42.
35. Christian Smith and Melinda Denton (2005), *Soul Searching,* Oxford University Press, 156–158.
36. The standard reply claims that capitalism is merely an economic institution, distinct from democracy as a political institution and religion, philosophy, and the humanities as cultural institutions—and that each of these can and should accomplish its own task within its own sphere without interfering with the others. This view is exemplified by an early neoconservative apologetics for the Reagan Revolution, Michael Novak's *The Spirit of Democratic Capitalism* (1982, Simon and Schuster). The idea is nice in theory but, ironically (for "realistic" neoconservatives), totally unrealistic. There may have been past times when such neat partitions of spheres of life held up. But fossil capitalism became so successful and powerful that it breached the bounds of mere economic activity to become *the* comprehensive, defining, and integrating institution of all of society. Capitalism has so thoroughly colonized the political and cultural spheres that we no longer simply have a capitalist economy but an entire *society* comprehensively organized, governed, and integrated by commercial capitalism's imperatives, ideologies, and images. In which case, the opposing cultural ontologies of neoliberal capitalism and traditional religion are a real issue for the latter. Indeed, neoliberalism has made its own mark on religion—see Matthew Guest (2022), *Neoliberal Religion,* Bloomsbury; Adam Possamai (2018), *The i-zation of Society, Religion, and Neoliberal Post-Secularism,* Palgrave Macmillan.
37. Harvey Cox (2016), *The Market as God,* Harvard University Press.
38. To be sure, many post-Boomers felt ambivalence about mass consumerism, reporting in interviews statements like, "I'm not too into material things." This reflected their diminished economic prospects of achieving the traditional American Dream (discussed in the following chapter) and the postmaterialist and expressive-individualist appreciation of experiences over objects. But ambivalent feelings did not make neoliberal consumerism go away; its macro-cultural influence still dominated. In the end, most post-Boomers found ways to enjoy materialism—especially its technological gadgets—even while critiquing it.
39. Paul McClure (2016), "Faith and Facebook in a Pluralistic Age," *Sociological Perspectives* 59: 818–834; Chelsea Starr, Kristin Waldo, and Matthew Kaufman (2019), "Digital Irreligion," *Journal for the Scientific Study of Religion* 58: 494–512; Paul McClure (2017), "Tinkering with Technology and Religion in the Digital Age," *Journal for the Scientific Study of Religion* 56: 481–497. Also see Paul McClure (2020), "The Buffered, Technological Self," *Social Compass* 67: 461–478; Allen Downey (2014), "Religious Affiliation, Education and Internet Use," Olin College of Engineering working paper; Emerging Technology (2014, April 4), "How the Internet Is Taking Away America's Religion," *MIT Technology Review*; Tyler Platz (2018), "From Pews to Profiles: The Impact of Facebook on Church Attendance," MA thesis, University of Wisconsin-Whitewater; Angela Patterson (2021), "Screening Faith," Doctoral dissertation, Fielding Graduate University. Other studies show more mixed results: Heidi Campbell (2010), *When Religion Meets New Media,* Routledge; Campbell (2005), *Exploring Religious Community Online,* Peter Lang; Jasmine Benjamin (2018), "The Influence of Smart Phones on the Faith of Young Adults from Christian Backgrounds and on Their Relationship with the Church," MA thesis, Regent University.
40. Pew Research Center (1998), "Event-Driven News Audiences," Pew Research Center, 3; Susannah Fox (2007, June 21), "The Internet Circa 1998," Pew Research Center; Frederic Lardinois (2009, December 23), "U.S. Internet Users Spend 13 Hours a Week Online," *New York Times*; Tech Crunch (2009, December 23), "The Rumors Are True: We Spend More and More

Time Online"; Harlan Lebo (2017), *The 2017 Digital Future Report*, Center for the Digital Future at USC Annenberg, 7–8, 21; Amy He (2019, June 4), "Average US Time Spent with Mobile in 2019 Has Increased," *Insider Intelligence*; Andrew Perrin and Jingjing Jiang (2018, March 26), "About a Quarter of US Adults Say They Are 'Almost Constantly' Online," Pew Research Center.
41. The actual times might be more, since I recoded all those who skipped these questions as 0 hours for each.
42. Regression results not shown here.
43. Including religious others: "17% of U.S. adults have unfollowed, unfriended, blocked or changed their settings to see less of someone on social media because of religious content the person posted or shared," reports the Pew Research Center; Jeff Diamant (2023, June 21), "One-in-Six Americans Have Taken Steps to See Less of Someone on Social Media Due to Religious Content"; see Robert Bellah, Richard Madsen, William Sullivan, and Ann Swidler (1986), *Habits of the Heart*, University of California Press, 71–75.
44. Sherry Turkle (2017), *Alone Together*, Basic Books.
45. Elisabeth Noelle-Neumann (1974), "The Spiral of Silence," *Journal of Communication* 24: 43–51.
46. Namely, that the more options people have to choose from, the more difficult their choices become and the less satisfied they turn out to be with *whatever* they chose. Barry Schwartz (2004), *The Paradox of Choice*, Ecco.
47. For some, private struggles with online pornography also proved damaging to their religious faith and relationships. See Samuel Perry (2019), *Addicted to Lust*, Oxford University Press.
48. Noelle-Neumann, "Spiral of Silence."
49. Nicholas Carr (2020), *The Shallows: What the Internet Is Doing to Our Brains*, Norton; Josh Firth, John Torous, and Joseph Firth (2020), "Exploring the Impact of Internet Use on Memory and Attention Processes," *International Journal of Environmental Research and Public Health* 17; Se-hoon Jeong and Yoori Hwang (2016), "Media Multitasking Effects on Cognitive vs. Attitudinal Outcomes," *Human Communication Research* 42: 599–618; Byeongsu Park, Doug Hyun Han, and Sungwon Roh (2017), "Neurobiological Findings Related to Internet Use Disorders," *Psychiatry and Clinical Neurosciences* 71: 467–478; Ming Peng, Xianke Chen, Qingbai Zhao, and Zongkui Zhou (2018, June 8), "Attentional Scope Is Reduced by Internet Use," *PLoS ONE* 13: 1–12; Joseph Firth et al. (2019), "The 'Online Brain': How the Internet May Be Changing Our Cognition," *World Psychiatry* 18: 118–129.
50. Research also suggests that the use of sophisticated vocabulary has declined between the mid-1970s and the mid-2010s across all levels of education, from less than high school to graduate school: Jean Twenge, Keith Campbell, and Ryne Sherman (2019), "Declines in Vocabulary Among American Adults Within Levels of Educational Attainment, 1974–2016," *Intelligence* 76: 101377.
51. See Mark Bauerlein (2008), *The Dumbest Generation*, Tarcher; Jeremy Adams (2021), *Hollowed Out*, Regnery.
52. Adam Alter (2018), *Irresistible*, Penguin; Anna Lembke (2021), *Dopamine Nation*, Dutton.
53. Tim Wu (2016), *The Attention Merchants: The Epic Scramble to Get Inside Our Heads*, Random House; Peter Horsfield (2015), *From Jesus to the Internet*, Wiley, chapter 13; Larry Rosen (2012), *iDisorder*, Palgrave.
54. Mingyue Fan et al. (2021, April 20), "Effects of Information Overload, Communication Overload, and Inequality on Digital Distrust," *Frontiers in Psychology* 12; Charlotte Huff (2022, November 1), "Media Overload Is Hurting Our Mental Health," *American Psychological Association* 53; Josephine Schmitt, Christina Debbelt, and Frank Schneider (2017), "Too Much Information? Predictors of Information Overload in the Context of Online-News Exposure," *Information Communication and Society* 21: 1151–1167; Jean Twenge, Thomas Joiner, and Gabrielle Martin (2017, November 14), "Increases in Depressive Symptoms, Suicide-Related Outcomes, and Suicide Rates Among U.S. Adolescents After 2010 and Links to Increased New Media Screen Time," *Clinical Psychological Science* 6; Donna Freitas (2017), *The Happiness Effect*, Oxford University Press.
55. Jeremy Earp and Sut Jhally (2018), *Advertising at the Edge of the Apocalypse*, Media Education Foundation.
56. Readers may wonder why, if it has become increasingly hard for people to sit in silence and pray in religious settings, as I claimed just above, the same people are sometimes willing and able to practice meditation, mindfulness, and yoga. Part of the answer is religion being an external structured authority versus the individual's control over the form and content of their

own meditation practices; religion's typical orientation to a divine Other versus mindfulness's concern with oneself; the usual need to practice religion within religion's schedule versus the ability to meditate on one's own personal timetable; and the larger negative associations many have with religious traditions versus the positive cultural sheen attached to mindfulness, exercise, meditation, yoga, and so on.

57. Fred Turner (2008), *From Counterculture to Cyberculture*, University of Chicago Press; Patrice Flichy (2008), *The Internet Imaginaire*, MIT Press; CACM Staff (2018), "Hippie Values Really Did Build the Internet," *Communications of the ACM* 61: 9–11; Richard Barbrook and Andy Cameron (2014), "The Californian Ideology," *Imaginary Futures* 1; John Barlow (1996), "A Declaration of the Independence of Cyberspace," Electronic Frontier Foundation.

58. Heidi Campbell and Stephen Garner (2016), *Networked Theology*, Baker Academic, 51; Peter Horsfield (2003), "Electronic Media and the Past-Future of Christianity," in Jolyon Mitchell and Sophia Marriage (eds.), *Mediating Religion*, T&T Clark, chapter 23.

59. Gabriele Cosentino (2020), *Social Media and the Post-Truth World Order*, Palgrave; Lee McIntyre (2018), *Post-Truth*, MIT Press.

60. Robert Cross, Salvatore Parise, and Leigh Weiss (2007), "The Role of Networks in Organizational Change," *McKinsey Quarterly*; John Kotter (2011, May 23), "Hierarchy and Network," *Harvard Business Review*; Gary Swart (2012, July 5), "How Internet Companies Are Changing Organizational Structure in the Workplace," *Business Insider*.

61. Theoretically, I am talking here about something like Max Weber's "elective affinities" and Pierre Bourdieu's "homologies" and the power of the "habitus." SeeMax Weber (1905/2002), *The Protestant Ethic and the Spirit of Capitalism*, Penguin; Pierre Bourdieu (1986), *Distinction*, Routledge.

62. One recommendation from a 2013 survey of 12,700 American Jews was that "Jewish institutions need to replace hierarchical and authoritarian structures with more fluid, flat, and open democratic systems of engaging people in non-authoritarian and even non-authoritative processes." SeeDavid Elcott and Stuart Himmelfarb (2013), "Generations and Regeneration: Engagement and Fidelity in 21st Century American Jewish Life," Berman Jewish Databank.

63. Search Amazon or Google on "postmodern" and "theology," "Christianity," or "church" for many examples.

64. Stuart Jeffries (2021), *Everything, All the Time, Everywhere: How We Became Postmodern*, Verso.

65. Christian Smith, with Patricia Snell (2009), *Souls in Transition*, Oxford University Press, chapter 2; Smith, with Kari Christoffersen, Hilary Davidson, and Patricia Snell Herzog (2011), *Lost in Transition*, Oxford University Press, chapter 1.

66. Peter Berger and Thomas Luckmann (1967), *The Social Construction of Reality: A Treatise in the Sociology of Knowledge*, Anchor Books. Elsewhere I have argued that moderate, realist forms of social constructionism are valid, revealing, and valuable. The problems come when constructionism is ridden off the rails into radical, post-Kantian, anti-realist forms. That mishap hijacks the valid insight that, for example, cultural *norms* about gender, sex, and motherhood are socially constructed (they are) and tries to fly us to a place where biological bodies, chromosomes, sexual intercourse, and childbirth are also socially constructed (they aren't; only the *beliefs* and *meanings* we have about them are). See Christian Smith (2010), *What Is a Person?*, University of Chicago Press, chapter 3.

67. The "neo" in neopragmatism refers back to the classical pragmatist movement in American philosophy led by C. S. Peirce, William James, and John Dewey. Rorty drew selectively on certain pragmatist themes to develop his own arguments, many of which did not follow the original tradition, especially that of Peirce.

68. Richard Rorty (1979), *Philosophy and the Mirror of Nature*, Princeton University Press. Other influential works of Rorty that followed included *Consequences of Pragmatism* (1982) and *Contingency, Irony, and Solidarity* (1989).

69. Thomas Kuhn (1962), *The Structure of Scientific Revolutions*, University of Chicago Press. Note, however, how *reality* has already snuck back into the anti-realist analysis.

70. Jaegwon Kim (1980), "Rorty on the Possibility of Philosophy," *Journal of Philosophy* 77: 588–597.

71. Rorty was a declared atheist but hardly disconnected from religion. He was the maternal grandson of Walter Rauschenbusch, a leading advocate of the Social Gospel movement of the late nineteenth and early twentieth centuries. He was married for 34 years to a practicing Mormon, Mary Varney Rorty. Rorty famously claimed that religion was a "conversation-stopper," which he saw as a vice for any good society. See Richard Rorty (1999), "Religion as a Conversation Stopper," in *Philosophy and Social Hope*, Penguin, 168–174, originally published

in 1994, in *Common Knowledge* 3: 1–6. However, later in his career he had something of a "spiritual turn," and while he did not personally embrace traditional faith, he softened his previous hostility toward religion and recognized the inevitability and conditional value of religious faith in a liberal society. Rorty also admitted that his own philosophical project was "ultimately spiritual" because, he said, "the adoption of my view would be a real change in people's self-image"; quoted in Jason Boffetti (2004, May), "How Richard Rorty Found Religion," *First Things*. He also acknowledged the theoretical validity of theism, defending the Reformed Epistemology of Alvin Plantinga, Nicholas Wolterstorff, and colleagues, saying that "Plantinga's *God and Other Minds* is quite convincing on many points, and I admire Wolterstorff's *Reason Within the Bounds of Religion.* . . . I admire them both as remarkable philosophers . . . [who] show why we atheists should stop praising ourselves for being more 'rational' than theists. On this point they seem to me quite right"; quoted in Stephen Louthan (1996), "On Religion—A Discussion with Richard Rorty, Alvin Plantinga and Nicholas Wolterstorff," *Christian Scholar's Review* 27: 179. Two years before his death, Rorty collaborated with Gianni Vattimo, a devout Catholic, to publish *The Future of Religion* (Columbia University Press), in which he recognized the viability of a non-essentialist religion in a post-metaphysical world that would emphasize solidarity, charity, and irony.
72. This is not to suggest that traditional religion would have done well to fight back in defense of modern presuppositions and commitments. Those who did (e.g., David Wells [1994], *No Place for Truth*, Eerdmans) did not get very far. Here traditional religion faced a "damned if you do, damned if you don't" situation that I describe in the Conclusion—there is not necessarily always a winning position when the terms of thought are defined by modernity and postmodernism.
73. Empirical evidence validates that expectation. I created a single linear scale combining answers to the six Millennial Zeitgeist Survey statements at the top of Table 6.4, then divided that scale into quartiles. Ninety-one percent of adults in the highest quartile of agreement with those statements attend religious services once or twice a year or less often, compared to 34% of those in the lowest quartile. Meanwhile, 48% of those in the lowest quartile of agreement attend religious service nearly every week or more often, compared to only 9% of those in the highest quartile. These differences remain statistically significant after controlling for age, education, income, sex, and race and ethnicity. The causal directions here may run both ways, but the association is strong and the mismatch causal mechanism of influence is sensible.
74. The best documentary history is Carl Grant and Thandeka Chapman (eds.) (2008), *History of Multicultural Education*, Volumes 1–6, Routledge.
75. Paul Gorski (1999), "A Brief History of Multicultural Education," *EdChange Critical Multicultural Research Room*.
76. Thandeka Chapman and Carl Grant (2010), "Thirty Years of Scholarship in Multicultural Education," *Race, Gender, and Class* 17: 43–44.
77. James Banks and John Ambrosio (n.d.), "Multicultural Education History," StateUniversity.com Education Encyclopedia.
78. Nathan Glazer (1998), *We Are All Multiculturalists Now*, Harvard University Press.
79. Dowell Myers (2016), "Peak Millennials," *Housing Policy Debate* 26: 928–947; Stephan Whitaker (2019), "Population, Migration, and Generations in Urban Neighborhoods," *Economic Commentary*, Federal Reserve Bank of Cleveland; Yongsung Lee, Bumsoo Lee, and Md Tanvir Hossain Shubho (2018), "Urban Revival by Millennials?" *Journal of Regional Science* 59: 538–566; Megan Benetsky, Charlynn Burd, and Melanie Rapino (2015), "Young Adult Migration," *American Community Survey Reports*, US Census Bureau; Hyojung Lee (2022), "Are Millennials Leaving Town?" *International Journal of Urban Sciences* 26: 68–86; Luke Juday (2015), "The Changing Shape of American Cities," *Demographics Research Group Report*, University of Virginia; Tim Nelson (2022, May 20), "Boomers Aren't Flocking to Cities After All," *Architectural Digest*; Greta Kaul (2022, May 29), "Millennials Get All the Credit for Embracing City Living," *MinnPost*; Beau Dure (2014, October 21), "Millennials Continue Urbanization of America," NPR; Richard Florida (2019, May 28), "Young People's Love of Cities Isn't a Passing Fad," *CityLab*; Joe Cortright (2020, June 15), "Youth Movement," *CityCommentary*; Tim Henderson (2015, July 23), "Millennials: Living on the Edge of the Big City," *Stateline*; Lucy Westcott (2014, March 27), "More Americans Are Moving to Cities," *The Atlantic*.
80. The mean percent religious adherence rate was 48.2% (standard deviation: 11.97%).
81. Sharon Hays (1998), *The Cultural Contradictions of Motherhood*, Yale University Press.
82. The mass media began to catch up in the 2000s. Between 1991 and 1999, the average number of references to intensive-parenting phrases per year was 1.4; between 2000 and 2006, that number

increased to an average of 7 per year, and then again to an average of 52.8 references per year between 2007 and 2020.
83. Fiona Shirani, Karen Henwood, and Carrie Coltart (2012), "Meeting the Challenges of Intensive Parenting Culture," *Sociology* 46: 25–40; Susan Kelley (2019, January 15), "Hands-on, Intensive Parenting Is Best, Most Parents Say," *Cornell Chronicle*. In 2003, sociologist Annette Lareau argued in her groundbreaking book, *Unequal Childhoods* (University of California Press), that parenting styles are class based—that what I here call the "old" model is the parenting style of poor and working-class families (what Lareau called the "accomplishment of natural growth" model) and that intensive parenting (what Lareau called "concerted cultivation") is a middle- and upper-middle-class style. I agree with Lareau's argument but think its scope of generalizability is temporally limited. Many middle-class Baby Boomers (including me) were raised by parents using the "natural growth" style; the "concerted cultivation" style appears since Lareau's book to be becoming increasingly normative among working-class families. Social class still matters, but its effects are likely becoming more subtle as intensive parenting spreads across some class boundaries.
84. Joe Pinsker (2019, January 16), "'Intensive' Parenting Is Now the Norm in America," *The Atlantic*; Justine Gunderson (n.d.), "The Historical Rise of Intensive Mothering and Its Implications for Women," Florida State University working paper. Intensive parenting arose in other countries, too: Lyn Craig, Abigail Powell, and Ciara Smyth (2014), "Towards Intensive Parenting?" *The British Journal of Sociology* 65: 555–579; Anne Gauthier, Caroline Bryson, Luisa Fadel, Tina Haux, Judith Koops, and Monika Mynarska (2021), "Exploring the Concept of Intensive Parenting in a Three-country Study," *Demographic Research* 44: 333–348; Trevor Tsz-lok Lee (2021), "Social Class, Intensive Parenting Norms and Parental Values for Children," *Current Sociology* 71: 964–981; Shira Maman, Danny Kaplan, and Shira Offer (2023), "'Going-with-the-Flow' or 'Getting-Things-Done'" *Journal of Family Issues* 45: 697–719.
85. Ciara Smyth and Lyn Craig (2017), "Conforming to Intensive Parenting Ideals," *Families, Relationships and Societies* 6: 107–124. As with the ideal emerging adult lifestyle discussed in the previous chapter, only parents with many resources are able actually to attain the intensive-parenting norm. Parents with less time, money, and energy can only attempt approximations. But the *norm* still remains the dominant cultural ideal.
86. Claire Cain Miller (2019, March 26), "The Relentlessness of Modern Parenting," *New York Times*; Casey Scheibling and Melissa Milkie (2023), "Shifting Toward Intensive Parenting Culture?" *Family Relations* 72: 495–514.
87. Despite evidence that intensive parenting may have no long-term effects and can potentially backfire with negative effects. Mara Yerkes, Marit Hopman, Marijn Stok, and John De Wit (2021), "In the Best Interests of Children?" *Critical Public Health* 3: 349–360; Holly Schiffrin, Hester Godfrey, Miriam Liss, and Mindy Erchull (2015), "Intensive Parenting," *Journal of Child and Family Studies* 24: 2322–2331.
88. Dingeman Wiertz and Chaeyoon Lim (2021), "The Rise of the Nones Across the United States," *Sociological Science* 8: 429–454.

Chapter 7

1. George W. Bush (2001), "'Islam is Peace' Says President," Remarks by the president at Islamic Center of Washington, DC, September 17.
2. The bump in reports on religious violence in 1981–1987 mostly concerned the war in Lebanon, including the bombing of US military personnel in Beirut on October 23, 1983.
3. George Lakoff and Mark Johnson (1980), *Metaphors We Live By*, University of Chicago Press.
4. Borrowing a metaphor from Galen Watts and Sam Reimer (2022), "How 'Religion' Became Polluted in Canada," Social Science History Association, 2022 Annual Meeting.
5. Most of the search hits in the early years refer to events in ancient, medieval, or early modern history, seemingly distant events not relevant to current life. Some of them also refer to specific recent conflicts—such as Catholics and Protestants in Northern Ireland, or Christians and Hindus in India—which, though very real, at the time seemed distant enough not to hold implications for American religion.
6. Other related search terms produced striking results reflecting this pattern. The number of books collected in the Library of Congress that answer to the search term "religious war," for example, grew hugely across these decades, from 102 published in the 1970s to 199 in the 1980s, 204 in the 1990s, 1,096 in the 2000s, and 2,507 in the 2010s. Americans in the first two decades of the twenty-first century had nearly 12 times more books on "religious war"

than those living in the 1970s–1980s. A similar pattern held for books on "jihad," which grew from 15 listed in the 1970s to 31 in the 1980s, 40 in the 1990s, 515 in the 2000s, and 793 in the 2010s—a 28-fold increase in books published on the topic from the 1970s to 1980s to the two decades after 2000. Similar patterns emerge from Google Ngram searches on "religious violence," "sectarian violence," and "religious terrorism" from 1980 to 2019 (results not shown).

7. Gary Wolf (2006, November 1), "The Church of the Non-Believers," *Wired*.
8. The automobile "fish wars" of the latter 1980s and after—in which the "Jesus" or *"ichthus"* written inside the early-Christian fish symbol decal that some Christians put on the backs of their vehicles was countered by the same fish shape sporting stubby evolving legs and "Darwin" (or sometimes "science") written inside—preceded the New Atheism as a pushback on evangelical and fundamentalist creationism, but that was decentralized and faceless, more snarky than aggressive.
9. Jerry Adler (2006, September 11), "The New Naysayers," *Newsweek*, 47–49.
10. In his 1995 book, *Darwin's Dangerous Idea*, Dennett had argued that design in nature needs no purposeful divine designer but is fully explainable by natural selection. Daniel Dennet (1995), *Darwin's Dangerous Idea: Evolution and the Meanings of Life*, Simon and Schuster.
11. Vox Day (2008), *The Irrational Atheist*, BenBella Books; Christopher Hitchens, Richard Dawkins, Sam Harris, and Daniel Dennett (2019), *The Four Horsemen*, Random House.
12. David Segal (2006, October 26), "Atheist Evangelist in His Bully Pulpit, Sam Harris Devoutly Believes That Religion Is the Root of All Evil," *Washington Post*.
13. For example, David Bentley Hart (2010), *Atheist Delusions*, Yale University Press; Terry Eagleton (2010), *Reason, Faith, and Revolution*, Yale University Press; Chris Hedges (2008), *When Atheism Becomes Religion*, Free Press.
14. Steven Poole (2019, January 31), "The Four Horsemen Review—Whatever Happened to 'New Atheism'?" *The Guardian*.
15. Elizabeth Bruenig (2015, November 6), "Is the New Atheism Dead?" *The New Republic*; David Sloan Wilson (2016, February 1), "The New Atheism as a Stealth Religion," *This View of Life*.
16. The isolated spike in 1994 represents an unlikely combination of miscellaneous publications that just so happen to contain the phrase "new atheism," some about the nineteenth century, some about religion in Israel, but none related to the movement discussed here.
17. The pre-internet-era hits are retro record counts of works by or about those authors from earlier years.
18. The phrase "new atheism" does not appear in books (in the Library of Congress, Google Books, Amazon.com) prior to 1991, except in two titles, one in 1984, the other in 1986—neither of which referred to the New Atheism of the twenty-first century. Even the more open-ended "atheism" shows up infrequently in book titles, subtitles, chapter titles, and summary descriptions in the 1970s, 1980s, and 1990s. In the last decade of the twentieth century, only 65 books in the Library of Congress system were overtly about atheism; an average of only 4.4 books per year (44 total) in the 1990s made normative arguments for and against atheism, most of those at a general philosophical level. The balance of 11 books about atheism in the 1990s were on historical or country case studies and intellectual histories of specific thinkers. The numbers in the 1980s were fewer. In the 1980s, 66 books in the Library of Congress system were about atheism; an average of 1.8 books per year (18 total) during that decade made normative arguments for and against atheism, most of those, again, at a general philosophical level. In short, book publishing in the last two decades of the twentieth century were not focused much on atheism, and the few books that were published then were about the "old atheism," even if at times they referred to their subjects as a "new atheism" (e.g., compared to atheism in the classical world). That all changed, however, by the mid-2000s.
19. Richard Dawkins (2006), *Root of All Evil*, Television movie.
20. David Allyn (2000), *Make Love, Not War*, Little, Brown; Kevin White (1992), *The First Sexual Revolution*, New York University Press.
21. Donna Freitas (2013), *The End of Sex*, Basic Books.
22. Elon Green (2016, June 23), "The Lost History of the 'Booty Call,'" *Esquire*; Peter Jonason, Norman Li, and Margaret Cason (2009), "The 'Booty Call,'" *Journal of Sex Research* 46: 460–470; Peter Jonason, Norman Li, and Jessica Richardson (2011), "Positioning the Booty-Call Relationship on the Spectrum of Relationships," *Journal of Sex Research* 48: 486–495; Jocelyn Wentland and Elke Reissing (2014), "Casual Sexual Relationships," *The Canadian Journal of Human Sexuality* 23: 167–177.

23. Tamar Lewin (2005, June 30), "Are These Parties for Real?" *New York Times*; Caitlin Flanagan (2006, January/February), "Are You There God? It's Me, Monica: How Nice Girls Got so Casual About Oral Sex," *The Atlantic*.
24. Kathleen Bogle (2007), "The Shift from Dating to Hooking Up in College," *Sociology Compass* 1: 775–788.
25. Tom Wolfe observed: "'Hooking up' was a term known in the year 2000 to almost every American child over the age of nine, but to only a relatively small percentage of their parents, who, even if they heard it, thought it was being used in the old sense of 'meeting' someone. Among the children, hooking up was always a sexual experience, but the nature and extent of what they did could vary widely" (Wolfe [2000], *Hooking Up*, Farrar, Straus and Giroux, 7).
26. Freitas, *End of Sex*; Christian Smith, with Kari Christoffersen, Hilary Davidson, and Patricia Snell Herzog (2011), *Lost in Transition*, Oxford University Press, chapter 4. This raises the important question of the relationship between public cultures and the personal experiences they foster, the negative unintended side of which can be suppressed from public recognition and discussion.
27. Breanne Fahs (2014), "'Freedom to' and 'Freedom from': A New Vision for Sex-Positive Politics," *Sexualities* 17: 267–290; Sophie Whitehead (2019, November 4), "What Is Sex Positivity?" School of Sexuality Education; Kelly Neff (2020), *Sex Positive*, Watkins.
28. Brittany Huckabee (2015), *Hot Girls Wanted*, Film documentary, Two to Tangle Productions.
29. Claude Fischer and Michael Hout (2006), *Century of Difference*, Russel Sage, 213.
30. I remind readers of my position expressed in the previous chapter: the critique that much of the increase here mirrors the growth of all internet websites during this time is correct but is also, for present purposes, irrelevant since the point is not that internet references to these terms grew faster than the internet itself, but rather that the exploding internet provided a crucial means by which interest in the new sexual culture was expressed and promulgated.
31. Janet Hardy (2009), *The Ethical Slut: A Guide to Infinite Sexual Possibilities*, Celestial Arts; Tristan Taormino (2008), *Opening Up: A Guide to Creating and Sustaining Open Relationships*, Cleis Press; Christopher Ryan and Cacilda Jetha (2012), *Sex at Dawn: How We Mate, Why We Stray, and What It Means for Modern Relationships*, Harper Perennial; and Franklin Veaux, Janet Hardy, and Tatiana Gill (2014), *More Than Two: A Practical Guide to Ethical Polyamory*, Thorntree Press.

    Following those came the predictable raft of how-to advice follow-ups, such as Eve Rickert, Nora Samaran, and Jessica Fern (2020), *Polysecure: Attachment, Trauma and Consensual Nonmonogamy*, Thornapple Press; and Lola Phoenix (2022), *The Anxious Person's Guide to Non-Monogamy*, Jessica Kingsley Publishers.
32. Jean Williams and Jasna Jovanovic (2014), "Third Wave Feminism and Emerging Adult Sexuality," *Sexuality & Culture* 18: 157–171.
33. On why sex is central in cultural struggles between transcendent religions and immanent cultures, see Steven Smith (2018), *Pagans and Christians in the City*, Eerdmans.
34. Chris Hedges (2009), *Empire of Illusion*, Nation Books, chapter 2.
35. Amy Lamé (2022), *From Prejudice to Pride: A History of LGBTQ+ Movement*, Wayland; Michael Bronski (2012), *A Queer History of the United States*, Beacon; Matthew Riemer and Leighton Brown (2019), *We Are Everywhere: Protest, Power, and Pride in the History of Queer Liberation*, Ten Speed Press.
36. Emily Zak (2013, October 1), "LGBPTTQQIIAA+: How We Got Here from Gay," *Ms. Magazine*; Jeffry Iovannone (2018, June 9), "A Brief History of the LGBTQ+ Initialism," *Medium*.
37. Justin McCarthy (2016, May 19), "Americans' Support for Gay Marriage Remains High," Gallup; Justin McCarthy (2021, June 8), "Record-High 70% in U.S. Support Same-Sex Marriage," Gallup. Also see Pew Research Center (2015, June 8), "Support for Same-Sex Marriage at Record High," Pew Research Center..
38. McCarthy, "Record-High"; McCarthy, "Americans' Support"; Pew Research Center, "Support."
39. At the Crossroads (2015, June 24), "Millennials' Feelings Towards Sexual Orientation and Gay Marriage," *At the Crossroads*.
40. Smith et al., *Lost in Transition*, chapter 1.
41. The puzzle here is that religious traditions, like liberal Protestantism, that have "updated" their beliefs and ethics to be more compatible with modern sexual sensibilities have not much attracted and retained the very youth who criticize religion for being outdated.
42. Diana Eck (2001), *A New Religious America: How a "Christian Country" Has Become the World's Most Religiously Diverse Nation*, HarperOne.

43. Eck had been researching US religious diversity since 1991, leading the Harvard University Pluralism Project (https://pluralism.org/), which over the years highlighted the realities of American religious diversity through many means.
44. By, respectively, Robert Wuthnow (2007), *America and the Challenges of Religious Diversity*, Princeton University Press; Daniel Cox, E. J. Dionne Jr., Robert P. Jones, and William A. Galston (2011), *What It Means to Be American: Attitudes Towards Increasing Diversity in America Ten Years After 9/11*, PRRI; Daniel Cox and Robert P. Jones (2017), *America's Changing Religious Identity*, PRRI; and Eboo Patel (2018), *Out of Many Faiths: Religious Diversity and the American Promise*, Princeton University Press.

    In 2014, the Public Religion Research Institute (PRRI) released an infographic, allegedly in response to a controversial Super Bowl commercial titled "America the Diverse," emphasizing growing religious pluralism across generations (for a critique, see https://religiondispatches.org/true-or-false-less-religion-means-greater-diversity/). Robert Putnam and David Campbell's 2010 book, *American Grace: How Religion Divides and Unites Us* (Simon and Schuster), emphasized in its subtitle religious division ahead of concord.
45. Richard Fry and Kim Parker (2018, November 15), "Early Benchmarks Show 'Post-Millennials' on Track to Be Most Diverse, Best-Educated Generation Yet," Pew Research Center.
46. Pew Research Center (2013), "The Religious Affiliation of U.S. Immigrants," Pew Research Center; Stephen Warner and Judith G. Wittner (1998), *Gatherings in Diaspora*, Temple University Press; PRB (2008), "Immigration Gives Catholicism a Boost in the United States," Population Research Bureau.
47. Peter Berger (1967/1990), *The Sacred Canopy*, Anchor.
48. Christian Smith and Melinda Denton (2005), *Soul Searching*, Oxford University Press, chapter 4. In following years, younger Millennials and Generation Z took this caution to a next level by demanding protective "trigger warnings" applied to a narrow range of things that trigger people, apparently believing that everybody has a right never to be upset or disturbed by anything.
49. Michael Emerson and Christian Smith (2000), *Divided by Faith*, Oxford University Press.
50. Brad Christerson, Michael Emerson, and Korie Edwards (2005), *Against All Odds: The Struggle for Racial Integration in Religious Organizations*, New York University Press.
51. Emile Durkheim, with Karen Fields (translator) (1912/1995), *The Elementary Forms of Religious Life*, Free Press.
52. Robert Bellah (1967), "Civil Religion in America," *Daedalus* 96: 1–21; Philip Gorksi (2017), *American Covenant*, Princeton University Press.
53. Samuel Huntington (2004), *Who Are We? The Challenges to America's National Identity*, Simon and Schuster.
54. Bruce Stokes (2017, February 1), "What It Takes to Truly Be 'One of Us.'" Pew Research Center; Neil Ruiz, Luis Noe-Bustamante, and Sono Shah (2023, May 8), "Diverse Cultures and Shared Experiences Shape Asian American Identities," Pew Research Center. For a comparison using different question wording in an earlier year, in 2002, the Pew Research Center asked, "All in all, do you think a person can be a good American if he or she does not have religious faith?" Eighty-four percent of all American adults said "yes." Responses varied by age, however, as 88% of 18-to-49-year-olds, 83% of 50-to-64-year-olds, and 77% of those 65 and older said "yes." Pew also asked, "All in all, do you think a person can be a good American if he or she does not believe in basic Judeo-Christian values?" Eighty-two percent of all American adults said yes. The spread between the youngest and oldest age group was 9%.
55. Stokes, "What It Takes," 22.
56. See, for example, Khalilah Brown-Dean (2019), *Identity Politics in the United States*, Polity; Yascha Mounk (2023), *The Identity Trap*, Penguin.
57. Lilliana Mason (2018), *Uncivil Agreement: How Politics Became Our Identity*, University of Chicago Press; for a broader view, Tobias Cremer (2022), "Defenders of the Faith?" *Religion, State and Society* 50: 532–552.
58. Joshua Mitchell (2020), *American Awakening: Identity Politics and Other Afflictions of Our Time*, Encounter; Andrew Sullivan (2018, December 7), "America's New Religions," *New York Magazine*; Michael Gerson (2019, March 18), "Politics Is Religion," *Washington Post*; Carl Trueman (2021, April 29), "Identity Politics, Opium of the People," *First Things*; Linda Feldmann (2021, May 12), "Is Politics the New Religion?" *Christian Science Monitor*; Daniel Mahoney (2018), *The Idol of Our Age*, Encounter.
59. Tobias Cremer (2023), *The Godless Crusade: Religion, Populism, and Right-Wing Identity Politics*, Cambridge University Press.

60. https://www.brown.edu/news/2021-09-01/costsofwar.
61. Mason, *Uncivil Agreement*.
62. By some accounts, the Bill Clinton presidency, and especially the Monica Lewinsky affair, was a watershed moment in these developments. Christopher Hitchens (1999), *No One Left to Lie To: The Triangulation of William Jefferson Clinton*, Atlantic Books.
63. Karla Vermeulen (2021), *Generation Disaster: Coming of Age Post-9/11*, Oxford University Press; also see Maxim Furek (2008), *The Death Proclamation of Generation X*, iUniverse; for a smart analysis of psychic harm, see Cassandra Sever (2024, September 3), "Not 'Coddling' but 'Rewiring': Explaining Psychic Harm," *Society* 61: 1–14.
64. Also see François Bourque and Ashlee Willox (2014), "Climate Change: The Next Challenge for Public Mental Health?" *International Review of Psychiatry* 26: 415–422; Inmaculada Boluda-Verdú, Marina Senent-Valero, Mariola Casas-Escolano, Alicia Matijasevich, and María Pastor-Valero (2021), "Fear for the Future: Eco-anxiety and Health Implications," *Journal of Environmental Psychology* 84: 2021 Bath University survey of 16-to-25-year-olds in 10 countries ($N = 10,000$) on young people's feelings about climate change reported that 75% say the future is frightening; 56% say they think humanity is doomed; two-thirds report feeling sad, afraid, and anxious about climate change; 83% agree humans have failed to care for the planet; 69% agree governments cannot be trusted; and 65% agree governments are failing young people. One respondent said, "I don't want to die, but I don't want to live in a world that doesn't care for children and animals," Caroline Hickman et al. (2021), "Climate Anxiety in Children and Young People and Their Beliefs About Government Responses to Climate Change," *Lancet Planet Health* 5(12): e863–e873.
65. For a generational comparison of trust in political leaders, see Daniel Cox, Kelsey Hammond, and Kyle Gray (2023), "Generation Z and the Transformation of American Adolescence," Survey Center on American Life, 12–13.
66. One supporting empirical finding: greater distress about climate change correlates strongly with lower religious service attendance. I created a single linear scale combining answers to the five statements in Table 7.7, then divided that scale into quartiles: 49% of adults in the highest distress quartile never attend religious services, compared to 21% of those in the lowest quartile. Comparatively, 40% of those in the lowest quartile of distress attend religious service two to three times a month or more often, compared to only 19% of those in the highest quartile. The differences remain statistically significant after controlling for age, education, income, sex, and race and ethnicity. The causal direction here certainly runs both ways: some religious communities discount the climate crisis, and religious involvement may help some cope better with climate distress; but greater climate anxiety may also, as I argued above, make traditional religion feel less tuned into important issues, relevant, and appealing.
67. Smith et al., *Lost in Transition*, chapter 5.
68. Steve Crabtree (2003, December 11), "Beyond the Dot-Com Bust," *Gallup Business Journal*.
69. Evan Cunningham (2018), "Great Recession, Great Recovery?" *Monthly Labor Review*, US Bureau of Labor Statistics.
70. Daniel Kurt (2022, November 22), "How the Financial Crisis Affected Millennials," Investopedia.
71. For example, Scott Berridge (2014), "Millennials After the Great Recession," *Monthly Labor Review*, Bureau of Labor Statistics; Pew Research Center (2012), "Young, Underemployed and Optimistic," Pew Research Center; Kevin Rinz. "Did Timing Matter? Life Cycle Differences in Effects of Exposure to the Great Recession," *Journal of Labor Economics* 40: 703–735.
72. Rob Ferrett (2020, May 27), *Washington Post*; Hillary Hoffower (2022, April 14), *Business Insider*; Annie Lowrey (2020, April 13), *The Atlantic*; Michael Hobbes (2017, December), *Huffington Post*; see Rabbi Sam Yolen (2021, April 14), "Jewish Millennials: The Lost Generation," *Community Review*.
73. Derek Thompson (2019, September 26), "Three Decades Ago, America Lost Its Religion. Why?" *The Atlantic*. "A culture that funnels its dreams of self-actualization into salaried jobs is setting itself up for collective anxiety, mass disappointment, and inevitable burnout."
74. Smith et al., *Lost in Transition*, chapter 5.
75. Miriam Forbes and Robert Krueger (2019), "The Great Recession and Mental Health in the United States," *Clinical Psychological Science* 7: 900–913; Hillary Hoffower and Allana Akhtar (2020, October 10), "Lonely, Burned Out, and Depressed: The State of Millennials' Mental Health," *Business Insider*; Ramin Mojtabai, Mark Olfson, and Beth Han (2016), "National Trends in the Prevalence and Treatment of Depression in Adolescents and Young Adults," *Pediatrics* 138: e20161878.

76. The reference group, "previous generations," does of course shift for each successive generation, although culturally what Gen Xers and Millennials will almost universally have in mind here are Baby Boomers.
77. Will Bunch (2022), *After the Ivory Tower Falls*, William Morrow; Jennifer Hochschild (1995), *Facing Up to the American Dream*, Princeton University Press; also see Erin Currier (2018, January 26), "How Generation X Could Change the American Dream," *Trend Magazine*.
78. Yolen, "Jewish Millennials."
79. For example, Glenn Tinder (1989, December), "Can We Be Good Without God?" *The Atlantic*; Phillip Yancey (1998, January), "Nietzsche Was Right: The Question Is Not Why Modern Secularists Oppose Traditional Morality; It Is on What Grounds They Defend Any Morality," *Books & Culture*.
80. Robert Buckman (2000), *Can We Be Good Without God?: Behaviour, Belonging, and the Need to Believe*, Viking Canada; Greg Epstein (2010), *Good Without God: What a Billion Nonreligious People Do Believe*, William Morrow; Walter Sinnott-Armstrong (2009), *Morality Without God?*, Oxford University Press; Robert Garcia and Nathan King (eds.) (2009), *Is Goodness Without God Good Enough?: A Debate on Faith, Secularism, and Ethics*, Rowman & Littlefield; Sam Harris (2010), *The Moral Landscape: How Science Can Determine Human Values*, Free Press; Philip Kitcher (2011), *The Ethical Project*, Harvard University Press; Robin Craig (2012), *Good Without God*, Thoughtware; John Figdor and Lex Bayer (2014), *Atheist Mind, Humanist Heart: Rewriting the Ten Commandments for the Twenty-First Century*, Rowman & Littlefield; Phil Zuckerman (2014), *Living the Secular Life: New Answers to Old Questions*, Penguin Press; Ronald A. Lindsay (2014), *The Necessity of Secularism: Why God Can't Tell Us What to Do*, Pitchstone Publishing; Surendra Sahu (2014), *Living a Good Life Without Religion*, eBook; and Katherine Ozment (2016), *Grace Without God: The Search for Meaning, Purpose, and Belonging in a Secular Age*, Harper.
81. Epstein was prodded to write his book by Diana Eck, Harvard Divinity School's Pluralism Project director, described above; see Sarah Sweeney (2009, October 29), "Rebel with a Cause," *The Harvard Gazette*.
82. That is, with cultures and civilizations, moral standards and norms accumulate and deplete, like bank account balances, over multiple generations, changing more slowly than individual beliefs by being embedded in laws, social institutions, and customs, but they are never permanent. Cultural and religious movements can thus build up collective moral "assets" (e.g., belief in universal human dignity) on which populations can live for a few generations, mistakenly taking them for granted as fixed, but which, without replenishment, are eventually "spent out," with resulting cultural deflations of moral standards and norms.
83. While the non-religious scored high (78%) on this, unsurprisingly, remarkable numbers of religious Americans did, too: 26% of white mainline Protestants, 59% of white evangelicals, and 62% of white Catholics said God was not necessary for morality. The main disagreement showed among Black Protestants, at 19%; see Gregory Smith (2017, October 16), "A Growing Share of Americans Say It's Not Necessary to Believe in God to Be Moral," Pew Research Center. By 2022, 42% of white evangelicals had come to agree that morality did not depend upon belief in God; see Janell Fetterolf and Sarah Austin (2023, April 20), "Many People in the U.S., Other Advanced Economies Say It's Not Necessary to Believe in God to Be Moral," Pew Research Center.
84. Smith, "A Growing Share"; Fetterolf and Austin, "Many People"; Pew Research Center (2007, October 4), "Views of Religion and Morality," chapter 3 in *World Publics Welcome Global Trade*.
85. From my calculations of original Pew survey data, not reported by Pew.
86. Stuart Rose (2001), "Is the Term 'Spirituality' a Word That Everyone Uses, but Nobody Knows What Anyone Means by It?" *Journal of Contemporary Religion* 16: 193–207; Penny Marler and Kirk Hadaway (2002), "'Being Religious' or 'Being Spiritual' in America," *Journal for the Scientific Study of Religion* 41: 289–300; Terry Gall, Judith Malette, and Manal Guirguis-Younger (2011), "Spirituality and Religiousness," *Journal of Spirituality and Mental Health* 13: 158–181; David Hodges and Charlene McGrew (2006), "Spirituality, Religion, and the Interrelationship," *Journal of Social Work Education* 42: 637–654; Boaz Huss (2014), "Spirituality," *Journal of Contemporary Religion* 29: 47–60; Brian Steensland, Xiaoyn Wang, and Lauren Schmidt (2018), "Spirituality: What Does It Mean and to Whom?" *Journal for the Scientific Study of Religion* 57: 450–472.
87. https://www.thearda.com/data-archive?fid=FAITHFAM.
88. Answer categories for each are "very," "moderately," "slightly," and "not."

89. Tom Smith and Benjamin Schapiro (2021), *Spirituality and Religion in the United States, 1998–2020*, NORC. By 2016, the number grew to 33%, up from 18.5% in 1998.
90. Michael Lipka and Claire Gecewicz (2017, September 6), "More Americans Now Say They're Spiritual but Not Religious," Pew Research Center; David Masci and Michael Lipka (2016, January 21), "Americans May Be Getting Less Religious, but Feelings of Spirituality Are on the Rise," Pew Research Center##; also see Becka Alper, Michael Rotolo, Patricia Tevington, Justin Nortey, and Asta Kallo (2023, December 7), "Spirituality Among Americans," Pew Research Center.
91. In the 2012 American National Election Survey (ANES), 28% of respondents mentioned "spiritual, not religious" as their religious identity. In 2014, 22.3% of respondents in the Chapman Survey of American Fears described their "religious identity" as "spiritual, but not religious," In the 2016 ANES, 22.2% described their "religious beliefs" as "spiritual but not religious," In 2018, 10.3% of GSS respondents selected, "I don't follow a religion, but consider myself to be a spiritual person interested in the sacred and the supernatural" (against three other combinations of considering oneself religious and/or spiritual)—most likely the explicit GSS mention of "supernatural," in which many "spiritual" Americans do not believe, suppressed the number who chose that option.
92. Joey Marshall and Daniel Olson (2018), "Is 'Spiritual but Not Religious' a Replacement for Religion or Just One Step on the Path Between Religion and Non-religion?" *Review of Religious Research* 60: 503–518.
93. Many other developments in the 1990s and 2000s, besides those discussed so far, could arguably also have contributed through various causal mechanisms to religion's obsolescence. While I do not have space to explore them, I suggest they could include the discovery of multiple non-human hominid species beside Neanderthals (e.g., *Homo floresiensis* in 2003), the emergence of transhumanism (1980s–2000s) and Anthropocene anti-humanism (2000s), and the mapping of the human genome (1990–2003)—each of which would require more discussion to explain why and how.
94. Joel Thiessen and Sarah Wilkins-LaFlamme (2017), "Becoming a Religious None," *Journal for the Scientific Study of Religion* 56: 64–82.

Chapter 8

1. Anson Shupe (2007), *Spoils of the Kingdom*, University of Illinois Press; Anson Shupe, William Stacey, and Susan Darnell (eds.) (2000), *Bad Clergy*, New York University Press; Claire Renzetti and Sandra Yocum (eds.) (2013), *Clergy Sexual Abuse*, Northeastern University Press; Anson Shupe (2008), *Rogue Clergy*, Routledge.
2. Jon Nordheimer (1985, June 20), "Sex Charges Against Priest Embroil Louisiana Parents," *New York Times*; Anson Shupe (ed.) (1998), *Wolves Within the Fold*, Rutgers University Press.
3. Pew Research Center (2010, June 11), "The Pope Meets the Press: Media Coverage of the Clergy Abuse Scandal," Pew Research Center; Frank Bruni and Elinor Burkett (2002), *A Gospel of Shame*, Harper; Mary Eberstadt (2002, June 17), "The Elephant in the Sacristy," *Weekly Standard*.
4. Katie Zavadski, Topher Sanders, ProPublica, and Nicole Hensley (2020, March 6), "Sins of Omission: Dozens of Catholic Priests Credibly Accused of Abuse Found Work Abroad, Some with the Church's Blessing," *Houston Chronicle*.
5. Claudia Lauer and Meghan Hoyer (2019, December 29), "Hundreds of Accused Priests, Clergy Members Left off Catholic Church's Sex Abuse Lists," *Time*; AP (2019, December 29), "Hundreds of Accused Clergy Left off Church's Sex Abuse Lists," *Los Angeles Times*.
6. Vivencio Ballano (2019), *Sociological Perspectives on Clerical Sexual Abuse in the Catholic Hierarchy*, Springer.
7. John Jay School of Criminal Justice (2004), "The Nature and Scope of Sexual Abuse of Minors by Catholic Priests and Deacons in the United States"; also see AP (2023, April 5), "Report Details 'Staggering' Church Sex Abuse in Maryland," AP News; Aidan Lewis (2010, May 4), "Looking Behind the Catholic Sex Abuse Scandal," BBC News; Mary Gail Frawley-O'Dea (2007), *Perversion of Power: Sexual Abuse in the Catholic Church*, Vanderbilt University Press.
8. State of Pennsylvania Grand Jury (2018, August 14), "40th Statewide Investigating Grand Jury (August 14, 2018)"; Isaac Stanley-Becker (2018, August 15), "'He's a Priest. I Trusted Him,'" *The Washington Post*.
9. Laurie Goodstein and Sharon Otterman (2018, August 14), "Catholic Priests Abused 1,000 Children in Pennsylvania, Report Says," *New York Times*.

10. Riazat Butt and Anushka Asthana (2009, September 18), "Sex Abuse Rife in Other Religions, Says Vatican," *The Guardian*; AP (2018, January 19), "Pope Francis Accuses Chilean Church Sexual Abuse Victims of Slander," *The Guardian*.
11. Tricia Bruce (2011), *Faithful Revolution*, Oxford University Press.
12. Michael Schaffer (2012, June 25), "Sex-Abuse Crisis Is a Watershed in the Roman Catholic Church's History in America," *The Philadelphia Inquirer*.
13. In the 2018–2019 audit year, alleged victims filed 4,434 new sex abuse allegations against US priests, involving $281.6 million in payouts that year. David Crary (2020, June 25), "US Catholic Bishops: Clergy Sex Abuse Claims Tripled in 2019," AP News. In 2023, the Catholic Archdiocese of Baltimore filed for bankruptcy. Ruth Graham (2023, September 29), "Baltimore Archdiocese, Bracing for More Abuse Claims, Files for Bankruptcy," *New York Times*.
14. Mark Clayton (2002, April 5), "Sex Abuse Spans Spectrum of Churches," *The Christian Science Monitor*; Pat Wingert (2010, April 7), "Priests Commit No More Abuse Than Other Males," *Newsweek*; Silviano Tomasi (2009, September 22), "Vatican Sets Record Straight on Sexual Abuse," Catholic Education Resource Center.
15. Because each of these cases and those named later are matters of public record with ample and easily accessible documentation available online, I will not add reams of footnotes here documenting the facts—readers can readily access details on any of them. Here I also focus on abuses garnering national attention. Many more of local and regional significance I do not document here.
16. AP (2022, May 22), "Top Southern Baptists Stonewalled and Denigrated Sex Abuse Victims, Report Says"; AP (2022, May 27), "Southern Baptist Leaders Release a Previously Secret List of Accused Sexual Abusers.".
17. Anson Shupe and Janelle Eliasson-Nannini (2012), *Pastoral Misconduct: The American Black Church Examined*, Routledge; Donald Matthews (2012), *Sexual Abuse of Power in the Black Church*, WestBowPress.
18. Gustav Niebuhr (1995, May 1), "Misuse of Money Totaled $2.2 Million, Church Says," *New York Times*.
19. For one argument for why "deviant" religious groups seem to suffer disproportionate numbers of allegations of religious abuse, see Megan Goodwin (2020), *Abusing Religion: Literary Persecution, Sex Scandals, and American Minority Religions*, Rutgers University Press.
20. The Bible refers to Cyrus in Hebrew as Koresh (כורש). David Bromley and Edward Silver (1995), "The Davidian Tradition," in Stuart Wright (ed.), *Armageddon in Waco*, University of Chicago Press.
21. Among other outraged anti-federal extremists, the perpetrators of the 1995 Oklahoma City bombing, Timothy McVeigh and Terry Nichols—which killed 168 people, including 19 children, injured 680, and destroyed much of the Alfred P. Murrah Federal Building—said that the deadly Waco siege motivated their attack, which they timed to coincide with the second anniversary of the failed federal Waco assault.
22. See Eviatar Zerubavel (2007), *The Elephant in the Room: Silence and Denial in Everyday Life*, Oxford University Press.
23. Since 1994, American evangelicalism has been engaged in something like "Evangelical Scandal Battles" of a different sort, in which different authoritative observers contend that evangelicalism suffers a particular kind of scandal that must be rectified for that tradition to reflect integrity in its mission. Historian Mark Noll began the contest with his 1994 book, *The Scandal of the Evangelical Mind* (Eerdmans), followed by ethicist Ronald Sider in his 2005 counter, *The Scandal of the Evangelical Conscience: Why Are Christians Living Just Like the Rest of the World?* (Baker), and again by historian Carl Trueman in his 2012 work, *The Real Scandal of the Evangelical Mind* (Moody). I find all three arguments persuasive and compatible, but sexual and financial scandals among evangelical leaders may need to be the next book to join that fracas.
24. Christianity Today (2023, August 17), Daily Briefing.
25. People often problematically assume "good old days" biases. But it perhaps may be worth noting the contrast between (a) the moral laxity in the age of televangelists and megachurches and (b) the "Billy Graham Rule" employed by the evangelist of the same name decades earlier—according to which the often-traveling Graham never allowed himself to be alone in a room with any woman not his wife. That rule helped keep him out of the scandal limelight, even if today it does seem highly legalistic by sexual revolution and even "hip" religious standards, the latter of which, however, may have something to do with a scandal that hit Graham's grandson in 2015. See Sarah Bailey (2015, June 21), "Billy Graham's Grandson Steps Down from Florida

Megachurch After Admitting an Affair," *The Washington Post*. This, however, is anecdote, not evidence. For an early empirical study of the effects of scandals, see Tom Smith (1991), "The Impact of the Televangelist Scandals of 1987–88 on American Religious Beliefs and Behaviors," NORC GSS Social Change Report. No. 34.
26. Anson Shupe (1995), *In the Name of All That's Holy: A Theory of Clergy Malfeasance*, Praeger.
27. Pew Research Center (2020, March 12), "White Evangelicals See Trump as Fighting for Their Beliefs," Pew Research Center.
28. Kevin Roose (2011, January 26), "The Last Temptation of Ted."
29. Haggard then shored up his position, adding, "Just like you're a heterosexual but you don't have sex with every woman that you're attracted to, so I can be who I am and exclusively have sex with my wife and be perfectly satisfied." Perhaps. But his previous behaviors revealed that to be apparently untrue, and, while that logic might work for married bisexuals, it is irrelevant for outright gays and lesbians.
30. For the measurable damaging effects on religious participation and financial giving, see Nicolas Bottan (2015), "Losing My Religion: The Effects of Religious Scandals on Religious Participation and Charitable Giving," *Journal of Public Economics* 129: 106–119; Dan Hungerman (2013), "Substitution and Stigma: Evidence on Religious Markets From the Catholic Sex Abuse Scandal," *American Economic Journal* 5: 227–253; Kate Shellnutt (2019, May 21), "1 in 10 Young Protestants Have Left a Church over Abuse," *Christianity Today*.
31. John Jay School of Criminal Justice, "Nature and Scope of Sexual Abuse."
32. George Marsden, (1980), *Fundamentalism and American Culture*, Oxford University Press.
33. Christian Smith et al. (1998), *American Evangelicalism*, University of Chicago Press.
34. Grant Wacker (2014), *America's Pastor: Billy Graham and the Shaping of a Nation*, Harvard University Press.
35. George Marsden (1987), *Reforming Fundamentalism*, Eerdmans; Joel Carpenter (ed.) (1988), *Two Reformers of Fundamentalism*, Garland. In fact, most evangelical attempts to engage the culture ended up primarily speaking to other evangelicals, not the outside world, with a few exceptions, such as Francis S. Collins (2006), *The Language of God*, Free Press.
36. From the 1976 book's ad copy. Francis Schaeffer (1976), *How Should We Then Live: The Rise and Decline of Western Thought and Culture*, Crossway.
37. Colin Duriez (2008), *Francis Schaeffer: An Authentic Life*, InterVarsity Press, 186.
38. Michael Hamilton (1997, March 3), "The Dissatisfaction of Francis Schaeffer," *Christianity Today*.
39. According to research by political scientists Paul Djupe and Ryan Burge, for instance, "the politics linked to evangelicalism have taken a toll on those who do not wish a political connection.... 3.4% of the [US] population is composed of *ex*vangelicals—those [who identified as] evangelical five years ago who no longer identified [as evangelical]," Djupe and Burge (2021, March 1), "Exvangelicals," Religion in Public. Emphasis added for clarity.
40. Isaac Sharp (2023), *The Other Evangelicals: A Story of Liberal, Black, Progressive, Feminist, and Gay Christians—and the Movement That Pushed Them Out*, Eerdmans.
41. Brantley Gasaway (2014), *Progressive Evangelicals and the Pursuit of Social Justice*, University of North Carolina Press; David Swartz (2014), *Moral Minority: The Evangelical Left in an Age of Conservatism*, University of Pennsylvania Press.
42. See Tim Alberta (2022, May 10), "How Politics Poisoned the Evangelical Church," *The Atlantic*.
43. This outcome was driven partly by formerly apolitical fundamentalists deciding, in the 1970s, to become politically active and, for strategic reasons, switching their identities from fundamentalist to "evangelical"—Jerry Falwell being a prime example of this tactic—thus moving into the evangelical identity space whole groups of former fundamentalists who brought with them all of their characteristically fundamentalist tendencies. Moderate evangelicals essentially had their tradition's identity hijacked for political purposes by former religious rivals and antagonists. Susan Harding (2001), *The Book of Jerry Falwell*, Princeton University Press; Frances Fitzgerald (2017), *The Evangelicals*, Simon and Schuster.
44. Which continued for years, with Jerry Falwell Sr., for instance, reportedly criticizing, in 1999, Tinky Winky, a character in the preschool children's television program *Teletubbies*, for being "a homosexual role model"; and, about September 11, claiming on television that "the pagans, and the abortionists, and the feminists, and the gays and the lesbians who are actively trying to make that an alternative lifestyle, the ACLU, People for the American Way, all of them who have tried to secularize America, I point the finger in their face and say 'you helped this happen.'"

45. Adam Gabbatt (2021, April 5), "'Allergic Reaction to US Religious Right' Fueling Decline of Religion," *The Guardian*.
46. Christian Smith (2004, January), "Religiously Ignorant Journalists," *Books & Culture*, 6–7.
47. A similar dynamic is at work as of this writing with the rise of Christian Nationalism, which places on steroids the turn-off of the Christian Right for most post-Boomers.
48. InterVarsity Press (since 2021 part of IVP's "Signature Collection"). Ct (2006, October 6), "Reviews—Best-of Lists: The Top 50 Books That Have Shaped Evangelicals," https://en.wikipedia.org/wiki/Knowing_God.
49. Published by Zondervan.
50. Of one evangelical quoted in the *New York Times*, for example: "She still identifies as an evangelical Christian, but she doesn't believe going to church is necessary to commune with God. 'I have my own little thing with the Lord,' she says"; Ruth Graham and Charles Homans (2024, January 8), "Trump Is Connecting with a Different Type of Evangelical Voter."
51. This, despite the widespread evangelical perception of being marginalized and embattled Smith et al., *American Evangelicalism*.
52. See Dan Kimball (2003), *The Emerging Church*, Zondervan; Brian McLaren (2004), *A Generous Orthodoxy*, Zondervan; Eddie Gibbs and Ryan Bolger (2005), *Emerging Churches*, Baker Academic; Doug Pagitt and Tony Jones (2007), *Emergent Manifesto of Hope*, Baker Books; Ray Anderson (2009), *An Emergent Theology for Emerging Churches*, IVP. For a sociological account, see Gerardo Marti and Gladys Ganiel (2014), *The Deconstructed Church*, Oxford University Press.
53. For example, Alvin Plantinga (2000), *Warranted Christian Belief*, Oxford University Press.
54. Sarah MacCammon (2018, December 17), "Evangelical Writer Kisses an Old Idea Goodbye," NPR; Alissa Wilkinson (2015, May 26), "Forget Tinder: Pop Culture Is Side-Hugging Courtship Hello," *The Washington Post*.
55. Alexandria Arritt (2017, November 13), "Damaged Goods: How Virginity Is Equated to Morality," University of Idaho Women's Center.
56. David Bario (2005, March 29), "Power to the Pure," *Rutland Herald*.
57. BBC (2004, June 29), "How Effective Are Abstinence Pledges?" BBC News.
58. Jennifer Baumgardner (2006, December 31), "Would You Pledge Your Virginity to Your Father?" *Glamour*; Nancy Gibbs (2008, July 17), "The Pursuit of Teen Purity," *Time*; Mark Oppenheimer (2012, July 21), "'Purity Balls' Get Attention, but Might Not Be All They Claim," *New York Times*.
59. Stephen Arterburn and Fred Stoeker, with Mike Yorkey (2020), *Every Man's Battle: Winning the War on Sexual Temptation One Victory at a Time*, WaterBrook.
60. For example, Peter Bearman and Hannah Brückner (2001), "Promising the Future: Virginity Pledges and First Intercourse," *American Journal of Sociology* 106: 859–912; Hannah Brückner and Peter Bearman (2005), "After the Promise: the STD Consequences of Adolescent Virginity Pledges," *Journal of Adolescent Health* 36: 271–278.
61. Jessica Valenti (2009), *The Purity Myth: How America's Obsession with Virginity Is Hurting Young Women*, Seal Press.
62. Joshua Harris (1997), *I Kissed Dating Goodbye*, Multnomah Books.
63. Leah Klett (2017, December 8), "Joshua Harris Apologizes for Mistakes in 'I Kissed Dating Goodbye' in Powerful TEDx Talk," *The Gospel Herald*; Joshua Harris (2018, November 23), "'I Kissed Dating Goodbye' Author: How and Why I've Rethought Dating and Purity Culture," *USA Today*; Leah Klett (2018, October 23), "Joshua Harris Says 'I Kissed Dating Goodbye' Will Be Discontinued," *The Christian Post*; Caleb Parke (2019, July 29), "Well-Known Christian Author, Purity Advocate, Renounces His Faith" Fox News; Tré Gions-Phillips (2019, August 29), "Film Distributor Drops Joshua Harris' Documentary After Being Blindsided by Author Saying He's No Longer Christian," *Faithwire*; https://en.wikipedia.org/wiki/I_Kissed_Dating_Goodbye#cite_note-14.
64. Respectively, Linda Kay Klein (2019), *Pure: Inside the Evangelical Movement That Shamed a Generation of Young Women and How I Broke Free*, Atria Books; Emily Joy Allison (2021), *#ChurchToo: How Purity Culture Upholds Abuse and How to Find Healing*, Broadleaf Books; Nadia Bolz-Weber (2020), *Shameless: A Case for Not Feeling Bad About Feeling Good (About Sex)*, Convergent Books; Matthias Roberts (2020), *Beyond Shame: Creating a Healthy Sex Life on Your Own Terms*, Fortress Press; Jamie Lee Finch (2019), *You Are Your Own: A Reckoning with the Religious Trauma of Evangelical Christianity*, independently published; Brenda Marie Davies (2021), *On Her Knees: Memoir of a Prayerful Jezebel*, Eerdmans; Alice Greczyn (2021), *Wayward: A Memoir of Spiritual Warfare and Sexual Purity*, River Grove; Rachel Joy Welcher

(2020), *Talking Back to Purity Culture: Rediscovering Faithful Christian Sexuality*, IVP; Sheila Gregoire, Rebecca Lindenbach, and Joanna Sawatsky (2023), *She Deserves Better: Raising Girls to Resist Toxic Teachings on Sex, Self, and Speaking Up*, Baker Books.
65. Respectively, Ellie Broughton (2022, November 11), "Tainted Love: Reckoning with the Damage of Purity Culture," *The Revealer*; Joe Forrest (2021, March 17), "Shame and Regret: How Evangelical Purity Culture Failed a Generation," *Interfaith Now*; Anonymous (2022, November 29), "Why Purity Culture Is Toxic: A Female Perspective," *The Cedarville Interpreter*; Elizabeth Baker (2021), "Why I Won't Raise My Children in the Purity Culture That Raised Me," *Houston Moms*. Also see Angie Hong (2021, March 28), "The Flaw at the Center of Purity Culture," *The Atlantic*.
66. Shannon Brown (2021, August 28), "How Purity Culture Messed Up Most of the Men I Know," *Medium*; Patrick Nouwen (2021, May 1), "Boys and Girls and the Scars of Purity Culture," Patrick Nouwen blog; Zachary Wagner (2021, March 17), "Broken Masculinity: How Purity Culture Sowed the Seeds of Violence and Abuse," Center for Pastor Theologians.
67. For example, Teresa Pasquale (2015), *Sacred Wounds: A Path to Healing from Spiritual Trauma*, Chalice Press; Carol Merritt (2018), *Healing Spiritual Wounds*, HarperOne; Marlene Winell (2006), *Leaving the Fold: A Guide for Former Fundamentalists and Others Leaving Their Religion*, Apocryphile Press.
68. https://www.religioustraumainstitute.com/, https://www.religioustrauma.gcrr.org/certification _enroll, https://www.reclamationcollective.com/.
69. Sarah McCammon (2024), *The Exvangelicals: Loving, Living, and Leaving the White Evangelical Church*, St. Martin's Press.
70. The debates around the role of politics for evangelicals are legion. Issues of race relations were prominent in the Promise Keepers movement of the 1990s (John Bartkowski [2004], *The Promise Keepers*, Rutgers University Press; Daniel Silliman [2021, June 21], "Promise Keepers Tried to End Racism 25 Years Ago. It Almost Worked," *Christianity Today*) and stirred up by critiques, such as Michael Emerson and Christian Smith (2000), *Divided by Faith*, Oxford University Press; and Brad Christerson, Michael Emerson, and Korie Edwards (2005), *Against All Odds: The Struggle for Racial Integration in Religious Organizations*, New York University Press.
71. Evangelical egalitarians and "complementarians" had, since the 1970s, disputed "the biblical role of women in the church and family." The purity culture experience shifted the focus and raised the stakes to a new level.
72. See, for example, Kristin Du Mez (2020), *Jesus and John Wayne*, Liveright; Jacob Cook (2021), *Worldview Theory, Whiteness, and the Future of Evangelical Faith*, Fortress; Constantine Campbell (2023), *Jesus v. Evangelicals*, Zondervan; Jon Ward (2023), *Testimony: Inside the Evangelical Movement That Failed a Generation*, Brazos; Marla Taviano (2022), *Jaded: A Poetic Reckoning with White Evangelical Christian Indoctrination*, Lake Drive Books; Randall Balmer (2021), *Bad Faith*, Eerdmans.
73. Nancy Ammerman (1990), *Baptist Battles*, Rutgers University Press.
74. Barry Hankins (2021, June 29), "America's Evangelical Church Is Being Torn Apart by Culture Wars," *The Guardian*.
75. The 48% positive Millennial interpretation of denominational fighting was likely bolstered by the question's inclusion of the focusing phrase, "like gender and LGBTQ issues." Some proportion of those "good" answers reflect an approval of religion on the specific issue of finally coming to terms with and correcting itself on issues of equality and affirmation across gender and sexual differences—on the assumption that the progressive side will eventually win, which most Millennials will take for granted, given their living through the rapid sea change in public opinion and law examined in the previous chapter.

Chapter 9

1. Robert Ellwood (1997), *The Fifties Spiritual Marketplace*, Rutgers University Press.
2. Daniel Bell (1976), *The Cultural Contradictions of Capitalism*, Basic Books, 134.
3. "A zeitgeist will affect some parts of social and geographical space and not others, and it will extend across social and geographical space to different degrees of intensity. Social space has different dimensions to it: we would expect a zeitgeist to affect some social groups . . . some . . . and some fields more than other" (Kraus [2019],"What Is Zeitgeist? Examining Period-Specific Cultural Patterns," *Poetics* 76: 6).
4. Cultural or movement "carriers" is a term from Max Weber describing specific demographic groups or types of people who tend to embrace, champion, embody, or represent particular trends or movements of cultural innovations or developments.

5. Winfrey is the exceptional Baby Boomer whose greatest cultural influence was in the 1990s and 2000s and on US spirituality culture.
6. https://www.christianpost.com/news/pamela-anderson-says-she-once-wanted-to-be-a-nun.html.
7. Janet Lowe (2001), *Oprah Winfrey Speaks*, Wiley & Sons, 122; https://www.celebinvestigator.com/jennifer-aniston/; https://www.learnreligions.com/why-julia-roberts-became-a-hindu-1769989; https://www.theguardian.com/music/2009/mar/02/snoop-dogg-nation-islam; https://en.wikipedia.org/wiki/Snoop_Dogg#:~:text=In%202012%2C%20after%20a%20trip,Jamaican%20experience%20in%20early%202013; https://www.cheatsheet.com/entertainment/what-religion-is-robert-downey-jr.html/.
8. See Thomas Shevory (1995), "Bleached Resistance: The Politics of Grunge," *Popular Music & Society* 19: 23–48; Karen Halnon (2005), "Alienation Incorporated: 'F the Mainstream Music' in the Mainstream," *Current Sociology* 53: 441–464; Seth Kahn (2000), "Kurt Cobain, Martyrdom, and the Problem of Agency," *Studies in Popular Culture* 22: 83–96; Mark Mazullo (2000), "The Man Whom the World Sold: Kurt Cobain, Rock's Progressive Aesthetic, and the Challenges of Authenticity," *The Musical Quarterly* 84: 713–755.
9. The song was never filmed as an MTV-style video, so only the audio can be studied.
10. Watch among the options the "Holymetalrob TV CCM:Channel" 5:12-length version.
11. Even the keys these songs were recorded in reflect their moods: the two CCM hits are in major keys, while "Smells . . . " is in F minor.
12. All song lyrics and a short bio of Nirvana's Kurt Cobain—who as a teen had become a born-again, church-attending Christian only later to renounce his faith—can be downloaded as Appendix C at https://global.oup.com/us/companion.websites/9780197800737/appendix/.
13. Naomi Quinn (ed.) (2005), *Finding Culture in Talk*, Palgrave Macmillan; Claudia Strauss and Naomi Quinn (1997), *A Cognitive Theory of Cultural Meaning*, Cambridge University Press; Roy D'Andrade and Claudia Strauss (1992), *Human Motives and Cultural Models*, Cambridge University Press; Giovanni Bennardo and Victor de Munck (2014), *Cultural Models*, Oxford University Press; Dorothy Holland and Naomi Quinn (1987), *Cultural Models in Language and Thought*, Cambridge University Press.
14. Discourse is "the best available window into cultural understandings and the way that these are negotiated by individuals. Culture in this sense of understanding encompasses the largely tacit . . . assumptions that people share with others in their group and carry around inside them, and draw upon in forming expectations, reasoning, telling stories, and performing a plethora of other ordinary everyday cognitive tasks. . . . Cultural analysis, then, refers to the effort to tease out, from discourse, the cultural meanings that underlie it" (Quinn, *Finding Culture*, 3, 4).
15. Allison Pugh (2013), "What Good Are Interviews for Thinking About Culture?" *American Journal of Cultural Sociology* 1: 42–68.
16. See Christian Smith, Bridget Ritz, and Michael Rotolo (2019), *Religious Parenting*, Princeton University Press, chapter 5.
17. It should go without saying that the following is meant to be descriptive and analytical, not normatively evaluative—different readers, holding their own cultural commitments, will have different judgments about the truth or value of these beliefs, but the sociological task here is simply to describe those beliefs well.
18. Our interviews, however, produced many more similar quotes, available in the aforementioned online PDF document for download and further study at https://global.oup.com/us/companion.websites/9780197800737/appendix/.
19. For readers younger than 40, yes, there was a time, for better or worse, when most Americans tended to trust authorities.
20. For a good exploration of American individualism's relationship to community, see Claude Fischer (2008), "Paradoxes of American Individualism," *Sociological Forum* 23: 363–372.
21. Derek Thompson (2024, April 3), "The True Cost of the Churchgoing Bust: Many Americans Seem to Have Found No Alternative Method to Build a Sense of Community," *The Atlantic*.
22. My research in the latter 2000s, when many Millennials were teenagers and younger emerging adults, showed that 75% of them disagreed with the statement, "For believers to be truly religious and spiritual, they need to be involved in a religious congregation," an 8% increase over what the same (teenage only) sample had said five years earlier; see Christian Smith, with Patricia Snell (2009), *Souls in Transition*, Oxford University Press, 135.
23. Following Christopher Partridge (2004), *The Re-Enchantment of the West*, T&T Clark.

24. Besides what I present here, I have a great deal of additional survey, interview, and other evidence to validate and elaborate the argument that spirituality and occulture have emerged to stake out major positions on the cultural field of beliefs and interests, rivalling both traditional religion and secularism. Those additional data and analyses are too much to fit into this book, however, so I will follow the little I present here with a separate book dedicated to making sense of this movement of re-enchantment. Consider Table 9.1 a preview of an elaborate, separate exploration to follow in a separate volume.
25. "Making Love to Music," in *D. H. Lawrence: Late Essays and Articles*, Volume 2, Cambridge University Press, 42.

Chapter 10

1. Two cautions to keep in mind: while we sampled these interview respondents from a nationally representative survey, the sample sizes of three of the four religious categories are not large, and the religious types are not sampled for interviews in proportion to their size in the population.
2. Most of the empty cells are due to relatively low *N*s in some column categories, which would fill out some with larger numbers of interviews conducted in those categories.
3. See Nancy Ammerman (2013), *Sacred Stories, Spiritual Tribes*, Oxford University Press
4. Evident here is postmodernism's general skepticism about metanarratives and aversion to embracing any set of constructive beliefs, and, simultaneously and ironically, a kind of quasi-verificationism, whereby if no religion is totally true then all religions must be rejected (as opposed to a fallibilist frame that acknowledges all human belief systems as incomplete and imperfect but at least some are nonetheless potentially warranted as embodying some or much truth).
5. Michael Lipka (2016, August 24), "Why America's 'Nones' Left Religion Behind," Pew Research Center.
6. Christian Smith and Amy Adamczyk (2021), *Handing Down the Faith*, Oxford University Press, chapter 3.
7. Jessica Grose (2023, June 7). "Why Do People Lose Their Religion? More than 7,000 Readers Shared Their Stories," *New York Times*.
8. Other similar investigations are worth considering, including David Kinnaman and Aly Hawkins (2011), *You Lost Me*, Baker; Phil Zuckerman (2012), *Faith No More: Why People Reject Religion*, Oxford University Press; Brandon Flanery (2022, December 13), "I Asked People Why They're Leaving Christianity and Here's What I Heard," *Baptist News*; Jim Davis and Michael Graham (2023), *The Great Dechurching*, Zondervan.
9. George Johnson (2017), "What Will the Jewish World Look Like in 2050?" *Moment Magazine*, Jewish Education Ventures.
10. Christian Smith and Melinda Denton (2005), *Soul Searching*, Oxford University Press, chapter 2; Christian Smith, with Patricia Snell (2009), *Souls in Transition*, Oxford University Press, 109.
11. Theodore Sasson, Janet Aronson, Fern Chertok, Charles Kadushin, and Leonard Saxe (2017), "Millennial Children of Intermarriage," *Contemporary Jewry* 37: 99–123.
12. American Jewish Committee, "AJC's Survey of American Jewish Millennials."
13. Ariela Keysar and Sergio DellaPergola (2019, May 6), "Demographic and Religious Dimensions of Jewish Identification in the U.S. and Israel," *Journal of Religion and Demography* 6: 149–188; Barna (2017), *Jewish Millennials*, Barna Group.
14. Barna, *Jewish Millennials*, 6, 95.
15. Benjamin Phillips (n.d.), "National Jewish Population Survey: 1990—Fifty-two Percent Intermarriage Rate Shocks Community," *My Jewish Learning*.
16. Sasson et al., "Millennial Children," 102–103. Also see Shual Kelner (2010), *Tours That Bind*, New York University Press; Jennifer MacLeod (2019), *Building a Better Birthright*, Safer Editions; https://www.birthrightisrael.com/about-us.
17. Dana Kaplan (2011), *American Reform Judaism*, Rutgers University Press; Samira Mehta and Brett Krutzsch (2020), "The Changing Jewish Family: Jewish Communal Responses to Interfaith and Same-Sex Marriage," *American Jewish History* 104: 553–577; Sasson et al., "Millennial Children."
18. Leonard Saxe (2014, December 3), "The Sky Is Falling! The Sky Is Falling!" *Tablet*; https://www.brandeis.edu/cmjs/birthright/publications.html.
19. For example, Lauren Markoe (2015, June 12), "US Jewish Numbers No Longer Declining, but Demographic Worries Persist," *Washington Post*; Arnold Dashefsky (2021), "A Half-Century (1970–2020) of the Social Scientific Study of Jewry," *Contemporary Jewry* 41: 289–312; Erin

Potts, Roger Bennett, Rachel Levin, and Stacy Abramson (2006), "'Grande Soy Vanilla Latte with Cinnamon, No Foam...' Jewish Identity and Community in a Time of Unlimited Choices," *Reboot*; Johnson, "What Will the Jewish World Look Like."
20. That said, during the time of final edits on this chapter a highly controversial war has broken out between Israel and Palestinian Gaza, the results of which, for this book's concerns, are at present anyone's guess.
21. To be clear, my limited finding about Jewish Millennials does not address their levels of commitment to *religious* Judaism, simply their lower rates of adopting not-religious identities.
22. One data point: I twice interviewed in the 2000s a teenager who had a Jewish mother and Protestant father; she was greatly affected by her Birthright Israel experience. When I first interviewed her in 2003, she was in high school and a self-professed moral relativist who, besides fighting a lot with her mother about Jewish observances, conceded as a self-described relativist that "if you lived in Germany in the 1930s you would believe Hitler was right, and who am I to say otherwise?" Five years later, having traveled to Israel and by then in college, the same young woman told me that her Israel trip had impressed her greatly and she was happy to embrace her Jewish heritage and observances and take them more seriously. Note, however, that, as of this writing, Israel is immersed in a war in Gaza in response to the Hamas terrorist attacks of October 2023. Any long-term effects on American Jewish connections to Israel are impossible to predict.
23. But see Presbyterian Heritage Tours, https://reformationtours.com/package/presbyterianheritagetour/. Emblematically, the grave of Reformer John Knox is buried under Bay Number 23 in a parking lot of the law court building in Edinburgh, Scotland. Maybe better, then, for Protestants to send their youth to Israel at least to see "where Jesus walked" than to visit particular heritage sites in Europe disconnected from the present by centuries of secularization.
24. "A little anti-Semitism, or at least anxiety about it, can go a long way in ensuring the Jewish future. In some ways, being loved to death via assimilation, as we have been in America, is more dangerous than being hated," observed Samuel Heilman, professor of sociology at Queens College, CUNY (in Johnson, "What Will the Jewish World Look Like").
25. C. Eric Lincoln and Lawrence Mamiya (1990), *The Black Church in the African American Experience*, Duke University Press; Henry Louis Gates Jr. (2021), *The Black Church*, Penguin; E. Franklin Frazier and C. Eric Lincoln (1974), *The Negro Church in America/The Black Church Since Frazier*, Schocken; Christopher Ellison and Darren Sherkat (1995), "The 'Semi-involuntary Institution' Revisited," *Social Forces* 73: 1415–1437.
26. Aldon Morris (1986), *The Origins of the Civil Rights Movement*, Free Press. Also see Shaonta Allen (2019), "Doing Black Christianity," *Sociology Compass* 13: 1–15.
27. Khari Brown, Robert Taylor, and Linda Chatters (2015), "Race/Ethnic and Social-Demographic Correlates of Religious Non-Involvement in America," *Journal of Black Studies* 46: 335–362.
28. Besheer Mohamed, Kiana Cox, Jeff Diamant, and Claire Gecewicz (2021, February 16), "Faith Among Black Americans," Pew Research Center; also see William Cooper and Rahul Mitra (2018), "Religious Disengagement and Stigma Management by African-American Young Adults," *Journal of Applied Communication Research* 46: 509–533.
29. Sandra Barnes (2023), "'Maybe I Need Christ or Maybe I Just Need Me,'" *Religions* 14: 1–20.
30. Shaonta Allen (2023), "Is the Black Church Dead?" *Religions* 14: 1–21; Rhys Williams, Courtney Irby, and Stephen Warner (2016), "'Church' in Black and White," *Religions* 7: 1–19; Keon McGuire (2018), "Religion's Afterlife," *Journal of Diversity in Higher Education* 11: 309–324; PBS (2021, July 23), "Millennials and Church," American Black Journal.
31. Brianna Parker (2018), *What Google Can't Give: The Relevancy of the Church for Black Millennials in the Tech Age*, Black Millennial Café; Erika Gault (2022), *Networking the Black Church*, New York University Press; Joshua Mitchell (2018), *Black Millennials and the Church*, Judson Press; Jacque Trim (2023), "The Mass Exodus of Black Millennials from the Black Church," Doctoral dissertation, George Fox University; Joy Challenger (2016), "Infused: Millennials and the Future of the Black Church," DMin. dissertation, Duke Divinity School; among many other graduate theses and dissertations.
32. Smith with Denton, *Soul Searching*, chapter 2.
33. Amorette Hinderaker (2020), "Leaving Mormonism," in Daniel Enstedt, Göran Larsson, and Teemu Mantsinen (eds.), *Handbook of Leaving Religion*, Brill, chapter 16; Hallie Golden (2017, April 13), "Why It's Not Easy Becoming an Ex-Mormon," *The Daily Beast*.
34. Jana Riess (2019, March 27), "How Many Millennials Are Really Leaving the LDS Church?" Religion News Service; Pew Research Center (2015, May 12), "America's Changing Religious Landscape," Pew Research Center.

35. Sadie Slikker (2019, June 26), "Are LDS Millennials Losing Their Faith?" *The Globe*; Eric Nelson (2016, January 12), "Leaving the Church," Personal manuscript; Ercan Koç (2023), "'I Don't Want the Church If the Church Doesn't Want Me,'" Master's thesis, Arctic University of Norway; Hannah Miet (2014, January 31), "When the Saints Go Marching Out," *Newsweek Magazine*; Emma Penrod (2020, April 20), "Growth in the LDS Church Is Slowing," *Religion Unplugged*; Katherine Taylor (2018, March 20), "Crossing Borders," Utah Public Radio; Hinderaker, "Leaving Mormonism."
36. Jana Riess (2019), *The Next Mormons*, Oxford University Press, 225.
37. Marissa Wenzke (2017, September 26), "How the Ex-Mormon Community Has Found a Home on Reddit," *Mashable*.
38. Hinderaker, "Leaving Mormonism," 200; also see truthandtransparency.org.
39. Paul Glader (2023, February 28), "Whistleblower Details New Allegations About $100 Billion LDS Fund," *Religion Unplugged*.
40. Rosemary Avance (2013), "Seeing the Light: Mormon Conversion and Deconversion Narratives in Off- and Online Worlds," *Journal of Media and Religion* 12: 16–24; Pauline Cheong and Megan Fisk (2013, October 31), "Leaving Church: Resisting Mormon Authority and Community in Online-Offline Dimensions," *AoIR Selected Papers of Internet Research*.
41. Jana Riess, quoted in Penrod, "Growth in the LDS Church."
42. Both quoted in Nicole Spearman (2023, March 24), "Gen Zers Leaving LDS Faith Find Community on Social Apps Like TikTok," *The Salt Lake Tribune*.
43. Hinderaker, "Leaving Mormonism," 207. See Nelson, "Leaving the Church"; William Barlow (2020, March 30), "Why My Generation Is Leaving the Church," *Times and Seasons*. For older Mormons' exit testimonies: Diana Ragsdale (2022, June 6), "It Took Leaving My Strict Religion at Age 57 to Realize That I Deserved Happiness," Today.com; Corey Miller, Lynn Wilder, Vince Eccles, and Latayne Scott (2017), *Leaving Mormonism*, Kregel Publications.
44. E. Marshall Brooks (2018), *Disenchanted Lives: Apostasy and Ex-Mormonism Among the Latter-Day Saints*, Rutgers University Press.
45. Seth Payne (2013), "Ex-Mormon Narratives and Pastoral Apologetics," *Dialogue*, 85–121; E. Marshall Brooks (2020), "The Disenchanted Self: Anthropological Notes on Existential Distress and Ontological Insecurity Among Ex-Mormons in Utah," *Culture, Medicine, and Psychiatry* 44: 193–213; J. Todd Ormsbee (2020), "'Like a Cord Snapping': Toward a Grounded Theory of How Devout Mormons Leave the LDS Church," *Critical Research on Religion* 8: 297–317; Kristina Scharp and Aubrey Beck (2017), "'Losing My Religion'—Identity (Re)constructions in Mormon Exit Narratives," *Narrative Inquiry* 27: 132–148; Ryan Gottfredson (2017, July 31), "An LDS Leader's Guide to Millennial Mormons," *Leading Saints*.
46. https://www.reddit.com/r/exmormon/comments/cdhi23/from_an_lds_source_one_study_h as_shown_that_55_of/?rdt=38699.
47. Ines Jindra and Justin Lee (2023), "Negotiating Leaving Religion, Family Relationships, and Identity: the Case of LDS Faith Transitions," *Clinical Social Work Journal* 51: 1–11.
48. Quoted in Penrod, "Growth in the LDS Church."

Conclusion

1. Forty years ago, in 1985, Berkeley sociologist Robert Bellah (and colleagues) warned in their book, *Habits of the Heart: Individualism and Commitment in American Life*, that individualism threatened to overrun American culture and choke off its other vital streams. Bellah observed that American culture is woven of four major traditions: the biblical, republican, expressive individualist, and utilitarian individualist traditions. Each, he argued, is quite different from and relates uneasily to the others, giving the larger culture a dynamic energy and creativity. Bellah was troubled, however, that utilitarian and expressive individualism were progressively stifling the biblical and republican traditions, impoverishing American civic and moral life. Bellah's analysis stressed the importance of cultural *discourse*, highlighting how the languages Americans use to talk about life and society enable and constrain our cultural imaginations and practices. Bellah was no postmodernist, but his emphasis on language and discourse fit well with that era's ascendant pomo fascination with "discursive formations." *Habits of the Heart* touched a sensitive nerve and sparked widespread discussion and debate. None of that, however, changed the force of what Bellah saw happening. Utilitarian and expressive individualism continued their takeover of American culture in the decades since. Traditional religion's obsolescence was, viewed through Bellah's lens, a significant advance in that larger takeover. Bellah's analysis was not incorrect, I think, but his privileging of discourse might have been misleading.

Readers could easily come away from *Habits* with the impression that, if Americans could only learn to tap into and confidently express the *languages* of the biblical and republican traditions, then cultural health and civic life might be restored. (In fact, to be clear, despite being fundamentally Durkheimian, Bellah also took institutions—especially capitalism—very seriously. For example, Bellah [1998], "Is There a Common American Culture?" *Journal of the American Academy of Religion* 66: 613–625).
2. One example: Stanley Hauerwas and William Willimon wrote presciently in 1989 about American Christians as "resident aliens" in a fundamentally post-Christian culture, but—despite talking about politics and lifestyles—their constructive proposals suffered from a "theological idealism" centered on the need to *think correctly* about ethics in light of "the true story" (*Resident Aliens: Life in the Christian Colony*, Abingdon Press). Stanley once told me he "does not believe in sociology." His prescriptions in that book suffer precisely from the lack of it.
3. Regarding "beyond doubt," see Isabella Kasselstrand, Phil Zuckerman, and Ryan Cragun (2023), *Beyond Doubt: The Secularization of Society*, New York University Press; David Martin has this right all along.
4. Christian Smith and Amy Adamczyk (2021), *Handing Down the Faith*, Oxford University Press, 117–160; Christian Smith, Bridget Ritz, and Michael Rotolo (2019), *Religious Parenting*, Princeton University Press.
5. Christian Smith, with Patricia Snell (2009), *Souls in Transition*, Oxford University Press, 140.

Appendix

1. As a reminder, the samples here are for all American adults surveyed across these decades—meaning that, since they represent a wide range of ages in each survey, this variable does not indicate their having been raised in these religions during the decade analyzed, but rather being an adult surveyed in that decade who had been raised in those religious traditions, however previously long before. Thus, for example, adults in the 1990s who were raised Black Protestant could have been so anytime between the 1930s and the 1980s, depending on their age.
2. All models include a dummy variable for having lived in a foreign country at age 16, the results of which, however, are not reported here because they are not related to my argument.
3. The religion-at-age-16 variable was not asked in 1971 or 2021, so the range of GSS years in analyses using that variable is 1973–2018.
4. See, for example, Christian Smith and Melinda Denton (2005), *Soul Searching*, Oxford University Press, chapter 2.
5. Jana Riess (2019), *The Next Mormons: How Millennials Are Changing the LDS Church*, Oxford University Press.

Index

For the benefit of digital users, indexed terms that span two pages (e.g., 52–53) may, on occasion, appear on only one of those pages.

4Him, 318
700 Club, 118–19, 120

Abbott, Andrew, 69–70, 116, 222
abortion, 214, 268–69
Abu Ghraib, 209, 282
adoption of innovations, 67–68
advertising, 88–89, 365–66
Afghanistan, 209–10
age of first marriage, 393–94n.70
AIDS epidemic, 262
al Qaeda, 174
Albrecht, Ritschl, 109
American Dream, 214–18, 308–9, 311
American National Election Survey (ANES), 410n.91
AmeriSpeak, National Opinion Research Center (NORC), 13–14, 15–16
Ammerman, Nancy, 36–37
analytical model, 297–98
Anderson, Pamela, 288, 289–91
Animals, the, 90
Aristotle, 259
Arnett, Jeffrey, 97–98
Association for Religious Data Archives (ARDA), 31
astrology, 3, 331, 334
atheism, atheists, 227–28, 316–17, 319, 324, 330, 337, 351
Augustine, Saint, 89–90
auras, 328
authenticity, 91, 300, 301
avalanche science, 61–62

Bakker, Jim and Tammy Faye, 118–19
Baldwin, James, 373
Baptists, 290, 325, 344, 355–56, 359
Baudrillard, Jean, 152–53t, 159
Beastie Boys, the, 393n.59
Beat Generation, 62, 90, 280

Beatles, the, 62, 121, 280
Bellah, Robert, 207, 418–19n.1
Belz, Joel, 33
Benny, Jack, 118
Berger, Peter, 155–56
Berlin Wall, 128–29
Bieber, Justin, 289–90
Billy Graham Rule, 411–12n.25
bin Laden, Osama, 175
birth control, 101–2, 183–84
Birthright Israel, 355, 417n.22
Black Protestant Millennials, 356–60
Black Protestantism, 2–3, 16, 31–32, 38, 339, 353
body piercings, 284
Bon Jovi, 393n.59
booty call, 185
The Boston Globe, 241
Bowman, Matthew, 363
Branch Davidian, 239–40
Brigham Young University, 362–63
Buddhism, 3–4, 45–46, 121, 183, 201, 325, 351–52
Burge, Ryan, 412n.39
Burning Man, 303–4
Bush, George H. W., 128–29
Bush, George W., 1, 173–74, 209–10, 213, 263, 282, 285
Butler, Judith, 191–92

cable television, 285–86, 365–66
carriers, of movements, 414n.4
Carter, Jimmy, 34, 129–30, 280–81
Catholic schools, 32, 105–6, 348
The Catholic Standard and Times, 114–15
Center for Sex Positive Culture, 187
Chabad campus organizations, 355
chakras, 325, 329
Chaves, Mark, 23–24, 26
Christian Broadcasting Network (CBN), 118–19

The Christian Century, 110–11
Christian Coalition, the, 119–20, 281
Christian Right, the, 58, 119–20, 205, 240–41, 250, 253–54, 296, 388n.33
Christianity Today, 110–12t, 114–15, 255
church closings, 31–32, 33
Church of England, 52–53
civil rights movement, 62, 119, 163–64
clergy honesty and ethics, 35–36, 36f
climate anxiety and grief, 211, 408n.64
Clinton, Bill, 130, 195, 208–9, 213, 281–82, 408n.62
Cobain, Kurt, 287–88, 415n.8
cognitive anthropology, 297–98
cognitive pluralism, 142–43
cohabitation, 77–78
Cohen, Michael, 240–41
Cold War, 18, 55–56, 95, 114–15, 119, 128, 172–73, 200–1, 280–81, 284, 287–88, 380–81
college majors, 399n.19
Columbine High School massacre, 281–82, 287–88
community, 84, 133, 135, 165–66, 314, 315, 320–21, 355
confidence in religion, 33, 34
consensual non-monogamy, 190–91
Contemporary Christian Music, 295
Cooke, Ellen, 237
COVID-19, 28, 31–32, 40, 215, 315, 346t, 386n.4, 387n.14
Crawford, Percy, 118–19
critical mass, 66, 365
crowding out, 68–69, 169–70
crystals, 329–30
cultural mismatch, 8, 62–64, 93, 138, 274–75
cultural models, 8, 44, 297–98
cultural wars, 210, 284, 285
culture, defined, 7–10

The Dallas Morning News, 230
Darwinism, 259, 397n.67
Davie, Grace, 52–53
Dawkins, Richard, 178–80t, 182–83
deep culture, 9–10, 124
DeGeneres, Ellen, 195
deinstitutionalization of marriage and family, 76–82, 125–26
Demerath, Jay, 102–3, 109–10
demythologizing Christianity, 108
Dennett, Daniel, 178–80t, 182
denominational battles, 205, 267–71t
depression, despair, 63, 69, 146, 208–14, 270
Derrida, Jacques, 152–53t

Dewey, John, 402n.67
Dickson White, Andrew, 122–23
digital revolution, 138–49, 172, 190, 243, 262
distrust of institutions, 305–6, 315, 322, 336
divorce, 79–80, 119, 262–63, 268–69, 340, 348
Dot.com bubble burst, 210, 214–15, 282, 287–88
Draper, John William, 122–23
Dungeons & Dragons, 287
Durkheim, Emile, 207, 418–19n.1

Eastern religions, 121, 325, 327
Eck, Diana, 200–2, 406n.42
Edwards, Jonathan, 109–10
Eisenhower, Dwight, 55–57, 116, 119, 280
emergent church movement, 261–62
emerging adulthood, 96–99, 125–26
emo, 281–82, 287, 308–9
Enlightenment, 73, 89–90, 369
Epstein, Greg, 220
esoteric, 3, 143–44, 308–9, 325, 331, 335
ethical non-monogamy, 188, 194
Europe, 1, 57, 120, 282, 398n.7
Every Man's Battle, 263–64
expressive individualism, 89–93, 125–26, 252, 365–66, 418–19n.1
exvangelical movement, 266

Facebook, 138, 144
Faith and Family in America Survey, 223–24
Faith Communities Today survey, 32–33
Falwell, Jerry Jr., 240–41
Falwell, Jerry Sr., 118–20, 249–50, 254, 412n.43, 412n.44
Family Research Council, 281
fear of missing out (FOMO), 317
Federal Council of Churches, 118
financial crisis of 2008–2009, 210, 282
Fosdick, Harry Emerson, 109
Foucault, Michel, 152–53t, 159, 399n.24
foundationalism, epistemological, 258–59, 262
Freud, Sigmund, 73, 183–84
Freundel, Barry, 237–38
friends with benefits, 184, 194
Fuller, Charles, 117–18
fundamentalism, 248–49, 268, 272

Gallup Organization, 16, 33, 34–36, 125, 198
gay rights, 119, 163–64, 343
General Social Survey (GSS), 16, 23, 24–26, 28, 30–31, 33–34, 83, 125, 223–24, 360–61, 375, 386n.4, 387n.15
geographical mobility, 135–36, 165–67t, 315

Girls Gone Wild, 194
Gleason, Philip, 103–4
global warming, 210–11
Golden Rule, 45
good life, 89, 304–5
good without God, 218–23, 228
Gore, Al, 210
goth, 281, 292, 308–9
GQ magazine, 245–46
Graham, Billy, 56, 117–19, 248–50, 252, 256, 260
Granda, Giancarlo, 240–41
Great Depression, the, 73–74, 86, 95, 129–30, 215
Great Recession, the, 18, 97, 210, 215–16, 282, 292, 398n.7
Grose, Jessica, 351–52
grunge, 281–82, 285–87, 290–92, 294–95, 308–9

Habits of the Heart, 418–19n.1
Haggard, Ted, 245–46
Hamilton, Michael, 249–50
Harris, Joshua, 264–65
Harris, Sam, 178–80, 182–83
Hauerwas, Stanley, 419n.2
Hegel, Georg W.F., 11
hell, 48–49, 110, 111–12, 238–39, 269, 271–72, 341*t*, 359
Henry, Carl F.H., 117, 248–51, 252
Hermann, Wilhelm, 109
Herzog, Jonathan, 57
higher education, 73–75, 98, 183–84
Hillel campus organizations, 355
Hinduism, 3–4, 45–46, 121, 201
hip-hop, 292
hipsters, 90, 292, 367–68
historical tradition, 313–14
Hitchens, Christopher, 178–80*t*, 182
hooking up, 187–89, 193, 194, 296–97
Hout, Mike, 31
Humanae Vitae, 106–7
Humbard, Rex, 118–19
Hunter, James, D., 285
Hurricane Katrina, 210, 287–88
hustle culture, 308–9, 310
hypocrisy, 120, 323, 341*t*, 346*t*, 348, 358, 359, 367–68

I Kissed Dating Goodbye, 264–65
identity politics, 208, 365–66
Im, Daniel, 31–32
Immigration and Nationality Act of 1965, 121, 200–1

inerrancy, 259–60, 268–69
Inglehart, Ronald, 94–96, 393n.64
intensive parenting, 168–70, 403–4n.82
invasion of Iraq, 209–10, 282
iPhone(s), 138, 282
Islam, 3–4, 173–74, 325
Islamic State, 209
Israel, 119–20
Israel and Palestine conflict, 210, 268–69

Jainism, 3–4, 121
James, William, 402n.67
Jewish Millennials, 353–56, 379, 417n.21
Jim Crow segregation, 204
Judaism, Jewish, 3–4, 49, 55–56, 137, 200–1, 325, 356–57, 359–60
Judeo-Christian, 55–56, 200–1

karma, 121, 327
King, Rodney, 284
kink-shaming, 187
Koresh, David, 239–40, 411n.20
Krause, Monika, 10–12, 19, 285–86, 414n.3
Kruse, Kevin, 56
Kuhn, Thomas, 158

L'Abri, 249
L'Arche, 240
Lareau, Annette, 404n.83
Lawrence, D.H., 337
leaving religion, reasons, 345–52
Lewinsky, Monica scandal, 281–82, 288, 408n.62
LGBTQ+, 192, 194–200, 245–46, 268–69, 270, 341*t*, 346*t*–40, 348, 359–60, 361, 414n.75
liberal Protestantism, 406n.41
Liberty University, 240–41
Lifeway Research, 31–32
Lindberg, David, 122–23
Lindsell, Harold, 259–60
loneliness, 63, 140–41, 372
Luckmann, Thomas, 155–56
Lundgren, Jeffrey, 238
Lyons, Henry, 236–37
Lyotard, Jean-Francois, 152–53*t*, 159

magic, 3, 284, 329, 332*t*, 334, 368–69
Maharishi Mahesh Yogi, 121
mainline Protestant decline, 100–3
Mannheim, Karl, 11
Mapplethorpe, Robert, 290–91
Martin, Edward, Pennsylvania Senator, 55–56
Marx, Karl, 128, 365

mass consumerism, 85–89, 98, 125–26, 293, 336
Matthew Shepard Hate Crimes and Prevention Act, 195
McConnell, Scott, 31–32
McCready, Bo, 5–6
McDowell, Josh, 259–60
McVeigh, Timothy, 411n.21
Meador, Jake, 137
me-and-God spirituality, 254–58
meditation, 37–38, 146, 329, 401–2n.56
Meeker, Meg, 185–87
membership organizations, declines in, 125–26
Menand, Louis, 51–52
Millennial Zeitgeist Survey, 41–42, 115–16, 135, 139–40, 162–63, 192–93, 206–7, 211, 217, 246–47, 270, 330–31, 403n.73
mindfulness, 37–38, 146, 401–2n.56
mission drift, evangelical, 248–54
modeling (religion as a source of), 52–53
moderation (religion as a source of), 54–55
modernist-fundamentalist split, 111
Mont Pelerin Society, 130
Moral Majority, the, 119–20, 250, 281
moral panic, 185–87
moralistic therapeutic deism (MTD), 388n.2
morality (religion as a source of), 44–47
moralizing religion, 107–16
Morissette, Alanis, 184
Mormon, Mormonism (LDS church), 2–3, 4, 144, 238–39, 286, 319, 353, 379–80
Mormon Millennials, 360–63, 379–80
MormonLeaks, 362
MTV, 287, 290–91
multiculturalism, 163–64, 285–86, 336
Muslims, 201, 216–17, 318
Mutual Radio Network, 118

National Association of Evangelicals, 100
National Baptist Convention, 236–37
National Council of Churches, 100
national identity, religion and, 200–7
National Jewish Population Survey, 355
National solidarity (religion as a source of), 55–59
Native American, 55, 325, 327
nature as sacred, 312
neoliberalism, 90–91, 129–38, 165, 168–69, 172, 190–91, 315, 365–66, 398n.7
Netflix, 40, 141–42
networks, 148, 149
New Age, 3–4, 90, 121, 328, 331
New Atheism, 178–83, 208, 219, 243, 267, 405n.8

New World Order, 128–29, 173, 281–82
Next Mormon Survey, 360–61
Nichols, Terry, 411n.21
Niebuhr, H. Richard, 109
Nielsen, Wendell Loy, 238
Nietzsche, Friedrich, 152–53
Nirvana, 285, 287–88, 294–95, 296, 322, 415n.12
Nixon, Richard, 129–30, 280–81
No Strings Attached, 184
not religious, the "nones," 1, 18, 30–31, 170, 171–72, 224, 226–28, 350t, 366, 368, 375
Novak, Michael, 400n.36
Numbers, Ronald, 121

Obama, Barack, 195, 213
obsolescence, defined, 2–7
occulture, occultic, 116, 284, 328, 330, 331, 335, 337, 368–69
Oklahoma, City bombing, 287–88, 411n.21
Olympic Park bombing, Atlanta, 238–39
OPEC oil embargo, 119
open marriage, 183–85
Operation Desert Storm, 285
Osama bin Laden, 175

Packer, J.I., 255
pagan, paganism, 3, 144, 284, 325, 328–29
paranormal, 3, 284, 328, 331
Parsons, Talcott, 388n.3
particulate matter, 64–65, 159–60, 182, 365
Peace Dividend, 128–29, 173, 281–82
Peirce, C.S., 402n.67
Personal-relationship-with-God discourse, 255–57, 322, 347
Pew Research Center, 16, 205, 223–24, 244–45, 349–50, 350t, 360–61, 407n.45
pietism, 257
Pink Floyd, 393n.59
Pinochet, Augusto, 131
The Pittsburgh Catholic, 114–15
Plantinga, Alvin, 402–3n.71
Pledge of Allegiance, 57
political polarization, 284, 315
polyamory, 185, 186f, 188, 193, 194
Pope John Paul II, 107
Pope Paul VI, 106
population ecology species decline, 60–61
pornography, 139, 190, 194, 262, 336
positive psychology (religion as a source of), 48–49, 321
postmaterialism, 94–96, 125–26, 365–66
postmodernism, 261–62, 281–82, 285–86, 366, 367–68, 403n.72, 416n.4, 418–19n.1

INDEX   425

Potter, Harry, 290–91
power hoarding Boomers, 272–75
precarity, 131–32, 282
Princess Dianna, 52–53
professional control over expert knowledge, 69–70
program idealism, 19–20, 367
psychological mobility, 84
punctuated equilibrium, 66–67
purity campaigns, 193–94, 262–67
Putnam, Robert, 84

R.E.M., 286
Rabin, Yitzhak, 281–82
rainbow party, 185–87
Rastafarianism, 290
Rauschenbusch, Walter, 402–3n.71
rave culture, 98, 292
Reagan Revolution, 26, 91, 95, 126
Reagan, Ronald, 57, 91, 95, 126, 130–31, 281, 400n.36
re-enchantment, 36–37, 330–35, 336, 369
Reinhard, Richard, 33
relativism, 124, 160–61, 162t, 164, 283
religion as a "concept," 116
religious abuse and scandals, 1, 35–36, 205, 210, 229–48, 281, 341t, 346t, 348, 412n.30
religious affiliation, 23–25
religious pluralism, 200–7
religious revival, 257–58, 369–70
Religious Right, the, 57, 95, 117–20, 125–26
religious service attendance, 26–27
religious trauma, 265, 266, 267, 372
religious turn-offs, 340–45
Riess, Jana, 360–61
Rinker, Rosalind, 255
Roaring Twenties, 11, 208–9, 282
Roberts, Oral, 118–19
Robertson, Pat, 118–19, 120, 249–50, 254
Robison, James, 118–19
Rogers, Everett, 67
Romanticism, 73, 90
Roosevelt, Franklin, 86
Roosevelt, Teddy, 129–30
Rorty, Richard, 157–59, 402n.68, 402–3n.71
Rousseau, Jean Jacques, 89–90
Rudolf, Eric, 238–39

sacralizing of partisan politics, 208
Saddam Hussein, 209
Saddleback Church, 38–39
Schaeffer, Francis, 249, 252
Schuller, Robert, 118–19

scientism, positivism, 11–12, 327, 330, 337
sci-fi, 327–28
Second Great Awakening, 257
secular humanism, 7, 249, 252
secularism, 219, 330, 335, 368–69
secularization theory, 2, 337–38, 369
Seinfeld, 285
selfies, 290–91
September 11, 9/11, 2001, 18, 124, 173–78, 181, 209, 213, 214–15, 226, 267, 282, 287–88, 412n.44
Serrano, Andres, 290–91
Servicemen's Readjustment Act of 1944, 74
Seventh-Day Adventist Church, 239–40
Sex in The City, 188, 290–91
sex positivity, 187, 188, 191–92
Shapin, Stephen, 122–23
Shepard, Matthew, 195, 287–88
Sikhism, 3–4, 121, 201
Silver Ring Thing (SRT), 263
situationships, 185
Sixties, the, 11
slut-shaming, 187–88
Smells Like Teen Spirit, 294–96
Smith, Tom, 31
Social Capital Project, 83
social constructionism, 155–56, 160–61, 402n.66
social media, 39, 140–41, 213, 308, 315, 365–66
sociological realism, 337, 365, 367
South, the, 167, 341, 375, 377–79
Southern Baptist Convention (SBC), 231–36, 239–40, 244, 263, 268, 344
Soviet Union, 57, 119, 128, 130, 280–82
spiral of silence, 142–43
spiritual abuse, 266–67, 372
spiritual but not religious, 1, 31, 223–26
spiritual, spirituality, 40, 116, 143–44, 146, 219, 297, 311, 327–29, 330, 331, 335, 337, 346t, 347, 350–51, 366, 368–69
Stephens, Jason, 55–56
Stetzer, Ed, 31–32
styles of attire, 291–93
sugar baby/sugar daddy relationships, 188–89, 194
Swaggart, Jimmy, 118–19
syncretism, 326

tarot cards, 334
Taylor, Charles, 89–90
Teena, Brandon, 195
televangelism, 117–20, 125–26, 281
Ten Commandments, 45, 219, 222, 271–72, 319, 323

Thatcher, Prime Minister Margaret, 130–31
The Be (Happy) Attitudes, 48–49
theological idealism, 19–20, 367, 419n.2
Thiemann, Ronald, 237
third sexual revolution, 183–94, 245–46
third-wave feminism, 191–92
threat-anxiety narratives, 37
threshold effects, 66
tipping point, 66, 365
tolerance, 102–3, 283
toxic faith, 266, –67
traditional religion, definition, 2–4
transcendence, 107–16
Transcendental Meditation, 121
transexual, transgender, 200, 268–69
True Love Waits (TLW), 193–94, 263
Trueman, Carl, 411n.23
Trump, Donald, 240–41, 318–19, 398n.7

unicorns, 185
US Religion Census, 165–66
utilitarian individualism, 90–91

Vampire: The Masquerade, 285, 287
van life, 98, 308–9
Vanier, Jean, 240
Vatican II, 103–5, 107
Veaux, Franklin, 185
Vermeulen, Karla, 211
vicarious religion, 52–53
vicarious thinkers, 181–82
Vietnam War, 62, 95, 119, 280
virginity pledges, 262–63
Voas, David, 23–24, 26
von Harnack, Adolf, 108–10

walk of shame, 188
war on terror, 282, 365–66
warfare between science and religion narrative, 122–24, 262
Watergate, 119, 210
Watson, Wayne, 295
Weber, Max, 365, 369, 414n.4
Western movies, 6–7
Wheaton College Billy Graham Center, 31–32
wiccans, Wicca, 3, 143–44, 325, 328
Willow Creek, 38–39, 241
Winfrey, Oprah, 185–87, 290
witchcraft, 3, 328
Wolf, Gary, 178
Wolfe, Tom, 406n.25
Wolterstorff, Nicholas, 402–3n.71
women in paid workforce, 75–76
world collapse, 363
World Council of Churches, 100
World Health Organization, 64–65
WORLD magazine, 33
World War I, 183–84
World War II, 73–74, 95–97, 130, 248–49
worship wars, 268–69
Wuthnow, Robert, 84
Wyrtzen, Jack, 118–19

Yeltsin, Boris, 128–29, 285, 398n.3
Yoder, John Howard, 240
yoga, 146, 401–2n.56
YOLO, 317
YouTube, 138, 187, 274, 295, 303

zeitgeist, defined, 10–12